# THE WESTERN EXPERIENCE

### FIFTH EDITION

### THE MODERN ERA

### VOLUME III

# PHYSIOGRAPHY OF EUROPE

Areas Below Sea Level

0    100    200    300    400 Miles

NORWEGIAN SEA

SCANDINAVIAN PENINSULA

ICELAND

KJÖLEN MOUNTAINS

GULF OF BOTHNIA

SHETLAND I.

Helsinki

Dal R.

ÅLAND I.

GULF OF FIN

FIN
LA
REC

HEBRIDES

ORKNEY I.

Oslo

L. Vänern

Stockholm

L. Peip

BRITISH
ISLES

GRAMPIANS

SCOTTISH
LOWLANDS • Edinburgh

NORTH
SEA

L. Vättern

GOTLAND I.

ÖLAND

Riga

JUTLAND
PENINSULA

Skagerrak

Kattegat

BALTIC SEA

IRELAND

PENNINE CHAIN

ATLANTIC OCEAN

IRISH
CENTRAL
PLAIN    Dublin

IRISH SEA

THE
WASH

HELIGOLAND

Copenhagen

Gdansk
(Danzig)

Masurian
Lakes

Niemen R.

St. George's
Channel

MIDLAND
PLAIN

FRISIAN I.

Elbe R.

NORTH GERMAN PLAIN

Warta R.

Vistula R.

Bug R.

Bristol Channel

Thames R.

Amsterdam

IJsselmeer

Berlin

Warsaw

London

Maas R.

Weser R.

Oder R.

SCILLY I.

Strait of Dover

Scheldt R.

HARZ
MTS.

Neisse R.

SUDETEN MTS.

CA

LAND'S END

ENGLISH CHANNEL

Meuse R.

Rhine R.

ERZ MTS.

Prague

USHANT I.

CHANNEL I.

Marne R.

ARDENNES

Main R.

BOHEMIAN
PLAIN

BRITTANY
PENINSULA

Paris

Seine R.

Moselle R.

VOSGES MTS.

BLACK FOREST

Danube R.

BOHEMIAN FOREST

Vienna

PLAIN OF FRANCE

Loire R.

JURA MTS.

Inn R.

Budapest

TISZA R.

BAY OF BISCAY

Vienne R.

Saône R.

L. Constance

L. Balaton

PLAIN OF
HUNGARY

CAPE FINISTERRE

Bordeaux

Lyons

L. Geneva

Drave R.

TRAN

Garonne R.

MASSIF
CENTRAL

Mt.
Blanc

PLAIN OF
LOMBARDY

Trieste

Save R.

Belgrade

Moreva R.

IBERIAN
PENINSULA

CANTABRIAN MTS.

PYRENEES

CÉVENNES

Rhône R.

Po R.

ISTRIA

DINARIC ALPS

DALMATIAN I.

Varda

Douro R.

SPANISH

Ebro R.

LIGURIAN SEA

Arno R.

APENNINES

ADRIATIC SEA

BALKAN
PENINSULA

Lisbon

GUADARRAMA

Madrid

PLATEAU

Tagus R.

CORSICA

ELBA

Rome

Tiber R.

ITALIAN
PENINSULA

CORFU

PINDUS MTS.

Guadiana R.

SIERRA MORENA

Guadalquivir R.

BALEARIC I.

MINORCA

SARDINIA

Mt. Vesuvius

IONIAN I.

SIERRA NEVADA

IVIZA

MAJORCA

TYRRHENIAN SEA

IONIAN SEA

MOREAN
PENINSUL

CAPE TRAFALGAR

Strait of Gibraltar    Gibraltar

Mt. Etna
SICILY

Strait of Messina

Algiers

Tunis

PANTELLERIA

LITTLE ATLAS MOUNTAINS

Fez

MALTA

MEDITERRANEAN SEA

MIDDLE ATLAS MOUNTAINS

GREAT ATLAS MOUNTAINS

SAHARAN ATLAS MOUNTAINS

Tripoli

GULF OF SIDRA

ALGERIAN SAHARA

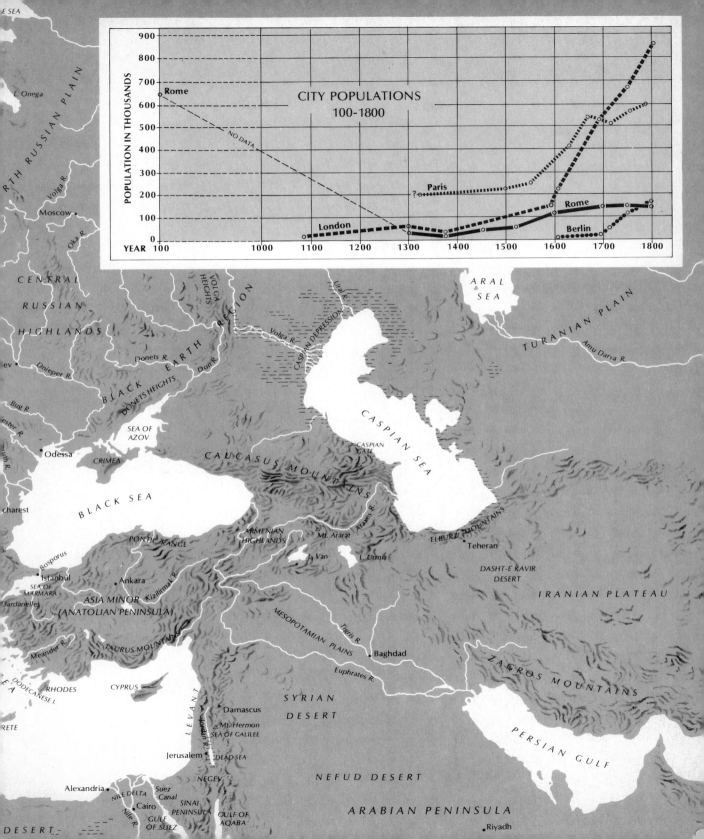

## CITY POPULATIONS
### 100–1800

POPULATION IN THOUSANDS

900
800
700
600
500
400
300
200
100

Rome

NO DATA

? Paris

London

Rome

Berlin

YEAR 100    1000    1100    1200    1300    1400    1500    1600    1700    1800

❄ ❄ ❄

ART ESSAYS BY THE LATE
*H. W. Janson*

# THE WESTERN EXPERIENCE

FIFTH EDITION · THE MODERN ERA · VOLUME III

## MORTIMER CHAMBERS
*University of California,
Los Angeles*

## RAYMOND GREW
*University of Michigan*

## DAVID HERLIHY
*Brown University*

## THEODORE K. RABB
*Princeton University*

## ISSER WOLOCH
*Columbia University*

### McGRAW-HILL, INC.

*New York   St. Louis   San Francisco   Auckland   Bogotá
Caracas   Hamburg   Lisbon   London   Madrid   Mexico   Milan   Montreal
New Delhi   Paris   San Juan   São Paulo   Singapore   Sydney   Tokyo   Toronto*

This book was set in Palatino by Ruttle, Shaw & Wetherill, Inc.
The editors were David Follmer and Scott Amerman;
the designer was Joan E. O'Connor;
the production supervisor was Leroy A. Young.
The cover was designed by Joan E. O'Connor and Karen K. Quigley.
The photo editor was Deborah Bull/Photosearch.
R. R. Donnelley & Sons Company was printer and binder.

COVER PAINTING:
Lyonel Feininger American, 1871-1956
*In a Village Near Paris* (Street in Paris, Pink Sky), 1909
Oil on canvas
39 3/4 × 32 (101.0 × 81.3)
The University of Iowa Museum of Art, Gift of Owen and Leone Elliot

THE WESTERN EXPERIENCE
Volume III
The Modern Era

1 2 3 4 5 6 7 8 9 0 DOC DOC 9 5 4 3 2 1 0

ISBN 0-07-010621-5

**Library of Congress Cataloging-in-Publication Data**

The Western experience / Mortimer Chambers . . . [et al.].—5th ed.
    p.     cm.
    Includes index.
    Contents: v. 1. Antiquity to the Middle Ages—v. 2. The early
modern period.—v. 3. The modern era.
    ISBN 0-07-010619-3 (v. 1)—ISBN 0-07-010620-7 (v. 2)
    ISBN 0-07-010621-5 (v. 3)
    1. Civilization—History.     2. Civilization, Occidental—History.
I. Chambers, Mortimer.
CB59.W38        1991c
909—dc20                                                90-20181

# ❆ CONTENTS ❆

## 29 WORLD WAR II AND THE SURVIVAL OF EUROPE 1941–1958    1218

## 30 THE PRESENT IN HISTORICAL PERSPECTIVE    1266

## ART ESSAY

## Maps

# ❄ INTRODUCTION ❄

Everyone uses history, and all of us use it in many ways. We use it to define who we are and to connect our personal experience with the history of the groups we belong to and with the history of a particular region, nation, and culture. Both individually and collectively we use the past to explain our hopes and ambitions and to justify our fears and conflicts. The Charter of the United Nations, like the American Declaration of Independence, is based on a view of history. When workers strike or armies march, they cite the lessons of their history. Because history is so important to us psychologically and intellectually, historical understanding is always shifting and often controversial. Indeed, the process of historical understanding is in itself circular: We are shaped by values, interests, and customs that (like our churches, universities, and political parties) have been formed by past experience. At the same time, the way we look at the past and what we see there—the questions we ask and the problems we pose—arise out of current concerns. Today we are likely to ask what industrialization did to the environment; in the 1950s scholars more often asked about the conditions that led to economic growth; a generation earlier the central question was how workers had gained a larger share of industrial wealth. Conservatives were more likely to study industrialization's effects on community and values, liberals to explore its relation to political freedom and education. Similarly, whether the undying interest in ancient Rome focused on civic virtue in the Republic, on Roman law, on the strength of the Roman Empire, or on its decline, the interest usually reflected some pressing issues of the historian's own era.

The circularity helps to keep the study of history alive, stimulating new interest and fresh research. We, who have been formed by the past, ask of history questions from our own time in order to learn more about both past and present. Some questions must be asked repeatedly, some issues arise again and again; but much of this knowledge is cumulative, for while asking new questions, historians integrate the answers learned from previous studies, and historical knowledge grows. History is not merely a subjective exercise in which all opinions are equally valid. No matter what motivated a particular historical question, the answer to it stands until overturned by better evidence. We now know more about the past than ever before and understand it as the historical figures whom we study could not. Unlike them, we know how their history came out; we can apply methods they did not have, and often we have evidence they never saw. This knowledge and the ways of interpreting it are the collective achievement of thousands of historians.

We also use history for pleasure—as a cultivated entertainment. The biographies of great men and women, dramatic accounts of important events, colorful tales of earlier times can be fascinating in themselves; and in enjoying them we share a pleasure felt by those who lived before us and by thousands of our contemporaries, thereby rooting ourselves more deeply in our common culture. In general the deeper our understanding of an historical era the richer our response to its art and thought is likely to be. That is not the least of the reasons for studying history. The historically well-educated person is like a privileged tourist, who can turn from the inspiring prospect of a great cathedral to the bustle of a simple village market or from the organization of a city to a single painting, able to see in each the achievements of particular eras, the expression of specific social and political arrangements, and the formation of a tradition still alive in our own time.

We also use history to discover about human behavior by discovering its variety, its similarities, and its limitations in different times and circumstances. In what kind of God or gods did people believe? What customs and institutions sustained those beliefs? How did people obtain food and protect human life? What tasks in each society were assigned to men and to women, to young and old, to rich and poor? Did formal beliefs, economic activities, established institutions, and social classes sustain each other or did they conflict? Can we estimate for any particular moment the countervailing pressures for change and for continuity? These types of questions concern all the social sciences, and all of them make use of historical examples in seeking answers. Historians, however, tend to emphasize how in a specific place at a particular moment the various aspects of social life were interrelated.

Readers of the fifth edition of *The Western Experience* will find themselves using this book in all these ways: to learn history as a subject in itself, to enrich their culture, and to test their ideas of social behavior; but they will also want to bear in mind how the authors selected what history to include. The very concept of a Western civilization is itself the result of history. The Greeks gave the names east and west to those points on the horizon where the sun rises and sets. Because the Persian Empire and India lay to their east, the Greeks were the first "westerners," their continent, Europe, was considered the west and Asia the east. The distinction between Western civilization and others—ethnocentric, often arbitrary, and frequently exaggerated—continued even as that civilization changed and expanded with the Roman Empire, Christianity, and the European conquest of the New World. The view that this is one civilization with America tied more closely to ancient Greece than Greece is to Egypt or Spain to Islam can be easily challenged in every respect save the conscious tradition that has shaped our culture.

*The Western Experience,* then, honors that tradition and gives primary attention to a small part of the world. That focus provides the opportunity to observe the processes of change and continuity over a long period of time. It includes important examples of city and of rural life; of empires and monarchies and republics; of life before and after industrialization; of societies in which labor was organized through markets, serfdom, and slavery; of cultures little concerned with science and of ones that used changing scientific knowledge; of non-Christian religions and of all the major forms of Christianity in action. All these types can be found in many other civilizations, but in a single civilization they can be seen evolving, influencing, and borrowing from each other.

Far more is known about Western history than can be put into a single book. Each paragraph is therefore, in some sense, a synthesis of scores (and sometimes more) of valuable books that have treated these same topics in greater depth. This new edition thus incorporates much new research that has modified views held only a few years ago, particularly in the greater awareness of women's roles, of the lives of ordinary people, of the lasting structural arrangements by which society is organized, of social conflicts often ignored and subtle changes easily overlooked.

At the same time one of the important aspects of the Western tradition is a general sense that certain great thinkers and artists, certain leaders, certain movements and events have been particularly important. That importance may lie in the trends they epitomize, the changes they brought, the influence they have exercised or the inspiration they provide. Whatever its basis, this tradition of Western history is generally acknowledged here, helping to determine the information included. For a long time historians emphasized politics as the activity that summarized a whole society and determined its course, a view reinforced by emphasis on the development of the national state; and that familiar perspective with its convenient chronological framework is generally maintained in this account.

But this book also reflects the influence of a distinctive kind of historical writing, commonly called "social history," which has greatly affected historical understanding in the past twenty years or so. Neither the name nor the impulse behind it is altogether new. As early as the eighteenth century many historians (of whom Voltaire was one) called for a history that was more than chronology, more than an account of kings and battles. In the nineteenth century even while historical studies paid dominant attention to past politics, diplomacy, and war (taking the evidence primarily from official documents found in state archives), there were important and systematic efforts to encompass the history of intellectual and cultural trends, of law and constitutions, of religion, and of the economy.

Social history, as a field of study, emerged as one among these efforts at broader coverage. For some it was primarily the history of the working class, often narrowed to be the history of labor movements. For others it was the history of daily life—daily life in ancient Rome or Renaissance Florence or old New York as reflected in styles of dress, housing, diet, and so on. This "pots and pans history" was the sort of history featured in historical museums and popular magazines. Appealing in its concreteness, it tended (like the collections of interesting objects that it resembled) not to have any theoretical or interpretative point to make.

Modern social history is an approach to history that pays attention to society in all its aspects (including institutions, culture, all social groups, economic ties, daily life, demography, and climate).

It has come to be distinguished by a certain point of view, particular methods and unusual sources, and a characteristic style. The point of view seeks to compensate for the fact that most historical writing has been about the tiny minority of the powerful, rich, and educated (who, after all, left behind the fullest and most accessible records of their activities). The new social history aims to be as mindful of popular culture as it is of formal or official culture, as interested in the family as it is in the state, in living conditions as it is in political theory. Social history tries to recover as much as it can of the experience of ordinary people, to look at the society from the bottom up as well as from the top down.

In method the new social history borrows theories, terminologies, and techniques from the social sciences—especially anthropology, sociology, economics, and political science. Thus social historians use models of "development," "modernization," and "cultural diffusion"; and they employ typologies of social stratification and family structure. They make sophisticated use of techniques developed by statisticians, demographers, behavioral scientists (especially survey researchers), and economists. Characteristically, such methods include a great deal of quantification, and social historians tend to be eager to count and ready to use computers whenever sufficient data can be uncovered. Careful sampling, statistical techniques, and computer analysis when combined with hard work and a new awareness have recently made it possible to discover information previously thought unobtainable about every period of the past. New interests and new techniques have in fact greatly expanded the range of useful historical sources, for important information can be gleaned from anything that records the pulse of human life: coins; pots and lamps; fiscal records and price lists; parish records of births, deaths, and marriages; weather reports and crop records; travel accounts and private letters; minutes of meetings and petitions; police and journalists' reports; and personal diaries. The social history written with these concerns, sources, and formal methods tends to be analytical rather than narrative in structure.

The authors of this book have been active in these new approaches, and they are thus particularly aware of some of the difficulties they raise for a general textbook. Those mainstays of historical organization, clear chronology and periodization, have been made more complex. The periodization of history based on the rise and fall of dynasties, on the formation of states, and on the duration of wars and revolutions usually does not fit the periodization most appropriate for changes in culture and ideas, economic production, or science and technology. Historical surveys have therefore frequently been organized topically as well as chronologically, with special chapters on economic or intellectual de-

velopments. But the history of ordinary life, especially in the period before industrialization, moves on a still different scale. A history of social processes that tend to move at a glacial pace, it often lacks sharp chronology. A history of structures more than events, it tends to be organized around problems rather than the biographies of individuals or the story of a nation.

In *The Western Experience* an effort has been made to combine the approaches and needs just discussed. The tradition of the introductory course in European history (and our cultural tradition as well) is recognized by keeping the book's chapters essentially chronological in sequence, sometimes using groups of chapters to cover a particular period of Western history. At the same time each chapter is presented as an interpretative essay, introducing a set of historical problems important to the understanding of the period treated. The "facts" that follow include the events and figures that all interpretations must take into account—the famous names and dates that are an important part of our historical lore—but the "facts" also include basic information about social organization, about modes of production and of exchange, and about cultural activity that is crucial to understanding the way of life of a particular society. All this information—much of it narrative after all, some of it good stories and accounts of dramatic events—is used to explore the problems on which a particular chapter focuses. There is also explicit attention to the kind of evidence on which these interpretations rest and the controversies that accompany them.

This edition includes, within most chapters, short essays on experiences of daily life. These essays present some concrete and colorful details about the fabric of ordinary life—subjects which, because of the nature of this textbook, are best highlighted in a special feature instead of included in the main body of each chapter. The topics of these essays have been chosen to illustrate themes significant for various periods of Western history, but the essays have another purpose as well. Professional historians think concretely even when arguing abstractly. They read discussions of the factors that led to the crusades or to industrialization having in mind a picture of what people wore and where they lived, of what preachers said, how wars were fought, and how goods were made. Descriptions of the experience of daily life should help students to remember that the analysis of history, like the narrative of events rests on the details of what real people really did and thought at a particular time in history.

Many of the users of earlier editions of this book have contributed to changes in the fifth edition. Professors have pointed to passages that could be clearer, to emphases that might be reconsidered, and sometimes to errors to be corrected. The timelines in each chapter have been expanded and improved because students requested it. Historians, determined that history should not be conceived as a string of dates, are likely to be uncomfortable with chronological tables. They tend to emphasize events rather than interpretation and political "facts" rather than cultural ideas or economic and social trends. The timelines produced for this edition seek to overcome these limitations; and, for students who have read a chapter thoughtfully and imaginatively, the timelines should provide a useful review of major points as well as events and a helpful sense of the larger chronological framework.

The readers of this text, then, can use the book as an introduction to historical method and will find within it a framework to which they can attach whatever else they know about Western society, a framework on which in the future they can build a richer appreciation of Western culture. History is essentially an integrative enterprise in which long-term trends and specific moments, social structure and the actions of particular individuals can all be brought together in the understanding of a given society. Readers should find some of their preconceptions—about the past, about how societies are organized, and about how people behave—severely challenged. Some will want to compare the response to historical problems in different societies and across time (for history is essentially a comparative mode of thought). Others will want to compare other civilizations as they ask themselves what qualities have characterized the Western world.

A college course is not the only way to build a personal culture. Nor is history the only path to integrated knowledge. Western history is not the only history one should know, or an introductory survey necessarily the best way to learn it. Still, as readers consider and then challenge interpretations offered in this text, they will exercise critical and analytical skills. They can begin to erode parochialism that views only the present as important, to acknowledge the greatness of their Western heritage and the value of familiarity with it, and to recognize the injustice, cruelty, and failures it includes. To be able to do these things is to experience the study of history as one of the vital intellectual activities by which we come to know who and where we are.

## ACKNOWLEDGMENTS
❊

We wish to thank the following reviewers and users for their helpful suggestions for *The Western Experience:* Catherine Albanese, Wright State University; Thomas M. Bader, California State University-Northridge; B. D. Bargar, University of South Carolina; Edward E. Barry, Montana State University; Iris Berger, State University of New York-Albany;

Alan E. Bernstein, University of Arizona; Charles R. Berry, Wright State University; Stephen Blum, Montgomery County Community College, PA; Jack Bournazian; Elspeth Brown, Hamilton College, NY; Paul Chardoul, Grand Rapids Junior College; Craig A. Czarnecki, Baltimore, MD; Ronnie M. Day, Eastern Tennessee State University; Bradley H. Dowden, California State University-Sacramento; Veron Egger, Georgia Southern College; Elfriede Engel, Lansing Community College, MI; R. Finucane, Georgia Southern College; Willard C. Frank, Jr., Old Dominion University, VA; Ellen G. Friedman, Boston College; James Friguglietti, Eastern Michigan College; Robert Gottfried, Rutgers University; Carl Granquist, Jr., Keene State College; Katherine J. Gribble, Highline Community College, WA; Margot A. Haberhern, Florida Institute of Technology; Drew Harrington, Western Kentucky University; Patricia Herlihy, Brown University; Neil M. Heyman, San Diego State University; Deborah L. Jones, Lexington, KY; Nannerl O. Keohane, Wellesley College; Thomas E. Kaiser, University of Arkansas-Little Rock; Donald P. King, Whitman College, WA; William J. King, Wright State University; Ellen E. Kittell, University of Oregon; Steven P. Kramer, University of New Mexico; Gordon Lauren, University of Montana; Phoebe Lundy, Boise State University; Gilbert H. McArthur, College of William and Mary; Edward Malefakis, Columbia University; Vesta F. Manning, University of Arizona-Tucson; William Carl Matthews, Ohio State University; Edgar Melton, Wright State University; Julius Milmeister, Pittsburgh, PA; Frederick I. Murphy, Western Kentucky University; Linda J. Piper, The University of Georgia-Athens; Carl Pletsch, Miami University; Ronald A. Rebholz, Stanford University; John F. Robertson, Central Michigan University; Louisa Sarasohn, Oregon State College; Judy Sealander, Wright State University; Ezel Kural Shaw, California State University-Northridge; Alan Spetter, Wright State University; Richard E. Sullivan, Michigan State University; George Taylor, University of North Carolina-Chapel Hill; Armstrong Starkey, Adelphi University, NY; Richard Weigel, Western Kentucky University; Robert H. Welborn, Clayton State College; Michael J. Witt, FSC, Christian Brothers College, TN; and Richard M. Wunderli, University of Colorado.

*Mortimer Chambers*
*Raymond Grew*
*David Herlihy*
*Theodore K. Rabb*
*Isser Woloch*

# ❆ CHAPTER 20 ❆

# REVOLUTIONS OF THE EIGHTEENTH CENTURY

# ❄ CHAPTER 20 ❄

# REVOLUTIONS OF THE EIGHTEENTH CENTURY

❅ ❅ ❅ ❅ ❅

The eighteenth century forms a bridge in Western history between two fundamentally distinct epochs. Europe in 1700—the Europe of the "old regime"—
largely preserved the institutions and the way of life that it had acquired over the
long centuries of the past. In 1700 the economy remained based predominantly upon
agriculture. People were aided in their labors by animals, wind, and water, but their
technology offered them comparatively little help. In social and political life, inequality
was the rule. Kings and emperors, who claimed to hold their authority directly from
God, presided over realms that were composed of distinct orders or estates, each
with its own obligations and privileges.

In contrast, the European society of 1800 was witnessing violent upheavals at every
level. Western peoples had begun a radical transformation of their methods of raising
food and producing goods. This Industrial Revolution, which continues in our day,
achieved a stunning conquest of the material world, restructured society, changed all
aspects of Western life in its early phases, and now offers similar promises and poses
similar problems to all the peoples of the earth.

Concurrently with the inauguration of the Industrial Revolution, profound changes
were undermining the stability of Western society. As we have seen, the leaders of
the Enlightenment broke with traditional religious assumptions; they denied that
morality and social order had to be based on divine revelation and supernatural grace.
Human reason could replace or was equivalent to the word of God. In a larger context,
growing numbers of people—not only from the middle classes but from the older
privileged orders as well—had come to believe that society was ill-served by traditional
institutions, and they agitated powerfully to reform them. The demand for reform
bore as its principal fruit the great revolutions that swept across wide areas of both
Europe and North America in the late eighteenth century.

❅

The latter 1700s thus initiate the great age of revolutions in the West. Of course, all
periods of the Western past have experienced change, and all have contributed to the
making of our present society. But the economic changes and popular revolts begun
toward the end of the century hold a pivotal position in the growth and transformation
of Western civilization. Perhaps no other movements have left such visible marks on
the character of our modern life—our government, our economy, and our social ideals.

## I. THE INDUSTRIAL SYSTEM

❖

Since the eighteenth century, the economy of the Western world has been in nearly continuous transformation. Humankind has achieved spectacular efficiency in raising food, producing goods, amassing wealth, multiplying itself, and changing the face of the earth. While no one can be certain, it is probable that more human beings are alive today than inhabited the earth over all the millennia before 1700. In a series of lectures given in 1880–1881, a young sociologist and economist at Oxford University named Arnold Toynbee chose (though he did not coin) the phrase "Industrial Revolution" to describe this metamorphosis.[1]

### Characteristics of an Industrial Economy

With a fund of information unavailable to Toynbee, it is easy to criticize the term that he, more than anyone else, made part of the historical vocabulary. It does not, for example, encompass changes in agriculture or transportation, without which the Industrial Revolution, properly speaking, would not have occurred. The traditional dates for it in Great Britain, 1760 to 1815 or 1830, are much too confined. If great factories are the mark of an industrial society, Britain and, even more, the Continent would have to be considered still underdeveloped by 1830. The revolution did not end in 1830. Indeed, the great advances based on the spread of the railroads, the application of chemistry to manufacturing, and the development of electrical power and the internal combustion engine did not affect the economy until the middle and late nineteenth century; moreover, computers, atomic power, and biotechnologies carry the changes forward into our own future. There are then many industrial revolutions, and they cannot be considered as marked off by precise dates.

While the term must be used carefully, most historians would still concur that from the late eighteenth century, initially in Great Britain, profound changes took place in the production of goods and food. Those changes eventually equipped a significant part of the Western world with a kind of economy unknown in all prior historical ages.

What essentially distinguishes an industrial, or modern, economy from the traditional economies of previous epochs? Arnold Toynbee and many later writers equated the Industrial Revolution with the application of steam power to manufacturing, which brought about the factory system. The steam engine, used to drive mills from the 1780s on, replaced the putting-out system of domestic industry, in which artisans worked at home with their own tools on materials delivered to them by merchants or entrepreneurs. The use of steam power required that the workers congregate in great mills or factories, and they thus came to form a new social unit. But the emergence of the factory system does not seem today an adequate explanation of this economic transformation. In agriculture and transportation there were no factories; yet the progress in these economic sectors was an essential component of the Industrial Revolution, as noted before.

Perhaps the most distinctive feature of an industrial economy is its capacity for sustained growth. Its productivity is so great that it is able not only to meet its current consumption needs and replace its worn tools but also to invest in new capital equip-

---

[1] Arnold Toynbee was the uncle of Arnold J. Toynbee, the distinguished author of *A Study of History,* perhaps the most ambitious effort at developing a philosophy of history to appear in recent years. His own lectures on the Industrial Revolution were compiled and edited by friends after his death in 1883, at the age of 30.

ment, which expands its means of producing. In short, the wealth produced, the capital equipment, and the economy will not be the same at the end of a given period as they were at the beginning. The essential feature of an industrial economy—we might say of a modern society, in contrast to all societies we have studied so far—is that it never stays the same. Since the eighteenth century, far more than in any other age, continuous, rapid, and all-pervasive change has been the law of Western life.

## Protoindustrialization

Of course, the whole of European economic history before the Industrial Revolution cannot be regarded as stable and changeless. Many historians now distinguish an intermediate phase of "protoindustrialization," falling between the establishment of manufactures in the medieval towns and true industrialization from the late eighteenth century. Under protoindustrialization, rural families devoted time not needed for agricultural labors to industrial work—spinning, weaving, and other forms of cloth work. Protoindustrialization was particularly advanced in the rural areas of the Low Countries and the Rhineland, but it was also characteristic of many regions of early modern Europe close to large cities. The cities remained sources of capital, materials, and marketing services.

Protoindustrialization had important economic, social, and demographic repercussions. Economically, it strengthened marketing networks, generated additional revenue for rural populations, and increased their demand for products and services of the towns. Socially, it familiarized rural inhabitants with industrial processes and discipline and with cash relationships. Demographically, it loosened restraints on marriages and births, and

stimulated population growth in the countryside. This, in turn, led to increased immigration into the cities and contributed to their growing size in the early modern age.

On the other hand, protoindustrialization did not lead to significant technological improvements nor to marked advances in productivity; it could not therefore sustain continuous economic growth. Protoindustrialization prepared but did not produce the Industrial Revolution.

## Toward the Industrial Order

How did the Industrial Revolution happen? In analyzing any economic system—traditional or modern, capitalist or socialist—economists distinguish between performance and structure. Performance is measured by output—the total or gross product, and the amount produced per individual in the community. This per capita productivity is, in fact, the best measure of an economy's performance. Structure refers to all those characteristics of a society that support or affect performance. Economic, legal, and political institutions; fiscal policies; technology; demographic distributions and movements; even culture and ideology—all make up the structure of a society, in the language of economic theory.

The Industrial Revolution was, in essence, a revolution in technology, which dramatically and continuously raised per capita productivity. In older treatments, historians stressed the numerous inventions that ushered in the factory era (see pp. 786–794). But technology alone does not offer an adequate explanation for the advent of industrialism. It was not an independent, or "exogenous," factor, to use again the language of economic theory. Social structure profoundly influences technological development, in any age. To ask why the revolution occurred is thus to pose two deeper questions: what were the structural obstacles to technological innovation and entrepreneurship in traditional European society? And what were the changes that, from the late eighteenth century, produced a structure that promoted and rewarded innovation?

One major early obstacle was the small size of many European markets, which were cut off one from the other by physical barriers, political frontiers, tariff walls, and different laws, moneys, and measurements. Small markets slowed the growth of specialized manufacture, and they limited the mobility of capital and labor. Then, too, the highly skewed distribution of wealth, characteristic of many European communities, distorted the structure of demand. In many countries, a narrow aristocracy absorbed nearly all the disposable income, and the economy organized itself largely to serve the wealthy few. Catering to the desires of the rich, the economy produced expensive goods, often exquisite in quality and workmanship, but always in small quantities. Small markets and skewed demand could not easily support a change in the mode of production, which aimed at producing an abundance of cheap goods.

Even when markets were large, organizational faults weakened their power to promote specialization and mobilize labor and capital. Big markets and advancing specialization augmented the number of market transactions and their associated costs. To lower these "transaction costs" (again in the language of the economist) required efficient business and banking institutions.

Crucial to the industrializing process was a set of property rights, which raised the rate of return to technological innovation. Many institutions in traditional Europe (especially bearing on property) did the opposite: they repressed inventiveness and entrepreneurship. Through feudal or seigneurial rents and tolls, lords throughout Europe collected payments for which they rendered no service in return. Increased production was likely to benefit these parasites as much as the entrepreneurs. In the villages of northern Europe, under the open-field system (see pp. 782–783), cultivators had to follow the same routines of working the soil; they were not free to change farming methods without the agreement of neighbors. In the towns, the guilds presented a major obstacle to economic innovation. Guild regulations, which in the eighteenth century were more exactly government regulations enforced by the guilds, prescribed the techniques to be used in production and often dictated the terms and conditions under which goods could be sold, apprentices taken on, or workers hired. In their policies, both urban guilds and rural villages tended to favor the poor and inefficient over the rich and entrepreneurial. They also tended to block innovation, freeze technology, and discourage effort.

Governments, too, helped sustain these restrictive practices, principally by exploiting them for their own fiscal benefit. For example, governments frequently collected fees from guilds and other privileged institutions and parties. Another governmental policy that obstructed innovation was the licensing of monopoly companies, with exclusive rights to trade in certain regions, such as the East Indies, or to manufacture certain products. With assured markets and profits, these companies were not likely to assume the risks of new ventures, and they blocked others from doing so.

Cultural attitudes may also have discouraged entrepreneurial efforts. Many persons, particularly in the aristocratic classes, still regarded money made in trade or manufacture as somehow tainted. Particularly on the Continent, the highest aspiration of the successful businessman seems often to have been the purchase of a noble title.

Although these institutions and attitudes still marked European life in the eighteenth century, they were subject to ever sharper criticisms. From midcentury on, social thinkers associated with the Enlightenment—the physiocrats in France, Adam Smith and the liberal economists in England—attacked the communal management of land in the countryside, the guild control of industry in the towns, and privilege and monopoly in all forms. In the name of economic rationalism, they denounced both the special advantages held by a favored few and special consideration extended to the poor and the weak. No privilege, no pity: This was the appropriate policy for enlightened society. Their hard but telling logic slowly affected policy. Guilds were already weak in the countryside and in towns of recent growth, like Manchester and Birmingham in England. Also, new industries, such as cotton manufacturing, largely escaped their supervision. The government of revolutionary France, in the Le Chapelier law of 1791, permanently outlawed guilds and trade associations. In the Corporation Act of 1835, the British Parliament similarly abolished the guilds, but they had long since become ineffective in their function of regulating the economy. The government policy of chartering monopolies was gradually abandoned (the English East India Company, for example, lost its exclusive trading rights in India in 1813). Legally and socially, the entrepreneur was winning unprecedented freedom.

## England

Of all the nations of Europe, England was the first to develop a social structure strongly supportive of innovation and economic growth. Its advantages were many, some of them deeply rooted in geography and history. This comparatively small realm contained an excellent balance of resources. The plain to the south and east, which contained the traditional centers of English settlement, was fertile and productive. The uplands to the north and west possessed rich deposits of coal and iron, and their streams had given power to mills since the Middle Ages.

The sea too was a major natural asset. No part of the island kingdom was distant from salt water. At a time when water transport offered the sole economical means for moving bulky commodities, the sea brought coal close to iron, raw materials close to factories, and products close to markets. And the sea gave Britain's merchants easy access to the much wider world beyond their shores.

Efficiency of transport was critical in setting the size of markets. From the late eighteenth century, Britain witnessed a considerable expansion of canals and turnpikes. Usually short in this compact land, they were cheap to build and profitable to operate. By 1815 the country possessed some 2600 miles of canals. In addition, there were few institutional obstructions to the movement of goods. United under a strong monarchy since the Middle Ages, Britain was free of internal tariff barriers. Merchants everywhere counted in the same money, measured their goods by the same standards, and conducted their affairs under the protection of the common law.

Other characteristics of Britain's society favored innovation. The population had a long tradition of valuing labor and could adapt rather easily to the personal and collective discipline required by the factory system. In about 1700, the standard of living of the English masses was probably the highest in Europe. English society was also considerably less stratified than that on the Continent, and the propertied classes tended to be oriented toward innovation. Primogeniture was the rule among both the peers (the titled members of the House of Lords) and the country gentlemen or squires, and the need to provide for their frequently large families encouraged them to increase their estates and revenues. From their ranks came the so-called improving landlords. Their younger sons, left without lands, had to seek careers in other walks of life, many of them in commerce and manufacturing. They frequently recruited capital for their ventures from their landed (and sometimes titled) fathers and elder brothers. Capital, therefore, like people, frequently crossed class lines in England. Another important pool of entrepreneurs was the considerable number of English religious dissenters, chiefly Calvinists and Quakers, who concentrated their energies on business enterprises because they were denied careers in government or the church.

The responsiveness of the propertied elements to investment opportunities was a remarkable feature of English society in the eighteenth century and one of the chief reasons why Britain was the home of the Industrial Revolution. These entrepreneurs and investors had a relatively greater influence on government than comparable groups on the Continent. Since the revolution of 1688, the government had been particularly sensitive to the interests of the propertied classes. They, in turn, had confidence in the government. The close ties between property and power facilitated the economic growth of the realm and was one important reason for the relative stability of the British regime in this age of revolutions.

Historians are not sure exactly what precipitated the takeoff of the eighteenth-century British economy or even what sectors led others in the industrializing effort. At one time scholars stressed the work of individual leaders, the improving landlords in agriculture or inventors, and entrepreneurs in the cotton industry. Today it is generally recognized that agricultural changes came only slowly and that the growth of the cotton industry, however rapid, still accounted for

## THE GROWTH OF ENGLAND'S FOREIGN TRADE IN THE EIGHTEENTH CENTURY

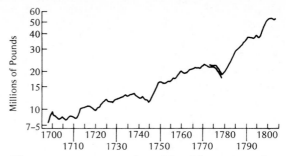

**Three-year averages of combined imports and exports.** (Adapted from Dean, Phyllis, and Cole, W. A., *British Economic Growth, 1688–1959*, 1964, p. 49.)

only a small part of England's gross national product. Historians are thus inclined to lay greater emphasis on broad economic stimuli felt in several sectors simultaneously. One recently formulated theory, partially Marxist in inspiration, stresses the economic and political exploitation of overseas colonies as the critical stimulus in early industrialization. Colonies offered a huge market for inexpensive goods, especially cotton fabrics, which the new machines produced most efficiently. They provided cheap raw materials, and the large profits of the colonial trade promoted the formation of industrial capital.

Overseas trade was certainly booming in the eighteenth century, and certainly gave a powerful thrust to industrialization. Still, the possession and exploitation of a colonial empire could not of itself assure early industrialization—witness Spain, Portugal, or Holland. Probably no less important was the growth of home population, which assured an enlarged domestic market and an abundance of cheap labor. Cultural changes may also have had an effect in that many people were willing to risk replacing old methods with new, and on other planes were questioning and transforming traditional ways of thought and behavior. Then, too, the industrial growth itself, once initiated, seems to have exerted a reciprocal influence on trade, population, and attitudes.

The processes of this first industrialization are thus highly complex and still not entirely understood. What seems certain is that a strong demand for cheap goods was growing at home and abroad in the eighteenth century, and that important segments of the British community perceived this opportunity and responded to it. English law and policy gave them crucial support, by ensuring a high rate of return for innovation and enterprise.

## France

Structural obstacles to economic growth were more deeply entrenched in France than in England. The kingdom of France in the early modern period did not form a single national market; rather, it was a federation of regional markets. France was large, and the expense of transportation grew rapidly with distance. Waterways were not conveniently distributed, and roads were miserable even in the age of Louis XIV's minister Colbert. Internal tariffs at provincial borders continued to restrain trade. In 1664 Colbert had created an area of free trade that embraced the older central provinces of the monarchy, but beyond these "five great farms," tariffs, tolls, and seigneurial dues burdened commerce. Merchants in the northeastern provinces of the Franche-Comté and Alsace, for example, found it easier to trade with the imperial cities of the Rhineland than with Paris. Contrasts in legal systems and in weights and measures further complicated and slowed exchange. As Voltaire sarcastically remarked, the traveler in crossing France by coach changed laws as frequently as horses.

Guilds and other forms of monopoly exerted a harmful influence within these regional markets. They paid fees to the central government in return for their privileges. In effect, the government was forgoing freer markets and more efficient economic performance in return for present revenue.

In spite of these obstacles, the French economy was not stagnant during the eighteenth century. After 1715 France enjoyed some 75 years nearly free from foreign invasions and internal uprisings; this was the calm before the terrible storms of the Revolution. The period of peace saw a remarkable proliferation of communications arteries. By 1738 the Picardy Canal linked the Somme and Oise rivers in the north. The Central Canal, built between 1783 and 1793, joined the Loire and Saône. Work was begun in 1777 on the Burgundy Canal, which enabled barges to move from the English Channel to the Mediterranean. The improvement of French roads, given major attention by Philibert Orry, a chief financial officer under Louis XV, was perhaps even more impressive. In 1738, Orry imposed a heavy *corvée* on the parishes, requiring from them contributions in labor for the construction and maintenance of roads. About a decade later the government founded the École des Ponts et Chaussées ("School of Bridges and Roads"), which soon became probably the best engineering school in Europe and which still functions today. By the late eighteenth century, France had acquired a magnificent system of royal highways that many contemporaries considered unsurpassed in Europe.

Foreign trade expanded too, especially with the West Indies and the Levant, despite the military reversals in North America and India. The number of French ships engaged in foreign commerce increased about fourfold between 1716 and 1789; on the eve of the Revolution, some 1800 vessels showed the French flag. In the same period exports of manufactured products rose by 221 percent and all other commodities by 298 percent. The great ports of Bordeaux and Marseilles enjoyed a period of prosperity unequaled since the Middle Ages.

Stable coinage aided the financing of enterprises. In 1726 the government fixed the value of the principal gold coin, the louis, and kept it stable for the remaining years of the old regime—a remarkable feat in light of the monarchy's desperate financial needs. The collapse of John Law's investment scheme in 1720 had a regressive effect on French banking, to be sure. French investors developed a lasting suspicion of banks, paper money, and joint-stock companies. Businesspeople tended to rely on resources that they or their close relatives could muster and preferred to deal in hard cash rather than commercial paper. Small size, small capital, and conservative management worked to hold back French business enterprises. But this only dampened, not suppressed, the expansion of the eighteenth century. That expansion, in turn, created powerful pressures to reform the archaic structure of the French society and government.

## II. ECONOMICS AND DEMOGRAPHY

❖

The birth of the new economic system required the development of effective ways of recruiting, managing, and channeling capital into those enterprises with the greatest potential for profit. The commercial capitalism of the previous centuries was thus gradually being transformed into industrial capitalism. Changes in monetary practices affected trade and prices, and price movements had a major impact not only upon the economy but upon government as well. At a still more fundamental level, these economic changes influenced the patterns of marriages, births, and deaths in European society. In fact, they helped stimulate a population explosion, which, in turn, had a powerful repercussion on European life.

## Financial Management

Critical to the takeoff of the industrialization process is a high rate of reinvestment, which, in turn, depends on the skillful management of money by both individuals and public institutions. Here again, Great Britain was the most advanced country of Europe. From the sixteenth century on, the demands of overseas trade promoted the formation of joint-stock companies. By the seventeenth century, great concerns controlling trade with India, the South Seas, Africa, and the Levant were dominating England's overseas commerce. The financial panic in 1720 caused by the collapse of the South Sea Bubble prompted Parliament to pass the so-called Bubble Act, which required that all joint-stock ventures secure a royal charter. This limited the formation of stock companies, for a charter was difficult and expensive to obtain. Eventually, however, the joint-stock company was to become as much the child of modern capitalism as the factory.

The early industrial enterprises, chiefly partnerships, could rely on a growing banking system to meet their capital needs. In the seventeenth century the goldsmiths of London had assumed the functions of bankers. They accepted and guarded deposits, extended loans, transferred upon request credits from one account to another, and changed money. In the eighteenth century banking services became available beyond London; country banks, of which there were 300 in 1780, numbered more than 700 in 1810. The English businessperson was familiar with bank notes and other forms of commercial paper, and his confidence in paper facilitated the recruitment and flow of capital.

The founding of the Bank of England in 1694 itself marked an epoch in the history of European finance. The bank enjoyed a phenomenal success in the eighteenth century as it has since. It assumed responsibility for managing the public debt and sold shares in the debt (equivalent to shares in the bank) to the public. It faithfully met the interest payments due to the shareholders, with the help of government revenues it was given to administer, and simultaneously placed at the disposal of the government financial resources unavailable to any Continental state. The bank was so well run that it may have attracted investments away from the private sector of the economy. However, stability in government finance assured a measure of stability for the entire money market. Moreover, the system also enlisted the tax powers of the government in the cause of industrialization. Taxes and interest payments took money from the mass of the people, who were likely to consume it, and gave it to the wealthy, who were likely to invest it. Some type of forced societal savings was probably essential to industrialization, as it preserved the necessary high rate of reinvestment.

## Prices

The eighteenth century in Britain and in France, and in other regions of the West as well, was thus an age of increasing wealth, but the economy did not expand steadily. Rather, it experienced periods of sharp fluctuation, of rapid growth and severe decline, of boom and bust. French scholars have made particularly rigorous studies of the economic cycles of the period in France as revealed primarily through the history of prices. Their analyses have provided a new

and powerful, if sometimes controversial, tool for investigating social change in eighteenth-century France and for interpreting the French Revolution itself.[2] We are less well informed concerning price movements and business cycles in other parts of Europe and in North America, but the available information suggests that the economy in these societies was behaving comparably to that of France.

For the first 30 years of the eighteenth century, prices in France and apparently in England, too, remained stable. The economy similarly remained relatively stagnant, one reason being the exhaustion of the European states during the War of the Spanish Succession and the difficult decade and a half of readjustment following it. The economic eighteenth century, as some French scholars call it, began about 1730 and lasted until about 1817, the time of the peace settlements following the Napoleonic wars. Inflation in prices dominated the era. Since French money was kept stable after 1726, the strong upward movement must be attributed to other causes. The great increase in foreign trade brought a new abundance of precious metals to Europe, especially gold from Brazil. But primarily, as we shall see further, the price rise reflected the pressures of a growing population and a growing demand for food, land, goods, and employment.

The present-day reconstruction of price movements in the eighteenth century distinguishes four periods:

1. Phase A: inflation. After 1730 prices moved slowly upward. The movement accelerated between 1758 and 1770, bringing

---

[2] The French historian E. Labrousse has written the fundamental studies on price movements in eighteenth-century France; see especially his *La crise de l'economie français à la fin de l'Ancien Régime et au début de la Révolution,* 1944.

prosperity to some segments at least of French society and making these years the "splendor of Louis XV."

2. Phase B: depression. Prices leveled off about 1770 and began to move downward after 1778. The next decade was one of hard times, which aggravated the financial difficulties of the government.

3. The Revolution cycle. From 1787 to 1791 a series of bad harvests raised the prices of grain. Striking after a protracted period of hard times, these shocks helped precipitate the social and political crisis that ended France's *ancien régime,* the old regime.

4. Continuation of phase A. Inflation and prosperity, after 1791.

Over the long term, the inflation did not affect all products, all sectors of the economy, and all segments of society equally. Prices in France between 1726 and 1789 increased by an average of about 65 percent. The cost of cereals, the basic food for the poor, rose slightly more than the average and considerably more than other agricultural products, such as wine and meat. Rents rose sharply, suggesting a shortage of available land; in relation to averages for the decade of the 1730s, rents paid in money had grown by 98 percent in the years 1786–1790. Wages, on the other hand, increased by a meager 22 percent in the same period, which would point to a glut of workers competing for employment.

These differentials had important social and economic effects. High rents in the countryside and low wages in the city took wealth from the poor and delivered it to the landlord and employer. This movement of money particularly benefited the entrepreneurial groups. Inflation helped drive many of the poor from the soil, to the advantage of their better-off neighbors, who were eager to expand their holdings; it was thus a principal

cause of acute rural unrest. In the city it enabled the industrial entrepreneur to sell goods for more and pay workers less. Burdening the poor, it also worked against the economically inactive members of society— the nobles, for example, who lived from fixed rents or dues set in money. Inflation hurt the government too, for its revenues did not grow as fast as its expenditures. A large portion of French lands, owned by the aristocracy or the clergy, was tax-exempt. The government therefore relied primarily on indirect taxation that weighed on the lower classes, which group controlled less and less of the national wealth. Inflation was thus shrinking the traditional tax base of the French monarchy and paving the way for financial crisis.

These price changes were influenced by another factor, which also helped make the eighteenth century an age of revolutions—an enormous increase in the numbers of Europeans.

## Population

What some French historians now call the demographic eighteenth century began about 1730. Reasonable estimates put the population growth of Europe at between 60 and 80 percent over the following 100 years. Probably never before had Western Europe experienced so rapid and substantial an increase in its people, and never has it since. (In Eastern Europe, especially the lands of the Russian Empire, a comparable population explosion occurred after 1860.) The growth was particularly marked in Great Britain and France. England grew from an estimated 5 million people in 1700 to more than 9 million in 1801, the date of the first British census. Swelled by continuous immigration and a high birth rate, the population of England's North American colonies grew at probably twice the English rate—from an estimated 275,000 in 1700 to 3.93 million in 1790. The French, according to various estimates, numbered 16 to 19 million at the death of Louis XIV, in 1715, and probably 26 million or more in 1789. With an estimated 18 percent of the total population in Europe about 1750, France was by far the most populous nation in the West; the Russian Empire alone surpassed it, and only by a few million. France's proportion of Europe's inhabitants reached its peak in the age of the Revolution and Napoleon, after which it fell continuously until the present generation. The country's military and political dominance of Europe under Napoleon was in no small measure founded on this demographic preponderance.

Spain increased from perhaps 7 to 10 million and the Italian states from 9 to 13 million. Prussia was growing more rapidly, from perhaps 1.7 to 3.1 million. But all these countries remained thinly populated in comparison with France, and they were not to feel the full pressures emanating from population growth until the following century.

In explaining this population explosion, historians once spoke with confidence of a "demographic transition." According to this simple theory, the population in traditional societies reproduces itself at a rate close to the biological maximum, but its growth is impeded by an equivalently high death rate. The immediate impact of industrialization is a reduction of the death rate, principally through improved measures of public health. The opening gap between the steady birth rate, which continues high, and the dropping death rate results in substantial expansion of total numbers. Eventually, however, in the later stages of industrialization, the birth rate declines, settling to equilibrium with the death rate, and this slows to a halt the further growth of population.

The most recent research in historical demography has questioned and modified,

without entirely discrediting, this classical model. This research has focused primarily on England, but the pattern it has uncovered probably applies to most of Western Europe.[3]

In the current view, two types of controls, or "checks," limit the growth of populations. One set of checks is "positive" and consists of epidemics, famines, wars, and other events that reduce the size of an already swollen population by dramatically increasing deaths. But at least from the middle sixteenth century, England escaped crises of overpopulation through relying on a second set of checks, called "preventive." The preventive check could involve the limitation of births within marriage. But, more commonly in traditional societies, it worked by requiring young people to delay marriage or to eschew it altogether. The key restraint on population growth was thus control of marriages. The system operated in the following fashion. A growing population drove up food costs, and this reduced real wages, as the workers had to spend a greater portion of their earnings on subsistence. But declining real wages obstructed marriages, as workers could not afford to support a wife and family. A falling population had the opposite effect. It reduced food costs, increased real wages, and encouraged marriages and births. The regime of the preventive check, characteristic of English society in the early modern period, operated like a homeostatic or self-regulating mechanism. It kept the population well within the limits its resources could support.

The immediate impact of industrialization was to lift traditional restraints on marriage and procreation. The booming commerce and new industries created jobs. Jobs, in turn, enabled young persons to depart early from the homes in which they grew up, to marry,

[3] See especially E. A. Wrigley and R. S. Scofield, *The Population History of England, 1541–1871*, 1981.

and to begin families sooner than would otherwise have been possible. Ready employment also stimulated births; children could earn wages at early ages and were more an asset than a burden to their families. But the real novelty in English demography under industrialism seems to have been that the population growth did not drive up food costs, as it had always done in the past. It did not therefore reduce real wages and prevent marriages. The old link between rising population, rising food costs, declining real wages, and declining number of marriages was, for the first time, broken. This indicates that the new industrial economy had achieved a breakthrough to unprecedented levels of efficiency, in the production of food and goods.

The impact of industrialization upon deaths was slow in appearing and equally complex. In many ways, the industrial system increased life expectancy. Established trading networks and cheap transport allowed food to be carried efficiently over great distances, and took the edge off most years of famine and dearth. Living standards, fluctuating but slowly improving, led to better care for children and the sick and better nutrition and hygiene for all. Cheap, plentiful, and washable cotton garments allowed new levels of personal cleanliness. Soon, cheap iron pipes brought clean water into households and carried sewage away, both moved by the cheap power of steam. Medical advances such as the development of vaccination helped protect the population. On the other hand, the growth of large cities introduced millions into a biologically unfavorable environment. In many great European cities, death rates did not sink below birth rates until the second half of the nineteenth century. In most great European cities, infant mortality remained stubbornly high well into the twentieth century.

Still, over the long term, the death rate was declining, and it fell more rapidly than the relative number of births. The theory of a demographic transition retains a certain crude validity. But it is not at all a full description of the behavior of the population in the period of industrialization, one of the great turning points in Western history.

## III. AGRICULTURE
❈

In England in 1700, an estimated 80 percent of the population lived directly from agriculture; by about 1800 that portion had fallen to approximately 40 percent. This massive shift of labor and resources from agriculture to industry would have been inconceivable had the countryside not been able to supply a greater abundance of food with a reduced amount of labor. To be sure, change came only slowly to rural areas, especially on the Continent; the peasant cultivators clung tenaciously to traditional ways. But significant improvements were still achieved in agricultural methods, and these, in turn, enabled the countryside to supply the industrial towns with food, labor, capital, and markets.

### The Enclosure Movement in Great Britain

The considerable improvement that Britain experienced in agricultural technology in the eighteenth century contributed greatly to its industrialization. In any agricultural system the central problem is the restoration of fertility to the soil, especially after repeated harvests. Since the Early Middle Ages, farmers in Europe had relied principally on resting their lands periodically under the two- and three-field system of crop rotation (see Chapter 6). This allowed bacteria in the soil to take needed nitrogen from the air. A quicker method, heavy manuring, could not be used

## THE VITAL REVOLUTION IN IRELAND

| Year | Millions of Persons | Year | Millions of Persons |
|------|------|------|------|
| 1712 | 2.8 | 1781 | 4.0 |
| 1718 | 2.9 | 1785 | 4.0 |
| 1725 | 3.0 | 1788 | 4.4 |
| 1732 | 3.0 | 1791 | 4.8 |
| 1754 | 3.2 | 1821 | 6.8 |
| 1757 | 3.5 | 1831 | 7.8 |
| 1772 | 3.6 | 1841 | 8.2 |
| 1777 | 3.7 | | |

Ireland, thinly settled in the seventeenth century, experienced one of the highest rates of population growth in Western Europe from circa 1700 until 1841. The increase was closely associated with the spread of potato cultivation, but it cannot be determined whether the potato removed previous limits on population size, or whether the population, growing for other reasons, turned more and more to that easily cultivated plant. The figures to 1791 are adopted from K. H. Connell, *The Population of Ireland*, 1950, p. 25. The later figures are from official censuses.

widely because the poorly productive farms could not support sufficient animals.

The secret of improving agricultural productivity lay in suppressing the fallow periods. This required that more animals be raised to provide the necessary fertilizer. One of the first of the British landlords to seek a solution was Jethro Tull, an agriculturist and inventor. Much of his work was impeded by false assumptions prevalent in the first half of the eighteenth century—for example, that plants actually devour the soil and that animal fertilizer is bad for them. But the zeal with which he conducted his experiments proved infectious. Tull also designed a horse-drawn hoe and a mechanical seeder, early steps in the mechanization of agriculture.

By the late eighteenth century, Norfolk, in the east of England, had achieved particular prominence for its techniques of "high farming." In the 1730s Tull's contemporary Charles "Turnip" Townshend stressed, as his nickname suggests, the value of using turnips and other field crops in a rotation system of planting instead of letting the land lie fallow. Some five decades later Thomas William Coke wrote extensively on field grasses, new fertilizers such as oil-cake and bone manure, and the principles of efficient estate management. The eighteenth-century high farmers also experimented with the selective breeding of animals. Coke improved the Suffolk breed of pigs, adding to the advances made by Robert Bakewell, a generation his senior, who had developed the Leicestershire breed of sheep and dramatically increased the weight of marketed cattle.

To make use of the new methods, the improving farmers had to be free to manage the land as they saw fit. This was all but impossible under the open-field system, which had dominated the countryside since the Middle Ages. Characteristically, even the largest landlords held their property in numerous elongated strips that were open to the land of their neighbors. Owners of contiguous strips had to follow the same routines of cultivation. One could not raise grasses to graze cattle when another was raising wheat. The village as a whole determined what routines should be followed and was thus the effective manager of each holding. The village also decided such matters as how many cattle each member could graze on common meadows and how much wood each could take from the forest. The open-field system froze the technology of cultivation at the levels attained in the Middle Ages. The landlord who wished to form a compact farm and apply new methods could not function within this framework, but needed the freedom to innovate.

The landlord could gain that freedom only by enclosing property. But both common law and cost considerations ruled out fencing the long, narrow strips. The entire village had to be enclosed, and this required the agreement of all its members, even the poorest. Voluntary enclosures were thus nearly impossible to arrange. There was an alternative, however: an act of Parliament, usually passed in response to a petition, allowing the enclosure of a village even against the opposition of some of its members. The procedure was difficult and expensive. The lands of the village had to be surveyed and redistributed in compact blocks among the members in proportion to their former holdings. Frequently, too, roads had to be constructed to ensure access to the fields. But over the course of the eighteenth century, the high rents and returns that could be earned with the new methods were making enclosures very desirable investments.

The first parliamentary act authorizing the enclosure of a village was registered in 1710, but this recourse was not exercised often until after the 1750s. Then the number of acts soared: 156 passed in 1750–1760 but 906 in 1800–1810. This sweeping change all but eradicated the traditional village and the open-field system from the British countryside.

While the enclosure movement was clearly rational from an economic standpoint, it brought much human misery in its wake. The redistribution of the land deprived the poor of their precious rights in the commons and often left them with tiny, unprofitable plots. Frequently, they were forced to sell their holdings to their richer neighbors and seek employment as landless laborers or urban workers.

Historians have interpreted the importance of enclosures in English economic and social history variously. They have viewed the system as a counterpart or even a precondition of industrialization in the cities. The peasant cultivator, thrown off the soil, provided the factories with cheap labor; the productive fields yielded the needed food; the prosperous gentry and its tenants purchased the manufactured products and helped provide industrial capital. Today research is showing that enclosures did not perhaps mesh quite so neatly with industrialization. There was no massive rural depopulation in their wake; the industrial labor force seems to have recruited its members as much from artisans already established in the towns as from the dislodged rural poor.

On the other hand, it would be unwise to discount the importance of this movement. It transformed the English countryside even in a physical sense, giving it the appearance it retains today: the large, verdant fields, neatly defined by hedges and walls. It resulted in the near-disappearance of the peasant cultivators, working their own land in the village of their ancestors. If enclosures did not violently push people to the towns, neither did they encourage growth in rural settlements. They were therefore a major factor in the steady shift of population from countryside to city and in the emergence of the first truly urban, truly industrial society in the modern world.

## Agriculture on the Continent

Change came more slowly to the countryside in Continental regions. The centers that witnessed the most active development were the Netherlands, the Paris basin and the northeast of France, the Rhineland, and the Po valley—all areas of dense settlement where high prices for food encouraged investments in agricultural improvements. Many great landlords emulated the British in improving methods of cultivation.

Continental farmers also waged a battle for managerial freedom, though it was by no means so sweeping as the English enclosure movement. For example, many French villages worked the land under a system similar to the open-field arrangement known as *vaine pâture* ("empty pasture," or fallow). This too required owners to follow the same routines of cultivation as their neighbors, with the village determining the rights of its members on common lands. From the middle of the century on, the representative assemblies of several provinces outlawed obligatory *vaine pâture* and allowed individual owners to enclose their land, and some authorized the division of communal properties. But the French monarchy did not adopt enclosures as national policy, and after 1771 even the provincial governments no longer seem to have authorized or required them. Traces of the medieval village and the medieval countryside thus lasted longer in France and other Continental regions than in England.

There is a further contrast between Great Britain and the Continent that is of considerable interest in social history. Enclosures in Britain led to the domination of rural society by great landlords and prosperous tenant farmers, who usually held the land under long leases. In France on the eve of the Revolution, probably 35 percent of the land was owned by the peasants who worked it. In this regard, the French peasants were more favored than those of any other European country, Britain included.

If the soil had been worked efficiently and if the population had remained stable, the distribution of the land would clearly have been socially advantageous. But, in fact, small peasant proprietors rarely had the resources to adopt new techniques, and their very numbers, apparently growing rapidly, obstructed their efforts. The society of small farmers was therefore vulnerable to population pressures and was easily disturbed by violent movements in prices—two major characteristics of eighteenth-century economic history, as we have seen. Because of poor transportation, one region could easily suffer a food shortage or even famine while neighboring areas were enjoying relative plenty. The pattern of land distribution in France and the character of rural society, superficially so favorable to the peasant, was thus also a source of acute unrest in the countryside.

In the regions close to the Mediterranean Sea, difficult geographical and climatic conditions—the often rugged terrain, thin soil, and a dearth of summer rain—did not readily allow the introduction of new techniques. The peasants continued to work their lands much as they had in the Late Middle Ages and for the same poor reward. The eastern regions of the Holy Roman Empire, Poland, and Russia had participated hardly at all in the commercial expansion of the early modern period; capital remained scarce and interest rates high. The political fragmentation of the empire and a paucity of transportation in Poland and Russia limited the size of the markets and the incentives to higher production. Areas close to the Baltic Sea, such as east Prussia, benefited from the growing demand for cereals in Western countries, but on the whole, Eastern Europe was not to experience the full force of agricultural change until the next century.

## IV. THE NEW SHAPE OF INDUSTRY
❈

In manufacturing, the essential achievement of the Industrial Revolution was an enormous increase in the productivity of labor. This was attributable to two innovations: the development of more efficient tools and machines, and the exploitation of new sources of energy. Economists would call this process "factor substitution," whereby capital, represented by the new tools and machines, was substituted for the skills and energy of workers. Initially, the new tools were cheap and simple enough to be used by artisans in the home or in small workshops. But the growing complexity of machinery, in particular the application of steam, called into being a new social unit—the factory. This new system of production changed the face of the great European cities and brought in its wake acute new social and political problems.

## Coal and Iron

The most successful innovations of the Industrial Revolution were dependent upon efficient utilization of raw materials, particularly cheap metals such as iron, which could be formed into machines, and cheap fuel such as coal. Countries poorly endowed with these resources (as, for example, the Mediterranean lands of Europe) faced formidable obstacles in their industrial growth. England, on the other hand, was well supplied, and its deposits of coal were found in convenient proximity to its iron ore.

Since the Late Middle Ages, the English economy had been handicapped by a shortage of wood, as the once-great forests had been progressively cut down. Consequently England increasingly turned to the use of coal as fuel, to heat homes, brew beer and ale, heat the vats for dyeing cloth, or fire the furnaces for making glass, pottery, or bricks. As miners began taking coal from deeper veins, they often penetrated beneath the water table and faced the critical task of pumping out the water. The need for powerful pumps stimulated experiments to harness steam in the late seventeenth century. A successful solution came with the development of the Savery and Watt engines. In the nineteenth century when steam was used to propel ships and trains, coal could be transported cheaply from mine to furnace. This allowed the price of coal to plummet.

In one process, however, coal was not satisfactory: the smelting of iron. Here the fuel had to be burned in direct contact with the iron ore, and mineral impurities in the coal combined with the iron to make an unsatisfactory product. Ironmasters traditionally used charcoal in the making of high-quality, malleable or wrought iron, but charcoal was expensive and the output of wrought iron consequently limited. In 1709 Alexander Darby succeeded in smelting ore with coke prepared from coal, but his invention had little immediate impact on the industry. Ironmasters used coke for smelting pig iron, which could be cast but not worked or machined. To refine the metal into wrought iron or steel, they continued to use charcoal.

But the demand for and price of iron rose after 1760, and this stimulated the development of new techniques. In the early 1780s Henry Cort devised the puddling process, the first commercially feasible effort to purify iron using coke alone. This invention freed ironmaking from dependence on forests. Ironmasters were simultaneously growing more adept at utilizing the metal. Perhaps the most skilled of them was John Wilkinson, a man with boundless faith that iron would become the basic building material of the new age. His improved techniques for boring cylinders made both better steam engines and better cannons possible. He built the first iron bridge in the world over the Severn River in 1779, experimented with iron rails, launched an iron boat, and at his death was buried in an iron coffin.

Low-cost metal, which could be precisely machined, and low-cost fuel, in turn, removed the chief obstacles to major and continuing improvements in the techniques of making goods.

## Inventions in Textile Production

In Great Britain the industry that led all others in growth and technological improvements was the manufacture of cotton cloth. Its beginnings were modest; wool had been

One visible marvel of early industrial progress was the first iron bridge, constructed near Coalbrookdale, England, in 1779 by the metalurgists Abraham Darby and John Wilkinson. (Photo: Ironbridge Gorge Museum)

the traditional basis of urban industry everywhere in Europe. Spinners could not produce a sturdy thread from cotton fiber, so weavers used it principally in combination with other threads, such as linen or wool.

In the early eighteenth century, several factors gave a powerful stimulus to both technological development and investment in cotton manufacturing. Trade with India had brought large quantities of muslin, calico, madras, and other fine cottons to England and built a healthy market. Wool could not be painted or printed, and cotton fabrics with bright designs appealed to the tastes of the age. To limit the competition that Indian cottons offered to domestically produced wool, in 1700 Parliament prohibited the importation of printed calicoes from India, Persia, and China and in 1721 even tried to prohibit the wearing of certain kinds of cotton cloth. By obstructing imports the government unwittingly provided a marvelous opportunity for the domestic entrepreneur. Fortune awaited

those who could market cottons comparable in quality and price to those once imported from the East.

The industry thus had a double task: to speed its production processes and to improve the quality of the finished cloth. Spinning could be done by women in conjunction with their daily chores, but weaving was slow and difficult work, almost always done by men. In 1738 John Kay of Lancashire, by profession a clockmaker, invented a flying shuttle, propelled by hammers instead of passed by hand. It accelerated the weaving process, removed restrictions on the width of the cloth, and reduced the number of workers needed on a broadcloth loom.

Now the weavers could work more quickly and efficiently than the spinners. To speed the production of thread and restore

**The developing market economy in Western Europe depended in part on improvement in transportation routes. In old-regime France, highways were maintained by royal engineers who used unpaid peasant labor under a much-resented system known as the** *corvée.*
(Photo: Giraudon/Art Resource)

equilibrium among the processes of manufacture, James Hargreaves devised his spinning jenny in the mid-1760s. The jenny, like the flying shuttle, required no source of power beyond the worker's muscle, and it could spin between 6 and 8 threads simultaneously; later models could make as many as 80. About the same time Richard Arkwright produced a spinner called the water frame that drew cotton fibers through rollers and twisted them into thread. Much dispute surrounds Arkwright's claim to this invention; it is likely that he pirated its basic design. But if his originality is questionable, he did possess qualities of imagination, daring, and

drive. He was an entrepreneur, one of the first self-made men to lead the Industrial Revolution.

The water frame, as its name suggests, was too large to be driven by human exertion. Arkwright first used horses, but within a few years he built a factory powered by a water mill. In 1785 he adopted the steam engine as his source of power, and the modern factory was born. Technical advances kept apace. A weaver named Samuel Crompton combined the features of the jenny and the water frame into a spinning mule—so called because it was a hybrid—which spun a fine and strong thread, exceeding in quality the best Indian product. Once more the equilibrium of the productive processes was disrupted, and the now-slower work of weaving restricted output. In 1784 Edmund Cartwright designed a power loom, though technical difficulties and the violent opposition of weavers limited the use of the loom until after the Napoleonic wars.

Other inventions accelerated other processes in cotton manufacturing during the last two decades of the century. An American, Eli Whitney, produced the cotton gin, which mechanized and enormously accelerated the separation of seed from fiber in the raw cotton. Sir Thomas Bell developed a method for printing the cotton cloth on cylindrical copper presses, and British and Continental inventors improved the chemical processes of bleaching and tinting the cloth.

Cotton production soared. Lancashire, with its great city of Manchester, and the neighboring counties became the great centers of cotton manufacture, soon serving the entire world. These were thinly settled areas before the eighteenth century, with few incorporated towns and no established guild systems to obstruct innovation. Lancashire offered the further advantages of water power, coal, and a good harbor, Liverpool. In 1743 England had imported about 1 million pounds of raw cotton; the figure was over 60 million by the turn of the century. And by the early 1820s cotton exports made up 46 percent of Britain's export trade.

## Harnessing Steam

Arkwright's water frame, Crompton's spinning mule, and Cartwright's power loom all required energy beyond the ability of people or horses to provide. Even earlier, as we have seen, the mining industry had developed a critical need for cheap power. Since ancient times people had noticed that steam exerts strong pressure. The third-century Greek scientist Hero of Alexandria had employed a jet of steam to spin a small wheel; the account of his experiments, translated into English in 1575, helped alert scholars to a simple means by which heat could be converted into motion. However, the first experiments with engines powered by fire were based on another principle: the pressure the atmosphere exerts against a vacuum.

In the seventeenth century several scientists—among them Pascal in France and Otto von Guericke in Germany—proved that the atmosphere has weight. Guericke used atmospheric pressure to push a piston through a cylinder, overcoming the efforts of 20 men to restrain it. Sensational experiments like this one led directly to efforts to construct an "atmospheric engine." To create the vacuum, some inventors tried gunpowder, but the fuel was too unstable to control. Steam was more manageable, and before the end of the century, atmospheric machines that utilized the condensation of steam to create the needed vacuum were being designed both in England and on the Continent.

The inventor of what must be considered the first commercially successful atmospheric engine was an Englishman, Thomas Savery, who described his invention to the public in a book published in 1702 and significantly entitled *The Miner's Friend*. Working as a pump, Savery's engine allowed the steam to come into direct contact with the water it was moving; this condensed the steam, dissipated heat, and rendered the pump woefully inefficient. However, Savery's engine at least proved that a fire pump was a practical possibility. A decade later another Englishman, Thomas Newcomen, returned to the piston and cylinder design and completely separated the engine from the pump. Although it still wasted a great deal of power, its reintroduction of the piston made it more efficient than Savery's by a third, and Newcomen engines were soon being used not only in Great Britain but in Hungary, Austria, France, and Denmark.

In the 1760s a young mechanic and instrument maker working at the University of Glasgow, James Watt, was given the task of repairing a small Newcomen engine used in scientific lectures. He recognized its two major inefficiencies: its great weight in relation to its power output and the quantities of fuel it required. Fascinated by the problem, he redesigned the machine and made the fundamental change of providing a separate chamber for the spent steam to condense in. His first engine, patented in 1769, was essentially an improved Newcomen engine, still relying on atmospheric pressure for its principal motive force.

But Watt had also recognized the advantage of using the pressure of expanding steam directly. The implementation of this idea took many years and required new levels of precision in machining cylinders and pistons, new designs for valves, and new knowledge of lubricants and the properties of steam itself. Watt's first practical model incorporating this principle, patented in 1782, was nearly three times more efficient than the Newcomen engine, its distant parent. He also devised a system of gears, called the sun and planet, for converting the reciprocating motion of the piston to the rotary motion needed to drive most machines. A still more important invention was the governor, or flywheel, which smoothed the movements of the engine.

Watt's partner, the industrialist Matthew Boulton, shared the merit of placing the inventions at the service of the economy. The site of Boulton's plant was Birmingham, which became the first great center for the manufacture of these new and powerful machines. From the 1780s on, the steam engine was giving power to factories as well as pumps; some 500 were built before 1800.

Even these early machines represented a remarkable improvement over traditional sources of power, ranging as they did between 6 and 20 horsepower. The average man working hard can muster about one-tenth horsepower, or about 75 watts. This would not be enough to drive most of the major appliances in American homes today, such as washers, vacuum cleaners, dryers, even beaters and blenders. The horse itself works continuously at a power output of only one-half horsepower. James Watt himself first defined the unit of horsepower as 33,000 foot-pounds per minute, but this could be achieved only by the strongest horses and only for short periods. So poor in power output are animals—people and horses—that even before the advent of the steam engine they were far surpassed by windmills and water mills.

The largest windmills in the eighteenth century could develop probably as much as 50 horsepower, but perhaps two-thirds of this was lost in friction as the power was transmitted from the rotors to the pump or mill. The best water mills of the period seem to have produced 10 horsepower, but most of them rarely surpassed 5. Still, this would replace 10 or more horses and save the miller the expense of feeding and caring for so many animals. With such advantages the construction of water mills rapidly quickened over the course of the eighteenth century; flowing water rather than steam powered the early phases of the Industrial Revolution. But then, too, sometimes winds ceased and streams froze, and water and wind power could not be transmitted from where it was harnessed to where it was needed. Steam engines could both produce more power more reliably and be placed where they were needed. To the traditional power-starved economy of Great Britain as of the world, the steam engine offered an enormous increment in its capacity to do work. More than any other invention, its appearance marks the advent of a new era.

## Industry on the Continent

Industrial growth was much slower on the Continent than in England. The numerous

In this design of a blast furnace, taken from a
French copper engraving of the eighteenth century, the large water wheel powers the bellows,
which, in turn, supply the needed jets of air to
raise the temperature of the furnace. The continued importance of water power was a principal reason many early factories were built in
rustic settings.   (Photo: The Granger Collection)

# ❄ EXPERIENCES OF DAILY LIFE ❄
## *An Artisan of Paris*

The working people of the eighteenth century are, for the most part, silent people; we learn of them chiefly from what their rich and educated contemporaries wrote about them. One salient exception is a journal written by a Parisian artisan named Jacques-Louis Ménétra. Begun in 1764, revised and enlarged continuously up to 1803, the journal is written in a deliberately misspelled and ungrammatical French without punctuation or even paragraphs. Ménétra seems to have been intent on putting distance between his autobiography and the literary conventions of his age. He wanted to be his own person, in literature and in life.

Born in 1738, he was, like many babies of his times, dispatched to the countryside to be nursed. But unlike many babies so dispatched, he survived. His mother died before his second birthday, and his grandmother took chief responsibility for rearing him. He attended the neighborhood parochial school (there were more than 500 such schools at Paris, and literacy was widespread even among the poor). There he learned reading and writing, his Catholic catechism, and singing. According to his boastful journal, he excelled in all scholastic activities and particularly in music. At school he also developed a lifelong antagonism toward the clergy and a philosophical aversion to Catholic dogma. He became a self-taught free thinker, a *philosophe* of the faubourgs.

The tenor of eighteenth-century life, as depicted in the journal, was violent, even for children. He once suffered a broken jaw when his father beat him. After completion of parish school, Jacques-Louis was apprenticed to a glazier (this was also his father's trade), and in this art, too, he claims to have excelled. Young French artisans, upon completion of their apprenticeship, became "companions" (*compagnons*) or journeymen, skilled workers who worked for wages in another's employ. The companions formed their own associations, a kind of trade union, which gave them solidarity in confronting competitors and bosses.

**Page from the journal of Jacques-Louis Ménétra, an artisan of Paris.** (Photo: Bibliothèque Historique de la Ville de Paris

Young *compagnons* also commonly made a tour of France, moving from town to town to gain money and experience. Ménétra made two such tours, extending over seven years. His wanderings took him from Brest to Bayonne, to Marseilles, even to Geneva in Switzerland. His journal boasts of his achievements in working glass; it also describes innumerable "pranks"—tricks he played on employers, companions, Jews, almost anyone. Although physically a small man, he frequently participated in brawls. But most notably, the memoirs include a long list of sexual exploits. Ménétra seemingly never met an attractive woman who could just say no.

Ménétra on his journeys claims to have had sexual relations with 52 women, not including his frequent visits to prostitutes. He names none of his conquests. His cool and factual list of sexual encounters is not pornographic; it is not even titillating. Among his loves were a marquise, three nuns, three peasant women, and six serving girls; all the other women he seduced were widows, wives, or daughters he met in the course of his daily labors. His sexual chronicle, recorded without passion, may reflect a kind of artisan animosity against those who employed and exploited him. The companions traveling together also often shared prostitutes or seduced the same women; sex served as a kind of male bonding. But this was also, in a way, staid, conventional sex; not a hint of sexual deviancy, on his part or the part of any companion, ever colors his narratives.

Upon returning to Paris in 1764, Ménétra married at age 27. This was again typical for males of the period. His journal does not even mention his bride's name. By 1770 he was the father of two living children, a girl and a boy, but his relations with his children seem hardly more loving than the relations his father had had with him. After marriage, the sexual affairs with other women declined to a modest 13. With the aid of his wife's dowry, he set up his own glass shop; he was now, like his father before him, a master glazier.

He was 51 when the Revolution broke out in 1789. As the Revolution turned toward greater radicalism, Ménétra moved into the ranks of the Parisian radicals known as the *sans-culottes*. He participated in several revolutionary assemblies and held several offices. But as the radical tide ebbed, Ménétra changed too. The last pages in his journal, written in 1802 and 1803 (it is not known precisely when he died), sang the praises of the Napoleonic regime.

The journal is deeply puzzling. Several incidents he describes could not have happened (the persons involved were already dead at the dates he gives); others he took from familiar folk tales and wove them into his life, as if he had witnessed them himself. Was he really so irresistible to anonymous women? He claims to have conversed with and even to have played checkers with the famous *philosophe* Jean-Jacques Rousseau. This is highly unlikely. Ménétra wrote his journal in an apparent effort to justify his life. It is hard to know who he thought would be his judges. It is hard even to see what standards he was applying. He seems to have acted without principle, without commitment to family, profession, or regime. He did it his way. Nonetheless, his journal preserves the authentic voice of a common man of eighteenth-century France—a captivating voice, even when it relates only dreams, even when it does not tell the truth.

Ménétra's chronicle is available in English translation by Arthur Goldhammer under the title *Journal of My Life*, with an introduction and commentary by Daniel Roche, foreword by Robert Darnton (1986). ❈

political divisions, tolls and tariffs, and the difficulties of transport restricted the size of markets. Continental society was more stratified than the English and did not develop effective mechanisms for recruiting the sons of nobles and gentry for business careers. It was also apparently less wealthy and could not initially generate a strong demand for industrial products. Business enterprises tended to be small, largely restricted to members of the same family, and cautious in policy. Cultural attitudes still placed high prestige on the life of the country gentleman, and this blocked the flow of people and capital from agriculture to manufactures.

Yet the Continental countries were experiencing important industrial changes, if not a revolution, in the eighteenth century. In France, cotton industries were taking root in Alsace, Normandy, and the region of Lille on the borders of the Austrian Netherlands. At Rouen, in Normandy, the largest center of cotton manufacture, production grew by 107 percent between 1732 and 1766. John Kay introduced his flying shuttle at Rouen in that period, and toward the end of the century the industry, while still comparatively backward, was adopting English-model mechanical spinners. The silk cloth industry, first promoted by Colbert, enjoyed a comparable boom, benefiting from the growing affluence of eighteenth-century fashionable society. At Lyons, the center of silk manufacture with a population of perhaps 143,000, the silk shops alone came to employ some 30,000 workers.

Coal production was also expanding. At Anzin, in northeastern France, one of the earliest centers of large-scale coal mining, output grew by 681 percent between 1744 and 1789. Iron manufacture at first lagged behind. The first foundry utilizing coke rather than charcoal went into operation only in 1769, and the industry's total output increased by only 72 percent in the half-century preceding 1789. Nonetheless, the iron as well

as the coal works furnished France early, if still restricted, examples of the factory system; they also equipped it with an armaments industry destined to serve it well during the wars of the French Revolution.

Switzerland, too, was a region of early industrial growth. Its ancient mercantile traditions, abundant resources in water power, and strategic position on the passes linking northern and southern Europe gave it distinct advantages in developing cotton manufactures and other forms of light industry. French Flanders (the southern half of the Austrian Netherlands), the valley of the lower Rhine, Silesia (acquired by Prussia in 1741), and Bohemia-Moravia were other centers of modest but real industrial growth, especially in textiles. In Germany and Central Europe the wars and reforms of the French revolutionary period, while frequently disruptive, also served to eradicate many of the institutional obstacles to trade. Growth still came slowly, and no Continental region could challenge the industrial supremacy of England before 1850. But well in advance of that date, these areas were laying the basis for a strong leap forward.

While changing its basic methods of raising food and producing goods, European society was also reforming its fundamental institutions and principles of government.

## V. CONSTITUTIONAL CONFLICTS
❈

The great expansion in population, the growth of the economy, and changes in other aspects of eighteenth-century life disturbed the political structures of European society. Groups within various states believed, often with good reason, that their governments were unresponsive to their needs. They agitated for constitutional reforms, which would ensure them a stronger voice in the determination of policy. The latter half of the century was a period of high political tension, constitutional crises, and spirited debate over the proper functions and organization of government.

## The Estates

To understand the nature of the constitutional crises, we must first recall a salient characteristic of government under the old regimes. In virtually all the governments of Europe, a role of major importance was assigned to the corporations of citizens known as estates. By definition an estate was a functional group within society—clerics, who prayed; nobles, who fought and counseled; merchants, who traded; and artisans and peasants, who labored. Birth or appointment gave people admission to the various estates, and membership conferred certain distinctive rights and obligations. Through parliaments, assemblies, or diets, the estates were also supposed to play a role in making government decisions.

Traditionally, the clergy constituted the First Estate and the nobles the Second, but usually these two groups maintained a common aristocratic viewpoint. The ruler was also an estate, considered a corporation of one in his or her person—or rather, office; the ruler had, in the political imagery of the day, another body that never died. This is implied in the usual acclamation of subjects at the death of their sovereign: "The king is dead. Long live the king!" Beneath these privileged orders was the estate of the common people, the Third Estate in France or simply the commons in England. In most European domains this was the most amorphous and the least influential of the constituent bodies of society.

The estates were developing self-awareness and political ambition in the eighteenth century, and most remarkably, in the latter half even the Third Estate came to exert its latent power. The rise to prominence and power of the common people at the expense of the hitherto dominant aristocratic orders makes this period, as one historian calls it, the "age of the democratic revolution."[4]

## Monarchical Reforms

In the great eighteenth-century struggle over the exercise of power, the rulers were often the first to seek and effect constitutional change. The rights and immunities of the separate estates, primarily the aristocratic orders, reduced their fiscal resources and often deprived them of authority in conducting foreign affairs and pursuing internal reform. The privileges and monopolies enjoyed by provinces, towns, and guilds restrained trade, hampered economic growth, and militated against the common welfare, of which eighteenth-century heads of state increasingly believed themselves the chief defenders.

The enlightened absolutists of the period made an attack on obstructive privilege a usual part of their policy, and many of them may be considered crowned constitutional reformers. Sweden offers perhaps the best example. A constitutional reform, dated 1720, had established a four-house Diet, or Riksdag. (Uniquely, in Europe, the peasantry in Sweden formed the Fourth Estate.) The reform of 1720 severely limited the king's powers. He could not tax, change the laws, or make war, peace, or alliances without the Diet's agreement. The Diet itself offered no effective leadership because it was divided into hostile factions, especially among the nobles, who spent their energies in ceaseless battles for office and patronage and readily

---

[4] See especially R. R. Palmer, *The Age of the Democratic Revolution,* 1959–1964.

sold their support to foreign powers eager to influence Swedish policy, notably France or Russia.

In 1771 a new king trained in France and imbued with liberal ideas, Gustavus III, ascended the throne. The following year, with the aid of the army and French support, he mounted a coup d'état against the Diet. At the point of bayonets, he forced a constitution on the houses—the first comprehensive, written document of its kind adopted by a European state. It gave the king broader, if still limited, powers: The Diet could assemble only on royal summons and could discuss only what the king proposed, though its agreement was still necessary for new taxes and laws.

Gustavus then proceeded to remake Swedish institutions, almost without the Diet's participation. He changed the laws governing ownership and inheritance of land, opened offices to all classes, reformed the courts, tried to suppress corruption, established freedom of the press and of religion, and lifted restrictions on trade in grain. Stung by the reforms, which often touched their privileges, the nobles grew ever more disgruntled and from 1786 on, openly challenged the king's authority. In 1788 they refused to support him in a war he had declared against Russia. In response, through the Act of Union and Security the next year, Gustavus once more altered the constitution, allocating to the king sole authority in foreign affairs and still further diminishing the role of the aristocracy in the Swedish state. Deprived of constitutional means of expressing their dissent, the dissatisfied nobles conspired against the king, who was shot dead at a masquerade in 1792.

If Gustavus's career offers an excellent example of fundamental reforms imposed from above, it also shows the violent opposition such policies could evoke from the aristocracy. In many European states the aristocracy was not content simply to defend its traditional privileges but agitated for a still larger share in the exercise of power.

## Aristocratic Resurgence

Europe's aristocracies had understandable cause for discontent with the changes occurring in the eighteenth century. The growth of trade, the expansion of capital, and pervasive inflation left many nobles hardpressed economically, and as a countermeasure, many of them tried to reactivate their ancient and half-forgotten feudal prerogatives over the peasants. In the political sphere as well, monarchs were allocating a progressively smaller place to the nobles in the business of government.

Aristocracies all over Europe thus sought to advance their fortunes and consolidate what they took to be their rightful place under their countries' constitutions. Armed with the ideas of Montesquieu, they claimed that nobles had the exclusive right to serve as the chief counselors of the king as well as the obligation of leading the community in the conduct of its important affairs. By the last decades of the century, the aristocracy had, in fact, secured a near-monopoly over high offices in both the state and the Church. In 1781, for example, the rank of commissioned officer in the French army was limited almost exclusively to those who could show four generations of nobility. And on the eve of the Revolution, the 18 archbishops, 118 bishops, and 8000 canons (high ecclesiastics) in the French Church were all of noble extraction. Simultaneously, aristocrats demanded that local assemblies of estates, which they dominated or hoped to dominate, be granted a larger share of political power.

Perhaps the best example of a revolution led by the aristocracy in support of such claims arose in the Austrian Netherlands

**Joseph II's bold agrarian reforms stirred up a hornet's nest of opposition among noble landlords. The monarch is shown here visiting a peasant's field.** (Photo: Austrian Press & Information Service)

(Belgium). The 10 provinces were governed under charters granted by the Hapsburgs and other rulers, which dated back to the Middle Ages. Representative assemblies, which controlled governments in all the provinces, largely determined the laws and imposed the taxes, apparently the lightest in the whole of Europe. Guilds, whose privileges similarly dated from the Middle Ages, were particularly strong in the Flemish towns and tightly regulated the economy.

In the 1780s Holy Roman Emperor Joseph II of Austria, as part of a general reform of his realm, sought to centralize and modernize Hapsburg administration of the southern Netherlands. He tried to abolish the special privileges enjoyed by the 10 provinces, and in the interest of freeing the economy, he also sought to break the guild monopolies. Much to the alarm of the United Provinces and Britain, he tried as well to reopen the port of

Antwerp, which had been closed to international trade since 1648. These changes were coupled with other liberal reforms—the abolition of torture, the introduction of religious toleration, the suppression of some monasteries, and the important social reforms for the rural population that were discussed in Chapter 19. Finally, in 1787 he overhauled the court system, under which the estates had exercised their chief judicial and administrative prerogatives.

The patricians protested these reforms. In late 1788 the representative assemblies of two provinces refused to grant Joseph money, and the emperor retaliated by revoking their ancient charters, with the aim of bringing them under the direct and unlimited powers of the crown. The frightened aristocrats organized secret societies, called Pro Aris et Focis ("For Altars and Hearths"), the name implying an objection to Joseph's treatment of the Catholic Church. The following year, doubtless encouraged by the defiance of the Estates General in France, the provinces declared their independence. In the face of concerted opposition, Austrian rule collapsed. But the revolutionaries now found themselves divided. One party, led by a Brussels lawyer, held that independence from Austria sufficed and no further changes were required. The provinces should be ruled by their assemblies, which meant by their traditional aristocracies. But a second party, led by another lawyer, sought to limit the privileges of the provinces, guilds, and assemblies. These democrats, as they were called, now faced the aristocrats in a struggle over the constitution of the land. In 1790, with the support of the Church and most of the peasants, the conservatives prevailed, and the leaders of the democratic faction were forced into exile.

The death of Joseph II the same year and the succession of his brother, Leopold II further complicated the picture. Leopold was about as sympathetic to reform as a monarch could be in the eighteenth century, and he energetically sought to make a common front with the democrats against the aristocrats. The coalition was successful, and Austrian rule was restored in the provinces in December. The democrats flocked back, but the coalition between the monarch and the people never had the opportunity to reform the government freely. The increasing radicalism of the Revolution in France made Leopold progressively suspicious of the intentions of his own democratic allies. Finally, in 1792 French revolutionary armies poured into the Austrian Netherlands and ended all possibility of peacefully wrought change.

## Popular Movements in the British Empire

In Great Britain a conflict arose involving the king, the aristocracy, and the people in the late eighteenth century. As elsewhere, a major role in initiating a popular movement was played by a reforming monarch, George III (1760–1820). Unlike his namesake grandfather and great-grandfather, George had been born in England and knew the land, its language, and its political system well. He was also intent on advancing royal authority. He did not seek to bypass Parliament but rather tried, much as the Whig ministers had before him, to control its members through patronage and influence. The Whigs saw royal ambition and the system through which it worked as a threat to their own traditional hegemony. Not only did they oppose the king and his ministers in Parliament, but they enlisted the support of reform elements originating outside of Parliament itself.

One such group, known as the Radical Dissenters, was led by such men as the clergyman Richard Price and the scientist Joseph Priestley. The appearance of daily newspapers (*The Morning Post* was founded in 1772 and *The Times* in 1785) gave them a marvelous means of spreading their views, and they leveled destructive criticism against the defects of the British political system. Characteristically, they called for representation proportionate to population, stricter laws against corruption, exclusion of royal officeholders from the Commons, and freedom of the press.

The most notorious of popular agitators was a journalist named John Wilkes. Ambitious, eloquent, and ruthless, Wilkes purchased a seat in Parliament with the aid of an opportune marriage. But success through traditional channels came too slowly, and he assumed the risky but promising role of a popular champion for reform. He viciously attacked in print the king's prime minister, and indirectly the king himself, over the terms of the Treaty of Paris in 1763, which he considered unfavorable to Britain's imperial interests. The government arrested him for sedition and libel on a general warrant—that is, with the name of the accused omitted. During his trial crowds in London marched in his support shouting "Wilkes and liberty," and the courts quashed the indictment. The government then accused Wilkes of having authored a pornographic poem, and this time he fled to France. There he stayed for four years, but in 1768, still under indictment, he returned to stand once more for Parliament. At his second attempt he was elected. Three times the Commons refused to seat him, and three times he was reelected. With the ardent support of radicals and to the acclaim of the London crowds, Wilkes finally took his seat.

The agitation for parliamentary reform in Great Britain was soon swept up in the larger issues raised by the outbreak of the French Revolution. The events of 1789 across the Channel naturally frightened certain social groups, but the Revolution's opponents were initially drowned out in a chorus of enthusiasm that swept the literate classes in Britain as on the Continent. It was hard, after all, to defend what was taken to be the traditional despotism of the French monarchy. But the increasing radicalism of the Revolution generated disenchantment and hostility.

The Wilkes affair and the agitation for parliamentary reform characterized the reform movements in a British context; revolutionary action did not. Wilkes and other radicals appealed not only to the London crowds but also to traders, craftsmen, and the like who did have the franchise and were thus able to express their political dissatisfaction by voting Wilkes and other men displeasing to the government into Parliament. Most radicals called only for the reform, not the replacement, of the British political system. They still retained some measure of respect for the nation's political traditions.

## Ireland and North America

Great Britain did face revolutionary agitation in her overseas possessions, notably Ireland and North America. In Ireland a largely Protestant gentry was demanding autonomy for the country's Parliament under the British king and reform in the trade laws, which injured the Irish economy. But the religious and cultural gulf that divided the Protestant gentry from the Catholic people prevented an effective alliance between them, and the throne was usually able to purchase the loyalty of the upper classes with relatively minor concessions. In 1782, for example, in response to agitation led by the Protestant patriots Henry Flood and Henry Grattan, Britain gave the Irish Parliament the sought-for autonomy. This assured the loyalty of Irish gentry during the final phase of the American Revolution and the more difficult struggle with revolutionary France.

In its 13 North American colonies, Britain faced a much different situation. George III and his prime minister, Lord North, attempted to force the colonies to pay the costs, past and present, of their own defense. The policy would have meant a pronounced centralization of authority within the government of the British Empire.

The prominent landlords and merchants of the Eastern seaboard took the leadership in opposing the fiscal measures and the constitutional changes they implied. Like the upper classes in many European lands, they too appealed to the people. But the resistance in North America differed profoundly from comparable movements in Europe. The American social leaders could not appeal to a body of corporate privileges that the actions of the king were allegedly violating. They therefore appealed to the traditional rights

**The committee that drafted the Declaration of Independence included John Adams, Thomas Jefferson, and Benjamin Franklin, all shown here standing at the desk.** (Photo: Yale University Art Gallery)

enjoyed by all British subjects, regardless of rank, and to theories of popular sovereignty advanced particularly by John Locke; the Declaration of Independence was to give eloquent expression to these broad concepts. The same lack of a true estate system in colonial American society, the amorphous and fluid margins separating the social strata, further blunted the development of conflicts between patricians and the lower social orders, which so often occurred in Europe.

These differences partially explain the unique character of the American Revolution. Its effects on society were limited. But in the theory that supported it and in the close and continuing alliance between the upper and lower classes, it was perhaps the most democratic of the revolutions of the eighteenth century. It created the first state and government in which the exercise of power was explicitly declared to be based not on divine right or inherited privilege but on the consent of the governed. It also represented the first successful revolution of an overseas colony against a European country. The example and effects of the American Revolution were thus of major importance in the dissolution of Europe's old regimes.

# VI. THE FRENCH REVOLUTION
❊

The pivotal event of European history in the eighteenth century—some would say in the modern epoch—was the French Revolution. From its outbreak in 1789, the Revolution touched and transformed social values and political systems in France, in Europe, and eventually throughout the world. France's revolutionary regime conquered much of Western Europe with its arms and with its ideology, though not without considerable opposition at home and abroad. Its ideals defined the essential aspirations of modern liberal society, while its bloody conflicts posed the brutal dilemma of means versus ends. The revolutionaries advocated individual liberty, rejecting all forms of arbitrary constraints—guild monopolies on commerce, feudal charges laid upon the land, vestiges of servitude such as serfdom, and even (in 1794) black slavery overseas. They held that political legitimacy required constitutional government, elections, and legislative supremacy. They demanded civil equality for all, denying the claims of privileged groups, localities, or religions to special treatment and requiring the equality of all citizens before the law. A final revolutionary goal was expressed by the concept of fraternity, which meant that all citizens regardless of social class, region, or religion shared a common fate in society, and that the well-being of the nation sometimes superseded the interests of individuals. The resounding slogan of *Liberty, Equality, Fraternity* expressed social ideals to which most contemporary citizens of the Western world would still subscribe.

## Origins

Those who made the Revolution believed they were rising against tyrannical government, in which the people had no voice, and against inequality in the way obligations such as taxes were imposed and benefits distributed. Yet the government of France at that time was no more tyrannical or unjust than it had been in the past. On the contrary, a gradual process of reform had long been underway. What, then, set off the revolutionary upheaval? What failed in France's long-standing, long-accepted political system? What had changed?

An easy answer would be to point to the incompetence of King Louis XVI (1774–1792) and his queen, Marie Antoinette. Good-natured but weak and indecisive, Louis was a man of limited intelligence who lacked self-confidence and who preferred hunting deer to supervising the business of government. Worse yet, his young queen, a Hapsburg princess, was frivolous, meddlesome, and tactless. But even the most capable ruler could not have escaped challenge and crisis in the late eighteenth century. The roots of that crisis, not its mismanagement, claim the principal interest of historians.

In eighteenth-century France, as we have seen, intellectual ferment preceded political revolt. For decades the philosophes had bombarded traditional beliefs, institutions, and prejudices with devastating salvos. They undermined the confidence that traditional ways were the best ways. Yet the philosophes were anything but revolutionaries. Harboring deep-seated fears and suspicions of the uneducated masses, they never for a moment contemplated drastic change or upheaval. Nor did they question the fact that elites should rule society, but wished only that the elites should be more enlightened and more open.

Indeed, the Enlightenment had become respectable by the 1780s, a kind of intellectual establishment. Diderot's *Encyclopedia*, banned in the 1750s, was reprinted in a less

The Faubourg St.-Antoine was one of Paris's working-class quarters. In 1789 a dispute broke out between the workers and the owners of the Reveillon workshop, and the workers sacked both the shop and the owners' house. The French and Swiss Guards dispatched to punish them were met with stones and pieces of tile rained down from the rooftops. The soldiers fired on their attackers, killing several. The incident, here depicted in a slightly later etching, illustrates the high social tension prevailing at Paris before the convocation of the Estates General. (Photo: New York Public Library/Picture Collection)

expensive format with government approval in the 1770s. Most of France's 30 provincial academies—learned societies of educated citizens in the larger towns—had by that time been won over to the critical spirit and reformism of the Enlightenment, though not to its sometimes extreme secularism. Among the younger generation, the great cultural hero was Rousseau, whose *Confessions* (published posthumously in 1781) caused a sensation. Here Rousseau attacked the hypocrisy, conformity, cynicism, and corruption of high society's salons and aristocratic ways. Though he had not exemplified this in his personal life, Rousseau came across in his novels and autobiography as the apostle of a simple, wholesome family life; of conscience, purity, and virtue. As such, he was the great inspiration to the future generation of revolutionaries, but the word "revolution" never flowed from his pen.

More subversive perhaps than the writings of the "high enlightenment" was the underground literature that commanded a wide audience in France. The monarchy's censorship tried vainly to stop these "bad books," which poured in across the border through networks of clandestine publishers, smugglers, and distributors. What was this fare that the reading public eagerly devoured? Alongside a few banned works by the philosophes, there was a mass of gossip sheets, pulp novels, libels, and pornography under such titles as *Scandalous Chronicles* and *The Private Life of Louis XV*. Much of this material focused on the supposed goings-on in the fashionable world of Paris and Versailles. Emphasizing scandal and character assassination, this literature had no specific political content or ideology. But indirectly, it portrayed the French aristocracy as decadent and the French monarchy as a ridiculous despotism.

Royal officials and philosophes such as Voltaire alike regarded the authors of this material as "the excrement of literature." Indeed, writers who were forced to earn their living by turning out such stuff must have been embittered by the need to waste their talents and ideals in this way. Their resentment at being stuck on the bottom rung in the world of letters would explode once the Revolution began in 1789. In itself, however, the "literary underground" was not the cause of that explosion.

Did the structure of French society, then, provoke the Revolution? Karl Marx, and the many historians inspired by him, certainly believed so, seeing it as the necessary break marking the transition from feudalism to capitalism. In the words of historian Georges Lefebvre, "The clergy and nobility preserved the highest rank in the legal structure of the country, but in reality economic power, personal abilities and confidence in the future had passed largely to the bourgeoisie. Such a discrepancy never lasts forever. The Revolution of 1789 restored the harmony between fact and law." In this view, the French middle classes, gaining in wealth during the eighteenth century, resented the privileges of the nobility and the obstacles that the social order placed in the path of their ambition. Though they framed their ideology in universal terms, the middle classes actually fought in 1789 to change the political and social systems in their own interests.

Three decades of research have rendered this theory of the Revolution's origins untenable. Its critics question the coherence or even the veritable existence of a sizeable capitalist bourgeoisie in eighteenth-century France, and point out that the leaders of the Revolution in 1789 were lawyers, administrators, and liberal nobles, rarely merchants or industrialists. Secondly, the barrier between the Second and Third Estates was porous, the lines of social division frequently (though not always) blurred. Many members of the middle class identified themselves as "living nobly"—as substantial rural property owners who did not work for a living. Conversely, wealthy nobles often invested in mining, overseas trade, and finance. Even more important, the gap between nobles and the middle classes was as nothing compared with the gulf that separated these groups from the common people of town and country. In this "revisionist" view, the bourgeoisie did not make the Revolution, so much as the Revolution made the bourgeoisie, in the sense that the reforms it achieved eventually bolstered their status and later helped stimulate growth in the market economy.

Yet the disruptive pressures at work in French society were numerous. Rapidly growing population produced both on the land and in the towns large numbers of young people seeking and often failing to attain a stable place in society. New ideas and attitudes rippled through the media of the day, despite the efforts of the censorship to curb the spread of material it deemed subversive. The nobility, long since banished by Louis XIV from an independent role in monarchical government, chafed at its exclusion, while the prosperous middle classes too aspired to a more active role. The monarchy struggled to contain these forces within the established social and political systems. Until the 1780s it succeeded, but then its troubles began in earnest.

## Fiscal Crisis

When he took the throne in 1774, Louis XVI tried to conciliate elite opinion by recalling the Parlements or sovereign law courts that his father had abolished in 1770. This concession to France's traditional "unwritten constitution" backfired, however, since the Parlements resumed their defense of privilege in opposition to reforms proposed by Jacques Turgot, Louis' new controller general of finances.

Turgot, a disciple of the philosophes and an experienced administrator, hoped to encourage economic growth by the policy of nonintervention, or laissez-faire. Thus he proposed to remove all restrictions on commerce in grain and to abolish the guilds. In addition, he tried to cut down on expenses at court, and to replace the obligation of peasants to work on the royal roads (the *corvée*) with a new tax on all landholders. Privately, he also considered establishing elected advisory assemblies to participate in local administration. Vested interests predictably viewed Turgot as a dangerous innovator. When agitation against him mounted at Versailles and in the Paris Parlement, Louis took the easy way out and dismissed his troublesome minister. With him went perhaps the last hope for significant reform in France under royal leadership.

The king then turned to a Protestant banker from Geneva with a reputation for financial wizardry, Jacques Necker. A shrewd man with a strong sense of public relations, Necker gained wide popularity. To finance the heavy costs of France's aid to the rebellious British colonies in North America, Necker avoided new taxes and instead floated a series of large loans at exorbitant interest rates as high as 10 percent. (England also financed its wars on credit, but because Parliament backed the Bank of England, which managed public finances responsibly and maintained public confidence in its notes, the English government could raise loans at 3 or 4 percent.)

By the 1780s royal finances were in a state of permanent crisis. Direct taxes on land, borne mainly by the peasants, were extremely high but levied inequitably. Great variations by province and numerous exemptions for privileged groups were regarded by those who benefited as "liberties" sanctified by tradition. Any attempt to revoke these privileges was bound to be attacked as tyranny. Meanwhile indirect taxes on commercial activity (customs duties, excise or sales taxes, and royal monopolies on salt and tobacco) hit hard at consumers, especially workers in the cities. Short of a complete overhaul of the tax system, little improvement in royal revenues could be expected, and the public would bitterly resist any additional tax burdens that the monarchy simply imposed. By the same token, the cycle of borrowing—the alternative to new or increased taxes—had reached its limits. New loans only raised the huge interest payments already being made. By the 1780s interest payments accounted for about half of the entire royal budget and created additional budget deficits of perhaps 150,000,000 livres each year.

When the king's new controller general, Calonne, pieced all this information together in 1787, he warned that, contrary to Necker's rosy projections, the monarchy was facing outright bankruptcy. Though no way had yet been found to win public confidence and forge a consensus for reform, the monarchy could no longer rely on old expedients to get by. Nor could it stand pat. New policies, bold innovations were essential. Calonne accordingly proposed to establish a new tax called the "territorial subvention," which would be levied on the yield of all landed property without exemptions. At the same time, he proposed to convene provincial assemblies elected by all large landowners to advise royal bureaucrats on the collection and allocation of revenues.

Certain that the Parlements would reject this scheme, Calonne prevailed on the king to convene an Assembly of Notables comprising about 150 influential men, mainly but not exclusively from the aristocracy. To Calonne's shock, the notables refused to endorse the decrees. Instead, they denounced the lavish spending of the court and insisted on auditing the monarchy's financial accounts. To save the day, Louis dismissed Calonne and appointed one of the notables, archbishop Brienne, in his place. Brienne now submitted the proposals to the Parlement, which not only rejected them but also demanded that Louis convene the Estates General, a body representing the clergy, nobility, and Third Estate, which had not met since 1614. Louis responded by dissolving the Parlement and sending its members into exile. But the outcry in Paris and the provinces against this arbitrary act was so loud that Louis backed down. After all, the whole purpose of Calonne's proposals had been to build public confidence and consensus for reform.

Facing bankruptcy and unable to float any new loans in this atmosphere, the king recalled the Parlements, reappointed Necker, and agreed to convene the Estates General in May 1789. In the opinion of the English traveler Arthur Young, France was "on the verge of a revolution, but one likely to add to the scale of the nobility and clergy." Determined opposition by the aristocracy was putting an end to absolutism. The question remained: What would take its place?

## From the Estates General to the National Assembly

The calling of the Estates General created extraordinary excitement across the land. When the king invited his subjects to express their opinions about this great event, hundreds did so in the form of pamphlets, and here the liberal or "patriot" ideology of 1789 first began to take shape. Patriots came from the ranks of the nobility and clergy as well as the middle classes, and they opposed the traditionalists whom they labeled as "aristocrats." Their top priority was the question of voting in the Estates General. While the king accorded the Third Estate twice as many delegates as the two higher orders, he refused to promise that the delegates would vote together ("by head") rather than separately in three chambers ("by order"). A vote by order meant that the two upper chambers would outweigh the Third Estate no matter how many deputies it had. The patriots hoped that the lines dividing the nobility from the middle class would crumble in a common effort by France's elites at reform. Instead, it appeared as if the Estates General might sharpen the lines of separation and enhance the role of the nobility.

It did not matter that the nobility had led the fight against absolutism. Even if they endorsed new, constitutional checks on absolutism and accepted equality in the allocation of taxes, nobles would hold vastly disproportionate powers if the Estates General voted by order. In the most influential of these pamphlets, Abbé Emmanuel Joseph Sieyès posed the question, "What is the Third Estate?" and answered flatly, "Everything." "And what has it been until now in the political order?" he continued, "Noth-

**Attacks on privilege were launched through the media of pamphlets and prints in 1789. The claims of the Third Estate easily translated into vivid imagery and caricature; this print was titled "The Awakening of the Third Estate."** (Photo: Collection VIOLLET)

ing." The nobility, he claimed, monopolized all the lucrative positions in society while doing little of its productive work. In the manifestos of Sieyès and other patriots, the enemy was no longer simply absolutism but privilege as well.

Unlike reformers in England, or the Belgian rebels against Joseph II, or even the American revolutionaries of 1776, the French patriots did not look back to historical traditions of liberty that had been violated. Rather they contemplated a complete break with a discredited past. As a basis for reform, they would substitute reason for tradition. This frame of mind helps explain why the French Revolution would be so radical.

For the moment, however, the patriots were far in advance of opinion at the grass roots. The king had invited citizens across the land to meet in their parishes to elect delegates to district electoral assemblies, and to draft grievance petitions (*cahiers*) setting forth their views. Highly traditional in tone, the great majority of rural *cahiers* complained only of particular local ills and expressed confidence that the king would redress them. Only a few *cahiers* from larger cities, including Paris, alluded to the concepts of natural rights or popular sovereignty that were appearing in patriot pamphlets. Very few demanded that France must have a written constitution, that sovereignty belonged to the nation, or that feudalism and regional privileges should be abolished. It is impossible, in other words, to read in the *cahiers* the future course of the Revolution. Still, they promoted widespread reflection on France's problems and encouraged the expectation that change would come. Their preparation was a stage in the rise of a revolutionary consciousness.

So too were the elections, whose royal ground rules were remarkably democratic. Virtually every adult male taxpayer was eligible to vote for electors, who, in turn, chose deputies for the Third Estate. The electoral assemblies were a kind of political seminar, where articulate local leaders emerged to be sent by their fellow citizens as deputies to Versailles. These deputies were a remarkable collection of men, though scarcely representative of the mass of the Third Estate. Dominated by lawyers and officials, there was not a single worker or peasant among them. In the elections for the First Estate, meanwhile, democratic procedures assured that parish priests rather than Church notables would form a majority of the delegates. And in the elections to the Second Estate, about one-third of the delegates could be described as liberal nobles or patriots.

Popular expectation that the monarchy would provide leadership in reform proved to be ill-founded. When the deputies met on May 5, Necker and Louis XVI spoke to them only in generalities, and left unsettled whether the estates would vote by order or by head. The upper two estates proceeded to organize their own chambers, but the deputies of the Third Estate balked. Inviting the others to join them, on June 17 the Third Estate took a decisive revolutionary step by proclaiming its conversion into a "National Assembly." A few days later 150 clergymen from the First Estate joined them. The king, who finally decided to cast his lot with the nobility, locked the Third Estate out of its meeting hall until a session could be arranged in which he would state his will. But the deputies moved to an indoor tennis court, and there swore that they would not separate until they had given France a constitution.

Ignoring this act of defiance, the king addressed the delegates of all three orders on June 23. He promised equality in taxation, civil liberties, and regular meetings of the Estates General at which, however, voting would be by order. France would be provided with a constitution, he pledged, "but the ancient distinction of the three orders will be conserved in its entirety." He then ordered the three orders to retire to their individual meeting halls. This, the Third Estate refused. When the royal chamberlain repeated his monarch's demand, the deputies' spokesman dramatically responded: "The assembled nation cannot receive orders." Startled by the determination of the patriots, the king backed down. For the time being, he recognized the National Assembly and ordered deputies from all three estates to join it.

Thus the French Revolution began as a nonviolent, "legal" revolution. By their own action, the delegates of France's districts and provinces ceased being the representatives of their particular constituents to the king, but became the representatives of the nation in its entirety. As such, they claimed to be the sovereign power in France—a claim that the king now seemed powerless to contest. In fact, however, he was merely biding his time until he could deploy his army to subdue the capital and overwhelm the deputies at Versailles. Twenty thousand royal troops were ordered into the Paris region, due to arrive sometime in July.

## The Convergence of Revolutions

The political struggle at Versailles was not occurring in isolation. Simultaneously, the mass of French citizens, already aroused by elections to the Estates General, were mobilizing over subsistence issues. The winter and spring of 1788–1789 had brought severe economic difficulties, as crop failures and grain shortages almost doubled the price of flour and bread on which the population depended for subsistence. Unemployed vagrants and beggars filled the roads, grain convoys and marketplaces were stormed by angry consumers, and relations between town and country were strained. This anxiety merged with rage over the behavior of "aristocrats" in Versailles. Parisians believed that food shortages and royal troops would be used to intimidate the people into submission. They feared an "aristocratic plot" against the Third Estate and the patriot cause.

When the king dismissed the still-popular Necker on July 11, Parisians correctly assumed that the counter-revolution was about to begin. Instead of submitting, they revolted. Protesting before royal troops (some of whom defected to the insurgents), burning the hated toll barriers that surrounded the capital, and seizing grain supplies, Parisian crowds then began a search for weapons. On the morning of July 14 they invaded the military hospital of the Invalides where they seized thousands of rifles without incident. Then they laid siege to the Bastille, an old fortress that had once been a major royal prison, where gunpowder was stored. There the small garrison did resist and a ferocious firefight erupted. Dozens of citizens were hit—providing the first martyrs of the Revolution—but the garrison soon capitulated. As they left, several were massacred by the infuriated crowd. Meanwhile, patriot electors ousted royal officials of the Paris city government, replaced them with a revolutionary municipality, and organized a citizens militia or national guard to patrol the city. Similar municipal revolutions occurred in 26 of the 30 largest French cities, thus assuring that the capital's defiance would not be an isolated act.

The Parisian insurrection of July 14 not only saved the National Assembly from annihilation but also altered the course of the Revolution by giving it a far more active, popular dimension. Again the king capitulated. Removing most of the troops around Paris, he traveled to the capital on July 17 and, to please the people, donned a cockade bearing the colors of white for the monarchy and blue and red for the city of Paris. This *tricolor* was to become the flag of the new France.

These events did not pacify the anxious and hungry people of the countryside, however. The sources of peasant dissatisfaction were many and long standing. Population growth and the parceling of holdings were reducing the margin of subsistence for many families, while the purchase of land by rich townspeople exerted further pressure. Seigneurial dues and church tithes weighed heavily upon most peasants. Now, in addition, suspicions were rampant that nobles were hoarding grain in order to stymie the patriotic cause. In July peasants in several regions sacked the castles of the nobles and burned the documents that recorded their feudal obligations. This peasant insurgency eventually blended into a vast movement known as the Great Fear. Rumors abounded that the vagrants who swarmed through the countryside were actually "brigands" in the pay of nobles who were marching on villages to destroy the new harvest and cow the peasants into submission. The fear was baseless, but it stirred up hatred and suspicion of the nobles, prompted a mass recourse to arms in the villages, and set off new attacks on châteaus and feudal documents. Peasant revolts and the Great Fear showed that the royal government was confronting a truly nationwide and popular revolution.

Peasant insurgency worried the deputies of the National Assembly, but they decided to appease the peasants rather than simply denounce their violence. On the night of August 4, representatives of the nobility and clergy vied with one another in renouncing their ancient privileges. This set the stage for the Assembly to decree "the abolition of feudalism" as well as the tithe, venality of office, regional privilege, and social privilege. Later, it is true, the Assembly clarified the August 4th decree to assure that property rights were maintained. While personal servitudes such as hunting rights, manorial justice, and labor services were suppressed without compensation, seigneurial dues were to end only if the peasants paid compensation to their lords. Most peasants, in fact, evaded this requirement by passive resistance, until pressure built in 1793 for the complete abolition of all seigneurial dues without compensation.

By sweeping away the old web of privileges, the August 4th decree permitted the Assembly to construct a new regime. Since it would take months to draft a constitution, the Assembly drew up a Declaration of the Rights of Man and Citizen to indicate the outline of its intentions. A rallying point for the future, the Declaration also stood as the death certificate of the old regime. It began with a ringing affirmation of equality: "Men are born and remain free and equal in rights. Social distinctions may be based only on common utility." The Declaration went on to pro-

claim the sovereignty of the nation as against the king or any other group, and the supreme authority of legitimate law. Most of its articles concerned liberty, defined as "the ability to do whatever does not harm another . . . whose limits can only be determined by law"; they specified freedom from arbitrary arrest; freedom of expression and of religion; and the need for representative government. The Declaration's concept of natural rights meant that the Revolution would be based on reason rather than history or tradition.

In his *Reflections on the Revolution in France*, published in 1790, the Anglo-Irish statesman Edmund Burke condemned this attitude, as well as the violence of 1789. In this most famous antirevolutionary tract, Burke argued that France had passed from despotism to anarchy in the name of misguided, abstract principles. Burke distrusted the simplicity of reason that the Assembly celebrated. In his view the complexity of institutions served the public interest: "prejudice [tradition] is the garb of hidden reason." Burke attacked the belief in natural rights that guided the revolutionaries; something was "natural," he believed, only if it resulted from long historical development and habit. Trying to wipe the slate of history clean was a grievous error since society "is a contract between the dead, the living, and the unborn." Society's main right, in Burke's view, was the right to be well-governed by its rulers. This argument did not, of course, go unchallenged in England or in France. In fact, Thomas Paine's tract, *The Rights of Man* (1792), written to refute Burke, won a far larger readership.

## The Restructuring of France

From 1789 to 1791, the National Assembly acted as a Constituent Assembly, laboring productively on a constitution for the new regime. While recognizing the civil rights of all French citizens, it effectively transferred political power from the monarchy and the privileged estates to the general body of propertied citizens, in which the former nobility remained as individuals without titles or privileges. At the center, the constitution created a limited monarchy with a clear separation of powers. Real sovereignty lay in the legislative branch, which would consist of a single house (the Legislative Assembly), elected for two years by a system of indirect voting. The king was to name and dismiss his ministers, but he was given only a suspensive or delaying veto over legislation; if a bill passed the Assembly in three successive years, it would become law even without royal approval.

The Assembly limited the franchise to "active" citizens who paid a minimal sum in taxes, but the property qualification was higher for those standing for public office. Under this system about two-thirds of adult males attained the right to vote for electors who would choose deputies, and also to elect certain local officials directly. Although it favored the wealthy, the system was vastly more democratic than the political structure in Britain.

Political rights did not extend, however, to women. In delegations to the Assembly and in pamphlets such as Olympe de Gouges' *Declaration of the Rights of Women* (1791), women's rights activists demanded suffrage for women without success. Sieyès spoke for most deputies when he answered that women contributed little to the public establishment and should have no direct influence on government. Besides which, he claimed, women were too emotional and easily misled. This weakness of character made it imperative that they be kept out of public life and devote themselves to their "natural" nurturing and maternal roles. Yet the formal exclusion of women from politics did not mean that they remained passive spectators.

Women were active combatants in the local conflicts over religious policy that will be discussed in the next section. In the towns they agitated over subsistence issues, formed auxiliaries to the local Jacobin clubs (and a handful of independent clubs), participated in civic festivals, and did relief work. Nor was the Revolution indifferent to women's rights. Its remarkably egalitarian inheritance law insisted that all children regardless of sex were entitled to an equal share of a family's estate. And in 1794 a national system of free primary education provided salaried teachers for both boys and girls.

While the Assembly excluded women from "active" citizenship without much debate, other groups posed a greater challenge on how to apply the rights of man to French society. In eastern France, for example, where most of France's Jews resided, public opinion scorned Jews as an alien race unentitled to citizenship. Eventually, however, the Assembly rejected that argument and extended civil and political equality to Jews. A similar debate raged over the status of free negroes or mulattoes in France's Caribbean colonies. In St. Domingue, it will be recalled, alongside the 35,000 whites and 500,000 slaves lived 28,000 free negroes, some of whom owned slaves themselves. White planters, in alliance with merchants who traded with the islands, were most concerned to preserve slavery. To this end, they demanded control over racial policy in the islands. Only by maintaining racial distinctions and disenfranchising free negroes, they argued, could they ensure the foundation of slavery. Despite Jacobin opposition, the Assembly adopted this view. In response, the mulattoes rebelled, and the unrest caused by their abortive uprising eventually helped ignite a slave rebellion, which, in turn, led to the independence of the island, now known as Haiti.

With regard to local government, the

In October 1789, the hungry women of Paris marched to Versailles and forced the king and the royal family to return to Paris with them. With the government now located in the city, the Parisian populace was able to exert a much stronger influence upon it. (Photo: New York Public Library/Picture Collection)

Constituent Assembly abolished the Parlements and intendants, and obliterated the political identity of France's historic provinces. The Assembly instead divided the nation's territory into 83 departments of roughly equal size (see Maps 20.1 and 20.2). Unlike the old provinces, each department would have exactly the same institutions. The departments were, in turn, subdivided into districts, cantons, and communes (the common designation for a village or town). On the one hand, this administrative transformation promoted local autonomy: The citizens of each department, district, and commune elected their own local officials, and in that sense political power was decentralized. On the other hand, these local governments were subordinated to the national legislature in Paris; they became instruments of greater national integration and uniformity.

The new administrative map also created the boundaries for judicial reform. Sweeping away the entire judicial system of the old regime, the revolutionaries established a justice of the peace in each canton, a civil court in each district, and a criminal court in each department. The judges on all tribunals were to be elected. While rejecting the use of juries in civil cases, the Assembly decreed that felonies would be tried by juries; if the jury convicted, judges would apply the mandatory sentences that were established in the Assembly's new penal code. Defendants also gained the right to counsel for the first time.

**MAP 20.1 FRANCE: PROVINCES AND REGIONS BEFORE 1789**
(From Breunig, Charles, *The Age of Revolution and Reaction, 1789–1850,* New York: Norton, 1970, p. 18.)

In civil law, the Assembly encouraged arbitration and mediation to avoid the time-consuming and expensive processes of formal litigation. In general, the revolutionaries hoped to make the administration of justice more accessible, expeditious, and popular.

The Assembly's clearing operations extended to economic institutions as well. Guided by laissez-faire doctrine, and by its complete hostility to privileged corporations, the Assembly sought to open up economic life to unimpeded individual initiative. Be-

**MAP 20.2 FRANCE: REVOLUTIONARY DEPARTMENTS AFTER 1789**
(From Breunig, Charles, *The Age of Revolution and Reaction, 1789–1850*, New York: Norton, 1970, p. 18.)

sides dismantling internal tariffs and chartered trading monopolies, it abolished the guilds of merchants and artisans, and proclaimed the right of every citizen to enter any trade and conduct it freely. Regulation of wages or of a product's quality would no longer concern the government. The Assembly also insisted that workers must bargain in the economic marketplace as individuals, and it therefore banned workers' associations and strikes. The precepts of economic individualism extended to the countryside too.

In theory, peasants and landlords were now free to cultivate their fields as they saw fit, regardless of traditional collective practices. In fact, however, communal restraints proved to be deep rooted and durable.

### Religious Issues

To address the financial problems that had precipitated the crisis of the old regime, the Assembly did something that the monarchy never dared contemplate. Since, under revolutionary ideology, the French Catholic Church could no longer exist as an independent corporation—a separate Estate within the state—the Assembly nationalized Church property, placing it "at the disposition of the nation," and simultaneously made the state responsible for the upkeep of the Church. On the basis of these "national lands" (to which the property of émigrés and the crown would subsequently be added), the Assembly issued paper notes known as *assignats,* which soon came to be treated as money. The national lands were sold by auction at the district capitals to the highest bidders. This favored bourgeois and rich peasants with ready capital, and made it difficult for needy peasants to acquire the land, though by pooling their resources some were able to do so.

The sale of Church lands and the issuance of *assignats* based on their value had at least three major consequences. First, it largely solved the financial problem and eliminated the need for constant borrowing. Second, the hundreds of thousands of purchasers gained a strong vested interest in the triumph of the Revolution, since a successful counterrevolution was likely to restore their properties to the Church. Finally, there was an unanticipated effect. After war broke out in 1792, the government greatly increased the volume of *assignats* beyond their underlying value, thereby touching off severe inflation and new political turmoil.

Apart from the question of Church property, the issue of church reform produced the Revolution's first and most fateful crisis. The Assembly intended to rid the Church of inequities that left much of the lower clergy impoverished while enriching the aristocratic prelates of the old regime. Many Catholics looked forward to such reforms, which would liberate the clergy to fulfill the Church's historic ideals. In the Civil Constitution of the Clergy (1790), the Assembly reduced the number of bishops to 83 and reshaped diocesan boundaries to conform with those of the new departments. Bishops and parish priests were to be chosen by the lay electors and paid according to a uniform salary scale favoring those at the lower end. Like other civil and military officials, the clergy was to take an oath of loyalty to the constitution.

The clergy generally objected to this reform because it was dictated to them by the National Assembly; they argued that it must be negotiated either with the Pope or a National Church Council. But the Assembly asserted that it had the sovereign power to order such reform since it affected temporal rather than spiritual matters. In November 1790 the Assembly forced the issue by requiring all existing clergy to take the oath forthwith; those who refused would lose their positions and be pensioned off. In all of France only seven bishops and about 54 percent of the parish clergy swore the oath; in the West of France a mere 15 percent complied. French Catholicism was torn by a schism, for the laity had to take a position as well. Should parishioners remain loyal to familiar priests who refused the oath (the refractory clergy), and thus be at odds with the state? Or should they accept the ministry of constitutional clergy sent in to replace them?

The Assembly's effort to impose reform without consideration of traditional Church procedures was a grave tactical error. The oath crisis polarized the nation. It seemed to link the Revolution with impiety, and the Church with counterrevolution. In local communities, refractory clergy began to preach against the whole Revolution. District administrations fought back by arresting them and demanding repressive laws. Thousands of local communities were rocked by civil strife between adherents of the two sides.

## Counterrevolution and War

Opposition to the Revolution had actually begun much earlier. After July 14 some of the king's relatives left the country in disgust, thus becoming the first *émigrés*. During the next three years thousands of nobles, including two-thirds of the officer corps, joined the emigration. Across the Rhine River in Coblenz many of these émigrés formed an army that threatened to overthrow the new regime at the first opportunity. The king himself, who might have provided a measure of stability to the new regime, publicly submitted to the Revolution but privately smoldered in resentment against it. Finally, in June 1791 Louis and his family secretly fled from Paris, hoping to cross the Belgian frontier, where they could enlist the aid of Austria. But Louis was recognized at the village of Varennes and forcibly returned to Paris.

Moderates hoped that this experience would finally end Louis' opposition. The Assembly, after all, needed his cooperation to make their constitutional monarchy viable. They did not wish to open the door to a republic or to further democratization. Radicals such as the journalist Jean-Paul Marat, on the other hand, had long thundered against the treachery of the king and the émigrés, and against the Assembly itself for allegedly betraying the people, as in the restricted suffrage of the new constitution. They now launched a petition campaign

against the king, which ended in a bloody riot—the massacre of the Champs de Mars on July 17, 1791—when the Paris national guard was ordered to disperse the demonstrators with force. This upheaval only strengthened the moderates' resolve to maintain the status quo. Adopting the fiction that the king had fled involuntarily, the Assembly reaffirmed his position in the new regime. But his traitorous act assured that radical agitation would continue.

The Assembly had earlier decided that no present deputy could stand for election to the new legislature. This self-denying ordinance meant that the Legislative Assembly would be composed of men less experienced and probably more daring than their predecessors. The new legislature was elected and convened on October 1, 1791. Almost from the start the question of war dominated its mood and work. By an odd coincidence, both the right and the left in France saw advantage in a war between France and Austria. The king and his court hoped that military defeat would discredit the new regime and restore full power to the monarchy. Most Jacobins—members of the leading political club in Paris—were eager to strike down the foreign supporters of counterrevolution at home and émigrés abroad.

When Francis II took the throne of the Hapsburg dominions in March 1792, the other half of the stage was set. Unlike his father, Leopold, who rejected intervention, Francis fell under the influence of émigrés and shortsighted advisers. He determined to assist the French queen, his aunt, and he hoped in alliance with Prussia to achieve territorial gains for Austria. With both sides eager for battle, France went to war against a coalition of Austria, Prussia, and the émigrés in April 1792.

Each camp expected rapid victory, but both were deceived. The French offensive was quickly driven back, and soon invading

| International and Military History | Political History |
|---|---|
| | |

1700

(1713–1714   Treaty of Utrecht; end of the War of the
Spanish Succession)*

(1715–1774   Louis XV king of France)

1750

(1756–1763   Seven Years' War)

1763   Peace of Paris; France loses most of colonial
empire

(1778–1783   France and England at war)

1760.1820   George III king of England
1763.1768   Wilkes affair in England
1774.1792   Louis XVI king of France
1774.1776   Minister of finance Jacques Turgot
attempts reforms
1777.1778   Swiss banker Jacques Necker minister
of finance
1782   Irish Parliament given autonomy
1783.1787   Calonne as minister of finance seeks land tax
1787   Assembly of Notables refuses to support reforms
1789, May   Convocation of Estates General
1789, June   Oath of the Tennis Court
1789, June   Estates General becomes National
Constituent Assembly
1789, July   Storming of the Bastile
1789, summer   Great Fear in countryside
1789, August   Feudalism abolished in France;
Declaration of
the Rights of Man and Citizen
1789, October   Paris mob forces king to Paris
1790   Civil Constitution of the Clergy;
death of Emperor Joseph II
1791   Constituent Assembly gives France a Constitution

1792, Feb.   Alliance of Austria and Prussia against
France
1792, April   France declares war against Austria
1792, July   Manifesto of the duke of Brunswick, threatening Paris if harm is done to the king
(1792   French victory over Prussians at Valmy)

1791   Louis XVI flees Paris; captured at Varennes
1791, October–1792, September   Legislative Assembly
(1792   September massacres)
1792   Gustavus III of Sweden assassinated by
disgruntled nobles

1800

*Events in parentheses are discussed in other chapters.

| Social and Economic History | Cultural and Intellectual History |
|---|---|
| **1694** Foundation of the Bank of England | (Voltaire [1694–1778]) (**1697** Bayle's *Dictionary*) |
| **c. 1700** English population 5 million; 80 percent of population lives from agriculture | |
| **1702** Savery's *The Miner's Friend* describes first practical steam engine | |
| **1709** Alexander Darby smelts iron ore with coke | (Rousseau [1712–1778]) |
| **1715** French population 16–19 million | (Diderot [1713–1784]) |
| (**1718–1720** John Law's financial scheme in France) | |
| (**1720** "South Sea Bubble" bursts in England) | |
| **1726** French government fixes value of gold louis | |
| **1732** Jethro Tull's *Horse Hoeing Husbandry* | (**1734** Voltaire's *Philosophical Letters*) |
| **1738** Flying shuttle invented by John Kay | |
| **1738** Philibert Orry initiates program of road construction in France | (**1740** Richardson's *Pamela*) |
| | (**1748** Montesquieu's *Spirit of the Laws*) |
| | (**1749** Buffon's *Natural History*) |
| **1750–1760** 156 enclosure acts enacted | (**1751–1772** *The Encyclopedia*) |
| | (Mozart [1756–1791]) |
| **c. 1765** Arkwright develops water frame | |
| **c. 1765** Hargreaves invents spinning jenny | (**1762** Rousseau's *Emile* and *Social Contract*) |
| | (**1764** Voltaire's *Philosophic Dictionary*) |
| **1779** John Wilkinson builds first iron bridge | (**1764** Beccaria's *On Crimes and Punishments*) |
| **1782** Watt's steam engine | (**1772** *Morning Post* published in England) |
| **1783–1793** Construction of Central Canal in France | |
| **1784** Cartwright designs power loom | (**1776** Gibbon's *Decline and Fall*) |
| **1785** Arkwright adopts steam engine in factory | (**1776** Smith's *Wealth of Nations*) |
| | (**1785** *The Times* published in England) |
| | (**1788** Mozart's last symphony) |
| **1789** French population 26 million | |
| **1791** Le Chapelier Law outlaws guilds and trade unions in France | |
| **1793** Whitney's cotton gin | |
| **1801** English population 9 million, 40 percent of population lives from agriculture | |
| **1800–1810** 906 enclosure acts | |

armies were crossing French borders. The Legislative Assembly ordered the arrest of refractory clergy and called for a special corps of 20,000 national guardsmen to protect Paris. Louis vetoed both measures and held to his decision in spite of demonstrations in the capital. This was, for all practical purposes, his last act as king. The legislature also called for a levy of 100,000 volunteers to bolster the French army and defend the homeland. As France mobilized for war, an officer named Rouget de Lisle composed a marching song for his volunteer battalion—a song eventually known as "The Marseillaise." Now the national anthem of France, it ranks among history's most stirring summonses to patriotic war.

"The Marseillaise" reflected the spirit of determination developing across the land. As Prussian forces began a drive toward Paris, their commander, the Duke of Brunswick, arrogantly demanded that Paris disarm itself and threatened to level the city if it resisted or if it harmed the royal family. When Louis XVI published this Brunswick Manifesto, it seemed the final proof that he was in league with the enemy. Far from intimidating the revolutionaries, the threat drove them into action. Since the Legislative Assembly had refused to act decisively in the face of royal obstructionism, Parisian militants, spurred on by the Jacobin Club, organized an insurrection.

On August 10, 1792, a crowd of armed Parisians stormed the royal palace at the Tuilleries, literally driving the king from the throne. The Assembly then had no choice but to declare him suspended. That night more than half its members themselves fled Paris, making it clear that the Assembly too had lost its legitimacy. The representatives who remained prepared to dissolve the Legislative Assembly permanently and ordered elections under universal male suffrage for a new body, to be called the National Convention. They left to the Convention the responsibility of declaring a republic in France, judging the former king, drafting a new constitution, and governing France during the emergency. What the events of 1789 in Versailles and Paris had begun, the insurrection of August 10, 1792 completed. The old regime in France had disappeared.

## SUMMARY

In the eighteenth century major transformations began in most aspects of Western life. The inhabitants of Europe and North America expanded at an extraordinary rate to unprecedented numbers, initiating a population explosion that has continued into modern times and now affects the entire world. The new industrial economy, if still of small size, created a new organization of production based on steam power and high engineering skill, factors that would sustain the economic growth of the following century. And the overall economic system took on a configuration that differed from the patterns of all prior periods in its capacity to transform itself and thus to lend a new dynamic quality to the society living from it.

These changes were accompanied by a crisis in social and political institutions. A tripartite struggle developed involving the ruler, the aristocracy, and the people over the proper allocation of power in the state. Several European monarchs sought to impose reform from above. The aristocracies, on the other hand, bitterly resented encroachments on their privileges, and some were willing to pursue the defense of their interests to the point of revolution. Both rulers and patricians appealed to the Third Estate, the people, often with unexpected results. The emerging claim to power of the unprivileged classes is the greatest change effected by the revolutions of the eighteenth century. No longer would the political history of the Western world focus exclusively on the elites.

The peoples of the West thus faced the task of building a new economic, social, and political order. What should its character be? How should power be managed, and how should wealth be distributed? What values should now govern human lives? These were the issues destined to occupy the Western nations as they entered the industrial and democratic age.

# RECOMMENDED READING

## Sources

Aspinall, Arthur, and E. Anthony Smith (eds.). *English Historical Documents, Vol. XI: 1783–1832.* 1959.

*Burke, Edmund, *Reflections on the Revolution in France.* 1969.

Higgins, E. L. (ed.). *The French Revolution as Told by Contemporaries.* 1939.

Horn, D. B., and Mary Ransome (eds.). *English Historical Documents, Vol. X: 1714–1789.* 1957.

Kirchberger, Joe H. (ed.). *The French Revolution and Napoleon: An Eyewitness History.* 1989. Includes many of the crucial documents and several contemporary accounts of the principal events.

*Ménétra, Jacques-Louis. *Journal of My Life.* 1986.

Roland, Manon Jeanne. *The Private Memoirs of Madame Roland.* Edward Gilpin Johnson (ed.). 2d ed. 1976. By a woman deeply involved in Revolutionary politics, guillotined in 1793.

*Smith, Adam. *Enquiry into the Nature and Causes of the Wealth of Nations.* 1961.

*Young, Arthur. *Travels in France During the Years 1787, 1788, 1789.* 1972. Critical view of French agriculture.

## Studies

Ashton, T. S. *The Industrial Revolution, 1760–1830.* 1968.

Bosher, J. B. *The French Revolution.* 1989. The Revolution that did not need to happen.

*Chartier, Roger. *The Cultural Origins of the French Revolution.* 1990. Surveys the ferment of ideas and attitudes before the Revolution and the channels in which they were expressed.

*Chaussinand-Nogaret, Guy. *The French Nobility in the Eighteenth Century: From Feudalism to Enlight-*enment.* 1985. A revisionist portrayal of the nobility as a progressive class.

Crafts, N. F. R. *British Economic Growth During the Industrial Revolution.* 1985.

*Deane, Phyllis. *The First Industrial Revolution.* 1975. Based on lectures, covering the years 1750–1850.

*De Tocqueville, Alexis. *The Old Regime and the French Revolution.* Stuart Gilbert (tr.). 1955.

*De Vries, Jan. *The Economy of Europe in an Age of Crisis. 1600–1750.* 1976.

————. *European Urbanization, 1500–1800.* 1984. The formation of great cities; covers all Europe.

Doyle, William. *The Oxford History of the French Revolution.* 1989. A recent attempt at synthesis.

Furet, François, and Mona Ozouf (eds.). *Critical Dictionary of the French Revolution.* 1989. A collection of short essays, some brilliant and some idiosyncratic, on selected events, actors, institutions, ideas, and historians of the French Revolution.

Gutmann, Myron. *Toward the Modern Economy: Early Industry in Europe.* 1988.

Egret, Jean. *The French Pre-Revolution, 1787–88.* 1978. A masterly account of the unraveling of the old regime.

Fairchilds, Cissie. *Domestic Enemies: Servants and Their Masters in Old Regime France.* 1984. Reflects the new interest in domestic and women's history.

*Flandrin, Jean-Louis. *Families in Former Times: Kinship, Household and Sexuality.* 1979. From demographic history to the history of the family.

*Hampson, Norman. *A Social History of the French Revolution.* 1963. Institutional rather than social; clearly organized and written.

Hohenberg, Paul M., and Lynn Holen Lees, *The Making of Urban Europe, 1000–1950*. 1985. The impact of protoindustrialization and industrialization on cities.

*Jones, Peter. *The Peasantry in the French Revolution*. 1988. A comprehensive study of the most important social issues raised by the French Revolution.

*Landes, David S. *The Unbound Prometheus: Technological Change and Industrial Development in Western Europe from 1750 to the Present*. 1969. Broad survey, effectively written.

*Lefebvre, Georges. *The Coming of the French Revolution*. 1967. Concise interpretation by a major French historian; should be compared to Doyle.

*Mantoux, Paul. *The Industrial Revolution in the Eighteenth Century*. 1962. Basic introduction, with stress on inventions and factories.

North, Douglass C. *Structure and Change in Economic History*. 1981. Stresses the importance of supportive legal institutions in the coming of industrialism.

*Palmer, Robert R. *The Age of the Democratic Revolution: A Political History of Europe and America, 1760–1800*. 1959–1962. Examines the common origins of revolutionary movements.

Rose, R. B. *The Making of the Sans-Culottes: Democratic Ideas and Institutions in Paris, 1789–1792*. 1983.

Rudé, George F. *Paris and London in the Eighteenth Century*. 1975.

Roberts, Michael. *The Age of Liberty: Sweden, 1719–1772*. 1986. Sweden as a case study in the crisis of the old regime.

Tackett, Timothy. *Religion, Revolution and Regional Culture in Eighteenth-Century France: The Ecclesiastical Oath of 1791*. 1986. An exhaustive archival study of the Revolution's first and most fateful crisis.

Venturi, Franco. *The End of the Old Regime in Europe, 1768–1776: The First Crisis*. R. Burr Litchfield (tr.). 1989. The crisis in thought and values leading to the dissolution of the Old Regime.

*Vovelle, Michel. *The Fall of the French Monarchy, 1787–1792*. 1984. A synthesis of recent research.

Wrigley, E. A., and R. S. Schofield. *The Population History of England, 1541–1871: Studies in Social and Demographic History*. A reconstruction of population movements by "backward projection."

* Available in paperback.

# ❄ CHAPTER 21 ❄

# THE TERROR
# AND NAPOLEON
# 1792–1814

# ❄ CHAPTER 21 ❄

# THE TERROR
# AND NAPOLEON
# 1792–1814

✼ ✼ ✼ ✼ ✼

The end of the eighteenth century is often called the age of the dual revolution—the Industrial Revolution beginning in England and the social and political revolution centering in France. But where the former unfolded gradually, the latter exploded. By 1791—just two years after the fall of the Bastille—the foundations of government and society in France had been profoundly altered. The estate structure, dominated by the monarch and the nobles, had been destroyed; middle-class values and leaders were in the ascendant; the peasantry had been freed from the seigneurial system; absolutism had been replaced by constitutional monarchy, legislative representation, and local self-government; freedom of religion and expression had been guaranteed.

✼

Yet the Revolution was far from over, and in the short view, one might say that it was only just beginning. True, the gains just enumerated ultimately proved to be the most enduring and doubtless the most important. But they had been won at the price of great opposition, and the old order was far from admitting defeat. Priests, émigrés, and royalists in France were seconded by old-regime monarchs, aristocrats, and armies elsewhere in Europe in their resistance to the Revolution. Moreover, within France itself vast sections of the population were hostile to the "patriots" of 1789 for a variety of reasons.

✼

Challenged in 1792 by war and counterrevolution, the patriots themselves were divided. Some were alienated by the leaders of the Revolution and ultimately joined its opponents. Others were radicalized and gave their allegiance to the Jacobins. These, in turn, were seeking allies among the urban popular classes—the sans-culottes. Building on the momentum of August 1792, when Louis XVI had been driven from the throne, the Jacobins forged a coalition with the sans-culottes, who sought to revolutionize the Revolution. The goals of this second revolution were more advanced than those of 1789: a democratic republic based on a broader definition of social equality. Its hallmark was a posture of relentless militancy.

✼

Each increment of revolution produced new opponents at home and abroad, but each increment of opposition stiffened the determination of the Revolution's supporters. An epochal confrontation was in the making that would engulf Europe. It began with a power struggle between revolutionary factions, a conflict of personalities as much as of political orientations; it ended in a coup that led France into a dictatorship under Napoleon Bonaparte.

## I. THE SECOND REVOLUTION

❊

The National Convention elected after the fall of the monarchy had a challenging mandate. It was supposed to consolidate the achievements of the first revolution and establish a democratic republic, in effect moving the Revolution into a second stage. It is impossible to say how this would have proceeded had the times been calm, but, of course, they were not. France was immediately beset by an emergency—a convergence of invasion, civil war, and economic crisis. This situation demanded new initiatives that affected the course of the second revolution. To save and expand freedom, it was argued, force and terrorism were necessary. Thus the ideals of democracy and social equality were confused with problems of national defense and with the brutal dilemma of means versus ends. Although the second revolution lasted for little more than two years (1792–1794), it challenged the very foundations upon which government and society had always been organized.

### The National Convention

The insurrection of August 10, 1792, had created a vacuum. Until the National Convention was elected and until it was able to govern effectively, the fabric of authority in France was extremely fragile. A revolutionary city government, or Commune, in Paris organized itself as one power center. But that bastion of radicalism could not control the course of events even within its own domain as evidenced by the September massacres—perhaps the bloodiest single event of the Revolution. As able-bodied volunteers left for the battlefront, Parisians nervously eyed the capital's jails, filled with political prisoners and common criminals. Seeing these prisoners as a potential counterrevolutionary striking force, and fearing a plot to open the prisons, radical journalists like Jean-Paul Marat warned of the threat. A growing sense of alarm finally exploded early in September. For three successive days groups of Parisians invaded the prisons, set up popular tribunals, and executed over 1000 prisoners. No official dared intervene to stop the slaughter.

The sense of panic soon eased, however, with the belated success of the French armies. Bolstered by units of citizen volunteers, the army halted the invading coalition at the Battle of Valmy in September. Two months later it defeated the forces of the old order at Jemappes in the Austrian Netherlands, which were now occupied by the French. Meanwhile, the National Convention, elected under universal male suffrage, convened at the end of September. It promptly declared France a republic, and set about trying to govern the country until a new democratic constitution could be drafted and implemented.

Louis XVI's fate was the Convention's first major business and it proved an extremely divisive issue. While the king was found guilty of treason unanimously, there was a sharp and prolonged debate over his punishment. Some argued for clemency, while others insisted on his execution as a symbolic break with the old order as well as a fitting punishment for his betrayal. Finally, by a vote of 387 to 334, Louis was sentenced to death, and efforts to reprieve this sentence or delay it for a popular referendum were defeated. On January 21, 1793, Louis was beheaded, put to death like an ordinary citizen. The French in general and the Convention in particular had become regicides—king-killers. This decision made compromise with the counterrevolution unlikely and total victory imperative. The Revolution would have to move forward.

France was now a republic, a country in which the influence of kings, priests, and

Tried and sentenced by the National Convention for treason, Louis Capet (formerly Louis XVI) stoically mounted the guillotine on January 21, 1793. His execution made it clear that the Revolution had taken a sharp turn and that it would deal implacably with its enemies. (Photo: The Granger Collection)

nobles was to be eliminated, in which regionalism was supposed to give way to unity, in which social justice and reform could advance. Yet in a few months everything began to go wrong, and the Revolution faced a new and more serious crisis. By the early spring of 1793 the republic was under siege, internally divided and foundering. At least five problems faced the Convention: factionalism and conflict within its own ranks; a new invasion by a coalition of anti-French states; peasant dissatisfaction and internal civil war; economic dislocation including inflation and scarcity of bread; and growing militancy among Parisian radicals.

From the Convention's opening day, two groups of deputies vied for leadership. The bitterness of their rivalry threatened to paralyze the republic altogether. Yet this conflict reflected a painful reality: opinion *was* divided by what had already happened, and a consensus or stable majority was extremely difficult to find. The factional conflict originated in 1791–1792 as a quarrel within the Paris Jacobin Club and intensified after the insurrection of August 10. A group of deputies and journalists centering on Jacques Brissot had helped lead the country into war, but had then shrunk back from the vigorous measures necessary to pursue it. (This group later would be labeled the "Girondists" since several of its spokesmen were elected deputies to the Convention from the department of the Gironde.) Advocates of provincial middle-class interests, fiery orators, and ambitious politicians, they gradually fell out of step with the growing radicalization of Paris.

Brissot and his friends were forced out of the Jacobin Club, while Parisian electors sent a deputation to the Convention that included leading members of the club such as Danton, Robespierre, and Marat. This Parisian deputation became the nucleus of a group called "the Mountain," since it occupied the upper benches of the Convention's hall. The Mountain attracted to its ranks the more democratically oriented provincial deputies, and attacked the Girondists as compromisers, as men unattuned to the new demands of the French people. The Girondists, in turn, denounced the Mountain as would-be tyrants who were captives of Parisian opinion to the detriment of the provinces and the propertied classes.

Between these two factions stood several hundred deputies in the center (called the Plain, in contrast to the Mountain). Committed to the Revolution, they were uncertain whom to trust and would support those men or policies that promised success in consolidating the Revolution. They disliked and feared popular agitation, but they were reluctant to turn against the popular movement, agreeing with the Mountain that the Revolution depended on it. In the debate on the king the center was split, but a majority finally embraced the Jacobins' demand for execution, whereas a few prominent Girondists had argued for clemency. Military and economic problems eventually propelled the majority to support the Mountain.

## The Revolutionary Crisis

Within a few months the Convention faced a perilous convergence of invasion, civil war, and economic crisis that demanded new policies and imaginative responses. The military victories of 1792 were quickly forgotten when Austria and Prussia mounted a new offensive in 1793, an alliance soon strengthened by the addition of Spain, Piedmont, and England. Between March and September reversals occurred on every front, while the regular army was weakened by poor leadership. In fact, the French commander, General Dumouriez, the Revolution's first military hero the year before, sought—unsuccessfully—to bring his army back to Paris in order to topple the Convention.

The Convention's first response to the deteriorating military situation was to introduce a form of conscription. But this, in turn, touched off a peasant rebellion in western France. Long-simmering resentments by a traditional peasantry, who hated the small patriot middle class in the towns for monopolizing political power and who resented the Revolution's persecution of their priests, finally ignited when the republic tried to conscript them. Peasants and weavers in the Vendée region south of the Loire River attacked the government's supporters in the region's isolated towns. Gradually, this insurrection was influenced by priests and émigrés who organized the rebels into guerilla bands and finally into what called itself the Catholic and Royalist Army. Wherever it triumphed, the Bourbons were proclaimed kings again and patriots were massacred. Several major cities were occupied briefly. For a while the rebels threatened the port city of Nantes, which could have been used for a landing of British troops if it had fallen.

The bitter factionalism in the Convention had meanwhile generated conflict elsewhere in the country. Various provincial centers that sympathized with the Girondists hovered on the brink of rebellion against the Convention's leadership and against Parisian radicalism. In Normandy and Brittany forces were raised to threaten Paris, while in the south local Jacobins lost control of Marseilles, Bordeaux, and France's second-largest city, Lyons. Like the Vendée rebellion, the Lyons resistance to Paris was eventually taken over by royalists who hoped to ignite the entire south of France against Paris. This was an intolerable challenge to the Convention. Labeling the anti-Jacobins in Lyons and elsewhere "federalists," the Convention sent out armed forces to suppress them. Ironically, in the United States at this time the word "federalist" referred to those who advocated a strong central government. In France it was used in the opposite sense, meaning those who seemed to challenge the republic's unity. As such, the federalists were considered counterrevolutionary, for to disavow Paris meant to disavow the Revolution itself.

Parisian radicalism—against which the federalists were reacting—was in large measure provoked by severe economic troubles. By February 1793 the Revolution's paper money, the *assignats*, had declined to 50 percent of its face value in the marketplace. It continued steadily downward after that, to as low as one-third. This disastrous devaluation was compounded by a poor harvest. Panic over the scarcity of grain and flour swept across France, especially in the cities. Municipal leaders attempted to fix the price of bread so as to make it available to the masses, but they could not secure adequate supplies. Likewise, the central government could not supply its armies under these conditions. Human greed, of course, made matters worse; uncivic-minded people attempted to profit from the situation by hoarding scarce commodities or by speculating in *assignats*.

The strongest impetus for taking vigorous measures against all these problems, military, political, and economic, came from the urban populace in Paris and other cities. But the vehemence of certain Parisian militants posed yet another threat to the Convention: the threat of excessive radicalism and anarchy. The ultraradicals, like their enemies the federalists, were unwilling to defer to the Convention. Spokesmen for the people, or sans-culottes, as they were called, communicated the view that the Convention, the Jacobin Club, and even the Paris city government were not sufficiently responsive to popular demands. They therefore demanded a purge of the Convention to rid it of moderates; a program of revolutionary public safety; and radical economic intervention to break through the laissez-faire immobility of the government: (1) price control (called a law of the Maximum) for all necessary commodities, (2) severe laws against hoarding and speculation, and (3) forced requisitions on the peasantry, to be carried out with the assistance of an armed force or revolutionary army of the interior. Behind these demands lay the threat of armed insurrection. For the Jacobins, the pressure from the sans-culottes provided aid in their struggle against the Girondists and federalists, but it posed the danger of spilling over into anarchy.

In a sense, all elements of the revolutionary crisis hinged on one problem: the lack of a strong, effective government that would not simply respond to popular pressure but organize and channel it into constructive action. The first step in the creation of such a government seemed to be the purge demanded by the radicals. On May 31 the sans-culottes launched a demonstration to force home their demands. The Plain at this point decided that the Mountain must be supported against the Girondists, who were thundering against the "tyranny" of the sans-culottes. On June 2, 23 Girondists were expelled by the Convention and placed under house arrest; they would subsequently be tried for treason. A turning point had come, but the future course of the Revolution was still in question.

## The Jacobin Dictatorship

The popular movement in Paris had brought the Mountain to power in the Convention. The question now was which side of the coalition would dominate. Popular demands swelled for terrorism against counterrevolution and for vigorous provisioning policies. The conviction was spreading among the sans-culottes that the sovereign people could dictate its will to the Convention by demonstrations and the threat of insurrection. At the same time, federalism exploded in the provinces in response to the purge of the Girondists; Lyons and Marseilles were now in full-scale rebellion.

The high point of popular agitation came on September 5, when a massive demonstration in Paris placed demands for drastic measures before the Convention. The demonstrators' main slogans were "Food—and to have it, force for the law" and "Let terror be placed on the order of the day." Concretely, they won the passage of laws imposing general price control, forbidding hoarding, creating revolutionary armies of the interior, and empowering local revolutionary committees to incarcerate citizens whose loyalty was suspect or who seemed to threaten the public safety—the so-called law of suspects.

### *The Revolutionary Government*

Back in June the triumphant Jacobins had drafted a democratic constitution, one of the original purposes for which the National Convention had been called. It had been sub-

mitted to a referendum and overwhelmingly approved by 2 million voters; thus it provided the cornerstone for a new legitimate government. But the constitution could not be implemented in the throes of such a crisis as now faced the nation, particularly in view of its internal divisions. In October the Convention acknowledged this, formally placed the constitution aside, and proclaimed the government "revolutionary until the peace." Such rights as elections, local self-government, and guarantees of individual liberty promised in the constitution would be enjoyed only after the republic was secure from its enemies within and without.

An array of revolutionary laws and institutions now existed; it remained for a group of determined and skillful political leaders to take the reins and make them effective. Such men were to be found on the Committee of Public Safety, appointed by the Convention to supervise military, economic, and political affairs.

The committee's leading personality and tactician was Maximilien Robespierre. An austere bachelor in his mid-thirties and a provincial lawyer before the Revolution, Robespierre had been a prominent spokesman for the left in the Constituent Assembly where he had advocated the rights of women, Jews, and free blacks, and had crusaded for the democratization of the regime. In 1792 he was an official of the Paris city government and a newspaper editor. But his principal political forum was the capital's Jacobin Club, which by 1793 he more or less dominated. Elected to the Convention from Paris, he was selfless and self-righteous in his dedication to the Revolution. He sought to guide the sans-culottes and serve their interests as much as possible, but he placed the survival of the Revolution above their particular grievances. Thus his leadership struck a delicate balance between his sense of responsibility

The Paris Jacobin Club was founded by a group of progressive deputies to the Constituent Assembly of 1789. After August 1792 and the elections to the Convention, it became a forum for democratic deputies and middle-class Parisian radicals, as well as a "mother club" with which popular societies in the provinces affiliated themselves. As such, it was the closest thing the French revolutionaries had to a party apparatus. (Photo: New York Publish Library/Picture Collection)

and his sympathy for popular aspirations. The two were not always compatible. His main object was to bring the republic through the emergency by creating confidence and efficiency in the revolutionary government, and in this he succeeded. His hope of reconciling class interests in the cause of democracy was ultimately frustrated.

The legislation for creating a centralized revolutionary government was passed in December 1793, at last filling the vacuum left by the fall of the monarchy. Under a law enacted December 4—or 14 Frimaire year II, according to the new French calendar—revolutionary committees in towns and villages were made responsible to the Committee of Public Safety. Local officials were redesignated national agents, their initiative was curbed, and they, too, were subject to removal by the Committee. Revolutionary tribunals, representatives on mission (deputies sent to the provinces as commissars), and revolutionary armies of the interior were all placed under the Committee's scrutiny and control.

Local Jacobin clubs were crucial links in this chain of revolutionary dictatorship. They, too, were organized into a centralized network, led by the Paris Jacobin Club. They nominated citizens for posts on revolutionary committees and exercised surveillance over them. The clubs were to be "arsenals of public opinion," to support the war effort in every way possible, and to denounce uncivic behavior among their fellow citizens.

No serious dissent was tolerated under the Jacobin reign. Freedom of expression was limited by the government's demand for unity during the emergency. The politically outspoken were purged. The first to fall were a group of ultraleftists led by Jacques René Hébert, a radical journalist and Paris official. They were accused of a plot against the republic. In reality, they had questioned what they considered the Convention's leniency toward "enemies" of the people. Next came the turn of the so-called indulgents, among them Danton. They had argued—prematurely, in the government's view—for a relaxation of terrorism and centralization. They were arrested, indicted on trumped-up charges of treason, and sentenced to death by the revolutionary tribunal. This succession of purges, starting with the Girondists and later ending with Robespierre himself, seemed to suggest, as one contemporary put it, that revolutions devour their own children.

## The Reign of Terror

Most of those devoured by the French Revolution, however, were not its own children. They were rather an assortment of armed rebels, counterrevolutionaries, and unfortunate citizens swept into the vortex of war and internal strife. The Reign of Terror developed in response to the multifaceted crisis described on the previous pages. The Terror reflected a revolutionary mentality that saw threats and plots all around (some real, some imagined). The laws of the Terror were designed to intimidate a wide range of people perceived as enemies of the Revolution. They included the law of suspects, which led to the incarceration of as many as 400,000 prisoners, and laws against the life and property of refractory priests and émigrés. They included also the price-control regulations and other laws aimed at preventing the collapse of the Revolution from economic chaos or food shortages.

The Terror was the force behind the law—the determination and techniques to make these laws work. Its purpose was to coerce French people into accepting certain sacrifices of self-interest to permit the republic and the Revolution to survive. By the same token, the emphasis on organizing the Terror, on supervising it from some central point of authority, was designed to prevent anarchic violence like the Paris prison massacres of September 1792 and the infamous events at Nantes, in which hundreds of Vendée rebels and priests were brutally drowned in the Loire River. The Committee of Public Safety prevented the indiscriminate condemnation of federalists and put a stop to violent de-Christianization. The Terror was meant to impress by the severity of examples, not by the liquidation of whole groups.

Statistical analysis of the death sentences during the Terror suggests a relationship between executions and clear-and-present danger. A total of 17,000 death sentences were handed down by the various revolutionary tribunals and commissions, and an estimated 10,000 additional armed rebels were executed without trial. Over 70 percent of the sentences were passed in the two zones of intense civil war: 19 percent in the southeast (the Lyons region) and 52 percent in the west (the Vendée region). Moreover, 72 percent of these were for armed rebellion. Conversely, one-third of the departments had fewer than 10 death sentences each and were relatively tranquil. While much of the revolutionary rhetoric and some of its legislation were aimed at the upper classes, the death sentences of the Terror hit hardest at the largest groups in the population: urban and rural common people who actively participated in the rebellions.[1]

Apart from the repression of the Vendée revolt, the Terror's bloodiest episode took place in Lyons. The Convention laid siege to the city until it capitulated in October 1793. Unbending in its hostility, the Convention declared that "Lyons has made war against liberty and thus Lyons no longer exists." The entire population was disarmed, and the houses of many wealthy citizens were burned. On-the-spot courts-martial were held and executions followed immediately. Some were carried out gruesomely, with the encouragement of irresponsible commissars. Almost 2000 people were put to death, two-thirds of them from the upper classes. The fanaticism of the Parisian sans-culottes sent against Lyons reflected their revolutionary fanaticism during the months of crisis.

## The Sans-Culottes and the Popular Revolution

The sans-culottes not only propelled the insurrectionary movements in 1789 and 1792, but also became ardent proponents of further revolutionizing in the social, political, and economic spheres. Their participation in the second revolution was essential to its success.

[1] These statistics are drawn from Donald Greer, *The Incidence of the Terror*, 1935.

The role of the people in the Revolution has always been noted, but until recently they have not been studied directly and in their own right. Instead, their actions and concerns have been portrayed through the eyes of their enemies or their spokesmen, themselves middle or upper class and far removed in their own life style from the common people. Inspired by Georges Lefebvre's classic studies of the peasants, historians have recently been writing about the French Revolution "from below"—about specific groups of ordinary people. These studies convey their social identity, their aspirations, attitudes, and revolutionary activity as they tried to place their collective stamp on what they regarded as their Revolution.

The most dramatic impact made by the sans-culottes on the Revolution came during the famous insurrectionary *journées*, or "days" of crowd actions, demonstrations, and uprisings, that marked most turning points in the Revolution's course (see table). The participants in these crowds and striking forces were not criminals and drifters, as antirevolutionary writers have claimed. They were Parisian tradespeople and workers— carpenters, cobblers, wine sellers, clerks, tailors, cafe keepers, stonemasons—mainly artisans, shopkeepers and journeymen. The sans-culottes varied in their relationship to the means of production: Some, such as workshop proprietors, owned them; others provided their labor. But most shared the life style of Paris's popular neighborhoods and had a strong sense of community.

### Popular Attitudes

Though many sans-culotte activists were prosperous tradespeople, they spoke for working people whose modest livelihood was threatened by rises in the cost of living. Accordingly, they were extremely concerned

Amidst elaborate arrays of symbolism, revolutionary iconography generally used the figure of a woman to represents its ideals—the example here depicting the notion of equality. During the brief period of revolutionary government in 1793–1794, however, the Jacobians introduced the more aggressive male figure of Hercules to represent the republic.   (Photo: *left*, Photographie Bulloz; *right*, Collection VIOLLET)

over the availability and prices of basic commodities like bread, candles, and fuel. As consumers, they faced the economic crisis of the revolutionary period with distress and anger. Their most basic demand was for government intervention to assure the basic necessities of life. This is one reason that women were prominent among revolutionary activists: They were most directly concerned with putting food on their family's table. By 1793 the Revolution's leaders were compelled to recognize this concern, and the right to subsistence was prominently proclaimed in the Jacobin constitution of 1793. Concretely, it meant a combination of government price control and requisitioning that

## CHRONOLOGY OF THE FRENCH REVOLUTION

July 14, 1789:     Storming of the Bastille and triumph of the Third Estate.

August 19, 1792:     Storming of the Tuileries and end of the constitutional monarchy.
September 2–5, 1792:     Paris prison massacres.

January 21, 1793:     Execution of Louis XVI.

March 1793:     Vendée rebellion begins.

May 31–June 2, 1793:     Sans-culotte march on the Convention and purge of the Girondists.

September 5, 1793:     Demonstration before the Convention and enactment of terroristic legislation and economic controls.

9 Thermidor year II
(July 27, 1794):     Fall of Robespierre.

1–2 Prairial year III
(May 20–21, 1795):     Unsuccessful insurrection by the Parisian sans-culottes for "Bread and the constitution of 1793."

18 Brumaire year VIII
(November 9, 1799):     Coup d'état by Napoleon Bonaparte and the revisionists.

violated the laissez-faire view of how the economy should work.

The sans-culottes, while firm believers in property rights, insisted that they must be limited by considerations of social utility. They denied that anyone had the right to "misuse" property by hoarding, speculating, or accumulating far more than he or she needed. Concepts of freedom and equality had a practical economic side in their opinion. As one petition put it, "What is the meaning of freedom, when one class of men can starve another? What is the meaning of equality, when the rich, by their monopolies, can exercise the right of life and death over their equals?"

Under the stress of soaring inflation and economic dislocation, the sans-culotte call for the right to subsistence and the middle-class call for laissez faire clashed dramatically. The willingness of the Mountain and the Jacobin Club to regulate the economy, at least during the war emergency, won them support among the urban people.

Bitterly antiaristocratic, the sans-culottes displayed their social attitudes in everyday behavior. Advocating simplicity in dress and manners, they attacked opulence and pretension wherever they found or imagined them to be. Under their disapproving eye, high society and fancy dress generally disappeared from view. There was a revolution too in manners and morals. Vices like prostitution, pornography, and gambling were attributed to aristocrats and were denounced in the virtuous society of the Revolution; drinking was the common people's vice and was tolerated.

The sans-culottes symbolized their break with the past by changing the names of their streets, cities, and public places to eliminate signs of royalism and aristocracy. The Palais Royal became the Palais d'Égalité ("Equality Palace"). Many people underwent debaptizing, exchanging their Christian names for the names of secular heroes like Gracchus, the ancient Roman reformer. Titles like "monsieur" and "madame" were dropped in favor of the simple, uniform designation of "citizen"—just as revolutionaries of a later generation would call each other "comrade."

### Popular Politics

The Convention believed in a system of parliamentary or representative democracy, with an active political life at the grass roots. But during the emergency the Jacobins were willing to impose a virtual dictatorship in the form of the highly centralized revolutionary government. The sans-culottes, on the other hand, favored a popular scheme of participatory democracy. They believed that the local voters, or in larger cities the local section assembly of citizens, was the ultimate sovereign body. It could never permanently delegate its authority, even to the elected Convention. In short, they wanted the decision-making power actively lodged with the people rather than their deputies. To Robespierre, this ideal of direct democracy appeared unworkable and akin to anarchy.

At the beginning of the revolutionary year II (1793–1794), the 48 sections in Paris functioned almost as tiny autonomous republics in which local activists ran their own affairs directly in the general assembly, a system an American would call town-meeting democracy. At times the sections cooperated with one another to exert collective pressure on the government. On the various *journées,* the sans-culottes demonstrated their conviction that the people, if necessary in a state of armed insurrection, ought to be the ultimate arbiter of the republic. Political life in those months, especially but not exclusively in Paris, had a naïve, breathless quality, generating high enthusiasm among thousands of sans-culottes, making them feel that for the first time the power of self-government was theirs.

The Convention looked on with mixed feelings. On the one hand, they were uneasy allies, committed to the ideals of democracy and equality. On the other hand, they were pragmatists who feared the anarchic force of this popular movement—its unpredictability, its disorder, and its inefficiency. The Mountain attempted to steer a difficult course between encouraging this civic participation and controlling it. The sans-culotte militants did a great deal for the war effort: They rooted out counterrevolutionaries, spread revolutionary usages, recruited soldiers, and formed committees for public relief. Like the Jacobin clubs in the provinces, the Parisian sans-culottes promoted the ideal of self-help.

From the sections, however, there came an endless stream of demands, petitions, denunciations, and veiled threats to the government. In the end, the Convention decided that the direct democracy of the sections had to be disciplined. In the spring of 1794, it passed a series of measures restricting the meeting times, activities, and rights of the sections that removed most of their effective powers. What the government failed to realize was that once the ardor of the sans-culottes was forcibly cooled off, that group's support of the Convention, and their willingness to sacrifice, would also diminish. The results would leave these leaders vulnerable to reaction.

## The Victories of the Year II

Even while the Mountain was curtailing the powers of the sans-culottes, however, it continued to bank on their support for the military defense of the nation. For the Revolution's more far-sighted leaders knew that France's ultimate fate rested in the hands of its armies. Drawing on the citizenry at large, the Convention forged a new armed force that overcame the coalition of hostile states arrayed against France.

### *Revolutionary Foreign Policy*

As initially formulated in 1789, revolutionary ideology had offered no direct threat to the European state system. French power was not to be felt across the country's borders except as persuasion. Indeed, the orators of the National Assembly had argued that the best foreign policy for a progressive and free society was peace, neutrality, and isolation from the diplomatic intrigues of monarchs.

But peace did not imply pacifism. When counterrevolution at home coalesced with threats from abroad, the revolutionaries were eager to resort to war against both. The hostilities that broke out in 1792 were for the most part defensive in origin as far as the French were concerned. But, as in all major wars, the initial objectives were rapidly forgotten. As the conflict spilled over large parts of Europe, it disrupted the political organization and boundaries of many Continental states.

The revolutionary wars involved considerations that were constant in international conflicts as well as certain new and explosive purposes. On the one hand, the French adopted traditional objectives such as rounding off and extending their frontiers and exacting agreements from adjoining states

Ever alert to conspiracies, real or imagined, Hébert's *Père Duchêsne* was a favorite newspaper of the sans-culottes. Lively, slangy, and blasphemous, its targets included moderates, "aristocrats," and clergy. During 1793 and 1794 it was distributed in vast quantities among the republic's armies. (Photo: The Research Libraries, The New York Public Library)

aimed at protecting those frontiers. At the same time, they pursued revolutionary principles such as the right of a people to self-

In February 1794, the National Convention decreed the abolition of slavery in all French colonies. Slaves on the largest island of St.-
Domingue (later Haiti) had already won their
freedom in a violent uprising led by Toussaint
Louverture.   (Photo: Collection VIOLLET)

determination. As early as September 1791,
the National Assembly had declared that
"the rights of peoples are not determined by
the treaties of princes."

As we have seen in the previous chapter,
there were people in many areas of Western
Europe who were eager to challenge the ancient arrangements—"the treaties of
princes"—that determined their political des-

tiny. Particularly in the zone of Europe lying
west of the Elbe River, several internal conflicts had already arisen before 1789, and the
success of the French revived liberal and revolutionary sentiment. Patriots in Geneva, the
United Provinces, and the Austrian Netherlands had already tasted repression. They
were eager for another round in their struggles and looked to France for assistance.

Refugees from these regions had fled to
France and formed pressure groups that lobbied with French leaders. Their fondest
hopes rested on the chance that in fighting
against the coalition, the French might liberate their own lands. If they were contiguous
to France (as were the Austrian Netherlands,

Savoy, and the Rhineland), France might then annex them to its own republic; elsewhere (in Holland, Lombardy, Ireland, and the Swiss Confederation) it might help set up independent republics by overthrowing the ruling princes or oligarchies. In the wake of war and revolutionary enthusiasm, the foreign patriots induced the Convention to declare in November 1792 that it "accords fraternity and aid to [foreign] people who wish to recover their liberty," though the French had in mind only those whose governments were actively leagued against France.

While there had been some talk of mounting a universal crusade to bring freedom to oppressed peoples, French leaders were in reality committed to a pragmatic policy. As the war spilled over into the Austrian Netherlands and Germany, they had to organize their forces and ensure a base of support abroad. This required that the aims of war embody the spirit and stated objectives of the revolutionary society, not the age-old motive of aggrandizement and domination. Thus in December of 1792 the government proclaimed further that it would establish the freedom of those to whom it had brought or would bring armed assistance. This meant that in each land where the French prevailed, feudal practices, hereditary privileges, and repressive institutions would be abolished. A provisional government would be established to cooperate with the French forces in supervising and paying for the liberation. Full independence was a long-term promise; more immediately, the occupied territory would be obliged to pay the expenses of French troops.

These intentions were greeted enthusiastically by progressive elements in the middle and noble classes and in some instances by artisans. But most nobles, priests, and peasants and large sections of the middle class were hostile or indifferent to them. They resented the requisitions and special taxes, though they did not necessarily wish a restoration of the old order.

By 1794 France had a permanent foothold in the Austrian Netherlands, which was shortly to be annexed to the Great Nation, as France now called herself. Apart from this, however, Robespierre proved to be relatively isolationist. Arguing that freedom had to be secured at home before it could be exported abroad, the Committee of Public Safety declined to intervene in behalf of a Polish revolutionary movement, refused to invade Holland, and designed a strategy that precluded any involvement in Italy. In short, while occupying the Austrian Netherlands and hoping to annex the left bank of the Rhine, the Convention renounced any drive for the establishment of new "sister republics."

## The Revolutionary Armies

The fighting men who carried the Revolution abroad were a very different body from the corps inherited from Louis XVI. The royal army had undergone major reforms since 1789, which opened military service as a decent career to all kinds of Frenchmen. At the same time, the organization of militias and national guards, with their elected officers, introduced a new concept of the citizen-soldier as against a professional army apart from civil society.

The army's chief problem came after the war began, when large numbers of royalist officers either deserted altogether or behaved disloyally. At the crucial Battle of Valmy, a remnant of the old army showed that it could fight effectively, but its numbers were too reduced by desertion and neglect. A hasty call-up of volunteers proved inadequate both in numbers and effectiveness.

The coalition launched its second major assault in 1793, and the poor performance of the French troops made it clear that drastic innovations were required. The Convention initiated far-reaching conscription and mobilization, the so-called mass levy of August 1793 (*levée en masse*). All unmarried men between the ages of 18 and 25 were drafted for combat service. All social classes were affected, and in a short time almost half a million French citizens were placed under arms. With elected officers at their head, the citizen-soliders marched off to the front under banners reading, "The French People, risen against the tyrants."

The Convention had already decided to combine these blue-uniformed recruits with their white-uniformed counterparts from the old professional army in units called demibrigades. In the future, noncommissioned officers would be elected by all troops, but higher ranks would be chosen by superior officers according to merit and seniority. The expectation was that military skills would be taught to the new troops by the professionals, who in turn would absorb a spirit of patriotism from the recruits. Although the actual amalgam took several years to complete, its spirit proved immediately successful.

One reason for this success was the Convention's attitude toward military discipline in a revolutionary society. Civilian control over the military was firmly established, and discipline now applied to officers as well as troops. The government insisted that generals show the will to win, confidence in the republic, and talent. A large number of young men were raised quickly through the ranks to command positions. Lazare Hoche, perhaps the most spectacular case, led an entire army at the age of 25 and died a military hero at 27. Other generals were less fortunate. The commander of the ill-fated Rhine army in early 1793 was branded a traitor, tried, and guillotined. The revolutionary slogan, "Win or die" was a serious matter.

A dramatically new approach to military life was thus taking shape: citizen-soldiers recruited through conscription, concern for their needs and morale, generous veterans' benefits if they were wounded, quick promotions for loyal and capable men, exemplary discipline for officers who wavered on the battlefield. The question still remained of how the new army would be used in the field, and the answer reflected the combination of revolutionary spirit and hard-headed practicality that prevailed in the republic.

The mass of soldiers in the new demibrigades did not have the training to be deployed according to the traditional tactics of old-regime armies. Yet they were infused with a sense of patriotism that it would be well to utilize. Hence strategists perfected the new battle formation of massive columns that could move quickly without much practice in drilling. Mass and mobility characterized the armies of the French Revolution. As General Hoche put it, "No maneuvers, no art; only fire and patriotism." The Committee of Public Safety advised its commanders: "Act offensively and in masses. Use the bayonet at every opportunity. Fight great battles and pursue the enemy until he is utterly destroyed." In this spirit the Jacobins and sansculottes demanded "all-out war."

The Jacobins did not neglect the home front, whose contributions to the war effort were crucial for victory. Economic mobilization, directed by the Convention and the Jacobin clubs, produced the necessary material support for the armies. Weapons, ammunition, clothing, and food were all produced or requisitioned in extraordinary quantities by herculean effort. Without them the military reforms would have achieved no purpose.

In late 1793 and early 1794, the armies won a series of decisive battles. They culminated in the Battle of Fleurus in June 1794, when the Austrian Netherlands was once again occupied; the annexation, officially conceded by the Hapsburgs in 1797, would last until 1814. At the Pyrenees and the

Rhine, French armies were victorious, forcing their enemies one by one to come to the peace table—first Spain and Prussia, then Piedmont, and finally Austria. An army crippled at the outset by treason and desertion, defeat, lack of training and discipline, and collapsing morale had been forged into a potent force in less than two years. Militarily the second revolution was a brilliant success.

## II. FROM ROBESPIERRE TO BONAPARTE
❊

To its most dedicated supporters, the revolutionary government had two major purposes: first, to surmount a crisis and steer the republic to victory; second, to democratize France's social fabric. Only the first objective won the widespread adherence of middle-class republicans. It is not surprising, therefore, that after the victories of the year II, the revolutionary government was overthrown and the second revolution dismantled. Jacobinism and democracy, however, had become a permanent part of the French experience, as had royalism and reaction. The political spectrum of modern Europe had been created. Within this spectrum the men of 1789 attempted to command a centrist or moderate position, but they proved inadequate to the task. During the four unsteady years of the Directory regime, however, revolutionary expansion outside of France proceeded aggressively. It triumphed briefly but soon precipitated a second anti-French coalition. This challenge brought the weaknesses of the Directory regime to a head and opened the way to the ascendancy of Napoleon Bonaparte.

### The Thermidorian Reaction (1794–1795)

The National Convention held a polarized nation together, consolidated the republic, and defeated the Revolution's foreign enemies. But in achieving these successes, the ruling Jacobins increasingly isolated themselves, making enemies on every side. Moderates and ultrarevolutionaries alike resented the rule that they imposed. Wealthy peasants and businesspeople chafed under the economic regimentation. The pressure of events and the relentless necessity to make hard and unpopular decisions wore out the Revolution's most prominent leaders.

After the decisive victories of the year II, the Convention's unity disintegrated. As the fifth anniversary of the Bastille's fall approached, Robespierre's enemies were emboldened to rise against him. Long-standing rivalries, differences over policy, and clashes of temperament now exploded. Robespierre girded himself to denounce yet another group of unspecified intriguers, presumably to send them to the fate of Danton and Hébert. But his rivals, both left and right, formed a hasty coalition and struck back, denouncing Robespierre to the Convention as a tyrant and would-be dictator.

The plotting of these individuals was crucial, but Robespierre's downfall is attributable also to the fact that he was no longer needed by the Convention. Having supported him with reluctance during the emergency, the moderate deputies were now willing to abandon him. The Parisian sans-culottes might have maintained Robespierre in power despite this desertion, but as we have seen, the Jacobins had alienated some by curbing the autonomy of the sections. Many sans-culottes were therefore indifferent to the struggle of personalities that took place in the Convention that July.

On the twenty-seventh—9 Thermidor—the Convention declared Robespierre an outlaw. Efforts to rally a popular force in his defense that night proved ineffective, and on the following day he and several loyal associates were seized and guillotined. French people perhaps did not realize it at the time, but 9 Thermidor thus became one of those crucial days on which the Revolution's course was decisively altered.[2]

After Robespierre's fall the Revolution's momentum was broken, and the apparatus of the Terror was dismantled. Soon the anti-Jacobins attacked the revolutionaries in turn. Their calls for retribution eventually produced a "white terror" aimed against Jacobins and sans-culottes that resulted in street fighting, assassinations, and, in the south of France, massacres.

To survey the unfolding of the Thermidorian reaction is equivalent to viewing a film of the preceding half-decade run backward through the projector. Suspects were released, the revolutionary committees abolished, defendants before the revolutionary tribunals acquitted, and their former accusers indicted in their place. The Paris Jacobin Club was closed, while in the provinces the affiliated clubs gradually withered away under harassment and restrictive legislation. Amnesty was extended to the Girondists and to the Vendée rebels; Mountain deputies were now denounced. In Paris the section leaders of the year II were driven out of political life and threatened with arrest. At all levels those who had borne the burden of responsibility and action in the year II suddenly found themselves attacked.

Paralleling these political reversals was a marked change in the state of public morals and social behavior. For those who sought a life of pleasure and luxury, Thermidor was a reprieve from the austerity and restraint of the year II. Public virtue gave way before indulgence and license. Luxury not only reappeared but by all contemporary accounts

was also flaunted with vulgarity. High society, with its balls, salons, and fancy dress, was reestablished. The titles "monsieur" and "madame" replaced the republican designation "citizen."

This social reaction occurred at a time of mass suffering. In keeping with free-trade ideology, the Thermidorians abandoned the legislation regulating the economy. The marketplace was again permitted to operate by its "natural laws" of supply and demand, producing a skyrocketing inflation. Worse yet, France experienced a harvest in 1795 more meager than in the crisis years of 1788–1789 and 1793. But despite such ill luck, the Thermidorians declined to intervene to protect small consumers from economic ravages. They were unable to provide a minimum supply of bread at an affordable price. In the face of near-famine, every index of social welfare now revealed disaster. Suicide and mortality rates rose markedly; police reports spoke of little else besides popular misery, discontent, and destitute people collapsing in the streets from undernourishment.

Since the government would not help, the former militants attempted to spark a political reversal to halt the reaction. Their hopes centered on the constitution of 1793, whose prompt and full implementation they now demanded. The slogan of sans-culottes in the sections during the spring of 1795 was simply "Bread and the constitution of 1793." The Thermidorians, however, were moving in precisely the opposite direction. Viewing that constitution as far too democratic, they were looking for an excuse to scrap it altogether.

The militants began demonstrating in April, and the government countered by ordering local authorities to disarm them. The only recourse left was insurrection, and it began on 1 Prairial year III (May 20, 1795). It was a grim, mournful uprising, a rear-guard action against disaster. The sans-culottes took over the Convention briefly in cooperation

---

[2] "Thermidor" has become a generic term to denote the phase in a revolution when the pendulum swings back toward moderation or reaction. It has been argued that the drafting of the United States Constitution in 1787 was the Thermidor of the American Revolution.

with a handful of sympathetic deputies. But their hours were numbered, for the Thermidorians had retreated merely to organize their armed forces. In two days of street fighting, the sans-culottes were driven back, cut off, and defeated. Severe repression followed: 36 people were executed, some 1200 imprisoned, and an additional 1700 interrogated and disarmed. Probably the majority of these had not even taken part in the insurrection but had been activists during the Terror.

Those days were the end of the popular movement, the last time that the Parisian revolutionary crowd would be mobilized in the 1790s. The democratic republic of the year II was lost. Whatever the possibilities had been for achieving some form of social democracy (and the issue remains ambiguous), they were now foreclosed.[3]

## The Directory (1795–1799)

By the end of 1795, the remaining members of the Convention assumed that the Revolution was over. The extremes had been vanquished, and the time for the "peaceable enjoyment of liberty" was at hand. They had drafted a new constitution—the constitution of the year III—proclaimed a general amnesty, and were prepared to turn a new page. The revolutionary government, which had replaced the fallen constitutional monarchy, was, in turn, replaced by a constitutional republic. It was known as the Directory, after its five-man executive body.

The Directory's proponents, concerned

[3] The Convention's measures to promote social democracy included the abolition of slavery, the final abolition of seigneurial rights without compensation to the lords, and equal division of estates among heirs. Legislation for a system of free public education, a progressive income tax, a war veterans' bonus, and the distribution of the property of convicted suspects to indigent patriots aborted.

above all with retaining power, declared that the republic would "be governed by the best citizens, who are found among the property-owning class." Accordingly, the constitution abandoned the universal suffrage of 1793 and restored the propertied franchise of 1791 and the multilayered system of indirect elections. Its elected two-house legislature was designed to moderate the political process, while it guarded against the rise of a potential dictator by installing the five-man Directory. Equally important, it omitted devices to facilitate active democracy, such as referendums, and said nothing of popular rights, like the right to free education and to subsistence, all of which were specified in the 1793 constitution. The elimination of popular democracy was balanced by measures to prevent a royalist resurgence. Fearing that free elections at this point might swing the republic too far to the right, the Convention decided to coopt two-thirds of its membership into the new legislature established by the constitution. A royalist attempt to oppose this with an armed protest was crushed.

The government thus repudiated both the royalist movement and the second revolution. As regicides, the directors necessarily opposed royalism; on the other hand, they were determined that popular democracy and terrorism would not recur. Apart from these considerations they were inclined to forgive and forget. They attempted to command a position somewhere near the hypothetical center of the political spectrum, which one historian has aptly called the mirage of the moderates.

To maintain themselves in power, the Directory politicians were obliged to remove with one hand freedoms that they had granted with the other. They repeatedly purged locally elected officials; they periodically undermined freedom of the press and of association, ostensibly guaranteed in the new constitution, by suppressing new Jacobin clubs and hostile newspapers. Above all, they refused to acknowledge the legitimacy of organized opposition, whether rightist or leftist. This explains the succession of coups and purges that marked the Directory's four years. Although the repressive measures were mild compared with those of the second revolution—deportation was generally the harshest punishment meted out—their net effect was to make the regime dysfunctional. In the end a significant number of Thermidorians were obliged to abandon their own creation.

## The Political Spectrum

For all its dictatorial qualities, however, the Directory regime was free enough to allow most shades of the political spectrum some visibility. Obliterated previously by the Jacobin commonwealth and later by the Napoleonic dictatorship, the full range of opinions and divisions in France was clearly revealed during the years of the Directory and would persist with certain modifications into the twentieth century.

The most important legacy of all was probably apathy, born of exhaustion or cynicism. Most citizens, especially peasants, were weary of controversy, distrustful of politicians, and hostile to administrators and tax collectors, whatever government they served. As a result, participation in the Directory regime's annual elections was extremely low.

Within this context of massive apathy, politically conscious French people were deeply divided. The ultraroyalists were uncompromising enemies of the Directory, dedicated to overthrowing it. They included émigrés, armed rebels, and refractory priests, along with their peasant followers, and many of them cooperated with the exiled Bourbons and English spies. Shading off from the ul-

traroyalists were the monarchists, mainly from the middle and peasant classes. They hoped to alter the republic's foundations and to drift gradually back toward royalism without necessarily overthrowing the republic by force. Their goals included allowing the émigrés to return, restoring the position of the refractory clergy, and stamping out entirely the last vestiges of Jacobinism. Since Napoleon largely carried out these changes, they formed a major base of his support.

On the left of the spectrum stood the Jacobins, or democrats. They were committed to preserving the Revolution of 1789 and the republic, but also identified positively with the second revolution. They did not advocate a return to the Terror, hoping rather, like the constitutional royalists, to work legally within the new institutions of the Directory to regain power. The Neo-Jacobin policy was to promote grass-roots activism through local political clubs, petitions, newspapers, and electoral campaigns. The clubs attracted a small cross section of middle-class revolutionaries and sans-culotte militants, thus keeping alive the egalitarian social ideals of the year II. In addition to calling for the implementation of existing laws against counterrevolutionaries, the Jacobins advocated free public education, a veterans' bonus for soldiers, the right to subsistence, and progressive taxation.

At the far end of the spectrum emerged a tiny group of collectivists whose significance would loom much larger in the nineteenth century than it did in 1796. This was the circle of Gracchus Babeuf. They viewed the year II as simply a stage in the revolutionary process that had to be followed by a final revolution against the middle-class republic in the name of the masses. Their objectives were a vaguely defined "real equality" and a "community of goods," a distributive type of communism. Believing that the middle-class republic was simply a new form of tyranny, they plotted its overthrow by means of a highly centralized secret conspiracy.

The Directory's adherents stood somewhere in the center of this broad spectrum, shifting their ground uncertainly and unsuccessfully. They were hostile to the royalists, but possibly even more antagonistic to the Jacobins. They sometimes collaborated with the reactionaries, as when they used the Babeuf plot as a pretext for repressing the entire left, though most democrats had rejected Babeuf's calls for insurrection and did not take his communism seriously. This propelled the Directory into a tentative alliance with the right, and the climate of public opinion became increasingly reactionary. However, when the first regular elections held in the year V (1797) produced a royalist victory, the moderates reversed themselves. Backed by General Bonaparte's Army of Italy, they purged the legislature of the most notorious royalists, annulled numerous elections, suppressed about 40 royalist newspapers, restored the sanctions against priests and émigrés, and allowed the Jacobins to open new clubs.

But after a few months, as the clubs began to revive a democratic spirit, the Directory grew fearful. During the elections of the year VI (1798), democratic and conservative republicans began to campaign against each other in what almost amounted to party rivalry. The Directory again intervened, closing the clubs, manipulating the electoral assemblies, and where this failed, purging the democrats elected. It is revealing to note that almost at the same time the American republic was going through a similar process, but there organized opposition was accepted as part of the legitimate political system. In France organized opposition was not tolerated, and that crucial decision contributed to the republic's demise.

## The Rise of Bonaparte

While France was retreating from its Revolution internally, however, it supported and spread it more forcefully than ever abroad. For the Revolution in Europe, the Directory years marked a high point of success. Under the Directory France gradually encouraged wars of liberation and the establishment of sister republics (see Map 21.1). This eventually led to the creation of progressive governments in the United Provinces and the Swiss Confederation, which became known respectively as the Batavian and Helvetic republics. It led also, despite the Directory's attempt to prevent it, to the spread of war and liberation to the entire Italian peninsula. This, in turn, came about because certain commanders in the field began to create their own diplomacy. Among them was a young brigadier general, Napoleon Bonaparte.

### The Making of a Hero

Bonaparte personifies the world-historical figure—the rare person whose life decisively affects the mainstream of human events. Born in 1769 of an impoverished but well-connected family on the French-controlled island of Corsica, he scarcely seemed destined to play such a role. His youthful ambitions were limited to Corsica itself, and most of his adolescent fantasies seem to have involved leading the island to independence from France. He was sent to French military academies, where he proved a deligent student, adept at mathematics, and an eager reader of history. Aloof from his aristocratic classmates, whose pretensions he resented, young Bonaparte was self-reliant and energetic. Imagination and energy would remain among his chief personality traits, but before the Revolution he lacked any notable objec-

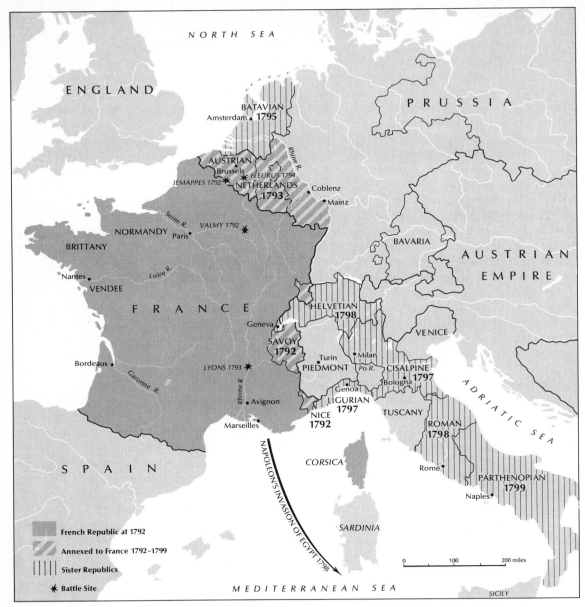

**MAP 21.1 THE REVOLUTIONARY REPUBLICS 1792–1799**

tive. Meanwhile, he became an expert in artillery.

The Revolution saw him return to Corsica, but his ambitions ran afoul of more conservative elements on the island. Eventually, the heat of provincial factionalism drove him and his family off Corsica altogether. At that juncture Napoleon moved onto a far larger stage of action. His rise as a military officer was steady and rapid; it was based in part on the luck of successive opportunities but equally on his ability to make fast, bold decisions and carry them out with efficiency. On leave in Paris in 1795, he made important contacts among the leaders of the Directory and was assigned to the planning bureau of the war ministry. This put him in a position to advocate a new strategy—the opening of a major front in Italy for a French strike at the Hapsburg forces from the south, pushing into Germany while armies on the Rhine drove in from the west. The strategy approved, he was given command of the Army of Italy in 1796.

The Austrian forces outnumbered the French, but Bonaparte moved his troops rapidly to achieve surprise and numerical superiority in specific encounters. The end result was a major victory that brought the French the Hapsburg province of Lombardy with its capital, Milan. Bonaparte's overall plan almost miscarried, since the army of the Rhine was unsuccessful in its part of the offensive. But this fact made his own victories all the more important to the Directory. Moreover, Napoleon ensured his popularity with the Paris government by making his campaign self-supporting through organized levies on the Italians instead of allowing his troops the customary looting.

On the scene in Italy, Bonaparte brought a great sense of excitement and showmanship to the French occupation. His personal magnetism and his ability to manipulate men and policies won him popularity among the Italians. He encouraged them to organize their own revolutionary movement, seeing the liberation of North Italy as a means of solidifying support for his army among them and enhancing his own reputation. This distressed the Directory since its own objective was to trade off conquests in Italy for security on the Rhine frontier. But in the end the government had to accept the fruits of the young general's victories over Austria and the Treaty of Campo Formio, which he personally negotiated in October 1797. Austria recognized a new and independent state in northern Italy, the Cisalpine Republic, and made peace with France, leaving the Rhine question to future negotiations.

Patriotic aspiration in France now focused on defeating the last member of the coalition—the hated British enemy. Bonaparte naturally yearned for the glory of accomplishing this feat, and he was authorized to prepare an invasion force. Previous seaborne landings directed at Ireland had failed, and Napoleon, too, was finally obliged to abandon the scheme because of insufficient naval capability.

In the spring of 1798 Bonaparte instead turned southward to launch an expedition to Egypt. The objective was to strike at Britain's colonial interests, ultimately including the approaches to India. But British naval superiority, in the form of Admiral Horatio Nelson's fleet, turned the mission into a debacle. At the Battle of the Nile, the French fleet was destroyed, and the army was marooned without support in North Africa. In addition, Napoleon suffered reversals in engagements with Turkish forces. Only skillful news management prevented the full dimensions of the defeat from being known in France; the expedition's exotic details—including the much-publicized element of scientific exploration—dominated the version of the events that most French people learned. Napoleon extricated himself from this mess by slipping off through the blockade alone, abandoning his army. Since important things were happening in France, he was confident that this would be overlooked.

### The Brumaire Coup

While Bonaparte was in Egypt, the Directory was faltering under the political pressures discussed earlier. Charges of tyranny and ineffectiveness accumulated against the executive. Its diplomacy had proved a failure. Further expansion in Italy, which had produced several new sister republics on the peninsula, had precipitated a new coalition against France—Great Britain, Russia, Austria, Naples, and Turkey. Facing a new war in the spring of 1799, the government was denounced for tolerating corruption by war contractors and for harassing patriotic generals.

In the elections of that spring, the widespread discontent was manifested in the defeat of many government-sponsored candidates. Shortly thereafter the legislature ousted four of the five directors and replaced them with a coalition led by Sieyès. The pretext for toppling the incumbents came from military reversals in June, when ill-supplied French forces were compelled to evacuate most of Italy and were yielding in the Helvetic Republic. Sieyès's supporters were secretly eager to alter the constitution itself. They had lost confidence in the institutions of the Directory regime and disapproved of the instability caused by its annual elections. They were "revisionists," hoping to redesign the republic along more oligarchic lines. Their main enemies were the Jacobins, who wished to democratize the Directory gradually. The centrist position had virtually disappeared.

The military crisis briefly favored the Jacobins, who responded with a battery of emergency measures to rally the country. Simultaneously, they urged legislation to guarantee freedom for newspapers, political clubs, and other forms of organized dissent. The revisionists opposed these proposals, stalled, and ultimately succeeded in having them rejected. Meanwhile, the autumn brought success for the French forces in the Helvetic state and in the Batavian Republic, where they repulsed an Anglo-Russian invasion. Most of Italy was lost, but the real threat to France itself had passed. At this point the revisionists began a concerted offensive at home against the democrats, closing down their clubs and newspapers and preparing for a coup d'état against the constitution, whose main supporters were now the powerless Jacobins.

Bonaparte's return to France seemed most timely. True, no dire military threat remained to propel the country into the arms of a general; the revisionists wished to scrap a relatively open-ended regime that might evolve in a democratic direction and to establish a more centralized, oligarchic republic. But they did need a general's cooperation, for generals were the only national heroes in this demoralized period. A general could organize whatever force might be necessary to ensure the success of the coup. Bonaparte was not the revisionists' first choice, but he proved to be the only one available. In addition, his trip up from the Mediterranean was greeted with a hero's welcome; the people had only a dim knowledge of the Egyptian fiasco and saw him in his well-earned role of victor in the Italian campaign.

Contrary to the intentions of Sieyès and his coconspirators, Bonaparte proved to be the tail that wagged the dog. As the plans were prepared, he thrust himself into a prominent position, emerging as the most ambitious and boldest of those involved. It was he who addressed the legislature to denounce a mythical Jacobin plot and to demand emergency powers to set up a new provisional government. These powers were granted, and Bonaparte joined with the two remaining directors to form a new executive, charged with bringing in a new constitutional draft. Soldiers were present to prevent any resistance. The legislature was then purged, with a cooperative rump left to ratify the new arrangements. This was how the *journée* of 18 Brumaire year VIII (November 9, 1799) unfolded.

The Brumaire coup had not been designed to create a dictatorship, but that was its eventual result. In the ensuing maneuvering among the revisionists, Bonaparte's ideas and personality prevailed. The general came out of the coup as the strong man in a triumvirate of consuls, and Sieyès's elaborate plans for a republican oligarchy ended in the wastebasket. He himself accepted a pension and retired to the country.

In other respects the plotters' plans succeeded. Elections and legislative power were limited. The social ideals propounded in the revolution of the year II were blocked, while those of 1789 were protected. The price was a surrender of popular sovereignty and parliamentary liberalism. On one final point the revisionists were to be particularly deceived. With Bonaparte's cooperation they had held out the promise of obtaining a durable peace through victory. Instead, the new regime promoted expansion and continuous war of unparalleled dimensions.

## III. THE NAPOLEONIC IMPERIUM
### ❊

Bonaparte rapidly became a forceful and skillful dictator. Certain of his institutional and social reforms proved so durable that they survived his downfall by well over a century. At the time, however, it was his success on the battlefield against France's foes that gave him a free hand domestically. And it was again on the battlefield that his ambitions began to grow, transforming him from a general of the Revolution to an imperial conqueror of the Continent. Bonaparte's occupation of Italy, Germany, Spain, and other lands set contradictory forces of change in motion. Nationalism, liberalism, and reaction alike were sparked by his presence.

### The Napoleonic Settlement in France

Napoleon's prime asset in his rapid takeover of France was the resignation of its citizens. Most French people were so weary politically that they were inclined to see in Napoleon what they wished to see. The Committee of Public Safety had won grudging submission only through its terroristic policies; Napoleon achieved the same result almost by default. That he was practical, an effective propagandist for himself, and a man of great personal magnetism helped placate a divided France. Ultraroyalists and dedicated Jacobins were never reconciled to his regime, but most citizens fell between those extremes and were able to find something to cheer about in the general's accomplishments.

Napoleon's attitudes are not easily classified: He was not a reactionary or a Jacobin, not a conservative or a liberal, though his opinions were flavored by a touch of each persuasion. The things he was most concerned with were authority and justification of his actions through results. The people of 1789 could find in him an heir of the Revolution because of his hostility toward the old regime. The corporate system, the creaking institutions of absolutism, and the congealed structures of aristocratic hierarchy were all distasteful to him. He considered them unjust and ineffective. Apart from these negative perspectives, Napoleon valued the Revolution's positive commitment to equality of opportunity. This was the major liberal concept of 1789 that he continued to defend.

Other rights and liberties he curtailed or ignored.

Ten years of upheavals had presented a grim paradox: The Revolution had proceeded in the name of freedom, yet successive forms of repression had been mounted to defend it. Napoleon fitted comfortably into this mold; unlike the Directory, he made no pretense about it. The social gains of the Revolution would be preserved through the exercise of strong control. His field of action was far greater than that of the most powerful eighteenth-century monarch, for no entrenched aristocracy existed to resist him. Benefiting from the clearing operations of the Revolution, he could reconstruct far more than any previous ruler and thus could show more results in justification of his authoritarian measures.

Tragically, however, Napoleon drifted away from his own ideal of rationalization. Increasingly absorbed in his personal power, he began to force domestic and foreign policies on France that were geared to his imperial ambitions. As a result, he increasingly directed his government toward raising men and money for the military machine, abandoning the fragile revolutionary legacy in the process.

### Political and Religious Settlements

Bonaparte imposed a constitution on France that placed almost unchecked power in the hands of a single man, the first consul, for 10 years. It also called for his own appointment to that position. Two later constitutional revisions, which were approved in plebiscites, further increased executive authority while diminishing the legislative branch until it all but disappeared. The first, in 1802, converted the consulship into a lifetime post; the second, in 1804, did away with the republic by proclaiming Napoleon emperor of the French with hereditary title. The task of drafting legislation was transferred from elected representatives to appointed administrators in the Council of State. This new body was charged with advising the emperor, drafting legislation under his orders, and supervising local authorities and public institutions. This marked the birth of government by experts that remained an alternative to parliamentary government throughout subsequent French history.

The system of local government established in 1800 came ironically close to restoring the centralized bureaucracy of the old regime, which had been unanimously condemned in 1789. Under Bonaparte, local elections, which the Revolution had emphasized, were virtually eliminated. Each department was now administered by a prefect appointed by Paris. The 400-odd subprefects on the district level as well as the 40,000 mayors of France's communes were likewise appointed. With minor changes the prefect system survived in France until the socialist victory of 1981, severely limiting local autonomy and self-government.

Police-state methods finished what constitutional change began: the suppression of genuine political activity in French life. Inheriting a police ministry from the Directory, Napoleon placed it under the control of a former terrorist, Joseph Fouché, directing him to eliminate organized opposition and dissent. Newspapers were reduced in number and drastically censored;[4] the free journalism born in 1789 was replaced by government press releases and news management—the propaganda techniques Napoleon had adopted in Italy and Egypt became standard procedure for the consulate and empire. Clubs were prohibited, certain dissidents deported, and other presumed opponents

---

[4] Before the Brumaire coup, Paris had had 73 newspapers; by 1811 it had only 4, all hewing to the official government line.

placed under surveillance by police spies. All this wrested submission from the whole range of political activists—royalist diehards, sans-culotte militants, and liberal intellectuals. Opposition was reduced to clandestine plotting or passive resistance.

Napoleon's actions in the religious sphere were designed to promote stability at home and popularity abroad. By 1800 revolutionary policy amounted to half-hearted secularism, with Catholicism tolerated but severely restricted. Continuing proscription of the refractory clergy made the free exercise of the religion difficult, and the orthodox Catholic world continued to consider the entire Revolution as antichurch.

Napoleon judged that major concessions to Catholic sentiment were in order, provided they could be carefully controlled by the state. In 1801 he negotiated a concordat or agreement with Pope Pius VII. It provided that Catholicism was the "preferred" religion of France, but protected religious freedom for non-Catholics. The Church was now permitted to operate in full public view. Primary education would be more or less turned over to the clergy, and clerical salaries would be paid by the state. Bishops would again be consecrated by the pope, but they would be nominated by the consul. Most important, the concordat reserved to the state the power to regulate the place of the Church within French society. One major revolutionary change was sustained: Lands confiscated from the Church and sold during the Revolution were to be retained by their purchasers. Another major change was abandoned: The 10-day week was dropped and the Gregorian calendar restored.

The balance of church-state relations was firmly fixed in the state's favor, for it was Napoleon's intention to use the clergy as a major prop of the new regime. With priests now responsible to the government, the pulpit and the primary school became instru-ments of social control, to be used, as the imperial catechism put it, "to bind the religious conscience of the people to the August person of the Emperor." Napoleon summarized his approach to religion in his statement that the clergy would be his moral prefects. Eventually, devout Catholics came to fear that this highly national version of church organization would be detrimental to true Catholicism. Pius renounced the concordat—to which Napoleon responded by removing the pontiff to France and placing him under house arrest.

## The Social System

With old-regime obstacles to civil equality removed, Napoleon believed that the Revolution was complete. It remained now to erect an orderly, hierarchical society to counteract what he regarded as the excessive individualism of revolutionary social reforms. The foundation stones of social change—the transfer of Church lands, the end of the guild system, the abolition of feudalism—would be consolidated. At the same time, the authority of state and family would be reasserted.

In the absence of electoral politics, Napoleon used the state's vast appointive powers to confer status on prominent local figures or *notables*, thus associating them with his regime. These regional dignitaries were chosen from among the prosperous landowners, ex-nobles, and middle class. A new source of status was added to enhance the prestige of those who served the regime well: the Order of the Legion of Honor, nine-tenths of whose members were military men. "It is with trinkets that mankind is governed." Napoleon is supposed to have said. Legion of Honor awards and local appointments under the patronage system were precisely such trinkets, and they endured long after their creator was gone.

Napoleon helped consolidate the place of

the notables in more practical ways. A system of compulsory labor "passports" gave employers control over their workers' movements; trade unions and strikes were strictly prohibited. Leading bankers realized their long-standing ambition to have a national bank chartered that they fully controlled and enjoyed the credit power derived from official ties to the state. In education Napoleon created elite secondary schools, or *lycées*, to produce high civil servants and officers. They were joined to a rigidly centralized academic system that survived intact into the twentieth century.

An equally durable legal codification covered social relations and property rights. The Civil Code, renamed the Napoleonic Code in 1807, was a revolutionary document that progressives were pleased to see exported throughout Europe. Feudal aristocracy and the property relations deriving from it were obliterated. Instead, all citizens could now exercise unambiguous contractual ownership of land. The code established the right to choose one's occupation, to receive equal treatment under the law, and to enjoy religious freedom. At the same time, it confirmed the Thermidorian and Directory retreat from the social policies of the second revolution. Property rights, for example, were not matched by anything resembling a right to subsistence.

Revolutionary legislation had emancipated women and children by establishing their civil liberties. Napoleon undid most of this progress by restoring the father's absolute authority in the family. A wife owes obedience to her husband, said the code, which proceeded to deprive her of property and juridical rights that had been granted during the Revolution. The rights of illegitimate children were also eliminated, and the husband's options in disposing of his estate were enlarged, though each child was still guaranteed a portion. Napoleon insisted on rela-

tively liberal provisions for divorce—but only as far as the husband was concerned. Penal codes and criminal procedures also rolled back revolutionary libertarianism. Defendants' rights and the role of juries were both curtailed.

The Napoleonic Code, the concordat, the education system, and the patronage structure all proved extremely durable institutions. They fulfilled Napoleon's desire to create a series of "granite masses" on which French society could be permanently reconstructed. His admirers emphasize that these achievements contributed to social stability despite France's chronic lack of stable governments. One can argue that they were skillful compromises between revolutionary equality and libertarianism on the one hand and a sense of hierarchy and authority on the other. Detractors point out that they were class-oriented, withdrawing from the mass of French people promises held out by the second revolution, and that they created an overcentralized, rigid institutional structure that sapped French vitality in succeeding generations. Whatever their merits or defects, these institutions did take root, unlike Napoleon's attempt to create a hereditary empire and a French-dominated Europe.

## Napoleonic Hegemony

Although Bonaparte was not needed to repel an invasion at the time of the Brumaire coup, he was expected to provide strategy and command for a successful conclusion of the war against the second coalition. Accordingly, the first consul left France at the earliest opportunity in late 1799 with an army to engage Hapsburg forces in northern Italy. The outcome of this campaign would confirm or destroy the settlement he had imposed on France. A decisive victory would make him impregnable; a rout would obviously destroy his political future.

This etching of the Battle of Austerlitz (December 1805) dramatically captures the two faces of Napoleonic warfare: the glory and the gore. In the background an Austrian flag is being presented to the emperor—the mark of his brilliant victory in that engagement. But in the foreground the mangled corpses of the casualties are plainly evident. As the years went on, the glory became more and more dubious, while the dead and disabled grew too numerous to contemplate.   (Photo: Culver Pictures, Inc.)

Napoleon's strategy called for a repeat of the 1797 campaign: He would strike through Italy while the army of the Rhine pushed eastward against Vienna. This time it worked. Following French victories at Marengo, in Lombardy, and Hohenlinden, in Germany, Austria sued for peace. The Treaty of Lunéville, in February 1801, essentially restored France to the position it had held after Napoleon's triumphs in 1797.

In the British Isles a war-weary government, now standing alone against Napoleon, decided to negotiate a treaty also. The Peace of Amiens, March 1801, ended hostilities and reshuffled territorial holdings outside Europe. But it was a precarious truce because it did not settle the future of French influence and expansion or commercial relations between the two nations. Napoleon soon showed that he was willing to violate the spirit of the treaty while abiding by its letter. The British and Austrians alike were dismayed by the continued expansion of French influence in Italy, the Helvetic Republic, and North America. Most important perhaps, France made it clear that it would exclude British trade rather than restore normal trading relations. Historians generally agree that the Peace of Amiens failed because neither side was strongly interested in making it last. Their century-long struggle for preeminence had yet to be decided.

A third coalition, a replay of its predecessors, formed as the treaties broke down. France's ostensible war aims were still the preservation of the regime at home and the sister republics abroad. The third coalition had the ideological and diplomatic objectives of restoring the Batavian Republic and Italy to "independence," dissolving French influ-

**Among its other functions, the Napoleonic Empire provided great spoils for the Bonaparte siblings. With Napoleon now an emperor, it was only fitting that his sisters were married off to princely husbands, and that his brothers were provided with thrones of their own in French-occupied Europe. Here, Prince Jérome Bonaparte marries Princess Catherine of Württenberg.** (Photo: Bulloz)

ence elsewhere, and if possible, reducing France to its original borders. But like most alliances of its sort, the third coalition was to be dismembered piecemeal.

French hopes of settling the issue directly by invading England proved unrealizable. At the Battle of Trafalgar, in October 1805, an already outnumbered and outmanned French navy was crushed by Admiral Nelson's fleet. An innovative tactician who broke rule-book procedures on the high seas as French generals had been doing on land, Nelson ensured the security of the British Isles for the remainder of the Napoleonic era.

Napoleon turned now against the Austro-Russian forces. Moving 200,000 French soldiers with unprecedented speed across the Continent, he took his enemies by surprise and won a succession of startling victories. After occupying Vienna he proceeded against the coalition's main army in December. Feigning weakness and retreat at the moment of battle, he drew his now numerically superior opponents into an exposed position, crushed the center of their lines, and inflicted a decisive defeat. The Battle of Austerlitz was Napoleon's most brilliant tactical achievement, and the Hapsburgs were compelled to jump for the peace table. The resulting Treaty of Pressburg was extremely harsh and humiliating for Austria. Not only was a large indemnity imposed on it, but it was also required to cede its Venetian provinces.

## The Conquest and Reorganization of Europe

By this time Napoleon had far surpassed his role of general of the Revolution and was beginning his imperial march toward the conquest of Europe. The French sphere of influence had increased dramatically to include most of southern Germany, which was organized into the Confederation of the Rhine, a client realm of France. At the moment only Prussia stood outside this sphere. Its neutrality during the war with Austria had been effected by skillful French diplomacy and Prussian miscalculation. Only after Austria had been forced to the peace table did Prussia recognize the threat it had allowed to rise by failing to combine effectively with its neighbor to the south. Belatedly, Prussia mobilized its famous but antiquated army; it was rewarded with stinging defeat by France in a number of encounters culminating in the Battle of Jena in October 1806. With Prussian military power proved a paper tiger and the conqueror settled in Berlin, the prestige of the ruling class disintegrated. Napoleon was now master of the northern German lands and the south. For a while it appeared that he would obliterate Prussia entirely, but in the end he restored its sovereignty after amputating part of its territory and imposing a crushing indemnity.

The subsequent reorganization of Central Europe brought Napoleon considerable gratification and prestige. He formally proclaimed the end of the Holy Roman Empire in 1806—Francis II had already changed his own title to Emperor Francis I of Austria two years earlier—and liquidated numerous small German principalities. In their place he erected two new states: the Kingdom of Westphalia, on whose throne he placed his brother Jérôme; and the grand duchy of Berg, to be ruled by Joachim Murat, his brother-in-law. His ally Saxony was proclaimed a full-scale kingdom, while a new duchy of Warsaw was created out of Prussian Poland. This "restoration" of Poland had major propaganda value; it made the emperor appear a champion of Polish national aspirations in view of the fact that the rulers of Prussia, Russia, and Austria had dismembered Poland in a series of partitions ending in 1795. Moreover, Napoleon could now enlist a Polish army and use Polish territory as a base of operations against the last Continental member of the coalition, Russia.

In February 1807 Napoleon confronted the colossus of the East in the Battle of Eylau; the resulting carnage was horrifying but inconclusive. When spring came Napoleon was in a desperate position. Only a dramatic victory could preserve his conquests in Central Europe and vindicate the extraordinary decisions of the past two years. Fortunately for the emperor, the Battle of Friedland in June was a French victory that demoralized Tsar Alexander I and persuaded him to negotiate.

Meeting at Tilsit, the two emperors buried their differences and proceeded to create a mighty alliance of two superstates that would dominate Europe, essentially partitioning it into Eastern and Western spheres of influence. Each would support the other's conquests and mediate in behalf of the other's interests. The Treaty of Tilsit of July 7 sanctioned Napoleon's reorganization of Europe as well as the dramatic expansion of French territory eastward. Apart from outright annexations, the chief vehicle for Napoleon's rearrangements was the creation of satellite kingdoms. The old sister republics now became kingdoms just as France itself had. And it happened that Napoleon had a whole family of brothers ready to assume royal crowns.

The distorted shape of Napoleonic Europe at its high point, around 1810, is best appre-

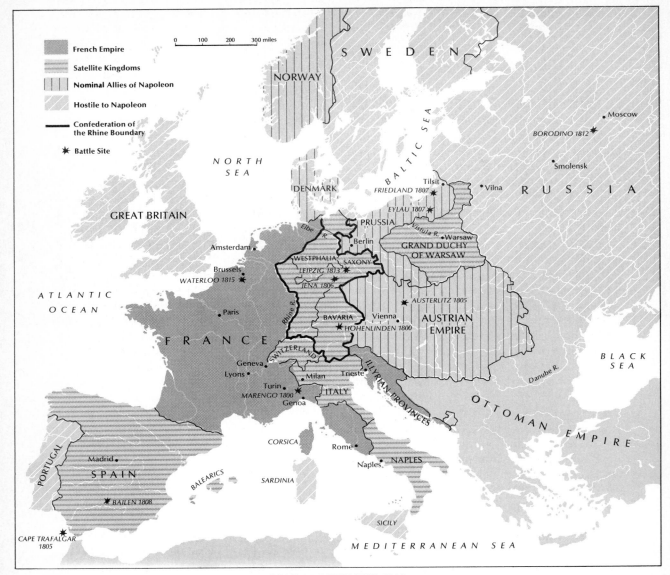

**MAP 21.2 EUROPE 1810**

ciated on a map (see Map 21.2). His chief satellites included the Kingdom of Holland, comprising the Batavian Republic, with brother Louis on the throne; the Kingdom of Italy, with Napoleon himself as king and stepson Eugène de Beauharnais as viceroy; the Confederation of the Rhine, including brother Jérôme's Kingdom of Westphalia; the Kingdom of Naples, covering southern Italy, with brother Joseph wearing the crown until he was transferred to Spain and passed it to brother-in-law Murat; and the duchy of Warsaw. The old Austrian Netherlands, the Rhineland, Tuscany, Piedmont, Genoa, the Illyrian provinces, and the Ionian Islands had been directly annexed to France. Switzerland persisted as the Helvetic Republic but under a new constitution dictated by France. In 1810, after yet another war with Austria, a marriage was arranged between the house of Bonaparte and the house of Hapsburg: Napoleon, having divorced Joséphine de Beauharnais, married Marie Louise, daughter of Francis I.

### The Continental System

Only Britain remained to be vanquished; meanwhile, it stood between Napoleon and his dream of complete hegemony over Europe, not to mention the world beyond. Since Britain was invulnerable to invasion, Napoleon's objective was to destroy its influence by means of economic warfare.

Unable to blockade British ports directly, the emperor sought to close the Continent— to blockade Britain from its markets, stop its exports, and thus ruin its trade and credit. In mercantilist fashion he reasoned that if Britain had nowhere to sell its manufactured goods, no gold would come into the country, which would eventually bankrupt it. At the same time, overproduction would cause unemployment, and the ensuing labor unrest might turn the British people against the government and force it to make peace with France. On the other hand, French advantages in Continental markets woud naturally increase with the elimination of British competition.

Accordingly, Napoleon mounted his so-called Continental System: He would prohibit British trade with all French allies and all commerce by neutrals carrying British products, prevent all ships coming from British ports from landing in Europe, and have any goods coming from or belonging to the British Isles seized.

The British responded in 1807 with the Orders in Council that in effect reversed the blockade: They *required* all neutral ships to stop at British ports to procure trading licenses and pay tariffs. In other words, they intervened in all trade between neutrals and most European ports. Violators would be seized. Napoleon's angry answer to this was the threat simply to capture any neutral ship that obeyed the Orders in Council by stopping at British ports.

Thus a total naval war involving neutrals grew out of the Continental System. Indeed, there scarcely remained such a thing as neutral immunity, since every ship was obliged to violate one system or the other and thus run afoul of naval patrols or privateers. While the British took only about 40 French ships a year after 1807 (for few were left to sail the seas), they seized almost 3000 neutrals a year, including many American ships.

Britain was hurt by the Continental System. British gold reserves dwindled, and internal strife did erupt in 1811, a year of widespread unemployment and rioting. France was affected adversely by the counterblockade, which cut it off from the raw materials necessary for industrial production. But the satellite states probably suffered the most, becoming economic vassals of France. In Amsterdam, for example, shipping volume declined from 1350 ships entering the port in 1806 to 310 in 1809; as a result commercial revenues dropped calamitously. Out of loyalty to the people whom he ruled, King Louis Bonaparte tolerated smuggling. This so infuriated Napoleon that he ousted his brother from the throne and annexed the Kingdom of Holland to France. Smuggling was in fact the weak link in the system, creating holes in Napoleon's dike of economic sanctions that constantly needed plugging. This, in turn, drove Napoleon to more drastic adventures.

## Resistance to Napoleon

Having vanquished every major European power on the battlefield except Britain, Napoleon now felt that nothing stood in his way. Since Spain and Russia did not seem responsive enough to his will, the emperor chose to deal with each of them by force, assuming that his plans against Britain could then be pursued to their conclusion. On all counts he was mistaken. Napoleon's confrontations with Britain, Spain, and Russia proved in various ways that his reach had exceeded his grasp.

### The Spanish Ulcer

Spain and France had a common interest in weakening British power in Europe and the colonial world. But their alliance after 1795 brought only reversals for Spain, including the loss of the Louisiana Territory and (at the Battle of Trafalgar) most of the Spanish fleet. Domestically, things were no better. The royal household had been the scene of scandalous and bitter controversy for some time. A lover of Queen Maria Louisa, Manuel de Godoy, had achieved astonishing power as prime minister and proved to be a corrupt opportunist who was extremely unpopular with the people. He was despised by Crown Prince Ferdinand, who was equally hostile to Godoy's protectors, the king and queen.

Napoleon looked on with extreme irritation. At the zenith of his power, he easily drifted toward the solution of reorganizing Spain himself. As a pretext for military intervention, he put in motion a plan to invade Portugal, supposedly to partition it with Spain. Once the French army was well inside Spain, it could impose the political solution to Spain's instability that Napoleon desired.

The squabbling King Charles IV and his son were tricked, threatened, and bribed into abdicating, one after the other. A group of Spanish notables was gathered to petition Napoleon to provide a new sovereign, preferably his brother Joseph, and Joseph was duly proclaimed king of Spain. With French troops already settled around Madrid, Joseph prepared to assume his new throne, sincerely eager to rule well under a liberal constitution. But as he took up the crown, an unanticipated drama erupted.

Faced with military occupation, the disappearance of their royal family, and the crowning of a Frenchman, the Spanish people rose in rebellion. It began on May 2, 1808, when an angry crowd rioted against French troops, who responded with brutal reprisals. This bloody incident, known as the Dos de Mayo and captured in Goya's famous paintings (see Plate 48), has been preserved in Spanish legend. The kidnaping of Prince Ferdinand a short time later galvanized the uprising into a sustained offensive against the French and pro-French Spaniards. Local notables created juntas to organize the rebels, mainly peasants and monks, and coordinated them with regular Spanish troops.

The troops were generally ineffective against the French but did produce one victory: Two French divisions were forced to surrender at Bailén in July, an episode that broke the aura of Napoleonic invincibility. The brunt of professional military operations was borne by the British in what they called the Peninsular War. Their expeditionary force first drove the French out of Portugal and eventually rolled them back across Spain under the inspired command of Arthur Wellesley, later duke of Wellington. All the while, as many as 30,000 Spanish guerilla fighters were providing another dimension to the conflict and contributing to its brutality. Their harassment of the French kept the foreign invaders in a constant state of anxiety and led to reprisals that, in turn, escalated the war's bitterness.

All told, the juntas, the guerillas, and the British held a massive French army of up to 300,000 men pinnned down in Spain and made it impossible for Napoleon to mobilize fully elsewhere on the Continent. He referred to the war as the "Spanish ulcer." Though Napoleon had contempt for the rebel monks and peasants, other Europeans were inspired by their example that resistance to the French emperor was possible.

Meanwhile, the war proved a disaster for Spanish liberals. Torn between Joseph, who would have been a liberal ruler, and the nationalist rebels, they ended by falling into an unviable position between the two. Those who supported Joseph found that he was never able to rule independently. It was Napoleon who gave the orders in Spain, relying on his generals to carry them out. Those who stood behind the rebels were able to organize a provisional government in 1812 by convening the ancient parliament, the Cortes, in the town of Cádiz. There they drafted a liberal and nationalist constitution, which pleased the British and therefore was tolerated by the local juntas. But in reality, the bulk of rebel sympathizers disdained the liberals. They were fighting rather for the Catholic Church and the Spanish Bourbons. When in 1814 the French were finally expelled and Ferdinand VII took the throne, the liberals' joy was short-lived. Ferdinand tore up the constitution of 1812, restored the monasteries and the Inquisition, closed down the universities, revived censorship, and arrested the leading liberals. The main beneficiaries of the Spanish rebellion and the Peninsular War were thus Spanish reactionaries and the British.

### The Russian Debacle

In 1811 Napoleon did not yet realize how his entanglement in Spain would drain French military power and encourage intellectuals and statesmen in Central Europe to contemplate nationalist uprisings against him. On the contrary, never were Napoleon's schemes more grandiose than in that year. Surveying the crumbling state system of Europe, he imagined that it could be replaced with a supranational empire, ruled from Paris and Rome and based on the Napoleonic Code. He believed that the era of the balance of power was over and that nationalist strivings would not stand in his way. On both counts he was mistaken.

The key obstacle to imperial reorganization and French domination was Russia. Wishing to retain its sphere of interest in Eastern Europe and the Baltic region, and increasingly discontented with the restrictions of the Continental System, Russia was a restive ally. Alexander was being pressured on the one hand to resist France by British diplomats, French émigrés, anti-Napoleonic exiles such as Baron Stein of Prussia, and nationalist reactionaries. On the other hand, Russian court liberals, more concerned with domestic reforms, were eager for him to maintain peace with France; but by 1812 their influence on Alexander had waned. On his side Napoleon wanted to enforce the Continental System and reduce Russia's capacity to interfere with Europe's destiny. As he put it with characteristic bluntness, "Let Alexander defeat the Persians, but don't let him meddle in the affairs of Europe." Once again two major powers were facing each other with progressively less interest in maintaining peace.

Napoleon decided to strike, and he embarked on his most ambitious military campaign. His objective was to annihilate the Russian forces or to conquer Moscow and chase the army to the point of disarray. Almost 600,000 men (many drawn from the satellite states), long supply lines, and repeated forced marches were his principal weapons.

# ❊ EXPERIENCES OF DAILY LIFE ❊
## *The Napoleonic Conscription Machine*

In its initial phase, the French Revolution made no demands on French citizens for military service. Rejecting the idea of conscription, the National Assembly opted instead for a relatively small professional army of long-term volunteers. When the war began in 1792, the Republic at first relied on one-year volunteers to bolster the line army. But as the scale of hostilities expanded to a five-front war, the Convention decreed a mass levy of able-bodied men between the ages of 18 and 25 (see p. 838). This unprecedented mobilization was meant as a one-time-only emergency measure, a temporary "requisition" of manpower. There was no implication that subsequent cohorts of young men would face conscription into the army as part of their civic obligations. Thus married men were exempted from the *levée en masse*—an exemption that would have provided a wholesale loophole for draft avoidance in the future if the levy had been intended to inaugurate a regular system of conscription.

As the war dragged on, however, the Directory regime put in place a conscription law in September 1798, which made various "classes" of young men (that is, those born in a particular year) subject to a military draft should the need arise. The Directory almost immediately implemented this law and called up three such classes. The results alarmed the government. Local officials in most departments reported that youths found the prospect of military service "repugnant," and that draft evasion was massive. Yet from this shaky foundation the Napoleonic regime developed a highly efficient conscription machine.

After much trial and error with the details, timetables, and mechanisms, the system began to operate smoothly within a few years. Napoleon's Ministry of War Administration assigned an annual quota of conscripts for each department. Using parish birth registers, the mayor of every community compiled a list of men reaching the age of 19 that year. These youths were then led by their mayor to the cantonal seat on a specified day for a draft lottery. A preliminary examination screened out the manifestly unfit as well as those below the minimum height of about 5'1". Panels of doctors at the departmental capitals later verified or rejected these exclusions, as well as other claims for medical exemptions. In all, about a third of French youths avoided military service legally as physically unfit: because they were too short, lame, deformed, or suffering from poor eyesight, "weak constitutions," chronic diseases, or other infirmities. This was an avenue of escape available to rich and poor alike, and was obviously open to wide abuse, corruption, and attempted fraud. It also served the useful purpose of filtering out individuals who would be of no use whatever to the army.

In the draft lottery, the children of widows automatically received the highest numbers, while the others picked numbers out of a box; married men were not exempt, for obvious reasons. Those with high numbers were passed by for the time being, while the physically fit who drew low numbers were designated to fill the local quota for induction. But two other means of avoiding the draft remained open to them: The wealthy could purchase a replacement, while the poor could flee.

Initially, the regime had a bad conscience about allowing replacements, for this possibility made its rhetoric about the duties of citizenship sound hollow. Nonetheless, to placate prosperous peasants (who were desperate to keep their eldest sons on the farm) as well as wealthy notables, the regime did permit the hiring of a replacement under strict guidelines that made it difficult but not impossible to do so. The proportion of replacements was somewhere between 5 and 10 percent of all draftees, though the cost to the families more than doubled as the size of draft calls escalated.

For Napoleon's prefects, the annual conscription process was the top priority, and draft evasion was the number one problem. Dogged persistence, bureaucratic routine, and various forms of coercion gradually overcame this chronic resistance. From time to time, columns of national guards or regular troops swept through the areas where evasion and desertion from military units were most common, arresting culprits by the hundreds. But draft evaders usually hid out in remote places—mountains, forests, marshes—so coercion had to be directed against their families as well. Heavy fines levied against the parents did little good since most were too poor to pay them. The next step was to billet troops in their homes, and if they could not feed the troops, the community's wealthier taxpayers were required to do so. All this created pressure on the youths to turn themselves in. By 1811 the regime had broken the habit of draft evasion. Conscription was being accepted as a disagreeable civic obligation, much like taxes. Just as draft calls were beginning to rise sharply, draft evasion fell dramatically. In 1812 prefects all over France reported that the annual levies were less contentious and more successful than ever.

Napoleon had begun by drafting 60,000 Frenchmen annually, but by 1810 the quotas had risen steadily to 120,000 and they continued to climb. Moreover, in 1810 the emperor ordered the first of many "supplementary levies," calling up men from earlier classes who had drawn high numbers. In January 1813, after the disaster in Russia, Napoleon replenished his armies by calling up the class of 1814 a year early, and by repeated supplementary calls on earlier classes and on older national guardsmen. At first these enormous levies went smoothly, even in former bastions of draft resistance. With long faces and tears, parents had resigned themselves to conscription and bade their sons farewell, hoping, no doubt, that the emperor would soon force a peace settlement.

Precisely because he could rely on his conscription machine, however, Napoleon consistently rebuffed offers by the allies to negotiate peace. But, in fact, he had reached the end of the line with his desperate call in November 1813 for 300,000 more men. Difficulties were inevitable, wrote one prefect, "when the number of men required exceeds the number available." Another reported: "There is scarcely a family that is not oppressed by conscription. . . . All these levies will not leave an able-bodied bachelor in the department, and also necessitate the mobilization of many family men."

Altogether—along with sizeable levies of Italians, Germans, and other foreigners from the annexed territories and satellite states—nearly 2.5 million Frenchmen were drafted by Napoleon. About one million of these conscripts never returned. ❈

**Napoleonic conscription machine.** (Photo: Musée Carnavalet/Photographie Bulloz)

The Russian response was to retreat in collected fashion and avoid a fight. Many nobles abandoned their estates and burned their crops to the ground. At Borodino, however, the Russians made a stand. In the battle that ensued, they sustained 45,000 casualties but managed to withdraw in order. The French lost 35,000. At this price they were able to enter Moscow on September 14, 1812, but the Russian army was still intact and far from demoralized.

On the contrary, Moscow demoralized the French. They found the city deserted, bereft of badly needed supplies. The next night it was mysteriously set ablaze, causing such extensive damage as to make it unfit for winter quarters. Realistic advisers warned the emperor that his situation was dangerous, while others told him what he wished to hear— that Russian resistance was weakening. For weeks Napoleon hesitated. Militarily it was imperative that the French begin to retreat immediately, but that would constitute a political defeat. On October 19 Napoleon finally ordered a retreat, but it was too late.

The delay forced an unrealistic pace on the army that it was in no condition to sustain. Supplies had been outrun, medical care for the thousands of wounded was nonexistent, horses were lacking. French officers were poorly organized for the march, and the soldiers were growing insubordinate. Food shortages compelled foraging parties to sweep some distance from the main body of troops, but these men fell prey to Russian guerillas. And there was the weather—a normal Russian winter in which no commander would wish to find himself on a march of several hundred miles, laden with wounded and loot but without supplies, horses, and food. Napoleon's poor planning, the harsh weather, and the operation of guerilla bands made the long retreat a nightmare of suffering for the Grand Army. It is estimated that no more than 100,000 troops sur-

vived the ordeal. Worse yet, the Prussian contingent took the occasion to desert Napoleon. This opened the possibility of mass defections from the empire and the formation of a new coalition.

## German Resistance and the Last Coalition

It is testimony to Napoleon's fortitude—if also to his imperviousness to the horror around him—that he was unshaken by all this. On the lonely sleigh ride back to his main lines, he was already planning how to recoup his losses, raise new armies, and set things aright. Other statesmen were equally determined to capitalize on Napoleon's defeat and destroy the empire once and for all.

Napoleon's credibility with liberal reformers in Central and Eastern Europe still stood, but it was now challenged by ringing cries for a nationalist revival in the Confederation of the Rhine that would throw off the tyrant's yoke. This type of thinking reinforced the continuing efforts of statesmen like the Prussian Stein and the Austrian Prince Klemens von Metternich to revive the struggle against Napoleon. Military reformers in Prussia had adopted French methods of conscription and organization, the better to oppose France. On the level of propaganda and the symbolic gesture, German publicists talked of a popular war of liberation—the ultimate tribute to the French Revolution.

Against this background of growing nationalist sentiment and military reform, the diplomats worked and waited. Finally, in March 1813, Frederick William III of Prussia signed a treaty with Russia, forming the nucleus of an offensive coalition against Napoleon. A great struggle for Germany ensued between the Russo-Prussian forces and Napoleon and his allies. Austria continued to claim neutrality and offered to mediate the dispute. At a conference in Prague, Napoleon

**Just as Goya's brilliant paintings "The Horrors of War" captured the unique ferocity of the Spanish campaign (see Plate 48), this picture evokes the particular agonies of the Russian debacle. One writer would later call Napoleon "The greatest fabricator of disabled men in modern times."** (Photo: Photo Archives, Nationalbibliotek Austria)

was invited to restore all conquests made after 1802. Napoleon rejected this, and the allies sighed with relief, since the proposal was merely a stalling tactic until Austria could be persuaded to enter the war.

In August, Emperor Francis I finally declared war on his son-in-law, while Napoleon learned of new defeats in Spain. Calling up underage conscripts, Napoleon was able to field one last army, but he found that his major southern German ally, Bavaria, had finally changed sides. At Leipzig a major battle raged for three days in October, at the end of which Napoleon was defeated. His last German allies deserted him.

With Napoleon driven back into France, the British reinforced the coalition to assure that it would not disintegrate now that Central Europe had been liberated. Final terms

were offered to the emperor: He could retain his throne, but France would be reduced to her "normal frontiers." (The precise meaning of this was purposely left unclear.) Napoleon counted on a dramatic reversal and chose to fight. With some reluctance the allies invaded France. Napoleon led the remnants of his army skillfully but to no avail; the French had lost confidence in him, and no civilian spirit of resistance to invasion developed as it had in 1793. Paris fell in March 1814. The price for this last defeat was the demand for un-

| International and Military History | | Political History | |
|---|---|---|---|
| | | 1789–1792 Constitutional Monarchy | |
| **1790** | | | |
| 1792 War declared | | | |
| 1792 Battle of Valmy | | 1792–1795 National Convention | |
| 1793 Levée en masse | | 1793–1794 Jacobin Dictatorship | 1789–1799 The French Revolution |
| 1794 Battle of Fleurus | 1792–1797 First Coalition | 1794–1795 Thermidorian Reaction | |
| 1795 Annexation of Belgium and the Rhineland | | 1795–1799 Directory | |
| 1796–1797 Bonaparte's Italian Campaign | | | |
| 1797 Treaty of Campo Formio | | | |
| 1798 Bonaparte's Egyptian Expedition | | 1799–1804 Consulate | |
| | 1798–1801 Second Coalition | | |
| 1801 Treaty of Lunéville | | 1801 Concordat | |
| 1801 Treaty of Amiens | | | |
| | | 1802 Legion of Honor | |
| | | 1804–1814 Empire | |
| 1805 Battle of Trafalgar | | | |
| 1805 Battle of Austerlitz | 1805–1807 Third Coalition | | 1799–1814 Napoleon's Dictatorship |
| 1806 Battle of Jena | | | |
| 1807 Tilsit Treaty | | 1807 Napoleonic Code | |
| 1808 Invasion of Spain | | | |
| 1810 Annexation of Holland | | | |
| 1812 Invasion of Russia | | | |
| 1813 Battle of Leipzig | 1813–1814 Fourth Coalition | | |
| 1814 Napoleon abdicates | | | |
| **1815** | | | |

conditional surrender and the emperor's abdication. Napoleon was removed to the island of Elba, between Corsica and Italy, and was granted sovereignty over it. After 22 years of exile, the Bourbons returned to France.

## SUMMARY

The second revolution, guided by the Jacobin dictatorship and propelled by the sans-culottes, lasted little more than two years in 1792–1794. When the crisis had been surmounted and counterrevolution vanquished, France disavowed the Jacobin leaders. The National Convention put an end to the Terror and also to the promise of social democracy. It attempted to install a moderate republican government. While France exported revolution to receptive states in the years of the Directory, however, the revolution at home foundered.

In supporting a coup whose leadership was taken over by General Bonaparte, conservatives did not foresee that his solution to the problem would be a dictatorship. But France soon succumbed to Bonaparte's one-man rule as his prestige grew, thanks to his feats on the battlefield. Before long the republic disappeared, replaced by the Napoleonic Empire.

Under the empire, confrontation of France with old-regime Europe engulfed the entire Continent. France still embodied the specter of revolution, but by this time it amounted to little more than Napoleon's contempt for the inefficiency and irrationality of the old order. Even so, this was a powerful challenge to the status quo. Napoleon also believed that the state system was dead, that Europe must be reorganized under French hegemony, and that administrative reform and the Napoleonic Code should be spread to the new realms. His conquests eventually overreached his ability to maintain them except by increasingly tyrannical measures. These, in turn, provoked a whole range of responses in Europe. Resistance grew, the empire came crashing down, and the Bourbons returned to France. But the clock could not really be set back from Europe's experience of revolution and Napoleonic transformation. The era of modern political and social conflicts had begun.

## RECOMMENDED READING

See also titles listed for Chapter 20.

### Sources
*Beik, Paul H. (ed.). *The French Revolution.* 1971.
De Caulaincourt, Armand. *With Napoleon in Russia.* 1935.
*Herold, J. C. (ed.). *The Mind of Napoleon.* 1961.
Stewart, J. H. *A Documentary Survey of the French Revolution.* 1951.
Thompson, J. M. (ed.). *Napoleon Self-Revealed.* 1934.

### Studies
The best general history of this period is *Donald Sutherland. *France 1789–1815: Revolution and Counter-revolution.* 1986.

Anderson, Eugene. *Nationalism and the Cultural Crisis in Prussia, 1806–1815.* 1939.
*Bergeron, Louis. *France Under Napoleon.* 1981. A fresh evaluation of the Napoleonic settlement in France, which supersedes most older works.
Bertaud, Jean-Paul. *The Army of the French Revolution.* 1988. A political and social study of the citizens and professional soldiers who formed the Republic's armies.
*Cobb, R. C. *The People's Armies.* 1987. On the para-military battalions of sans-culottes, an "instrument of the terror" in 1793–1794.
———. *The Police and the People: French Popular Protest.* 1970. A study of peasants and sans-culottes that should be compared to Soboul's.
Connelley, Owen. *Blundering to Glory: Napoleon's*

*Military Campaigns.* 1988. An irreverent but incisive account of Napoleon's military leadership.

——. *Napoleon's Satellite Kingdoms.* 1965. A study of the states conquered and ruled by the Bonaparte family.

Forrest, Alan. *Conscripts and Deserters: The Army and French Society During the Revolution and Empire.* 1988. A detailed examination of one of the chief causes of popular hostility to the revolutionary and imperial regimes.

——. *The French Revolution and the Poor.* 1982. A history of good intentions and disappointing results.

Gershoy, Leo. *Bertrand Barère, a Reluctant Terrorist.* 1962. Perhaps the best English-language biography of a revolutionary figure.

Geyl, Pieter. *Napoleon, For and Against.* 1949. Napoleon and the historians, as interpreted by a noted Dutch scholar.

*Herold, J. Christopher. *The Age of Napoleon.* 1963. A lively popular history.

*Hunt, Lynn. *Politics, Culture, and Class in the French Revolution.* 1984. The imagery and sociology of revolutionary politics.

Kennedy, Emmet. *A Cultural History of the French Revolution.* 1989. The Revolution's impact on cultural institutions and artistic activity.

Kennedy, Michael. *The Jacobin Club of Marseilles.* 1973. On the second most important center of Jacobinism.

Levy, D., H. Applewhite, and M. Johnson (eds.). *Women in Revolutionary Paris, 1789–1795.* 1979. A documentary history of women activists.

Lyons, Martyn. *France Under the Directory.* 1975. A brief topical survey of the Revolution's later, unheroic phase.

*Markham, Felix. *Napoleon.* 1966. Perhaps the best biography in English.

Palmer, Robert R. *The Improvement of Humanity: Education and the French Revolution.* 1985. A history of good intentions and mixed results.

——. *Twelve Who Ruled: The Year of the Terror in the French Revolution.* 1941. A modern classic, which remains the best book on the subject.

*——. *The World of the French Revolution.* 1971. A survey emphasizing the interplay of French revolutionary power and native revolutionary movements outside of France.

*Rudé, George. *The Crowd in the French Revolution.* 1959. Description and analysis of popular participation in the Revolution's crucial turning points.

——. *Robespierre: Portrait of a Revolutionary Democrat.* 1975. An extremely admiring portrait.

Schama, Simon. *Patriots and Liberators: Revolution in the Netherlands 1780–1813.* 1977. An exhaustive but lively account.

——. *Patriots and Liberators: Revolution in the Netherlands 1780–1813.* 1977. An exhaustive but lively account.

*Soboul, Albert. *The Parisian Sans-Culottes and the French Revolution.* 1964. An abridgement of a landmark French thesis; should be compared to Cobb's treatment.

*Sutherland, D. M. G. *France, 1789–1815: Revolution and Counterrevolution.* 1985. Emphasizes widespread counterrevolution.

Woloch, Isser. *Jacobin Legacy: the Democratic Movement Under the Directory.* 1970. On democratic activism after the Terror.

\* Available in paperback.

# ❋ CHAPTER 22 ❋

# THE POLITICS OF RESTORATION AND REFORM 1815–1850

# ❄ CHAPTER 22 ❄

# THE POLITICS
# OF RESTORATION
# AND REFORM
# 1815–1850

Peace brought the chance to build again. After a generation of fighting, the victorious alliance had established once more that no one state should dominate the Continent. The first task, then, was to preserve that balance. The wars against France, however, had been about more than territory or balance of power; they were also battles for monarchy and against revolutionary ideas. To the victors, peace and security required that revolution as well as French aggression be prevented in the future. Painfully aware that political order was fragile and that rulers could be toppled from within, the allies sought to restore the social as well as the international equilibrium of prerevolutionary Europe.

❄

To protect their hold on power, the regimes reestablished would need to be more effective than before the Revolution—to maintain large armies and collect more taxes, to support a better-trained bureaucracy, dispense justice more evenly, and provide more services. Governments would affect the lives of their people more directly and thus depend upon popular acquiescence more heavily than in the past. For even the most reactionary rulers, restoration would always mean some compromise between refurbishment of the old and acceptance of the changes brought by revolution, war, and Napoleonic occupation.

❄

Politics was the vehicle for reestablishing social order and for effecting the required compromises. The organization of the state, it seemed, could shape society as well as maintain order. In the nineteenth century people divided with religious intensity over questions of government, its proper form, powers, and policies. Conservatives and the liberals who fought them shared this focus on politics and made it a hallmark of the era.

❄

But political conflict proved hard to contain either by repression or by reform. Where the revolutions of 1830 brought moderate, reforming governments, they suffered no less dissension than their more conservative predecessors; and France's liberal monarchy was the first to fall in the wave of revolution that swept the Continent in 1848. In their democratic aims and then in their divisions and defeats, the revolutions of 1848 exposed the fact that recent changes in society went even deeper and were more problematical than the changes in political forms.

## I. THE CONSERVATIVE ORDER

❄

In setting the terms of peace, allied leaders sought stability above all else. Proper political arrangements were expected to accomplish that. International agreements would establish an intricate balance of power as a guarantee of peace. Conservative monarchies,

**The Congress of Vienna. In this watercolor, the fashionable artist J. B. Isabey presents the congress as a kind of elegant salon in which the very clothes the statesmen wore mix the styles of the old regime and the new century.** (Photo: The Granger Collection)

maintaining order in their own lands, would cooperate to stamp out the threat of revolution anywhere in Europe.

## The Congress of Vienna

The most pressing issue was the future of France. Some of the allies, including the tsar of Russia, were willing to accept a conservative republic, but most favored some sort of monarchy. The Treaty of Paris, signed in May 1814, recognized Louis XVIII, a brother of Louis XVI, as king and granted France her "ancient limits"—the frontiers she had gained by 1792. A settlement covering all the territory affected by the Napoleonic wars would take longer. Warily watching one another, the allies agreed to call an international congress where their respective interests could be carefully weighed and balanced.

The congress met in Vienna in September 1814, an occasion for serious deliberations and elaborate pomp. The crowned heads of Austria, Prussia, Russia, and dozens of lesser states, ministers of nearly every government, advocates of special causes, expert advisers, princesses and countesses, dancers and artists, and the ambitious of every rank flocked to the Austrian capital. Their contrived gaiety made the Congress of Vienna a symbol of aristocratic restoration from the first.

The business of the congress remained the responsibility of the four great powers—Austria, Great Britain, Russia, and Prussia—an inner circle to which France was soon admitted. Prince Klemens von Metternich, who had led the Austrian Empire to this triumph, conducted the affairs of the congress with such skill that its provisions can be seen as largely his work. Handsome, elegant, and arrogant, Metternich was an eighteenth-century aristocrat embattled in a revolutionary age. Fluent in all the major European languages and a dandy who dabbled in science, he was as proud of his success with women as of his dissembling diplomacy. More consistently than any other single figure, he had understood the extent of Napoleon's ambitions and had welded the international alliance that defeated the French emperor. Named foreign minister of Austria in 1809, he would hold that position for nearly 40 years, associating his vision of Europe as an international community built upon order, balance, and restraint with his protection of Austria's vital interests and his personal career.

Metternich was generally supported by the reserved and able Lord Castlereagh, who made his broad view of British interests a major factor throughout the negotiations. Tsar Alexander I, who acted as his own chief diplomat, was more unpredictable. Educated in the ideas of enlightened despotism, but now more given to mysticism and conservative fear, he was attracted to grand visions likely to upset the careful calculations of self-interest by which the congress reached agreement. By contrast, Prince Talleyrand moved comfortably in these circles. The former bishop who had served the First Republic and then the Directory, who had helped Napoleon to power and been his foreign minister for eight years, Talleyrand was now the indispensable servant of Louis XVIII, using all his famous shrewdness to regain for Bourbon France its former influence.

The concerns of these men focused on Continental Europe, for only Great Britain among the victors had extensive holdings

In the tradition of aristocratic portraits, Prince Metternich is conveyed as a polished courtier; the medals, symbolic of his position and power, are also a reminder of the purpose of his policies. (Photo: The Mansell Collection)

overseas, and British designs on South Africa, Ceylon, and Malta were modest enough to be accepted with little dispute. Europe was considered the sphere of the great powers; each closely weighed the claims of the others, and all especially watched Russia, with her mammoth armies, undefined ambitions, and quixotic tsar.

Disposing of Polish and Saxon territory proved the thorniest issue. Napoleon's creation of the Duchy of Warsaw suggested one solution: an independent but greatly reduced Poland. The three partitions of Poland in the eighteenth century suggested another: to keep the balance of power in Eastern Europe by dividing Poland among the three Eastern monarchies. Their own conflicts made that difficult. Because the king of Saxony had remained loyal to Napoleon too long, Prussia claimed his realm as compensation for past suffering; Russian armies, however, now held the land in question. For Austria, the expansion of Russia and Prussia was an ancient nightmare no more acceptable after Napoleon than before. Its fears drove Austria closer to Great Britain, and the rift among the allies made room for France to play a major part.

In the final settlement, a triumph of diplomacy in eighteenth-century style, everyone got something (see Map 22.1). Russia received most of Poland as a separate kingdom under the tsar. Prussia got about half of Saxony and as compensation for the rest was given greatly enlarged territories in the Rhineland. Thus formidable Prussian armies would stand along the French border. The Austrian Netherlands were absorbed in a new independent Kingdom of the Netherlands, which created another strong buffer against France and met the British desire that no major power control the Low Countries' important river ports. In return for her loss of the southern Netherlands, Austria acquired Venezia, which with Lombardy greatly strengthened her dominance of northern Italy. The other duchies of northern Italy went to dukes with close Austrian ties (in a touch of chivalry, Marie Louise, Napoleon's now throneless Austrian wife, was given Parma to rule).

By these and similar exchanges in less pressing cases, the most extensive European settlement since the agreements at Westphalia in 1648 established the balance of power as an interlocking system.[1] Each of the victors had gained territory, and the areas that France might easily overrun were now held by states—the Kingdom of the Netherlands, Prussia in the Rhineland, and Austria in northern Italy—capable of resisting future French aggression. The final act was signed in June 1815 by the five great powers and by Sweden, Spain, and Portugal, a gracious recognition of their past importance.

## The Hundred Days

The deliberations of the Congress were interrupted in March 1815 by the terrifying news of Napoleon's escape. He had tried to make the best of ruling Elba and even showed something of his old flair as he designed uniforms, held receptions, and inquired into the local economy. But the island principality was far too small to contain an emperor's ambition. Landing in the south of France, he made his way to Paris. Important parts of the French army defected, and Louis XVIII, after hoping for support that did not develop, once again climbed into his carriage and headed for the eastern border. Napoleon had become the ruler of France without firing a shot. He then tried to negotiate with the allies, but they declared him an outlaw and quickly assembled their troops. After several minor battles he was defeated for the last time at Waterloo on June 18 and surrendered to the British. They dispatched him to the more distant island of St. Helena, in the South Atlantic.

Napoleon's dashing venture lasted only a hundred days, but its effects were felt far longer. The terms of peace were altered, the possibility of a stable restoration questioned, and the meaning of Bonapartism redefined. France seemed once more a threat, and a new treaty reduced her boundaries to those of 1789 (which entailed the loss of much of the Saar to Prussia) and required her to pay the allies an indemnity. The Bourbons, of course, returned to the throne of France, but their

---

[1] The Kingdom of Sardinia would have liked Lombardy but got Genoa, the last of the ancient Italian republics to fall. Russia took Finland from Sweden, which in turn got Norway from Denmark.

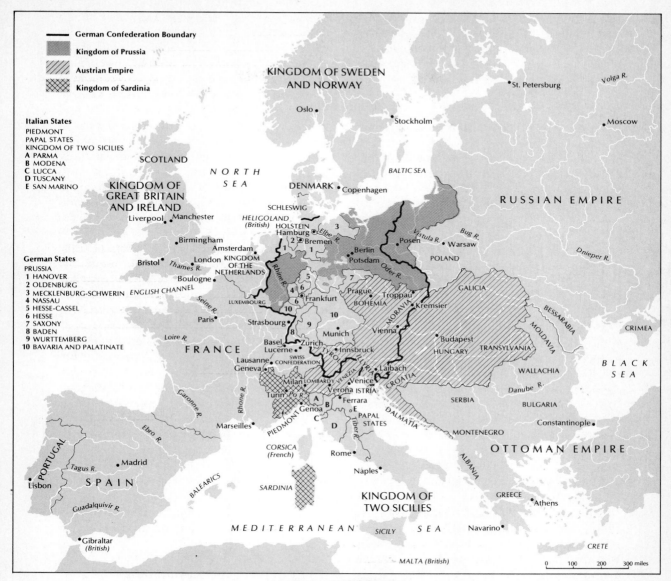

**MAP 22.1 EUROPE 1815**

claims to popularity were embarrassed by the ease with which Napoleon had regained power, and they lived with the specter of renewed revolution. During his Hundred Days, Napoleon had offered a liberal government that softened the memory of his despotism (he even banned slave traffic in the French colonies), and from St. Helena he continued to propagandize for Bonapartism as the best means of achieving both liberty and order. Allied diplomats, less expert in playing to popular opinion, planned instead for frequent meetings to maintain by international force the settlement so carefully contrived.

### The Nature of the Settlement

The Congress of Vienna had not attempted simply to restore the prerevolutionary world but rather to institute a system that would assure social and political order. A Bourbon ruled again in France, but he was a king with a constitution. Despite past glories, the Republic of Venice was not reestablished. Nor were the Holy Roman Empire and hundreds of its minor German principalities; instead, the reorganization effected under Napoleon was kept, with modifications, and 39 German states, including Prussia and Austria, were joined in a loose and ill-defined German Confederation. The aristocrats at Vienna sought advice from teams of experts on matters of history and law, a very modern use of specialists. They laid down rules of diplomatic conduct useful to this day, and in provisions such as those establishing free navigation on international riverways, displayed their enlightened reasonableness. For a century Europe would be free of universal war, and something of that stability was due to the wisdom at Vienna, which left twice-defeated France a respected power and the interests of other states intricately connected. The Congress of Vienna has been admired ever since, especially by those who consider statecraft to consist of the restrained use of power for the maintenance of order.

The congress was less impressive, however, in the realm of ideas. Talleyrand had proposed the concept of legitimacy as a general principle that would dignify the deliberations. The powers, he argued, should favor regimes that had lasted and proved acceptable to their subjects; this would obviate the need to restore every shaky and petty throne. But even so vague a principle

proved inconvenient. Tsar Alexander aimed for something grander and proposed a Holy Alliance, based on an agreement that all states would conduct their affairs according to Christian teachings. Three governments refused: The sultan cared too little for Christian teachings and the pope too much, and Britain would not be committed to Continental ties. All the others signed but with public skepticism, and historians have similarly tended to dismiss the Holy Alliance as a meaningless product of Alexander's mysticism. Yet there was something modern and maybe wise in the tsar's awareness of European public opinion.

The next generation of Europe's liberals, reformers, and nationalists would remember the Congress of Vienna not as the occasion of realistic compromise but as a brutal shuffling of territory by men indifferent to the claims of nationality or promises of constitutions, where aristocrats danced while foisting reactionary regimes on the people of Europe. For 50 years every revolution and every war in Europe would include among its goals the dismantlement of the arrangements made at Vienna. The plan to hold frequent congresses among the great powers implied that the wartime alliance would be continued. For Castlereagh, this would be the means of accommodating inevitable change. But Metternich sought instead a Concert of Europe, under his leadership, to snuff out the flames of revolution wherever they occurred.

## The Pillars of the Restoration

The new international order expressed conservative principles and required conservative governments throughout Europe. This major political experiment depended on the guardians of the restoration—Russia, Austria, and Prussia. Only they could shore up the less secure regimes established elsewhere, but to sustain that role, they themselves needed effective governments and domestic stability.

## The Russian Empire

By 1820 Tsar Alexander had abandoned an earlier enthusiasm for new ideas to become Metternich's staunchest ally. In his last years censorship was harsher, universities were more restricted, and the constitution granted the newly organized Kingdom of Poland was largely ignored. On Alexander's death, in 1825, a group of young army officers, the Decembrists, attempted a coup in the name of a constitution. Poorly planned, their isolated conspiracy was easily defeated, but they would later be remembered as part of Russia's radical tradition; Nicholas I, Alexander's younger brother who succeeded to the throne, believed that only a loyal army and his own decisiveness had prevented revolution.

Under Nicholas, Russia became Europe's strongest pillar of reaction. A diligent administrator, he gave close attention to the army and extended the influence of the police into every aspect of Russian life. The bureaucracy, made more independent of the nobility, became more efficient and centralized but still could barely meet the demands of overseeing a vast land of varied peoples where communications were poor and educated people scarce. Petty corruption, the arrogance of local officials, and fear of change seriously weakened the government's capabilities.

The growth of a European market for Russian grain stimulated the economy, and many large estates became more prosperous and more specialized as they produced for export. Industry, primarily small-scale and domestic, was also growing; but the smaller lord suffered in a money economy, and the growing indebtedness of many a Russian noble became another source of social tension. Most thoughtful people including the highest officials of the state, agreed that serfdom had

become a hindrance, but the commissions ordered to study the matter could propose no solution not likely to increase unrest. Thus information was collected, and hundreds of peasant uprisings were noted with concern and suppressed with force, but the few steps taken to improve the lot of peasants remained thoroughly inadequate.

Sensing the importance of public attitudes, the government attempted to establish a kind of official philosophy based on the teachings of the Orthodox Church and utilized censors and police to enforce these precepts of autocracy. Despite fears that education bred discontent, schools were built (to provide a literate minority). Discussion of Russia's destiny became a compelling theme. Those who expected it to develop along familiar European lines were called Westernizers. Slavophiles, though making use of many Western (especially German) ideas, stressed rather the uniqueness of Russia. Its religion, peasant communes, and traditional culture, they argued, were the source of a unique mission in world civilization. Neither group was entirely consistent or well defined, but within a great culture an urgent questioning had begun about Russia's place in a changing world, giving shape to an intellectual ferment that lasted through the century.

The authority of the Russian state, however, continued to tower over the social tensions and intellectual debates. Despite loquacious exiles, bitter Poles, angry peasants, and its own immobility, the Russian government seemed enormously solid. Nicholas would watch with pride as his empire remained secure while revolution swept over most of the thrones of Europe in 1848.

## The Hapsburg Monarchy

The German, Italian, and Eastern European lands under Hapsburg rule were administered by a well-organized and centralized bureaucracy. Forged by Maria Theresa and Jo-

This Viennese drawing room of the 1840s shows the influence of the Biedermeyer style and of the values associated with it. The elaborate wallpaper, patterned upholstery and tablecloth, richly varnished wood, plants, and pictures, which required substantial means, used current taste to convey the warm solidity of the middle-class urban life.  (Photo: Direktion der Museen der Stadt Wien)

seph II, it had enabled Austria to survive the Napoleonic wars without the dramatic reforms that transformed Prussia and had become a source of conservatism. Metternich and others recognized the need for more coherent and far-reaching domestic programs, but their projects—for a strong Imperial Council, for more influential diets of local landholders, and for an administration that reflected national differences—came to noth-ing. It was easier to guarantee order through bureaucratic restrictions, police surveillance, and energetic censorship.

Hungary, with its independent traditions and a powerful aristocracy, proved particularly troublesome to the Hapsburgs. Emperor Francis I was forced in 1825 to convene the Hungarian Diet when the counties refused to pay needed taxes, and Hungary's traditional privileges of partial autonomy were grudgingly acknowledged then and again in 1830. Finding it easier to relinquish some authority rather than make the changes that might have assured the empire's prosperity and power, Austria remained locked in a stalemate between a cautious central bureaucracy and a selfish local aristocracy. Both rested on a peasant society that had no direct voice in politics. By the 1840s Magyar had been made the official language of the Hungarian administration and schools, but this was followed, in turn, by demands for a more representative parliament and a campaign conducted by Lajos Kossuth in newspapers and meetings for the full panoply of liberal and national reforms.

The agitation in Hungary, stimulated by nationalist ferment in Italy, encouraged others under Hapsburg rule to claim their "natural rights." A revolt in Polish Galicia in 1846 was defeated by Austrian arms, aided by the bitter divisions between Polish peasants and their masters, and new signs of restlessness appeared in Croatia and Bohemia.

The confusion of conflicting claims was one of the monarchy's assets, for the national and religious groups opposed to Hapsburg rule were equally hostile to one another. Divided by class, religion, and language, they were not often politically effective. The growing consciousness of nationality was, however, a significant change. These movements, which enabled lawyers and merchants to seek popular support in their cry for governmental reform, reflected economic developments and intellectual currents sweeping Europe. People who sought merely to strengthen noble privilege or local authority (the Magyars, for example, were determined to dominate the other peoples of Hungary) joined with those who wanted better administration, parliaments, and schools in opposing the authorities in Vienna.

At the center weak Ferdinand I, who had inherited his father's crown in 1835, presided over an aristocratic government that found inaction the safest compromise of internal differences. Metternich saw the need to acknowledge national sentiment within the empire and worried about Prussia's growing dominance in Germany. His chief antagonist among Ferdinand's ministers, Count Kolo-wrat, stressed the desperate need for fiscal reform. Their insights, like the advantages of the well-structured imperial bureaucracy, were slowly dissipated in an isolated, divided, and frightened court accustomed to relying on the effectiveness of tradition and Metternich's foreign policy.

## The German Confederation and Prussia

Germans called their battles against Napoleon the Wars of Liberation; and after that common, national experience, talk of "Germany" meant more than it had before. But the German Confederation, a tacit acknowledgment of the changes Bonaparte had wrought, was one of the Congress of Vienna's more cautious compromises. The rivalry of Austria and Prussia, distaste for reform, and the claims of German princes combined to prohibit a politically strong union. Nearly 40 sovereign entities, ranging in size from the Austrian Empire and Prussia to four free cities, were made members of the loose league under the permanent presidency of Austria. Its diet, which was to meet at Frankfurt, was more a council of ambassadors than a representative assembly, and a unanimous vote was required on fundamental questions. Primarily another buffer against France, the confederation was permitted to legislate only on certain matters—restriction of the press was characteristically among them. If such advisory councils seemed unavoidable (each member of the confederation was expected to establish one), they were to be kept limited. In practice, the German Confederation was important in German politics largely when Metternich wished to make it so.

He used it, for example, to suppress student agitation. University fraternities, especially *Burschenschaften*, were generally nationalist and reformist, full of rhetoric about mystic brotherhood. In 1817 they celebrated the tercentenary of Luther's theses with a

rally, the Wartburg Festival. Several hundred representatives gathered to drink, listen to speeches, sing songs, and cheer as a corporal's cane and a Prussian military manual were tossed into a bonfire. The symbolism was clear enough. Alarmed, governments in both Berlin and Vienna investigated and concluded that closer censorship and more careful surveillance of universities were needed. After the assassination of a reactionary writer, the confederation was pressed into issuing the Carlsbad Decrees of 1819, which intensified censorship, proscribed dangerous professors and students, outlawed fraternities and political clubs, and required each state to appoint commissioners to certify the ideological reliability of the universities.

Despite these alarms, there was less agitation in Germany than in most of the rest of Europe. Rather, the cultural life of these largely rural lands thrived in complacent university and market towns that seemed to eschew politics on a larger scale. The universities were strongest in philosophy and theology, and German Romanticism, when political at all, tended to become more conservative. In the last days of Beethoven and Schubert, Goethe and Hegel, German politics remained quiescent. The German states most influenced by France did adopt constitutions, but the diet Frederick William III promised for Prussia was never called, and the Council of State established in its place included only the most important military men, officials, and aristocrats. Prussian strength was not associated with representative government.

Prussian influence increased, however, as an efficient state continued to sponsor education and to spur economic growth. A uni-

---

**Students, burghers, and common folk were brought together in song and drink to celebrate national feeling (note the German tricolor) in festivals like this one at Wartburg in 1848.** (Photo: The Bettmann Archive)

fied tariff established in 1818 included all its territory, east and west; lowered duties (in part to discourage smuggling); and allowed free entry to raw materials. These progressive measures worked so well that within a decade many of the smaller states nearly surrounded by Prussia adopted them; and by 1833 most German governments except Austria had joined Prussia's customs union, the *Zollverein*, whose revenues, collected by Prussian inspectors, were shared and used primarily for better roads. One of the most important steps toward German unification under Prussia had been taken without nationalist intent by the government that knew how to win the benefits of liberal institutions without paying the price of liberal practice.

Germany had few modern factories, but the Zollverein proved a remarkable spur to commerce. Moreover, by 1848 manufacturing and trade would be stimulated by one of the best railroad networks in Europe, built with considerable state support, especially from Prussia. These developments caused serious social dislocations. Some old trades found it difficult to compete with factory production and cheaper goods from other countries. The revolt of Silesian weavers in 1844, bloodily put down by Prussian troops, is only the most famous of many desperate and fruitless protests. Caught between rural immigrants competing for their jobs and the increased competition their products faced in the marketplace, workers looked to local governments for help; but the governments, too, were caught between their conservative social base and centralizing pressures from state bureaucrats eager to impose efficiency and uniformity.

Constitutional issues depended in part on accidents of dynasty. In Hanover a reactionary king set aside a four-year-old constitution in 1837, but in Prussia the reign of Frederick William IV, which began in 1840, raised prospects of significant constitutional reform. The new king, the least militaristic of Prussian monarchs, had a liberal reputation; and though he was no friend of constitutions, in 1847 he reluctantly called for a United Landtag, to be composed of representatives of the eight provincial diets meeting in two houses. Short of revenue, in part because of its heavy investment in railroads, the government seemed in a situation like France's in 1789.

The Landtag optimistically insisted on regular sessions and some authority over the budget, but the king replied that a Prussia made by the sword would never allow petty legalisms to come between her monarchs and her people. After two months the delegates were sent home, leaving Prussia without a constitution or new taxes. Some serious ferment continued, particularly in Rhineland cities, where meetings and manifestoes demanded representative government, civil liberties, and sometimes—most frightening of all—a graduated income tax and guarantees of the right to work.

Demands for constitutional change gathered force as they combined with nationalist aims. Talk of German unification became so acceptable that both the Hohenzollern and the Hapsburg rulers paid it verbal respect. Western German reformers, and particularly those in exile, like the poet Heinrich Heine, associated their dreams of a German nation with their desire for a liberal government. Despite the difficulty of defining what territory a German nation should include or determining how it could be organized, political programs accompanied the spread of education, railroads, and economic modernization. Dismissing the Landtag did not do much to settle anything.

## Order Imposed

While the governments of Russia, Austria, and Prussia dealt with serious domestic challenges, Metternich led the effort to maintain the status quo through international cooperation and force. But even conservative powers had conflicting interests, and the political systems they had restored in Spain, Italy, and France proved dangerously vulnerable.

### The Declining Concert of Europe

Uprisings much like the Decembrist revolt in Russia, took place in Italy and Spain in 1820 and 1821, led by young army officers who were influenced by memories of Napoleonic reforms and convinced that personal advancement and efficient government required a constitution. In Italy especially, their movements won some brief popular support and measured the weakness of restoration regimes that had to be sustained by outside force.

The availability of that force was Metternich's achievement. When representatives of Great Britain, Prussia, Russia, and France met at Aix-la-Chapelle in 1818 (to acknowledge payment of the French indemnity and to ratify the withdrawal of foreign troops from France), they embodied the concept of Europe the Austrian prince had envisioned at the Congress of Vienna. By the time of their meetings at Troppau and Laibach in 1820 and 1821, however, the tenor had changed. Metternich, determined to guard against the virus of revolution anywhere in Europe, called for action against the revolt in Naples, but Great Britain disapproved of such direct intervention in the domestic affairs of European states, and France, unwilling to antagonize opinion at home, was hesitant. Only Metternich interpreted the Congress of Laibach as a mandate for Austrian troops to march to Naples.

The breach among the powers became more apparent when they met the following year—without British representation. They approved French intervention in Spain, a royal parade to display the French monarchy's revived prestige. But the subsequent hope of reestablishing European authority in Latin America brought stern warnings from Britain and the proud declaration of the Monroe Doctrine from the United States. The sphere of Metternich's concert was being delimited.

It was hardly evoked at all when the Greeks revolted against Ottoman rule in 1821. Russia was restrained from declaring war on the Ottoman Empire by Metternich's strenuous warnings. But the cries for freedom from the ancient home of democracy excited liberals throughout Europe. By 1827 the sultan seemed at last about to subdue the Greeks; but the British and French fleets intervened, and Russia declared war a few months later. Greece was granted independence in 1829 on terms arranged by the European powers, who carefully stipulated that a king should be chosen from one of the Continent's lesser ruling families. The response to revolution within the Ottoman Empire had been more like the diplomacy of imperialism that would emerge later in the century than the concert's commitment to the status quo. Diplomacy, despite Metternich's skill, proved an uncertain weapon against political change.

## The Restoration Regimes in Spain and Italy

In Spain the Bourbon king Ferdinand VII had regained his throne with the expulsion of Napoleon's army. Strong enough to denounce the constitution he had promised, he was too weak to do much more. Ferdinand enjoyed some popularity because of patriotic resentment against French rule, but his government found no solution for its own inefficiency or the nation's poverty. In Spanish America the revolts led by José de San Martín

and Simón Bolívar gained strength,[2] and the army that was assembled in Spain to reconquer the colonies mutinied and marched instead on Madrid in 1820.

This revolution forced the king to grant a constitution, and for three years the constitutional regime struggled to cope with Spain's enormous problems, weakened by its own dissension and its uncooperative king. But restrictions on religious orders raised powerful opposition from the Church; freedom of the press produced more devastating criticism; and having a constitution was no help with the colonies. When a French army once again crossed into Spain in 1823, this time in the name of order, the Spaniards, who had fought French invasion so heroically just 10 years earlier, were strangely acquiescent. With the rebellion defeated, the constitution disappeared again. Yet Ferdinand's repression neither ended the threat of revolution nor satisfied the more reactionary monarchists.

Restoration in Italy meant the return of the aristocracy, the reestablishment of old political boundaries, and the overwhelming dominance of Austria.[3] Yet the years of French rule had struck deep roots in Italy. The new regimes won acceptance with promises of constitutions, enlightened administration, peace, and lower taxes; but the rulers who headed them were frightened and often

[2] The history of these uprisings and of the impact of European events on Latin America is discussed in Richard Graham, *Independence in Latin America*, 1972, a companion volume to *The Western Experience* in the Studies in World Civilization series.

[3] Italy was divided into the Kingdom of the Two Sicilies; the Papal States; the grand duchy of Tuscany; the duchies of Lucca, Modena, and Parma; the Kingdom of Sardinia (Piedmont and Sardinia); Lombardy-Venezia, annexed to Austria; the principality of Monaco; and the republic of San Marino. All the duchies were held by friends or relatives of the Hapsburgs. The disappearance of Venice and Genoa as independent states left tiny San Marino, safe on its mountaintop, the oldest republic in the world.

bitter. Unimaginative, harshly or moderately repressive, and conveniently corrupt, the governments provided the sleepy stability Metternich thought appropriate for Italians.

Such an atmosphere bred some conspiracy and rumors of far more. Across Italy secret groups, known collectively as the Carbonari, began to meet; their name, which means charcoal burners, evoked the image of Christ's poverty. Some talked of tyrannicide, some of equality and justice, and some of mild reform. They had in common the excitement of secret meetings, terrifying oaths, and ornate rituals.

The news of the revolution in Spain in 1820 was enough to prompt revolt. In Naples young army officers led the demand for a constitution, but royal concessions were followed by a more amorphous uprising in Sicily, which the Neapolitan revolutionaries then helped defeat. Their own constitutional regime died with the invasion of an Austrian army less than a year after revolution had broken out.

While the Austrians were marching to Naples, a similar revolt erupted in Piedmont. The king abdicated and the prince regent, Charles Albert, hastily granted a constitution before the new monarch arrived. When he came, the Austrian army was with him; Piedmont's constitution lasted two weeks.

The revolutions of 1821 in Italy left reactionary governments more rigid and Austrian influence more naked. They showed the inadequacies of loose, romantic conspiracies. But they contributed something as well to a radical and patriotic tradition.

### The Bourbon Restoration in France

The crucial test of postwar stability, however, was the domestic tranquility of France. More than elsewhere, restoration there was a complex compromise carefully designed to build from political forms the means to maintain a balance between the old regime and the changes that followed from revolution. The charter that Louis XVIII granted by grace—not as a right—allowed the legislature more authority than Napoleon had permitted but made cabinet ministers directly responsible to the king. The old estates were now ignored, but membership in the Chamber of Peers was hereditary, and the right to vote in elections to the Chamber of Deputies was limited to men of landed wealth. Napoleon's centralized administration was kept and his taxes enthusiastically maintained.

Supporters of the new regime, shaken by how easily Napoleon had displaced it during the Hundred Days, returned to power determined to crush their enemies, and the Chamber elected after Waterloo was too reactionary even for Louis XVIII. In parts of the countryside a violent "white terror" broke out, in which some of those tainted with a revolutionary past were ousted from office or even killed. Yet Louis XVIII resisted as best he could the more extreme demands of the ultraroyalists. Land confiscated from the aristocracy and the Church during the Revolution was not returned, and most of those who had benefited since 1789 were allowed quietly to live out their lives. The king and his ministers, moderate and able men, pursued a course of administrative efficiency and political restraint. From 1816 to 1820 they governed well in a relatively peaceful and prosperous country, and Paris became again Europe's most brilliant center of science and the arts.

The Catholic Church, weakened by the loss of property and still more by a scarcity of new priests in the postrevolutionary generation, revived remarkably. Missions of preachers toured the countryside calling for a return to the faith, praising the monarchy, and planting crosses of repentance. The nobles, traditionally rather skeptical, were now more pious; and so, too, for the first time in more than a century were France's leading writers. To the surprise of many Catholics, however, the Concordat of 1801 remained in effect, another of Napoleon's institutional arrangements to prove remarkably durable.

Despite its achievements, the regime remained insecure and uncertain, satisfying relatively few, neither all Catholics nor anticlericals, neither ultraroyalists nor liberals. The assassination of the duke of Berry in 1820 reminded everyone of how fragile the monarchy was. The son of Louis's younger brother, the count of Artois, he was the last Bourbon likely to produce an heir, and the royal line seemed doomed until the widowed duchess gave birth to a son eight months later. Louis XVIII feared the radicalism that appeared to be reviving throughout Europe, and he reacted to his nephew's assassination by naming more conservative ministers, increasing restrictions on the press, and dismissing some leading professors.

The air of reaction grew heavier in 1824 when the count of Artois succeeded to the throne as Charles X. A leader of the ultraroyalists, he had himself crowned at Reims in medieval splendor, a ceremony redolent with symbols of the divine right of kings and the alliance of throne and altar. The new government, led by a skillful but impolitic ultra, passed measures that gave the Church fuller control of education, declared sacrilege a capital crime, and granted a cash indemnity to those who had lost land in the Revolution.

In fact, the law against sacrilege was never enforced, and the indemnity, which helped end one of the most dangerous issues left from the Revolution, was a limited one. France remained freer than most European countries, but Charles's subjects worried about the intentions of a regime that disliked the very compromises on which it rested.

Public criticism grew, leading figures passed over to the parliamentary opposition, and secret societies blossomed. Disturbed by liberal gains in the elections of 1827, Charles X dutifully tried a slightly more moderate ministry, but he could not conceal his distaste for the increasingly hostile left nor offer enough concessions to win its support. By 1829 the king could stand no more. While political disputes grew more inflamed, he appointed a cabinet of ultras, but the Chamber of Deputies refused a vote of confidence. He called new elections, but instead of regaining seats the ultras lost still more.

Determined not to make the mistakes of Louis XVI, Charles X reacted with firmness. In 1830 he and his ministers suddenly issued a set of secretly drafted decrees, the July Ordinances, which dissolved the new Chamber even before it met, further restricted suffrage, and muzzled the press. Having shown his fiber, the king went hunting. A shocked Paris slowly responded; crowds began to mill about, some barricades went up, and stones were thrown at the house of the king's premier. Newspapers breached the ordinances to charge that the constitution had been violated, and the government responded with troops enough to raise tempers but too few to enforce order. By the time Charles acknowledged the need to appoint more acceptable ministers, people were being killed (nearly 700 died in the three days of Paris fighting). Many troops began to mingle with the crowds, and liberal leaders started planning for a new regime. Paris was again the scene of a popular uprising, and Charles X, once again victim of what he most detested—revolution—abdicated on August 2.

For 15 years, and for the only time in its history, France had been administered by its aristocracy, which had performed with probity and seriousness. The crown had won the Church's enthusiastic support, and the nation had prospered at home and enjoyed some success in foreign affairs. But the monarchy was meant above all to provide political stability, and that, the restoration's most important experiment had failed to do.

## The Battle of Ideas

Political ideas, social theories, and new movements in the arts were all closely interconnected in the early nineteenth century. New work reshaped every field of thought, through the work of leading intellectuals and artists and international movements that altered the way pictures were painted, poetry was written, statistics were collected, society was analyzed, biology was studied, and history was understood. Several elements served to connect all this creative diversity and increase its impact. The professors, writers, scientists, and artists whose works were most influential increasingly saw themselves as having a special place in society. Primarily but not exclusively male and largely from the middle class, they prided themselves on their unique talents and special knowledge. They depended less on patronage than on their connections to established institutions such as academies, universities, publishing houses, magazines, and newspapers. There they made their careers and their reputations. Through exhibitions, public lectures, and their writings, they sought to reach other people like themselves and then a broader educated public. They were also, almost without exception, deeply affected by the French Revolution and the lessons it seemed to teach about the likelihood of sweeping change. Their professionalism, official or semi-official connections, public role, and concern for change connected intellectual life to politics and to burning debates about the nature of society.

## Romanticism

The major cultural current was Romanticism. The term encompasses so many diverse and often contradictory elements that historians have despaired of giving it a single clear definition. It is possible to argue endlessly, and often very fruitfully, about the elements in any single artist or writer that were or were not romantic. Diversity was part of its dynamism. The roots of Romanticism lie in a reaction, during the latter part of the eighteenth century, against much that was associated with the Enlightenment and the classical forms then in favor. Thus Romantic painters emphasized vibrant color and swirling lines more than perfect proportion and control; Romantic novelists favored vivid, personal description and singular settings over balanced sentences and lucid prose; Romantic musicians more freely broke conventional rules of harmony, shifting keys and rhythmic structure. Thus certain themes emerge as characteristically romantic: an emphasis upon feeling, emotion, and direct experience more than universality and logic; a fascination with Nature understood as raw and unpredictable; interest in the momentary and the unique in human affairs and in history; a search for the organic relatedness of life that can be sensed through experience and expressed aesthetically but cannot be captured by reason.

Such values and such an emphasis would not seem to require any particular view of society; yet for most Romantic writers in this political age, it did. Attracted by rural life and customs, Romanticists often treated folk culture and language as the expression of a people; and Romanticism would play a central role in nineteenth-century ideas of nationalism. The Romanticism of Rousseau, which had emphasized the contrived and destructive quality of established society, was radical in its political implications. And many young Romantics (including William Wordsworth in England and Ludwig van Beethoven in Germany) not only welcomed the French Revolution but saw in it the release of new forces, a liberation of genius, and the dawn of a new era of creativity. In the Restoration, Romanticism was no less political, although now predominantly conservative, for Romantics of every stripe tended to insist that art had a social function and a public purpose. The great stimulus to the spread of Romanticism lay in the cultural explosion in Germany, marked by the works of Georg Friedrich Hegel and Friedrich Schlegel in philosophy, of F. W. J. Schelling in literature, and of an outpouring of compositions that saw German music surpass Italian music as the European model and the works of the later Beethoven, Franz Schubert, Robert Schumann, and Felix Mendelssohn become the most admired in the current literature.

Associated with a pride in things German, and with a rejection of French universalism, this German Romanticism was taken up in France by figures like Réné de Chateaubriand, who evoked the moving beauty and social necessity of religion, and in England by Samuel Coleridge, who wrote at length of the organic society that would preserve order and grant a special place to the vision and mystical inspiration of its geniuses.

## Conservative Thought

In the long battle against the French Revolution, conservatism had become what today would be called an ideology, a coherent view of human nature, social organization, political power, and the roots of change that was intended to justify social hierarchies and established institutions. Conservatives might disagree about particular policies, but conservatism had become a broad school of thought that would help shape political discourse throughout the nineteenth century.

The eloquent reasoning of Edmund Burke, whose writings appeared throughout the latter half of the eighteenth century, provided perhaps the most influential formulation of the conservative position. Society, he argued, depends on continuity. By granting special privileges to certain groups, it adapted to social needs in a way conducive to order, achieving a delicate arrangement in which rank was related to social role and differences of status, having evolved through time, were acceptable to all. This "natural" order was far wiser than the "artificial" plans of radicals, however well-intentioned, who necessarily would disrupt more than they intended and ultimately threaten society itself.

The Burkean view thus allowed for gradual change, at least in theory, but in practice, such arguments could be used against any plan for general reform. And that resistance was strengthened by a distrust of reason, a turning away from the Enlightenment, expressed in the argument that humanity's highest achievements and deepest understanding do not result from cold calculation. While rejecting the French Revolution, conservatives were in touch with much of contemporary thought. Romanticism, which was primarily literary and artistic rather than political, affected radicals as well as conservatives; but in its appreciation of human experience as unique, subjective, and emotional, it made an important contribution to conservatism. Romantics yearned for absolute values and ultimate meanings, and whether they found the source of these in God, historical process, or nature, they agreed that human knowledge is a puny thing compared with the great forces outside it.

Conservatives thus considered that schemes for a more just society are simply beside the point and that nations cannot be ruled merely by human constitutions or law. Society was seen as a great interconnecting web, an organic whole not suitable for piece-meal restructuring, and phrases about individual rights seemed dangerous abstractions hiding selfish interests and encouraging false hopes.

The early nineteenth-century fascination with history and the contemporary interest in Christian philosophy gave further stimulus to conservatives, who found in history a record of how painfully civilization had evolved and how fragile it remained, and they often sought, particularly in recent events, evidence of human error and divine will to give larger meaning to their political battles. They viewed Christianity as the source of Europe's strength and Christian fear as a necessary restraint on humanity's selfish and prideful nature. Without it, society would dissolve into revolution and anarchy. Conservatives tended therefore to connect religion with their own politics and to attach the Church to aristocracy and monarchy. They regarded political battles as merely part of a far larger and millennial conflict.

Such views gave conservative thought both a militancy and a depth to which German contributions were perhaps the most original and lasting. For Europeans used to receiving radical ideas from France, however, two of the most striking exponents of conservatism in the restoration period were men who wrote in French, Joseph de Maistre and Louis de Bonald. Society's first task, they argued, is self-preservation. Authority alone can check the selfish wills of individuals, and authority requires undivided sovereignty, social hierarchy, and the vigilant suppression of dangerous ideas. Having experienced revolution, they were fascinated by power and demanded its vigorous use by an unfettered monarch. They declared that church and state must be closely linked, and de Maistre

held the international authority of the papacy to be a social necessity. Revolution he explained as divine retribution for false ideas.

Conservatism in this form contained little that was humane or tolerant. With its praise of hangmen and censors, it spoke only to those who already shared its fears. It left little space for compromise and lambasted every concession as a dangerous weakening of the dikes restraining revolution. Like liberalism, republicanism, and socialism, nineteenth-century conservatism became an ideology that divided while calling for unity and that emphasized political power while speaking of the social good.

## II. THE SPREAD OF LIBERAL GOVERNMENT
❊
### Political Liberalism

The revolution that arose in France in 1830 and the revolt that created Belgium were not put down by conservative powers, and the differences between the representative monarchies of the West and the autocratic governments of Central and Eastern Europe sharpened. The great age of liberalism began in 1830, with England as its model. Liberal movements in this period would come to seem very moderate by later standards, in part because they focused rather narrowly on politics, and sought institutional and legal change even at the risk of revolution, while defending private property.

### The Revolutions of 1830

After Charles X's speedy abdication, the provisional government, organized largely in newspaper offices, had a faintly republican coloration. But the issue had been largely settled in favor of what most people of influence preferred—a liberal monarchy—when the

Marquis de Lafayette, still a republican and a popular hero, presented Louis Philippe from the balcony of the Hôtel de Ville as the candidate for the throne. The new king headed the House of Orléans, a radical branch of the royal line (his father had voted with the Jacobins for the death of Louis XVI). His posters proclaimed him citizen-king, and the flag he chose—the Revolution's tricolor in place of the Bourbon fleurs-de-lis—signified a return to revolutionary traditions. Pressures from the people of Paris had led Louis Philippe to appear more liberal than he was, and the new government hastened to assure Europe's other monarchs that this French revolution would send no militants to sponsor or support revolution elsewhere.

The revolution, brief and largely limited to Paris, was a revolution nevertheless, and any uprising in France was a European event. Minor revolts occurred in central Italy, Spain, Portugal, and some of the German principalities, and revolution broke out in Poland. But Austria, though somewhat inhibited by France, once again extinguished revolt in Italy, and the Russian army crushed Poland's rebels. Closer to France, the Swiss cantons were forced to liberalize their constitutions. And in the southern Netherlands, Catholics and liberals took the occasion to rise against Dutch rule. Once assured that France had no territorial designs on the region, Britain led in winning international guarantees for the independence of the southern Netherlands with a mounting show of force that brought Dutch acquiescence. The new state of Belgium was born.

### Liberal Thought

Liberalism was not a compact doctrine but rather a set of attitudes closely tied to ideas of social progress, belief in economic development, and values associated with the middle class. It varied considerably by country and changed everywhere over the course of the nineteenth century.

Liberal political values were rooted in the writings of John Locke and the philosophs; and liberals generally honored the French Revolution, despite its excesses, as a great moment in the history of freedom. For many, Romanticism, too, tended to become liberal once again. Emphasis upon genius could lead to demands for freedom and individualism; respect for the customs and traditions of a people could lead to demands for a national state. This was the Romanticism of writers like Percy Bysshe Shelley in England and, by 1830, of Victor Hugo in France. A leading French liberal during the restoration, Benjamin Constant, put his case unequivocally: "The liberty of the individual is the object of all human association; on it rest public and private morality; on it are based the calculations of industry and commerce, and without it there is neither peace, dignity, nor happiness for men." By this creed, freedom itself would be the source of morality, prosperity, and progress. The freedom liberals sought was primarily political and legal (their views on economic rights were frequently far more limited), and they favored those in any country who fought for a constitution and representative institutions, freedom of the press and of assembly, an extension of the jury system, separation of church and state, public education, and administrative reform. Most liberals were not democrats, feeling that education and leisure were necessary for political wisdom, but nearly all believed that policies beneficial to everyone would follow from allowing ideas a free hearing and propertied voters a free voice.

## Liberal Politics in Britain

Britain's withdrawal from Metternich's Concert of Europe in the 1820s and its growing

*Massacre at S.ᵗ Peter's or "BRITONS STRIKE HOME"!!!*

**This cartoon of the 1819 Peterloo Massacre captures the sense of class hatred it evoked. The hungry poor, peaceably seeking reform, are wantonly trampled by His Majesty's overfed officials.** (Photo: The Mansell Collection)

sympathy for Continental reform represented more than insular habit. Britain was becoming the world's leading example and advocate of liberalism, but that identification with a particular ideology came only after years of acrimony.

The end of war against Napoleon brought a depression to the British Isles as wartime markets collapsed and Europe's most developed economy stumbled before the problems of demobilization. The government's policies clearly favored the rich; it rescinded the wartime income tax and raised the tariff on grains, which increased the price of bread. These measures provoked agitation in town and country, and newspapers, political clubs, and popular meetings echoed with cries of class resentment. In 1816 a crowd demanding parliamentary reform grew violent, and the next year an alarmed government suspended habeas corpus for the first time in English history. A mass meeting for reform at St. Peter's Field, Manchester, in 1819 so terrified the local magistrates that they called out troops. In the ensuing charge, hundreds of demonstrators, including women and children, were wounded, and several were killed. With bitter mockery people called it the Peterloo Massacre.

Parliament decided to preserve order by

passing the Six Acts of 1819, which restricted public meetings, facilitated the prosecution of radicals, and imposed a stamp tax intended to cripple the radical press. In 1820 the discovery of a clumsy plot to blow up the cabinet at dinner added to the sense of danger. When George IV followed his succession to the throne in 1820 (he had been prince regent since 1811) by instituting divorce proceedings against Queen Caroline on the ground of adultery, the public used the scandal to demonstrate its contempt. Even the Church of England was attacked as a bastion of privilege in a land where Protestant dissenters and Roman Catholics could not hold public office. Gradually, agitation focused on the Corn Laws, which set tariffs on grains, of which the most important was wheat; the Combination Acts, which made it illegal for workers to organize; and Parliament itself, criticized as the unrepresentative protector of inefficient administration by a closed ruling caste.

Even an unreformed Parliament could be sensitive to public opinion, however. In 1822 George Canning replaced Castlereagh as foreign secretary and leader of the House of Commons, and he was joined by other Tories who favored temperate reforms that taken together marked a new direction. As president of the Board of Trade, William Huskisson, a member of the commercial community of London and Liverpool and an admirer of liberal economic theories, reduced some tariffs. At the Home Office Sir Robert Peel quietly ceased the prosecution of newspapers and the use of political spies. Uniformed police, instituted in London in 1829, made law and order the responsibility of civil authority, and the list of capital crimes was halved. Radicals even won the repeal of the Combination Acts; and though subsequent violence brought an amendment effectively outlawing strikes, the legality of workers' associations was preserved.

Such reasonable reforms were intended to make the government both more efficient and more popular, but they also reflected a widening acceptance of liberal ideas that disturbed many Tories. Increasingly, they came to depend on the conservative duke of Wellington, the prestigious victor over Napoleon at Waterloo, to hold their party together. Expected to resist change, he, too, found further concessions unavoidable. Agitation over religious freedom and other issues swelled in Ireland, and Wellington pushed through Parliament a measure he himself disliked, allowing Catholics and dissenters to vote and to hold public office. But radicals, workers, merchant reformers, and doctrinaire liberals demanded more—the reform of Parliament itself. Elections in 1830, required by the death of George IV and the accession of William IV, only raised the political temperature, and in the countryside laborers set haystacks afire by night while by day stern magistrates ordered laborers accused of seditious activity transported to Australia.

### The Reform Bill of 1832

As public turmoil rose and British leaders watched with concern the course of revolution in France, a new cabinet—the most thoroughly aristocratic of the century—proposed the reform of Parliament. Initially defeated in the House of Commons, the measure passed only after a new election increased the number of reformers and after the king reluctantly threatened to create enough new peers to get the measure through the House of Lords, where it had been defeated several times. Each setback for reform made the public mood uglier, and the king's intervention came amid demonstrations, the burning of the town hall and the bishop's palace in Bristol, and much dark talk about the French example.

The bill, far from radical, offered much

# ❋ EXPERIENCES OF DAILY LIFE ❋
## *Town Life*

Towns with more than 2000 inhabitants were usually considered urban; and those with between 2000 and 20,000 people, although smaller than the famous cities, held a special place in European life during the nineteenth century. More Europeans lived in the countryside and in small villages than in towns, and the growth of much larger cities brought startling changes; but towns were an important link between tradition and change. In the Rhineland, German towns were likely still to claim considerable autonomy in running their own affairs; in Italy they often continued to be restive at the dominance of the larger local capitals. These were not such important issues where strong national government had been long established; English towns were closely tied to the local gentry and aristocracy and connected through them to national politics; French towns were supervised by officials who reported to their superiors in a national civil service. Everywhere, however, these towns were centers of communication and markets, and they provided services, administrative and professional, that reached deep into rural life—the sights and smells of which were present in their streets. They were places of local dialects and regional customs; yet their town halls, squares, and parish churches had an urban flavor and often reflected a proud civic history. The residents knew each other, their background and their status; yet social relations expressed tensions and conflicts that increasingly reflected larger differences of class and ideology.

For town dwellers, the Restoration meant, above all, a return to stability. It promised relief from increased taxes to pay for war and, in much of Europe, relief from the threatening and costly presence of foreign troops. It also brought the revival of old organizations and customs. Whether called guilds or corporations or some newer name, organizations of skilled craftsmen revived. In Germany they renewed their efforts to control production and prices and to ban goods made by outside competitors; in France they were more likely to be brotherhoods of skilled craftsmen. In small towns everywhere, the ancient trades were

the core of the productive economy. The master shoemaker or blacksmith or weaver lived in a room next to his shop where his wife and children were likely to assist him and a few hired laborers and an apprentice or two. The hierarchy among these workers was clear; and although wages, conditions of work, and training could vary considerably, such matters were rooted in custom and overseen by societies that restricted admission to a trade and helped journeymen learn their craft by working at it in different towns (called tramping in England, doing the tour in France). Artisans and tradesmen might belong to mutual-aid societies organized by occupation; members paid small amounts weekly or monthly with the hope of receiving help with expenses when they were sick or to be buried. Mutual-aid societies often had religious connections, serving as parish and social organizations as well. Charities and such schools as existed were also often tied to the church, and they, too, tended to be paternalistic and to exclude outsiders. The lawyers, notaries, clergy, and property owners who often sat on the boards of these organizations were, in turn, acquaintances of the officials and members of the commissions that ran the town. Each group had its favorite meeting places, sometimes special halls or the parish church, more often taverns or cafes. Towns also followed a seasonal calendar of holidays, saints' days, religious holidays, fair days and market days; for each there were characteristic processions, games, and entertainments that reinforced a sense of community but also of hierarchy, established order, and traditional conflicts between families, sections of towns, and trades.

These structures, which encouraged suspicion of outsiders and distrust of change, proved less stable than they seemed. Much had been undermined by the period of revolution and war and by Napoleonic rule. Many of these organizations and customs had then been banned or suspended. Restored after 1815, their functions were changing. Endowments, small in any case, had largely disappeared. Above all, the structure of town life was challenged from the outside. Displaced peasants, day laborers, and migrants had little place within this system; but they arrived in increasing numbers. Old policies for repressing vagrants no longer worked. Traditional charities with their offers of bread and soup or tiny doweries for orphan girls were quaintly inadequate. German towns often tried to ban newcomers, restrict peddlers or Jews or certain kinds of trades, and control the right to marry; Italian towns continued to shut their gates at night and attempt to regulate the commerce that entered during the day. The towns of France and England did not have such options, but for them, too, policing was a problem. From the British Isles through central Europe, improved communication brought the competition of new products and additional workers willing to accept low wages. Prices fluctuated with growing regional and national markets, beyond local control. New inventions challenged old modes of production and often undermined the local economy. Those who favored paved streets and better lighting—let alone improved roads, new canals, and eventually, railroads—turned to regional and national governments for help; and these governments, even when conservative, acted as agents of change with their censuses and inventories and investigations as well as their legislation and official policies. In prosperous towns, leaders sought to overcome the disadvantages of provincialism by sponsoring newspapers, civic buildings, theaters and libraries; but for that, too, they increasingly looked outside the town to region and nation.

In the process, town life was politicized. Officials feared that workers' organizations would discuss political goals and sponsor strikes, as they often did. Frustrated by repression and restriction, some artisans joined secret societies. So did some lawyers and teachers and merchants. Rumored to be in correspondence with similar societies in other towns, these secret organizations obsessed police and administrators. Many a tavern was denounced as a hotbed of radical plots, and even traditional processions and celebrations could easily become an occasion for political demonstration. Thus the news in 1830 or 1848 of revolution in the capital city quickly brought to light, in very personal and immediate terms, the cleavages within town life. Whatever the subsequent outcome, local residents would long remember who joined which cheering crowd, which newspaper took what stand, who paraded or spoke under what flag, and who gained or lost office. The personal, social, and ideological divisions of town life were becoming aligned in lasting ways with national politics. ❄

**Burghers hiring servants on Servants Market Day in Alsace.** (Photo: Archiv für Kunst und Geschichte, Berlin)

less than the more outspoken radicals had wanted, but it marked a fundamental change. Suffrage was increased, especially in the counties, allowing some 800,000 men of substance to vote, well-to-do property-owners in the boroughs, property-owners and some tenants in the counties.[4] More important still, however, was the abolition of local variations, for a uniform national standard could, as many Tories complained, be easily broadened in the future. Before the Reform Bill of 1832, many boroughs that had solemnly been sending representatives to Parliament were barely villages; the most notorious, Old Sarum, was uninhabited. The bustling cities of Birmingham and Manchester had had no representatives at all, while perhaps a third of the members of Parliament had owed their seats to the local influence of some lord. Now such "pocket boroughs" were abolished; 22 larger cities were assigned two representatives each and 21 smaller ones, one apiece. Although landed interests would continue to dominate Parliament, the worst abuses had been corrected, representation was at least crudely related to population, and the voices of commerce and manufacturing were both more numerous and louder.

Restricted suffrage and social tradition (and the open ballot) still assured the dominance of the upper classes. But the political mood was different, and a series of other reform measures followed the 1832 bill. Slavery was abolished in Britain's colonies in 1833, a victory for Protestant reformers and humanitarian radicals. The Factory Act soon followed, limiting children's workweek to 48 hours for those 6 to 13 and 69 hours for those

14 to 18, and a new Poor Law was passed in 1834 (see Chapter 23). The Municipal Corporations Act the next year established a uniform system for the election of town and city officials and allowed all those who paid taxes in a municipality to vote in its elections—a more direct attack on aristocratic privilege than the Reform Bill of 1832.

Grave political and social problems remained to be faced, but most Britons could now reasonably hope that these might be resolved within Parliament. When the young Victoria ascended the throne in 1837, she commenced a reign of more than six decades that would rival Queen Elizabeth I's as a period of glory and power. Like Louis Philippe, Victoria was well informed and determined to play an active role in affairs of state. Like him, too, she had some of the tastes and many of the values of a good bourgeoise. But she was subordinate (often against her wishes) to an increasingly flexible political system.

## The 1840s in Britain

Two great popular movements in Britain agitated for change. Chartism was a huge, amorphous movement that grew out of disappointment with the reforms of the 1830s and the frustrations of workers' organizations. Its central aim, spelled out in what was called the People's Charter, was political democracy.[5] Chartists' meetings were watched with suspicion in 1839, 1840, and 1848; but their petitions to Parliament were summarily rejected. Their propaganda circulated widely, and riots on behalf of Chartist demands ended in scores of deaths. Yet by 1842 the movement was weakening. It failed, despite

---

[4] This was a considerably broader electorate than in France or Belgium, though Belgium, the only country to give elected representatives a salary, had in many respects Europe's most liberal constitution. About 1 Frenchman in 160 could vote in 1830, 1 Briton in 32 after the Reform Bill of 1832, and 1 Belgian in 95 by 1840 and 1 in 20 by 1848. Universal male suffrage permits approximately 1 in 5 to go to the polls.

[5] The six points of the People's Charter were universal manhood suffrage, a written ballot, abolition of property qualifications for members of Parliament, payment of the members, constituencies of equal population, and annual elections. All but the last of these were adopted by 1918.

its size, to find a program that could for long mobilize the masses struggling for survival; and it failed, despite its emphasis on political rather than more threatening economic goals, to stir the consciences of those in power. Angry or desperate workers could riot here or there, but in England they were too isolated from one another and from other classes to gain even their political goals.

The other great movement, against the grain tariff, was victorious. The Anti-Corn Law League grew out of urban resentment over the high cost of bread, maintained by a tariff that benefited the landowning classes. From Manchester the movement spread throughout the country, becoming a kind of crusade, an attack on the privileges of aristocracy in the name of the "productive orders" of society, the middle and working classes united. The league propagandized with the new techniques of popular politics:

**Mass meetings had been one of the Chartists' most effective devices, and this one held on Kennington Common in London on April 10, 1848, was one of the most publicized. With revolution on the Continent and famine in Ireland, radical hopes were as high as conservative fears. The 20,000 who attended the meeting had passed thousands of armed soldiers, policemen, and special constables. The risk of violence explains the small number of women and children in this photograph of an attentive throng. The crowd was unaware that its leaders had already agreed not to follow their speeches with the advertised march on Parliament or that the throng would soon disperse in peace from what was the Chartists' last national demonstration.** (Photo: Royal Archives Windsor Castle)

parades and rallies, songs and speeches, pamphlets and cartoons. Its slogans were printed on trinkets for children, ribbons for women, drinking cups for men. Two manufacturers, Richard Cobden and John Bright, effective writers and orators, became among the best-known and most influential men in British life, spreading the gospel of liberalism across the land. To the upper classes, such activity seemed in terrible taste; and conservatives argued from conviction that the nation's greatness was rooted in its landed estates. Nevertheless, Sir Robert Peel's government twice passed measures lowering duties on a wide range of items, including grain. The league demanded more.

Finally, in 1845, Peel announced his support for outright repeal of the Corn Laws. The threat of famine in Ireland had decided the issue for him. Almost simultaneously, the Whig leader, Lord John Russell, affirmed his conversion to the principles of free trade. Yet neither man was eager to carry the fight through the houses of Parliament. Only when Russell was unable to form a government did Peel undertake the task, and in 1846 he shepherded the measure through both the Commons and Lords. The grain tariff was reduced to almost nothing, and nearly all duties were abolished or greatly lowered.

As in 1832, the political system had bent when demands for reform gained widespread support among the middle class, but Peel's courage split his party and ended his ministry. He was jeered by angry Tories as a young backbencher, Benjamin Disraeli, rose to decry Peel's treachery to the aristocracy. Britain's adoption of free trade had not come easily, but it signified the growing weight of both public opinion and the liberal creed. In their very triumph, however, liberals broadened the sphere of political attention from questions of suffrage, efficiency, and formal justice to more difficult ones of social well-being.

## Liberal Monarchy in France

Louis Philippe's regime, known as the July Monarchy, was another compromise between order and liberty. The new constitution, with stronger guarantees of political freedom, was presented as a contract the king swore to keep, not a gift he granted. Similar to the one it replaced, it lowered property requirements for voters, nearly doubling their number—though suffrage was still safely restricted to some 170,000 men of means—and the hereditary upper house was replaced by lifetime peers. More important, most of the old aristocracy resigned their offices, never to return to public life. Those who replaced them, professional people and bearers of newer (often Napoleonic) titles, differed from their predecessors more in outlook than social origin.

In France the overriding political question of the 1830s was the July Monarchy itself, attacked from left and right. A mass held in Paris in memory of the duke of Berry became a legitimist (pro-Bourbon) demonstration, in turn prompting an anticlerical crowd to sack and loot the archbishop's palace and a nearby church. The duchess of Berry tried to spur an uprising in 1832 on behalf of her son, now the legitimist claimant to the throne; on the other hand, the strike of silk workers in Lyons was considered a republican revolt and was suppressed with the bitterness of class hatred by the bourgeois National Guard. Secret republican organizations with provocative names like the Society of the Rights of Man spread nonetheless, and Louis Napoleon, Bonapartist heir after the death of the emperor's son in 1832, attempted to stir a revolt in 1836 and again in 1840.

Yet all these attempts failed; and the July Monarchy, having established itself as a vehicle of monarchist stability, could even appeal to the cult of Napoleon I by bringing the emperor's body back from St. Helena and placing it with patriotic pomp in the marble crypt of the Invalides. A little self-consciously claiming its place in the revolutionary tradition of France, Orléanist rule did not usher in a period of great reforms like those in Britain in the 1830s, but the administrative system developed under the Revolution and Napoleon made such reforms less necessary. The provision for a nationwide system of public education in 1833 was a step English liberals would long envy. Gradually, as the regime benefited from the enthusiasm for railroads and visions of economic growth, its ministries became more confident and stable; the press, under some restrictions, grew more tame. And many who had made their reputations under Napoleon or had been moderate republicans rallied to its support.

### The 1840s in France

Within government circles, political conflict in the 1840s largely involved two factions, led by Adolphe Thiers and François Guizot. Both men were journalists and historians of great talent. With Thiers stood those who considered the revolution of 1830 one step in a process of evolution toward increased suffrage and constitutional reform. Those associated with Guizot, including the king himself, believed the constitution of 1830, having achieved a proper balance between liberty and order, should be preserved intact. Neither party was organized in any modern sense, and the differences between Guizot and Thiers were not very great, being at least as subtle as those between Peel and Russell, but their competition (legitimists and republicans had little voice in parliament) appeared to guarantee free and stable government. Later, it would seem a weakness that the skillful verbal duels of Guizot and Thiers failed to evoke in the nation at large the resounding echoes of English agitation over the Corn Laws.

From 1840 to 1848 the government of France was dominated by Guizot, Louis Philippe's premier during those years. A Protestant in a Catholic country, an intellectual in

politics, a man who held broad principles rigidly, Guizot had in excess failings common to many liberals of the nineteenth century. He spoke of liberty, progress, and law in eloquent terms that made his cautious practices seem hypocritical. The policies he pursued were, like Louis Philippe himself, lacking in the idealism that excites or the sense of larger purpose that gives dignity to compromise. When defending himself, he thought he was defending liberal government, and he cleaved to his positions to the point where rigidity itself became a principle.

The two freest and most prosperous of Europe's great nations had developed similarly since 1830. In both, liberal governments led by able men sought through reasonable compromise, the rule of law, and parliamentary government to unify their nations and to make "progress" compatible with stability. Discontent and workers' misery, though frightening, were understood in the councils of government primarily as a threat to order. In England there was a powerful aristocracy from whom reform had to be painfully wrung, but they conceded under pressure, in part because they felt secure. In France the aristocracy counted for little after 1830, but more radical visions of democracy and social justice, finding little to hope for within the system, flourished outside it more strongly than across the Channel. The July Monarchy, which felt the insecurity of its recent and revolutionary origins, held to its narrow political forms until in 1848 it fell with the ease of incumbents losing an election. England and France had never been politically more alike than during the reign of Louis Philippe.

## Liberal Victories in Other Countries

The political victories of French and British liberalism seemed part of a general trend, not only because of the prestige and influence of those countries but because of similar developments elsewhere. In Belgium, and Switzerland also, liberal political institutions accompanied notable economic growth. And the strength of liberal movements in Spain and Italy further measured the weakening of that conservative dominance Metternich had sought to assure.

## Belgium

The Belgian monarchy established in 1830 was one of the triumphs of liberal constitutionalism. The next year the new state, which owed its existence to French restraint and British protection, took as its king Leopold I, who had lived long in England (he was an uncle of Queen Victoria) and who soon married the daughter of Louis Philippe. The constitution went further than France's in guaranteeing civil rights and the primacy of the Chamber of Deputies, and politics continued to revolve around the coalition—rare in Europe—of Catholics and liberals, aristocrats and members of the upper-middle class who had led the revolt against the Netherlands.

Rapidly becoming the most industrialized nation on the Continent, Belgium was prosperous; and if its lower classes were more miserable and more largely illiterate than those of France, that very fact made the social isolation of the leaders politically less dangerous. Self-confident and satisfied with the new order of things, they built on the administrative traditions left from Austrian and French rule and proved themselves remarkably adept at planning railroads, reforming taxes and schools, and making timely political concessions.

## Switzerland

Liberal institutions spread to Switzerland, too, as part of the international trend and were spurred by the revolutions of 1830. Beginning in 1828, some cantons adopted such measures as representative government and freedom of the press, and 10 cantons formed a league in 1832 to agitate for religious freedom and for a stronger, secular central government within the Swiss confederation. These policies were resisted by seven largely Catholic cantons, dominated by their aristocracies; and the conflict, combining religious and political issues, became passionate. In 1845 the seven conservative cantons formed an alliance, the Sonderbund; two years later the leagues were at war. The Sonderbund looked for support from conservative and Catholic states, but none came—the papacy, Austria, and Piedmont had their hands full in Italy—and the liberal sympathies of Britain and France once again proved decisive. With the Sonderbund's defeat, Switzerland adopted a new constitution in 1848 influenced by the example of the United States and providing for universal male suffrage; the old union of cantons was transformed into a federal state.

## Spain

In Spain the monarchy itself had turned to liberals to seek support against attacks from the right. King Ferdinand VII, who died in 1833, had carefully arranged for the succession of his three-year-old daughter, Isabella; but his brother, Don Carlos, claimed the throne.[6] Rural, regionalist, and reactionary, Carlism was a loosely organized and badly divided movement that found its support primarily in the more isolated regions of the

---

[6] Salic law, dating from Merovingian times, prohibited the accession of women to royal thrones. Generally followed on the Continent, it meant that in 1837 Queen Victoria could not also assume rule over Hanover as her father had, and it passed to the duke of Cumberland. In Spain Ferdinand VII had abolished the Salic law by a pragmatic sanction in 1830 so that Isabella could be his heir.

north—Navarre, the Basque country, and parts of Catalonia and Aragon. The Carlists, who favored autocracy and the traditional claims of Spanish Catholicism, began a limited civil war on Isabella II's succession that ended only in 1839 with their defeat. But Don Carlos won a place in Spanish legend as a dashing and chivalric hero, the protector of old Spanish virtues, and Carlism would remain a factor in every subsequent Spanish revolution as a conservative rallying cry.

To win liberal support, the regency granted a constitution in 1834. Cautiously modeled on the French constitution of 1814, it allowed narrow suffrage and protected the monarch's prerogatives, but it established representative institutions as a lasting feature of Spanish politics. Even so modest a step was enough to place Spain in the liberal camp, and Isabella's government relied on extensive support from Britain and France. Similar developments in Portugal under young Queen Maria II led to an alliance of the four countries in 1834, a league of constitutional regimes to offset the interventions of young princes sent from Italy and Germany to fight for Don Carlos.

Internal war led generals to engage in politics and divided the liberals. The moderates supported the constitution of 1834 and admired Guizot's France, while the more anticlerical progressives called for a democratic constitution and the election of local officials. The progressives won a more radical constitution in 1837 and in 1840 led an uprising on behalf of General Baldomero Espartero, who displaced the queen mother as regent and established a dictatorship. Three years later General Ramón María Narváez brought a government of the moderates into power that lasted until 1854. In Spain, too, regimes needing popular support turned to parliamentary forms; in the 1840s Spain seemed to be taking its place among the liberal nations of Europe.

In his portraits, as in much of his private life, Giuseppe Mazzini seemed more a romantic poet than a revolutionary agitator. (Photo: The Granger Collection)

## Italy and the Ideas of Giuseppe Mazzini

Ferment continued in Italy following the events of 1830, though order was restored throughout the peninsula and its governments remained staunchly conservative. Uprisings and demonstrations broke out in town after town, and most of them were related to the work of Giuseppe Mazzini.

A Genoese, Mazzini absorbed something of the republican and radical traditions of his native city. In exile most of his life, mainly in London, he ceaselessly conspired, corresponded with acquaintances all over Europe, and published highly effective propaganda. His intent was revolutionary, and his Young Italy movement was far more democratic and radical than the Carbonari or the discontented officials who led revolts in the 1820s. A united Italy was his first concern, but his influence was European-wide, for he incorporated romantic values with patriotic visions of national independence, democracy, social reform, and progress.

The French Revolution, Mazzini argued, overemphasized negative and individual rights, leaving "humanity" a weak abstraction. He stressed instead the moral duties that people owed each other and the role of the nation, which gives individuals a social purpose, humanity a concrete meaning, and liberty to all. While attacking privilege, he rejected socialism as materialistic, liberalism as lacking in social values, and conservatism as stiflingly paternalistic. Yet, like most leaders of his generation, he put politics first; with the right kind of government, social, cultural, even moral problems would find their solution. All nations should educate people to brotherhood; every nation has its mission. Italy, having given to Europe Roman law, the Roman Catholic Church, and the Renaissance, would now create the first of this new kind of nation.

Mazzini was vague about the sources of political power and imprecise about economic organization. His unquenchable faith in the moral potential of simple people and their readiness to rise spontaneously in a great cause approached delusion. Yet he wrote tellingly about the specific grievances of peasants, artists, professionals, and intellectuals. Most of the revolts he supported ended in tragic failure, but he educated a generation to share at least a part of his dream.

Especially in northern Italy, young lawyers, liberal landowners, and some members of the aristocracy began to find national implications in nearly all they did. Annual congresses of Italian scientists became quiet demonstrations; disputes over where railroad lines should be built became means of expressing discontent with Austrian rule. Literary journals and societies for agricultural improvement took up the national theme. Piedmont's efforts to win trade away from Austria by commercial treaties and projected railroads excited Italian patriots and worried the imperial government.

This ferment, more genteel than the revolution Mazzini envisioned, gained new force with the election in 1846 of Pope Pius IX. He was not the Austrian candidate, and he brought to the papacy a reputation for moderation, reformist sympathies, and deep Italian feeling. When he declared amnesty for all political prisoners in the Papal States, there were jubilant demonstrations in nearly every Italian city. Talk of administrative reforms in papal territory spurred demands elsewhere for further liberal measures, including citizen militias and the abolition of censorship in Tuscany and Piedmont. When Austria tried to exercise its traditional influence, new demonstrations broke out. In fact, the various Italian governments were embarrassed by their new popularity and were being pushed further than they had meant to go when they undertook to negotiate a common Italian tariff and allowed their citizens to jeer the Austrians and talk of constitutional union.

Southern Italy had been rather removed from this agitation, but in the fall some of its towns attempted revolt, and in January 1848 well-organized revolution broke out in Palermo. By the end of the month, Neapolitan armies had been swept from Sicily except for units in a few fortresses. The Sicilian revolt, which demanded the honored Spanish constitution of 1812, led to heightened demands in Naples itself. When the Bourbon monarch granted a constitution, the dikes were broken. Early in February Piedmont and then Tuscany gained similar constitutions, all resembling France's of 1830, and the Papal States were expected to follow suit. The demand for liberal institutions, when combined with the cry for a free and independent Italy, seemed invincible.

## III. THE REVOLUTIONS OF 1848
❈

Both conservatives and liberals had assumed that political measures of the proper sort could assure domestic order. But in 1848 revolution swept across Europe from France to Hungary. Within a few weeks of one another, very different regimes gave way before rather similar demands. Social and national issues— issues on which political liberals disagreed— now proved even more divisive than constitutional questions. One factor common to most of the uprisings was economic distress, marked by rising food prices after a poor harvest and a recession that struck many new industries after the expansion of the 1840s.

### Revolution in France

Economic crisis does not make a revolution; the death from starvation of more than a million people in Ireland during the famine years of 1846–1849 did little more than the Chartists to shake British rule. In France, however, a faltering economy added to political pressure for a more liberal and representative regime while Guizot held firm to the constitution he believed in and Louis Philippe to the minister he trusted.

To protest against the government's intransigence, a series of banquets took place across the country, the most important of which was scheduled for Paris on February 22. When a frightened government banned it, some deputies announced they would attend the banquet anyway. Crowds began to gather in the streets, occasionally clashing with police, and workers who could never have afforded banquet tickets started building barricades. Revolution had begun.

The government had careful plans, though perhaps not the right generals, for dealing with insurrection; but when even the respectable citizenry of the National Guard sullenly refused to cheer their king, Louis Philippe, like Charles X before him, abdicated in favor of his grandson and left for England. Once again, however, the Paris crowds had more revolutionary aims, and on February 24 the Second Republic was declared from the Hôtel de Ville.

Political clubs and pressure groups organized quickly, and members of the provisional government, "nominated" in the offices of two rival newspapers, were "confirmed" by cheers from the crowd outside the Hôtel de Ville. The leading figure was Alphonse de Lamartine, a handsome and eloquent poet, converted to Republicanism on the day of revolution. But the cabinet also included a scientist and several journalists; a radical republican, Alexandre Ledru-Rollin; a socialist, Louis Blanc; and even one worker, Albert Martin, always referred to with unconscious condescension by his first name only.

Despite their distrust of each other, moderates and radicals compromised with some skill. The republic adopted universal male suffrage, a degree of democracy allowed in no other large nation; declared the citizen's right to work a principle of government; and erected a commission to hold public hearings on problems of labor. Noting that each French revolution "owed it to the world to establish yet one more philosophic truth," the republic abolished the death penalty.

At the same time, pains were taken to demonstrate the new regime's restraint. Foreign war was rejected, Lamartine's eloquence persuaded the crowd to abandon a red flag in favor of the tricolor (with a red cockade), and new taxes were levied to balance the budget. Relations with the Catholic Church were the best in a generation, and the April elections for a Constituent Assembly, which the more radical had wanted postponed, took place in good order, with nearly 85 percent of the eligible electorate voting—striking evidence of political awareness. The result was an overwhelming majority for the moderate republicans and a serious setback for the left, which had fewer deputies than the monarchists. The Second Republic seemed solidly established.

### The Spread of Revolution

As news of the events in France sped across Europe, a conservative nightmare became a reality. Nearly every capital, it developed, had citizens who found exciting promise in words like "constitution," "rights," "liberty," "free press." In Hungary the Diet cheered Kossuth's call on March 3 for representative government, and revolution broke out at the same time in the Rhineland and later in Vienna (March 12), then in Berlin (March 15), Milan (March 18), and Venice (March 22).

As spontaneous and loosely organized as the rising in Paris, these revolts followed a similar pattern. The news from France would attract excited crowds; groups of men—especially journalists, lawyers, and students—would meet in cafés to discuss rumors, newspaper accounts, and their own aspirations. Governments, as ready as local radicals to believe that revolution was at hand, would call out troops to maintain order, and with a kind of inevitability, some incident would occur—a shot fired by a soldier insulted once too often or by someone in the crowd with an unfamiliar gun.

Now barricades would rise in the style that came from Paris, constructed of paving stones, a passing coach ceremoniously overturned, nearby trees, and furniture. Barricades became the people's voice, threatening but vague, as workers and doctors, women and children labored together through the night. When blood was shed, the crowd had its martyrs. In Paris corpses were carried around on a cart as a spur to revolutionary determination; in Berlin the king supported his fainting queen while bareheaded he paid the homage his subjects demanded to citizens his troops had killed.

When new concessions were won, the atmosphere would grow festive. New flags would fly, often a tricolor, symbolizing national union. In the almost universal dedication to politics, newspapers and pamphlets would appear in floods (100 new newspapers in Vienna, nearly 500 in Paris). Workers burst into the Tuileries and jovially ate the lunch prepared for a king who had no time to eat it. Republicans met at the police station to read with amusement (and sometimes the shock of betrayal) police reports on their activity. Radicals would seek ever after to recapture the unanimity, the joy, the power of a day of revolution. Others, and not just conservatives, would never quite forget the fearsomeness of the mob, fanatical faces, and ugly threats.

The revolutions had in common the psychology they manifested and many of the liberal goals they demanded. Scarcity of food, depression, and the economic dislocation caused by new industry played some part in all of them; in most cities so did the fact of recent and rapid growth in the numbers of the urban poor. Peasant discontent was critical in Central Europe. Yet the revolutions of 1848 were not a single phenomenon; specific issues, the personalities who expressed them, and the forces that resolved them varied from state to state.

## Revolution in Germany and Italy

Frederick William IV had been replying to growing agitation in Prussia with vague assurances, a promise to reconvene the united

**This contemporary engraving of the fighting in Frankfurt on September 18, 1848, contrasts the fighting styles of troops and the people.**
(Photo: The Granger Collection)

Landtag, and a strengthening of his troops. With the incredible news of revolt in Vienna and the fall of Metternich, the king softened, relaxing censorship and calling the Landtag. Fighting broke out despite these concessions, and Frederick William gave way to demands that the hated troops leave Berlin, using the magic word "Germany" in proclamations to "my dear Berliners" and even wearing the national colors: black, gold, and red. A constituent assembly was elected in May by universal but indirect suffrage, and when it met in Berlin, where a civic guard now kept order,

revolution in Prussia seemed to have triumphed.

Events in the rest of Germany confirmed that triumph. In March some 600 delegates had met in Frankfurt in a preparliamentary assembly, and no government dared oppose their call for elections by universal male suffrage to a national assembly. In May the national assembly convened at Frankfurt included 830 delegates, mostly from the smaller states of the more liberal west, more than half of them lawyers and professors. But there were businessmen, members of the liberal gentry, and even nobles suddenly awkward in such society. The great majority favored a monarchial German state with an almost democratic constitution, and the brilliant, difficult, and noisy assembly set about to write a constitution claiming for itself executive authority over a united Germany.

In the Austrian Empire, by mid-March the Hungarian Diet had established a free press and a national guard, abolished feudal obligations (with compensation to be paid the lords), and resolved to require nobles to pay taxes. Everyone noticed the parallel to 1789. The demands that Hungary be allowed to levy its own taxes and direct its own army, briefly resisted in Vienna, were soon granted, and a new cabinet, which included Kossuth, began to govern through established institutions.

A constitutional regime in Hungary alone, however, could hardly be secure; but its example encouraged students in Vienna to demand representative government for Austria and especially in the capital city. The crowds soon clashed with the troops and once fired upon became more militant. In rapid order Metternich resigned, censorship was abolished, a constitution was promised, and arms were passed out to the students. The government attempted again and again to circumscribe these concessions but quickly retreated before renewed outbursts. When students rejected the proposal that the vote be granted everyone but factory workers and servants, universal male suffrage was conceded in mid-May. At the same time, Hungarian autonomy brought similar demands from Czechs in Bohemia, Croats in Croatia, and Rumanians in Transylvania (these last two domains under Hungarian rule). The old Austrian Empire had all but collapsed.

In Naples, Tuscany, and Piedmont the measures won through the March Laws in Hungary and the March Days in Berlin had been gained a few days earlier. Then the Papal States were granted a constitution, though it awkwardly preserved a veto for the pope and the College of Cardinals. With revolution in Vienna, open revolt broke out in Milan; and after five days of bitter fighting, the Austrian army retreated from the city. The Five Glorious Days of Milan added their luster to the heroic legends of March. A people aroused, it appeared, could defeat a great army. Soon Venice, too, rose up to reestablish the Venetian republic.

Nationalist pressure then pushed Piedmont to declare war on Austria, and papal troops with papal blessing were sent to join a Neapolitan army in the common battle against Austrian rule in Italy. But a few days later Pius IX declared he could hardly fight against Catholic Austria, and Ferdinand II recalled his army from the front after his Swiss mercenaries defeated the revolutionaries in Naples. Piedmont was left alone to bear the brunt of the national war against Austria. Still, patriotic spirits remained high; and when at the end of May Piedmontese troops won a battle, the prospects for a free and independent Italy seemed good.

## The Fatal Dissensions

Political freedom exposed the disagreements among those who had fought for it. In France these divisions were primarily social—between Paris and the countryside, between middle class and workers. The moderate majority of the new assembly were satisfied with what their republic had already achieved and determined that liberty should not be threatened by disorders. Workers, on the other hand, found conditions little improved by revolution or the new republic and agitated for a social program.

Frightened, the government dissolved the national workshops, which had been established to provide useful work for the unemployed. Only a faint echo of ideas popularized by Louis Blanc, the workshops, in fact, offered more relief than employment. The good bourgeois saw in them a dangerous principle, outrageous inefficiency, and wasteful expense; but they symbolized the hope of the lower classes, and unemployed men from Paris and the countryside had joined them by the tens of thousands. On news of their dissolution, barricades went up in the workers' quarters of Paris, and the poor fought with the ferocity of hopelessness as republican troops under General Louis Eugène Cavaignac systematically crushed the threat to order. The accidental death of the archbishop of Paris, killed while trying to mediate, seemed to prove the inevitability of civil war. After three days of fighting, June 24–26, the government troops triumphed. More than a thousand people died, and thousands more workers would be sent to prison or into exile. Paris had never seen greater bloodshed in so brief a period.

For the young Karl Marx and for socialists ever since, the June Days were the classic example of open class conflict, and radicals never quite recaptured their faith that democracy would lead to social justice. Given almost dictatorial powers, Cavaignac took steps to restrict the press, suppress radical societies, and discipline workers. The creation of a French republic still seemed in itself a radical step, and Cavaignac remained a convinced republican. The assembly continued to write a constitution, which, announced in November, kept universal suffrage and provided for a unicameral parliament (with no conservative upper house) and a president elected directly by popular vote. But while its official acts might have been unexceptionably republican, after June there was something a little hollow about the representativeness of the Second Republic.

In Germany and Austria revolutionary change uncovered latent conflicts among artisans, peasants, and nobles as well as between workers and members of the middle class. Furthermore, revolts in these lands had not deposed their rulers, who kept control of loyal armies. Above all, nationalism, which evoked such popular enthusiasm, separated the constitution makers from each other.

Czech patriots had refused representation in the Frankfurt parliament, insisting that Slavs should not be subject to German rule. Instead, a pan-Slav congress met at Prague in June. When disorder resulted, the Austrian field marshal Prince Windischgrätz, long disgusted with his emperor's weakness, bombarded Prague, crushed all resistance, and established military rule. The Frankfurt parliament congratulated him on his German victory.

It was no more sympathetic to Italian nationalism. The Austrian general Count Joseph Radetzky had retreated from Milan only as far as the great fortresses that had dominated the Lombard plain since the Middle Ages. In July, disregarding orders to negotiate, he skillfully attacked the Piedmontese and overwhelmingly defeated them. Austrian troops, once more in control of Lombardy, marched back into Milan. Radetzky, too, won congratulations from Frankfurt.

The German parliament also acquiesced as Prussian troops put down a Polish rising in Posen, and it called on Prussia to fight Denmark in behalf of Germans in Schleswig and Holstein, who opposed the extension of Danish authority in these duchies. In September riots broke out in Frankfurt itself, an expression of both nationalist and economic complaints; and the assembly, without revenue or a military force of its own, invited Austrian and Prussian troops to restore order.

Meanwhile many Croats had been demanding autonomy from Hungary just as Hungary had from Vienna, and General Joseph Jellachich with his emperor's encouragement built on Croat sentiment to weld an effective army that overpowered desperate Hungarian resistance and marched almost to Vienna. Before that threat the city rose again in October, but the armies of Windischgrätz and Jellachich bombarded Vienna into submission. The emperor returned, his authority reestablished in all his empire save Hungary and the Venetian Republic.

Rome, too, witnessed another revolutionary outburst in November, and like the June Days in Paris, the September riots in Frankfurt, and the October revolt in Vienna, this rising showed a popular fury and frustration that had not been so apparent in February and March. For hungry and desperate people, freedom added political awareness to old suspicions, and turmoil had taught the usefulness of force. The pope had proved, of course, not to be a nationalist; and within Rome an entrenched and reactionary administration choked each effort at reform. The appointment of Count Pellegrino Rossi, who had been French ambassador to Rome and a friend of Guizot, to be prime minister of the Papal States would earlier have justified the wildest hopes; but now the cautious and rigid Rossi merely increased antagonisms. In November he was assassinated, Pius IX slipped away to the safety of Gaeta in the Neapolitan kingdom, and the eternal city under Mazzini's leadership assumed the ancient title of the Roman Republic.

Venice and France also remained republics, and assemblies were still busy drafting constitutions in Vienna, Berlin, and Frankfurt. There could be no doubt, however, that in general, the forces of order were gaining ground at the end of the year. Nationwide elections in December selected a president for the French republic. There were four candidates: Lamartine, the most prominent figure of government from February to June, received the fewest votes; Ledru-Rollin, leader of the republican left, fared somewhat better; Cavaignac, who had held executive powers

since wiping out the June uprising, made a respectable showing; and Louis Napoleon Bonaparte won 70 percent of the votes. All campaigned as republicans, but all save Napoleon symbolized disillusionment. The Louis Napoleon who once had fought with the Carbonari in Italy could claim to be the man of revolution. He was clearly also a man of order, and yet he had written more about social questions and workers' needs than any other candidate. He was supported by the Catholic Church and the monarchists, for want of anyone else. Above all he had his name.[7] In December he became the first and only president of the Second Republic.

Austria, too, found a strong new leader. Prince Felix von Schwarzenberg filled the place Metternich had left vacant, and in December he persuaded Ferdinand I to abdicate in favor of his 18-year-old-son, Francis Joseph I, who had made no embarrassing commitments during the year. In Prussia the king dissolved the Landtag and promulgated a constitution of his own, very similar to Piedmont's and Belgium's. Ten months of turmoil had led back to the arrangements of February.

### The Final Phase

Many of the revolutionary regimes nevertheless proved difficult to subdue. Not until May 1849 did Neapolitan armies reconquer all of Sicily, and the bombardment of Messina earned Ferdinand II the cruel nickname of King Bomba. The Roman Republic maintained better order than the regime it replaced, and for three months it fought with

---

[7] On trial for his attempted coup in 1840, Louis Napoleon had concluded his defense with these words: "I represent before you a principle, a cause, and a defeat: The principle is sovereignty of the people; the cause, that of the Empire; the defeat, Waterloo. The principle you have recognized; the cause you have served; the defeat you want to avenge."

heroic tenacity before bowing to French troops sent by Louis Napoleon to restore the pope. In March, Piedmont, pressed by radical demands and Austrian provocation, had again declared war, only to be immediately defeated. Charles Albert abdicated, and for its efforts in the Italian national cause, all the kingdom had was an enormous debt and an unpopular government, a new ruler, a constitution, and the red, white, and green flag of Italian nationalism. Ten years later the constitution and the flag would seem quite a lot; for the time being, Austria's position in the Italian peninsula was secure.

Austria invaded Hungary in January, but her forces were pushed back; and when Schwarzenberg rejected its draft constitution, the Hungarian Diet declared a republic. The Hungarians continued to battle against the armies of Austria and against Croatians, several groups of Slavs, and Rumanians as national animosities reached new heights of fury. In June Russian intervention sealed the fate of the Hungarian republic; the conservative powers were coming to cooperate once again.

By March 1849 the Frankfurt Assembly had completed the constitution so carefully debated and elected Frederick William IV of Prussia German emperor; but after brief hesitation, he announced that the crowns he recognized came by grace of God. The Frankfurt constitution, with its universal male suffrage and touching list of old abuses to be abolished, its promises of civil rights and education, would never be tested. The assembly dissolved, and new revolutions broke out in the Rhineland, Saxony, and Bavaria (Baden's third revolution in a year led to a brief republic there), all of them quashed in June and July with the aid of Prussian troops.

The last of the revolutionary regimes to fall was that of the Venetian republic, defeated in August 1849 more by starvation and cholera than by Austrian artillery, though it accomplished the unprecedented feat of lobbing shells three miles from the mainland into the city.

A famous liberal historian has called 1848 "the turning-point at which modern history failed to turn,"[8] and his epigram captures the sense of destiny thwarted that still colors the liberal view of 1848. Historical analyses of that year, concerned with explaining the failure of the revolutions, generally include five broad points. First, liberal constitutions, new economic policies, and increased civil rights failed to pull strong and lasting support from the masses whose more immediate needs were neither met nor understood. Second, the revolutions of February and March were made primarily by the middle classes, strengthened by popular discontent; but when radicals sought more than representative government and legal equality, the middle classes were reminded of their concern for order and private property. Outside France the middle classes, once isolated from the masses, were too weak to retain power. In France they did so but turned on the urban poor, leaving themselves without support they would later need. Third, the leaders of the revolutions, inexperienced in practical politics, often mistook arguments for power and left intact the established authorities that would soon turn on them. Fourth, nationalism divided revolutionaries and prevented the cooperation that was essential for durable success. Fifth, while the military power of Austria and Russia remained formidable, no major nation was ready to intervene in behalf of change. Britain was sympathetic, France encouraging, and the United States, whose consulates were centers of republicanism, enthusiastic; but none offered the kind of help Russia gave the Austrian emperor.

From a different perspective, however,

---

[8] George Macaulay Trevelyan, *British History in the Nineteenth Century and After*, 1937, p. 292.

# 1815–1850/TIMELINE

| International and Military History | Political History |
|---|---|
| **1814–1815** Congress of Vienna | |
| **1815** | **1815** Napoleon's One Hundred Days |
| | **1817** Wartburg Festival in Germany |
| **1818** Conference of Aix-la-Chapelle | **1819** Carlsbad Decrees in Germany; "Peterloo" and Six Acts in England |
| **1820–1821** Conference of Troppau and Laibach: Austrian troops to Naples, French troops into Spain | **1820** Assassination of the duke of Berry |
| | **1820–1821** Uprisings in Italy and Spain |
| | **1821–1829** Greek revolution |
| **1823** Monroe Doctrine, Latin American revolts | |
| | **1824** Charles X king of France |
| | **1825** Decembrist revolt in Russia |
| **1830** Recognition of Belgium | **1830** Revolution in France; revolts in Belgium and parts of Italy and Germany |
| | **1830–1848** July Monarchy in France under Louis Philippe |
| | **1832** Reform Bill in Great Britain |
| **1834** Alliance of France, Great Britain, Spain, Portugal | **1833–1834** Isabella queen of Spain, new constitution and civil war |
| | **1837** Victoria queen of England |
| | **1840–1848** Ministry of Guizot in France |
| | **1840s** Agitation in Spain, Austrian Empire, Italy, Germany |
| | **1845–1848** Sonderbund and civil war in Switzerland |
| | **1847** Landtag in Prussia |
| **1848–1849** Revolutions in France, Germany, Italy, Austria | **1848** Revolutions in France, Italy, Germany, Austrian Empire |
| **1849** Russia joins in putting down revolt in Hungary | **1849** Revolutions defeated; Louis Napoleon president of France |
| **1850** | |

*Events in parentheses are discussed in other chapters.

# 1815–1850/TIMELINE

| Social and Economic History | Cultural and Intellectual History |
|---|---|

**1815**

**1817**  Suspension of habeas corpus in Great Britain

DeMaistre  (1754–1821)
Shelley  (1792–1822)

**1820**  White terror in France; Carbonari agitation in Italy

**1824**  Repeal of British Combination Acts

**1829**  Catholic emancipation
**1829**  London police

Beethoven  (1770–1829)
Schubert  (1797–1828)

Schlegel  (1772–1827)

(Hegel  (1770–1831))*

Coleridge  (1772–1834)

**1833**  German Zollverein
**1834**  Lyon silk workers rise

**1833**  Abolition of slavery in British colonies
**1834**  Poor Law; Factory Act, Municipal Corporations Act

British Reform Acts

**1838–1842**  Height of Chartist agitation

**1840s**  Railroad building on Continent

**1844**  Silesian weavers rise

**1846**  Repeal of British Corn Laws
**1846–1849**  Economic distress throughout Europe and famine in Ireland

Chateaubriand  (1768–1848)
Wordsworth  (1770–1850)
Mendelssohn  (1809–1847)
Schumann  (1809–1856)
Hugo  (1802–1885)

**1850**

the fact of revolution so widespread and tenacious was as significant as its collapse, for 1848 also measured the failures of restoration, displayed again the power of political ideas, and uncovered the effects of a generation of social change. Many of the gains won in that year endured: The peasants of eastern Prussia and the Austrian Empire, emancipated in 1848, remained free of servile obligations; and the new constitutions were kept in Piedmont and Prussia. On all sides, important lessons were learned. The monarchs triumphant in 1849 punished revolutionaries with execution, flogging, prison, and exile, but they gave increased attention to winning some popular support. Nationalists and liberals, on the other hand, would never again depend so optimistically on the spontaneous power of the people, and advocates of social reform learned to be more skeptical of political liberalism.

## SUMMARY

The period from 1815 to 1849 was an era of political experiments, each claiming to be permanent. For conservative regimes, the problem was to achieve the administrative efficiency necessary for survival while preserving as much of the old social order as possible. In Western Europe the problem was, in a sense, reversed. The benefits of regular justice, legal equality, and broader participation in politics came to be widely (although by no means universally) acknowledged; the question was how far society could go in this direction without undermining the stability and social distinctions on which, most educated people believed, civilization itself depended. The extent of suffrage aroused so much fury because it put political rights in social terms, defining by law (and therefore by conscious choice) who should participate, who constituted the political nation. Universal suffrage—few people in this period considered that the term might include both sexes—was radical because it seemed to declare men politically equal whatever their social differences. Constitutions, by making the rules of political life formal and explicit, acknowledged such rules to be made by human beings and subject to change.

The battles over these issues were fought in political terms, reflecting an almost universal assumption that political systems could determine the very nature of society. These conflicts, in turn, established the ideologies of conservatism and liberalism, which proved to be a lasting part of European public life. As these positions grew more complex, conservatives in countries like Britain, Belgium, and France learned to live with representative government while remaining determined to defend the principles of authority and social order. Liberals, while insisting that the proper political forms and legal procedures could guarantee liberty and assure progress, divided over the social responsibilities of the state. The focus of politics broadened.

Society, however, was changing independently of politics and in ways for which no political system was adequately prepared. Neither the political compromises of the restoration nor the timid liberalism of the 1830s managed to achieve the stability that was their primary aim. Seeking wider political support, some political leaders deliberately took up social issues, aware that peasants and workers were a potential force, or at least threat, that must be recognized. The nature of these social changes, only partially understood and seen as both promising and frightening, is the subject of Chapter 23. Although they engaged social issues more directly than their predecessors, the revolutionary governments of 1848 fared no better, falling in short order to social division and organized power. In the next generation, political leaders would greatly extend the authority of the state, and how they came to do that is the subject of Chapter 24. Politics after 1848 would be understood less as an autonomous sphere of activity and more in terms of the changes in social structure, economic organization, and style of life taking place in an age of industrialization.

# RECOMMENDED READING

## Studies

*Agulhon, Maurice. *The Republican Experiment, 1848–1852*. Janet Lloyd (tr.). 1983. Sensitive and authoritative study of politics and society.

Anderson, Eugene N., and Pauline R. Anderson. *Political Institutions and Social Change in the Nineteenth Century*. 1967. Comprehensive view of constitutional and legal change.

*Briggs, Asa. *The Making of Modern England, 1784–1867*. 1967. A wide-ranging and readable survey of English society and politics.

*Carr, Raymond. *Spain, 1808–1975*. 1982. The most balanced and comprehensive account in any language.

Church, Clive H. *Europe in 1830: Revolution and Political Change*. 1983. The first detailed study taking a pan-European approach.

Davies, Norman. *God's Playground: A History of Poland*. Vol. II. *From 1789 to the Present*. 1981. Effectively studies the development of a nation without a national government.

*Gash, Norman. *Aristocracy and People: Britain, 1815–1865*. 1979. An unusually balanced account of how British politics adapted to social and economic change.

Greenfield, Kent R. *Economics and Liberalism in the Risorgimento: A Study of Nationalism in Lombardy, 1814–1848*. 1978. A classic study of the connection between economic change and nationalism.

*Grew, Raymond (ed.). *Crises of Political Development in Europe and the United States*. 1978. Ten essays on the patterns of political modernization in major countries.

*Hamerow, Theodore S. *Restoration, Revolution, and Reaction: Economics and Politics in Germany, 1815–1871*. 1958. A complex analysis of the relationship of social classes and the state to economic change.

*Hobsbawm, E. J. *The Age of Revolution, Europe 1789 to 1848*. 1970. A sparkling, influential Marxist assessment of the period.

*Jardin, André, and André-Jean Tudesq. *Restoration and Reaction, 1815–1848*. Elborg Forster (tr.). 1983. Examines both the general trends and developments in the provinces.

Johnson, Douglas. *Guizot: Aspects of French History*. 1963. Insightful essays focusing on the dominant figure of the July Monarchy.

Kossman, Ernst H. *The Low Countries, 1780–1940*. 1978. Valuable and balanced treatment of a region that was an important participant in all the trends of modern European history.

*Langer, William L. *Political and Social Upheaval, 1832–1852*. 1969. Richly detailed, this study treats all of Europe in all its major aspects.

*Macartney, C. A. *The Hapsburg Empire, 1790–1918*. 1968. Detailed and authoritative.

Magraw, Roger. *France, 1815–1914: The Bourgeois Century*. 1986. A clear general account attentive to social change.

*Nicolson, Harold. *The Congress of Vienna. A Study in Allied Unity: 1812–1822*. 1970. A lively and balanced account of the process of peacemaking.

Pinkney, David H. *Decisive Years in France, 1840–1847*. 1986. The transformation to a liberal, bourgeois society.

Salvemini, Gaetano. *Mazzini*. 1957. Still the best introduction to Mazzini's thought.

Saville, John. *1848: The British State and the Chartist Movement*. 1987. The latest study of this important movement.

Seton-Watson, Hugh. *The Russian Empire, 1801–1917*. 1967. A solid, largely political survey.

*Smith, Bonnie G. *Changing Lives: Women in European History Since 1700*. 1989. Discussion of the major trends affecting all classes, with excellent bibliographies.

*Stearns, Peter N. *1848: The Revolutionary Tide in Europe*. 1974. Brings together important modern research.

*Stromberg, Roland N. *European Intellectual History since 1789*. 1975. A graceful and thorough presentation of the major trends.

*Wandycz, Piotr S. *The Lands of Partitioned Poland, 1795–1918*. 1974.

*Weiss, John. *Conservatism in Europe, 1770–1945: Traditionalism, Reaction and Counter-Revolution*. 1977. Treats this often ignored counterweight to the liberal position.

* Available in paperback.

# ❄ CHAPTER 23 ❄

# INDUSTRIALIZATION AND SOCIAL CHANGE 1800–1860

❅ ❅ ❅ ❅ ❅

The political conflict that marked the first half of the nineteenth century was part of a larger process of social change. Social relations, long governed by rank and custom, were increasingly treated as matters of free contract between individuals, a development that made it easier for some to seek new opportunities and left the poor more unprotected. Economic changes were the most obvious of all. Land had always been the primary and surest source of wealth, but technology and the spread of the industrial system were changing that, even though only a fraction of any population was directly engaged in industrial occupations. Economic growth became a continuing process in which inventions, the demand for more capital, factory organization, and more efficient transportation reinforced one another. Economic development, in turn, was intricately connected with population growth, urbanization, and new social groupings. The concentration of people, wealth, and power in great cities altered culture, social structure, and politics.

❅

These changes that justified optimistic visions of continuing progress also brought grave human distress. Slums, poverty, and unemployment appeared to be inseparable by-products of economic growth, and increasingly, society was perceived as consisting of antagonistic classes. The proper relations between rich and poor, worker and employer, men and women were called into question as established social patterns were undermined.

❅

Despite these changes, which deeply affected what people believed, where they lived, what they ate, and how they related to those around them, there was also much historical continuity. Traditional ways eroded slowly, and the institutions of government, culture, and religion maintained old forms while serving altered purposes, thereby adding to the painful dissonance between professed goals and everyday reality. While the middle class increased in size, self-confidence, and importance, the aristocracy remained socially and politically dominant in most of Europe. Western civilization once again showed its remarkable adaptability, but the strain was great.

❅

The fact of change became the focus of intellectual as well as economic life. Liberals and socialists offered contrasting visions of the sources of change and where it must lead. On all sides the growing interest in the study of history was part of the argument about what the future must bring. Reformers put their faith in the rational individual, freed to calculate his or her own best interest, and in a proper organization of society, one that would encourage flexible adaptation to ever-changing needs. The emphasis on social organization, which showed in the concern for charity and education as well as efficient production and responsive government, underscored the need for some social solution to the misery of the masses.

## I. PROGRESS OF INDUSTRIALIZATION

❋

The most obvious economic change was in the way goods were produced. Industrialization, which had begun in the eighteenth century, was then both stimulated and disrupted by the effects of the French Revolution and subsequent years of warfare. In the nineteenth century industrialization became a recognizable process spreading from industry to industry, involving governments as well as capitalists and workers, and spreading from nation to nation.

### The Effects of Revolution and War

The preconditions of industrialization discussed in Chapter 20 had continued to develop in much of Europe: The exploitation of resources had become more systematic, population was growing, transportation had generally improved, the means of recruiting capital had expanded, and the number of able political and business leaders concerned with speeding industrial growth had increased. These factors were especially evident in Great Britain, whose lead over Continental countries in goods produced, capital invested, and machinery employed had widened steadily from 1789 to 1815.

On the Continent the French Revolution and the Napoleonic era had, in important respects, cleared the way for future industrialization. In France, western Germany, northern Italy, and the Low Countries, land tenure was no longer the pressing economic and social issue; rural life was less restricted by traditional rights; and peasant proprietors, now relatively content, had become firm defenders of private property and were ready to be drawn into production for a national market. The abolition of old commercial restrictions and guilds had eliminated some obstacles to the free movement of workers and the establishment of new enterprises. Adopted on much of the Continent, French commercial law and the Napoleonic Code not only favored free contracts and an open marketplace but also introduced the advantages of uniform and clear regulations. The French government had exported a common and sensible standard of weights and measures, encouraged the establishment of technical schools (the Polytechnic School in Paris long remained the world's best), and honored inventors and inventions of every sort from improved gunpowder to new techniques for raising sugar beets. Under Napoleon, Europe had benefited from improved highways and bridges and a large zone of free trade; the Bank of France, as restructured in 1800, had become the European model of a bank of issue providing a reliable currency.

In the short run, however, the long warfare had slowed and disrupted economic growth. Vast resources in material and men were destroyed or consumed, and the Continental system, which had initially swung production and trade in France's favor, had collapsed with Napoleon's fall, bringing down many of the enterprises that it had artificially sustained. Both instability and renewed British competition discouraged daring capital investment. Great Britain, which had found compensation in American markets for its exclusion from the Continent and had avoided the shock of invasion, suffered a severe slump in the postwar years when the anticipated Continental demand for British goods failed to materialize and the transition to a peacetime economy proved difficult to achieve.

### Patterns of Industrialization

By the mid-1820s, however, British trade was reviving, and by 1830 rapid expansion was transforming the whole economy. No single industry was yet fully mechanized, but the pattern of industrialization was clearly recognizable. Cotton was the most important industry, its spinning mechanized, its weaving becoming so. Growth in one economic sector stimulated growth in others. Increased textile production, for example, accelerated the use of chemical dyes; greater iron production required more coal. A few factories in one place encouraged others in the same region where they could take advantage of the available work force and capital, and the concentration of production increased, in turn, the demand for roads, canals, and later railways (see Map A-26 in the Cartographic Essay). All this required more capital, and on the cycle went. In continuity, range of industries affected, national scope, and rate of increase, Great Britain's industrial growth was the greatest humankind had yet experienced; current estimates are that its gross national product was rising about 3 percent per annum.

With dazzling speed new inventions became whole industries and were integrated into the economy. The steam engine's application to rail travel is a classic case. When the patents expired on the Boulton and Watt steam engine in 1800, some 500 such engines were in use—and a number of British cotton mills had switched to steam power, although the less efficient Newcomen engines invented nearly a century before were also still being built. The first successful steam railway line was not built in England until 1825; a few years later an improved engine impressed spectators by outracing a horse, and in 1830 the first passenger line took its riders the 32 miles from Liverpool to Manchester in an hour and a quarter. There were 2000 miles of such rail lines in Great Britain just over a decade later and 7000 by 1851.

The product of a new industry, railroads also stimulated further industrialization.

Above the shops and bustling commerce of the Boulevard des Capucines in Paris, Nadar, the most noted photographer of the day, had his offices in this building, which shows the attractive side of economic growth in the 1860s. (Photo: Bibliothèque Nationale.)

They carried food and raw materials to cities and manufactured products to consumers more rapidly and cheaply, but they also carried news of national events and of jobs and made it possible for the men and women who crowded into dirt-stained railway cars to move great distances in their search for work.

Similarly, the telegraph, slowly developed by a generation of scientists in many countries, rapidly progressed from an adjunct of railroading to a military necessity and a conveyor of general news. The most impressive of the early long lines was Samuel F. B. Morse's from Philadelphia to Washington, opened in 1843. Less than a decade later, Britain laid 4000 miles of telegraph lines, and a cable to the Continent was in operation.

Yet the leap from new invention to industrialization was not necessarily direct or predictable. Often dozens of subsidiary inven-

**LENGTH OF RAILWAYS (IN KILOMETERS)**

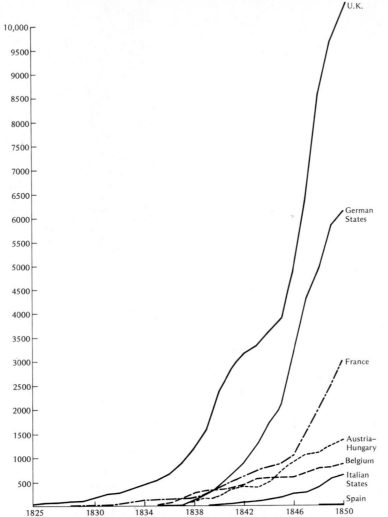

(Source: Mitchell, B. R., *European Historical Statistics, 1750–1970*, 1975, pp. 581–582.)

tions or improvements were necessary to make a new machine competitive. More often on the Continent even than in Britain, old manufacturing techniques and commercial methods persisted alongside the new. Machines themselves were usually made of wood and frequently still driven by wind, water power, or horses. But the water-driven mills, charcoal-fired smelters, and hand-powered looms that dotted the countryside would be gradually but relentlessly displaced as would hundreds of thousands of skilled artisans and rural families working in their homes to produce in the old ways—a transformation that accounted for much of the human suffering occasioned by industrialization.

In 1815 many regions of the Continent, including such traditional commercial centers as Barcelona and Naples, had seemed ready to follow the British example of industrial growth, but by the 1850s the zone of industrialization had narrowed to eastern and northern France, Belgium and the Netherlands, western Germany, and northern Italy. Within this area industrial change was more uneven than in Britain. Most of Germany remained an area of quiet villages in which peddlers and trade fairs were major avenues of commerce, though by midcentury German states were crisscrossed by the Continent's largest railway network. In the 1830s and 1840s, steamboats plied all the navigable rivers of Western Europe.

Belgium, which had prospered from its former connections with Holland, continued to build on technological skills, geographical advantages, and excellent supplies of coal. Extracting more coal than France or Germany and the first country to complete a railway network, Belgium was the mainland's first industrialized state. The French railway system, on the other hand, was not finished until after the German, for it was slowed by political conflict despite early and ambitious plans. France's canals, considered good in 1815, had trebled by 1848; and its production of iron, coal, and textiles increased severalfold in the same period. A generation earlier this would have been impressive growth, but Britain's expansion in each of these sectors was several times greater. In iron production, for example, the two countries were about equal in 1800, but Britain's output was six or seven times greater by 1850. Britain outstripped France still more in textiles and coal, producing by midcentury half the world total in these as well as iron.

Everywhere increased production led to

**This train traveled from Paris to Rouen about 1860, but note that the new technology had little effect on the laborers' tools.** (Photo: H. Roger Viollet)

more commerce and closer international ties as capital, techniques, workers, and managers moved across the Channel and from Belgium and France into the rest of Europe. The Bank of France granted an emergency loan to the Bank of England in 1825, only a decade after Waterloo; and the domestic banking policies of President Andrew Jackson of the United States in response to a financial panic there in 1837 led to a wave of crises in the financial centers of Europe.

## The Role of Government

Most observers of the new prosperity believed it followed from natural economic laws that worked their wonders more fully the freer the economy was from governmental intervention. Yet by midcentury the state was centrally involved in the process of economic growth. Railroads required franchises and

## PRODUCTION IN BELGIUM, FRANCE, GERMANY, AND THE UNITED KINGDOM

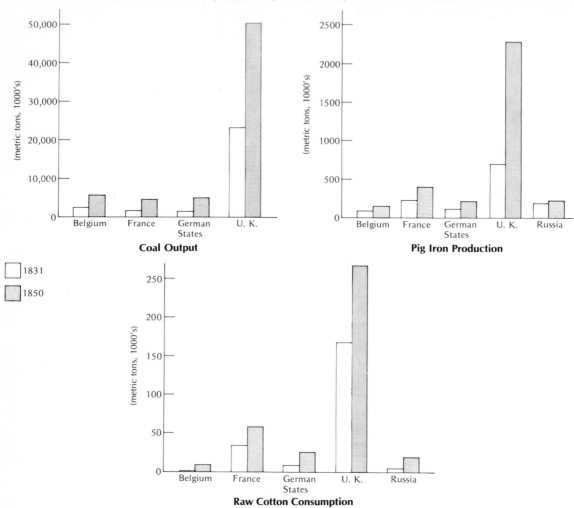

(Source: Mitchell, B. R., *European Historical Statistics, 1750–1970*, 1975, pp. 360–361, 391–392, 428–429.)

the power of eminent domain before a spike was pounded. Inevitably, routes, rates, and even the gauge of the track became political matters to be settled by parliaments or special commissions. In Belgium and in most of Germany, railroads were owned as well as planned by the state.

Tariffs, the dominant issue in British pol-

itics in the 1840s, became a critical question in every country. Britain's abolition of the Corn Laws in 1846 was not only an expression of confidence in its position as the world's greatest producer, but also a decision that industrial interests had become more important to the nation's welfare than agriculture. The German Zollverein and the unification of Italy in the 1860s created larger areas of free trade; and after the Cobden-Chevalier treaty of 1860 between Britain and France, mutually reducing tariffs, a general international reduction of trade barriers allowed goods to move across borders with unparalleled freedom.

Equally important was the role of governments in banking and currency. Just before the middle of the century, Parliament granted the Bank of England a monopoly on issuing money and, as a guarantee to investors, required companies to register with the government and publish annual budgets. Similar steps were taken across Europe. In 1852 Louis Napoleon established the Crédit Mobilier, a joint-stock bank for starting or assisting important companies, and the Prussian government offered benefits to banks and industrialists. Before industries could effectively tap private wealth, investors needed assurance that they risked only the money they invested, without being liable (as in a partnership) for all a firm's debts. That assurance required new legislation establishing limited liability and encouraging the formation of corporations, and every major country passed such measures.

The growth of cities and the benefits of new technology created additional social demands involving government. By the 1840s most cities had a public omnibus, some sidewalks, and gas lighting in certain areas. Usually provided by private companies, such services had to be subsidized, regulated, and given legal protection by government, and as their cost and importance increased, so did the state's participation in them, usually extending to full ownership.

The role of government, the economic importance of public facilities, and the possibilities of using new techniques were exemplified by postal service, which most states had provided since the seventeenth and eighteenth centuries. With few exceptions graft-ridden and unreliable, these postal systems became intolerable in the industrial age. In Britain agitation for improvement was led by an inventor and radical who argued in terms of the new economic analysis—reduced rates would make the service pay for itself by increasing volume—and the demands of progress. He also proposed standard envelopes, payment in advance, and an adhesive stamp as means of reducing costs and graft. Denounced as dangerous and impractical, his reforms were nevertheless passed in 1840. Within 20 years the volume of mail in Britain increased sixfold, and money orders, postal savings, and the telegraph were added to postal services. In France mail delivery was extended even to rural areas, and by the 1850s every major government was adopting the new system, including the postage stamp, which quickly became the object of a fashionable middle-class hobby.

Effective government, in short, was now expected to further industrialization—by subsidizing ports, transportation, and new inventions; by registering patents and sponsoring education; by encouraging investment and enforcing contracts; by maintaining order and preventing strikes. In the 1840s the leaders of Britain, France, and Belgium busily did these things—in Great Britain the number of government employees increased about fourfold in the first half of the century—and the desire for other states to more fully follow suit was elsewhere an important part of the revolutions of 1848 and the nationalist movements of the following period.

## The Relative Development of Different Nations

The British celebrated their position as the masters of industrialization in 1851 with the first international industrial exhibition. Prominent people from the aristocracy, business,

**London's imposing Crystal Palace was designed to house the first international industrial exhibition, held there in 1851. The building was constructed of cast iron and glass, a significant innovation in architecture.** (Photo: Radio Times Hulton Picture Library)

and government joined in the planning, and a specially designed pavilion was built in London, a sort of giant greenhouse called the Crystal Palace, that proved to be an architectural milestone. Many governments feared that Britain risked revolution by attracting huge mobs to London, but the admiring crowds proved well-behaved.

In fact, the exhibition provided a significant comparison of the relative economic development of the participating countries. Russia displayed primarily raw materials; Austria showed mainly luxury handicrafts. So did the Zollverein and the Italian states, but their appearance as single economic units foretold much. Although unable to fill all the space it had demanded, the United States impressed viewers with collections of fossils, cheap manufactured products for domestic use, mountains of dentifrice and soap, and a series of new inventions, including Colt revolvers, a sewing machine, McCormick's reaper, and a vacuum coffin. French machines, which ranged from a much-admired device for folding envelopes to a little-noticed submarine, were generally considered the most elegant. But British machines surpassed everyone's in quantity, size, and variety. It is, explained the *Morning Chronicle*, "to our wonderful industrial discipline—our consummately arranged organization of toil, and our habit of division of labour—that we owe all the triumph."

The wealthiest nation in history by 1850,[1] Great Britain increased its lead over other countries in goods produced during the next 20 years. Important changes were taking place, however. While textiles were still important, they were no longer the leading sector of industrialization, and steel replaced the less processed forms of iron as the metal adapted to the greatest variety of crucial industrial uses.

Economic expansion in France and the German states was now comparable to Britain's a generation earlier. France's rate of growth was greater than Britain's, but it was lower than that of Germany, which was just beginning to take advantage of rich resources (especially coal), a rapidly growing population, and traditions of technical education. During the 1860s Germany outdistanced France in the critical indexes of coal, iron, and steel production. A major shift in the locus of European economic and political power was part of the extensive social change that accompanied Europe's industrialization.

## II. THE STRUCTURE OF SOCIETY
❊

Economic growth on such a scale was accompanied and indeed promoted by changes in the fabric of society. Population was rapidly rising, and cities were increasing in size and importance. Society came to be perceived as consisting of a few classes rather than as a social pyramid built on intricate personal responsibilities up and down the social scale. The expanding middle class became increasingly prominent, while workers became more and more aware of their own distinct needs and interests. Industrialization and specialization affected all of society, from the state to the family, altering women's roles and the standard of living. At the same time, child labor, tyrannical foremen, teeming slums, and unemployment brought new social problems and required new efforts to meet them. The growing prosperity and security of the middle class contrasted all the more sharply with the destitution of the urban poor.

## The Growth in Population

Historians nowadays stress the far-reaching effects of the growth in European population, but its causes remain uncertain. For a long time industrialization itself was thought to have brought it about, the assumption being that prosperity and opportunities for employment, particularly of children, had induced a rising birth rate. That explanation is now doubted. In fact, the increase of population often occurred in rural regions, where the social effects of widespread industrialization were not likely to have been so deeply felt. There is, however, a connection between the growth of population and industry, for generally, the two phenomena appeared together as they did in Great Britain, Belgium, and western Germany. The most likely factors stimulating the rise in population were a decline in disease-carrying germs, an increase in the food supply, a lowering of the age at which people married, and after 1870 some improvement in public sanitation.

Although the data are spotty at best, the most recent research suggests that the world experienced a decline in some common dis-

---

[1] Although all estimates for this period are uncertain, it seems likely that in 1860 the per capita wealth of the French was about two-thirds and of Germans about two-fifths that of Britons.

# ❊ EXPERIENCES OF DAILY LIFE ❊
## *The Factory*

The factory quickly became the symbol of a new age. That in itself is revealing. In the preindustrial era there had been places where hundreds of laborers worked under one roof, and even with industrialization, most wage-earners did not work in factories. The noisy, smoking factory symbolized power—the power of steam and of technology, the power of capital to assemble machinery and work-force, the power of competition to drive down prices and wages, the power of markets to absorb ever more production yet determine what would be produced; above all, the power of this whole system to change the landscape, to erect or transform cities, and to reshape the lives of masses of men, women, and children.

The factory model was most clearly triumphant in the production of textiles. Spinning and weaving had always been domestic tasks; even in Europe's most important textile centers, where merchants collected the output from hundreds of looms, the actual work was done primarily in the home and involved all the family. The most successful weavers had also employed others, so that on average there had been about a half-dozen weavers in a domestic establishment. Thus pay and working conditions varied from place to place (weavers were often victimized by the middlemen who supplied their thread and purchased their cloth) and varied as well with the season and the disposition of the individual employer. This system, nevertheless, encouraged workers to take some pride in their reputation and skill, emphasized the importance of personal relations, and associated work with the environment of the family. The factory, on the other hand, required an investment in buildings, machinery,and raw materials far beyond the reach of most weavers; in return, production per worker increased more than a thousandfold with the efficient organization and power-driven machinery of the factory. By the 1830s cotton factories in Manchester averaged nearly 300 employees (they tended to be somewhat smaller elsewhere, as did those devoted to weaving silk or wool). These factories put enormous competitive pressure on older forms of production, slowly driving them out of business, although the weavers' hatred of factories and the flexibility of the domestic system allowed weavers to survive for a long time in particular regions and by making special products.

Those who came to work in the factory might be former weavers, but they were likely to be less skilled laborers (often migrants) driven by unemployment and fear of the workhouse (which the Poor Law of 1834 made a likely fate and which the factory rather resembled). Most of them were women and children, for the more numerous jobs went to them: splicing thread, tending power looms, snipping loose ends, oiling machines, doffing bobbins, sweeping the floor. Children were paid less than women and women less than men, who did the heaviest work and served as carpenters and mechanics. At first, even in the factories, children had usually worked with their parents; but increased specialization meant that, like their mothers and fathers, they came to be employed and supervised without regard to family ties. The family, however, increasingly required the combined income of all its members. Sometimes the father, with his preindustrial skills, remained unemployed and had to do housework while his wife and children earned wages, which in the eyes of Friedrich Engels was another source of "the righteous indignation of the workers at being virtually turned into eunichs."

The workday usually began at 5:30 or 6:00 and lasted for 12 hours of work plus whatever time was allotted for meals and recesses (when belts were replaced and machinery fixed). The workroom was often already hot and would become more so in summer. It was sure to be steamy and moist (the taut thread broke less readily in a humid environment; thus in domestic establishments the looms were often in the cellar). Soon the dust would be so thick that the windows had to be opened, which in winter meant the factory was cold and wet. For the employer, there was much at stake in seeing that the expensive machinery kept running and that all those workers worked; yet employers found their employees too often lethargic and sullen, prone to drunkenness and indifference. It fell to foremen to keep the operation running smoothly. They used whips and curses but most of all fines (fines for lateness, for slacking off, for flawed work, for talking, or sometimes even for singing or whistling) to establish the discipline efficient production demanded.

The best employers, like middle-class reformers or the inspectors who subsequently appeared as the result of factory legislation, were shocked by all this and at the way the workers lived, particularly their foul language, filth, poor health, ignorance, and promiscuity. They could find no solution beyond more regulation. At Lille, in the north of France, concerned employers let women off work a half-hour before the men and paid spies to report any malingering or secret trysts. Reform-

ers were upset that workers seemed to oppose restrictions on child labor (for fear that everyone's workday and income might be reduced). Employers were convinced that only notorious troublemakers agitated for the 10-hour law (finally passed in England in 1847). Among workers, those with established skills looked down on factory workers; and it was the skilled—hatters, masons, tanners, typesetters, bakers, and eventually also steam-engine makers—rather than factory workers who formed labor organizations and agitated for political redress. Yet factory workers were, in terms of income at least, better off than about half of all laborers. Their lot improved a bit as legislation limited hours, set some standards of sanitation and hygiene, and required fencing around the most dangerous machines (the belts distributing power could easily catch a piece of clothing and were the most frequent cause of injury), and as, by midcentury at least, their wages began to rise. A symbol of power, the factory was also a school of class resentment. ❊

**Power loom weaving at a nineteenth-century factory.**   (Photo: A. A. Knopf File)

eases beginning in the eighteenth century. Microbes have cycles (like those of locusts but less regular), and undoubtedly remissions had occurred many times before. Now, however, better supplies of food could allow the larger numbers surviving the perilous years of infancy to reach adulthood and form families of their own.

The food supply rose because of better transportation, more effective agricultural techniques, and the potato. Everywhere in Western Europe agricultural societies sprang up, experimenting with and advocating improved means of cultivation, better use of fertilizer, and by the 1840s some mechanization of farming. Primarily the work of enlightened aristocrats, these societies were aided by governments and churches in disseminating their doctrines through the countryside. The humble potato may have had particular importance, for it was easy to cultivate in a small space and yielded more calories per acre than any other single crop. Not common on the Continent before 1750, it became the staple of the peasant's diet in most of Europe by 1830.[2] While infant mortality remained enormously high by modern standards, even a slight decline in death rates could make a great difference, so close to subsistence did most Europeans live.

The reasons for the trend toward earlier marriage are less clear, but apparently peasants freed from servile obligations tended to set up new households at a younger age. The spread of cottage industry, before the development of great factories, allowed families to add to their income by spinning or weaving at home, and agricultural changes made it somewhat easier for the new family to find a piece of land sufficient for its survival. The

greater numbers of people in one generation—only a slight rise in a single decade or province—multiplied in the next generation and led to an enormous increase in the aggregate. As population grew, the proportion of young and thus fertile people within it grew still faster, which increased the ratio of births to total population. The net result was that the 188 million Europeans of 1800 had become 266 million by 1850 and 295 million in 1870.

The growth in population had broad ramifications. More people consumed more food, and this necessitated more intense cultivation of available soil and the use of much land previously left fallow. More people meant a larger potential work force readier to leave the countryside for industrial jobs, and that movement of population became a social change of immeasurable importance. To a lesser extent, an increasing population meant an expanding market for goods other than food, an element of growth that would have stronger impact later in the century. The greater prominence of the young was in itself significant, and there is some indication that they were more restive and that the educated among them were a potential source of radical leaders.[3] There was also a distinction in birth rate by social class, which demographers call differential fertility. On the whole, the higher a man stood on the social scale, the fewer the children in his family. The distinction became more notable in the course of the century as families became more concerned with providing education and wealth

---

[2] William L. Langer made an effective case for the potato's importance for the rise of population in "Europe's Initial Population Explosion," *American Historical Review*, 1963, pp. 1–17.

[3] In 1789 perhaps 40 percent of France's population was between 20 and 40 years old and another 36 percent under 20, the highest proportion of the young France has ever known. Mazzini limited membership in Young Italy to those under 40, and probably most of the leaders of the revolutions of 1848 would have met that standard. The relation of youth to revolution is interestingly discussed in Herbert Moller, "Youth as a Force in the Modern World," *Comparative Studies in Society and History*, April 1968.

## THE WORK FORCE IN INDUSTRIAL NATIONS MID-1850s

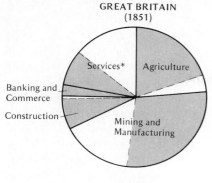

**GREAT BRITAIN**
**(1851)**

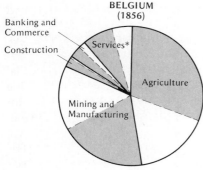

**BELGIUM**
**(1856)**

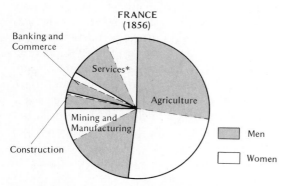

**FRANCE**
**(1856)**

☐ Men

☐ Women

**\* Including transport and communication, domestic servants, and armed forces.**
(Source: Bairoch, P., et al., *The Working Population and Its Structure*, Brussels, 1968.)

for their heirs. But to contemporaries it often suggested that the lower classes, lacking foresight and moral restraint, were likely to swamp society.

Indeed, one of the most influential books in the first half of the century was Thomas R. Malthus's *An Essay on the Principle of Population as It Affects the Future Improvement of Society*, first published in 1798 and reissued in many subsequent revisions. Observing the Britain of his time, Malthus argued that population increases faster than the supply of food unless checked either by death (through war, famine, or pestilence) or by deliberate sexual continence. A clergyman, he advocated continence but remained pessimistic that human beings were capable of such restraint. Malthus was also an economist well versed in contemporary theory, and for much of the century the demographic method and economic arguments in his controversial work deeply influenced social writing. For Malthusianism was presented as the scientific statement of a natural law containing the harsh but convenient corollary that the misery of the poor resulted from their own improvidence. The view that economic progress rested on immutable laws and that those laws allowed little hope for the masses became a central theme of early nineteenth-century liberalism.

## Urbanization

No demographic change was more important than the growth of cities. At the turn of the century, greater London was just reaching 1 million in population. No European city since imperial Rome had ever approached that size. Paris grew to that figure a generation later, but the third largest European city in 1800, Naples, had only 350,000 inhabitants. In all of Europe there were then only 22 cities with populations over 100,000. By midcentury there were 47. Great Britain was the leader, with 6 cities over the 100,000 mark; London's population had surpassed 2.5 million by 1856, Liverpool had grown from 80,000 to almost 400,000, and Manchester and Glasgow each had more than 300,000 people. By this time, half of Britain's population lived in towns or cities, making it the most urbanized nation since ancient times.

On the Continent the major capitals burgeoned. Paris reached a population of close to 1.5 million by 1850; Berlin nearly trebled, to 500,000; and a growth rate almost as great pushed Brussels to 250,000. St. Petersburg, Vienna, and Budapest all had populations between 400,000 and 500,000. Most of Europe's old cities increased by at least 50 percent in the first half of the century, and many a town became a city.

By the 1860s the English countryside was actually losing people, as were some sections of France; the tide of urbanization was overwhelming, and nearly all the subsequent increase in European population would go to swell the growth of cities, most of whose inhabitants were now immigrants as rural folk moved to nearby villages, villagers to towns, town dwellers to cities. Clearly, the tide of urbanization was strongest where industry was great, but the growth of ports and national capitals demonstrated the importance of great commercial, financial, and political centers as well.

Society had neither the experience nor the means to cope with such an expansion. Urban conditions for all but the reasonably prosperous were unspeakable. Narrow alleys were littered with garbage and ordure that gave off an overpowering stench. The water supply in Paris, better than in most large cities, offered access to safe water only at fountains dotting the city (the affluent paid carriers by the bucket), and in London the private companies that provided water allowed it to flow only a few hours a day. In most cities the water supply came from dangerously polluted rivers. Sewage was an even more serious problem. A third of Manchester's houses used privies in the 1830s, and a decade later the ratio of inside toilets to population was 1 to 212. In London cesspools were a menace to health overshadowed only by still more public means of disposal.

The most dramatic inadequacy, however, was in housing of any sort. A third of Liverpool's citizens lived crowded in dark, cold cellars, and conditions in Lille were similar. In every city the poor of both sexes crowded into filthy, stuffy, unheated rooms; and over the cities, especially manufacturing and mining towns, chemical smog and coal smoke darkened the sky. It is hardly surprising that crime was rampant, that often more than a third of the births were illegitimate, and that the number of prostitutes soared (reaching perhaps 80,000 in London, where 9000 were officially registered; 3600 were registered in Paris).

The maintenance of public order changed its meaning. For the restoration governments, the police were primarily secret agents whose job was to ferret out real or potential enemies. But the protection of lives and property in great cities, the effective handling of crowds, and the enforcement of local ordinances required something other than spies or the military. London's police force was established by Peel in 1829,[4] and Paris's Municipal Guard was created under Guizot a few years later.

For all their misery, cities continued to grow; and the worst conditions were slowly alleviated by housing codes, public sewers, and reliable water supplies. These improvements were made possible in part by industrialization, which provided iron pipes, water closets, gas lighting, better heating, and

---

[4] The role played by Sir Robert Peel is still honored in the nickname "Bobbies."

In this famous engraving of London by Gustave Doré, the rhythmic sameness and cramped efficiency of new housing suggest a machine for living appropriate to the age of the railroad. (Photo: New York Public Library/Picture Collection)

sounder buildings. Urban life developed a style of its own, increasingly distinct from life in the countryside. Towns clustered around factories and railway stations, and cities teeming with the poor and indigent were also the thriving centers of communication, commerce, politics, and culture.

## Social Classes

So many kinds of change necessarily affected social grouping. In the seventeenth and eighteenth centuries, people spoke of the "or- ders" or "ranks" in society, implying a social pyramid rising from the lowliest peasant to the ruler and assigning each person a position in it. That position in large part defined relations with those above and below.

By the beginning of the nineteenth century, the expression "middle" or "middling classes" had begun to appear, and by mid-century society was generally conceived in terms of broad strata, called classes. People's social class was thought to describe the status of their occupation but also something of the values they held, their style of life, and later the political and social interests they were likely to support. Descriptive of an expanding, fluid, national society, the concept of class expressed an important change in outlook and social reality.

## The Aristocracy

The class most easily identified was the aristocracy. It included all nobles and their immediate relatives, whether they held noble titles or not; members of the upper gentry, who were large landholders and lived like nobles; and (in the ancient commercial cities of the Netherlands, northern Germany, and northern Italy) the established and wealthy patrician families, who dominated the cities though they might not bear titles.

The aristocracy's privileges and influence had been challenged in the eighteenth century by the French Revolution; the class was threatened in the nineteenth century by new industrial wealth, which overshadowed the fortunes of large landholders and gave greater influence to leaders from the middle class. It lost some traditional authority with every increase in urbanization, every victory of constitutionalism or administrative reform. The decline of the aristocracy's privileges and power was so clear, in fact, that the continued importance of the class is easily overlooked.

In most countries aristocrats still controlled most of the wealth, were closely allied to an established church, and dominated the upper levels of administration and the military. By training and tone the most international of social classes, aristocrats remained the preeminent diplomats even under bourgeois regimes. They also stimulated some of the most influential critiques of nineteenth-century society, denouncing the middle class for selfishness and materialism, proclaiming urban life morally inferior to rural, and lamenting the loss of gentlemanly honor. The efforts of the aristocracy to defend its position, the means used, and the success achieved provide an important measure of social and political development in each country.

In much of Europe, especially the south and east, the aristocracy held on to local power and tremendous wealth, a social pattern exemplified by the Kingdom of Naples and by Russia. In both states the nobility, constituting only about 1 percent of the population, in effect ruled over most of the peasant masses. Three-fifths of the people in southern Italy lived on baronial estates. The Neapolitan aristocracy had lost many of its formal privileges under Napoleon, but with the restoration they reestablished their authority through cooperation with king and Church and by providing the leading professional men. In Russia just a fraction of the nobility held one-third of the land, and most of the rest was owned by the state and administered by nobles. Russia's aristocrats, tyrants on their estates and dominant over local administration, were the chief pillar of tsarist rule.

Where the nobles made up a higher proportion of the population, the pattern was somewhat different. In Poland, Hungary, and Spain, many of the nobility were extremely poor, and they tended to alternate between desperate allegiance to an empty title and sympathy for radical change, thus becoming another and important source of instability.

In some countries, however, aristocrats sought to strengthen their influence through representative government and decentralization, thereby cooperating with political and economic reformers. The confident Magyars took this position in Hungary, and so, even

Fashion magazines, with plates such as this from the 1830s, carried the latest fashions from Paris to England and from London to country houses, reassuring the socially ambitious as to how they should appear in public. The upper-class woman was expected to dress modestly except for evening wear, but even when walking or taking tea she might give as much attention to hat, gloves, apron, and shoes as to the dress she wore. (Photo: Ken Pelka, courtesy of the Cooper-Hewitt Museum, Smithsonian Institution/Art Resource, NY)

more generously, did the aristocrats of northern Italy, Belgium, and Great Britain. They were thus prominent during the revolutions of 1848 in Hungary and northern Italy and in the subsequent nationalist movements in those countries. The Belgian aristocracy cooperated with liberals in 1830 and after, accepting an endless string of concessions and reforms. Above all, in England the aristocracy proved willing to exchange formal power for general influence. Of the 100 men who served as cabinet ministers in Britain between 1832 and the reform of 1867, 64 were sons of nobles; and perhaps four-fifths of the members of Parliament were landholders or their representatives, closely tied to the aristocracy. On the other hand, younger sons and lesser aristocrats in England were more closely associated with the upper-middle class, lessening the sharpness of social division.

It was possible, of course, for an aristocracy to maintain its traditional hold over government even when the state became the instrument of dramatic and rapid change. This occurred in Prussia, where the most influential aristocrats were the Junkers, owners of great estates in east Prussia, some of which included sizable villages. Considered crude and ignorant by most of the aristocracies of Europe, which set great store by polished manners, elegant taste, and excellent French, the Junkers had a proud tradition of service to the state and loyalty to their king. In local government, in the bureaucracy, the army, and the court, their manners and their values—from rectitude to dueling, from arrogance to loyalty—set the tone of Prussian public life.

France is thus the European exception, for there the old aristocracy was reduced to a more minor role in national politics after 1830. Its members retained major influence in the Church, army, and foreign service, but those institutions were also on the defensive. Yet even in France, aristocrats maintained a strong voice in local affairs and a major influence on manners and the arts. Everywhere, however, they were in danger of being isolated from important sources of political and economic power. It was small compensation to be known for elegance and leisure or a famous name. Lineage was once of such importance that tracing family lines had been a matter of state; now even pride of family was becoming a private matter.

## The Peasantry

Closely related to the aristocracy in its dependence on the land and devotion to tradition, the peasant class encompassed the overwhelming majority of all Europeans. Always viewed as at the very bottom of society, peasants, too, were affected by the changes taking place around them. Agriculture was becoming more commercial, its production increasingly intended for a broad market rather than mere subsistence or local consumption. Profits increased with the cultivation of a single cash crop, the use of machinery, and improved fertilizers, changes primarily available to those with capital and a sizable piece of land. Large farms therefore became relatively more profitable, and landed nobles, bourgeois investors, and the richer peasants sought by every means to expand and consolidate their holdings, a trend encouraged by legislation in much of northern Europe.

The emancipation of peasants from "feudal" obligations—effected by the French Revolution and carried to much of Western Europe by Napoleon, decreed in Prussia as part of the reforms of 1806, and spread to most of Eastern Europe with the revolutions of 1848 (see Map A-25 in the Cartographic Essay)—encouraged their entry into the commercial market, but it also deprived them of such traditional protections against hard times as the use of a common pasture, the right to glean what was left after the first harvest, and the practice of foraging for firewood in the forest. Similarly, the decline of the putting-out system and of local industries took away critical income, especially during the winter months. Gradually and with considerable local variation, peasants were becoming more dependent on the little piece of land to which they had some legal claim or the wages that could be earned from labor. The available land increased as more of it was cultivated, especially in the west, but it was usually of poor quality and divided into small plots.

Improved communications increased the impact of more distant markets and brought peasants a keener sense of the opportunities and political events in the outside world. In addition, as governments became more efficient, they reached more deeply into peasant society for taxes and conscripts, enforcing regulations that often seemed alien and harsh. And the population of the now disturbed rural world was expanding, adding to economic pressure and restlessness.

Peasants are thus easily seen as passive victims of outside historical forces, but their response was also significant. The despair of reformers who were discouraged by their ignorance and illiteracy, who resented their opposition to change, and who were often defeated by their suspicion of outsiders, peasants tenaciously maintained old loyalties to their region, their priests, their habitual ways. Often they developed elaborate ties of family and patronage that absorbed state-appointed administrators into local social networks. Peasants were frequently shrewd judges of their short-term interests, cooperating with measures immediately beneficial to them and resisting all others with the skepticism of experience.

Their hunger for land, resentment of taxes and military service, and sense of grievance against those above them could also become a major political force. Their involvement made a crucial difference in the early days of the French Revolution and in the Spanish Resistance to Napoleon, the wars of German liberation, and the strength of nationalism in Germany and Italy. Rulers were kept on edge by eruptions of peasant violence in southern England in the 1820s; Ireland in the 1830s and 1840s; Wales, Silesia, and Galicia in the 1840s; and on a smaller scale in every country from Spain to Russia. The outbreaks of 1848 almost immediately brought feudal service toppling down in the Austrian Empire and eastern Prussia. At the same time, rural indifference to constitutional claims and workers' demands sealed the doom of the urban revolutions.

But the peasantry was far from united. The deepest division was betweeen those who owned land and those forced to sell their labor. Some of the former, especially in the west, grew relatively prosperous and joined the influential notables of their region. More of them lived as little dependent upon cash as possible, vulnerable to the slightest change in weather or market, supplementing their income by whatever odd jobs members of the family could find. In most of Europe tenant-farming was more common, with endless local variations as to who paid for seed or fertilizer and how the final crop was divided. At best, such arrangements provided the peasant with significant security, but they tended also to be inflexible, slow to adapt to changes in prices, markets, and technology.

Rural laborers were the poorest and most insecure of all, the tinder of violence and the recruits for factory work.

A central problem for nineteenth-century European society was how to integrate the agricultural economy and the masses dependent on it into the developing commercial and industrial economy. By the 1850s the process had gone farthest in France and Great Britain but through opposite means. In Britain the peasantry was largely eliminated as the continuing enclosures of great estates reduced the rural poor to laborers, shifting from place to place and hiring out for the season or by the day (see Maps A-22 to A-23 in the Cartographic Essay). The concentration of landholding in Great Britain was one of the highest in Europe: some 500 aristocratic families controlled half the land and some 1300 others, most of the rest. In France, on the other hand, peasants owned approximately one-third of the land, and their share was gradually increasing. Owners of tiny plots outnumbered the landless, and they supported themselves by favoring crops that require intense cultivation, such as grapes and sugar beets, and by maintaining small-scale craft industries.

Elsewhere the patterns lay between these two extremes, though rising populations everywhere made the landless the majority. The tradition of small landholding persisted in western Germany, northern Italy, Switzerland, the Netherlands, Belgium, and Scandinavia alongside a trend toward the consolidation of larger farms that reduced millions to becoming day-laborers. Emancipation in Germany usually required peasants to pay for their freedom with part (often the best part) of the land they claimed. New historical methods that can compensate for the lack of written records have also established the importance of local variations—the quality of the soil, the favored crop, government policy, and legal custom. The fate of many a national political movement turns out on a closer look to have depended, like the uprisings often misunderstood as simply the violence of the untutored, on peasants' understanding of how in a changing world they could best preserve what little they had.

There was a clear distinction, however, between these Western and Central regions and Eastern Europe, where Russian serfdom was the extreme. In the West the changes that increased agricultural productivity often left the life of peasants more precarious. In the East a heavy social price was paid for preserving the landholders' authority over their peasants and their claims to their labor, which ranged from a month or so a year to several days a week in Russia; the emancipation of Russian serfs in the 1860s (see Chapter 24) proved necessary in order to allow economic expansion and minimal military and administrative efficiency. As urbanization and industrialization advanced, many writers waxed nostalgic for the bucolic purity and sturdy independence of peasant life, but the problems of the peasantry were, in fact, some of the gravest and most intractable of European society.

### The Working Classes

Industrial laborers, however, attracted far more attention. In the 1830s and 1840s, serious French analysts wrote of the "dangerous classes" crowding into Paris. By midcentury industrial workers were the examplars of a growing social class, though even in Britain in the 1860s they made up a small fraction of all those who lived by wages paid for physical labor; there were more domestic servants than factory hands. The conception of a working class derived less from what people did for a living or their poor pay than from their dependence on others—for employment, for defining what their job entailed, and for setting the hours and conditions of their work.

The most independent workers were the artisans. Stripped of their tight guilds and formal apprenticeships by the French Revolution, a series of laws passed in Britain up to the 1830s, and a process in Germany completed by the revolutions of 1848, artisans nevertheless continued to ply their crafts in a hierarchy of masters, journeymen, and apprentices working in small shops where conditions varied as much according to the temper of the master as the pressures of the market. Skilled workers, from carpenters and shoemakers to mechanics, moved in a less organized labor market but were distinctly better paid than the masses of the unskilled. Although vulnerable to competition from machines and new products and above all to unemployment during the frequent economic slumps, these workers in general were among the beneficiaries of industrialization. Their real wages tended slowly to increase, and they could expect to earn enough to support their families in one or two bare rooms on a simple diet.

Factory workers on the whole earned too little to sustain a family, and thus the employment of women and children became as necessary to survival as it was advantageous to employers, who appreciated their greater dexterity and the lower wages they would accept. The largest factories were the cotton mills, where commonly, half the laborers were women and a quarter, children. In coal mines, where women and children were hired to push carts and work in the narrower shafts, they were a smaller proportion of the work force. A class was thereby formed of men, women, and children, clustered about a source of employment, dependent on cash for their subsistence, and subjected to the rigid discipline of the factory. Awakened before dawn by the factory bell, they tramped to work, where the pace of production was relentless and the dangers from machinery and irate foremen was great. Any lapse of attention during a workday of 14 hours or more, even stopping to help a neighbor, brought a fine and a harsh reprimand. Children were frequently beaten, as men had been before fines proved more effective, and all were spurred by threats of piece rates and unemployment. Life was still more precarious for the millions of men without regular employment, who simply did such tasks as they could find, hauling or digging for a few pence.

Industrial workers were thus set apart by the conditions of their labor, the slums where they lived, and special restrictions such as the *livret*, or passport, that all French workers were required to present when applying for a job and that recorded the comments of previous employers on their conduct and performance. Understandably, the powerful worried about the social volcano on which they lived, and the sensitive feared the effect of the immorality and degradation that accompanied industrial life.

Ignorant and exhausted workers, often strangers to one another, for the most part lacked the means necessary for effective concerted action. Their frequent outbursts of resentment and intermittent strikes usually ended in some bloodshed and sullen defeat. Sometimes the riots, demonstrations, and strikes became local revolutions, spreading across the north of England in 1811 and 1812, breaking out in Lyons in 1831 and 1834, Bristol in 1831, Lancashire in 1841, and Silesia in 1844. Significantly, most of these outbursts were led by artisans, who felt most keenly the threat of change and held clearer visions of their rights and dignity. Although the authorities usually blamed the sinister plots of a few agitators for such disturbances, they nevertheless stimulated the vision of a day when laborers of many kinds, both urban and rural, might concertedly demonstrate their power. The June Days in Paris were widely understood, by all sides and perhaps exaggeratedly, as an expression of the new working class.

Trade unions were banned everywhere except in England after 1824, and even there the laws against conspiracy restricted their activity; but various local organizations had developed since the eighteenth century to take the place of the declining or outlawed guilds. By midcentury more than 1.5 million British workers may have belonged to such groups, which tended, like the friendly societies, to form around a few of the more skilled workers and to meet in secret, often of necessity but also better to express a sense of brotherhood and trust. Although fond of elaborate rituals and terrifying oaths, their specific purposes were usually modest: burial costs for a member or assistance in times of illness. Equally important was the sense of community they fostered among those having in common their trade and neighborhood. In France workers' groups achieved state recognition as (carefully supervised) mutual-aid societies and were given some government subsidies under Louis Napoleon. Above all, these organizations were both expressions of and efforts to create a working-class culture with values, interests, and leaders of its own. In this sense, the authorities' fear that they would become hotbeds of radicalism had some basis.

There were also workers' political movements, of which Chartism was by far the largest, and cooperatives, which were intended to increase workers' control of their lives. Consumers' cooperatives were numerous by the 1830s in England, and producers' cooperatives, often established with church support in France and Italy, were the model for the French national workshops of 1848. For the most part, however, these expressions of workers' insistence on their rights and dignity remained small in scale and local in influence.

The hundreds of strikes that occurred throughout Western Europe in the first half of the century were rarely the result of any lasting organization, but they suggested what unions might accomplish and led to heroic efforts by leaders of the working class, particularly in Great Britain during the 1830s. Without funds, means of communication, or common experience, these early efforts at unionizing petered out after a few years or sometimes a few months. Not even the Workingman's Association for Benefiting Politically, Socially, and Morally the Useful Classes, launched with some fanfare in 1836, managed to survive for long or bring off the general strike the more radical dreamed of. Yet these organizations, which gave the more fortunate workers some effective voice and some valuable experience of national political life, did influence Parliament in favor of factory legislation. The meetings, torchlight parades, and special newspapers and tracts all contributed to the growing sense of class. So, above all, did the repression by police and courts that usually followed. By midcentury millions of workers in Britain, somewhat fewer perhaps in France, and smaller numbers elsewhere shared heroes and rituals, believed they faced a common enemy, and accepted organization as the prime means of defending themselves in a hostile world. In Britain the national trades unions of skilled workers formed in the 1830s and 1840s (with only some 100,000 members then) would steadily increase their size and influence, reaching more than a million members a generation later.

The vast majority of the working class, however, remained essentially defenseless, possessing meager skills, dependent upon unstable employment, and living in the isolation of poverty. Ideas of *fraternité* and *egalité*, of the rights of freeborn English people, and of simple patriotism, often expressed in Biblical prose, communicated a common sense of hope and outrage to millions of the men and women who attended rallies, met in dingy cafés, and read the working-class press (or listened as it was read to them).

Newspapers and pamphlets intended for workers became extensive in England after 1815, were less widespread in France in the 1830s and 1840s, and appeared everywhere in 1848. The common themes were people's natural rights, pride of work, and the claims of justice. They burst forth countless times in whole programs for change, phrases proudly tucked into petitions and posters, and anonymous gestures like the direct humor of the British coal miner who left a note to the man whose house he broke into during a strike in 1831:

> I was at yor hoose last neet, and meyd myself very comfortable. Ye hey nee family, and . . . I see ye have a great lot of rooms, and big cellars, and plenty of wine and beer in them, which I got ma share on. Noo I naw some at wor colliery that has three or fower lads and lasses, and they live in won room not half as gude as yor cellar. I don't pretend to naw very much, but I naw there shudn't be that much difference. . . .[5]

Outbursts of sabotage, strikes, and riots—most historians now agree—were rarely aimless but had specific targets reflecting immediate needs. Lasting gains, however, normally required some connection between the local crisis and larger, national movements. When that was not the case, and it usually was not, the workers and their families had nevertheless contributed to the creation of a subculture of which their betters knew little.

### The Middle Classes

Of all the social classes, the most confident and assertive was the middle class. At the top stood the great bankers, who in London and Paris were often closely connected to the liberal aristocracy and whose political influ-

---

[5] Cited in Edward P. Thompson, *The Making of the English Working Class*, 1966, p. 715.

ence after 1830 was considerable. More separate from and a little contemptuous of the traditional elites stood the great industrialists and the wealthiest merchants. At the bottom were the small shopkeepers, office clerks, and schoolteachers, often distinguishable from artisans only by their pretensions. This petite bourgeoisie comprised most of the middle class numerically, but the class was epitomized by those between these groups: most merchants, managers, and upper bureaucrats and nearly all lawyers, doctors, engineers, and professors. That such disparate people could believe they had common interests and values and therefore a similar position was the result of recent history. They opposed prescriptive privilege and saw themselves as the beneficiaries of social change that allowed the talented to gain security and influence.

They were primarily an urban class and intimately connected with the commerce and politics of city life. In Paris they constituted nearly all of that part of the population, between one-fourth and one-fifth, prosperous enough to pay some taxes, have at least one maid, and leave an estate sufficient to cover the costs of private burial.[6] In other cities their proportion was probably somewhat smaller; among nations they were most numerous in Great Britain, a sizable fraction in France and Belgium, and a smaller minority elsewhere. Belonging to the only class that it was possible to fall out of, middle-class people established their membership by economic self-sufficiency, literacy, and respectability. Their manner, their dress, and their homes were thus symbols of their status and meant to express values of probity, hard work, fortitude, prudence, and self-reliance (see Plate 49). No matter how favored by birth or for-

tune, they tended to think of themselves as self-made.

While industrial centers were notoriously drab, the middle-class home became more ornate, packed with furnishings that boasted of elaborate craftsmanship. Women's fashions similarly featured ornamental frills, and shops translated Parisian elegance into forms available to more modest purses. Masculine garb, by contrast, grew plainer, a point of some pride in a practical age; and clerk and banker tended to dress alike. Those who forged great industries out of daring, foresight, and luck; those who invented or built; those who taught or tended shop or wrote for newspapers came to share a certain pride in one another's achievements as proof that personal drive and social benefit were in harmony and as a harbinger of progress yet to come.

More than any other, the middle class was associated with an ideology; and the triumph of the middle class in this period—so heralded then and by historians since—related as much to constitutionalism and legal equality, individual rights and economic opportunity as it did to any explicit transfer of power. The conquests of the middle class were measured not just by its rise in importance but also by a more general adoption of its values. Even being in the middle, between the extremes of luxury and power and of poverty and ignorance, was seen as an advantage, a kind of inherent moderation. In the nineteenth century, most of Europe's writers, scientists, doctors, lawyers, and businesspeople would have felt no need to blush on finding themselves called by a London paper in 1807 "those persons . . . always counted the most valuable, because the least corrupted, members of society," or on hearing John Stuart Mill speak a generation later of "the class which is universally described as the most wise and the most virtuous part of the community, the middle rank."

---

[6] Perhaps the most detailed study yet made of the middle class in this period is Adeline Daumard's *La Bourgeoisie parisienne de 1815 à 1848*, 1963.

## Social Conditions

Industrialization and urbanization necessarily affected most aspects of social life. Not only were there new tasks to be performed but traditional ones also came to be accomplished in more organized and specialized ways. All of this, in turn, meant changes in the role of the family and of women, in the standard of living, and in public policies on matters of general welfare. Such changes at first sharpened the differences between social classes and became the subject of anguished debates, and they led to systematic efforts at reform.

### Differentiation

Sociologists use the term "differentiation" to describe increased specialization among groups and institutions, and that, too, was a trend increasingly apparent in the nineteenth century. Its effects were clearest in the division of labor within a large factory and in the tendency to separate production from the home. Thus social differentiation meant, in part, the increasing separation of family roles from work. It affected institutions too. Banks and markets became more specialized, and the reliance on legal contracts differentiated economic from personal or social relationships. Governments preferred to rely on their officials rather than traditional elites (even when, as frequently happened, local notables were the ones appointed to office), and governmental functions themselves became more specialized. Maintaining the peace, collecting taxes, inspecting factories and schools, and administering welfare fell to separate bureaus. In addition, social tasks once performed by others, such as the registering of births and deaths and the providing for education and charity, largely performed by the clergy before the French Revolution, were now increasingly absorbed by the state—another reason for the importance of politics in this period.

Just as each trade and each locality followed its own course of social change, so each nation differed in the pace and manner of institutional differentiation. Britain, more than Continental states, left many public matters to local government and private groups; in France the role of the national government increased, and the German states tended to combine centralizing bureaucracies with considerable local autonomy. Whatever the pattern, the growth of differentiation was a major source of conflict among institutions, between levels of government, and within communities.

### The Family and the Role of Women

To a great many nineteenth-century observers, social change appeared to threaten the continued importance of the family, and moralists of every sort warned that the institution most central to civilization was being undermined. Recent research, however, has suggested a different view: Heightened concern for the family was not only a response to real stress but also an expression of increased belief in the social importance of proper child-rearing; the family proved, on the whole, an extraordinarily adaptable institution, and the forms of adaptation varied greatly, especially by social class. So did the place of women, and the question of women's proper role joined the long list of social issues on which nineteenth-century society sustained rigid convention yet confessed itself increasingly troubled.

For the aristocracy, family included a wide network of relatives, valuable connections to land, privilege, and power within which women played a critical but subordinate role as carriers of the dowries that joined estates, managers of large domestic staffs, and centers of the social circles in which aristocrats

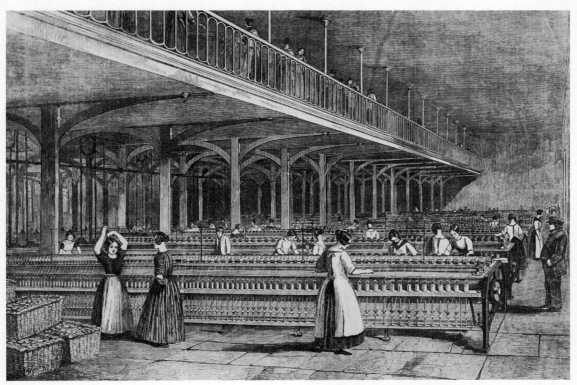

An etching of Dean Mills in 1851 shows cotton spinning as contemporaries liked to think of it: women working together with nimble industriousness under the watchful but gentle eye of a sturdy foreman, all in the iron grandeur of an immaculate, orderly, huge new factory. (Photo: The Mansell Collection)

met. The peasant family, on the other hand, varied with local tradition, social structure, and economy. Where plots were large enough, the family unit would be likely to include grandparents or even in-laws, cousins, and nephews. Particularly in Mediterranean regions, such extended families often shared housing in the village but worked in different nearby fields. When they could, however, a young couple generally set up a household of their own. Where peasants owned land, the problem of keeping it intact while giving something to all the children was difficult, a frequent source of dispute whether law and custom required equal division of inheritance as in France, primogeniture (inheritance by the eldest son) as in England, or ultimogeniture (inheritance by the youngest son) as in parts of Germany. The elderly feared dispossession, the children that they would not get their share in time.

Yet for peasants, the family remained the basic economic unit, pooling income from various sources, dividing labor in customary ways—with the women usually handling household chores and the smaller animals, the men responsible for the heavier work, and everyone working together in critical periods of planting and harvest. Often the women had more access than the men to additional sources of income—piecework from a nearby mill or domestic service for the well-to-do—and they played a central role in marketing. Men, on the other hand, were more likely to travel considerable distances, especially in difficult times, to pick up a bit of work on roads or docks or at some great landlord's harvest. As population increased, the children were more often pushed out to seek employment in the nearest mills and towns.

For artisans, too, the family was often the unit of production, although the division of tasks by sex was usually more explicit, and even small workshops had long tended to exclude women, at least from the better-paid tasks. For working-class women and children to labor long hours was thus not the change so many upper-class commentators made it seem. The strain on the family came rather from the lack of housing and the conditions of work. Not only did women and children have to supplement the father's income, but they were less and less likely to work as a family—although many employers in the early nineteenth century did prefer to hire (and fire) entire families. But they rarely worked side by side; if taught a trade, children were less likely to learn it from their parents. Hardened at an early age, adolescents in factory towns were probably more likely to leave home when their pay allowed, and urban conditions made it more difficult for the family to support the aged and the sick. Such factors did weaken family ties as did—at least in the eyes of the upper class— the common practice for working men and women to live together without the trouble or expense of formal marriage rites. Yet among workers, too, the family survived and the home remained a special place expected to provide protection for small children, a haven for wage earners, and temporary shelter for relatives seeking a job. The fact that women worked for pay may also have slowly lessened their subordination even if it did not lead very directly to the new and superior stage of family life that Karl Marx thought it might.

In the lower-middle class, especially in France, women were as important as and frequently more visible than men in operating small shops. The life of the middle-class woman, however, contrasted greatly with that of her poorer sisters, and the role allotted wife and mother became one of the most apparent and important indicators of social status. In earlier eras women had played some part in public life, in politics and business as well as high society, and they continued to be the organizers, patrons, critics, and ornaments of many of Europe's most cultivated circles. But the middle class isolated women from the harsh competition of business and politics. As the contemporary French historian Jules Michelet complained, "By a singular set of circumstances—social, economic, religious—man lives separated from woman." In Victorian England gentlemen met in their clubs or withdrew after dinner for their cigars and weighty talk. The nineteenth-century feminine ideal was an idle and pallid creature, encased in corset or bustle, whose most vigorous act of self-expression was fainting.

There are no proven explanations of why such customs should have developed. There was, of course, a kind of conspicuous consumption in allowing a wife to be idle even if her husband worked hard, a certain partial imitation of aristocratic elegance; but there were signs, too, of an unconscious effort at maintaining a sort of counterculture. If men must be competitive, hard, and practical, women should be tender, innocent, and gracious, the weak but pure upholders of virtue and aesthetic sensibility. The middle-class woman with no estate to manage and few servants to direct was almost literally placed on a pedestal. Neither her needlework nor her piano playing were viewed as serious, but her role in maintaining the protective calm of the home and as exemplar of the moral virtues was.

Clearly, these attitudes were related to the famous prudery of the age and the distrust of sexual passion. Thomas Bowdler produced in 1818 his *Family Shakespeare*, "in which . . . those words and phrases are omitted which cannot with propriety be read in a family," a strange sensitivity after 200 years; and "the anti-English pollution of the waltz . . . the most degenerating that the last or present century can see" was denounced in *The Ladies' Pocket Book of Etiquette* of 1840. The middle classes sought to maintain an orderly world through convention. At a time when prostitution and drunkenness were at new heights, this was more than repression; it was an effort to bend society to the self-discipline on which a thriving commerce, the advancement of knowledge, and personal fulfillment were thought to rest.

Unless they had (female) servants to do these things for them, wives of every class— no matter what their other burdens—were expected to prepare and serve the food, wash and mend the clothes, and clean the family dwelling. Middle-class concern with the family also emphasized, however, the special role of women within the home, which became a private citadel largely closed to the outside world. In the family the liberal dream of combining individualism and social order came closest to achievement, for the patriarchal father, devoted mother, and carefully trained children were meant to live in disciplined harmony. Childhood itself lasted longer in the middle class, where character, manners, and education required elaborate preparation. The mother made this home; and books, newspapers, magazines, and sermons were filled with accounts of the talents that role required. Motherhood had become an honored occupation, fondly depicted in novels and the new women's magazines founded, like the Parisian *Journal des Femmes* of 1832, to make women "skilled in their duties as companions and mothers."

Before winning fame with their novels, the Brontë sisters professed envy for the working woman, who at least had her own money, but respectable careers were slowly opening to women. The governess was, along with the butler, the chief domestic, and many a bright but poor young woman used that often lonely position to gain some knowledge of the world and establish a career or enhance her prospects for marriage. In England and increasingly on the Continent, most elementary-school teachers were women, and that occupation opened significant opportunities by the 1860s. Florence Nightingale offended her wealthy family by working as a nurse; but she returned from the Crimean War in 1856 a national heroine to become a major influence in public health and in the establishment of nursing as a secular profession for women. She was the first woman to win the British Order of Merit. On the Continent, George Sand (the masculine pen name says much about the status of women) was one of the most prolific and noted writers of the age, an important figure among the artists of France, who shocked and excited her contemporaries as much by her attacks on marriage and the treatment of women as by her free personal life. In England women writers proved keen and often caustic observers of society, from Jane Austen's deft analysis of genteel life in the countryside to Elizabeth Gaskell's sympathetic picture of industrial workers and the more complex novels of George Eliot (Mary Ann Evans), who was an active participant in the major intellectual and reform movements of the period. By the 1840s, when Flora Tristan traveled across France preaching to workers of the connection between their plight and women's, the emancipation of women had

(Scènes dans les **mines de houille**, en Angleterre. — Le Trapper.)

(Jeune fille traînant un chariot.)

(Jeune homme employé à l'extraction du charbon.)

become an important theme in the writings of nearly all the utopian socialists (see the next section), who found in women's role a key to the errors of middle-class society. John Stuart Mill's *Essay on the Subjugation of Women*, published in 1869, and his advocacy of suffrage for them thus stand as a milestone marking the growing strength of the women's movement.

## The Standard of Living

There is more agreement among historians about the general pattern of social change in the first half of the nineteenth century than about its specific effects on the standard of living, particularly of the working class. For this period, England is the critical case; and scholars agree that between 1790 and 1840 national wealth about doubled but that the upper classes were the principal beneficiaries. Did workers gain, too? Certainly they were poor, but poverty, even of the bleakest sort, was not new (and a growing desire to correct such destitution was in itself one of the important changes of the period). The poorest peasants of Sicily, who lived in caves, like those of Sweden or Ireland who lived in holes dug into the ground, may have been victims of the social system; they were hardly vicitms of industrialization.

What was new, then, was the terrible crowding and the workers' helpless dependence. The conditions in which workers lived made poverty more miserable, more obvious to all, and more threatening to the general welfare. In part the result of increased pop-

---

**These French illustrations from the 1840s of work in an English coal mine show the classic horrors—naked men, chained women, and straining children—that made industrialization in the English style something to be avoided.** (Photo: New York Public Library/Picture Collection)

ulation, the crowding followed directly from the sudden growth of factory towns. Even if the hurridly built housing was drier and cleaner than the peasant hovels that had served for centuries, the squeezing of whole families into a single room and the cramming of hundreds and thousands of people into areas with little light, with a single source of insalubrious water, and with no means for disposing of sewage created problems so different in scale as to be different in kind. Industrialization also added the special hazards of lead and phosphorous poisoning; and the assault of coal mining, cotton spinning, and machine grinding on the lungs made tuberculosis ubiquitous. Everywhere in Europe members of the working class were recognized generally to be thinner, shorter, and paler than other people.

Accompanying this was an often demoralizing dependence. Most new factories employed between 150 and 300 men, women, and children, which would mean many people whose well-being was largely tied to a single employer. A high proportion of these people were new to the area in which they lived, starkly dependent upon cash to pay their rent, purchase rough cotton for clothes, provide the bread that was the staple of their diet, and buy some candles and coal. For millions, employment was never steady; for millions of others, unemployment was the norm. It was common for a third of the adult males of a town to be without work, especially in the winter, and pauperism was acknowledged to be the social disease of the century, a condition that included some 10 percent of the population in Britain and only slightly less in France. Workers, of course, suffered most in the periodic depressions that baffled even the most optimistic. The depression of 1846 was nearly universal, and that of 1857 extended from North America to Eastern Europe. Layoffs in the Lancashire cotton industry ran so high as a result of the

American Civil War that at one time more than 250,000 workers, better than half the total, lived by what they could get on relief. The recipes for the watery soup handed out by the charitable agencies of every city define the thinness of survival.[7]

At the same time, there was a counter-trend. In some trades and places, workers were distinctly better off; in general, real wages—wages measured, that is, in terms of what they could buy—may have increased somewhat. Pay rose generally in the mid-1840s and notably again in the 1850s, though these gains meant less in new factory towns, where workers could be forced to buy shoddy goods at high prices in company stores. Alcoholism was so extensive that in many a factory town paydays were staggered in order to reduce the dangerous number of drunks, and this sign of alienation may also reflect an increase in available money. Technology, of course, brought benefits as well. The spread of the use of soap and cotton underwear was an enormous boon to health, and brick construction and iron pipes had improved housing even for many of the relatively poor by midcentury. Luxuries such as sugar, tea, and meat were becoming available to the lower-middle class and the more prosperous artisans.

The vigorous debate among historians over the standard of living in this period has become in large measure a test of the author's feelings about capitalism. But pessimists and optimists generally agree that whatever improvements occurred reached the masses slowly, that their effects often could not compensate for the added burdens of industrial employment, and that the chasm between the destitute and the regularly employed (who in England were called the deserving poor) became greater than ever before.

For in industrial Europe the urban poor remained a subject of baffled concern. Skilled workers and the middle classes were unquestionably more prosperous than even in the recent past, but that made the contrast with the poverty of those beneath them even more striking. A luxury restaurant in Paris (there were over 3000 restaurants of every type there by 1830 as contrasted to only 50 or so before the Revolution) might charge 25 or 30 times an average worker's daily wage for a single meal; even modest ones charged twice the daily wage to a clientele that ate three or four times a day in contrast to the two meals of many workers. Despite the subtle shadings of status and wealth, the great differences of class were palpable in every aspect of daily life.

## Public Welfare

The social questions of pauperism, public health and morals, and class divisions were debated in hundreds of speeches and pamphlets; and the parliamentary and private inquiries in Britain, like the elaborate social studies in France, expressed a humanitarian attempt to improve the lot of the lower class through the rational techniques that seemed to work brilliantly when applied to issues of profits and politics.

Some employers, especially in Britain and Alsace, built special housing, drab barracks that nonetheless seemed marvels of cleanli-

[7] The French chef of the Reform Club of London was much admired for his "good and nourishing" recipe: 1/4 lb. leg of beef, 2 oz. of drippings, 2 onions and other vegetables, 1/2 lb. flour, 1/2 lb. barley, 3 oz. salt, 1/2 oz. brown sugar—and 2 gallons of water! It was by no means the cheapest soup. Cited in Cecil Woodham-Smith, *The Great Hunger*, 1964, p. 173.

**Gustave Doré's engraving of a London slum captures both the sullen hopelessness of the poor and the sense of the dangerous classes continuously breeding children that frightened the upper classes.** (Photo: The Granger Collection)

ness and decency. Middle-class radicals supported the Society for the Diffusion of Useful Knowledge, founded in 1826 to carry enlightenment to the lower classes. They contributed to and gave lectures at night schools for the workingman, such as those run by the Mechanics' Institute (of which there were more than 700 in Great Britain by 1850) and by the Polytechnic Association of France (which had more than 100,000 participants on the eve of the revolution of 1848). Thousands of middle-class people personally carried the lamp of truth to the poor in the form of pious essays, moral stories, and informative descriptions of how machines worked. Bibles by the million added to this extraordinary testimony to faith in the power of the printed page and to the spread of literacy. Ambitious members of the lower-middle class were, however, more likely than workers to take advantage of these opportunities.

For the truly poverty-stricken, charities were established at an incredible rate; more than 450 relief organizations were listed in London alone in 1853, and whole encyclopedias were published in France cataloguing these undertakings. A revival of Christian zeal provided powerful impetus to such groups in Britain, and on the Continent new Catholic religious orders, most with specific social missions, were founded by the hundreds. They sponsored lectures, organized wholesome recreation, set up trade apprenticeships, provided expectant mothers with a clean sheet and a pamphlet on child care, opened savings banks that accepted even the tiniest deposit, campaigned for hygiene or temperance, gave away soup and bread, supported homes for abandoned children and fallen women, and ran nurseries, schools, and hostels. These good works were preeminently the province of women. Almost invariably, they presented themselves as models of social salvation, which required only that others follow their example. The Society

of St. Vincent de Paul, which was organized in Paris in 1835 and soon spread to all of Catholic Europe, required thousands of educated and well-to-do men regularly to visit the poor so they might teach thrift and give hope by their example as well as their charity. Important for some lucky individuals and a significant means of informing the comfortable about the plight of the poor, the heroic efforts of these organizations were never adequate to the social challenge. Most of Europe's urban masses remained largely untouched by charity or religion.

In matters of public health, standards of housing, working conditions, and education, governments were forced to take a more active role. By modern standards the official measures were timid and hesitant, and the motives behind them were as mixed as they were in factory legislation, favored not only by humanitarians but also by landed interests happy to restrain industrialists.

It is not surprising that conditions of health remained appalling. Vaccination, enforced by progressive governments, made smallpox less threatening after the turn of the century, but beyond that, any advances in medicine contributed little. The great work of immunization would come later in the century. The most important medical gain of the 1840s was probably the use of anesthesia in surgery, dentistry, and childbirth. Serious epidemics broke out in every decade. Typhus, carried by lice, was a constant threat, accounting for one death in nine in Ireland between 1816 and 1819, and typhoid fever was caused by infected water in city after city. Apparently beginning along the Ganges River in 1826, cholera spread through East Asia, reaching Moscow and St. Petersburg by 1830 (100,000 died of cholera in Russia in two years). From there it spread south and west, to Egypt and North Africa, to Poland, Austria, and into Germany, to be reported in Hamburg in 1831. Despite efforts to put ports in quarantine (a move opposed by shipping interests), the disease reached northern England and later France in the same year, continuing slowly to the south, taking a ninth of Palermo's population in 1836–1837.

The reaction to the epidemic of 1831–1832 in Britain, France, and Germany, however, revealed much about social change. An official day of fasting, prayer, and humiliation in England or the warnings of the archbishop of Paris that the cholera was Divine Retribution, expressed widespread distrust of an era of materialism and its belief in progress as well as the strength of traditional faith. But governments were expected to act, and, torn between two inaccurate theories of how the disease spread (contagion on contact and miasmic effluvia; the cholera bacillus was finally identified by Robert Koch in 1883), they did. Inspectors were mobilized to enforce such sanitary regulations as existed (and not infrequently were faced with riots by a populace fearful of medical body snatchers). In Paris and Lille tenements were whitewashed by the tens of thousands, food inspected, streets and sewers cleaned on administrative order. Similar steps were taken in the German states and in Britain, where after the inadequacy of local government became apparent, a national Public Health Commission was given extraordinary powers over towns and individuals. Statistics were gathered, and over a period of years doctors and inspectors (with consciences troubled) reported on the terrible conditions they had found among lower-class neighbors whose quarters they had never visited before. There was another such epidemic in the 1840s and lesser ones thereafter, but the shock and uncertainty of what to do was never again so great. Gradually, hospitals, too, came under more direct state supervision as the cost and complexity of medical treatment increased. By midcentury housing and sanitary codes regulated most of urban construction through-

out the West, and inspectors were empowered to enforce these rules. Liberalism showed its other face in England's handling of the terrible potato famine in Ireland. As the potato blight struck late in 1845, disaster for a population so dependent on a single crop was not hard to predict. For the next several years some of England's ablest officials struggled with bureaucratic earnestness to collect information, organize relief, and maintain order; yet they did so in a manner so inhibited by respect for natural economic forces and the rights of property that, in practice, only meager relief was offered while millions starved.

The 1830s and 1840s witnessed a series of restrictions on child labor, banning employment of those under 9 in textile mills in Britain and factories in Prussia, under 8 in factories in France, and under 10 in mines in Britain. By the end of the 1840s, similar measures had been adopted in Bavaria, Baden, Piedmont, and Russia. Generally, the laws held the workday of children under 12 or 13 to 8 or 9 hours and of those under 16 or 18 to 12 hours. In Britain and France there were additional requirements that the very young be provided with a couple of hours of schooling each day. To be effective, such regulations required teams of inspectors, provided for only in Britain, where earnest disciples of Jeremy Bentham (who is discussed in the next section) applied them diligently. This expansion of government authority had been vigorously opposed, but the appalling evidence presented to commissions of inquiry made the need apparent, and the ability to gather such evidence became one of government's most important functions.

The most bitterly controversial welfare measure of the period was Britain's Poor Law of 1834. The old system of relief required counties to supplement local wages up to a subsistence level determined by the price of bread. Expensive and inadequate to changing

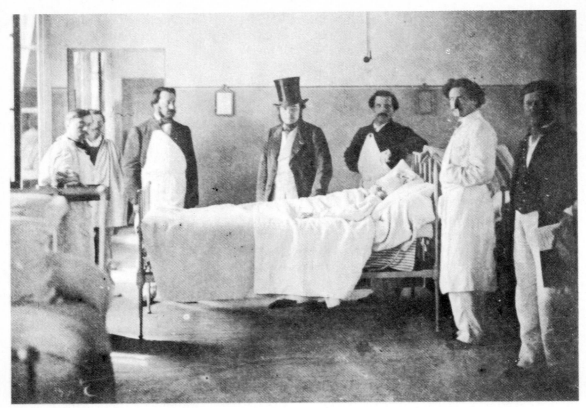

**Photography gained wide acceptance both as a mode of portraiture and as a scientific tool in the nineteenth century. Charles Negre's photograph of "The Doctor's Visit" to the Imperial Asylum at Vincennes in 1860 combines both of these in a stark display of the hospital environment of the era.** (Photo: Philadelphia Museum of Art; Collection of André Jammes)

needs, the system was attacked by liberal economists, who charged that it discouraged workers from migrating to new jobs and cost too much. An extensive campaign led to the Poor Law of 1834, based on the quaint Benthamite notion that unemployment must be made unattractive. Those receiving relief were required to live in workhouses, where the sexes were separated and conditions kept suitably mean. Resented as a cruel act of class conflict, the new law proved unenforceable in much of the nation, though recent studies have suggested that it was less harsh in either practice or intent than its critics charged. On the Continent welfare measures kept more traditional forms while steadily shifting the responsibility for them from local and religious auspices to the state.

Public education also became a matter of national policy. Prussia had made local schooling compulsory in 1716, and efforts to enforce and regulate that requirement culminated in 1807 with the creation of a bureau of education. In the following decades the government, with the cooperation of the Lutheran clergy, established an efficient system of universal education with facilities for training the needed teachers and guarantees that the subject matter taught would remain rudimentary and politically safe. The network of secondary schools was also enlarged but kept quite separate, in effect excluding the lower classes. Most of the German states had similar arrangements, establishing nearly universal elementary education. In France the Napoleonic structure provided the framework for public education, in principle although not in practice providing a substitute for the extensive but more informal and largely religious schools of the old regime. The law of 1833 required an elementary school in every commune. Despite many difficulties, the system steadily expanded, the quality of teachers improved, and the power of inspectors over tightfisted local authorities increased. By the revolution of 1848, three-fourths of France's school-age children were receiving some formal instruction. The conflict between the Church of England and the dissenting sects prevented the adoption of a state-controlled system of national education in Britain, a lack welcomed by those conservatives who opposed educating the masses. Nevertheless, the subsidy first voted in 1833 to underwrite the construction of private schools proved an opening wedge, and it increased in amount and scope each year. From Spain to Russia elementary schools were favored by every government. Inadequate and impoverished, the public schools of Europe offered little chance of social advancement to those forced to attend them, but few doubted that they could be a major instrument for improving society as well as a force for social peace.

## III. THEORIES OF CHANGE

❈

### Liberalism

The overwhelming fact of political and social change demanded interpretation; and liberalism not only produced change but explained it. It became an international movement, one led primarily by men of means and education, who watched the successes of their cause throughout Western Europe and encouraged one another in the conviction that history was inevitably advancing toward the fulfillment of their common vision. That confidence rested not only on political victories but also on the experience of economic growth. The gains of liberal politics—representative government, free speech, and laws applied equally to all citizens (see Chapter 22)—seemed to accompany the triumph of liberal economic theory and the application of liberal social policies. Liberal politics and liberal economic theory were thus closely related; yet these two aspects of liberalism have proved separable. The advocates of one were not always, and not necessarily, committed to the other, and the question of their relationship is still a matter of controversy, especially in the United States. The model of liberalism was nineteenth-century England.

### Economic Liberalism

Adam Smith and the physiocrats had argued that government intervention in the marketplace merely restricted the play of economic forces that if left to themselves would increase productivity and prosperity. This belief, which had become liberal dogma, was expounded systematically by David Ricardo, whose writings represented the keystone of modern economics for generations. Ricardo was one of England's self-made men, a financier who became wealthy during the Napoleonic wars and then retired from business, thereafter contributing enthusiastically to charity, taking part in politics, and developing his economic ideas, which England's leading liberals encouraged him to publish. First issued in 1817, his *Principles of Political Economy and Taxation* presented his theory in flat prose as a science, precise but highly abstract.

The wealth of the community, Ricardo argued, comes from land, capital, and labor; and these three "classes" are compensated by rent, profit, and wages. A product's value results from the labor required to make it—the labor theory of value, which socialists would later use for very different purposes. For Ricardo, this theory led to principles of property similar to Locke's and to an emphasis on labor saving as the source of profit foreshadowed by Adam Smith. Rents are determined not by individuals but by the poorest land in cultivation. The most fertile land produces more for the same labor, and that increment constitutes profit, received as rent. As population pressures bring more (and poorer) land into cultivation, rents rise because the difference between the best and worst land increases. Wages are subtracted from profit, but an "iron law of wages" (his phrase is characteristic) decrees that when labor is plentiful, the workers tend to be paid at the subsistence level. Short-term fluctuations in prices are the natural regulator within the system, pushing people to activities for which demand is high. Thus Ricardian economics extended the sphere of inexorable economic laws and riveted them to Malthusian ideas about pressures of population.

Both land and labor are commodities, Ricardo said, their value quite unaffected by sentimental talk about aristocratic values or craftsmanship, and society is a congeries of competing interests. Legislation cannot raise wages or prevent the marketplace from working in its natural way; but if people acknowledge economic laws and act in their own best interest, a natural harmony and progress follow.

Ricardo called his subject political economy, and from it, a powerful reform movement developed. Clearly, liberals argued, the landed interest had misused political power to benefit itself, depriving the rest of society. Throughout Europe liberal economic theory added important weight to demands that special privilege be eliminated and that governments be responsive to their citizens, who best know their own interests. With the impressive evidence of economic growth before them, it was natural for liberals to add that politicians might well adopt something of the openness, efficiency, and energy of the men of action who were transforming business.

## Utilitarianism

A second major stream of liberalism was utilitarianism, a complex and often contradictory philosophy elaborated by Jeremy Bentham. Although English, Bentham was in many respects a philosophe, ready to write a constitution for Russia or codify the laws of Latin American republics. Some of his most important writings before 1789 appeared first in French—the revolutionaries gave him French citizenship—and he combined plans of detailed reform with a theory of psychology in the Enlightenment tradition. At first Bentham stressed reform of the legal system, and he remained all his life an opponent of the precedent-bound, technicality-loving courts of England. In contrast to most philosophes, he rejected the doctrine of natural rights as a meaningless abstraction, and unlike most liberals, he did not hesitate to advocate heavy state intervention in society.

In Bentham's thinking, utility replaces natural rights as the test of proper policy, and it is measured by the standard of what provides the greatest good for the greatest number. The good is that which avoids pain and gives pleasure—a calculation that all people make for themselves anyway and that with education they can learn to make more wisely. (Bentham called this the "felicific calculus," but his verbal pomposity was famous; his after-dinner walks were "postprandial perambulations.'') The egocentrism that built great industry could also build a just and happy society. In Bentham's terms, the proper estimate of pain and pleasure leads one to behave like a prudent, middle-class Christian; and the task of government is to make sure that pain and pleasure are appropriately distributed for various kinds of behavior.

Bentham's followers, sober intellectuals who called themselves philosophic radicals, became even more influential. They pressed his doctrines in every sphere, and by his death in 1832, they were among the most important reformers of Parliament, law, prisons, education, and welfare. A special group within a larger liberal movement, they shared and contributed to the tendency of liberals everywhere to take pride in pressing for humane reforms on grounds of common sense and natural harmony.

## The Broader Liberalism of John Stuart Mill

Thus liberals appraised society primarily in terms of opportunities for individual growth and freedom of individual choice. Such an emphasis gave some ethical dignity to the pain of industrialization and social change. Confident and optimistic, their doctrines seemed universally valid.

Yet liberalism, to the perpetual surprise of its adherents, proved a creed of limited appeal, forever subject to attack and internal division. Enthusiasm for limited constitutional reform, so great in the 1830s, was harder to sustain in 1848. It proved difficult in practice to reconcile liberty with order and equal rights with private property, and the opportunities and freedoms proudly cited by men like Guizot seemed to others the selfishness of the well-to-do. Religious conflict in Catholic Europe, the need first to create national states in Central and Eastern Europe,

This photograph of John Stuart Mill shows a solid bourgeois (compare Ingres's portrait of Louis Bertin, Plate 49) who is also a sensitive intellectual. (Photo: The Granger Collection)

and the problems of the dispossessed everywhere inhibited the full application of liberal ideas.

Before such problems, liberals themselves divided. As maintained by some, liberalism became the narrow and, at times, mean justification of a social class; for others, it expanded until the need for social justice and equal opportunity largely obscured the principles of competitive economics and a non-interfering state that were its original strength. In each country its temper was different, shaped by a national history liberals never wholly dominated.

Its very malleability, however, enabled liberalism to endure as a doctrine and a political force; and its transition to a broader meaning is best exemplified in John Stuart Mill, the most important liberal spokesman of the nineteenth century. Mill's father was a leading Benthamite, and he raised his son in the strictest utilitarianism; but the younger Mill gradually came with searching candor to modify received doctrine. Extraordinarily learned, a philosopher, economist, and publicist, Mill's greatest influence has been through his political writings. Fearful of the intolerance and oppression of which any class or even the public at large was capable, he made freedom of thought a first principle, and he advocated universal suffrage as a necessary check on the elite and proportional representation as a means of protecting minorities. Influenced by Auguste Comte (see Chapter 25) and others, he acknowledged the critical role of institutions in social organization and admitted that those institutions, even liberal ones, best suited to one stage of development might not be appropriate for another.

Mill hoped for a beneficial influence from a more open bureaucracy, from organized interest groups, and from cooperatives. Moved by the problems of the industrial poor, he tried to distinguish between production (to which liberal economics could still apply) and distribution (in which the state might intervene in behalf of justice), and he came to see that collective action by the workers could enhance freedom rather than restrict it. He sought a place for aesthetic values within the colder doctrine he inherited and in later years courageously advocated causes, such as the emancipation of women and the confiscation of excess profit, that seemed fearfully radical to most contemporaries. His liberalism, thus modified and extended, remained firm; and his essay, *On Liberty*, published in 1859, stands as one of the important works of European political theory, a careful but heartfelt, balanced but unyielding declaration that society can have no higher interest than the freedom of each of its members.

## Early Socialists

Some men, however, envisioned a better society based on quite different principles. Among scores of socialist schemes, the ideas of Saint-Simon, Fourier, and Owen won an important place in the history of socialism by their comprehensiveness, their particular insights, and the intensity with which they were promulgated.

All three men lived through the French Revolution, had some personal experience of burgeoning capitalism, and began to develop systems for remaking the world in the early stages of industrialization, even before Napoleon's final defeat. Turning from political solutions to social problems, they developed economic and moral critiques of the contemporary world. Competition, they argued, is wasteful and cruel, induces hard-hearted indifference to suffering, misuses wealth, and leads to frequent economic crises. Differently organized, society can instead be harmonious and orderly, providing enough for all.

As a young French officer, Claude Henri de Rouvroy, comte de Saint-Simon, fought with George Washington at Yorktown. During the French Revolution he abandoned his title and built a fortune, which he quickly lost, through speculation in land, and under the empire he settled down to the difficult career of a seer. For a society divided between the propertied and the propertyless, Saint-Simon proposed to substitute the direction of experts standing above the conflict: scientists, men of affairs (*industriels*), priests, and artists. These specialists, chosen for their ability, would design plans for the benefit of all, increasing productivity and therefore prosperity. The new society would recapture the integrated, organic quality of Greek city-states and the Middle Ages but with scientists and managers holding the authority once granted priests and soldiers. In a world so structured, the state would have little independent importance; for skilled people would work together, planning and directing, as in an efficient business. The artists and priests of the new order could then lead humanity to self-fulfillment and love.

Saint-Simon's theories won little hearing among the powerful of his day, but they earned a significant following especially among the bright students of the École Polytechnique. An entire cult, the New Christianity, developed among his disciples after Saint-Simon's death in 1825, only to be dissipated by internal division and public ridicule by the 1840s. Nevertheless, an extraordinary number of France's leading engineers and entrepreneurs in the next generation fondly recalled the Saint-Simonian enthusiasms of their youth, and in their penchant

for planning, grand economic organization, and social reform, they carried elements of his teaching into the world of affairs and respectable politics. There were important Saint-Simonian movements in every country, and later socialists would maintain his conviction that proper planning would make an economy both more just and richer.

François Marie Charles Fourier had been a traveling salesman before dedicating himself, at the same time as Saint-Simon, to a theory which he firmly believed would rank among the greatest discoveries ever made. His cantankerous and shrewd writings on

A French engraving of Robert Owen's textile mill shows a model of order and calm in which everyone appears to have taken to heart the rules carefully posted along the wall.   (Photo: The Granger Collection)

contemporary society were so copious that his manuscripts have still not all been printed despite the devotion of generations of admirers. Largely self-taught, he committed to paper his fantasies of strange beasts and incredible inventions that would abound in a future age, which made him an easy target for critics.

His central concept, however, was an ideal community, the phalanstery (from "phalanx"). Once even one was created, the happiness and well-being of its members would inspire the establishment of others until all of society was converted. A phalanstery should contain some 1600 men and women, representatives of all the types of personality identified in Fourier's elaborate psychology. He listed a dozen passions that move human beings and proposed to organize the phalanstery in such a way that individuals would accomplish the tasks necessary to society by doing what they wanted. Everyone would perform a variety of tasks, engaging in no one for too long; pleasure and work would flow together. Members of the phalanstery would be paid according to a formula that recognized the capital, labor, and talent each contributed. Largely self-sufficient, a phalanstery would produce some goods for export according to its particular resources, and these would be traded with similar communities.

No phalanstery was ever established exactly as Fourier planned (he even offered designs for the architecture), but communities were founded on Fourierist principles from the United States to Rumania; and if few of them survived for long, the vision did of a society in which cooperation replaces compulsion and joy transforms drudgery.

Robert Owen was one of the success stories of industrial capitalism: A self-made man, he rose from selling cloth to be the manager and part owner of a large textile mill in New Lanark, Scotland. Owen's rule transformed the town, and by the end of the Napoleonic wars, distinguished visitors were traveling from all over Europe to see the miracle he had wrought. The workday was shortened from 17 to 10 hours; new housing was constructed, eventually allowing an employee's family several rooms; inspection committees maintained cleanliness; gardens were planted and sewers installed. In nursery schools with airy, pleasant rooms, children were given exercise, encouraged to sing and dance, taught without corporal punishment from books and projects designed to be attractive, and trained in the useful arts. Most impressive of all, the subjects of this paternalistic kingdom developed a pride in their community; productivity rose and profits increased.

Owen had, he felt, disproved Ricardo's dismal laws, and he turned to projects for establishing ideal communities throughout the nation. Like Fourier's, they would be placed in a rural setting and would supply most of their own needs. Members would take meals and enjoy entertainment in common, and children would be raised communally. Educated to the age of 8, the young would then engage in productive labor until they were 26; after five years in distributive or managerial jobs, adults would assume the tasks of government, cultivating the sciences and the arts in their increasing leisure. The controlled environment would assure good character among community members, and the division of tasks would provide them with varied and rich lives. Standardized production would offer more goods at lower cost (the snobbery that made luxuries attractive would disappear), and higher wages would increase the local market.

Even after losing most of his wealth with the failure of the community of New Harmony in Indiana, Owen continued to be the single most important figure in the labor movement and the workers' cooperatives that spread through England in the 1830s and 1840s. But by the time of his death, in 1858,

Owen, who had converted to spiritualism, was largely ignored by the world he had sought to remake.

The importance of these movements did not depend upon the outcome of specific projects. The values they stressed echoed those of working class movements everywhere. These early socialists imagined a society of cooperation and love, one enriched by new inventions and new means of production but based on new forms of social organization. Advocates of change, they were transitional figures seeking to combine the best of the old and new eras. Their indictment of capitalism, and their insights into the nature of productivity and exchange, and their call for social planning and education had an impact far beyond their relatively small circles of believers. A large number of Europe's best minds were touched by their theories. The vision of fulfilling work and the mystique of cooperation so strong in their writings remained part of the working-class movement, was repeated in socialist and anarchist calls to brotherhood, and from the 1840s on found an echo in many movements for democracy and social change. Yet nearly everyone ultimately rejected their ideas as impractical and too radical. Bucolic isolation and artisanal production became increasingly unrealistic, and these theories were incredibly vague about problems of politics and power.

The charge of radicalism, however, requires some further comment. The criticisms of liberal society mounted by Saint-Simon, Fourier, and Owen were not so different overall from the conservative attack. With some restrictions—Saint-Simon, for example, insisted on the abolition of inheritance—they even allowed private property, and none of them was a thoroughgoing democrat. What most shocked contemporaries were their views on the status of women, sexual mores, and Christianity. All rejected the place allotted women in bourgeois society, and Owen not only specified that they should share in governing but also believed their emancipation required a smaller role for them in the family. All wrote of sensual pleasure as good and its repression as a characteristic European error. The Saint-Simonians publicly advocated free love, and Fourier carefully provided that neither young nor old should be deprived of the pleasures of the flesh. Owen was only slightly less outspoken in his contempt for Christian marriage. Yet all three stressed religion as the source of community feeling, brotherhood, and human ethics. Their efforts to replace what they had eliminated therefore led to imitations of Christian ritual and foggy mysticism that not only contrasted with their concern for rational planning but invited easy ridicule from a society with many reasons for rejecting their utopias. By the end of the nineteenth century that is how these early socialists would be remembered, as "utopian socialists." By then, socialist thought would center instead on the more hard-headed and systematic theories of Karl Marx (see Chapter 25).

## The Sense of History

Change had become a central preoccupation of European thought. Since 1789 the French Revolution was the great example of how, beginning with politics, change could extend to all of society. By the 1830s, however, it was clear that industrialization was another source of sweeping and possibly inexorable change destined to affect most of Europe in some degree. The effort to understand these vast processes reinforced the interest in history, an interest further stimulated by romantic respect for the past and the conviction of nationalists that the historical record of each people revealed its uniqueness. Liberals and socialists, like conservatives, argued in terms of history, and its systematic study became the most honored of the human sciences.

Catholic town in 1440.

1 St Michaels on the Hill. 2. Queens Crofs. 3. St Thomas's Chapel. 4. St Maries Abbey. 5. All Saints. 6. St Johns. 7. St Peters. 8. St Allhallows. 9. St Maries. 10. St Edmunds. 11. Grey Friars. 12. St Cuthberts. 13. Guild hall. 14. Priory. 15. St Olaves. 16. St Botolphs.

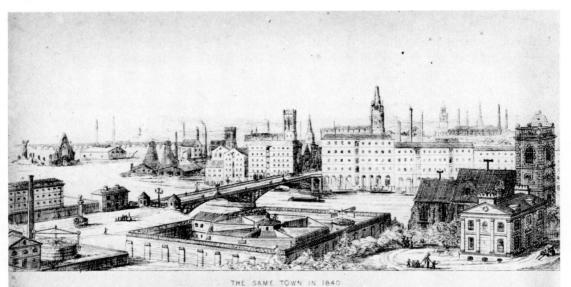

THE SAME TOWN IN 1840

1. St Michaels Tower, rebuilt in 1750. 2. New Parsonage House & Pleasure Grounds. 3. The New Jail. 4. Gas Works. 5. Lunatic Asylum. 6 Iron Works & Ruins of St Maries Abbey. 7. M. Evans Chapel. 8. Baptist Chapel. 9. Unitarian Chapel. 10. New Church. 11 New Town Hall & Concert Room. 12. Wesleyan Centenary Chapel. 13. New Christian Society. 14. Quakers Meeting. 15. Socialist Hall of Science.

In England, France, and Germany, national projects were launched for publishing historical documents and for training scholars to interpret them. Some historians were as widely read as novelists, among them Michelet, for whom French history was a dramatic story of the people's fight for freedom, and Thomas B. Macauley, for whom the history of England was a record of progressive change through moderation and compromise. In each country certain events and themes—in England, the Glorious Revolution of 1688; in France, the Revolution; in Germany, the rise of Prussia—were favored as part of an intense search for national roots, heroes, and patterns of development significant for the present. Many a political leader first gained fame as a historian.

This preoccupation with history, which affected all intellectual life, received its most powerful philosophic expression in the writings of Georg Wilhelm Friedrich Hegel. A Rhinelander who had felt the impact of French culture and watched Napoleon's career with fascination, thoroughly trained in philosophy and Lutheran theology, Hegel set out to establish a philosophy as comprehensive as that of Thomas Aquinas or Aristotle. He was determined to reconcile the contradictions between science and faith, Christianity and the state, the ideal and the real, the eternal and the temporal that plagued modern thought.

He sought to do so by establishing an undying purpose at the heart of history and by discovering the process of historical change. That process he described not as the simple increase of reason or wealth so often called progress, but something far more complex and subtle—the dialectic of thesis, antithesis, and synthesis. All the actions, the values, and social structures of a given society constitute a thesis, an implicit statement about life. The thesis, however, is never adequate to every need, and its incompleteness generates contrary views, institutions, and practices—the antithesis. Thus every society gives birth to conflict between thesis and antithesis until finally out of their battle a new synthesis is molded. The synthesis is a new thesis that generates another round of conflict. History moves by this dialectic in a steady unfolding of the World Spirit. Its direction is toward the fulfillment of human freedom and self-awareness. In the ancient East only one man was free; in Greece and Rome some were free; in the Germanic Christian kingdoms after the Reformation, all were free. Since the French Revolution people have consciously acted on history, knowing what they want and fulfilling the World Spirit at the same time. Thus cosmic and human reason work together; the meaning of history is essentially religious.

Hegel's complex and abstract philosophy was—as he would have said it had to be—an important expression of his age, and it has proved a lasting influence. Like most nineteenth-century thinkers, he was determined to find an eternal meaning at the core of historical change, and was convinced that his own nation was its highest articulation. After Hegel, philosophy and literary criticism tended to become increasingly historical, and historians sought more systematically for relationships among all aspects of a culture.

---

A convert to Catholicism and a leading student of Gothic architecture, Augustus Pugin was one of the architects of the Houses of Parliament. These illustrations, part of a book of *Contrasts* comparing Catholic and Protestant society, sum up the romantic and conservative critique of modern society for replacing church spires with smokestacks, cottages and craftsmanship with massive tenements and factories, and charities with prisons. (The new prison in the foreground is Jeremy Bentham's Panopticon, designed so that a single guard can see down all the cellblocks.) (Photo: New York Public Library/Picture Collection)

| International and Military History | Political History |
|---|---|
| | |
| **1800** | |
| | **1806** Partial emancipation of Prussian peasants |
| **(1814** Defeat of Napoleon)* <br> **(1814–1815** Congress of Vienna) | |
| **(1830** Revolutions in France, Belgium, parts of Italy and Germany) | **1830s** Reform legislation in Britain <br> **1830s–1840s** Child labor acts, Great Britain, France, Germany |
| | **(1846** Repeal of the British Corn Laws) |
| **(1848** Revolutions) | **1848** Peasant emancipation in Germany, Austrian Empire <br> June Days in Paris |
| | **1852** Crédit Mobilier, Napoleon III launches social program |
| **(1854–1856** Crimean War) | |
| **(1859** Piedmontese–French War against Austria) <br> **1860** Cobden–Chevalier Treaty reducing tariffs | |

*Events in parentheses are discussed in other chapters.

| Social and Economic History | Cultural and Intellectual History |
|---|---|
| | École Polytechnique (est. 1794) |
| | **1798**  Malthus (**1766–1834**), *On Population* |
| **1800**  European population 188 million | |
| **1800**  Bank of France restructured | |
| | **1807**  Prussian Bureau of Education |
| **1811–1812**  Wave of strikes and demonstrations in England | |
| **1816–1819**  Typhus epidemic in Ireland | |
| | **1817**  Ricardo (**1772–1823**), *Principles of Political Economy* |
| **1825**  First successful commercial railroad in England | Saint–Simon  (**1760–1825**) |
| | **1826**  Society for Diffusion of Useful Knowledge, movement for workers' night schools |
| | Hegel  (**1770–1831**) |
| | Bentham  (**1748–1832**) |
| **1831**  Workers revolt, Bristol | **1833**  French law for universal primary education |
| **1831–1834**  Workers revolt, Lyons | Fourier  (**1772–1837**) |
| **1830** Russia / **1831–** Germany / **1832** Britain / **1836–1837** Italy  ⎱ Cholera epidemics | |
| **1838–1850**  Chartists | |
| **1840s**  Rush of railway building, telegraph | |
| **1846–1849**  Bad harvests and depression | |
| **1850**  European population 266 million | |
| | **1851**  Crystal Palace exposition |
| | Owen  (**1771–1858**) |
| | Macauley  (**1800–1859**) |
| | **1859**  J.S. Mill (**1806–1873**), *On Liberty* |
| | Michelet  (**1798–1874**) |
| **1860** | |

And within a generation of his death in 1831, just after a wave of the revolutions he abhorred, some of his followers claimed to find in the Prussian state at war humanity's highest ethical expression, while others, led by Karl Marx, the most famous of the Hegelians, predicted the state's withering away. By then it was a European habit to approach any question of society, culture, or politics in terms of historical change.

Conservatism, liberalism, and socialism are broad terms for describing the central tendencies among the major theories and political movements of the nineteenth century. The ideological debate that enriched culture and divided politics was really about society; and it was not just a battle of theories, for conflicts and arguments were rooted in the immediate experience of local conditions and in the larger, partially shared, experience of revolution and industrialization. As workers organized to fight for better wages or for simple recognition, as merchants lobbied for the removal of restrictions or for improved roads, as property owners demanded that order be preserved, as citizens insisted on representative government, and as officials tried to justify their policies, all of them used the available ideologies to connect specific issues to general principles, a particular program to a vision of how society worked and of how change could be directed or controlled.

## SUMMARY

European society changed in many ways during the two generations following the Napoleonic wars. Factory organization and labor-saving machinery in 1815 showed their economic promise primarily in Britain, but by the 1850s an industrial revolution without apparent end was transforming much of Western Europe, where the population was increasing, cities expanding, and the way of life changing.

The effort to understand these changes dominated intellectual life, and the interpretations of contemporary trends and of history all promised a better future. Except for conservatives, few doubted that the path of progress was marked by liberalism: freedom of speech and representative government protecting the rights of the individual, the laws of competition and self-interest working their magic. These bustling, expanding societies produced a vigorous and varied culture that expressed both the confidence and the concerns of a tumultuous era. Individualism and values associated with the middle class—rationality, probity, thrift, hard work, and a close two-generation family—were the dominant ideals.

In such an atmosphere, the misery and subjugation of the lower classes seemed an intolerable contrast with the increasing wealth of society as a whole. Poverty, urban misery, and ignorance appeared no longer as natural conditions but as problems to be solved. More effective charities, better regulations, new institutions for education and welfare, or radical communities—the solutions proposed by the ideologies of change, whether piecemeal or sweeping, concentrated on improved social organization. In a civilization that expected so much of politics, this necessarily pointed to a more extensive and active role for state.

## RECOMMENDED READING

### Studies

*Briggs, Asa. *Victorian Cities*. 1970. Studies of the industrial cities and their impact on British life.

*Chevalier, Louis. *Laboring Classes and Dangerous Classes in Paris During the First Half of the Nineteenth Century*. Frank Jellinek (tr.). 1981. This study of the Parisian poor also says much about the reactions of those better off.

*Davidoff, Leonore, and Catherine Hall. *Family Fortunes: Men and Women of the English Middle Class, 1780–1850*. 1985. A good picture of the aspirations and concerns of middle-class life.

De Ruggiero, Guido. *The History of European Liberalism*. R. G. Collingwood (tr.). 1977. A classic comparison of liberal theory in major European nations.

*Gideon, Siegfried. *Mechanization Takes Command*. 1948. Provocative analysis of the social and aesthetic implications of the machine age.

*Heilbroner, Robert L. *The Worldly Philosophers*. 1972. A good introduction to the ideas of the economic liberals.

*Henderson, W. O. *The Industrialization of Europe: 1780–1914*. 1969. A general study contrasting developments in England and on the Continent.

Himmelfarb, Gertrude. *On Liberty and Liberalism: The Case of John Stuart Mill*. 1974. Penetrating and controversial analysis of the still-controversial philosopher of liberalism.

*Hobsbawm, E. J. *Industry and Empire*. 1969. Perceptively follows developments in Britain since 1750.

*Katznelson, Ira, and Artistide R. Zolberg (eds.). *Working-Class Formation: Nineteenth-Century Patterns in Western Europe and the United States*. 1986. Significant interpretative essays by some leading scholars.

*Landes, David S. *The Unbound Prometheus: Technological Change and Development in Western Europe from 1750 to the Present Day*. 1969. Emphasizes the role of technology.

*Lichtheim, George. *A Short History of Socialism*. 1975. Well-constructed treatment of the evolution of socialist ideas in their historical context.

*Lindemann, Albert S. *A History of European Socialism*. 1984.

*McLeod, Hugh. *Religion and the People of Western Europe, 1789–1970*. 1981. A well-conceived study of the impact of social change on religious practice.

*Manuel, Frank. *The Prophets of Paris*. 1965. An excellent discussion of French utopian thinkers.

O'Brien, Patrick, and Caglar Keyder. *Economic Growth in Britain and France, 1780–1914*. 1978. A thorough examination of statistical methods and data for the period, focusing in particular on wages and productivity.

*Pollard, Sidney. *Peaceful Conquest. The Industrialization of Europe 1760–1970*. 1981. A provocative new study that focuses on the importance of geographical regions and not political units.

Price, Roger. *An Economic History of Modern France, 1730–1914*. 1981. Underlines the importance of modes of communication and transportation in the development of the marketplace.

———. *A Social History of Nineteenth-Century France*. 1987. A clear synthesis of recent research.

*Rudé, George. *The Crowd in History, 1730–1884*. 1964. Argues that there was a fundamental change in the social composition and demands of crowds after industrialization.

*Sewell, William H., Jr. *Work and Revolution in France. The Language of Labor from the Old Regime to 1848*. 1980. Highlights the continuities within the culture of the early working class.

*Shanin, Teodor (ed.). *Peasants and Peasant Society*. 1987. Essays treating the varied aspects of a complicated subject, especially useful in Eastern Europe.

Snell, K. D. M. *Annals of the Laboring Poor: Social Change and Agrarian England, 1660–1900*. 1985. A pioneering look at the position of the rural underclass, transformed in the nineteenth century.

*Thompson, Dorothy. *The Chartists: Popular Politics in the Industrial Revolution*. 1984. A lively and sympathetic account that relates working-class action to the larger social context.

*Thompson, Edward P. *The Making of the English Working Class*. 1964. A remarkable work of sympathetic insight and exhaustive research.

*Tilly, Louise, and Joan Scott. *Women, Work and Family*. 1978. Discusses the impact of industrialization on women and on the family economy.

*Trebilcock, Clive. *The Industrialization of the Continental Powers, 1780–1914*. 1981. A synthesis that uses recent research to emphasize the political implications of industrialization.

Walker, Mack. *German Home Towns: Community, State, and General Estate, 1648–1871*. 1971. Sensitive and original treatment of the response of small-town life to political and social change.

* Available in paperback.

# ❄ CHAPTER 24 ❄

# THE NATIONAL STATE
# AND THE MIDDLE CLASS
# 1840–1880

❅ ❅ ❅ ❅ ❅

In the period following the revolutions of 1848, the issues of political freedom, social order, and economic growth all focused on the state. As principal arbiter among competing interests and contradictory goals, the state increased its own authority. The revolutions themselves had demonstrated both the critical importance of public opinion and the explosive potential in social conflict. After 1850, governments, especially those that kept some representative institutions, sought to enhance their popularity without sacrificing their centralizing power. Economic growth demanded a state able to protect national markets, improve communications, direct public works, assure financial stability, and maintain order.

❅

To fulfill such sweeping political and economic agendas, governments had to increase their capacity to administer and enforce new policies. That proved to be most feasible where the state was closely associated with national feeling and with the middle class. Nationalist movements promised political freedom through a national state conceived as the ultimate expression of the nation. The expanding national state, in turn, provided the middle class a larger field of action and looked to them to direct the economy, maintain the institutions, and sustain the cultural life of the nation. A strong state, tied to nationalism and the middle class, might make it possible to enjoy the benefits of growth, reform, and social change while preserving the established order.

❅

The cultural achievements of this expanding, changing European civilization were as remarkable as its economic growth and nation building. By midcentury, the high culture associated with the middle class was universally recognized as the admirable and exciting expression of a new age. That culture encompassed the arts and sciences and managed, more effectively than any other social activity, to balance continuity and variety, individualism and institutional strength.

❅

The government most willing to experiment with new combinations of public support, innovative programs, and central control was that of Louis Napoleon in France, but the most dramatic political changes of the period were the unifications of Italy and Germany. The governments of Britain, Spain, the Austrian Empire, and Russia faced similar demands as well as an immediate need for increased military power and administrative efficiency. The domestic political equilibrium achieved differed from nation to nation, but it was everywhere related to momentous shifts in international power. The Crimean War in 1854–1856 marked the breakdown of the old Concert of Europe, a change that opened the way for the wars that welded the Italian and German nations. Moreover, the Continental hegemony of France in the 1850s and 1860s ended with the unification of Germany. Europe's great nations found themselves faced with new dangers as they acquired unprecedented economic, military, and political power.

## I. A MIDDLE-CLASS CULTURE
❊
### Cultural Institutions

The European high culture of the nineteenth century can fairly be called a culture of the middle class. Not marked by any single style, this culture was national and urban rather than centered in courts, salons, or villages ("provincial" had become a pejorative term); and it was remarkable for quantity as well as quality, for there were more writers, artists, musicians, and scholars than ever before. For all its deliberate variety, European high culture of the nineteenth century remained distinctive in its institutionalization, the forms of its expression, the themes it emphasized, and the shifting styles it favored.

Before the nineteenth century most paintings were done for a specific commission and often for a particular room; most music was composed for a special (often religious) occasion and designed to fit the talents of performers available in one palace; most books were written for a particular audience whom the author could feel he or she knew intimately. In the new century this had largely changed. Music moved from palaces, churches, and private salons to public concert halls; artists sold their paintings to any purchaser and by midcentury, in galleries created for that purpose; and writers found themselves engaged in commerce.

If artists felt insecure in their dependence on an audience of unknown character and unproved cultivation, they had a larger public than ever before. That public was, for the most part, the same people active in politics, the professions, and business—or rather, such people and their wives. They bought tickets for concerts just as they frequented restaurants with famous chefs, enjoying in both cases pleasures once part of private society and now open to all who had the inclination and money.

Theaters, institutions accustomed to commercial operations, flourished in every city, and they ranged from the new music halls to the great stages and opera houses built (usually by the state) to rank with parliament buildings as monuments of civic pride. Most major cities supported choirs, bands, and symphony orchestras, which grew larger and technically more proficient (the "Mannheim crescendo" was a new marvel of instrumental synchronization and discipline that Beethoven required of every orchestra). Conservatories and museums became national public institutions, maintaining established taste against a sea of change and considerably increasing Europe's stock of skilled artists and musicians. Some of the greatest of these institutions—the British Museum in London, the Bibliothèque Nationale in Paris, the Hermitage in St. Petersburg, the Alte Pinakothek in Munich—opened to the public in the 1840s, usually in imposing new structures. The Louvre became the model museum of art, granting access to everyone and arranging its holdings by country and in chronological order. Lending libraries, charging a few pence per volume, were common even in smaller cities.

Those who sought self-improvement also flocked to public lectures on the sober implications of political economy or the wonders of science, among which photography ranked high. Daguerre announced his photographic process to the French Academy in 1839, which persuaded the French government to purchase the rights to the new technique so that it could be given to the world unencumbered by royalties. Important advances followed rapidly, and photography was enthusiastically applied to the needs of science and exploration, widely used for portraits, and recognized as the newest of the arts.

But no cultural institution was more important than the press. Before 1800 the news-

Increasing numbers of the public (note the middle-class families) flocked to the British Museum in the 1840s to view its exhibits on art and literature as well as natural history. (Photo: British Museum)

paper, of little importance outside of France and Britain, had been more like a newsletter, gossip column, or political pamphlet. By 1830 there were more than 2000 European newspapers, despite the censorship, special taxes, and police measures with which governments sought to restrict so awesome a social force. Where these restraints were eased, which was a central liberal demand in all countries, sales soared. By midcentury *The Times* of London increased its 1815 circulation of 5000 to 50,000, and two of the most popular French papers, the *Presse* and *Siècle*, both founded in 1836, had topped 70,000. In attaining such distribution, newspapers changed. The *Presse* and *Siècle* succeeded in halving their subscription rates (which remained substantial) by drawing their revenue primarily from advertising. Articles discussed commerce, the arts, and science as well as politics, and the papers competed for readers with serial novels by Honoré de Balzac and the elder Alexandre Dumas. The *London Illustrated News* created the picture magazine in 1842, which was copied immediately in every large country, and satirical magazines (*Punch* was founded in 1840, a few years after the *Caricature* and *Chiarivari* in Paris) made the cartoon a powerful political weapon. Honoré Daumier's biting pictures of fat bankers and complacent bourgeois raised social criticism to art.

Technology contributed to these developments. The *Times* had installed a steam press in 1814, and a flood of technical improvements increased the speed and quality of typesetting and printing. Press services such as the Agence Havas and Reuters switched from carrier pigeons to the telegraph to bring bulletins to a public increasingly eager for the latest news. And paper-making machines reduced the cost and increased the volume of printing in every form.

## The Cultural Professions

Newspaper work became a full-time occupation and gradually a profession—the terms *journalism* and *journalist* date from this period—and so did performing, painting, and writing. The virtuoso actor or musician could make an honored career. The violinist Niccolò Paganini, who transformed violin technique, commanded huge fees and enormous crowds wherever he played; Jenny Lind, "the Swedish Nightingale," was the rage of Europe; and Franz Liszt shaped international musical taste and standards of performance. The distinction between the amateur and professional musician became firm. Many a young man announced that he was a painter and proudly starved, in Paris if possible, out of loyalty to his career (there were 354 registered artists in Paris in 1789 but 2,159 in 1838); a few, among them England's great landscape painter J. M. W. Turner, became wealthy. The most popular writers—Balzac, Sir Walter Scott, Victor Hugo, Charles Dickens—were able to live by their pen alone, honored among the famous men of their age. Many responded to their new opportunities with appropriate industry. Scott wrote 28 novels in 18 years, and Balzac was equally prolific. Few went so far as Dumas, who employed scores of assistants to help crank out his profitable product. Artists making their way in a profession might hope for a prize or fellowship from one of the leading cultural institutions, but ultimately, their fate depended on the opinion of their fellow artists and of an often untutored public not sure of its own taste.

That problem of judgment led to still another profession: the critic. The best critics won places for themselves as literary figures in their own right. But their essential role was to extend the canons of taste to a public faced with kaleidoscopic variety, just as the popular books on etiquette and gastronomy taught manners to people of new means and prepared the bourgeois palate for *haute cuisine*.

## Cultural Forms

Although cultural life in the nineteenth century was full of uncertainties—about the role of the artist, the relationship of art to society, and the values art should express—middle-class culture remained essentially a formal one, proudly removed from the merely popular or customary. In music, the forms of the symphony, concerto, quartet, and sonata, established in the eighteenth century, had been enlarged and enriched, especially by Ludwig van Beethoven, whose creative amalgam of formal structure and personal expression became the dominant model for nineteenth-century composers. His music, in whatever form, had the quality of a philosophic yet poetic essay, conceived and presented as high art to be heard in concert, studied and savored for itself and not as part of some larger entertainment or social occasion. This seriousness, intellectual and emotional, and this separation of art from any single context fit well with the changing circumstances in which music was performed by professional musicians before a paying audience. Beethoven's successors maintained that sense of music as an autonomous art and created works of such vitality that to this day most of the concert repertoire consists of music composed between 1800 and World War I.

The novel, which had also achieved its identity in the eighteenth century when it was often written in an epistolary style as if from one acquaintance to another, became the most widely enjoyed of the arts in the nineteenth century. Most often presented through an omniscient but anonymous narrator, its most common theme was the conflict between individual feeling (especially romantic love) and the roles and conventions demanded by society. Balzac attempted in his novels to encompass all the "human comedy" (the phrase contrasted with Dante's divine concerns), showing the wealthy, the ambitious, and the poor, soldiers, bankers, politicians, and writers. The novelist analyzed society and individual psychology through concrete types, and sometimes, as with Dickens, challenged the public conscience more effectively than any preacher or politician. Scott's swashbuckling stories of romance and chivalry in an earlier age probed the connection between personal character and social tension in a way that influenced writers throughout Europe. Hugo, Alexander Pushkin, and Alessandro Manzoni promulgated patriotism as they taught their readers of national solidarity and the need to battle for liberty. Fiction presented the problems of poverty and family and city life, while deftly dissecting the frivolous aristocrat and the self-righteous middle-class merchant. A high proportion of the writer's public were women (as were some of the most popular authors),

and the issues of their lot, of love, dependence, or boredom, were more penetratingly presented in novels—Flaubert's *Madame Bovary* is the outstanding example—than anywhere else. Middle-class culture also had an intimate side, reflected in the popularity of poetry, the lithograph, and watercolor, and in the demand for piano music (industrial techniques made the piano, with its iron frame, economical enough to be a common sight in middle-class parlors)—all to be enjoyed in the home and with private emotion.

## Artistic Styles

The themes that run through the artistic work of the period, however, convey a tension. Romanticism's concern with the individual hero or genius—found in the paintings of Delacroix, the plays of Hugo, the poetry of Keats and Shelley—had stressed the artist's personal vision and the capture of a momentary feeling to be set like a precious stone in a carefully wrought piece of music, or poem, or painting (see Plates 51–53). A logically easy step led to the cry of art for art's sake, that the merit of a work lay in its purity, independent of purpose or message. But artists also became increasingly fascinated by society and historical change, seeking the nature of "modernity," in the words of Charles Baudelaire, by extracting "from fashion whatever element it may contain of poetry within history." Behind this lay the desire for an integrated vision encompassing all of life, a coherent understanding that would connect culture to society, economics, and politics. Many writers and painters turned to "realism," the effort to convey with sometimes shocking directness the lives of ordinary people (see Plates 54–57).

There was a wish as well to integrate the arts themselves; and Baudelaire, a leading poet and critic, writing on the death of Delacroix in 1863, proclaimed it "the spiritual

**Tearing down Vienna's old city walls in 1857 made way for one of the period's famous urban projects. The great circular boulevards, where the walls had been, embraced the old city and served as a gate to old palaces and new middle-class housing; and the boulevard was lined with public buildings, each in a symbolically appropriate architectural style (a Gothic church, Renaissance palaces for the university and museums, a baroque opera house), all of them monuments to civic and imperial culture.** (Photo: Direktion der Museen der Stadt Wien)

condition of our age that the arts aspire . . . to lend one another new powers."[1] This reciprocity was part of the vitality of lyric opera, another of the arts to reach its height in the nineteenth century. Opera was first of all theater, combining popular appeal with aristocratic elegance, and performances were important civic events. Elaborate plots, often in historical settings, and flowery poetic texts were taken as seriously as the varied, tuneful, and complex music, the whole further enriched by ballet, colorful sets, and special effects. The two leading operatic composers were Giuseppe Verdi and his exact contemporary Richard Wagner. Verdi was an Italian national hero, whose compelling and often patriotic music, with its paeans to human virtue and its portrayal of every human emotion, remains a staple of opera houses everywhere. Wagner, however, created a kind of revolution in music by carrying the search for an artistic synthesis still further, for he wrote his own texts, often building with patriotic intent on Germanic myths, and identified his major ideas and characters with specific musical themes to create a whole in which

[1] The comment on Delacroix's death is cited by Morse Peckham, *Beyond the Tragic Vision*, 1962, p. 215; the reference to the artist's search for modernity is from an essay on the painter Constantin Guys in Charles Baudelaire, *The Painter of Modern Life and Other Essays*, Jonathan Mayne, (tr. and ed.), 1965, p. 12.

voices, instruments, words, and visual experience were inseparable. In every form, serious art intended to uplift its audience, morally and intellectually and aesthetically.

Such varied goals and ambitions, diverse audiences, and numerous professional artists led to the frequent shifting of styles that was characteristic of nineteenth-century culture. Romanticism had gradually given way by midcentury to realism; and these approaches combined and divided into scores of schools and styles, creating a highly self-conscious art in music, painting, and writing. Innovation was in itself often taken for a sign of genius, and the belief that artists must be in an avant-garde, ahead of their duller public, became a cliché. If society honored the arts, the arts, in contrast, conveyed more confidence in the future or nostalgia for the preindustrial past than respect for the present. Yet in their universal criticism of the shallowness and materialism of the middle class on which they rested, the artists of the nineteenth century were spokespersons for the inner doubts that were an inherent part of middle-class culture.

### Religion

Both the confidence and the insecurity of this culture showed in attitudes toward religion. Most thoughtful people appear to have suffered religious shocks, felt the loss of faith, but also had some religious experience. On the Continent many of the middle class became bitter anticlericals, seeing in the church the barrier to progress. The Abbé Lamennais, one of the most admired of Catholic leaders, had broken in the 1830s from a Church that would not accept his program for associating the tenets of his faith with democracy. The Protestant David Strauss created a sensation across Europe with his *Life of Jesus,* which appeared in 1835, for it cast erudite doubt on the accuracy of the Gospel, frightening many

with the apparent need to choose between historical scholarship and Christ. More typically, especially in England, stern morality and propriety were substituted for theology. Yet people worried terribly that society would lose its direction and individuals their moral purpose without religion. Protestant and Catholic missions combated ignorance and indifference with an intensity not seen since the seventeenth century. The pious became more militant and turned to social action, preaching temperance, teaching reading, and establishing charities. In religion as in the arts, new organization was carrying contemporary confidence and internal conflicts more and more widely.

## II. THE POLITICS OF NATIONALISM
❊
### The Elements of Nationalism

This culture, associated with the middle class (its principal producer and consumer) and with the state (which supported it and benefited from the prestige it conferred), was also understood to be an expression of the nation. Nationalism is often listed as one of the important "'isms" of the nineteenth century, along with conservatism, liberalism, and socialism; but nationalism was significantly different. It presented itself as a natural expression of the people although its proponents were primarily middle class; ideologically malleable, it was used by both the left and the right; and politically, it proved to be immensely powerful. Why this should be so, why nationalism has assumed such importance remains one of the important questions of modern history.

Nationalism's deepest roots lie in a shared sense of regional and cultural identity, especially as those roots are expressed in custom, language, and religion. These had been greatly affected, even shaped, by the development of the state, whose power and importance had increased since the state building of the seventeenth century. But it was the experience of the French Revolution that established nationalism as a political force capable of mobilizing popular enthusiasm, of reforming society, of creating seemingly irresistible political movements, and thus of greatly adding to the power of the state. Napoleon had sought to appeal to national feeling wherever his armies took him, and somewhat more timidly the Allies had used that sentiment to recruit opposition to the French in Germany, Spain, and (less successfully) in Italy.

Nationalism was also a movement of self-conscious modernization, embraced by people who believed their societies might equal the industrial wealth of England and acquire political systems as responsive and efficient as those of Britain and France. Increased communication and mobility further stimulated the sense of belonging to a larger but definable community. Nationalism was thus a response to social and economic change, one that promised to bring middle classes and masses together in support of common goals. Nationalists, like socialists, stressed the values of community; like liberals, they tended to believe that change could bring progress. They emphasized the importance of culture and generally shared the attitudes of Romanticism, with its rejection of the universalism of the Enlightenment. Thus German intellectuals such as Johann Gottfried von Herder and Johann Gottlieb Fichte were characteristic in urging their countrymen to put aside values imported from France in favor of a uniquely German culture.

The exploration of ethnic origins took many forms. A group of German scholars made philology a science, and by the 1830s and 1840s an extraordinary revival of national languages had occurred across Europe. Gaelic was hailed as the national tongue of Ireland; in Finland the first public lecture in Finnish marked a break from the dominant Swedish culture; intellectuals in Bohemia began abandoning their customary German to write in Czech. More remarkable still were the number of languages consciously contrived out of local dialects and invented vocabularies. Norwegian became distinct from Danish, Serbian from other Slavic languages, and Slovak from Czech—all literary languages by the 1840s, each the work of but a handful of scholars for whom widespread illiteracy eased the task of establishing a national language.

This fascination with folk culture and a national past was reinforced by the emphasis on history, which fostered the discovery of a special national mission. French historians wrote eloquently of France's call to carry reason and freedom across Europe, and Mazzini proclaimed the destiny of the Third Rome. The poet Adam Mickiewicz, lecturing in Paris, inspired nationalists of many countries with his descriptions of how Poland's history paralleled the life of Christ and had yet to achieve Resurrection. Francis Palacky's pioneering work stressed the role of the Czechs as leaders of the Slavs. Such visions were repeated in poetry and drama, which now blossomed in the native tongue, and justified resistance to alien rule. Cultural nationalism thus served as a weapon of middle-class self-assertion whereby people who felt cramped by social hierarchy, an unsympathetic bureaucracy, and a stagnant economy could win broader support for their own dreams of progress.

In places subject to foreign rule, such as Hungary or much of Italy, movements for agricultural improvement, promoted by the liberal aristocracy, became centers of nationalism, and a national tariff, which would enlarge the area of free trade internally and protect native industry, became a nationalist battle cry. Friedrich List, a leading liberal economist, argued from the American example that only behind tariff barriers could a united Germany develop the industry and the vigorous middle class necessary for competitive strength and independence. Everywhere nationalist groups generally demanded public education, more political freedom, and efficient government. Strengthened by its promises of economic growth and its respect for native traditions, nationalism generated political movements of broad appeal, capable of mobilizing popular enthusiasm. Daniel O'Connell's inflammatory speeches won thousands to Young Ireland and its demands for the end of union with Great Britain; by the 1830s he commanded the largest movement of political protest Europe had yet seen.

Many governments in the 1830s and 1840s had made some appeals to patriotic and nationalist feelings, but nationalism remained strongly associated with revolutionary movements and secret organizations dedicated, like those of Mazzini, to popular uprisings that would create democratic republics responsive to the popular will. Nearly all the regimes that came to power with the revolutions of 1848 accompanied their plans for new constitutions and political freedom with the rhetoric, the symbols, and at least some of the programs of nationalism. During the course of those revolutions, however, nationalists and national movements found themselves doubly divided, divided between those who sought democracy and equality and those who emphasized the need to maintain order and preserve established institutions, but also divided, especially in central Europe, between conflicting nationalist claims. With the defeat of those revolutions, the political significance of nationalism changed as moderate nationalists, frightened by the social divisions revolution had revealed, showed increased respect for military power and a strong state and as even repres-

sive monarchies began to see in nationalist policies a welcome source of popular support.

## The France of Louis Napoleon

By 1850 those who held power in much of Europe were victors over revolution, and the waves of government repression that followed were hardly surprising. Yet Prussia, where reaction was harsh and the Junkers reasserted their influence, retained the constitution of 1850. In the Austrian Empire, where the emperor scrapped the constitution, peasants kept their new freedom from feudal obligations. But the most daring experiment in combining reform, popular participation, and unchallenged authority was the reign of Louis Napoleon in France. That striking venture in a new political style proved a disturbing influence as an example to others and as a factor in international relations, which along with domestic politics became increasingly sensitive to the demands of national prestige and public opinion.

With monarchists a majority in the Chamber of Deputies and Louis Napoleon the nation's president, the Second Republic was ruled by its enemies. Napoleon, often at odds with the deputies, continued the appeal to public opinion that had won him election. When, in the third year of his four-year term, the Chamber rejected a constitutional amendment that would have permitted him a second term, he decided to mount a coup d'état.

He struck on the eve of December 2, 1851—the anniversary of the first Napoleon's coronation as emperor in 1804 and of his victory at Austerlitz in 1805. Potential opponents, including 200 deputies, were quickly taken into custody; troops occupied the streets and overran the barricades that rose. At the same time, Napoleon restored universal manhood suffrage, which the conserva-

**Even official portraits sought to preserve a certain enigma about Napoleon III, both emperor and popular leader.** (Photo: Photographie Bulloz)

a representative assembly, the Corps Législatif, that could debate and vote on but not initiate or amend legislation and a Senate appointed by the president, who was assured a 10-year term and almost full powers. Tired of disorder, the French people were willing to settle for the façade of democracy. Exactly one year after the coup d'état, the Second Republic was transformed into the Second Empire under Emperor Napoleon III, a change even more overwhelmingly supported in another direct vote. Neither plebiscite allowed the citizen to do more than vote yes or no—accepting changes already effected or risking a rejection that might bring any number of unspecified perils in its wake.

The Second Empire found favor with most businessmen and the Catholic Church. It wooed monarchists, local notables, and peasants and played to popular opinion. The regime skillfully used the prefects who headed each *département* to strengthen its authority, and it managed to keep the press in line without official censorship. Throughout Europe people watched with surprise that a government which claimed a democratic mandate could so tightly hold the reins of power, could promise both peace and national glory, and could sponsor programs for social welfare as well as economic growth.

Varied and innovative, the Second Empire has been seen by some historians as a kind of early New Deal and by others as a precursor of fascism, but all consider it a significant effort to cope with the political implications of a mass industrial society. Napoleon III was influenced by Saint-Simonian socialism, attracted by liberal nationalism, and obsessed by belief in his own destiny, his Napoleonic star. Alternately decisive and weak, farsighted and misled by vague dreams of glory, he was Napoleon the Little to his opponents, Napoleon the well-meaning to his hardheaded critics, the Emperor to most of the French.

tive Chamber had restricted with a residence requirement aimed at excluding "unstable" workers, and promised a revised constitution. Hundreds were killed, and all told, between 20,000 and 30,000 were arrested with nearly 10,000 transported to Algeria. The resistance ended quickly.

Yet Louis Napoleon presented himself as the voice of the people; and three weeks after the coup his actions were ratified by more than 90 percent of the voters in a national plebiscite. The new constitution established

The decade of the 1850s witnessed an economic boom stimulated at least in part by the policies of the regime, which sought more systematically to foster economic growth than any other government of the period. Tax incentives and laws facilitating the formation of companies with limited liability encouraged investment. The state, in addition, created special investment funds (of which the Crédit Mobilier was the most famous), paid entrepreneurs a respect they had rarely enjoyed in France, and launched grand public works projects.

One of these was the elaborate rebuilding of Paris, ranging from a vast new sewer and water system to the city's great boulevards and parks, most of which date from this period. A pioneering venture in city planning, these undertakings typified the imperial style. The plans were reviewed by Napoleon III himself, who favored ostentatious and regular structures, and were carried out by his extraordinarily able prefect Georges Haussmann. Slums were cleared, often with painful dislocation for their residents; boulevards, planned for their aesthetic effect and as an aid to traffic, were also expected to make uprisings more difficult; façades often received more attention than the buildings behind them. And the whole project gave rise to rumors of political spoils and speculation. Yet the result was a city healthier and more convenient, envied and imitated throughout the world. The court of Napoleon and Empress Eugénie was brilliant, and French prestige in the arts and sciences (Louis Pasteur first achieved fame in this period) was never higher. In the Napoleonic tradition, the government rewarded talent with honors and promotions. The emperor, indefatigable patron and sponsor of educational and social reform, took credit for all this—more, in fact, than was his due.

Foreign policy, similarly meant to be popular, was marked more by public enthusiasm than by tangible gains. The Crimean War ended with a conference in Paris in 1856, and France's intervention in Italy's war against Austria in 1859 appeared to end in victory. While maintaining good relations with Great Britain, the empire proudly showed its radical roots by supporting the national aspirations not only of Italians but also of the Poles who, ever restive, rose against Russian rule in 1863.

By the 1860s, however, the empire's fortunes were changing. Support of Italy had antagonized French Catholics; the annexation of Nice and Savoy, France's reward for that support, had aroused British suspicions; and the French public was troubled by the cost of military glory. Eager to strengthen his domestic support, Napoleon welcomed the chance to intervene in Mexico as an inexpensive venture that would earn Catholic gratitude, but that imperial scheme ended in disaster. England, Spain, and France had sent troops there in 1861 to force payment of foreign debts; and the French remained when the others withdrew, defeating the liberal Mexican government and imposing the Archduke Maximilian of Austria as emperor of Mexico in 1864. Unexpected Mexican resistance and opposition from the United States forced the French to abandon Maximilian, who was defeated and executed in 1867. Napoleon's vague hope to benefit from the decline of the Ottoman Empire or the expansion of Prussia fared no better when confronted with the clearer and more consistent policies of Bismarck.

The regime was also losing support at home. The Church, resentful of the state's energetic intrusion into its traditional spheres of charity and public welfare, was angered by the government's close supervision of its affairs, and Catholics became more militant in their criticism of Napoleon's domestic and foreign policies. A far-reaching tariff agreement with Great Britain in 1860, followed by similar treaties with other countries, was a step toward free trade that appealed to liberal economists but upset many business people, particularly those dependent for survival on France's traditionally high tariffs. Laborers wanted more than public works and the government's support for mutual-aid societies. Restrictions of political freedom were increasingly resented, and ideological clashes became more intense.

Aware of these dissatisfied voices, Napoleon III sought new support by gradually making his government more responsive. In 1860 the Corps Législatif was granted permission to present resolutions and to reply to the emperor's annual address. By 1868 freedom of the press and the right of assembly had been reestablished, and the legislature was being allowed to interrogate ministers. The regime established public secondary schools for girls, encouraged the formation of worker's organizations, and acknowledged the right to strike. This liberalization, however, alienated some old supporters without mollifying the empire's critics. In each election the opposition, much of it republican, gained seats until it held nearly half the lower house in 1869. On the first of the year in 1870, a full-fledged parliamentary system was adopted, with ministers responsible to the bicameral assembly and a republican, Émile Olivier, as prime minister. Eager for public favor, the new administration took a nationalist stand against Prussia in a dispute, discussed below, that helped bring about the Franco-Prussian war of 1870 and the end of the Second Empire. The promise of progressive rule and social order, once enough to win middle-class support, was not enough to keep it.

## International Relations in the 1850s

Louis Napoleon was not the only ruler to recognize the political rewards of a daring foreign policy. Shortly after the Austrian Empire regained its authority with the defeat of the Hungarian revolution in 1849, Schwarzenberg sought to reassert Austria's influence over the other German states. His chance came when King Frederick William IV of Prussia, moved by the nationalist vision of leading a united Germany, called a meeting of German rulers. Many were reluctant to attend, and Schwarzenberg shrewdly reconvoked the diet of the old German confederation. This put the German states in the dangerous position of choosing between Austrian and Prussian leadership. Austria, with the clear support of Russia, then threatened Prussia with war, citing a number of issues at conflict. Before so grave a challenge, Prussia backed down, and in a conference at Olmütz in 1850, promised to abandon the scheme for a German union under its command. Hapsburg hegemony over Germany seemed assured, reestablished by a fearless minister.

The British foreign secretary also exploited the advantages of an assertive policy. Henry John Temple, Viscount Palmerston, was a flamboyant aristocrat, frequently at odds with his cabinet colleagues who disapproved of his outspoken sympathy for liberal regimes on the Continent. Often indifferent to procedural niceties, he was shrewdly alert to public opinion. Thus Palmerston saw a national issue in the claims made by one Don Pacifico against the Greek government. An Athenian mob had burned his house because he was a Portuguese Jew; but Pacifico, who was born in Gibraltar, held British citizenship. Palmerston vigorously supported his demands for compensation, sending notes, threats, and finally the British fleet to Greece until an indemnity was paid.

Responsible statesmen in Great Britain were outraged, but Palmerston defended himself in one of the great speeches in the history of the House of Commons. Dramatically, he recalled the pride of ancient Romans, who could say, *"Civis Romanus sum,"* "I am a Roman citizen," and know themselves secure throughout their empire. A British subject, Palmerston declared, "in whatever land he may be, shall feel confident that the watchful eye and strong arm of England will protect him against injustice and wrong." To the public at least, Palmerston was vindicated. Like Napoleon III, he recognized the appeal of nationalism.

### The Crimean War

The restless ambitions and search for prestige that had come to characterize international relations were a direct cause of the war of France and Great Britain against Russia in 1854–1856. Nothing less would have made so serious a conflict out of the opposing claims to Jerusalem's holy places put forth by Roman Catholic and Greek Orthodox monks in 1851.

France, citing traditions ranging from the Crusades to Richelieu, supported the Latin monks and pressed the Ottoman sultan, whose empire included Jerusalem, to grant them specific privileges. For Louis Napoleon, the issue provided a further chance to win Catholic support at home and to upset the balance of power established at the Congress of Vienna. Russia, rising to the defense of the Orthodox faith and anticipating the collapse of the Ottoman Empire, reacted strongly. It demanded a protectorate over Orthodox churches within the empire and in 1853 increased its pressure by occupying the Danubian principalities of Wallachia and Moldavia, lands under Ottoman suzerainty, which had last been occupied by Russia in 1848 to put down revolution there. That move increased the involvement of Britain, ever inclined to see a threat to its empire in any Russian expansion. The British encouraged the sultan to resist Russia's demands.

Diplomatic activity reached fever pitch, and Britain and France sent their fleets into the Aegean Sea. Repeatedly, negotiations broke down, and in October 1853 the sultan exuberantly declared war on Russia. After Russian forces destroyed an Ottoman fleet, Britain and France declared war on Russia in March 1854, a step greeted with patriotic enthusiasm in London and Paris. Austria, suspicious of a French emperor who supported nationalism in Poland and Italy and unwilling to bear the brunt of a Russian attack, remained neutral. But when Russia withdrew from the Danubian principalities in August 1854, Austria occupied them in turn, leaving the contending powers without a battlefield.

Six months after war was declared, British and French forces landed in the Crimea to continue the fighting against Russia in battles conducted with remarkable incompetence on both sides. Russia could not mobilize or effectively deploy the large armies that made it so feared, and Britain's supply system proved incapable of sustaining hostilities at such a distance. In 1855 the allies welcomed the aid of little Piedmont.

A full year after invading the Crimea, the allied forces finally took Sevastopol. That defeat, threats that Austria and Sweden might enter the war, and the accession of Alexander II led Russia to sue for peace in December. The final terms were to be set at a European congress in Paris, attended by the belligerents and by Austria and Prussia.

The foreign ministers who met in Paris in 1856 dealt amiably and easily with the specific issues arising from the war. Beyond establishing the prewar status quo, the treaty admitted the Ottoman Empire into the European concert, guaranteed its integrity, and greatly reduced Russian influence. Russia ceded some territory at the mouth of the Danube River, surrendered its claims to any protectorate over Christians, and accepted a ban on warships in the Black Sea. Only this last point really rankled.

Napoleon III was unable, however, to launch the full assault on the treaties of 1815

**The press did much to popularize the Crimean War. This illustration shows Florence Nightingale rushing to the front, where her service first made her famous.** (Photo: The Granger Collection)

he wished for; Austria and Great Britain distrusted his interest in reshaping Europe. Although the Emperor wanted to include it, the question of Polish independence never got on the agenda. The Italian question, on the other hand, was at least mentioned—the only concession Piedmont won, but even that was enough to produce patriotic outbursts in Italy and terror in Austria. The issue of the Danubian principalities with its implications of Balkan nationalism also frightened Austria. The possibility that the two provinces might be joined was too divisive to be settled then, but by 1858 they were, in effect, united, the basis for a Rumanian national state.

In many respects, the congress had be-haved like its predecessors, but it marked an important change in the prominence of nationalism and in the demise of that alliance of Austria, Prussia, and Russia that had preserved European peace and conservatism for so long. Russia and Austria had cooperated in opposing nationalism and revolution through the crises of 1848, but competition between them for influence in the Balkans now became one of the facts of European politics. Indeed, Russia now counted for less in purely European matters and found itself turning with gratitude to signs of sympathy from Napoleon III. The fact that the congress met in Paris rather than Vienna indicated the altered prestige of the European states. The old balance of power, the old concert of conservative nations, the old diplomacy of European aristocrats who largely ignored public sentiment—all this had been shaken.

Almost 500,000 soldiers died in the Crimean War, the highest toll of any European conflict between the Napoleonic Wars and World War I. Two-thirds of the casualties were Russian, and two-thirds of all losses resulted from sickness and bad care. Yet the outbreak of war produced a surge of enthusiasm no government could ignore. The diplomacy that led to it and the way it was conducted were shaped by concern for national prestige, and the parades of magnificently uniformed soldiers, like the heroic stories reported by an aggressive journalism for an eager public, underscored the political importance of the war. In those terms, France, Piedmont, and Great Britain all gained from it; the Ottoman Empire, under Western pressure, began to adopt the modernizing institutions of the West; and Russia, sobered by defeat, launched an era of fundamental reform unequaled since the days of Peter the Great. In Italy and Germany the way was opening for still more drastic changes.

## The Unification of Italy

Since the French Revolution, the sense of common nationality had grown stronger among Germans and among Italians, supported by common experience and economic change. That nationalism, exemplified by Mazzini, was fostered by numerous organizations, defined in propaganda that ranged from clandestine pamphlets to major literature, and expressed in many a local uprising. Especially among the middle class, nationalist feeling became intense, the core of campaigns for representative government, efficient administration, a dependable system of justice, and a national economy. And the regrouping of domestic forces after 1848, which gave greater prominence to the middle class, as well as the altered international situation following the Crimean War, provided new opportunities for the nationalist movements of Central Europe.

In Italy the revolutions of 1848 had established that nationalism was a powerful political force. Their failure made it equally clear that separate revolts were not enough to overcome the arms of Austria, the main opponent of Italian unification. The Mazzinian program was thus cast in doubt, but so were old dreams of papal leadership in the national cause. Of the several Italian states, only Piedmont, despite having been twice defeated by the Austrians, maintained an independent foreign policy, still flew the tricolor of Italian nationalism, and kept its constitution.

Piedmont had other strengths. Its aristocracy, narrow in outlook, Catholic, and conservative, was dedicated to the service of the state; and its monarch, Victor Emmanuel II, though no liberal, ruled with a parliament and longed for a patriotic war against Austria. Although a small state, the kingdom had a tradition of military strength and bureaucratic rectitude. More recently, its government had encouraged commerce and the building of railroads and had limited the privileges of the Catholic Church, setting Piedmont on the liberal course established earlier in Great Britain, France, and Belgium.

These policies acquired firmer purpose in 1852, when Count Camillo Cavour became prime minister. A member of the Piedmontese aristocracy, well traveled in France and England, Cavour was a gentleman-farmer who believed in economic and scientific progress, representative government with limited suffrage, the rule of law, and religious tolerance. Nationalism he understood primarily as an avenue to modernization, and he found in free trade, sound finances, and railroads a power that could remake Piedmont.

Cavour pursued his liberal goals with tactical brilliance, skillfully using newspapers and parliamentary debate to mold public opinion. With some disloyalty to the cabinet of which he was a member, he suddenly formed a new parliamentary coalition of the left center and right center, a base of power from which he dominated both king and parliament from 1852 until his death in 1861. In that brief time he established himself as one of the outstanding statesmen of the century.

Piedmont's internal strength was Cavour's first concern, but he also sought to make his state the center of Italy's resurgence, the Risorgimento.[2] He welcomed exiles from other parts of the peninsula, encouraged the nationalist press, and sought every opportunity for symbolic gestures of patriotism. He was aided in this by the Italian National Society, one of whose founders was Daniele Manin, the president of the short-lived Venetian republic in 1848. The National Society propagandized for Italian unity under Piedmont's king and established secret committees in most of the cities of Italy. Its members were predominantly liberal aristocrats, local lawyers, and professors. In calling for Italian unity, they freely borrowed and effectively used the ideas of Mazzini, but this idealism was combined with hard-headed insistence on the need for international alliances and military force to defeat Austria. Economic liberalism largely replaced more generous and vaguer social theories, and talk of revolution did not lessen the commitment to a national state that would protect private property, persecute no one, and maintain social order.

Most of all, Cavour depended on astute foreign policy. He had pushed for Piedmont's participation in the Crimean War and was rewarded with the discussion of the Italian question at the Congress of Paris. Using his state's enhanced international position, British sympathy, and Napoleon III's ambition, he hoped to gather the forces to defeat Austria.

This hope turned on Louis Napoleon, whose Italian connections, nationalist leanings, and restless search for prestige Cavour assiduously played upon. He was aided by liberal sympathy throughout Western Europe and even by Italian revolutionaries, whose activities helped convince many that an Italy unliberated would remain a dangerous source of European instability.

At last, in July 1858, Cavour and Napoleon III met secretly at the little spa of Plombières in eastern France to plot war against Austria. They agreed that Piedmont would acquire all of northern Italy and that the grand duchy of Tuscany would be enlarged and become the Kingdom of Central Italy. These two large states and the Kingdom of the Two Sicilies would then form a confederation under the pope. France would receive Nice and Savoy, thus strengthening her border, and Napoleon's cousin Prince Jérôme would marry Victor Emmanuel's reluctant 15-year-old daughter. In his desire to tie his throne to the legitimate monarchs of Europe, Napoleon III shared the old-fashioned concerns of Louis Philippe and Napoleon I, but he also hoped to satisfy nationalism while using monarchy as a bulwark against radicalism. The arrangement contrived at Plombières would provide multiple openings for Bonapartist influence while preventing the formation of a unified Italian state that could become a threat to France. The plan, too delicately balanced to be practical, sought cautious ends through cynical daring.

After Plombières, Cavour encouraged the nationalist demonstrations spreading throughout Italy but tried to prevent the kind of outbreak that might cause Napoleon to change his mind. While Cavour hunted for

---

[2] Risorgimento, now the historian's label for the whole period of Italian unification, was a term meaning "resurgence," often used by nationalists and made the title of a liberal newspaper that Cavour helped to found and edit.

an excuse for war, Great Britain pressured for peace and France hesitated. But Austria, watching young Lombards and Venetians escape conscription by streaming to Piedmont as volunteers, determined to end the nationalist threat once and for all. It sent Piedmont an ultimatum so strong that Cavour needed only to reply with cautious dignity in order to have his war. On April 29, 1859, Austria invaded Piedmont, and France went to the rescue of a small state attacked by her giant neighbor.

The rapid movement of large French armies was impressive, but thereafter the war was fought with little tactical brilliance on either side. In June the Austrians were seriously defeated at Magenta, in Lombardy; but the Battle of Solferino, three weeks later, was as indecisive as it was bloody. As the Austrians retreated to the fortresses controlling the Lombard plain, Napoleon lost his taste for war; and rather than face further losses, a long siege, the danger that Prussia would come to Austria's aid, and discontent at home, he unilaterally agreed to a truce. The emperors of France and Austria met at Villafranca in July to establish the terms of peace, which included ceding Lombardy but not Venezia to Piedmont and maintaining the other Italian states as before (see Map 24.1).

## The Formation of the Italian Kingdom

Those states, however, had not survived the excitement of a national war. Gentle revolutions accompanied the march of Piedmontese troops throughout northern Italy. When local patriots gathered in the streets, the dukes of Modena, Parma, and Tuscany simply fled. In these areas and in part of the Papal States (the Romagna), supporters of Cavour—usually members of the National Society—assumed dictatorial powers in provisional governments that adopted Piedmontese laws and currency and called for elections to rep-

resentative assemblies. Thus the terms of the Villafranca truce could not be carried out. The provisional regimes cautiously went their way, carefully maintaining order, and after a few months arranged plebiscites—a device Napoleon could hardly reject—on the question of annexation to Piedmont. Italians trooped to the polls with bands playing, and flags waving, peasants behind their lord and workers with their guilds. The result was as overwhelming as the plebiscites of France; and Victor Emmanuel quietly accepted the request to rule from the Alps to Rimini, on the Adriatic. The province of Savoy and the city of Nice were turned over to France.

The extension of the Piedmontese state was a triumph of moderate liberals with which more democratic nationalists were not altogether content, and sputtering revolts in Sicily gave them a chance to lead a different sort of Risorgimento. Former Mazzinians gathered guns in Genoa and laid plans for an expedition that Cavour dared neither support nor oppose. The leader of this daring venture was Giuseppe Garibaldi. Exiled for his Mazzinian activity in the 1830s, Garibaldi had spent 10 years fighting for democratic causes in South America, returning to Italy in time to take part in the wars of 1848. He had directed the heroic defense of the Roman Republic in 1849 and led the most effective corps of volunteers fighting for Piedmont in 1859. One of the most popular figures in Italy, he set sail for Sicily one night early in May 1860 with a thousand men, mainly middle-class youths from Lombardy, Venezia, and the Romagna.

No event in the nineteenth century so captured the popular imagination everywhere as that daring venture. The Expedition of the Thousand was like some ancient epic come to life in an industrial age: untrained men, wearing the red shirts Garibaldi had adopted in South America, fought with bravery and discipline, enthusiastically supported

**MAP 24.1 THE UNIFICATION OF ITALY 1859–1920**

in the countryside. Garibaldi's tactics confused and defeated the Bourbon generals, despite their far larger and better-equipped forces. In two weeks the Red Shirts occupied Palermo and within two months all of Sicily except Messina. Volunteers flocked from all over Italy, and money was collected for them in the streets, at theaters, and at special meetings from New York to Stockholm.

Garibaldi proclaimed his loyalty to Victor Emmanuel, but he was equally open about his distrust of Cavour, who, in turn, feared the undiplomatic brashness as well as the republican and radical sentiments of the Garibaldians. When in August Garibaldi sailed across the strait and landed on the Italian mainland, declaring Rome and not just Naples to be his goal, Cavour determined to recapture control. He encouraged uprisings in the Papal States and then sent Piedmontese troops into the region in the name of order. Carefully skirting the area around Rome, they moved south to meet Garibaldi. On September 18, between lines of suspicious men, Giuseppe Garibaldi and Victor Emmanuel rode out to shake hands. Piedmontese appointees quickly replaced the officials named by Garibaldi, who added to his legend by disdaining all proffered honors and quietly sailing with a bag of seed for his island retreat on Caprera. Plebiscites in the newly conquered provinces produced an almost unanimous vote for union, and in March 1861 the Kingdom of Italy was proclaimed before the first Italian parliament. The moderate liberalism of Cavour had triumphed.

### Political and Economic Problems 1860–1876

Cavour's death shortly afterward was the first of many setbacks the new kingdom suffered, though the problems Italy now faced were, in any case, less susceptible to political solutions. The great differences among the regions of Italy seemed to argue for a decentralized federal system, but wartime conditions and fear of separatism prompted the government simply to extend Piedmontese administration and law. Too often, especially in the south, officials with an alien accent applying strange laws seemed almost foreign occupiers. Southern poverty and traditions of local patronage and corruption hobbled the new regime. Outbursts of brigandage in the south, occasionally supported by exiled Bourbons, the papacy, and Spanish Carlists, were an inchoate social protest that the new government met with military suppression, expending more lives than in all the wars of the Risorgimento.

Thrilled to have accomplished so much, Italian patriots could not accept the exclusion of Rome and Venice from united Italy, but both were international problems. Catholics throughout the world, convinced that papal independence required territorial sovereignty, opposed the annexation of Rome, which Napoleon III was pledged to protect; and Austrian troops, massed in Venezia, threatened the new Italian state. Within Italy the constant agitation over Rome, sometimes led by Garibaldi, weakened and divided the government.

The new nation acquired Venezia as a by-product of the Austro-Prussian war of 1866 when both powers offered Venezia to Italy— Prussia as the reward for an alliance and Austria, at the last minute, in return for Italian neutrality. Italy honored its prior pledge to Prussia and went to war, suffering defeats on land and at sea off the Adriatic island of Lissa in the first naval engagement in Europe between ironclads. Prussia's quick victory ended the war, however, and the province of Venezia (without the Tyrol, though Garibaldi had won some of the few Italian victories there) was added to Italy. Rome, all that was left of papal territory, was annexed when

**The handshake of Victor Emmanuel and Garibaldi, which sealed the unification of Italy as their armies met in 1860, became a favorite subject for illustrations of the Risorgimento. This engraving is English.** (Photo: Culver Pictures)

French troops withdrew during the Franco-Prussian War of 1870. Italy had gained its capital.

These were impressive achievements, even if they were less glorious than patriots had hoped, but they brought other difficulties to the fore. Italy passed a Law of Guarantees, assuring the full independence of the Vatican and providing an annual indemnity, but it was rejected by Pius IX, who declared himself a prisoner, refused to recognize the Italian state, and forbade Catholics to take part in national elections. Conflict with the Church was a source of dangerous division, and Italy's governing class remained seriously isolated from the country at large. Because of the high property qualifications in Piedmont's constitution, now extended to all Italy, only 500,000 Italians out of a population of more than 25 million were able to vote; and this exclusion of the lower classes coupled with the abstention of Catholics made the subtleties of parliamentary conflict seem unreal.

Italy was poor, overwhelmingly agricultural, and the heir to generations of retrogressive policies; it had no coal or iron, and three-quarters of the population was illiterate. With liberal conviction the Italian government assumed the debts of the annexed states, accepted enormous military costs, and sought to balance the annual budget. Despite taxes among the highest in Europe, Italy necessarily continued to lag in schools, railways, and roads. The extension of Piedmontese law brought with it the confiscation of lands held by thousands of monasteries; but they commanded low prices because they were sold quickly, and the sale of land did not benefit the peasants as much as hoped. Free trade within the nation and the lower Piedmontese tariffs brought many long-term benefits but instant distress to hundreds of small producers. For millions of artisans and peasants suffering the dislocations of war and social change, few tangible benefits followed from replacing reactionary dukes with a liberal national state.

Steadfastly, Italy's leaders tried to foster the process of modernization. When the old Cavourians lost office to men of the left center in 1876, the change so dramatic to politicians was barely discernible to most Italians. A new generation of equally isolated middle-class leaders took charge in a country that was full of disappointments. But Italy was nonetheless free and reasonably stable, its national income rising. Its parliamentary institutions would be more severely tested later (Italy continues, p. 1041).

## The Unification of Germany

The unification of Germany was completed a decade after Italy's, the work of Prussia, noted since the eighteenth century for efficient institutions that enabled it to wring impressive military strength from limited resources (see Map 24.2). Like Piedmont, Prussia began the 1850s with a new constitution at home but forced to accepted Austrian terms abroad. Prussia was, however, a major European power with a long-recognized claim to economic and political leadership among the German states.

After Olmütz, Austria appeared to domi-

nate German affairs. But by 1853 all German states except those directly tied to Austria had joined the Zollverein; and Prussia's position had clearly changed by 1859, with Austria defeated in Italy and Napoleon III agreeing to a sudden truce, in part at least, out of fear of Prussia. Thus the Hohenzollern monarchy was the focus of nationalist opposition to Napoleon that spread through the German states. The German National Society, founded in the Rhineland in 1859 in direct imitation of the Italian National Society, propagandized vigorously for a Germany united under Prussia, citing its military power, the rapid industrialization underway in both the Rhineland and Prussia, and the liberal possibilities in Prussia's constitution.

Within Prussia the rule of William I, which began in 1858, was also a turning point.[3] After a long period of reaction in which the press had been muzzled, public meetings repressed, many political leaders imprisoned, and the upper house of the legislature dominated by officials and landowners, William permitted such restrictions to be eased and turned his attention to improving the army.

The new era opened with a constitutional crisis. General Albrecht von Roon was appointed minister of war, and Helmuth von Moltke, his chief of staff, proposed a major military reorganization that would double the army's size and provide it with extensive new equipment. The plan won William's support, but the lower house of the legislature, in which liberals had gained an unexpected majority, rejected it. Although the constitution of 1850 allowed universal male suffrage, it avoided democracy by dividing voters into three classes according to the taxes they paid, giving the two wealthier classes as many rep-

---

[3] William I (1797–1888) became regent in 1858, when his brother Frederick William was adjudged insane, and king on his brother's death in 1861.

**MAP 24.2 THE UNIFICATION OF GERMANY**

resentatives as the third class, to which the overwhelming majority of the electorate belonged. In addition, the king had the right to veto any legislation and to appoint the ministers he chose. Designed to assure conservative dominance, the three-class system had the unexpected effect of magnifying the voice of new industrial wealth, and the majority of the Landtag was now prepared to challenge the monarch head on.

Liberals, who distrusted Prussian militarism and an army dominated by the Junkers, preferred a citizen militia and opposed increased expenditures. To William and his advisers, royal authority in the form of control of the army and the budget was at stake. As the conflict dragged on, they went ahead with the reorganization despite promises not to, paying for it out of general funds. Elections in 1862, however, only strengthened the opposition, which firmly insisted that the Prussian government be responsible to the legislation. William, calling on God and conscience, threatened abdication and then hesitantly named Otto von Bismarck his chief minister.

Bismarck was a Junker, better educated than many, whose pride of caste and reactionary views were resented by liberals and whose intensity and imagination made him seem as erratic and dangerous as Napoleon III to most conservatives. For 30 years all of them would have to live with his stinging sarcasm, bruising contempt, and brilliance. Like Cavour, he saw more clearly than his king that nationalism could be used against revolution and made foreign policy the central concern as well as the justification of his program.

In the conflict with the Landtag, the power of parliament was at stake, and Bismarck gave the king firm support. He lectured the deputies on Prussia's national role and the chances too often missed in the past. If Germans looked to Prussia, it was because of its powerful army, not because of any liberal institutions; and he added, in the most famous statement he ever uttered, that "the great questions of the day will not be settled by speeches and majority decisions—that was the mistake of 1848 and 1849—but by blood and iron." He dissolved parliament and applied heavy government pressure in the subsequent elections. But despite conservative gains, the opposition increased still more. Bismarck then shifted tactics. He encouraged whatever divisions within parliament he could find, convoked it as little as possible, and ignored it whenever he could. He bribed the press with money and access to news, and he badgered and closed opposing papers. He made promotions in the civil service and judiciary dependent upon unquestionable loyalty to the government. Then, confident of the army and bureaucracy, Bismarck proceeded to spend funds and collect taxes without parliamentary authorization.

He sought to justify this defiance of Prussia's elected representatives through his foreign policy. He blocked Austria's continuing effort to reorganize the German Confederation, and his threat that perhaps the German Diet could be elected by universal suffrage stunned conservatives with its radicalism and liberals with its cynicism. While underscoring the limitations of Austria as a leader of any German national venture, he sought to win Russian friendship away from the Hapsburgs. When Russia repressed a Polish uprising in 1863 with such severity that Austria, France, and Britain joined in protest, Prussia supported the tsar. When conflict over Schleswig and Holstein flared up in the same year, Prussia used the occasion to assert leadership in German affairs. The Danish king outraged German nationalists by attempting to annex Schleswig and to extend his authority over Holstein. But Prussia thwarted any independent policy by the German Diet and persuaded Austria to join in war against Denmark in January 1864. Bismarck then foiled efforts at international negotiations until the Danes were defeated and he could win acceptance for a plan whereby Schleswig was placed under Prussian administration and Holstein, surrounded by Prussian troops, under Austrian. The awkward arrangement, a potent source of contention between Austria and Prussia, was clearly impermanent.

Friction with Austria increased almost daily, and Bismarck prepared for war and made sure that Austria would stand alone. He dangled visions of adding territory along the Rhine before Napoleon III, won Italy's support by promising it Venezia, and gained

Russia's assurance of neutrality. Both Austria and Prussia were already mobilizing when Austria convened the Holstein diet to discuss the duchy's unclear future. Bismarck denounced the move as a violation of their understandings, and Prussian troops marched into Holstein in June 1866.

Austria won the support of most of the German Confederation, but Prussia forced Hanover to surrender within two weeks. Three Prussian armies swept into Bohemia, and at the Battle of Sadowa, Austria suffered overwhelming defeat. The Austro-Prussian War lasted just seven weeks. Expert opinion had predicted a long fight, but Prussia, well equipped and ready, applied the lessons of the American Civil War, using railroads and telegraph to move with a speed for which Austria was unprepared.

Many Prussian conservatives had been shocked at Bismarck's disrespectful and belligerent treatment of Austria, but now they were eager to avenge Olmütz and to make heavy territorial demands on Austria. Against the wishes of his king and generals, Bismarck insisted that the Hapsburg monarchy be treated leniently; Austria surrendered no territory. But Prussia's gains elsewhere changed the face of Europe; it annexed Hanover, Nassau, Electoral Hesse, and Frankfurt, all of which had sided with Austria in the quarrel, and then established a confederation of North German states under Prussian leadership. Austria was excluded from the new union. On being told of Napoleon's hope (which Bismarck had encouraged) of some territorial gains for France, the South German states agreed to a military alliance with Prussia.

### The North German Confederation

The constitution of the North German Confederation was in itself a triumph of Bismarckian policy. The basis for a new national state, it left member states free to regulate their local affairs while joined together through a bicameral federal parliament. Its upper house, the Bundesrat, was composed of 43 delegates sent in varying numbers from the separate states, with Prussia's 17 more than the one-third necessary for a veto. The lower house, the Reichstag, was elected by universal male suffrage. A political structure that seemed to protect local interests and point toward democracy in practice assured the dominance of Prussia and the subordination of parliament. The confederation's chief executive was the king of Prussia, and he appointed the chancellor, who, responsible to no one, shared with him full authority over foreign and military affairs. The armies of the separate states were combined under Prussian leadership.

In Prussia itself, elections held during the war had strengthened the conservatives in the Landtag. The liberals still maintained a majority, but they could hardly reject Bismarck's amazing achievements. After Prussia's victories, the Landtag voted a bill of indemnity, retroactively legalizing the taxes and expenditures Bismarck had imposed. Unwilling to appeal to the masses, the liberals were as soundly defeated as Austria. They were pleased that the new Reichstag would be elected by universal male suffrage, impressed that many conservatives detested Bismarck's acceptance of any parliament at all, and grateful to have a strong national state. Most of them joined a new (more pro-Bismarckian) party, the National Liberals. Conservatives unwilling to accept gestures toward constitutionalism countered by banding together as the Free Conservatives. Prussian politics focused on Bismarck; and Germany was set on Bismarck's course, directed by men determined to strengthen the state and to maintain its autonomy.

The North German Confederation represented an enormous expansion of Prussian power and a great step toward unification. While the South German states preserved their separate status, no German nationalist could think Bismarck's federation a satisfactory or permanent solution. Instead, it seemed that the unification of Germany, like that of Italy, was to be achieved in stages, in part through diplomacy. There were other reasons, too, for stopping halfway. North Germany, Protestant and more industrial than the south, offered a sound base for the kind of Germany Bismarck envisioned, as different from the largely agricultural and Catholic south as northern Italy was from Naples. With their own rich cultural traditions and ancient dynasties (which still viewed the Hohenzollerns of Prussia as upstarts), Germany's southern states looked more to Vienna and Paris than to Berlin and remained suspicious of Prussia's militarism and cold efficiency.

Overcoming these differences was a central task of the North German Confederation, and Bismarck found the threat from France his strongest weapon. Napoleon wished to acquire Luxembourg (all parties appeared willing), and Bismarck manipulated the emperor's designs into a crisis that produced protests against cession to France of an "ancient German land" and brought France a serious diplomatic defeat. But neither such maneuvers nor the benefits of the Zollverein overcame southern resistance. A majority of the southern delegates elected to the Zollverein, led by Bavaria and Württemberg, opposed any further "Prussianization" of Germany. Something more than elections and trade were necessary if Germany was to be quickly united.

## The Franco-Prussian War

That something more was war with France. Historians once hotly disputed who was to blame for that war and whether it was "nec-

essary." New research and changing perspectives have lessened the controversy; the war was wanted by Bismarck but first declared by France, the result of nationalism in both nations more than long-range calculation. It was provoked by competition over influence in Spain. The provisional government there was seeking a replacement for Queen Isabella II, who had been forced to abdicate in 1868. It picked Leopold, prince of Hohenzollern-Sigmaringen, but under heavy French pressure he finally declined. Eager to curry public favor and to score a point against Bismarck, the French government sought more. In a famous interview at the western German spa of Ems, where William I was taking the baths, the French ambassador demanded that the Prussian king give a public guarantee that the Hohenzollern candidacy would never be brought forward again. The king refused and later telegraphed a report to Bismarck of the difficult though formally correct interview. Bismarck carefully edited the Ems dispatch to make French demands seem even more imperious and the king's refusal even more abrupt, and released it to the press. Bismarck, Roon, and Moltke correctly assumed that war would follow. The French government, which could hardly afford further humiliations, responded to the patriotic fury it had helped ignite and declared war on July 19, 1870.

France hoped for support from Italy and Austria but had failed to establish any formal agreement with either, and they remained neutral. The French army, more formidable than Austria's had been, possessed modern equipment in some respects superior to the German, but the forces of the confederation were more carefully prepared and far more decisively led. In rapid movements the Germans pushed through Alsace and encircled a French army at Metz in August. With heavy losses on both sides, another French army, attempting to relieve Metz, was severely defeated at Sedan in September. There Napoleon III surrendered and was taken prisoner. Major fighting was over, but French resistance continued. Paris, quickly surrounded by German troops, held out under a long siege, and a provisional French government continued efforts to maintain a French army in the field. For the rest of the year, German troops were subjected to a kind of guerrilla harassment, and an armistice came only at the end of January, when Paris capitulated.

The brief war had profound effects. A German national state was created. The Second Empire fell; and after bitter internal conflict, the Third Republic was established in France. Even more than defeat itself, the harsh terms of peace—France was required to pay an indemnity of 5 billion francs and to cede Alsace and Lorraine—assured that the enmity between France and Germany would be a central fact of international relations.

### The Second Reich 1871–1879

The decision to annex Alsace-Lorraine was primarily a military one, intended to provide Germany with the strongest possible fortifications in case of future conflicts with France. But it also responded to a popular demand of German nationalists, and Bismarck still needed their support. His major concern was to complete the unification of Germany, and well before the final French surrender, he began intricate and difficult negotiations with each of the South German states. They had joined in fighting France with a mixture of enthusiasm and fear, but it took concessions, secret funds, threats, and all his skill before Bismarck got the German states, Prussia's generals, and the king to accept his terms for permanent union. When they did, William I was crowned German Kaiser (emperor) in the Hall of Mirrors at Versailles on January 18, 1871, the anniversary of the founding of the Prussian monarchy.

With modifications, the constitution of the North German Confederation was extended to all the new nation. The upper house of parliament, the Bundesrat, received increased powers, including the right to declare war, but many domestic affairs were reserved to the 25 states that made up the Reich and special privileges were granted Baden, Bavaria, and Württemberg. There was no doubt, however, that the great new nation created by the popular will, Bismarck's ability, and Prussian arms would be dominated by Prussia.

The Second Reich was from its inception a powerful nation.[4] Germany in 1871 was already more populous than France, and its rate of demographic growth was the fastest Europe had ever known. Germany's industrial production increased at an astounding rate, and less than half the population was engaged in agriculture after the first decade of unification. Because it had developed later than Great Britain and more rapidly than France, its industrial equipment was more modern. The French indemnity added to the available capital, and the government aided industrial efficiency by making heavy investments in railroads, granting tax privileges, establishing tariffs, and encouraging the formation of large combines, the famous German cartels. German universities became the leading ones of Europe in the application of scientific method to every discipline.

Such rapid growth was disruptive in Germany, as elsewhere. Nationalists stressed the traditional values of the *Volk*, the people, and nowhere were materialistic, commercial, and urban values more intensely attacked than in industrial Germany. This conflict could stimulate achievements as lasting as the work of Richard Wagner, who combined daring musical innovations with old Teutonic myth and genius with mere prejudice; but it increased

---

[4] The old Holy Roman Empire was patriotically honored as the first Reich.

**The halls of Versailles ring as Prussian officers hail the proclamation making King William emperor of Germany.** (Photo: The Granger Collection)

the dangerous tensions between powerful conservative circles, a growing but defensive middle class, and workers increasingly aware of their distinct interests. The great achievements of the German state rested on its ability to satisfy industrialists and appeal to nationalists by operating liberal institutions through autocratic means.

Bismarck, who wanted not to offend local interests and who left the army essentially autonomous, worried very much about the internal dangers to the new nation. He therefore sought to establish the supremacy of the state by moving against two apparently vulnerable groups likely to oppose Prussian policies: first the Catholic Church and then the socialist party.

Rather grandiosely named the *Kulturkampf* ("Struggle for Civilization"), the con-

flict with the Catholic Church centered on new laws requiring state approval of Church appointments, state supervision of Catholic education even in seminaries, and the abolition of religious orders. Many of these measures were part of the secularization common throughout Europe, but others were an effort at "germanization" (Poland and Alsace were heavily Catholic) intended to weaken anti-Prussian sentiment. Passed in the period from 1871 to 1875, they came at a time when the Church appeared intransigently opposed to modern society, and they won the support of National Liberals, many conservative Lutherans, and much of the left.

Yet the *Kulturkampf* was not a success. The severity of the laws and the harshness with which they were carried out made martyrs of many a priest and nun. As a majority of bishops lost their sees and many went into exile, Catholics rallied to their Church; and many others began to fear so intrusive a state. The Catholic Center party steadily gained votes in Reichstag elections. Thus when the more flexible Leo XIII became pope, in 1878, Bismarck sought an understanding with the Vatican. Many of the laws most offensive to Catholics were allowed to lapse, and the battle of civilization subsidied as the state turned toward the repression of other enemies.

Socialism did not offend Bismarck either in its attacks on laissez faire or in its emphasis upon the social role of the state, and he had gotten on well with the leading German socialist of the 1860s, Ferdinand Lassalle. But as socialists sought to win a mass following, founding the Social Democratic party in 1875, their attacks on autocracy, the military, and nationalism seemed more dangerous. In 1878 two attempts to assassinate the Kaiser (neither by a socialist) gave Bismarck his chance, and he called for laws repressing socialism. The Reichstag refused, and the election of 1878 was fought largely on that issue, with conservatives and the Center party gaining some seats. As a result, the Reichstag banned most socialist publications, prohibited socialist meetings except under police supervision, and forbade public collections for socialist causes. The Social Democrats were, in effect, forced underground, and another important element of society learned to hate and fear the German state. Within the Reichstag, however, socialists remained free to speak, and their party gained support with every election.

The abandonment of the *Kulturkampf* and the offensive against socialism were part of a larger realignment in German politics. Having preserved their strength, the conservatives and Catholics who had resisted the new Germany came to accept it, while liberals, torn between Bismarck's accomplishments and their old principles, grew weaker. Economic troubles, the effect of both the nation's rapid growth and a European agricultural depression, also helped forge a pro-Bismarck coalition more durable than any based on persecution. In 1879 demands for a higher tariff led the chancellor to propose and the Reichstag to grant strong protective tariffs on both manufactured and agricultural goods. The majority supporting that measure included Junker landlords, Rhineland industrialists, and the more nationalist liberals, split once again from their doctrinaire comrades. Bismarck was finding a formula to draw together the most powerful interest groups in German society in support of a conservative state under his strong leadership. (Germany continues, p. 1044.)

## III. RESHAPING ESTABLISHED STATES

The Second Empire in France, the liberal monarchy of unified Italy, and the Bismarckian system of the Second Reich were all, in their different ways, efforts to build strong national states by combining nationalism, representative institutions, the dominance of established groups, and industrial growth. In the international system that resulted, war more than ever stood as the ultimate test of the state's efficiency. The defeats of Russia in 1856, of Austria in 1859 and 1866, and of Napoleon III's France in 1870 were understood to require drastic governmental changes. In less developed countries like Russia, Austria, and Spain, however, essential reforms threatened established interests and became possible only as new compromises (less extensive than those that had brought about the unification of Italy and

Germany) were worked out. In France, on the other hand, national unity, effective institutions, and middle-class dominance were already assured; and there conflict centered rather on the issue of what other groups should participate in and benefit from the policies of the state—questions that led to civil war and the Third Republic. France (and to a lesser degree, Spain and Italy) became more like Great Britain, where continued reform and economic growth maintained a triumphant model of the prosperity and stability that liberal institutions could produce.

## Russia 1855–1881

Immediately after the Crimean War and only a year after assuming the throne in 1855, Tsar Alexander II issued a manifesto promising improvements in justice, education, and employment. Goals once envisaged only by liberals were adopted in defeat by the Russian autocrat. The critical reform was the abolition of serfdom. Discreetly but firmly the nobles were told to bring the institution to an end from above rather than wait for its destruction from below.

Months passed in silence while secret committees drafted proposals and most nobles dragged their feet. Intellectuals had argued against serfdom for generations, and peasants spoke through more frequent uprisings. Economic developments—a money economy, foreign trade, new industry—had further weakened the old system. Yet landowners could always argue against taking revolutionary risks just yet. Only in 1861 was serfdom abolished—by the tsar's decree.

The law of 1861 gave legal rights to more than 22 million serfs, providing in general that peasant farmers should gain title to the land they worked or its equivalent. They could either contract a long-term debt to the state, which would, in turn, compensate the owner, or accept one-quarter of that land free

and clear. During an interim of two years, they would continue to owe all former obligations to their masters.

In practice, the lord usually kept the best land for himself and through inflated land prices received additional payment for the loss of his serf labor. On the whole, former serfs found themselves with less land than they needed to support their families and also make their payments; and provisions for pasture, forest, and water rights were rarely satisfactory. Thus some wage labor, usually for the former master, remained a necessity for subsistence.

The law of 1861 also gave important responsibilities to the *mir,* or village commune. Its elected officials assigned plots, determined the crops to be planted, and paid taxes to the state for which each plot of land was assessed by the *mir.* The former serfs could not leave the commune or sell their land without permission; and even after leaving, they remained liable for taxes. In this way, the state made sure that the debts owed to it would be met and that the new peasant society would maintain structures with which the state could deal. Indeed, the commune, which came to be considered a characteristic Slavic institution, tended to resist change in favor of traditional ways; similarly, few lords really became modern farmers. But this conservatism to some degree eased the adaptation to a social change immense in itself.

A few years later the government liberated all state peasants—nearly 25 million—on more favorable terms, granting on the average more land at a lower price than that available to former serfs. Still sharply segregated from more privileged members of society, with special laws and punishments, including flogging, applicable only to them, peasants remained a caste distinguishable in dress, speech, and customs.

Although the emancipation of the serfs, who constituted about 47 million of Russia's

# ❄ EXPERIENCES OF DAILY LIFE ❄
## *Schooling*

Universal schooling was an invention of the nineteenth century. In 1815 most European children did not go to school at all; of those who did, most attended irregularly and briefly. By 1900 governments were expected to provide schooling for every boy and girl of school age (usually 6 to 11 or 6 to 13). That change was the result of an enormous effort. Revenue had to be raised to build schools, pay teachers, and provide supplies. New attitudes and institutions were needed to train teachers, establish some norms of what would be taught, and compel parents to enroll their children. That often led to dangerously bitter conflicts over the role of churches, the different needs of boys and girls, and the training appropriate for peasants and workers. Despite all the obstacles, in a few generations going to school became a universal part of childhood.

In the old regime elementary instruction varied greatly. Some areas had established schools; more often teaching was offered as a kind of supplementary social service by ministers or their assistants or by members of religious orders or by people who were retired and literate. The fate of most schools depended upon local traditions and talents of a single teacher. In a number of German states, including Prussia, governments had sought to establish a universal primary system in the eighteenth century. Such efforts were redoubled early in the new century by governments in Germany and the Netherlands, by state and Church in France, and by competing churches in Great Britain. In Protestant areas, including much of Germany, Scandinavia, and Scotland, local schools and school boards were supervised by the pastor. In Catholic countries, and especially in France, there was an extraordinary growth in religious orders devoted to teaching. Still, most teachers were lay men or women, increasingly so as the number of schools grew. Not only was their pay poor but much of it came in contributions of food or wood or a rent-free room. Teachers were expected to supplement their income with other activities; many farmed a small plot or were shepherds in the summer, assisted the priest or minister (especially as janitors and bell ringers), or served as town scribes. Similarly, widows, wounded veterans, and retired sailors and peddlers often set up schools as a means of earning a little money at home. By the latter third of the century, however, state-supported public schools with licensed (and modestly trained) teachers became the norm.

With similar gradualness, the school itself emerged as a distinctive place, separate from the teacher's quarters; and late in the century many an adult could still recall learning to read amid the noises and smells of kitchens, laundry, or stables. As a distinctive space, the schoolroom developed its own equipment. The box of sand in which students could trace their letters with a stick gave way to individual slates and a larger blackboard on an easel. Long benches with desk attached became standard furniture, to which further refinements, such as porcelain inkwells, eventually were added. The teacher's desk and armchair on a raised platform came to dominate classrooms that tended to become more and more crowded (a regulation in France limiting urban classes to 130 students was a progressive measure in the 1860s). Greater attention to students' health led school inspectors, whose number was growing, to insist that classrooms be adequately heated, to recommend a kettle of water on the stove for satisfactory humidity, and to make sure that windows allowed for the proper amounts of light and fresh air. By late in the century in nearly every classroom there would be some maps, a small library, perhaps a scientific instrument or two and some sort of abacus for learning arithmetic. By then the dunce cap was disappearing, along with corporal punishment, and students did exercises in notebooks and read from textbooks specially designed for the public schools. The school itself was more and more likely to be in its own distinctive building, with the national flag flying above it and also proudly tacked to the wall of the classrooms. On the outside of the building a dignified name, a patriotic or learned quotation, or a table of metric weights and measures expressed a communal sense of education's social importance.

Whatever its local roots, the school had become a symbol of the nation as well as an instrument for creating patriotic citizens. The language taught was the national tongue (earlier schools had often begun with Latin), with regional variations and dialects rejected as inferior and incorrect. Schools were also expected to inculcate values of sobriety, work, cleanliness, and respect for the family as well as patriotism. The academic content remained elementary, with reading, writing, and arithmetic at the core, to which was added some (primarily national) geography, history, and literature, and probably some singing and drawing. Science and physical exercise became more important as the century progressed. "Individual" instruction, in which one student read aloud to the teacher while the others remained idle, gave way to newer pedagogies, as did the inexpensive "monitorial system" popular in the 1830s and 1840s, in which more advanced students drilled the younger ones. Wherever the size of the population permitted it, the boys and the girls were taught in separate schools. Although the elementary curriculum was very similar for both, the separation of the sexes was generally considered an important step in preparing them for their adult roles. Girls' schools devoted a good deal of time to sewing, needlework, and uplifting stories of how—through order, well-managed accounts, and the proper tone—the wife could create a strong family and a sober husband. Boys' schools spent comparable time on carpentry, land measures, perhaps the rudiments of some trade, and later in the century on military drill. For the most part, this elementary education was expected to lead directly to apprenticeship, the first job, and marriage. Secondary education, which provided either the classical education that gave access to the university or a preprofessional training, remained quite distinct from the primary school. Still, the very success of the latter began in the course of the century to open the socially sensitive question of who should have access to further education and on what terms. ❈

**A nineteenth-century German school.**
(Photo: Culver Pictures)

**In this 1861 photograph a Russian official is reading to peasants on a Moscow estate the "Regulations Concerning the Peasantry," the decree that abolished serfdom.** (Photo: Novosti Press Agency)

74 million people, did not establish a laissez-faire economy, it provided the basis for institutions allowing some popular participation in public life. Within each district, communes supported their own courts, selected their own judges, and administered the regulations on taxes and conscription. In 1864 district and provincial councils—the zemstvos, elected through a three-class system like Prussia's—were made responsible for primary schools, local roads, and measures of local welfare. Generally cautious, the zemstvos gave important political experience and a sense of political responsibility to many

professional men and other members of the middle class. Cities, too, were granted increased autonomy and allowed to elect representative bodies.

The number of primary schools, though always inadequate, increased dramatically. In addition, the government encouraged secondary and university education, relaxed censorship, and adopted a number of military reforms. The system of requiring 25 years of service from selected serfs was altered until by 1874 universal service, with generous exemptions and only 6 years of active duty, approached the concept of a citizen army.[5]

As each reform uncovered more that needed to be done, the government became more cautious. Concessions to Poland had prompted demands that culminated in the revolution of 1863. Harshly quelled by 1865, it lost Poland its separate status and strengthened conservatism in Russia. The repression extended into Russia, where the police remained independent of local controls. By 1875 the zemstvos had been forbidden to discuss general political issues, and restrictions on what could be taught or printed had been tightened.

As a consequence, the movements of radical opposition flourished. The famous division of the generations, expressed in Ivan Turgenev's *Fathers and Sons,* showed in the rejection of leaders like Alexander Herzen, who from exile in London had once inspired reform but whose views belonged to the era of Mazzini and the utopian socialists. New spokesmen, called nihilists by their enemies, rejected compromise within the system and accepted the uility of violence advocated in

---

[5] Most soldiers were, of course, recruited from the peasantry. A provision reflecting the social importance of education stipulated that those who completed primary school were liable for only four years of duty, those who finished secondary school for two years, and those with university education for just six months.

the anarchism of Mikhail Bakunin (discussed in Chapter 25). Populists talked of going to the people, educating the peasants to a more revolutionary view. Socialism, too, was spreading in the 1870s. All these doctrines were affected by pan-Slavist views, which stressed Russia's peculiar destiny and disdained the liberal parliamentarianism of the West. The intelligentsia of Russian society remained isolated and, increasingly disenchanted with a tsar liberator, moved further left. In an atmosphere of conspiracy, terrorists attempted assassination as a way to shake an oppressive regime. Usually they missed their target, but in 1881 a bomb killed Alexander II. Alexander III, his son, took the reigns of power smoothly. However inadequate, the reforms of Alexander II assured that imperial Russia could survive an assassination. (Russia continues, p. 1037.)

## The Hapsburg Empire 1859–1875

Following the revolutions of 1848, the Hapsburg monarchy had sought to meet its political and economic problems by creating a modern, unitary state. Under the young Franz Joseph I, the emphasis on administrative efficiency was renewed, and for the first time in its history, the entire empire was subjected to uniform laws and taxes applied by a single administration. The emperor and the aristocracy, however, were never comfortable with their earnest bureaucrats, and the innovation of centralization was not accompanied by the zeal for reform the policy required. Mounting debts and defeat in Italy in 1859 were accepted as proof that it had not worked, and in 1860 Franz Joseph's October Diploma announced a new federal constitution giving considerable authority to regional diets.

Intended to reduce resentment against high-handed government, the constitution was a failure from the start. It prompted dangerous arguments among the various nationalities over what their "historic" provinces really were and won the determined opposition of liberals and bureaucrats alike. The emperor therefore reversed himself the next year in the February Patent, which established an imperial bicameral parliament. Having stirred his people to visions of local self-government and autonomous nationalities, he was now again asking for their subordination to rule from Vienna. Furthermore, representatives to the lower house were to be elected by a four-class system that assured the dominance of the German-speaking middle class.

In Hungary the liberal nationalist Ferencz Deák led a campaign to reject these arrangements and reestablish instead the constitution of 1848, a far more liberal instrument. The imperial government tried the traditional tactic of recruiting support from the empire's other nationalities against the dominant Magyars, but the response was unenthusiastic. Although not strong enough to force its will, Hungary was able to prevent the new constitution from having its intended effect. Deák then worked for a compromise, which became acceptable after the empire's defeat in the Austro-Prussian War.

In 1867 Franz Joseph was crowned king of Hungary, an autonomous state joined to Austria only in the person of the emperor and by common policies of defense and diplomacy. Thus he preserved his authority in the matters of foreign policy he cared about most by conceding to one nationality what he denied to others. Thereafter two critical issues of Hungary's domestic politics were the treatment of the non-Magyar majority of its population and the divergent economic interests of Austrian industry and Hungary's great landholders (a conflict that centered on the tariff). On both questions the Magyar landowning aristocracy generally had its way, and after 1875 the dominant Liberal party, led by Kálmán Tisza, made Magyar the language of school and government and protected Magyar economic interests.

In the Austrian parliament the emperor turned for support first to the German liberals, who offended him by their anticlericalism, and then to Czechs and Poles, who disturbed him with their nationalist demands. Each group won some concessions, but fundamental, lasting reforms were difficult, and government depended increasingly on a reliable, conservative bureaucracy dominated by Germans more than on parliamentary policies. Still, the Hapsburg monarch presided after 1867 over responsible ministers in both halves of his empire, who enjoyed a determining voice in public affairs.

An awkward compromise, the Dual Monarchy gave power to wealthy landlords and merchants and rested on the dominance of Magyars (over Rumanians, Croatians, and Serbs) and of Germans in cooperation with Czechs and Poles (over Slovenes, Slovaks, and Ruthenians). It lasted for 50 years as one of Europe's great powers, an empire of diversified peoples and cultures, threatened by nationalism, changing even while resisting change, but with more freedom in practice than in principle, and sustained at its center by the graceful civilization of Vienna. (Austria-Hungary continues, p. 1039.)

## Spain 1854–1876

In Spain the compromises stability required proved difficult to maintain, and governments were weakened by their inability to risk losing the support of the army, the Church, big business, or regional interests. By emphasizing the economy, a liberal coalition under General Leopoldo O'Donnell ruled for nine years (having replaced General Narváez in 1854). And during that time Spain experienced on a smaller scale the waves of speculation, railroad building, economic growth, and ostentation associated with the Second Empire in France. The government fell in 1863 before changing demands it could not meet and palace intrigue it could not stop. Its conservative replacement then sought security through repression and electoral manipulation, which ended in revolution in 1868 and the unpopular Queen Isabella II's flight to France.

Disaffection of the military in 1868 was its immediate cause, but the revolution also won support from workers, radicals, liberals, professional groups, and businessmen. The new regime, led by General Juan Prim, sought to combine the moderation implied by constitutional monarchy with the liberal appeal of universal manhood suffrage, trial by jury, and freedom of religion and the press. It proved easier to adopt a new constitution, however, than to find a new king, as each candidate decided against entanglement in Spanish politics and the sort of international complications that precipitated the Franco-Prussian War.

The son of Victor Emmanuel II of Italy, who finally agreed to accept the throne in December 1870, ruled for just two years as King Amadeus I. The Italian royal house was anathema to Catholics because of its clashes with the pope, and the king was treated as an upstart and foreigner by grandees and courtiers. As republican agitation and Carlist uprisings became more serious, Amadeus abdicated in 1873 rather like a prime minister who had lost a vote of confidence.

The king had been neither a symbol of unity nor a political leader, and the Cortes declared Spain a republic. That lasted a year. Divided between centralists and federalists, Republicans were further weakened by Carlist revolts and Catholic distrust. The government alienated much of its following by repressing constitutional liberties in its quest for order, and the military again stepped forward to place Isabella's son, who had just come of age, on the throne as Alfonso XII.

He began his reign in 1875 under a new constitution that was closer to the one in effect from 1845 to 1869 than the more democratic ones that had succeeded it. The court never again meddled in politics as Isabella had done, and the ringing freedoms proclaimed during the republic were honored at least in theory. Spain thus found stability in a parliamentary government whose majority was largely determined by manipulated elections with limited suffrage. The Conservative and Liberal parties, as they came to be called, alternated in power with little change in policy. Both provided sensible and mildly corrupt governments that offered something to most influential groups. By not trying to strengthen the state, they were able to mask the bitter divisions between regionalists and centralists, Catholics and anticlericals, the poor and the propertied. (Spain continues, p. 1040.)

## France 1870–1878

The complicated system of the Second Empire could not survive military defeat. With the rout of French troops, a republic was announced to cheering crowds for the third time in France's history. Neither the state nor the nation, however, was called into question. As the Government of National Defense, republic leaders tried valiantly to turn 1870 into another 1792, when a republic had mobilized the nation against the monarchical armies of Europe. But German forces had already broken the back of France's army, and they surrounded Paris on September 19, less than three weeks after the capture of Napoleon III at Sedan. The new government sent some of its members to Tours to organize resistance from there, but even the ur-

**In this cartoon from the siege of Paris in 1870, a butcher prepares to deal with the hungry Parisians waiting in the rain for a bit of horsemeat.** (Photo: New York Public Library/Picture Collection)

gency of war barely covered the divisions between moderate and radical republicans, who were determined to continue the fight at all costs. Their leader, the fiery orator Léon Gambetta, daringly escaped from Paris in a balloon to accomplish remarkable feats of organization from Tours. Enthusiastic national guards and peasants boys were recruited and somehow equipped; Garibaldi arrived to help, and the French seriously harassed German troops, even recapturing Orléans, but by December the overmatched French forces were pushed back. The government retreated to Bordeaux while Paris held out against a German siege. During a winter as severe as any on record, Parisians cut the trees of their boulevards for fuel, slaughtered pets, and emptied the zoo as a starving city continued to resist. But heroism and patriotic fervor could not defeat a modern army, and at the end of January Paris capitulated. German troops marched down Haussmann's boulevards into a denuded and quiet city.

Although Gambetta wanted to continue the fighting, few others did; the armistice called for elections to establish a government that could ratify the terms of peace. In the absence of political parties or extended campaigning, the successful candidate was usually someone already well known, a local leader committed to ending the war, and thus two-thirds of those elected to the National Assembly that met in February 1871 were monarchists. Some were legitimists, who longed for a Bourbon restoration and were already calling the count de Chambord King Henry V; more were Orléanists. But there were also some republicans, mostly moderate, and a handful of Bonapartists.

Despite the moving speeches of delegates from Alsace and Lorraine, peace on German terms was accepted, and approval was quickly given for an interim government under Adolphe Thiers. The eloquent critic of Guizot, in exile during the 1850s and the empire's public opponent in the 1860s, Thiers gained at 73 the power he had long coveted. By naming him chief of the Executive Power, the Assembly avoided declaring whether France's permanent government would be a monarchy or a republic. It then agreed to meet next at tranquil Versailles rather than radical Paris, and adjourned.

### The Paris Commune

Determined to consolidate his position, Thiers recognized Paris as the greatest threat to the sort of compromise between Orléanists and moderate republicans he represented, and one of his first acts was to disarm the city's National Guard. At the end of the German siege, many of the well-to-do had left Paris, but the poor and the radical remained, hardened by months of fighting. When troops arrived to take the city's cannons, they were met by an angry crowd; shots were fired, and by day's end two generals lay dead and most of the soldiers had joined the side of their urban brothers. Faced with insurrection, Thiers followed the advice he had given Louis Philippe in 1848: He withdrew the army to let Paris taste its revolution so he could first isolate and then crush it.

The municipal council of Paris declared a commune, once again evoking the great Revolution, and called on other cities to do the same. The Paris Commune included moderate and radical republicans, some followers of Pierre Joseph Proudhon and Louis-Auguste Blanqui, militant socialists in the tradition of Saint-Simon and Fourier, and a few members of the Marxist First International. Its program, favoring democracy and federalism, was not very specific on other matters; and it had little time to experiment with egalitarian and anticlerical measures. Its efforts to make peace with the government at Versailles were rejected, and the Assembly there replied to the threat of a radical government and the Parisian "mob" by suddenly ending the moratorium on debt payment (including rents) that had been in effect in Paris during the siege and by ceasing to pay the National Guard, the only income for many Parisians. While German armies watched, troops from Versailles began their assault on Paris.

The civil war between the democrats of Paris and the Assembly at Versailles fed on the distrust and despair that accompanied the French war effort, the siege of Paris, and defeat. The city's isolation during that year of anguish, when rumors of treachery were heard at every hand, had amplified other divisions: between industrial and rural France,

Civil War broke out on March 18, 1871. Distrusting the citizens of Paris who were loyal to their national guard, angry at defeat, and resentful of its conservative policies, France's nervous new government sent troops to seize artillery left in the city from the siege. Onlookers reacted with fury. Shouts and stones led to shots and bloodshed; wildly furious men, women, and children overpowered the soldiers; then someone recognized generals Lecomte and Clément-Thomas. They were lined up and shot. The Paris Commune had begun.   (Photo: Collection VIOLLET)

between urban democrats and middle-class moderates. The two sides fought out of fury for competing visions of what the nation should become now that the Second Empire had fallen. Hostages taken by the communards to win release of some of their captured leaders were killed, among them the Archbishop of Paris. On both sides prisoners were shot, and the bitter and bloody fighting lasted nearly two months before troops broke into the city in May. Even then the battle continued, barricade by barricade, into the working-class quarters, where the group commanded by Louise Michel—the most famous of hundreds of militant *citoyennes* who would later tell her captors, "I belong entirely to the Social Revolution"—was among the last to fall. Solid citizens shuddered at revolutionary excess (and especially the part played by women), but on the whole, the victors were more brutal. Tens of thousands of Parisians died in the streets, and summary courts-martial ordered execution, imprison-

ment, or deportation for tens of thousands more.

The commune raised the red specter throughout Europe. From the first, Marxists hailed it as a proletarian rising, the dawning of a new era, though Marx was indignant with the communards' respect for property and legality and their lack of revolutionary daring. Former communards became the heroes of socialist gatherings for the next generation, and to this day the cemetery where many of them were executed remains a shrine honored by socialists and communists.[6]

Historians have been at great pains to show how little socialism, still less Marxism, there was in the Paris Commune (it respectfully left the Bank of Paris intact); yet myth has its historical importance too. This indisputably was class conflict, and the rage on both sides was more significant than mere differences of program. After 1871 a communist revolution became a credible possibility to radical and conservative alike, and working-class movements pointed to the martyrs of the Commune as evidence of the selfish cruelty of bourgeois rule.

## The Founding of the Third Republic

Thiers's government quickly reestablished effective administration, thanks to a state apparatus stronger than any political group, and the loan needed to pay the indemnity to Germany was soon oversubscribed. As by-elections produced victories for moderate republicans, monarchists feared that their chance for a restoration might be slipping away. They rallied in 1873 to defeat Thiers in a close vote and united behind the Bourbon claimant, the childless count of Chambord, with the understanding that he would be succeeded by the claimant from the House of Orléans. His intransigent refusal to accept the tricolor, the flag of revolution but also nationalism, left the monarchists afraid to attempt a restoration yet. They borrowed time by electing Marshal Marie MacMahon as Thiers's replacement for a seven-year term. A monarchist who had fought under Napoleon III, he accepted from a sense of duty and brought to his post a dislike of politics that helped him act like the constitutional monarch for whom he was holding the throne.

While the conservatives appointed by MacMahon risked defeats in the Assembly[7] and the monarchists grew more divided, the republicans gained in confidence. In 1875 a bill passed by one vote provided that the president of the republic should be elected by the votes of two legislative houses, and these, in turn, were established by laws stipulating that the Senate would be indirectly elected by local officials and the Chamber of Deputies by direct universal male suffrage.

The Third Republic was thus established without ringing phrases as the government that, in Thiers's epigram, divided the French least. A regime of compromise, for which republicans led by Gambetta had worked hard, it had earned acceptability by crushing the Commune and accepting a conservative Senate. Created by the most reluctant of founding fathers, it endured longer than any French regime since 1789.

In the elections of 1876, the republicans captured two-thirds of the seats in the Chamber and almost half those in the Senate. Although MacMahon chose a conservative republican, Jules Simon, as premier, tension between the president and the Chamber predictably grew. The republicans accused the Catholic Church of being the political agent of legitimists and criticized the military and the Orléanist prefects. MacMahon, in turn, reproved Simon, whereupon Simon resigned, denouncing presidential interference. This was the crisis of "seize mai" (May 16, 1877), which precipitated the final step in the establishment of the republic, for MacMahon, who had previously rejected every hint that he attempt a monarchical coup, now reacted strongly. He dissolved the

---

[6] A century later a Russian sputnik proudly carried not only a Soviet flag but a red flag from the Commune of 1871.

[7] MacMahon's ministers, led by the able Orléanist, the duke de Broglie, were so rich in noble names that the period has come to be called the Republic of the Dukes from a study published by Daniel Halévy in 1937.

Chamber, called new elections, and named a new ministry to manipulate their outcome. Although the republicans lost some seats, they preserved an overwhelming majority. Never again in the Third Republic did a French president use his power of dissolution; and the presidency, so strong under Thiers, declined further in authority.

When MacMahon resigned, in 1879, the two houses elected Jules Grévy, a republican who in 1848 had argued there should be no president at all. A good old man who frightened no one, Grévy exemplified the caution, the compromises, and the republican tradition on which the Third Republic rested. French public institutions preserved the remarkable continuity that characterized them after 1800 despite the changes of regime. Successive republican governments guaranteed political freedom and deferred to the middle class. Economic growth, less dramatic than in Great Britain or Germany, was also less disruptive. Like its European neighbors, France had painfully found an awkward balance, one peculiarly its own, between the demands for order and the need for change. (France continues, p. 1042.)

## Great Britain 1854–1880

The moderation and flexibility of Great Britain's parliamentary system contrasted with the dramatic changes in Continental regimes. And that, like prosperity and empire, was a source of Victorian confidence. Many claimed that special qualities in the English character—respect for tradition, the emphasis on law and Parliament, habits of toleration and deference—accounted for the combination of industrial advance and political order.[8] Yet

---

[8] Walter Bagehot, one of the most noted political writers of the period, especially praised the English sense of deference to social betters. Inequality and individual morality, he argued, allowed Britain to enjoy order without coercion and justice without anarchy.

overwhelming social change as well as the reforms of the 1830s and 1840s had required the state to become more active in a wider range of activities and more responsive to a broader public. Ultimately dependent on elections, the government nonetheless remained the province of the upper classes, who found it difficult and sometimes repugnant to reach the masses.

Even in matters of foreign policy, however, public opinion was increasingly important. The Crimean War evoked a patriotic enthusiasm astute politicians would seek to recapture, and the ineptitude with which it was conducted forced investigations into administration and the military that increased the cry for new reforms. During the American Civil War, many liberals favored the South, for resisting central government, as did most of the English upper classes, who viewed Southern culture with aristocratic sympathy. John Bright and many radical and working-class leaders, on the other hand, saw the cause of human dignity and democracy represented by the North. The revival of British radicalism was closely connected with the willingness of the very textile workers who suffered from the scarcity of American cotton to cheer for President Abraham Lincoln's war.

Confronted by many pressures, the British political system maintained a remarkable capacity to generate limited but effective reforms. Lord John Russell built an effective coalition of liberal Tories and Whigs, and Lord Palmerston, prime minister from 1859 to his death in 1865, could at least arouse public affection—a quality that made him more popular in the nation than in Parliament. They presided over ministries of able men who soberly and sometimes imaginatively sought to lead a more efficient state to address some of the more pressing social and political problems. Competitive examinations for entry into a restructured civil service marked an important departure achieved in

1855 after years of effort. Legal disabilities for Jews were removed, and the special taxes in behalf of the Church of England were dropped. British rule in India was thoroughly reorganized following a great mutiny in 1857 among native soldiers in the Indian army. In the same spirit the important act of 1867, which made Canada a dominion with its own representative institutions, was passed with little resistance.

## The Parties of Gladstone and Disraeli

Such repsonsible accommodation was not sufficient, however, to meet the needs and aspirations of the lower-middle class and workers. More fundamental change came only when a major realignment made possible the establishment of modern political parties, the extension of suffrage, and the emergence of two brilliant leaders who combined democratic appeal with masterly management of the established political system.

One of them was William Gladstone, who made his mark as chancellor of the exchequer under Palmerston. A skilled parliamentary tactician, a man of impeccable background, he was also a personal friend of some of the more doctrinaire liberal reformers and showed open sympathy for the left-wing liberals known as radicals. Gladstone was one of the former Tories who followed Sir Robert Peel in leaving the party upon their conversion to free trade in 1846, and he was instrumental in transforming the Whigs into the Liberal party. In liberal principles he found a moral cause around which to build a strong political movement.

Gladstone became an advocate of increased suffrage as that question, in the air since 1832, became compelling. Cautiously, he and Russell sponsored a complicated bill, which was defeated. The issue was then snatched from them by the rising star of the Conservatives (as the Tories were now called), Benjamin Disraeli, who led his rather startled party to support a more generous measure, passed in 1867. The right to vote was extended to all men who were borough (town) residents and paid taxes either directly or indirectly through rent. An electorate that had risen to almost a million was now doubled (including about one adult male in three), and two great parties were coming systematically to compete for popular favor in terms of national issues. As the parties became better organized and disciplined, they reached far deeper into society with greater awareness of the people's concerns, and the great parliamentary clashes of Gladstone and Disraeli became a dramatic part of British public life.

Despite Disraeli's remarkable role in promoting the Reform Bill of 1867, the enlarged electorate produced a great Liberal victory the following year, and for six years Gladstone's first and perhaps most successful ministry did much to improve British society. Great Britain, well after most other European nations, at last established the basis for a national educational system by providing state aid to both church schools and locally supported secular schools. Education was compulsory only by local option and was not yet free, but a giant step had been taken. It was accompanied by important reforms in the two great universities. Oxford and Cambridge, which encouraged new curricula and allowed men not Anglican to compete for fellowships and teaching posts. The Liberals also reformed the army, limiting traditional privileges, improving training, and establishing shorter terms of service on the Prussian model. Even the purchase of commissions was abolished despite great resistance from the House of Lords. Ireland, too, received their attention. Here the Liberal government disestablished the Anglican Church of Ireland, restricted the abuses of absentee landlords, and provided guarantees that the peasants would receive some credit for improvements they made, some protection

An international flotilla marked the grand opening of the Suez Canal in 1869. As part of the elaborate ceremonies, for which both the Empress Eugénie and Emperor Franz Joseph came to Egypt, the khedive commissioned Verdi to write an opera, *Aïda*. The opera received its formal premiere in Cairo two years later. (Photo: © BBC Hulton Picture Library)

against eviction, and some help in purchasing land for themselves.

Few doubted that Great Britain would become more democratic, and many suspected that the Conservative party was doomed. Yet the elections of 1874 returned it to power, for Disraeli more than Gladstone had inherited Palmerston's appeal to nationalism. Belief in the glory and wealth of empire and willingness to expand the authority of the state in matters of public welfare were to become the strong foundation for a modern Conservative party.

Under Disraeli colonial matters received greater and more public attention, and his purchase in 1875 of a large block of shares in the Suez Canal provided the basis for subsequent British domination in Egypt. When "Empress of India" was added to Victoria's title in 1876, it sounded foreign and flamboyant to many in the upper classes but caught the imagination of citizens proud of their national power and their queen. A public health act in 1875 took the important step of establishing a national code for housing and urban sanitation. Trade unions, their legality questioned by a court decision, had been recognized in a Liberal bill of 1871, but it was the Conservatives who removed restrictions that had prohibited picketing and kept strikes ineffectual.

This conception of Tory democracy was a British parallel to the policies of Bismarck and Napoleon III. Through the party system the sphere of politics was being extended and the role of the state increased beyond the intention of the upper-class men who made the system work. Its effectiveness, in addition to the wealth of industry and empire, made Britain the most powerful and most envied nation of the world. (Great Britain continues, p. 1046.)

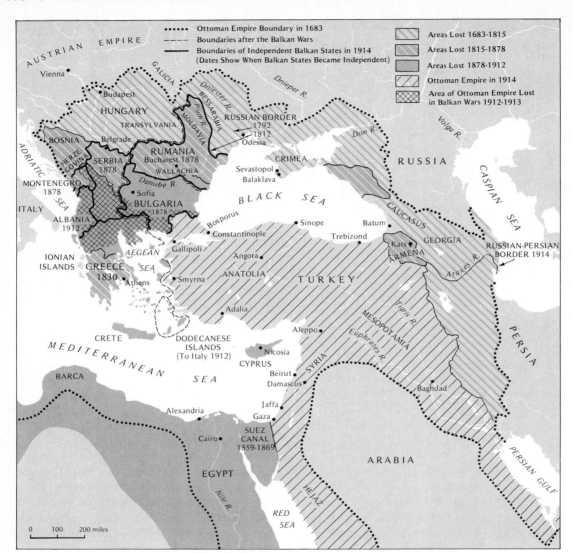

**MAP 24.3 THE DECLINE OF THE OTTOMAN EMPIRE 1683–1914**

## Stabilizing International Relations 1870–1881

The unification of Italy and Germany and the defeat of France had fundamentally altered the relations of the European powers, and nationalist movements within the Austrian and Ottoman empires raised the possibility of further change. The European powers were quick to perceive new opportunities and dangers in the Balkans.

Russia, eager to undo defeat in the Crimean War, snatched the occasion of the Franco-Prussian War to renounce the treaty clauses banning its navy from the Black Sea and looked hopefully for chances to extend its influence. The Hapsburg monarchy, hoping to compensate for its losses in Italy and Germany and aware of the threat nationalism posed to its rule, watched the Balkans with growing concern. Great Britain's interest also increased with the political popularity of empire and the opening of the Suez Canal in 1869. Built by French engineers, it offered a shorter route to India and made the eastern Mediterranean appear all the more vital.

Most of the Balkan peninsula was nominally under Ottoman rule (see Map 24.3), but throughout the area there was a ferment of nationalism, constitutionalism, and modernizing reform. Especially strong in the autonomous countries of Serbia and Rumania, it reached into the Ottoman Empire itself, where a proclamation of 1876 established, at least in theory, a constitution guaranteeing parliamentary government and individual liberties. The Bulgarian uprising against Ottoman rule in 1876 was thus not an isolated event, and it won immediate support from Serbia, which had long hoped for a Balkan federation against Ottoman power and for the acquisition of Bosnia and Herzegovina. After Ottoman forces put down the revolt with shocking brutality, Russia intervened, moved by traditional ambitions and pressure from its own pan-Slav movement, which had actively encouraged Balkan nationalists.

Russia's military campaigns were poorly conducted, but its gains were sufficient within the year to force the sultan to accept the treaty of San Stefano in 1878. Russia was to acquire territory across the Caucasus Mountains (from Batum to Kars), extending its centuries-long advance southward. Both Montenegro and Serbia were to be enlarged and granted full independence and, most important, the treaty provided for a large and autonomous Bulgaria. That new state, it was universally thought, would be a Russian

puppet looming over the Balkan peninsula; and the European concert, which had exercised so little voice in the unification of Italy or Germany, the fall of the Papal States, or the cession of Alsace-Lorraine, was called into action.

The combined pressure of the great powers forced Russia to agree to an international conference to establish new terms of peace in the Balkans, and at the subsequent Congress of Berlin in 1878, as at the Congress of Paris in 1856, they administered a sharp rebuff to Russia. They granted autonomy to a greatly reduced Bulgaria, and lessened the gains given Serbia and Montenegro. Austria-Hungary was authorized to occupy Bosnia and Herzegovina, which nevertheless remained under Ottoman rule, and the British occupation of Cyprus, previously agreed to by the Ottoman Empire, was confirmed.

The balance thus established in the Balkans was precarious, achieved only by extending Russian, Austrian, and British interests at the expense of a weakening Ottoman Empire, while ignoring the nationalist ambitions of many Greeks, Bulgarians, Rumanians, and Serbians.[9] This was a pattern for preserving peace that outside Europe would become characteristic of imperialism.

That the congress was held in Berlin reflected Germany's prestige and its new commitment to maintaining the balance of power. Germany and its chancellor had become preeminent in Continental relations. Russia, the offended power, had nowhere to turn for allies but Berlin, for France was too radical and Great Britain a consistent foe. Bismarck

---

[9] The southern part of Bulgaria, Rumelia, remained under Turkish rule as a separate province. Serbia, Montenegro, and Rumania received independence but less territory than they claimed. The Rumanian provinces of Wallachia and Moldavia had been joined in 1862 and received their own prince two years later. A Hohenzollern, he became King Carol in 1881. The tsar's nephew was elected to the Bulgarian throne.

| International and Military History | Political History |
|---|---|
| 1840 | |
| | |
| 1846–1878   Pope Pius IX | |
| | 1848   Franz Joseph Austrian emperor (to 1916) |
| 1849   Defeat of revolutionary movements | |
| 1850   Austria's "humiliation" of Prussia at Olmutz | 1851   Louis Napoleon's coup d'état |
| | 1852   Second Empire of Napoleon III |
| | 1852–1861   Cavour prime minister of Piedmont, then Italy |
| 1854–1856   Crimean War, Conference of Paris | |
| 1859   Piedmontese–French war against Austria: North Italian kingdom | |
| 1860   Garibaldi's expedition to Sicily  } Unification of Italy | 1860–1861   Constitutional changes in Austrian Empire |
| 1861   Kingdom of Italy | |
| 1861–1865   U.S. Civil War | 1862–1890   Bismarck Prussian, then German chancellor |
| | 1863   Revolution in Poland |
| 1864   Schleswig–Holstein Crisis | |
| 1864–1867   Maximilian in Mexico | |
| Unification of Germany | 1867   Dual Monarchy, Hungary autonomous; Second Reform Bill in England |
| 1866   Austro–Prussian War (Venezia to Italy) | 1868   Revolution in Spain |
| 1869   Suez Canal opened | |
| 1870   Franco–Prussian War (Italy takes Rome, Alsace-Lorraine to Germany) | 1870–1871   Paris Commune |
| (1870   Vatican I) | 1871–1875   Height of *Kulturkampf* in Germany |
| 1871   German Reich | |
| | 1876   Fall of "Old Right" in Italy |
| | Queen Victoria becomes empress of India |
| 1878   Congress of Berlin | |
| 1878–1903   Pope Leo XIII | 1879   Tariff and beginning of antisocialist campaign in Germany |
| 1879   Dual Alliance Germany–Austria | |
| 1880 | |
| | 1881   Assassination of Alexander II of Russia |

*Events in parentheses are discussed in other chapters.

| Social and Economic History | Cultural and Intellectual History |
|---|---|
| **1840** | **1840s** Growth of cultural nationalism |
| | **1842** *London Illustrated News* |
| | *Liszt* **(1789–1846)** |
| **1850s** Social programs of Second Empire; rebuilding of Paris directed by Haussmann | Balzac **(1799–1850)** |
| | Lamennais **(1782–2854)** |
| **1860** Cobden–Chevalier Treaty on tariffs | |
| **1861** Emancipation of Russian serfs | |
| | Delacroix **(1798–1863)** |
| **1870s** Legal protection of British trade unions | Dickens **(1812–1870)** |
| | Manzoni **(1785–1873)** |
| **1875** British public health act | (Sand **[1804–1876]**) |
| **1880** | (Eliot **[1819–1890]**) |
| | Flaubert **(1821–1880)** |
| | Wagner **(1813–1883)** |
| | Verdi **(1813–1901)** |

thus laid the groundwork for a system of alliances to isolate France and secure Germany's position. In 1879 Austria-Hungary and Germany signed a mutual defense pact that remained the foundation of German diplomacy, promising that the two countries would fight together in case either was attacked by Russia. Then Bismarck daringly turned to isolated Russia in 1881, reviving the Three Emperors' League he had attempted a decade earlier: Austria-Hungary, Germany, and Russia swore neutrality in the event of war between any of them and a fourth power.

More important than the precise provisions were the fear of international anarchy and the new relationship these alliances implied. Bismarck used Prussia's connections with both Eastern European empires, based upon an unstable balance in the Balkans, to re-create the conservative alliance of the three powers. At the same time, he sought the friendship of Great Britain and Italy, leaving Germany supreme and France alone upon the Continent—an arrangement to be sealed by dangerously explicit treaties as if solemn contracts could check the forces of domestic change or define the ambitions of national states.

## SUMMARY

By 1880 many of the aims of the revolutionaries defeated in 1848 had been accomplished. Italy and Germany were sovereign nations, and Hungary was autonomous. Serfdom had been abolished in Russia and religious disabilities largely removed in the United Kingdom. France and Germany enjoyed universal manhood suffrage. Representative government was firmly established in Britain, France, Italy, and Spain, and everywhere the state accepted a larger responsibility for social welfare. A dynamic middle-class culture flourished, and in a broad sense, nationalism had triumphed outside Eastern Europe (few denied its potential importance there), though the policies of nationalists seemed to promote conflict, a strong army, and a vigorous state more than liberalism.

Political changes after 1850 were a response to ideas and to new economic and social conditions that radicals had been among the first to recognize, but these changes were brought about largely by the state, which radicals had failed to capture. Everywhere stronger and more specifically secular, the state increased its authority, its social role, its sovereign claims, and its expenditures. Bureaucracies expanded, their officials copying the Junkers in Germany, carrying the voice of Germanic Vienna through the Hapsburg Empire, following in France the rational style of the great state schools, and carrying an upright liberalism deeper into British life. If social tension only occasionally burst into the open violence of the Paris Commune, that stability depended upon an intricate balance of forces—different in each nation—maintained by the state.

In general, Europeans faced the last third of the nineteenth century with increased confidence, impressed with the evidence of economic and social progress and hopeful that institutional and moral improvement would naturally follow. They could point, and often did, to evidence that in all the ranges of human thought, they enjoyed one of history's greatest civilizations. But even as this optimism flourished, there were rumblings of discontent from intellectuals who found the fashionable faiths shallow and from groups lower in society who were only just beginning to make themselves heard. The combination of an emphasis on politics, rapid social change, and the expansion of the state could prove explosive as conflicting interests fought to see who would command the enormous power Western society had assembled.

# RECOMMENDED READING

## Studies

*Anderson, Benedict. *Imagined Communities: Reflections on the Origin and Spread of Nationalism.* 1983. An important and provocative analysis of modern nationalism around the world.

*Barzun, Jacques. *Classic, Romantic, and Modern.* 1961. One of Barzun's many famous essays in defense of Romanticism.

*Beales, Derek. *The Risorgimento and the Unification of Italy.* 1982. Concise, skeptical introduction to the history of Italian unification.

*Chadwick, Owen. *The Secularization of the European Mind.* 1975. Perceptive, careful introduction to changing patterns of thought affecting religious attitudes.

*Gellner, Ernest. *Nations and Nationalism.* 1983. An effort to build a theory by analyzing the relation of industrialization to nationalism.

*Hamerow, Theodore S. *The Social and Economic Foundations of German Unification, 1858–1871.* 2 vols. 1969–1972. The politics and ideas of unification placed in the context of a developing economy.

*Hauser, Arnold. *The Social History of Art.* Vols. III and IV. 1958. Suggestive if sometimes mechanical effort to relate artistic trends to social change.

*Howard, Michael. *The Franco-Prussian War.* 1969. Exemplary study of how war reflects (and tests) an entire society.

*Jelavich, Barbara. *History of the Balkans.* 2 vols. 1983. An impressively thorough recent survey of both society and politics, from the eighteenth century to the present.

*Lukács, Georg. *The Historical Novel.* Hannah and Stanley Mitchell (trs.). 1962. Insightful and learned study of the social significance of the nineteenth-century novel by one of Europe's leading Marxist scholars.

*Mack Smith, Denis. *Cavour.* 1985. An expert and well-written assessment of the personalities and policies that created an Italian nation.

*Mosse, George L. *The Nationalization of the Masses: Political Symbolism and Mass Movements in Germany from the Napoleonic Wars Through the Third Reich.* 1975. One of the most recent and complete efforts to find the roots of Nazism in popular nationalism.

*Pinkney, David. *Napoleon III and the Rebuilding of Paris.* 1958. Interesting essay in urban history.

*Plessis, Alain. *The Rise and Fall of the Second Empire, 1852–1871.* Jonathan Mandelbaum (tr.). 1985. A balanced assessment in the light of recent scholarship.

*Read, Donald. *England 1868–1914. The Age of Urban Democracy.* 1979. Political change presented in terms of economic and social conditions.

Rich, Norman. *Why the Crimean War? A Cautionary Tale.* 1985. A concise synthesis and engaging interpretation of the political and diplomatic problems involving the major powers.

*Smith, Anthony D. *Theories of Nationalism.* 1983. A complex, comparative analysis of the structure of nationalist movements.

Szporluk, Roman. *Communism and Nationalism: Karl Marx versus Friedrich List.* 1988. Competing ideologies established in the nineteenth century seen as a key to modern politics.

*Williams, Roger L. *The French Revolution of 1870–1871.* 1969. An introduction to the current findings and long-standing controversies about the Paris Commune.

*Zeldin, T. *France: 1848–1945.* 2 vols. 1973–1977. Reissued in 5 paperback vols., 1979–1981. Excellent on the society and the attitudes of the middle class.

* Available in paperback.

# ❋ CHAPTER 25 ❋

# THE AGE OF PROGRESS
# 1860–1914

�֍ ✖ ✖ ✖ ✖

The half-century from the 1860s to 1914 saw the flowering of nineteenth-century civilization. In economic organization, technology, the arts and sciences, and politics, the revolutionary changes that had occurred before 1850 had now taken root, and in some respects the result was an almost incredible success story. European power, wealth, and prestige reached new heights and spread around the world; the benefits from increased knowledge, political freedom, and unfettered capitalism in most respects exceeded the early claims made for them. The pace of change seemed to increase in every domain of human activity, and the idea of historical progress became almost an obsession.

✖

Paradoxically, an age that described itself in such tones of optimism and confidence also subjected itself to internal criticism of extraordinary severity. Literacy spread, but intellectuals denounced the mass culture it fostered. The arts flourished, but they expressed conflicting values and attitudes that made modern civilization seem lacking in coherence. The standard of living rose, but working people formed militant organizations to combat their employers, and socialists considered the very success of capitalism to be evidence of its imminent collapse. Conservatives assailed the threat to civilized values posed by excessive faith in reason, rampant avarice, and purposeless tolerance of every idea and faction. Christians continued to decry materialism and the exclusion of religion from its rightful role. The late nineteenth century is often described as the triumph of the middle class and the age of liberalism, but it was characteristic of that triumph and that age that many were moved to reject it.

✖

These conflicts placed an added strain on political life at the very time that the state was expected to wield unequaled power. Each nation developed its own pattern for meeting this challenge, and remarkably, each of these political systems escaped the revolutionary upheaval that often seemed likely. That fact, like the continuation of international peace and the spread of European empire, appeared to be evidence of the health of European civilization, but the period closed in the cataclysm of World War I. From the perspective of the troubled 1930s the late nineteenth century seemed an almost idyllic period remembered nostalgically as the "belle époque" of happy stability. Yet it was also the breeding ground of twentieth-century conflict and doubt.

## I. ECONOMICS AND POPULATION

✖

### The Second Industrial Revolution

Economic growth in the second half of the nineteenth century resulted from a contin- uation of processes already under way, but with important differences that have led historians to call this the second industrial revolution. It was characterized by rapid economic growth, by accelerated industrial change (notably in steel, in the chemical in-

## ECONOMICALLY ACTIVE POPULATION CA. 1900

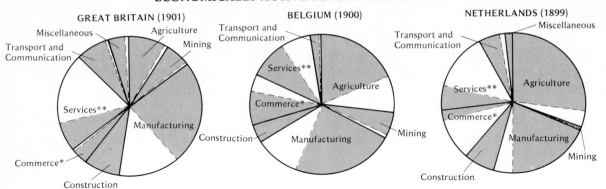

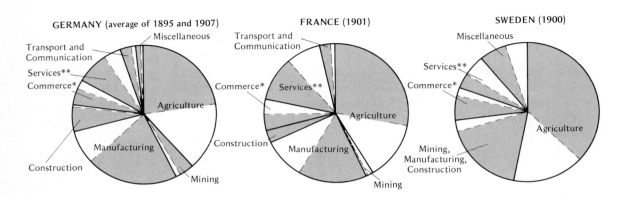

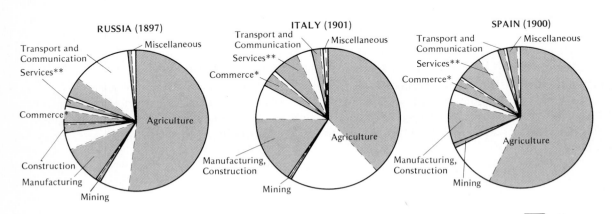

*Commerce includes banking, utilities, real estate, and insurance.
**Services includes armed forces and domestics.

(Source: Bairoch, P., *The Working Population and Its Structure*, 1968, p. 119.)

☐ Men
☐ Women

dustry, and in the applications of electricity), by an emphasis on large-scale production, by the spread of industrialization in central and eastern Europe, and by ever-expanding markets at home and abroad. While Europe's population grew more rapidly than ever before, the value of manufacturing went up three times as fast. Prosperity spread beyond the favored groups to affect all classes, and for the first time in history, economic growth was expected to continue year after year.

The expansion of the German economy following unification was the most spectacular. Everything seemed to foster the new nation's industrialization. Already rich in natural resources, Germany acquired more raw materials as well as factories with the annexation of Alsace-Lorraine. Its system of railroads provided excellent communications; the famous educational system produced ample numbers of the administrators and engineers the commercial sector now required. The government, which had played an active role in every facet of industrialization, continued to cooperate with business interests. Military needs stimulated basic industry, and a growing population provided an eager domestic market. Being newer than those of Britain or France, German factories employed the latest and most efficient equipment, obtaining the necessary capital through a modern banking structure. By 1900 those plants were far bigger than anyone else's, and firms engaged in the various stages of production often combined in huge cartels dominating an entire field of enterprise as Germany became preeminent in new fields such as chemicals and electricity. German salesman appeared all over the world with catalogs in native languages and products suited to local conditions, selling with a drive and optimism British merchants resented as bad manners.

The older industrial economies of Great Britain, Belgium, and France continued to grow but more slowly; yet by 1900 France's industrial production, despite the loss of important textile and iron centers in Alsace, about equaled Great Britain's a generation earlier, when Britain had led the world. French iron production more than doubled in the first 25 years of the Third Republic, and new processes made the nation's ore output second only to that of the United States. In value of production per capita, a figure that suggests something of a nation's standard of living, France remained ahead of Germany, though behind the British Isles.

By the turn of the century, Great Britain, whose industrial superiority had seemed a fact of nature, was clearly being surpassed in some of the critical indexes of production by the United States and Germany. Although the economy did continue to expand, its state of health became a serious issue in English public life, and economic historians remain fascinated by the question of why its growth became sluggish.

There are almost too many explanations. British plants and equipment were old and owners hesitated to undertake the cost of modernizing or replacing them. Well-established firms often made it hard for new companies to get a start. British schooling was weak in technical subjects, and education provided less opportunity for social mobility than on the Continent. Indeed, social attitudes, always difficult to analyze, may explain more than strictly economic factors. British industrialists, slow to appreciate the specialist and resistant to new ways, became less venturesome and perhaps a little complacent. Even so, London remained the financial capital of the world—a world in which industrialization was rapidly spreading to Sweden and Italy, Russia and Japan.

That important change was tied to others. Industrialization no longer depended so directly on the possession of critical natural resources like coal and iron ore but benefited from foreign investment and imported tech-

## INDUSTRIAL PRODUCTION (THOUSANDS OF METRIC TONS)

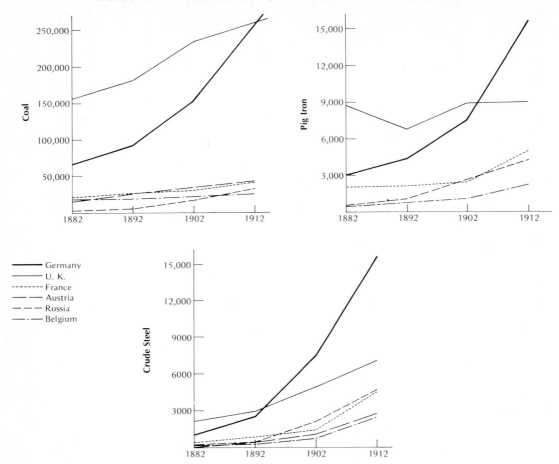

nology. Newly industrializing countries did not necessarily adopt liberalism but expected large banks to play a central role and accepted heavy state involvement.

### Technological and Market Developments

Industrial expansion in this period was closely tied to new technology. By 1890 Europe was producing even more steel than iron, using the Bessemer converter developed in the 1860s, which permitted far higher temperatures in smelter furnaces; and subsequent discoveries made lower-grade ores profitable. British, German, and French maritime shipping, which doubled between 1870 and 1914, depended on faster and larger steamships. New chemical processes and synthetics led to improved products ranging from dyes, textiles, and paints to fertilizers and explosives. A whole new industry developed to produce and supply electricity. The incandescent lamp created a demand for large generating stations to distribute power over a wide area, and by 1900 the manufacture of generators, cables, and motors, in turn, allowed increased and cheaper production in scores of other fields.

As striking as the new technology itself was the speed with which it was adapted to commercial uses. The telephone, invented in 1879, became a business necessity and an established private convenience within a few decades. The steam turbine, shown in the 1880s to be more efficient than the reciprocating engine, was widely employed for a variety of tasks, and it could soon be fueled by oil as well as coal. Home sewing machines and bicycles were created directly for the consumer market—in itself a significant reflection of the growing purchasing power of the masses. Inventions were now expected to change people's lives; the automobile in the 1890s, the airplane in the 1900s, and the radio a decade later were all greeted with enthusiasm even before their commercial possibilities were established.

Although greater prosperity and growing populations increased the demand for food, the percentage of the population that made its living in agriculture continued to decline, down to only 8 percent in Britain, 22 percent in Belgium, and 35 percent in Germany. In France, which maintained a more balanced economy (as did the Netherlands and Sweden), 43 percent of the population lived off the land. But everywhere the wider use of machinery and chemical fertilizers increased the capital investment required for farming, and improved transportation intensified international competition. These factors encouraged much greater specialization. The most famous example is Denmark, where agriculture began to center on a highly capitalized and profitable dairy industry. But in France, too, wheat and sheep production declined in favor of wine grapes and sugar beets, which farmers could raise more profitably. Britain now imported almost all its grain and Germany, a great deal.

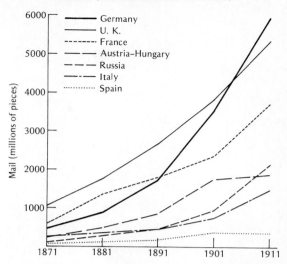

**MAIL (MILLIONS OF PIECES)**

Germany
U. K.
France
Austria–Hungary
Russia
Italy
Spain

The volume of mail has been used by some scholars as an indicator of modernization, reflecting increased literacy, internal communication, and commercial activity. In these terms, then, the relative position of the several nations on this chart is suggestive of more than gross population, as are the points at which Germany surpasses first France and then the United Kingdom or at which Russia surpasses Italy and then Austria-Hungary.

The influx of agricultural produce from the Americas and Eastern Europe, especially Russia, pushed prices down at the same time that farmers desperately needed cash for the improvements required to make farming profitable, and more young men were forced to leave the countryside. European agriculture was caught in recurrent crises, and landed interests pressed their governments for help. The most common response was protective tariffs, increased by France, Germany, Austria, Russia, Italy, and Spain. Initially applied primarily to agriculture, the new tariffs were soon extended to manufactured goods as well, reversing the earlier trend toward the liberal policy of free trade.

*The Great Eastern,* **combining steam and sail in massive square lines, looms over all other vessels in this print of 1861.** (Photo: The Granger Collection)

But the trade barriers did not stop the general decline in prices. Strangely, the second industrial revolution occurred in one of the longest and most severe periods of deflation in European history. From the 1870s to 1896, prices, interest rates, and profits fell, with far-reaching effects. Handicraft industries, which had survived side by side with mechanized manufacturing throughout Europe, were forced out of business. So were numerous smaller and less efficient industrial firms. As competition sharpened, many industrialists welcomed the support governments could give through tariffs, state spending, and colonial empire. The great boom in railroad building ended, and governments had to save socially useful lines deserted by bankrupt companies. Economic demands became a central theme of politics as more and more of economic life centered on great factories owned by large corporations (and closely tied to banks and government) that employed hundreds of workers who, in turn, increasingly organized into industrial unions.

## The Demographic Transformation

The growing population that sustained the second industrial revolution evolved a quite different demographic profile from that of any previous period. Europe's population increased—from 295 million in 1870 to nearly 450 million by 1914—although in most of Europe birth rates had begun to decline. By the 1880s, however, mortality rates were falling

## THE TRANSFORMATION FROM SAILING VESSELS TO STEAMSHIPS

Three stages of conversion to steam power

——— from the first date on which steamships first equaled sailing ships in tonnage to the date on which the ratio was 2:1.

‒‒‒‒ from the date on which the ratio of the tonnage of steamships was twice that of sailing ships to the date on which the ratio was 5:1.

·········· from the date on which the ratio of tonnage of steamships to sailing ships was 5:1 to the date on which the ratio was 10:1.

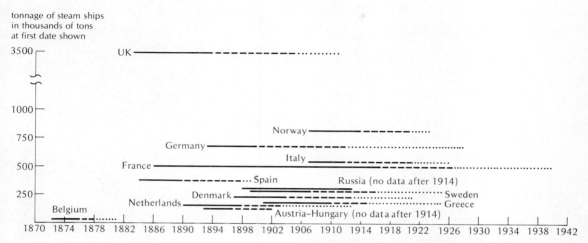

still more steeply. This pattern of falling birth rates combined with a sharper decline in mortality rates has been named the demographic transition. Continuing in our own time, it has become one of the marks of modernity that has spread from Europe to the rest of the world.

Infant mortality, in particular, was reduced by improved sanitation, better diet, and the virtual elimination of diseases such as cholera and typhus. By the turn of the century, improvements in medical care were lowering mortality rates still further. This left a net population growth despite a declining birth rate.[1]

Declining death rates, then, reflect the

This chart suggests several points about the conversion to steam from sail that are indicative of the process of industrialization in general: (1) most nations began the process at about the same time except for one or two early leaders, and (2) nations with a smaller investment in a preindustrial economy could convert to new technology more rapidly (Belgium and Spain, for example) so that even late-starters (such as Norway, Italy, and Greece) caught up with the others in the proportion of their ships driven by steam. Note the characteristic contrast between the United Kingdom and France. Britain, with a much larger fleet, converted to steam at a brisk pace, whereas France did so very slowly.

benefits of industrial prosperity, but the declining birth rates indicate a subtler change. The number of children a family had was becoming more a matter of choice, aided by the spread of contraception; and where bourgeois values took root and child labor declined, workers followed the upper classes in the trend toward later marriage, fewer births,

[1] "Birth rate" is used here as the more familiar term, but "fertility rate"—the ratio of the number of children born to the number of women of child-bearing age—would be more precise.

and smaller families. Although the issues are complicated and the statistics uncertain, the estimates of crude birth rates in about 1910 suggest the social significance of this changing pattern: They were highest in Rumania, Bulgaria, Portugal, Hungary, Italy, and Spain, and lowest in Switzerland, Belgium, and France. Parents who were confident their children would live, who wanted them to inherit property and receive some education, chose to have fewer of them. Before 1850 population growth had been higher in Western than in Central and Eastern Europe. That now was reversed, and the enormous increases in the populations to their east gave the French added reason to fear Germany's larger and younger population and Germans cause to worry about the Russian giant.

## Migration

Another extraordinary demographic change resulted from the greatest voluntary movement of peoples in human history. Like the second industrial revolution, this wave of migration continued a century-old trend, but once again the scale of the change was unprecedented. Between 1875 and 1914 some 26 million Europeans emigrated overseas, more than half of them to the United States. The growth of population, an established pattern of internal migration to cities, unemployment in Europe and burgeoning opportunities in the New World, larger boats and cheaper fares, and visions spread by literacy of a better life all pushed Europe's lower classes to crowd into the steerage of ship after ship. More people left the United Kingdom than any other countnry; in proportion to population the greatest exodus was from Ireland. Before 1890 the United

**Launching an early version of a French airplane.** (Photo: J.-H. Lartigue from Rapho Guillumette)

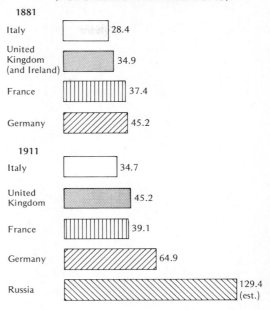

**THE CHANGE IN NATIONAL POPULATIONS AT THE TURN OF THE CENTURY (POPULATION IN MILLIONS)**

**1881**

| | |
|---|---|
| Italy | 28.4 |
| United Kingdom (and Ireland) | 34.9 |
| France | 37.4 |
| Germany | 45.2 |

**1911**

| | |
|---|---|
| Italy | 34.7 |
| United Kingdom | 45.2 |
| France | 39.1 |
| Germany | 64.9 |
| Russia | 129.4 (est.) |

Kingdom, the Scandinavian countries, and Germany sent migrants in the highest proportion to their population. After 1890 the leaders were the United Kingdom, Italy, Spain, and Portugal. But every nation except France (Europe's major receiver of immigrants) contributed significant numbers to the movement.

Perhaps a third of those who left their native land to go overseas eventually returned home, but for every one who took a ship, countless more moved from countryside to town and town to city (see Map A-27 in the Cartographic Essay). Mainly the young and the poor, they were responding to new ambitions as well as perennial misery. In doing so, they added to the restless change within Europe—in most cities a majority of residents had been born elsewhere—and carried European languages and cultures around the world. This economic and de-

**EMIGRATION FROM EUROPE**

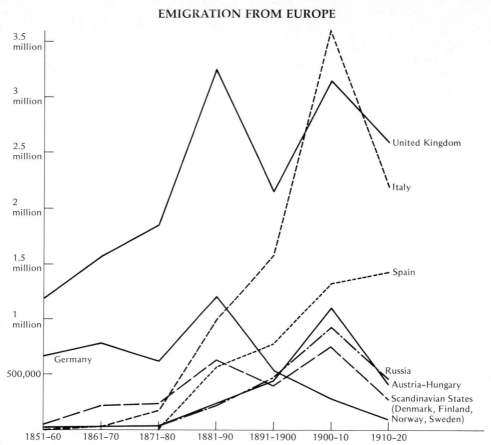

(Source: Mitchell, B. R., *Europe Historical Statistics, 1750–1970*, 1975, p. 135.)

mographic growth reinforced the dynamism of late-nineteenth-century society. New products, new businesses, new careers flourished everywhere, along with more freedom, education, and social mobility. Industrial civilization and progress reached into the peasant hut and the urban slum.

Even the lower classes benefited from the new prosperity. Meat and white bread became an expected although not daily part of the diet for most people in the industrialized countries. Commerce offered cheap products at fixed prices, and jobs in sales and distri-

bution brought new opportunities to rise into the lower-middle class. As they became better paid, industrial workers were pleased to see their wives give up their factory jobs, and unions argued for a "family wage" to make that possible. Women, particularly those between the ages of 15 and 25, still constituted about one-third the work force, concentrated in poorly paying jobs. Most working-class women continued to supplement family income by such tasks as taking in washing, sewing, making artificial flowers, or forming matchboxes, usually with the aid of their

**The new electric tram scoots above the ordinary bustle of the streets of Paris in the 1880s.** (Photo: The Granger Collection)

small children. If domestic service remained the primary occupation for young girls, those with some education could increasingly consider teaching, nursing, or clerical work.

City crowds in London, Paris, and Berlin in 1900 were strikingly different from those of 1850. They were larger—for cities were bigger (8 European cities had a population of half a million or more in 1880, 29 by 1910) and even workers had some free time—and they were healthier and cleaner. Their costumes told less about their trade or region; the worker could afford a dress suit, and the shopgirl could wear clothes that were not a mere uniform of her class. Fewer pickpockets and almost no beggars circulated in the streets. By 1900 nearly every city had its

electric tramway, rapidly expanding the city beyond the circumferential boulevards that had replaced medieval walls, incorporating suburbs into a metropolitan area, and opening the prospect of better housing even for workers. The more fortunate of these could even aspire to an apartment with indoor plumbing.

There was good reason then for belief in progress. Yet such rapid changes were unsettling, fatal for some occupations and hard on whole regions. In this turbulent society, misery and insecurity were less tolerable and harder to excuse. Seen as the by-products of

## DEMOGRAPHIC TRANSITION

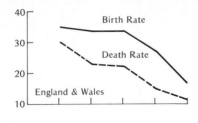

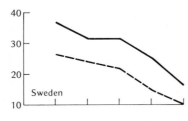

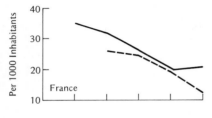

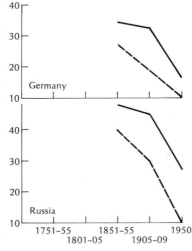

Per 1000 Inhabitants

(Source: Cipolla, Carlo, *The Economic History of World Population*, 1962.)

Note that everywhere both birth rates and death rates decline. The declining death rates reflect improved distribution of food and better hygiene and health care. The decline in birth rates reflects a change in social behavior. The space between them suggests the rate of population growth, very slight in the case of France, steady in England and Sweden, and sudden in Germany and Russia.

the very social system that produced so much wealth, they stimulated renewed efforts to change society itself.

## II. THE CULTURE OF INDUSTRIAL SOCIETY
❊

The 50 years before World War I was one of the great periods in the history of music, painting, and writing. Yet much of the artistic expression most admired today was disturbing to contemporaries, different from what they expected, and hard to understand. Instead, the public, though now more prosperous and literate, preferred commercial entertainments that offended intellectuals who found them wanting in either spontaneity or seriousness. But the expansion of knowledge, especially in the sciences, was such reassuring evidence of general progress that social theorists turned again, as the philosophes had done during the Enlightenment, to explaining it.

### Theories of Progress: Comte, Darwin, and Spencer

The philosophy of Auguste Comte (1798–1857), enormously influential from midcentury on, was itself characteristic of much nineteenth-century thought. Clearly rooted in the ideas on the Enlightenment, it gave greater attention to the process of historical change. Like Hegel, Comte sought to erect a comprehensive philosophical system that would encompass all of human knowledge, and like him, Comte believed that his own era had opened the final stage of historical development. Comte was especially impressed, as were most contemporary intellectuals, by the social role of religion, the conquests of natural science, and the possibilities of human progress. For many years private secretary to Saint-Simon, Comte retained the confidence of the early socialists that society would soon be reorganized on rational principles.

He systematically elaborated his positive philosophy in 10 volumes published between 1830 and 1845, and these, with his other writings, established positivism as an international movement even before his death, in 1857. The key to civilization, he argued, is humanity's understanding of the world, which has developed through three historical stages. In the first, the theological stage, humankind interpreted everything in terms of gods who lived in nature. In the second, or metaphysical, stage, people learned through Christianity to think in more abstract terms. In the third, or positive, stage now dawning, human understanding was becoming scientific through objective and precise observation followed by generalization in the form of scientific laws. Every science, he argued, has already passed through the first two stages and into the third—astronomy first, then physics, chemistry, and biology. Now a new science, sociology (Comte coined the term), must crown the progression.

While thus honoring the role of established religion, Comte announced its demise, substituting a "religion of humanity" of his own invention. Some devoted followers accepted his complex scheme whole. But his importance rests rather in the wider agree-

ment with his view that civilization progresses with increased knowledge discovered through scientific method and that the great contemporary need was for the scientific study of society and of humankind itself. This creed inspired and shaped much of the rapid development of the social sciences— economics, political science, anthropology, sociology, and psychology—achieved in the late nineteenth century.

A more concrete and more shocking theory of human progress emerged from Charles Darwin's *On the Origin of Species*, whose publication in 1859 was a milestone in the history of science.[2] With sober caution, Darwin (1809–1882) had worked much as Comte said a scientist should. Born into a well-known family of clergy and doctors with ties to many of England's leading intellectuals, Darwin had difficulty in finding a suitable career. But his respect for facts led him to collect evidence in matters of natural history from every available source—his own observations from travel in the South Seas, the work of others, the lore of farmers. He first formulated his concept of natural selection in 1838, but not until Alfred R. Wallace independently developed a very similar theory could he be persuaded to publish his findings. Although Darwin's presentation was the more fully and carefully developed, the parallel theories of the two men suggest how much both owed to ideas already current. Biologists had shown the relationship between biological form and function in impressive detail; geologists had begun to analyze the earth in terms of natural forces, without recourse to sudden cataclysms or divine intervention; classical economists, especially Malthus, had

---

[2] The full original title of Darwin's work suggests its broad and provocative implications: *On the Origin of Species by Natural Selection, or the Preservation of Favoured Races in the Struggle for Life.* The first edition sold out on the day of publication.

**With self-conscious art, the photographer of old Charles Darwin suggests some timeless mystery.** (Photo: New York Public Library/Picture Collection)

stressed the importance of the cruel conflict for food, which Darwin made the essential key to natural selection.

Darwin established that the variety of species is potentially infinite—rejecting the Classical and Christian idea of immutable forms in nature—and argued that there is an almost constant modification of species, each tested in the universal struggle for existence. He not only presented detailed evidence for evolution but described its mechanism: Those best adapted to their environment survived to reproduce, as did their progeny. Over millions of years more complex or "higher" forms of life emerged, each expanding as the environment and competition for food allowed.

This scientific theory, expressed with caution and supported by massive evidence, almost instantly became the center of controversies that raged throughout Europe for a generation. Evolution, mutable species, survival determined by brute conflict rather than divine will—each of these challenged established assumptions in science and theology. Nor did Darwin hide his belief that the same laws apply to the development of man and beast. This seemed to many a scandalous disregard of divine providence and Christian teaching. Nowadays, except for fundamentalists, theologians and scientists generally agree that there is no necessary conflict between the concept of evolving species and Christian doctrine, but such tolerance required a distinction between the study of natural laws and religious tradition that in the nineteenth century few were willing to make.

These principles were nevertheless quickly extended to more current concerns, a tendency that came to be called "social Darwinism." Few of the claims of social Darwinism were logically necessary extensions of Darwin's views; but reference to his grand theories added a universal meaning, scientific prestige, and a new vocabulary to contemporary debate. This usage tended to ignore the unimaginably long time span in which Darwinian theory operated and to extend by loose analogy the formal concept of species to groups, classes, nations, or civilizations. An invitingly tough-minded way to argue, social Darwinism could be used to support reform (improved education or social welfare represent a higher stage of evolution that will produce a stronger species) or revolution. More commonly, it was used to justify competition in the marketplace or between nations (as the mechanism of

**Building a monument to progress: Gustave Eiffel's bold engineering showpiece begins to rise in front of the more traditional (and temporary) structures of the World's Fair of 1889.** (Photo: The Bettmann Archive)

evolution) or to explain the dominance of Europeans over "colored" peoples or of men over women (as a natural expression of their relative positions on the evolutionary scale). At its most extreme, social Darwinism presented the law of the jungle as realistic, scientific, and beneficial. It was usually not so unmodulated, but the assumptions of social Darwinism infiltrated to some degree most aspects of late-nineteenth-century social thought.

One of the grandest statements of the laws of progress was the *Synthetic Philosophy* of Herbert Spencer (1820–1903), published between 1860 and 1896. Spencer's ideas were closely tied to those of Comte and Darwin, and his contemporaries ranked him among the major philosophers of all time.

Spencer's central principle, which made progress "not an accident, but a necessity," was the evolution of all things from simplicity to complexity, from homogeneity to diversity. With heavy learning, he traced this process in physics and biology, sociology and psy-

chology, economics and ethics. Such comprehensiveness was part of his appeal, and he applied his theses to physical matter, to human understanding, and to social institutions. He was admired for his claim to be hard-headed and practical; but while he refused to worry about the metaphysical abstractions of traditional philosophy, he maintained the assumptions of a narrow and rigid liberalism. He argued that the marketplace is the true test of the fittest, and that it must be uninhibited by state intervention even in behalf of welfare or public education.

When Spencer died, in 1903, much of his work was already outmoded by new developments in the several disciplines, strict laissez faire had been abandoned even by most liberals, and his sort of rationalism had come under heavy attack. His confidence that universal laws of development enshrined the values of middle-class English Protestants would soon seem quaint to most people.

## The Natural Sciences

Discoveries in the natural sciences in this period supported the belief that a few universal principles underlie all existence. And in the nineteenth century these principles could still be understood, however imprecisely, by the educated public. The findings of science were expected to improve civilization through both their immediate application to technology and their contributions to general philosophy. Thermodynamics, the study of the relationship between heat and mechanical energy, provides an excellent example.

Building on theorems stated by Nicolas Sadi Carnot early in the century, thermodynamics became the core of nineteenth-century physics. It developed in many directions at once, treating practical problems of steam engines as well as fundamental properties of matter. By midcentury the combined work of scientists in many countries had established that formulas predicting the behavior of gases could be applied to the field of mechanics. This culminated in the mathematical formulation of the two fundamental laws of thermodynamics. One states the principle of the conservation of energy: Energy can be transformed into heat or work and back again but can be neither created nor destroyed. The other declares that any closed physical system tends toward equilibrium, a state in which heat is uniformly distributed and therefore cannot be used to produce work.[3] In practical terms, this means that heat can be made to do work only when connected through an engine to a cooler body. Philosophically, it invites speculation about the universe as a giant machine in which the level of energy must inexorably decline.

The study of magnetism advanced in a similar way from the work of Michael Faraday. He had shown in the 1830s and 1840s that lines of magnetic force are analogous to gravity and that electricity can induce magnetism (and vice versa—the principle of the dynamo). In 1873 James Clerk Maxwell published equations that described the behavior of electricity, magnetism, and light in terms of a single, universal system. Thus gravity, magnetism, electricity, and light were all related. By the end of the century, physics had established mathematical laws of theoretical beauty and practical power extending from the universe to the atom, which was then conceived of as a miniature solar system.

The fundamental generalizations of chemistry are contained in the periodic law and periodic table published by Dmitri Mendeleev in 1869. Compounds and elements had been clearly distinguished for only half a century, and the difference between molecules and atoms came to be generally accepted only in 1860. Yet Mendeleev's table established a marvelous symmetry, so precise that the elements could all be charted by atomic weight, with similar elements occurring at regular intervals. This regularity even allowed for the prediction of unknown elements that would, when discovered, fill the gaps in the table.

Such achievements resulted from the efforts of hundreds of scientists, freely exchanging ideas across national boundaries, working with precise methods and the logic of mathematics. Experiments admired in the 1820s seemed crude by the 1870s, and science became the province of carefully trained professionals rather than inspired amateurs. Research demanded even more systematic organization and larger and more expensive laboratories. The success of science stimu-

---

[3] The measure or amount of energy unavailable for work is called entropy, a term coined by the physicist Rudolf Clausius in 1865.

lated a general expansion of education, and most of the disciplines that constitute the modern university achieved their separate identity, establishing professional organizations and scholarly journals, in the late nineteenth century.

Much of the theoretical scientific knowledge opened the way to very practical benefits. Thermodynamics led to the development of more efficient sources of power. The investigations of electricity led to the telegraph by midcentury and to electric lights and motors for hundreds of uses a generation later. Proof that germs were not spontaneously generated as was generally believed came from the Frenchman Louis Pasteur's studies in the 1860s of why wine spoiled, which led to techniques of pasteurization, of crucial importance in the wine, dairy, and silk industries. His work on immunology enabled him to find a preventive vaccine for rabies. In England Joseph Lister discovered that germs could be killed by carbolic acid, and the application of that knowledge made surgery a reasonable remedy rather than a desperate gamble. A decade later Robert Koch in Germany showed that different diseases were caused by distinct microbes, discovered the microorganism responsible for tuberculosis, and opened the way to new techniques in bacteriology and in the battle against communicable diseases. Advances such as these not only improved agriculture and medicine but stimulated the drive to make sanitation and public health into systematic sciences. Tangible evidence, as well as intellectual pride, supported the view that science progressed at an unprecedented pace for the benefit of all humankind.

## Formal and Popular Culture

The creative arts continued to flourish, benefiting from high prestige and ever larger and more sophisticated audiences. Yet the forms and styles employed grew so diverse that the arts hardly seemed to speak for a single civilization. One reason, and the one that disturbed contemporaries least, was the trend toward national styles. The use of folk elements and distinct traditions gave an instantly recognizable national identity to English or Russian novels and French, German, or Russian music. Another reason for the variety of artistic styles was the tendency for artists to act as social critics, thereby bringing issues of politics and values that troubled society into the realm of aesthetics. Thus the tension between the individual and society, between the artist's personal perceptions and the unstable conventions of a world undergoing rapid change, remained a central theme of nineteenth-century art. These concerns and then the reaction against them in favor of a "purer" art led to the bewildering variety of competing movements. "Naturalism," the "Pre-Raphaelites," "Impressionism," the "Decadents," "Symbolism"—such self-conscious labels were frequently proclaimed with angry manifestoes against previous art and present culture.

Naturalists claimed that the artist, like a scientist, should present life in objective detail after careful research. This aim was particularly suited to the novel; and Emile Zola, with descriptions precise as acid of industrial and Parisian life, was a master of the school. Determinism, through blood inheritance or social class, was a favorite and related theme in this Darwinian age. It proved especially effective on the stage where the protagonists' destiny inexorably unfolded before the new audience slowly won over to realistic drama in the two decades before World War I.

For the realistic painters of midcentury or the Pre-Raphaelites of England (who took their name from the pious and simpler art of the early Renaissance), much of a painting's importance lay in its subject matter and message. Then a new generation of painters broke with this tradition to concentrate on capturing the effects of light and color almost as if the artist's brilliance in analyzing and recreating such effects was in itself the purpose of painting. Artists denied exhibition at the annual Paris Salon in 1867 established the Salon des Refusés, proudly contesting the validity of official taste. These are the painters we remember, for they included some of the leaders of Impressionism (see Plates 58–59), whose golden age was the 1870s and 1880s, among them Auguste Renoir and Claude Monet. They and the Post-Impressionist Paul Cézanne were recognized in their own lifetime as ranking among the great artists of Western history, but painters only slightly younger, like Paul Gauguin and Vincent van Gogh, turned to still newer and more personal styles (see Plates 60–62).

Thus each of the arts tended to develop on its own terms, independent of established judgments. Art nouveau, turning its back on the practical and efficient industrial world of the turn of the century, delighted in applying ornamental arabesques to everything from wrought iron to poster lettering and printed cloth. Poetry, like painting, became an increasingly private expression indifferent to conventional morality, often obscure, and constructed in terms of complex aesthetic doctrines. The fashionable fascination with death, languid despair, and perfumed aestheticism was called decadent by its critics, a label willingly accepted until it gave way to Symbolism. A movement of French poets that spread throughout Europe, Symbolism interpreted the things one sees and describes as symbolic of a deeper and more spiritual reality. Art, like life itself, was to be complexly understood on several levels of meaning at once, and individual style had become a personal conquest, a private bridge between the identity of the artist and the external society. Still more radical changes in the arts occurred in the decade preceding World War I. These were changes that further separated the artist from the broader public, but they would shape the art of the twentieth century.

In contrast, architecture, the most immediately social of all the arts, was the least innovative until the very end of the century. Only then were the structural and aesthetic possibilities hidden in railroad sheds, bridges, and exhibit halls developed into the skyscraper and a new architectural style. Perhaps the tension between individual and society so fruitful elsewhere was stultifying to so public and functional an art. Even when they achieved real beauty, the great buildings of the nineteenth century were eclectically dressed in the styles of other periods. Churches evoked the spiritual coherence of the High Middle Ages; banks and public buildings expressed in stone the civic virtues of Greece and Rome. Even apartment houses usually imitated some earlier epoch, as if to make new wealth feel more secure.

## Popular Culture

European popular culture changed radically in the second half of the century. Traditional festivals and games, once tied to the local region, gradually gave way to public amusements reflecting an increasingly urban life and the greater leisure and wealth of the masses. With each change to a new popular medium, from operetta to music hall to vaudeville and—after the turn of the century—silent films, a larger part of the population shared in public entertainment. Popular culture thus tended to become more uniform within each nation and across Europe. It also became more formal (the Marquis of Queensberry rules for boxing, for instance, date from 1867) and increasingly commercial, both in the music hall and on the athletic field. Leading actors and actresses became stars whose offstage lives were part of their fascination. Light enter-

**For this picture of Berlin published in 1908 by Germany's leading illustrated paper, *Illustrierte Zeitung*, the artist emphasized the romantic excitement of a modern city, knitted together by speeding trolleys, boats, and trains.** (Photo: Polster Archive)

tainment, along with the circus and amusement parks, was an important business, whose clientele included families from the lower-middle and working classes. Soccer, once the sport of the English public school, became professional (most of Europe's famous teams were formed around the turn of the century), attracting huge, noisy Sunday crowds. While workers shared these urban entertainments, the middle classes began to crowd summer resorts and to play recently formalized games like golf and tennis. This profitable popular culture assumed and to some extent created an audience with common tastes and in doing so helped bridge the social gap between workers and the middle class, between town and city. Newspapers had similar effects as publishers learned to

increase their circulation (several now approached daily sales of a million copies) through sensational articles and colorful features written in a direct and less literary style. Like the millions of popular novels (now more specialized into women's romances, adventure stories especially for children, and penny thrillers), such writing abandoned any pretense to cultivated taste, further separating formal from popular culture.

These changes were related to another of immeasurable importance: For the first time in Western history, in the major nations at least, a majority of the adult population could read and write. By the 1880s governments almost everywhere, recognizing the importance of literacy to politics and industry, had made education universal and compulsory; and school fees had been reduced or eliminated. In 1850 only in Prussia could most of the adult population read or write; by 1900 more than 90 percent of the adult population of Germany, France, and Great Britain was literate, and the proportion elsewhere was climbing rapidly. Mass schooling was usually limited to a few years of the most elementary subjects, and aside from special supplementary instructions in workers' classes, night schools, and special vocational institutes, few of the poor had any opportunity for further training. The amount and kind of education they received was one of the clearest distinctions between the middle class and those below it. Nevertheless, the schooling available to everybody was steadily extended, and the barriers separating mass education from the preparation that led to secondary school and university were gradually lowered.

For most contemporaries, society's extraordinary commitment to education ranked with liberty, industrial prosperity, and scientific knowledge as proof of social progress. But there were some who saw in the quality of popular entertainment and mass journalism an ominous new threat to Western culture.

## III. ATTACKS ON LIBERAL CIVILIZATION
❈

Much of liberalism's promise was being fulfilled in the last quarter of the nineteenth century. After 1870 new constitutions made governments more representative and civil rights more secure; expanding trade and production lifted the standard of living, and individuals enjoyed greater social opportunities; laws became more humane; peace, foreign and domestic, seemed more certain. Yet many intellectuals expressed contempt for middle-class society, radicals sought the end of the capitalist system, and conservatives and Christians mounted new attacks on liberal values. As liberalism itself broadened into greater concern for social justice, its optimistic assumptions about the nature of progress and humanity's rationality were strongly challenged.

## Marxism

No criticism of contemporary society has proved more influential, no nineteenth-century theory more lasting than the work of Karl Marx. Marx was born in 1818 into a middle-class Rhineland Jewish family that had prospered with the emancipation from civil disabilities brought by the revolutionary armies from France. He was an able student and received an excellent education at the leading German universities. Too radical to be permitted an academic career, he turned to journalism and became editor of a famous liberal newspaper, the *Rheinische Zeitung*. But his attacks on censorship and his views on economics led the Prussian government to demand his removal, and in 1843 Marx left for Paris. There he met other exiles and leading French radicals, men to whom he would later give the enduring label of "utopian" socialists, and he established a friendship with Friedrich Engels that would become a lifetime's collaboration.

Trained in German philosophy, abreast of contemporary economics, and in touch with the currents of radicalism, Marx began in Paris the systematic development of his own ideas. He outlined his theory in a powerful, apocalyptic tone in the *Communist Manifesto*, written jointly with Engels, which was published just before the revolutions of 1848. Little noticed at first, it proved to be one of the great pieces of propaganda of all time, a specific program and a general call to action combined with a philosophy of history. Marx devoted the rest of his life—from 1849 to 1883, which he spent in poverty-stricken exile in London—to the painstaking elaboration of his ideas in essays, letters, and the first volume of *Das Kapital,* published in 1867. Engels, who shared Marx's exile in Britain, edited the second and third volumes, which appeared in 1885 and 1894.

Marx wrote with verve on contemporary affairs—his essays on the revolutions of 1848 and Louis Napoleon's coup d'état are classics—but fundamentally he wanted, like so many thinkers of his time, to build a comprehensive philosophical system. Later in the century his followers would compare him with Darwin as the "discoverer" of the "law" of history, dialectical materialism. The dialectic came from Hegel, the struggle between thesis and antithesis leading to a synthesis as the next stage in historical evolution. Marx, however, rejected Hegel's idealism—the view that the dialectic works through ideas that constitute the spirit of the age—insisting instead that any society rests fundamentally on the organization of its economy, the mode of production.

Political systems, Marx said, grow from these material underpinnings, and in each, the dominant social class expresses the needs, the values, and the interests associated with that particular mode of production. The agricultural economy of the Middle Ages required the feudal system with its particular social values and laws, upheld by the landowning aristocracy. That system produced its antithesis in the middle class, which is based on capitalism. But capitalist and industrial society dominated by the middle class was, in turn, producing a new antithesis through its own contradictions and embodied in the

Something of the power of his personality shows through this photograph of Karl Marx, the scholar (with reading glass) and bourgeois. (Photo: The Granger Collection)

rising proletariat. Class conflict is the mechanism of historical progress, and the triumph of the proletariat will bring a new synthesis, a classless society. History would thus lead, by its own inevitable laws, to a world similar to the one envisioned by other socialists. In the classless society, people would no longer be forced into the inequality required for capitalist production. At present, compulsion is the primary purpose of the state, but in the new era the state would wither away, unneeded.

Revolutions, in this analysis, mark the arrival to power of a new class. They are, however, more than mere transfers of power. A new class brought changes in law, religion, and customs, which it then maintained in its own interest. The middle class, in Marxist terms, has represented a great, progressive force. But capitalism, despite all the ideologies and social institutions designed to shore it up, will fail through its own internal contradictions.

Marx's detailed analysis of capitalism took much from the classical economists (at a time when they were beginning to be outmoded). The value of a product, he insisted somewhat obscurely, comes from the value of all the labor required to produce it—to transform raw materials into manufactured goods. The capitalist makes a profit by keeping part of the value added by others' labor, by exploiting the working class. But capitalists must compete with each other, and to do so, they are forced to lower prices, which, in turn, reduces profits. This has two effects. First, the capitalist must exploit labor more harshly, cutting wages to the minimum required for subsistence. Second, the smaller producers will fail, which will lead to increased concentrations of capital and force more and more members of the middle class into the proletariat, composed of people with nothing but their labor to sell. Thus a shrinking capitalist class suffering from declining profits will face a growing proletariat. Capitalism therefore lays the basis for socialism by depriving all but a few of property. The contradictions will be resolved when the whole system fails.

Many of Marx's specific predictions now seem wrong. Although some of the rich have grown richer, the poor are not poorer. Marx simply did not see much that is central to the modern economy—ever-expanding technology, the spread of ownership through public sale of stocks, and mass consumption. He did not anticipate the social effects of literacy, popular democracy, and mass communication. Marxist psychology is inadequate, with little acknowledgment of the loyalties and the irrationality so important in human personality. He sought to combine in one system Hegel's most difficult ideas, the economic theories of liberalism, the "scientific" method of positivism, and the moral vision of socialism—a combination awkward at best. Such critical terms as "class" and "state" remained ambiguous, and the concept of class struggle, applied elastically to a petty event as well as centuries of history, lost its analytic force. The goal of history, according to Marx, is the classless society; yet he sketched that condition only vaguely and left unanswered fundamental questions about it and about the means of obtaining it.

## The Appeal of Marxism

Despite such weaknesses, and the theory's every flaw has been widely broadcast, Marxism has deeply affected all modern thought, shaped the policies of all sorts of governments, and provided a core for some of the most powerful political movements of the last century. Such impact requires explanation, and perhaps four points can capture something of the answer.

First, Marxism not only sees society as a whole and explains historical change but demands systematic and detailed analyses of the interrelationship of social values, institutions, politics, and economic conditions. It also suggests methods for conducting such analyses, which accounts for its continuing importance in all the social sciences.

Second, Marxism accepts and indeed hails industrialization as inevitable and beneficial even while accepting most criticisms of industrial society. Many reformers dreamed of green gardens and simpler days; but Marx believed the machine can free human beings from brute labor and through greater productivity provide well-being for all. Industrialization could be made to provide solutions to the very problems it created. Thus Marxism has special appeal for societies eager to modernize.

Third, the theory is rich in moral judgments without having to defend any ethical system. Although social values are considered relative, and those of his opponents denounced as hypocritical, Marx's own rage at injustice rings out in a compelling call to generous sentiments that rejects sentimentality.

Finally, Marxism claims the prestige of science and offers the security of determinism. Knowing where destiny leads, its believers can accept the uneven flow of change, confident that any defeats are temporary. Opponents are to be recognized and fought less for what they say or do than for what they represent—for their "objective" role in the structure of capitalism. Accepting concessions does not compromise the fight, for tactics can be very flexible when the only requirement is that they assist the inevitable movement of history toward the victory of the proletariat. Marx believed that small social changes may lead to sudden qualitative ones, and Marxists thus can favor immediate reforms as well as revolution.

The variety inherent in Marx's system has been a source of bitter division as well as strength among socialists, but it has helped keep Marxism more vigorous and coherent than any other of the grand theories spawned in the nineteenth century.

### The First International

Marx and Engels intended to be not merely authors of a theory but leaders of a political and social movement. When in 1864 a group of English labor leaders called a small international conference in London, Marx readily agreed to come as a representative of the German workers. The International Working Men's Asssociation, usually called the First International, was founded at that meeting, and Marx dominated it from the start. He did his best to replace traditional radical rhetoric about truth and justice with the hard language of Marxism, and during the eight years of the First International's life, he gradually succeeded in expelling those who disagreed.

The French members were generally followers of Louis-Auguste Blanqui and Pierre Joseph Proudhon, socialists for whom Marx had little use; he dismissed the Blanquists, with their fondness for violence and dreams of conspiracy, as romantic revolutionaries. His first socialist writing had been a critique of Proudhon's plans for workers' cooperatives and sympathy for anarchy. The International's English members did not accept Marx's emphasis on revolution or his claim that the Paris Commune was "the glorious harbinger of a new society."

The most important conflict, however, was with Mikhail Bakunin. A Russian anarchist, Bakunin had established himself as one of Europe's more flamboyant revolutionaries in 1848. Later sentenced to exile in Siberia, he escaped in 1861, eventually joining the International in 1867. Bakunin respected Marx and understood his materialist philosophy, while Marx seems to have felt some of the fascination of Bakunin's personality. But Bakunin supported nationalism and praised the revolutionary spirit of countries like Italy and Spain, whereas Marx insisted that the revolutionary cause was international and most promising in more industrial lands. The Russian's delight in conspiracies and plots seemed childish to the German expatriate; and Bakunin, who distrusted any state, found a dangerous authoritarianism in Marx and Marxism.

The 1872 meeting, at which Bakunin was expelled, was the First International's last, for

# ❄ EXPERIENCES OF DAILY LIFE ❄
## *Women at Work*

The latter part of the nineteenth century brought great changes in the daily lives of ordinary men and women, but changes specifically affecting women came more slowly and unevenly. As women lived longer and bore fewer children, aspects of life beyond marriage and motherhood assumed increased importance; the legal and cultural constraints placed upon women solely because of their sex became more apparent. In every industrial country women's movements demanded greater opportunity and equality for women, and everywhere resistance was formidable.

The most widespread changes came with greater industrialization and urbanization, which created more jobs for women. By the second half of the nineteenth century, most women worked for wages from the early teens until marriage. Increasingly, they continued to do so after marriage, an often essential contribution to the income of families that could not pay city prices for rent and food on one man's wages. The increase in the number of women workers was especially noticeable in Germany, Italy, and the Scandinavian countries, where industrialization was more recent; and the proportion of women who worked for pay was highest in France (about 40 percent of all women; the proportion of married women who worked was twice as high there as in England). Jobs, however, remained tightly tied to gender. More women in England and Germany were employed as domestic servants than in any other field. Next came work as a laundress, seamstress, chambermaid, or waitress. Only about one-fifth of working women were employed in factories, and there women were usually assigned tasks associated with domestic skills, or older, preindustrial forms of labor. The proportion of women workers in textile industries steadily rose, from a third to nearly half of those employed in English wool, from more than half to two-thirds of those in Italian silk, from less than half to a majority of those in the cotton industries of England, France, and Germany.

Women were less numerous in the burgeoning industries of the second industrial revolution (the metal industry or transportation, for example, hired few women) than in more stagnant industries where pay was lower. Women were paid less than men in any case, from half to two-thirds as much even for quite comparable work. And far more women than men did piecework, making buttons or cardboard boxes in shops or working at home. The garrets of every city were filled with women living in tiny rooms where they worked at making hats, artificial flowers, and lace late into the night. Isolated, such workers found it hard to resist ruthless entrepreneurs who demanded rapid work and then subtracted from their miserable pay for every flaw. There were also many new jobs in the service sector. As cities grew, more women were needed to wash, iron, and mend clothes, the classic job for a girl newly arrived in the city. Small shops, and more slowly, the great department stores hired women as clerks, preferably women from the lower middle class who could speak and dress in the ways expected by a bourgeois clientele. A few of the famous stores provided dormitories for their employees, including the women who handled correspondence or prepared catalogues. There, they might be provided with books to read and singing groups to join while kept under strict curfew. The city life of single women who supported themselves and lived alone worried moralists and titillated readers of the sensational press.

Bit by bit women took over as bookkeepers, office clerks, and secretaries; and as an occupation came to be seen as women's work, pay, prestige, and opportunities for advancement declined. Such positions required elementary schooling; universal public instruction did make a difference. Some professions also opened to women, especially nursing (primarily provided by nuns in Catholic countries) and teaching in elementary school (by the end of the century three-quarters of the elementary school teachers in England were women, more than half of them in Sweden and France, and one-fifth of them in Germany). Many middle-class women devoted a great deal of time to charitable activities; and as social work became more professional, government agencies readily hired women to do it. Universities, never closed to women in Italy, slowly opened to a special few in France and England and, after the turn of the century, in Germany. Girls' secondary schooling became more institutional and substantial.

Everywhere, from the 1860s on, women began to organize. Often divided over goals and tactics, these movements tended to fall into three types. The first and largest were led by middle-class women and quite cautious in outlook, but they could effectively demonstrate the contradiction between cultural ideals that emphasized female purity and motherhood and social reality that subjected millions of women to desperate poverty and sometimes brutal conditions. By the 1880s and 1890s, more explicitly feminist and radical organizations came to the fore, particularly in England and Germany. Aware that their demands required fundamental social change, they were often drawn toward the Labour and Social Democratic parties, where they met a mixed response. And many feminists worried that laws regulating women's work would tend to preserve paternalistic attitudes and to close off new opportunities. A third response centered in the growing women's trade union movement, more concerned with immedi-

ate problems of pay and working conditions. Employers' resistance, the nature of women's work, and low pay made unionization difficult, however, as did the resentment of men who saw women as a threat to their jobs and higher wages. When a British trade union leader declared it their "duty as men and husbands . . . to bring about a condition of things where wives should be in their proper sphere at home," he spoke for most of his sex of every class (and quite possibly for a majority of women).

By 1910, however, mosts European nations had passed laws protecting women workers, increasing women's rights to dispose of property, to share in decisions affecting their children, and to take part in civic life (the ban forbidding women to attend public political meetings in Germany was lifted in 1908), allowing wives independent control of the money they earned (1884 and 1910 in France), and even establishing a minimum rate for piece work (England, 1910). Dominant attitudes had changed only a little, but all the talk of the new woman, women in schools, on bicycles, speaking at public meetings and demonstrations, and the examples of outstanding achievements by individual women—in science, medicine, education, literature, art, economics, and social reform—indicated that the ice of necessity and custom was breaking up. ✳

**Women at work in a Coventry cycle factory in the 1890s.** (Photo: the Mansell Collection)

Marx and Engels then let the association die. Its membership had never been large or even clearly defined. Yet it played a part in building a workers' movement by disseminating Marxism, by teaching others to view each strike or demonstration as part of a larger conflict, by stressing the international ties of workers in a period of nationalism, and by exemplifying the advantages of militant discipline. In these ways and in its intolerance of doctrinal error and its intemperate polemics, the First International helped set the tone of the growing socialist movement.

## Socialism and Anarchism

Between 1875 and World War I, socialist parties became an important part of political life in nearly every European country. Except in Great Britain, most of them were at least formally Marxist. As they began to win elections, socialists disagreed over whether to follow a more moderate policy aimed at electoral success or adhere rigidly to the teachings of Marx. The most common compromise combined moderate policies with flaming rhetoric, and the Second International, formed in 1889 with representatives from parties and unions in every country, sought to maintain doctrinal rigor and socialist unity. Thus the Marxian critique of liberalism and capitalism was spread through books, newspapers, and magazines; in parliamentary debate; and in every election.

Labor organizations outside Germany were not often consistently Marxist, but their growth was another dramatic change of the period. Unions were everywhere class-conscious, frequently tempted by anarchism and suspicious of politics. Their membership soared, with millions of workers paying dues in the industrialized countries, and the strike became the common expression of social protest. Skilled artisans, threatened by new modes of production yet strengthened by their own traditions of cooperation, were often still the leaders in militant action; but the organization of labor spread especially in larger factories despite the forceful resistance of employers and of the state. In the last decades of the century European society faced the most extensive labor agitation it had ever known. Yet strikes were coming to be better organized and more orderly as well as larger, and they sometimes won important public sympathy.

Most people did not distinguish very clearly among the various radical movements and associated anarchist "propaganda of the deed" with socialists and labor organizers. Certainly anarchists were in the headlines; they assassinated the president of France in 1893, the prime minister of Spain in 1897, the empress of Austria in 1898, the king of Italy in 1900, and the president of the United States in 1901. In the 1880s and 1890s, bombs were thrown into parades, cafés, and theaters in cities all over Europe, and such incidents were followed by the arrest of radical suspects and spectacular trials.

But bomb throwers and assassins were only a tiny wing of the broad anarchist movement. Its intellectual tradition was continuous since the time of the French Revolution, and its most famous figure after Bakunin was Prince Peter Kropotkin, an exiled Russian aristocrat. Kropotkin was a theorist whose gentleness and compassion made him a kind of spiritual leader, but his descriptions of anarcho-communism did not unify the movement. Some anarchists stressed individualism, some pacifism, and some the abolition of private property; all rejected imposed authority and denounced the state as a repressive machine serving the interests of wealth. They won their largest following among the poor who felt themselves crushed by industrialization: immigrants to the United States, peasants in southern Spain,

**John Burns, leader of a dock laborers' strike, addressing a crowd in London's East End in 1889.** (Photo: The Bettmann Archive/BBC Hulton Picture Library)

artisans and some industrial workers in Italy and France. Anarchism was influential in the opposition to bureaucratic centralization and to militarism, and it appealed to artists and writers who shared the anarchists' contempt for bourgeois values, while contributing heroes and martyrs to the growing mystique of the radical left.

These ideas and organizations contributed to the growing strength of the radical left. Vigorous debate sustained an intellectual energy in party meetings and newspapers that attracted many workers and intellectuals alike. More numerous, larger, and better-financed unions and political parties were active locally as well as nationally. Often they sponsored meeting places where workers could relax or study as well as plan concerted

action. All this activity did not produce unanimity. Disagreements over principles and tactics often exposed differences between skilled and unskilled workers, between workers in established trades and new industries, between men and women, and between labor unions and political parties. These conflicts have received a great deal of scholarly attention, partly because working-class leaders insisted so much on the importance of class unity; but there was a cultural and social basis as well for the growth of radical movements. Socialism, anarchism, and trade unions addressed feelings of brotherhood, justice, and common interest that had developed within working-class life. Expressed in songs and speeches, meetings, demonstrations, and strikes, they reflected shared values and experiences developed over generations. This common culture was reinforced by the fact that the conditions of wage labor became more similar across different industries and by housing patterns that created working-class districts. Radical ideas and labor movements linked the immediate issues of working-class life to broad principles and to national politics, generating responses and having effects on society that were significantly different in each nation. The common element was that everywhere a vigorous challenge to the established system had in some way to be met.

### The Christian Critique

The attack on liberalism came not only from the left but also from the pulpits of every Christian denomination. Individualism, the charges ran, is often mere selfishness; religious tolerance masks indifference to moral issues; progress is another name for materialism. Churches tended to reject the growing claims of the state, especially in education and welfare, and many Protestants and Catholics denounced the values and the injustices of capitalist society as forcefully as did the socialists.

The Roman Catholic Church was particularly hostile. In 1864 Pius IX issued an encyclical, *Quanta Cura*, with a syllabus of "the principal errors of our time" attached. Taken from earlier statements by the pope, its 80 items were written in the unbending tones of theological dispute. The syllabus listed false propositions, for example, declaring erroneous the opinion that ". . . it is no longer expedient that the Catholic religion should be held as the only religion of the State, to the exclusion of all other forms of worship."

Catholics more politic than the pope were quick to point out that this denunciation of formal error was not the same as advocating religious intolerance, but such subtleties were easily lost. The syllabus denounced total faith in human reason, the exclusive authority of the state, and attacks on traditional rights of the Church; but its most noted proposition was the last, which declared it false to think that "The Roman Pontiff can, and ought to, reconcile himself, and come to terms with progress, liberalism and modern civilization."

The Vatican Council of 1869–1870, the first council of the Church in 300 years, confirmed the impression of intransigence. It was a splendid demonstration of the Church's continued power, and prelates came from around the world to proclaim the dogma of papal infallibility. It declared that the pope, when speaking *ex cathedra* (that is, formally from the chair of Peter and on matters of faith and morals), is incapable of error. This had long been a traditional belief, and its elevation to dogma confirmed the trend toward increased centralization within the Church and affirmed the solidarity of Catholics in the face of new dangers. Even as the council met, the outbreak of the Franco-Prussian War allowed the Italian government to take the city of Rome for its capital, and governments throughout Europe wondered if Catholics could now be reliable citizens of a secular state.

The expanding role of government, especially in matters of education and welfare, made conflicts between church and state a major theme of European life. While theories of evolution, positivism, and biblical criticism put defenders of traditional belief on the defensive, politicians worried about the influence of the churches, particularly in rural areas and among national minorities, as anonymous masses of people were increasingly called to the polls.

In the United Kingdom the Church of England had steadily been stripped of its special privileges in moves opposed at every step by the clergy, most peers, and conservatives; but religious differences continued to inflame the Irish question. Bismarck launched and then abandoned the *Kulturkampf* as the German government relied more and more on the Catholic Center party. In Russia the Orthodox Church became, in effect, a department of state, used to strengthen the dominance of Russians in the multinational empire, while the Austrian government, in contrast, broke its close ties (and its concordat) with the Roman Catholic Church in an effort to lessen opposition to Viennese rule. The conflict between church and state was most open and bitter, however, in Spain, Italy, and France, where it was the central political division of the 1880s and 1890s.

Generally, these conflicts subsided somewhat after the turn of the century. Relatively secure states, having established the breadth of their authority, tended to become more tolerant; and anticlericalism came to seem outmoded as governments faced the rising challenge from the left. The churches, too, responded more flexibly, in the style of Pope Leo XIII (1878–1903), who established an understanding with Bismarck and encouraged French Catholics to accept the Third Republic.

At the same time, Christianity displayed renewed vigor. There was a general revival of biblical and theological studies, marked in the Roman Catholic Church by emphasis on the theology of St. Thomas Aquinas, whose arguments for the compatibility of faith and reason brought greater clarity and confidence to Catholic positions. Christian political and social movements learned to mobilize enormous support and became more active in social work (the Salvation Army, for example, was founded in 1865).

This engagement in charity, religious missions at home and overseas, education, labor unions, and hundreds of special projects not only strengthened Christian social influence but led to outspoken denunciations of immoral and unjust conditions. In his social encyclicals, especially *Rerum Novarum* issued in 1891, Leo XIII added a powerful voice to the rising cry for reform. He restated Catholic belief in private property, the sanctity of the family, and the social role of religion but went beyond these well-known views to speak to modern industrial conditions. The Catholic Church, he wrote, not only recognizes the right of workers to their own organizations and to "reasonable and frugal comfort" but warns the state against favoring any single class and society against viewing human beings as merely a means to profit.

The churches recognized the altered circumstances that left neither public institutions nor private habit reliable supports of religion. Strongest in rural areas and with more women communicants than men, they strove to improve their position in the cities among workers and the middle class. The adjustments were neither easy nor smooth, but by 1910 Christianity was more respectable among intellectuals, more active in society, and more prominent in politics than it had been since the early nineteenth century. Whether of the political left or right, Lutherans, Catholics, Anglicans, and Methodists found in Christianity a whole arsenal of complaints against liberalism and industrial capitalism.

## Beyond Reason

Until World War I European political thought remained predominantly liberal, but some of the optimism was fading. Liberals themselves made less of simple individualism and worried more about problems of community and social justice, and some writers even doubted that politics was much affected by the free exchange of ideas so dear to John Stuart Mill. Newer strains of thought questioned the power of human reason and argued for leadership by a small elite.

The Frenchman Georges Sorel shared the growing suspicion that public opinion owed more to prejudice than to reason. Like many intellectuals, he felt contempt for middle-class society but argued that its overthrow would not come in the way predicted by Marx. His most important book, *Reflections on Violence* (1908), postulated rather that historic changes like the rise of Christianity or the French Revolution come about when people are inspired by some great myth that stands beyond the test of reason. As a myth for his times, he proposed the general strike, a possibility then much discussed by European unions. Sorel thus contributed to the widespread syndicalist movement, which called on workers' organizations, *syndicats,* to bring down bourgeois society; his larger significance was his rejection of bourgeois rationalism in favor of violence and the will. Like many contemporary writers in Italy and Germany, he found the energy for change in humanity's irrationality.[4]

Sorel's countryman Henri Bergson, the most eloquent and revered philosopher of his day, expounded a gentle, abtruse set of theories. In touch with contemporary movements in the arts, psychology, and religion, he, too, pictured much that is best in human understanding as arising not from reason but intuitively from subjective and unconscious feelings. Society therefore should encourage a spirit of energy and common endeavor, favoring the spontaneity that translates feeling into action.

The revolutionary challenge such ideas

---

[4] Vilfredo Pareto and Sorel, both trained as engineers, are usually grouped together with Robert Michels as leading theorists of the new political "realism."

---

contained became clearer in the works of Friedrich Nietzsche. He, too, stressed the will in a philosophy that lashed contemporary civilization on every page. His disdain for ideas of equality and democracy was balanced by his hatred of nationalism and militarism; he rejected his society not only for what it was but also for what it meant to be. The only hope for the future was the work of the few, of supermen who would drop the inhibitions of bourgeois society and the "slave morality" of Christianity.

Nietzsche's tone had the violence of a man trying to bring everything crashing down, but he was no mere nihilist. He wrote his passionate aphorisms as a man in terror for himself and his world. A deeply original thinker, he was a child of his times in his approach to culture and history but above all in his anger.

## Anti-Semitism and the Right

Like Nietzsche's philosophy, anti-Semitism, which he detested, was part of the rising current of opposition to liberal society. Anti-Semitism in the 1890s was more than a continuation of centuries-old prejudices, and it was surprisingly universal. Venomous assertions of Jewish avarice and lack of patriotism were used to discredit the entire republic in France and opponents of imperial policy in Great Britain. Anti-Semitic parties elected 16 deputies to the Reichstag in 1893, and the prestigious Conservative party in Germany added anti-Semitism to its program. The lord mayor of Vienna from 1895 to 1910 found anti-Semitism invaluable in winning his electoral victories, and it was an official policy of the Russian government from the terrible pogroms of 1881 on.

There is no simple explanation for a phenomenon seemingly so contrary to the major trends of the century. One reason relates to the perception of Jews as a ready symbol of liberal, capitalist society; they had received their civil rights at the hands of Napoleon and in liberal revolutions, lived primarily in urban environments, and found their opportunities for advancement in the expanding professions and businesses of the nineteenth century. They were prominent leaders in many of the most venturesome enterprises, most important scientific discoveries, and most striking social theories. Nationalism, especially in Germany, had come to stress folk culture and race; by attacking Jews, conservatives could make the liberal, capitalist world itself seem alien to national traditions. Crude adaptations of Darwinism gave racial theories a pseudoscientific panache,[5] and indeed quack science generally flourished, for credulity was encouraged by the fact that much of academic science, especially physics, was no longer comprehensible to laymen. Theories of conspiracy gave concrete and simple explanations for the baffling pace of social change, offering the hope that by circumscribing specific groups—such as the Jews—society could resist change itself.

Neither irrationalism nor anti-Semitism belongs inherently to a single political persuasion, but both were used primarily by the political right in the decades preceding World War I. Rightist movements revived notably in these years, building on those social groups that felt most harmed by the changes of the century: aristocrats, rural people, members of the lower middle class whose status was threatened, and many Christians. Often incongruously, they defended established constitutions—the House of Lords in

Britain, the concordat with the Roman Catholic Church in France, three-class voting and government independent of the Reichstag in Germany, limited suffrage and an intrusive monarchy in Italy, the authority of the tsar in Russia. They added to this conservatism contemporary concerns about the shallowness of middle-class culture and the need for government intervention in behalf of a stable economy. A reinvigorated Right tried, frequently with success, to make patriotism and national strength their battle cry, learning to make an effective mass appeal. Denounced by Marxists as defenders of reactionary capitalism, they declared socialism the menace of the hour and the natural consequence of liberal error.

Thus critics from the right and the left gained vigor from attacking the very changes that most people still labeled progress. So many simultaneous assaults created grave political crises in many states, yet most achieved an altered equilibrium in which government accepted more responsibility for social justice, politics became more democratic, and society grew more tolerant. Never before had Europeans generally been so free to move about as they wished and say what they liked.

## IV. DOMESTIC POLITICS
❈

Growing populations and the second industrial revolution necessitated new policies, and every government had to meet the challenge. Each nation, building on its own traditions, had to readjust the relationship of its political system to its changing social structure. The element of continuity in progressive change particularly impressed contemporaries, but it is easier with hindsight to see the turn of the century as a period of conflicts that predicted much about the twentieth century.

[5] An important example is Houston Steward Chamberlain's *The Foundation of the Nineteenth Century,* published in Germany in 1899. A Germanophile Englishman and intense admirer of Wagner, Chamberlain traced all that was best in European civilization to its "Aryan" elements. The work was widely admired until the collapse of the Nazi regime.

**By the end of a century, the daring young woman was even encouraged to take to the motorcycle. Demurely dressed for the city, she could commute from the country, scattering the geese of an earlier era and passing the peasants by.** (Photo: Musée de la Publicité Union Centrale des Arts Decoratifs)

## The Broad Issues

These conflicts often revolved around four broad issues. One was the question of access to political life, of who would be allowed to participate and in what way. Most nations adopted some form of universal male suffrage operating through highly organized, mass political parties. A second question was the definition of the national community. Nearly everywhere the charge was made that some groups—ethnic minorities, foreigners,

Catholics, Jews, anarchists, or socialists—were of uncertain loyalty, a cause of the social disruptions that threatened the life of the nation. Such fears often provided the basis for recruiting groups previously excluded to new political activity. How those charges were handled took the measure of national traditions and in political terms of the relative strength of left and right. Usually, these clashes established bitter cleavages. Occasionally, there was an amicable resolution. When Norway voted for separation from Sweden in 1905, the decision was accepted peacefully, and the two nations lived thereafter in harmony, among the most democratic in the world.

A third issue was one of social justice, specifically the rights to be accorded workers and the role of the state in providing for social welfare. Generally, conflict over these matters led to recognition of union organization and the right to strike and also to national legislation and new state agencies to provide minimum guarantees for the welfare of all. The trend, then, was toward large organizations—parties, nationalist movements, and labor unions, all in direct contact with an enlarged and highly organized state.

A fourth issue, the place of women, was somewhat different. It touched on all these issues as well as sensitive ones of family and religion. Wherever society was urban and industrial, women's movements multiplied. Usually led by middle-class women, they were active on every front, seeking access to education, political rights, and control over their own earnings and property even if married. The scores of women's organizations were relatively small, and they often disagreed about what their primary goals should be. Nevertheless, the meeting of the International Congress of the Rights of Women, which brought together representatives from 12 countries in conjunction with the Paris exposition of 1878, can be taken as a signal that women's issues were becoming a regular part of the public agenda. Feminists found themselves combating customary attitudes in every social class, as well as the prejudices of doctors who insisted on women's physical weakness and psychological instability and of social Darwinists who declared that civilization required women to concentrate on their biological function. Although only piecemeal, their gains were important, and increasingly, women's demands were added to the fundamental questions at conflict. In many instances political liberalism attempted to meet these diverse challenges, offering partial solutions and a process for continued change. Often social conflict seemed to result in a kind of political stalemate, and in each nation international ambitions and dangers both increased domestic tension and were ominously used to preserve domestic order.

## Russia 1881–1914: Liberal Revolution

To Europeans, no proof that progress favored representative institutions was more impressive than their sudden introduction into Russia. Even there political crises led to liberal concessions. Alexander III became tsar in 1881 on his father's assassination, an event he attributed to excessive talk about further reform following the abolition of serfdom. He used the Orthodox Church and the police to extend an official reactionary ideology through public life and gave nobles an increased role in regional zemstvos and rural administration. Local governors were authorized to use martial law, restrict or ban the religions and languages of non-Russian peoples, and persecute Jews.[6] This "Russifica-

[6] One of history's famous forgeries, the *Protocols of the Elders of Zion*, was published (and written) by the Russian police in 1903. The protocols purported to be the secret minutes of a Jewish congress that revealed a conspiracy to control the world.

tion," meant to create a united nation, was continued with equal conviction but less energy by Tsar Nicholas II, who ascended the throne in 1894. Unrest increased, and many in the government welcomed war as a means of achieving the solidarity repression had failed to create.

War came in 1904, when Japan suddenly attacked the Russians at Port Arthur, which they had leased from China in 1898 as part of their expansion into East Asia and Manchuria. For years these moves had troubled the Japanese, and Russia had neither kept promises to withdraw nor acknowledged Japan's proposals for spheres of influence. The war was a disaster for Russia. Surprise attack was followed by defeats in Manchuria, the fall of Port Arthur, and the annihilation of a large Russian fleet that had sailed around the world only to be sunk in Japanese waters. In the treaty, signed at Portsmouth, New Hampshire—the United States, like Japan, wished to demonstrate its status as a world power—Russia ceded most of its recent gains, including Port Arthur and the southern half of Sakhalin Island, and recognized Japanese interest in Korea.

So dramatic a defeat increased pressure for major reforms as had the Crimean War 50 years before, but the pressure came this time from deep within society. Peasant agitation had been on the rise since a terrible famine in 1891, secret organizations had arisen to defend subject nationalities, and industrialization had begun to fill St. Petersburg and Moscow with workers organizing to improve their miserable lot. The Social Revolutionaries, a party combining the traditions of populism and terrorism, grew more active; and the Marxist Social Democrats, hitherto composed of rather disparate groups, now organized in exile and strengthened their ties within Russia.

In this atmosphere liberal members of the zemstvos held a national congress in 1904,

**On the morning of January 22, 1905 (Sunday, January 9 on the Russian calendar), protesters petitioning the tsar marched to the Winter Palace and were fired upon by Russian soldiers. The event, known as "Bloody Sunday," triggered a series of strikes and mutinies among the military.** (Photo: Soviet Life from Sovfoto)

though forbidden to by the government, and insisted on civil liberties. Then in January 1905 striking workers in St. Petersburg, demanding a national constitution as well as the recognition of labor unions, announced they would petition the tsar. They marched on the Winter Palace carrying icons and singing, "God save the tsar"; and when they had assembled, the troops opened fire, killing scores and wounding hundreds more.

"Bloody Sunday" led to agitation so widespread that in March the tsar both promised to call an assembly of notables and announced immediate reforms: religious toleration, reduced restrictions on Jews and non-Russian nationals, and cancellation of part of the payments peasants owed for their land. Agitation for a constitution only grew stronger, expressed through urban strikes, peasant riots, and mutinies in both the army and navy. In August the tsar conceded more, declaring he would call a national assembly, the Imperial Duma, which was to be merely consultative and elected by limited suffrage. Many of those close to the court were shocked by so radical a step; few outside it were satisfied. The public's response was a wave of strikes beginning in Moscow and spreading from city to city and trade to trade. For the last 10 days of October, Russia's economic life came to a halt, the most effective general strike Europe had ever seen. It won from the tsar the October Manifesto granting a constitution.

The manifesto provided for a Duma vested with legislative authority, elected by broad suffrage, and guaranteed freedom of speech and assembly. Crowds danced in the streets. For the first time the regime's opponents were divided: Those willing to work with this constitution became known as Octobrists; liberals who insisted on a constituent assembly and broader guarantees formed the Constitutional Democratic party, called Cadets for short; on the left socialists and revolutionaries rejected compromise, and the St. Petersburg Soviet, a committee of trade union leaders and socialists, called another general strike. It was only partially successful, however, for revolutionary fervor was dying down. Emboldened, the government arrested the leaders of the St. Petersburg Soviet in December, and when Moscow's workers rose in revolt, they were bloodily defeated.

Before the first Duma met in May 1906, Fundamental Laws announced more fully the form the constitution would be allowed to have. An upper house, half its members appointed by the tsar, would be added to the national legislature, thus making the Duma the lower house; the tsar would keep the power of veto, the right to name his ministers, and full command of the executive, the judiciary, and the armed forces. In elections boycotted by the left, the Cadets gained a large majority of the seats in the Duma, and they began the new era by demanding representative government. The Duma was dissolved after two months, but new elections, in which the left took part, produced a more radical assembly, also soon disbanded. The stalemate was broken by a new electoral law favoring the propertied classes that created a conservative majority in subsequent legislatures.

The Revolution of 1905 had nevertheless brought important changes. Russia now had parliamentary institutions and organized parties; the power of the aristocracy had been greatly reduced; and the nation was clearly set on a modern course. The prime minister from 1906 to 1911, Peter Stolypin, reformed education and administration and strove to stimulate economy with programs that abandoned the *mir* system in favor of full private ownership of land and that created land banks and social insurance. With the aid of foreign capital, the pace of industrialization rapidly increased. Radical movements were sternly repressed, and while discontent among workers and poorer peasants remained serious, Cadets were finding it possible to work with the new system. Liberals throughout Europe rejoiced that the giant of the East had at last begun to follow the path of Western progress.

## Austria-Hungary 1879–1914: Political Stalemate

The Dual Monarchy did not experience the kinds of crises that set Russia on a new course and led to a more democratic equilibrium in France and Italy. Rather, social and national tensions no less grave resulted in political stalemate. Count Eduard von Taaffe was prime minister from 1879 to 1893, replacing German liberals who had sought reforms more generous than aristocracy or court could abide. His government was a coalition of German conservatives, Czechs, and Poles, but concessions to these nationalities antagonized the bureaucracy and the aristocracy, who were the pillars of the empire. The spread of education and its increased social importance made the language used in schools a divisive issue, one that exacerbated the conflicts among nationalities, eventually broke up Taaffe's coalition, and led to his downfall. Industrialization in Austria increased economic conflicts with agrarian interests in Hungary and brought workers' agitation that Taaffe barely held in check by harshly repressing socialists while pushing through welfare measures that conservatives detested.

Subsequent governments tended to be even less venturesome, and after 1900 they relied increasingly on decree powers and the support of the crown rather than the Austrian parliament. Universal manhood suffrage, introduced without conviction in 1907, established the Christian Socialists and the Social Democrats as the two largest parties, neither of them acceptable to the leadership of the empire. Thus they clashed to little purpose in a parliament largely ignored and with rising anger in the city of Vienna, where the Christian Socialists held sway by combining welfare programs with demagogic anti-Semitism.

Conflict with the autonomous regime of Hungary remained critical until the turn of the century. There Magyars maintained their dominance by requiring their language to be used in government and education, tightly controlling the electoral system, and maintaining administrative corruption. Their efforts to protect the interests of large landowners and to increase their independence of Vienna, however, led to contention that weakened the empire. When in 1903 they demanded greater autonomy for their own army and the adoption of Magyar as the language of command, they touched one issue about which Emperor Francis Joseph I cared too much to yield. He suspended the Hungarian constitution, ruled without parliament, and frightened the Magyars into submission by threatening to establish universal suffrage, which would leave them a political minority in their own country.

Magyars and the empire needed each other, and the new Hungarian government—led by István Tisza, son of Kálmán Tisza and a member of one of the leading Magyar families—sought to cooperate in strengthening the Dual Monarchy and lessening the open conflict of nationalities within Hungary. Magyar politics, which in the 1840s had won European admiration as a model of liberal nationalism, had turned by 1906 into the shrewd defensive strategy of a threatened aristocracy. Tisza became one of the most influential figures in imperial politics by recognizing that mutual survival depended on avoiding dangerous changes whenever possible and by using imperial foreign policy to strengthen from the outside a political system in danger at home.

## Spain 1875–1914: The Problems of Modernization

As in Russia and Austria, Spain's pockets of urban industry (especially in Barcelona) existed in a larger society only partially affected by modern change. From the adoption of the constitution of 1875 until the Spanish-American War 23 years later, conservative and liberal parties held power alternately, tolerantly manipulating elections to assure one another's survival. Neither party, however, provided a consistent program for dealing with rising discontent at home or in the colonies. Unrest in Cuba was exacerbated by alternating policies of repression and laxity, and Cuban resistance had become guerrilla war by 1898, when the United States entered the conflict with an imperialist enthusiasm of its own. The brief war was a disaster for Spain that forced it to withdraw from Cuba and to cede Puerto Rico, Guam, and the Philippine

Islands to the United States. That ferment brought to the fore a group of Spanish intellectuals known as the generation of 1898, and the question of what was wrong with the nation became the preoccupation of public life in Spain.

From 1899 to 1909 the Conservatives held power, but they grew increasingly intolerant, and they could not sustain the old political compromises. Then the liberals, already badly divided, launched a series of reforms; but these measures—restrictions on religious orders, taxation of the church's industrial properties, a progressive income tax, and toleration of strikes—hardly lessened conflict. Economic growth, particularly in the industrial centers of Bilbao and Barcelona, made old problems of rural poverty, poor communications, and regionalism more serious. Politics had become more unwieldy with the introduction of universal manhood suffrage in 1890, and while the Church denounced liberals, the anarchists and socialists increased in strength. In Barcelona these conflicts burst forth in a week of violence in 1909 during which private citizens were murdered and churches were burned and looted. The revenge that followed reestablished Spain's reputation for brutality. A weak government caught between left and right and a king (Alfonso XIII had come of age in 1902) whose prestige declined with each ineffectual call for compromise could not resolve the problems tearing at Spanish society.

## Italy 1878–1914: Crisis Survived

The new nation of Italy, less prosperous and more divided than its patriots had promised, maintained a creaky but relatively stable political system. The transition was smooth to the reign of Humbert I, in 1878, and to government by the anti-Cavourian "left," which soon repealed the hated grain taxes, estab-

lished the principle of compulsory education (with a modest requirement for three years of schooling not always enforced), and extended suffrage to about one adult male in eight.

The prime minister maintained his majorities through an informal system called *trasformismo*, in which he built alliances that shifted with the issue at hand and used patronage to bargain for votes. Taking office in 1887, Francesco Crispi, a hero of the Risorgimento, sought popularity through outspoken anticlericalism, mild reforms, and above all, concern for Italy's prestige. He drew Italy closer to Germany and met the general agricultural depression by repressing rural revolts and establishing high tariffs that led to a harmful trade war with France. As the economic crisis deepened and public order deteriorated, Crispi's ministry fell.

His successors, dedicated to balancing the budget, were weakened by a banking scandal that, like the collapse of the Panama Canal enterprise in France, sullied the entire parliamentary system. Returned to office in 1894, Crispi frankly relied on the army and martial law to maintain order while seeking an Italian protectorate in Ethiopia. At Aduwa in 1896, however, 25,000 Italian troops were nearly wiped out by well-prepared Ethiopian forces four times their number, the first major defeat of a European army by African forces. Crispi fell again, and subsequent governments sought to salvage what they could, preserving Eritrea as an Italian colony and easing tensions with France.

At the same time, domestic unrest increased, marked by agrarian agitation and in northern Italy (which was rapidly industrializing) by anarchist bomb throwing, socialist demonstrations, and waves of strikes culminating in riots that reached revolutionary scale in Milan in 1898. Order was restored at the cost of bloodshed, the suppression of scores of newspapers, and a ban on hundreds of socialist, republican, and Catholic organizations. A frightened Chamber of Deputies nevertheless refused to authorize continued restriction of civil liberties, and its stand was supported in the critical elections of 1900. In Italy, as in France, the political campaign of a revitalized right was defeated by parliament and public opinion.

From 1903 to 1914 Prime Minister Giovanni Giolitti sought to give Italian politics a broader base. He prevented violence but not strikes, and socialists grew optimistic about parliamentarianism as the government nationalized railroads and life insurance, sponsored public health measures, and in 1911 accepted universal suffrage. Giolitti also encouraged Catholics to take part in national politics, which they had boycotted since 1870. In the decade before 1914, the Italian economy, less developed than that of the great industrial powers, experienced the fastest growth rate in Europe.

In an age of imperialism, Italian nationalists (and some industrialists) had yearned for an empire that would make Italy more nearly the equal of the other European powers. Their designs on Tunisia frustrated by the French in 1881, they had turned to the ill-fated venture in Ethiopia. After the clash of French and German interests in 1911 over dominance of Morocco (see Chapter 26), nationalist groups in Italy pressured the government to take Libya before someone else did. Libya was formally part of the Ottoman Empire, but Italy had carefully staked its claim through years of cautious diplomacy, and in 1912 Giolitti found the excuse for war against the sultan. Italian troops landed at the port city of Tripoli and took Rhodes and the other major Dodecanese Islands, also Ottoman possessions. The sultan ceded Libya, and the year of war produced an enthusiasm Italian governments had rarely won, a moment of unity many would want to recapture.

Giolitti's accomplishments, however, rested on his skill at obscuring political issues, influencing elections, and using silent deputies. The economic problems of the south remained grave and the discontent of more and more organized and militant workers largely unappeased. A dull and sometimes corrupt government proved an easy target for increasingly vocal critics from the left and the right. In the elections of 1913, the first under the broadened suffrage, these critics achieved notable gains.

## France 1878–1914: The Triumph of the Republicans

By the 1880s the Third Republic had established its political style: The executive was relatively weak, the presidency reduced to a ceremonial office; most cabinets lasted only about a year in office; and the many parties had little authority over deputies tied to local interests, who were proudly independent on national issues. Stability came from the frustrating fact that shifting majorities produced new governments not very different from their predecessors—most ministers served in several cabinets—and from an able civil service.

For 20 years, from 1879 to 1899, the leading politicians were moderate republicans who found in lack of daring the best guarantee of the republic's durability and in anticlericalism their most popular plank. Strong defenders of free speech and individualism, they recognized unions but initiated few projects of public works or social welfare. In the 1880s they made elementary education in state schools compulsory and established restrictions on the Catholic Church intended to weaken its political influence, a view of progress that carried national political divisions into the villages of France.

Moderate republicans had little gift for winning popular enthusiasm, however, and

Inaugurated in 1900, the Paris subway, the *Metropolitain,* was a huge success. Technology and art were invitingly combined in Hector Guimard's dramatic entranceways constructed of elegant ironwork in the *art nouveau* style and topped by a shimmering glass roof. (Photo: Collection VIOLLET)

political crises occurred frequently. In 1889 General Georges Boulanger gained so much popularity by his appeal to patriotism and his sympathy for workers that there was danger of a coup d'état. Then in 1892 companies planning a canal through Panama similar to their successful Suez venture went bankrupt. Investigations uncovered political graft and provoked a stormy campaign against the corruption of Jewish financiers, liberal newspapers, and republican politicians. Only as the republic's opponents seemed close to toppling the regime did its defenders pull together.

The Third Republic's great trial came with the Dreyfus case. Captain Alfred Dreyfus, a Jew and a member of the General Staff, was convicted by court-martial in 1894 of providing the German military attaché with secret French documents. Although the sensational press shouted Jewish treachery, the issue became the center of public attention only three years afterward, when evidence appeared suggesting a different officer had been guilty. Generals, refusing to reopen the case, spoke darkly of honor and state secrets, and the right-wing press hailed their patriotism. The case was marked by revelations in parliament and the press, a series of sensational trials, and huge public demonstrations. The majority of Catholics, monarchists, and conservatives joined in patriotic indignation against Jews and socialists allegedly conspiring to sell out France and weaken a loyal army. The left—intellectuals, socialists, and republicans—came to view Dreyfus as the innocent victim of a plot against republican institutions. They won the battle for public opinion, though barely, and Dreyfus was given a presidential pardon in 1899.[7] That victory set the tone of subsequent French politics, cementing traditions of republican unity on the left and greatly reducing the political influence of the Church and monarchists. Years of polemics and confrontation, however, left deep scars.

From 1900 until World War I, government was in the hands of firm republicans who, despite their cautious position on social issues, called themselves the Radical party. They set about purging the army of their opponents and launched new attacks on the Church that subsided only with the passage of a law separating church and state in 1905. Yet they administered with restraint. Solicitous of the "little man," of small businessmen

---

[7] Zola was twice convicted of libel. Courts-martial in 1898 acquitted the man who forged the principal evidence against Dreyfus and convicted Dreyfus a second time in 1899 but "with extenuating circumstances," which added new confusion and led to the presidential pardon. A few Dreyfusards continued collecting evidence and finally won acquittal in a civil trial in 1906. Dreyfus was then decorated and promoted to the rank of major.

A French newspaper headlined Émile Zola's now-famous "J'Accuse . . . !," a denunciation of the corrupt handling of the Dreyfus affair. The case became the cause célèbre of the nineteenth century; opinion as to Dreyfus's guilt or innocence led to demonstrations, propaganda, street fighting, lawsuits, and political realignments. (Photo: René Dazy)

and peasant farmers, they solidified support for the republic.

Indeed, part of the Third Republic's achievement was its ability to draw radical politicians to moderate policies. A socialist even entered the cabinet in the aftermath of the Dreyfus affair (thereby earning the condemnation of the Second International for cooperating in a bourgeois state). The labor movement, more syndicalist than Marxist, doubled its membership in this period, but despite frequent strikes from the 1890s on, it never produced the more revolutionary general strike so much talked of. As prime minister from 1906 to 1909, Georges Clemenceau, once associated with the radical left, effectively combined policies of reform and con-

ciliation. On the eve of world war, France, prosperous and stable, appeared to have surmounted its most dangerous divisions.

## Germany 1879–1914: Tensions Following Unification

German political life reflected a fragmented society in which the court, army, bureaucracy, and business were semi-independent centers of power and in which social classes were sharply demarcated. Yet Bismarck ran it until 1890 with an authority few modern figures have equaled, establishing a pattern his successors would strain to maintain.

The architect of so successful a system was understandably scornful of criticism, and a chancellor so overweening won many enemies; but Bismarck was untouchable until William II ascended the throne in 1888. Twenty-nine years old, bright but ill-prepared, William was infatuated with all things military, anxious to make himself loved, and eager to rule. He disagreed with parts of Bismarck's foreign policy and opposed the antisocialist laws, but theirs was primarily a conflict of wills. In 1890 the emperor, impatient with Bismarck's paternal arrogance, forced his resignation.

Succeeding chancellors (there were four between 1890 and 1917) served until the dissatisfaction of some powerful faction led to their replacement. In 1909 Theobald von Bethmann-Hollweg, the last peacetime chancellor of the Second Reich and the first of bourgeois origin, was chosen in part out of concern over a restive parliament, but that cautious bureaucrat was hardly the man to tame the forces of German politics.

The fundamental problems of the Second Reich were inherent in the system itself. A dynamic foreign policy whose successes could dazzle opponents at home proved impossible to sustain. Foreign policy and the political importance of the army required increases in armed strength that kept militarism at the center of politics. In 1887, when a seven-year renewal of the army bill fell due, Bismarck asked for its enlargement. Resisted in parliament, he made this an electoral issue and won a sizable victory, the last stable majority any chancellor enjoyed. Similarly in 1893, 1898, and 1911–1913, military appropriations were a source of intense conflict and propaganda; each time the army grew larger and the government's statements more nationalist.

Strident propaganda was also the mainstay of the political leagues—the Landlords', Peasants', Pan-German, Colonial, and Naval Leagues—organized in the 1890s. Well-financed by Junkers and some industrialists, they campaigned for the military, overseas empire, and high tariffs with attacks on socialists, Jews, and foreign enemies. As pressure groups, they won significant victories—notably in the naval bill of 1898, which proposed to create a fleet that could compete with Britain's. Germany's conservative classes appealed to public opinion more effectively than their anti-Dreyfusard counterparts in France or the militant right in Italy.

Under Bismarck, Germany had adopted comprehensive programs of health, old age, accident, and disability insurance that established a model of social welfare legislation unequaled elsewhere for a generation. William II was hailed as "the Labor Emperor" for supporting social security, labor arbitration, the regulation of workers' hours, and provisions for their safety. The workers, however, would not be wooed.

The Social Democrats, having been forced by harassment to rely on local organization, became powerful: They won more votes than any other party in every election from 1890 on, becoming in 1912 the largest party in the Reichstag (and the strongest socialist party in Europe) despite the distortions of the electoral system. Socialists also dominated Germany's vigorous labor unions, which had 2.5 million members by 1912. A movement detested by the authorities, German socialism created its own subculture of newspapers and libraries and recreation centers.

The German political system, which offered them no chance of sharing in government, did not make compromise tempting. In practice, the Social Democrats were attentive to the concrete concerns of their constituents, but in principle and in tone, they remained firm revolutionaries. One of their leading theorists, Eduard Bernstein, proposed a modified doctrine in a daring book, *Evolutionary Socialism* (1897). He argued that many of Marx's predictions had proved wrong, that parts of his economic analysis were faulty, and that socialists should place less emphasis on economic determinism and revolution and seek instead to improve working conditions and strengthen democracy. Bernstein's revisionism became the focus of international debate and affected socialist movements everywhere, but it was formally rejected by the Social Democrats, who made Karl Kautsky's rigorous Marxism their official policy.

While organized factions glared and threatened, Bethmann-Hollweg presided over a bureaucracy rife with cabals and tried to hold in check a court where people spoke openly of using the army against radicals. Germany remained strong, prosperous, and apparently stable, but major political change proved impossible; even the attempt to make taxes more equitable was defeated. Thus Bethmann-Hollweg's mild program for modifying the political system came to nothing. When the Continent's most powerful nation entered into world war, the Reich was still dominated by Prussia, where voting continued by the three-class system, and ministers remained responsible to the crown and not the Reichstag.

## Great Britain 1880–1914: Imperialism and Democracy

Gladstone returned to power in 1880 after a campaign that, in its effort to carry serious issues to the public, was a further step toward democracy; and in 1885 the Liberal majority led Parliament to adopt measures accepting the principle of universal manhood suffrage, known as the Third Reform Bill (it says much about the life of the poor that the requirement of an independent place of residence—which excluded domestic servants, sons living with fathers, and those without a permanent address—was enough to disqualify roughly one-third of all adult males). Gladstone's foreign policy, however, was decried as weak, and his popularity, which increased when Britain stumbled into the occupation of Egypt in 1882, was dissipated a few years later. As the Irish question became more heated, Gladstone responded with re-

forms that fixed fair rents and prevented the eviction of paying tenants; but Irish nationalists demanded home rule, an independent Irish parliament. When Gladstone acquiesced in 1886, his party split as badly as the Tories had a generation before over the corn laws. Joseph Chamberlain, a radical in social matters who had adopted the popular cause of imperialism, led an important group of Liberals into alliance with the Conservatives. Gladstone's perpetual compromises were beginning to seem old-fashioned.

Conservative governments would hold office for 16 of the next 19 years, most of them under Lord Salisbury, successor to Disraeli, who had died in 1881. An able diplomat, Salisbury continued his party's emphasis on the importance of the empire and led the nation through a bitter conflict with the Dutch-speaking Boers of South Africa.

Many Boers had left Britain's Cape Colony in the 1830s, eventually establishing independent and frankly racist republics recognized in the 1850s as the South African Republic and the Orange Free State. In 1877, however, the British government had violated previous treaties by annexing the Transvaal. This produced a revolt in 1880 and Gladstone's concession of domestic autonomy in 1881. Almost constantly at war with neighboring African peoples, the republics were also at odds with the expanding British interests in South Africa. The unstable situation became explosive with the discovery of diamonds in the Orange Free State and gold in the South African Republic in the 1870s and 1880s. (See maps and the discussion of imperialism in Chapter 26.) New settlers poured in, and companies amassed enormous wealth; railroads were rushed to completion and natives driven away or forced to work for meager wages.

In violation of existing treaties, the British annexed the South African Republic in 1877, then granted it independence (with some strings attached) a few years later in the face of the Boer's resistance. Frequently at war with adjacent native societies, especially the Zulus, the British were drawn in more and more deeply. Cecil Rhodes, an Englishman who had gained a near-monopoly over the world's diamond production before he was 30, used his position as prime minister of the Cape Colony to further schemes for a South African federation, and the Boers found themselves resisting raids by whites as well as blacks. By 1890, the Boer republics were surrounded by British colonies and swarming with British citizens, whom the Boers taxed heavily but excluded from voting. Negotiations broke down in 1899, and the Boers declared war. The British rapidly occupied the major cities, but they subdued the Boers' expert guerrilla resistance only after two more years of destroying farms and herding the homeless Boers into concentration camps. This embarrassing war, with its heavy price in blood and prestige, stirred a fierce patriotism in England that increased the Conservatives' strength.

Despite public enthusiasm for their imperial policy, the Conservatives faced growing opposition at home which they attempted to meet by sponsoring major reforms. In 1888 and 1894 they restructured local government, a major source of the aristocracy's political power, making county councils elective. They made an expanding civil service more accessible to the middle class, and an act of 1902 established a far stronger national education system that for the first time included secondary schooling.

Yet these important changes did not appease the working class, whose rising dissatisfaction was expressed in dramatic strikes by London match girls in 1888 and dock workers the next year. The strikes had won public sympathy and marked the beginning of a "new unionism" of unskilled workers organized on an industrywide basis and prepared

for political activism. The formation of the Labour Representation Committee in 1900 marked the beginning of what quickly became the Labour party. Its greatest strength came from the unions, but it included the Fabian Society, a group of prominent intellectuals whose propaganda in behalf of reformist, democratic socialism gained an influence far beyond its numbers. Twenty-nine Labour members of Parliament would be elected in 1906, and within a few years the Liberals, now back in power, would come often to depend on Labour votes in the House of Commons. British labor was further pushed to political action by a court decision, upheld by the House of Lords in 1902, which made unions liable for losses caused by strikes. Overturning a verdict that could cripple unions became a central issue of the 1906 election.

In that election the Liberals won the most one-sided victory since 1832. They immediately passed measures establishing workers' compensation, old age pensions, and urban planning. Since this legislation and the expanding arms race required new revenues, David Lloyd George, the chancellor of the Exchequer, proposed the "people's budget" in 1909. A skilled orator who delighted in the rhetoric of class conflict, he promised to place the burden of social welfare costs squarely on the rich.

In an unprecedented act an aroused House of Lords rejected the government's budget, forcing new elections and bringing on a constitutional crisis. Although the Liberals lost many seats, they retained office with Irish and Labour support, and King George V's threat to appoint hundreds of additional peers finally forced the upper house to accept not only the hated budget but also a constitutional change forbidding the Lords to veto money bills and permitting any measure to become law when passed by the Commons in three sessions.

| International and Military History | Political History |
|---|---|
| | |
| **1860** | |
| | |
| **1870**  Franco–Prussian War | |
| | **1875**  Constitutional monarchy in Spain |
| **(1881**  France occupies Tunisia)* <br> **1882**  Britain occupies Egypt | |
| | **1885**  Third Reform Bill in Britain <br> **1886–1914**  Issue of home rule in Ireland |
| | **1890**  Fall of Bismarck; universal manhood suffrage in Spain <br> **1890s**  Height of anarchist agitation <br> Rise of political anti–Semitism |
| **1896**  Italian defeat at Aduwa, Ethiopia | **1894–1899**  Dreyfus case in France |
| **1898**  Spanish–American War <br> **1899–1902**  Boer War | **1898**  German naval bill |
| **1904–1905**  Russo–Japanese War | **1905**  Revolution in Russia <br> **1907**  Universal manhood suffrage in Austria |
| **1912**  Italian–Turkish War | **1911**  Universal manhood suffrage in Italy <br> **1912**  Social Democrats become largest party in Reichstag |
| **1914** | **1914**  European population 450 million |

*Events in parentheses are discussed in other chapters.

| Social and Economic History | Cultural and Intellectual History |
|---|---|
| | Comte (1798–1857) |
| | **1859** Darwin (1809–1882), *Origin of Species* |
| **1860s** Bessemer converter | |
| | **1862–1877** Pasteur's major work on germs |
| **1864–1872** First International | **1864** Syllabus of Errors |
| | **1867** Salon des Réfusés; Marquess of Queensberry rules; Marx (1818–1883), first volume of *Das Kapital* |
| | **1869** Mendeleev's periodic table |
| **1870** European population 295 million | **1869–1870** Vatican I |
| **1870–1896** General decline of prices, new tariff barriers | **1873** Maxwell's equations |
| **1878** International Congress of the Rights of Women | |
| **1879–1885** Development of telephone, incandescent lamp, internal combustion engine, and steam turbine | |
| | Monet (1840–1926) |
| **1888** London match girls strike | van Gogh (1853–1890) |
| **1889** Second International; British dock workers strike | **1891** *Rerum Novarum* |
| | **1897** Bernstein, *Evolutionary Socialism* |
| | **1897 and 1906** Bergson's most noted books |
| **1898** Milan riots | Nietzsche (1844–1900) |
| | Zola (1840–1902) |
| | Gauguin (1848–1903) |
| | Spencer (1820–1903) |
| **1903** Heavier–than–air flying machine | Cézanne (1839–1906) |
| | **1908** Sorel, *Reflections on Violence* |
| **1909** House of Lords loses right of veto over budget; Barcelona riots | *Koch* (1843–1910) |
| **1914** Parliament votes Irish home rule | |
| | Renoir (1832–1919) |

The peers' intemperate outburst, which cost them so much, was part of the general rise in social tension. From 1910 to 1914 strikes increased in frequency, size, and violence; a general strike became a real and much-talked-of threat. Women campaigning for the right to vote interrupted public meetings, invaded Parliament itself, smashed windows, and planted bombs. Arrested, they went on hunger strikes until baffled statesmen ordered their release. Such behavior from ladies was shocking in itself; but as the movement gained strength, recruiting women (and some men) from every social class, its outraged attack on smug male assumptions reinforced the rising challenge to a whole social order.

Nor was the threat of violence limited to the left. In 1914 the Commons gave a bill for Irish home rule its third passage, which made it immune to a veto in the House of Lords.

The Protestants of northern Ireland, with support from many English, openly threatened civil war. Squads began drilling, and the British officer corps gave frightening indications that it might mutiny rather than fight to impose home rule on Protestant loyalists.

Only the outbreak of world war generated the national unity that neither imperialism nor social reform had been able to create. If the death of Queen Victoria in 1901 had symbolized the end of an age of British expansion, the ascent of George V to the throne (1910–1936) marked the opening of new conflicts. Edward VII's brief reign (1901–1910) would soon be remembered a little sadly as the Edwardian era, a happy time of relaxed confidence that prosperity and democracy were the natural products of progress and a guarantee of peace.

## SUMMARY

As the nineteenth century ended, Europeans seemed preoccupied with the future. A great many of the most optimistic predictions from the past were being fulfilled. In general, productivity and prosperity, at levels never achieved before, continued to rise. Science and technology promised still greater wonders. In most countries there was greater freedom of expression, political participation, and leisure, increased literacy and education, and better health care than in the past. Even in retrospect, the level of creativity in the arts and scholarship and the growth of knowledge and professional standards in every field remain impressive. Yet the civilization that achieved all this was bitterly denounced not only for injustices, which by contrast seemed all the more blatant, but more fundamentally, for its lack of coherent values, for its materialism, for the ugliness of industrial society, and for the privileged position of a middle class portrayed as self-serving and philistine.

The progress measured by general prosperity, knowledge, and freedom was shared within limits by common people through rising standards of living, social mobility, universal education, and increased democracy. Yet millions of Europeans chose or were forced to emigrate. Class conflict and clashing interests clearly threatened the social system. As each nation confronted these tensions, it fell to the state to balance repression and reform, social justice and special interests. Often such compromises, usually sought through the political process, made conflict and discontent more explicit.

For good or ill, the trend toward greater democracy and large-scale organization seemed irresistible. There had been no revolutions save in backward Russia for a generation and no European war, facts often cited as proof of progress. There was some reason to believe that the problems of the late nineteenth century might also be resolved through political freedom, social responsibility, and economic growth. Then suddenly in 1914 the very compromises that had held society together and kept the peace exploded—not in revolution, but in total war.

# RECOMMENDED READING

## Studies

*Arendt, Hannah. *The Origins of Totalitarianism.* 1958. This important study begins with a profoundly pessimistic application of hindsight to the imperialism and anti-Semitism of the late nineteenth century.

*Avineri, Shlomo. *The Social and Political Thought of Karl Marx.* 1971. An important and fresh study.

Berlanstein, Lenard R. *The Working People of Paris, 1871–1914.* 1984. The impact of social change on the nature of work and on the lives of wage earners, both in the workplace and out.

Boxer, Marilyn, and Jean Quataert. *Socialist Women: Socialist Feminism in the Nineteenth and Twentieth Century.* 1978. Treats the most important figures in all the major countries.

Clark, Ronald W. *The Survival of Charles Darwin.* 1984. A detailed biography, which also discusses the impact of Darwin's work.

*Dangerfield, George. *The Strange Death of Liberal England.* 1935. Skillfully and argumentatively written description of a society in crisis.

*Derfler, Leslie. *Socialism since Marx: A Century of the European Left.* 1973. Thoughtful discussion of the movements that stemmed from Marx.

*Gay, Peter. *The Education of the Senses.* 1984. A sensitive treatment of sexuality during the Victorian Age, and the first part of a major new study of the bourgeoisie.

Gillis, John R. *Youth and History: Tradition and Change in European Age Relations, 1770 to the Present.* 1981. An original study of youth transformed by social change.

*Himmelfarb, Gertrude. *Darwin and the Darwinian Revolution.* 1968. Relates Darwinian ideas to the intellectual currents of the age.

Hobsbawm, Eric. *The Age of Empire, 1875–1914.* 1987. Argues for the importance of imperialism in domestic life.

*Hughes, H. Stuart. *Consciousness and Society: The Reorientation of European Social Thought, 1890–*1930. 1958. A gracefully written and indispensable analysis of the currents of modern thought in a time of transition.

Johnson, Douglas. *France and the Dreyfus Affair.* 1966. An account of the affair that explains its extraordinary impact.

*Joll, James. *The Anarchists.* 1964. Discusses the ideas and motives of very disparate gruops.

*———. *The Second International, 1889–1914.* 1966. A good general history of this period of the socialist movement, with striking portraits of the major figures.

Kern, Stephen. *The Culture of Time and Space 1880–1918.* 1983. Finds that ideas and experience relating to the most basic dimensions of life were fundamentally transformed by technological and cultural change.

Lidtke, Vernon. *The Alternative Culture: Socialist Labor in Imperial Germany.* 1985. Analyzes Europe's most organized working class subculture.

*Löwith, Karl. *From Hegel to Nietzsche: The Revolution in Nineteenth-Century Thought.* 1964. A sober essay on the transformations in modern thought.

Lyons, Francis S. *Ireland Since the Famine.* 1971. A broad social history.

*McLellan, David. *Karl Marx. His Life and Thought.* 1977. Brings out the essential unity of Marx's writings.

*Mayeur, Jean-Marie, and Madeleine Rebérioux. *The Third Republic from its Origins to the Great War, 1871–1914.* J. R. Foster (tr.). 1984. A balanced synthesis of recent scholarship.

Miller, Michael. *The Bon Marché: Bourgeois Culture and the Development of the Department Store.* 1981. A fascinating study of an important cultural institution.

Milward, Alan S., and S. B. Saul. *The Development of the Economies of Continental Europe, 1850–1914.* 1977. Excellent study of the second great wave of industrialization.

Pugh, Martin. *The Tories and the People, 1880–1935.* 1985. A study of the basis for and limitations of the Conservatives' mass appeal.

*Pulzer, Peter G. *The Rise of Political Anti-Semitism in Germany and Austria.* 1964. A clear and balanced survey of a difficult topic.

Ralston, David B. *The Army of the Republic, 1871–1914.* 1967. On the problem of the military in France both before and after the Dreyfus affair.

Rearick, Charles. *Pleasures of the Belle Epoque.* 1985. Captures the cultural and social vitality of the period.

*Robertson, Priscilla. *An Experience of Women: Pattern and Change in Nineteenth-Century Europe.* 1982. A social and intellectual history of middle- and upper-class women in Western Europe.

*Schorske, Carl E. *Fin-de-Siècle Vienna: Politics and Culture.* 1980. Unusually sensitive and imaginative assessment of one of the important moments in European cultural history.

Seton-Watson, Christopher. *Italy from Liberalism to Fascism.* 1967. A thorough general account.

*Shattuck, Roger. *The Banquet Years.* 1968. A brilliant account of the role of artists in late-nineteenth-century Paris.

Stone, Norman. *Europe Transformed, 1878–1919.* 1984. An insightful and fresh new survey of the period, outlining the weaknesses of the liberals.

Tannenbaum, Edward R. *1900: The Generation Before the Great War.* 1976. Interesting essays on the major facets of society.

*Wagar, Warren W. *Good Tidings: The Belief in Progress from Darwin to Marcuse.* 1972. A wide-ranging account of the period's principal theme.

*Weber, Eugen. *Peasants into Frenchmen: The Modernization of Rural France, 1880–1914.* 1976. Provocative treatment of the resistance of rural France to the pressures for change.

*Wohl, Robert. *The Generation of 1914.* 1979. Theories of generations in conflict are related to the intellectual and political discontent preceding World War I in this important book.

* Available in paperback.

# THE IMAGE
# OF HUMANITY

❄ ❄ ❄

# IN MODERN ART

❀ ❀ ❀ ❀ ❀

The birth of the modern world is linked with two revolutions—the industrial revolution, symbolized by the invention of the steam engine, and the political revolution, which began in America and France under the banner of democracy. Both are still going on. Industrialization and democracy, as goals, are sought all over the world. Western science and political ideology (and, in their wake, all the other products of our civilization) are spreading to the remotest corners of the globe. Their impact has transformed every facet of our lives, at a rate so rapid and violent that many of us are said to be suffering from "future shock."

❀

How have these twin revolutions affected artists? Their position in the modern world, when measured against the standards of the past, can only be called paradoxical. Industrialization has produced vast new wealth, but the share of our income, public or private, spent on art patronage is very much less than it was in earlier times. Yet the artist's public has grown tremendously in comparison with the past; museums, most of them founded within the past hundred years, attract millions of visitors today, and books on modern art are available in every bookshop. The artist's prestige, too, if not financial condition, is higher than ever before. In antiquity and the Middle Ages there had been no distinction between art and craft; the Renaissance invented the concept of artistic genius but reserved it for a very few such as Leonardo da Vinci and Michelangelo, and even they were dependent on the wishes of their patrons. From the early nineteenth century on, however, artists have been acclaimed as superior to any established authority, subservient to nothing but their own impulses. They assumed, in fact, a role as exalted and as independent from the rest of society as the prophets of the Old Testament. But, like prophets, artists now had to face the prospect of being without honor in their own country. Indeed, they were expected to be. The modern artist's ideal is the bohemian, the "glorious failure" who goes through life neglected and ridiculed, only to be hailed as a genius by posterity. Actually, few of them have had careers exemplifying this pattern—Vincent van Gogh is the most famous case—yet there can be no doubt that the modern artist's lot has been more troubled than that of artists in earlier periods. Freedom has had to be purchased at the expense of security. Even artists who were financially successful have often felt it incumbent upon them to live as if they were not, so as to avoid becoming dependent on the public's favor which to them seemed a betrayal of their calling.

❀

In a world without the framework of traditional constraints, the artist's latitude of action is both more frightening and more exhilarating than anybody else's. One of the modern artist's risks—and at the same time an acknowledgment of importance—is suppression for ideological reasons. In Hitler's Germany any artist who did not work in the government-approved style was declared "degenerate" and forbidden to exhibit; a similar lack of freedom recently prevailed in Russia, where the dogma of "socialist realism" was enforced, even though in the early years after the Revolution of 1917 modern artists were welcomed as kindred spirits since they, too, were revolutionary. In the West, too, there have been times when artists working in unfamiliar idioms are denounced by conservative politicians as "subversive." Such experiences only tend to reinforce the modern artist's distrust of the Establishment. Nor can the creative person rely on public opinion, which is swayed all too often by the tides of taste and fashion. The modern artist, thus, seems to be forever cast in the role of the outsider, regardless of fame or prestige.

This basic change in the artist's condition may help to account for the fact that no coherent image of humanity has emerged in modern art. The shared values which enabled the artists of earlier ages to coin such an image have either disappeared or lost their reality; Jupiter (as Karl Marx once observed) could not survive against the lightning rod. Even portraiture, a continuous and vital tradition since the Early Renaissance, succumbed to the invention of photography in the mid-nineteenth century (see Plate 49). What, then, could take the place of traditional subject matter? The answer is summed up in such nineteenth-century slogans as "art for art's sake" or Walter Pater's claim that "all art aspires to the condition of music." Music, needless to say, is nonrepresentational; it arouses emotion through the harmonious and rhythmic manipulation of sound. Once it was acknowledged as the highest of the arts, painters began to think of their work as a kind of "visual music," governed by laws that could not be derived from observation of the outside world. At first they were content to give their works "musical" titles, with the subject mentioned only in second place as a sop to the public (the picture popularly known as "Whistler's Mother" was exhibited as "Arrangement in Black and Grey: The Artist's Mother"), but by 1910 some painters had gone completely "nonobjective" by eliminating representation altogether, and their successors are still with us today.

Wherever we do encounter images of men and women in nineteenth-century art, the human condition is seen as shaped by the environment, physical or social, as in Daumier's "Third-Class Carriage" (Plate 55), Brown's "The Last of England" (Plate 56), Courbet's "The Stone Breakers" (Plate 57), and Degas's "The Glass of Absinthe" (Plate 58). The sympathy these pictures evoke has been consciously avoided by Seurat, whose "Bathers" (Plate 59) are so depersonalized that we perceive them only as a part of their setting rather than as individuals. A "musical" title would seem entirely appropriate to such a painting. It is only in what may be broadly termed the expressionist tradition of modern art that the human image retains a central importance; but its goal is to probe extreme states of the psyche, not to define the nature of mankind. The beginnings of this line of development go back to the great French Romantics of the early nineteenth century: Géricault's "The Madman" (Plate 50) leads to Munch's "The Scream" (Plate 61) seventy years later, and ultimately to Kienholz's

"The State Hospital" (Plate 64), just as Delacroix's "Frédéric Chopin" (Pate 51) is prophetic of van Gogh's "Self-Portrait" (Plate 60), Rouault's "Head of Christ" (Plate 62), and Picasso's "Weeping Woman" (Plate 63). Such images invite a twofold interpretation. They are surely signs of a general and continuing crisis due to the revolutionary changes we have been experiencing ever since the end of the eighteenth century. At the same time, they afford an insight into the cause of these changes: the West's heightened awareness of personal intellectual, moral, and emotional powers. Having so vastly expanded our range of thought, action, and feeling, we are faced with the task of redefining our own identity, to give meaning to our existence, outside the metaphysical framework that sheltered our ancestors. The modern artist senses, more sharply than the rest of us, that this is indeed a time to try our souls.

Ingres, whose long career spans the first two-thirds of the nineteenth century, was the greatest disciple of David (see Plate 46). He is usually called a Neoclassicist and his opponents Romantics. Their quarrels recall the old debate between "Poussinists" and "Rubenists" (see Plates 43–45), with Ingres insisting that drawing is superior to color while the Romantics maintained the contrary. Actually, the views of both factions were far more doctrinaire than their pictures. In his portrait of *Louis Bertin,* Ingres's allegiance seems to be to observed reality pure and simple rather than to any theoretical convictions. There is so little "style" here that at first glance the picture looks like a superior kind of photograph. Had it been painted a decade later Ingres might well have been accused of working from a daguerreotype. In fact Ingres's realism and the development of photography sprang from the same impulse: a demand for the unvarnished scientific truth. Nothing less would do for the age of the industrial revolution. When the first practical photographic processes became available in the late 1830s, they were hailed as "the pencil of nature," and portraiture became their chief task. Thus Ingres was the last great professional in a field soon to be monopolized by the camera. His *Bertin,* however unvarnished it may seem, is a masterpiece of interpretation, endowing the sitter with a massive force of personality that is almost frightening. Individualistic, self-reliant, aggressive, Bertin seems the perfect image of the bourgeois entrepreneur, the hero of "free enterprise."

*Plate 49. Dominique Ingres*
LOUIS BERTIN
*1832, canvas, height 46"*
*Louvre Museum, Paris*

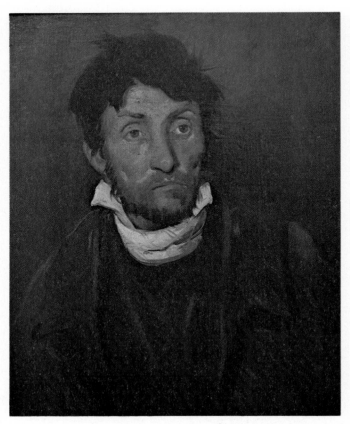

*Plate 50. Théodore Géricault*
THE MADMAN
*1821–1824, canvas, height 24"*
*Museum of Fine Arts, Ghent*

If Ingres's *Bertin* represents the class of men that shaped the character of post-Napoleonic Europe, the two portraits on these pages—one of a madman, the other of a great composer—seem more closely related to each other than to the forces and events of their time. Ingres shows his sitter as he wanted to be seen, squarely facing his public; Géricault's and Delacroix's subjects, in contrast, are so completely caught up in their private worlds that they remain unaware of the observer. They are indeed not portraits in the traditional sense but studies of extreme states of the human condition, and it is this that stamps them as Romantic.

Romanticism refers to an attitude of mind, rather than to a specific style, and is therefore harder to define. The word derives from the vogue for medieval tales of adventure, called "romances" because they were written in a Romance language, not in Latin. This interest in the long-neglected "dark ages," however, sprang from a revulsion against established values of any kind and had its roots in a craving for emotional experience. Almost any experience would do, real or imaginary, provided it was intense enough. The declared aim of the Romantics was to tear down the artifices barring the way to a "return to nature"—nature the unbounded, wild and ever-changing, nature the sublime and picturesque. Were man to act "naturally," giving his impulses free rein, evil would disappear. In the name of nature the Romantics worshiped liberty, power, love, violence, the Greeks, the Middle Ages, or anything that aroused their response, but actually they worshiped emotion as an end in itself. At its extreme this attitude could be expressed only through direct action, not through works of art, for the creation of a work of art demands some detachment and self-awareness. What Wordsworth, the great Romantic poet, said about poetry—that it is "emotion recollected in tranquillity"—applies also to painting. To cast his fleeting experience into permanent form, the Romantic artist needs a style. It is hardly surprising that painters such as Géricault and Delacroix preferred the vivid color, broad, open brushwork, and spontaneous emotion of Rubens, Hals, Velázquez, and Goya (see Plates 37–39, 48) to the meticulous draftsmanship and painstaking detail of Poussin, David, and Ingres (see Plate 43, 46, 49). Géricault, the older of the two, began his career as an admirer of Gros (see Plate 47), at a time when Napoleon was at the height of his glory. He died in 1824, at the age of 33. His interest in people's emotional life led him to befriend the director of the Paris insane asylum, for whom he painted a series of portraits of individual patients illustrating various types of derangement. Our picture belongs to this group. Géricault's sympathy toward the subject, his ability to see the victims of mental disease as fellow human beings rather than as accursed or bewitched outcasts, is one of the noblest fruits of the Romantic movement.

Delacroix had his first great public success in the year of Géricault's death. Until his own death almost forty years later, he remained the foremost Romantic painter of France and the acknowledged antagonist of Ingres. He rarely did portraits other than those of his personal friends and fellow victims of the "Romantic agony" such as the Polish composer Frédéric Chopin. Here we see the image of the Romantic hero at its purest: a blend of Gros's *Napoleon* and Géricault's *Madman,* he is consumed by the fire of his genius.

*Plate 51. Eugène Delacroix*
FRÉDÉRIC CHOPIN
*1838, canvas, height 18"*
*Louvre Museum, Paris*

Landscape had been part of the Western tradition of painting as early as Roman times (see Plate 6). In the seventeenth century it became an important subject in its own right. The Romantics, with their worship of nature, raised it to a new level of significance; landscape painting conveyed some of their most profoundly felt emotions. The *Monk at the Seashore* by the German painter Caspar David Friedrich, an early and memorable example, embodies an experience central to the Romantic imagination: that of the sublime. The tiny, lonesome figure contemplating the immensity of sea and sky becomes a moving symbol of man's insignificance when confronted with the cosmos. Turner's *Slave Ship* seeks to achieve the same effect in more dramatic fashion. First entitled *Slavers Throwing Overboard the Dead and Dying—Typhoon Coming On,* the painting is, on one level of meaning, a protest against the inhumanity of the slave trade: threatened by a storm, the captain casts his human cargo overboard. The typhoon appears to be nature's retribution for his greed and cruelty, but it is also

*Plate 52. William Turner*
THE SLAVE SHIP
*1839, canvas, height 36"*
*Museum of Fine Arts, Boston*

more than that, a catastrophe that engulfs everything, not merely the slaver and his victims but the sea itself with its crowds of fantastic and oddly harmless-looking fish. While we sense the force of Turner's vision, most of us today, perhaps with a twinge of guilt, tend to enjoy this explosion of color for its own sake rather than as a vehicle for the awesome emotions the artist meant to evoke. The English art critic John Ruskin, who owned *The Slave Ship,* saw in it "the true, the beautiful, and the intellectual"; to modern eyes it seems, rather, "an airy vision, painted with tinted steam" (to cite the uncharitable but acute characterization of Turner's work by John Constable, another important English landscape painter of the early nineteenth century). The very simplicity of Friedrich's *Monk at the Seashore,* painted three decades earlier, strikes us as more convincing than do the pyrotechnics of Turner.

*Plate 53. Caspar David Friedrich*
MONK AT THE SEASHORE
*1808, canvas, height 43¼"*
*Schloss Charlottenburg*
*Berlin (West)*

*Plate 54. Camille Corot*
**SELF-PORTRAIT**
*ca. 1835, canvas, height 13½″*
*Uffizi Gallery, Florence*

This self-portrait by the great French landscapist Camille Corot is so cool and straightforward that we can hardly think of it as Romantic. It contains no hint of the emotionalism we have come to associate with the movement. Yet in at least one important respect it mirrors a characteristically Romantic attitude—it is painted out-of-doors, in brilliant sunshine. Until the early nineteenth century, painting had been confined to the studio; artists would record their impressions of nature in drawings or watercolors, but to paint out-of-doors was regarded as undesirable, technically as well as aesthetically. The equipment it demanded was far too cumbersome to be carried about, and the process itself was too slow to record the ever-changing conditions of directly observed nature. The Romantics, sensitive to transitory moods, upset this centuries-old tradition; while some of them continued to paint landscapes indoors, others insisted on working under the open sky so as to capture all the subtle gradations of light and atmosphere they experienced at a particular moment. Soon industry came to their aid by producing ready-to-use oil paints in tubes, packed in convenient boxes, as well as portable easels and stools. The pictures produced on the spot with the aid of such equipment were small in size and lacked the precise detail of earlier landscapes, but they had a freshness and immediacy never achieved before. Corot was a pioneer in this novel kind of landscape painting; it is hardly a surprise, therefore, that he should have chosen to do his self-portrait in the same way. We see him in his working clothes, observing himself with the same directness and clarity that distinguish his views of the French and Italian countryside. The result is strangely timeless—it might have been painted yesterday rather than in the heyday of Romanticism.

Within a few decades after its beginnings in the last eighteenth century, the industrial revolution had profoundly disturbed and transformed every facet of man's existence in the Western world. It was not until the middle of the nineteenth, however, that artists began to reflect these changes in the themes they chose for their work. *The Third-Class Carriage,* by the French cartoonist and painter Honoré Daumier, is a powerful early example. It captures a peculiarly modern human condition, "the lonely crowd": these people have in common only that they are traveling together in the same railway car. They take no notice of one another— each is alone with his own thoughts. Daumier explores this state with an insight into character and a breadth of sympathy worthy of Rembrandt, whose work he revered. His feeling for the dignity of the poor also suggests Louis Le Nain (see Plate 42), whose work had recently been rediscovered by French critics. Ironically, Daumier found no public for his paintings, even though he was famous for his satirical cartoons. Only a few friends encouraged him and, a year before his death in 1879, arranged his first one-man show.

*Plate 55. Honoré Daumier*
THIRD-CLASS CARRIAGE
*ca. 1862, canvas, height 26"*
*The Metropolitan Museum of Art, Bequest of Mrs. H. O. Havemeyer, 1929*
*The H. O. Havemeyer Collection, New York*

*Plate 56. Ford Madox Brown*
THE LAST OF ENGLAND
*1852–1853, wood panel, height 32½"*
*City Museum and Art Gallery*
*Birmingham, England*

Although Daumier's *Third-Class Carriage* has a contemporary theme, its style is akin to that of the great Romantic, Delacroix (see Plate 51), whose sweeping brushwork and dramatic lighting derive from the Baroque. Other mid-nineteenth-century painters reacted against Romanticism not only in their choice of subject matter but by adopting a radically different style, as evidenced on these two pages. As early as 1846, the French poet and art critic Charles Baudelaire had called for paintings that would express "the heroism of modern life." His friend, the painter Gustave Courbet, made an artistic creed of this demand. A socialist in politics who was deeply affected by the revolutionary upheavals of 1848, Courbet came to believe that the Romantic stress on emotion and imagination was merely an escape from the realities of the time. The modern artist must rely on his own direct experience alone, he must be a realist ("I cannot paint an angel because I have never seen one," he said). Courbet's realism recalls the art of Caravaggio (see Plate 33); like Caravaggio, his work was denounced for its supposed vulgarity and lack of spiritual content. The storm broke when he exhibited *The Stone Breakers* (Plate 57), the first canvas fully embodying his goals. Courbet had seen two men working on a road and had asked them to pose for him in his studio. He has painted them solidly and matter-of-factly, without any pathos or sentiment; the young man's face is averted, the old one's half-hidden by a hat. Yet Courbet cannot have picked them casually; their contrast in age is significant—one is too old for such heavy work, the other too young. Endowed with the dignity of their symbolic status, they do not turn to us for sympathy. Another of Courbet's friends, the socialist Proudhon,

*Plate 57. Gustave Courbet*
THE STONE BREAKERS
*1849, canvas, height 22½″*
*Collection Oskar Reinhart, Winterthur, Switzerland*

likened them to a parable from the Gospels.

Meanwhile, a concern with the "heroism of modern life" asserted itself quite independently in England as well, although the movement lacked a leader of Courbet's stature and assertiveness. Its best known product is probably *The Last of England* (Plate 56) by Ford Madox Brown, which enjoyed vast popularity in the English-speaking world during the latter half of the century. The subject— a group of emigrants watching the coast of their homeland disappear as they set out on their long overseas journey—may no longer carry the same emotional charge it once did, yet there can be no question that Brown has treated an important modern theme and that he has done so with touching seriousness. If the pathos of the scene seems a bit theatrical to us, its documentary quality gains conviction from the impersonal precision of detail, which strikes us as almost photographic; no hint of subjective "handwriting" is permitted to intervene between us and the subject.

*Plate 58. Edgar Degas*
THE GLASS OF ABSINTHE
*1876, canvas, height 36"*
*Louvre Museum, Paris*

For realists such as Courbet or Ford Madox Brown, subject matter was a primary consideration; style was a means to an end, the end being to present significant aspects of modern life as concretely as possible. During the last third of the nineteenth century, this relationship came to be reversed: the "how" now overshadowed the "what." A group of painters in Paris, dubbed Impressionists by a hostile critic (because their work looked so sketchy and unfinished to him), painted "slices of life" that might or might not include human beings and that no longer claimed to be significant in themselves. What gave them importance was the way they were painted, their brilliance of light and color, their freshness and originality of vision. Often the scenes the Impressionists chose were studiedly casual, like *The Glass of Absinthe* (Plate 58) by Edgar Degas. The disenchanted pair at the café table is sharply observed but, as it were, out of the corner of the artist's eye. The design, at first glance, seems as accidental as a snapshot (Degas was an enthusiastic amateur photographer), yet the longer we look, the more we realize that everything has been made to dovetail precisely, that the zigzag of empty tables between us and the luckless couple reinforces their brooding loneliness. Degas had been trained in the tradition of Ingres (see Plate 49); this may account for his strong sense of human character, which sets him apart from his fellow Impressionists. Had he been born fifty years earlier, he might well have become the greatest professional portraitist of his time.

In one respect *The Glass of Absinthe* is uncharacteristic of Impressionism: its subdued color scheme. Seurat's *Bathers* (Plate 59), in contrast, shows the brightness and intensity which led one conservative critic to complain that such

*Plate 59. Georges Seurat*
BATHERS
*1883–1884, canvas, height 79"*
*The National Gallery, London*

pictures hurt his eyes. The choice of subject—people enjoying their leisure on a sunny midsummer day—is equally typical of Impressionist painting. So is its shimmering surface, which results from the way the paint has been applied in separate dots or flicks of pure color. Otherwise, however, Seurat's picture hardly conforms to what we would expect of a quick "impression"; the simplified, smooth contours and the deliberate spacing of these immobile figures give the scene a timeless stability such as we have not encountered since the time of Giotto and Masaccio (see Plates 14, 19). The triumph of Im-

pressionism had indeed been short-lived. Within less than twenty years after its creation in the late 1860s, some of its chief exponents began to search for a style that would combine the virtues of Impressionism with the solidity and durability of the Old Masters. Seurat was the most consistent and methodical of these "Post-Impressionists" (as they have come to be called for lack of a more striking term). The very fact that *Bathers* is a very large canvas, carefully prepared by numerous preliminary studies, demonstrates his ambition to rival the great wall painters of the Renaissance.

*Plate 60. Vincent van Gogh*
SELF-PORTRAIT
*1889, canvas, height 22½"*
*Collection Mr. and Mrs. John Hay Whitney*
*New York*

While Seurat was reshaping Impressionism into a more severe, classical style, Vincent van Gogh pursued the opposite direction, for he believed that Impressionism did not give the artist enough freedom to express his emotions. His early interests were in literature and religion; profoundly dissatisfied with the values of industrial society and imbued with a strong sense of mission, he worked for a while as lay preacher among poor coal miners before he took up painting. Van Gogh's early work has the dark tonality of Daumier and Courbet (see Plates 55 and 57). In 1886, however, he went to Paris, where he met Seurat and other leading artists who opened his eyes to the vital importance of color. His Impressionist phase, although brief, was of key importance for van Gogh's further development; Paris had taught him to see the sensuous beauty of the visible world, yet painting continued to be a vessel for his personal emotions. In order to explore this inner reality with the new means at his command he went to Arles, in the south of France. It was there, between 1888 and 1890, that he produced his greatest pictures. The sectarian Christianity of his early years now gave way to a mystic faith in a creative force animating all forms of life—the missionary had become a prophet. We see him in that role in the *Self-Portrait* on this page, his emaciated, luminous head set off against a whirlpool of darkness. "I want to paint men and women with that something of the eternal which the halo used to symbolize," van Gogh had written, groping to define the human essence that was his aim in pictures such as this. Clearly, the methodical color dots of Seurat were inadequate for his purpose. Van Gogh's brushwork is inalienably personal, each stroke filled with so much movement that it becomes not merely a deposit of

*Plate 61. Edvard Munch*
THE SCREAM
*1893, canvas, height 36″*
*National Museum, Oslo*

color but an incisive graphic gesture. At the time of this *Self-Portrait* the artist had already begun to suffer fits of mental illness. Despairing of a cure, he committed suicide a year later, for he felt very deeply that art alone made his life worth living.

Van Gogh's discontent with the spiritual ills of Western civilization was widely shared toward the end of the nineteenth century. It pervades the early work of a gifted Norwegian, Edvard Munch, who came to Paris in 1889 and was influenced by van Gogh, among others. *The Scream* is an image of fear, the terrifying, unreasoned fear we feel in a nightmare. Its long wavy lines seem to carry the echo of the scream into every corner of the picture, making of earth and sky one great sounding board of fear.

*Plate 62. Georges Rouault*
HEAD OF CHRIST
*1905, oil on paper, mounted on canvas*
*height 54", Collection of the Chrysler Museum at Norfolk*
*Gift of Walter P. Chrysler, Jr.*

The twentieth century may be said to have begun several years late, so far as art is concerned. Between 1901 and 1906, several comprehensive exhibitions of the work of the great Post-Impressionists were held in Paris, making their achievements known to a broad public for the first time. The young painters who had grown up in the morbid mood of the 1890s were profoundly impressed, and several developed a radical new style full of violent color and bold distortions. They so shocked critical opinion that they were dubbed the Fauves (the wild beasts), a label they wore with pride. What brought them together was not a common program but a shared sense of liberation; their work was only loosely related, and the group dissolved after a few years. Nevertheless, its members exerted a lasting influence on that broad stream of modern art which we call expressionism. Among the Fauves, Georges Rouault was the only one for whom the image of man remained a central concern, the true heir of van Gogh. The savage expressiveness of his huge *Head of Christ* mirrors his anguish at the corrupt state of the world. But this expressiveness does not reside only in the "image quality" of the face; the slashing strokes of the brush speak with equal eloquence of the artist's rage and compassion. If we cover up the upper third of the picture, it ceases to be a recognizable image, yet its expressive power is hardly diminished.

Picasso's *Weeping Woman*, by comparison, strikes us as far more disciplined but at the same time more daringly distorted, as if the artist had first carved up this woman's head and hand and then reassembled the anatomical details in a new order, making them spiky and sharp-edged in the process. The inner logic of the method is attested by its success: Picasso has created an image of almost unbearable intensity, reflecting his horror and despair at the time of the Spanish Civil War, which he saw as the prelude of a still greater holocaust. The First World War had produced no such emotional involvement in Picasso; he spent those years perfecting a severely formal, semi-abstract style known as Cubism. It took the agony of his own country to turn him into an expressionist. In his *Weeping Woman* he found a way to put the austere precision of Cubism to new use, forging it into a tool for the creation of images that have lost none of their shattering force during the intervening decades. It was the finest moment in an artistic career without parallel in this century.

*Plate 63. Pablo Picasso*
WEEPING WOMAN
*1937, canvas, height 23½″*
*Collection Mrs. Lee Miller Penrose, London*

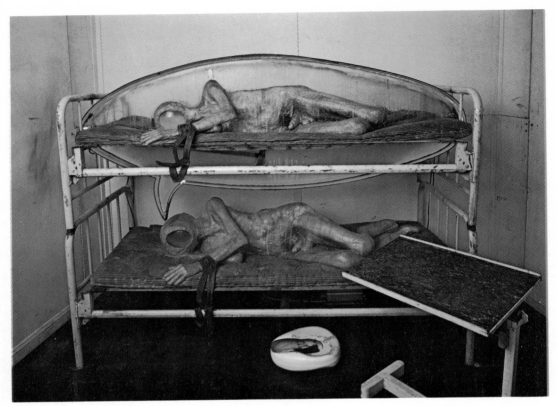

*Plate 64. Edward Kienholz*
THE STATE HOSPITAL
*1966, mixed mediums, height 12'*
*Moderna Museet, Stockholm*

Since the 1950s, we have been witnessing an artistic movement whose name, "Pop Art," derives from its use of popular imagery such as comic strips. To the Pop artist, our visual everyday world, shaped by the mass media and commercial culture and hitherto disdained as vulgar, is a fascinating source of raw material. The most radical results of this tendency to break down the barriers between art and reality are the so-called "environments," full-scale models of real-life situations that combine painting, sculpture, and stagecraft. Kienholz's *The State Hospital* is such an "environment": a cell in a ward for senile patients, with a naked old man strapped to the lower bunk. Neglect and mistreatment have reduced what little mental life he had almost to the vanishing point—his head is a glass bowl with live goldfish. But why the figure in the upper bunk? It duplicates the one below, but since it is enclosed within a comic-strip balloon it must be a mental image, the patient's awareness of himself. The balloon and the metaphoric goldfish bowl are alien to the horrifying realism of the scene, yet they play a vital part in it, for they make us think as well as feel. Kienholz's means may be Pop, but his aim is that of Greek tragedy.

# ❆ CHAPTER 26 ❆

# IMPERIALISM AND THE GREAT WAR 1870–1920

# ❄ CHAPTER 26 ❄

# IMPERIALISM AND
# THE GREAT WAR
# 1870–1920

✿ ✿ ✿ ✿ ✿

The political and economic changes transforming Europe since the eighteenth century had now been carried throughout the world, and all civilizations were forced in important ways to grow more alike. Imperialism carried Western power around the world, and initially, the flow of culture and communication was primarily one-way: European technology, dress, etiquette, ways of doing business, wage payment, religion, and political ideas spread everywhere. Wherever they went and whether they came for gain or out of humanitarian concern, Europeans taught their Christianity and their ways of controlling power, the utility of their roads and railways and medicine, the lure of profit through international trade. Other cultures slowly developed their own ways of using European ideas of education, justice, and nationalism. In return, Europeans enjoyed prestige, power, and wealth. Confident in their superiority, they were slow to borrow from non-Western cultures; but gradually, from strange foods, Eastern and African art, to Oriental religions and philosophy, European civilization came to be enriched by the cultures it had been so quick to overpower.

✿

Imperialism had deep roots within European society, and so did the arms race among Europe's most industrialized nations. This threatening competition had long been held in check by a complicated system of diplomacy. Then suddenly that system broke down, and in 1914 the nations of Europe willingly went to war. For the first time since the Napoleonic era, all the major powers engaged in battle on continental soil, and during more than four years of unrelieved horror, the total energies of society were committed to the bloodiest conflict Europe had ever known. World War I strained the technological and organizing skills developed by the most industrialized and democratic states of the late nineteenth century. It ended with the collapse of the Russian, Austro-Hungarian, and German empires, defeated in war and torn by revolution. The new nations carved from them remade the map of Europe, and in Russia, Communists established a government whose very existence altered political life throughout the West. On the winning side, the liberal Italian state never really recovered from the war, and victorious France and Great Britain emerged significantly changed.

✿

Scholars have pondered the origins of World War I for half a century, and we can now see how a diplomatic system that seemed a triumph of flexible realism led to the disaster. Behind international relations lay domestic pressures within each country. Aggressive imperialism and nationalism were both used by conservative groups to preserve their power at home. In its causes as well as its conduct, the war was also closely tied to the economic and social changes of the preceding 40 years. The machine guns, tanks, airplanes, and submarines that transformed military tactics were products of recent technology. The incredible quantities of armaments and ammunition consumed depended on modern methods of production and management. This war required the mobilization of the population to an extent possible only because of the levels of mass communication, literacy, popular participation, and efficient bureaucracy reached since the mid-nineteenth century.

❈

The effects of the Great War were like those of a revolution. When it ended, fallen governments were replaced, buildings were rebuilt, and in the West, at least, groups previously dominant still held power; but the relations between town and country, peasant and landlord, worker and capitalist, citizen and government had been forever altered in most of Europe. The war thus had a significance beyond the immediate issue of victory and defeat. At the peace conference the desire to make sure so disastrous a conflict could never recur was strengthened by the suspicion that in 1914 a great civilization had come close to suicide.

## I. EUROPEAN IMPERIALISM

❈

### The Meanings of Imperialism

The great model of empire throughout European history lay in the memory of ancient Rome, and in modern times the term *empire* was employed in a related sense by both Napoleons, Austria-Hungary, and Russia up to 1918. To most Europeans in the late nineteenth century, however, those very examples suggested that empire as a form of government was distinctly on the wane. Imperialism came to mean, instead, European rule overseas, and nowadays the term commonly includes economic and cultural domination that may or may not involve direct political control. Thus current students of imperialism stress the spread of a world market, from the trade in luxuries and slaves of the seventeenth century to the multinational corporations of today.

European imperialism, understood in this sense, increased enormously throughout the nineteenth century but especially from the 1860s on. Trade expanded both in value and in geographical range. Wherever commerce took them, Europeans built docks and warehouses, established companies, and made new investments. Whether directed from Europe, by European settlers, or by local merchants, these commercial enterprises adopted European techniques of management, accounting, and technology. Businesses expanded by attracting European capital, and much of the profit they generated was returned to European banks and investors. Thus tied to foreign markets, such enterprises, in turn, transformed local economies through their labor policies and their purchases of local goods and services. This complex process was further stimulated by improved communication. Steamships required better ports, more reliable and expensive provisions, and larger cargoes. Telegraph lines connected India to Europe in 1865, and a cable ran from Vladivostok to Shanghai, Hong Kong, and Singapore by 1871. By the 1880s rail lines operated on every continent; and more were being built, all requiring European equipment, engineers, and investment. By the turn of the century the automobile began to generate a demand not only for highways and bridges but also for a steady flow of petroleum, the basis for new international corporations.

Western influence was not limited to investments and trade. In the same period universities on the European model were established from Constantinople to India; and students from China, Japan, India, and the Middle East became familiar figures in European and American centers of learning. All these developments had fundamental social and political implications for daily life and for traditional elites in Latin America, Asia, and Africa. It is the cumulative effect of this process—a process that increases Western wealth and prestige while disrupting and transforming non-Western societies, that corrodes non-European traditions and cultures while feeding Western interests and power— that the term *imperialism* evokes today.

For the generation preceding World War I, the spread of empire was dramatic evidence of Europe's dynamism; and it was justified on grounds of progress—carrying higher civilization and Christianity to backward lands—as well as national interest. When they spoke of imperialism then (and they spoke and wrote about it a great deal), Europeans generally used the term somewhat more narrowly to mean direct intervention and domination by a European state outside Europe. (The British Empire was the most important example.) This late-nineteenth-century fascination with imperialism revealed a characteristic emphasis upon politics and the state, and it reflected a striking new reality as well. In the past most liberals had considered overseas empire to be both impractical and undesirable, and they had cited the benefits of free trade and the obvious lesson of the American and Latin American revolutions. Then, rather suddenly, imperialism became an important issue in domestic politics and a stimulus to the international rivalries that would culminate in world war.

## Explanations of Imperialism

In 1875, after centuries of close contact with Africa, European powers laid claim to no more than a tenth of Africa's land. Twenty years later, seven nations had established dominion over almost the entire continent. And they had carried their competition to most of Asia and the small islands of the Pacific Ocean. Won in open conquest, through protectorates, and by treaties granting special trading privileges, most of the newly acquired lands at first had few European settlers (the primary means of exploiting local wealth in the past) and most of them lay in tropical zones Europeans had heretofore found unappealing and unhealthy.

Such rapid and far-reaching developments demand explanation, and by the turn of the century, the opponents of imperialism in particular had an explanation for the pervasive imperial fever. In 1902 J. A. Hobson, a British economist, published *Imperialism: A Study*, a critical tract that has been heavily attacked by subsequent scholars but that remains the starting point of modern analysis. Writing during the Boer War, Hobson was eager to show that imperialism offered little to restless populations or to commerce. Emigrants, he noted, preferred to go to the Americas, and Britain's trade with the European continent and the Americas was far greater and growing faster than its trade with its colonies.

The economic explanation of imperialism Hobson found in financiers, small numbers of people controlling great wealth and looking for quick profits. They used their social and political connections to induce the government to protect their investments through political dominance over undeveloped lands. Similarly, they exploited the missionaries, soldiers, and patriotic dreamers who glorified empire. Imperialism thus stemmed from the manipulation of public opinion in the interest of certain capitalists.

Hobson's analysis inspired the still more influential theory of Lenin. The leader of Russia's Marxist revolutionaries, Lenin provided a Marxist interpretation of a subject on which Marx had written little. In *Imperialism: The*

*Last Stage of Capitalism* (1916), Lenin agreed that the stimulus behind empire building was basically economic and that the essence of colonialism was exploitation. Imperialist ventures, Lenin argued, grew not just from the policies of a few but from the very dynamics of capitalism itself. Competition produced monopolies and lowered profits, forcing surplus capital to seek overseas investments. The alternative, to enlarge the domestic market by raising wages, would be uncompetitive and thus further reduce profit. Imperialism was therefore the last "stage" of capitalism, the product of its internal contradictions. Lenin would add during World War I that imperial rivalries, involving whole nations, led to wars that further hastened the end of capitalism. "Imperialist" became an empithet for a system considered decadent as well as immoral.

Although influenced by these views, most historians have remained uncomfortable with them. They contribute little to an understanding of the actual process of imperial conquest, in which capitalists were often reluctant participants. They do not explain why imperialists called for political control beyond treaty rights or for the swift spread of European power into areas that offered small financial return; investment, like trade, remained heavier in more developed noncolonial countries. Nor do economic arguments tell us much about the role of the popular press, explorers, earnest missionaries, and ambitious soldiers in pressing hesitant politicians to imperial conquest.

Many factors help explain the sudden increase in the pace and importance of European imperialism, although all analysts today would agree that economic interests, at least in the long run, were among the most important. Even early in the century the European economy was closely tied to imports of raw materials such as cotton, tea, and timber, and policies to guarantee these supplies had

been welcome. A general increase in trade and the growing demand for rubber, oil, and rare metals spurred the search for natural resources. Stiffening competition in international commerce and rising tariffs taught businessmen to seek the backing of their governments. By the late nineteenth century a society familiar with self-made men was readier to believe that new lands offered the chance to make a quick fortune. Technology, too, played a part. Not only was regular trade with distant places made easier, but dynamite lessened the difficulty of building roads, while modern medicine reduced the dangers of the tropics. Coaling stations and telegraph posts acquired strategic as well as commercial importance, a fact that argued for military and political protection.

Beyond such rational calculations, imperialism was rooted in the values Europeans held and in their domestic society and politics. Mass-circulation newspapers gloried in imperialism, writing of adventure and wealth, Christianity and progress in the virile language of force. To the people of the late nineteenth century, exploration and conquest were high and noble adventure. Press reports made popular heroes of daring men like Henry M. Stanley, who followed the rivers of South Africa and penetrated the interior of the Congo, and Pierre de Brazza, who traveled up the Congo River, overcoming hardship and danger after dismantling a steamship so it could be carried around the rapids. Exploration seemed, in itself, an expression of progress, the brave adventurer the personification of individual initiative. If the explorer also gained wealth, that completed the parable.

The missionaries who risked their lives to build a chapel in the jungle and convert the heathen were as symbolically appealing as the explorer. For churches often at odds with the culture of their day and in conflict with the state, here was a dramatic outlet and a welcome reassurance of their importance in modern life. Hundreds of Social Darwinists preached the inevitable conflict of race with race and hailed the resultant spread of civilization, by which they meant, of course, their own. Geographical societies became prominent in every European country, proudly acclaiming yet another association of new knowledge with increased power.

Where class tensions were high and domestic conflict serious, colonial expansion offered all citizens a share in national glory and gain. Rudyard Kipling's poems of imperial derring-do in exotic lands hail the simple cockney soldier; whatever his lot at home, he was a ruler abroad. Thus in politics, imperialism, like nationalism, cut across social divisions. It was an important part, especially in Great Britain and Germany, of the political resurgence of the right, allowing conservative groups strong in the army, the Church, and the aristocracy to ally themselves with commercial interests in a program of popular appeal. Employment as well as glory was promised as the fruit of a policy of strength. Significantly, imperialism never achieved comparable political effect in France, the nation with the second largest of the European empires, though this empire, too, was built principally by soldiers and priests. The right fumbled its effort at mass appeal in the Dreyfus affair; patriots were preoccupied with avenging the loss of Alsace and Lorraine to Germany; and French nationalism retained ideas associated with the Revolution that often conflicted with those of imperialism. Still, imperial triumphs were welcomed when they came. Everywhere empire offered the appeal of individual daring and direct action in a society becoming more bureaucratized. It gave openings to groups, such as the military and the clergy, often disparaged at home, and it supplemented popular theories with concrete tales of risk, gain, glory, and conquest. It fit conceptions of European racial and cultural superiority, and it proved useful in domestic politics.

## Patterns of Imperialism

Despite the general popularity of imperialist ideas, few wholehearted imperialists held high political office even in Great Britain. The history of colonial conquest in this period was less one of long-range schemes than of particular decisions that appear almost accidental when viewed singly. Frequently, individual explorers, traders, or officers established their claims in a given region by treaties with native leaders won to agreement by fear, the lure of profit, the promise of investment, or the hope of help against some nearby enemy. Once so involved, European interests proved difficult to dislodge. The Europeans on the scene obtained recognition, often after the fact, from their home government. In the process of enforcing contracts and maintaining order, they tended to exceed their original authorization and to extend their territorial claims. Governments anxious not to appear weak before their public or before other powers then supported such moves; trading concessions and protectorates became colonies. This pattern of expansion required little premeditation. Applying their own laws and practices to other cultures, Europeans were shocked when natives failed to honor Western rules, and they responded with increased force.

Even Europeans attracted by non-Western cultures or devoted to helping local populations, in the name of Western religion and medicine, undermined their host societies—introducing alien ideas, institutions, and technology and overwhelming them by sheer wealth and power. There is, in fact, a whole other history of imperialism just now being written from the perspective of the indigenous peoples that shows how native political,

economic, and religious organization was disrupted by the arrival of outsiders. To the confident people of empire, such conditions left no alternative but further European control.

## Africa

From a few coastal posts, European involvement in Africa began in the 1670s a rapid spread inland that would end in the partition of the entire continent by 1895 (see Map 26.1). Early signs of the domination to come were the collapse of Egyptian finances, the energetic exploration of the Congo sponsored by King Leopold II of Belgium, and the increasing conflicts between the British and the Boers.

The Suez Canal was completed in 1869, the shares in its ownership held by French investors and the khedive of Egypt, who ruled as a monarch representing the nominal suzerainty of the Ottomans. When the debt-plagued khedive sold his shares in 1875, they were purchased by the British government in one of Disraeli's most dramatic coups. Determined to protect their investments, the British and French then established joint control over Egyptian finances. In 1882, however, a nationalist revolt by the Egyptian army against both the khedive and foreign influence threatened this arrangement. The British government decided to mount a show of strength (in which the French parliament refused to allow France a part), and the Royal Navy bombarded Alexandria to teach Egyptians that contracts must be met. In the resulting chaos, the British attempted to restore order, a process that quickly led to their occupying Egypt, and the country remained

---

**A German cartoon of 1896 lampoons African people and the Teutonic order brought to Africa by German imperialism.** (Photo: The Granger Collection)

under their rule until after World War II. In Tunisia a similar pattern of increased foreign investments followed by a financial crisis and intricate diplomatic maneuverings brought about French occupation in 1881. Both events accelerated the competition for African empire.

Although reluctant to accept responsibility for all their citizens did, European governments nevertheless found themselves drawn piecemeal into scores of treaties that prescribed for societies little understood and fixed boundaries in areas whose geography was barely known. The International Association for the Exploration and Civilization of Central Africa, founded in Brussels in 1876, quickly became a private operation of Leopold II. The association paid less attention to its lofty aims of furthering science and ending slavery than to the vast territorial claims it might make by sponsoring Stanley's explorations. From their outposts along the west coasts, the French, the English, Spaniards, and Portuguese hurried to push into the hinterlands of what are now Senegal and Nigeria.

French gains in West Africa were the most extensive of all, and in 1898 a group of soldiers who had pushed two-thirds of the way across the continent at its widest point arrived at Fashoda, on the Nile, a few days before the British, who were moving into the Sudan. Both nations considered the encounter of their troops at Fashoda a matter of national honor, and imperialists plotted on maps how dominance over Africa was at stake. The French imagined holdings stretching from west to east across the continent, controlling the headwaters of the Nile. The British talked in terms of territory and maybe even a railway from the Cape of Good Hope to Cairo, a north-south axis through the continent. Thus for weeks Great Britain and France were on the brink of war over the obscure outpost at Fashoda, sought by no

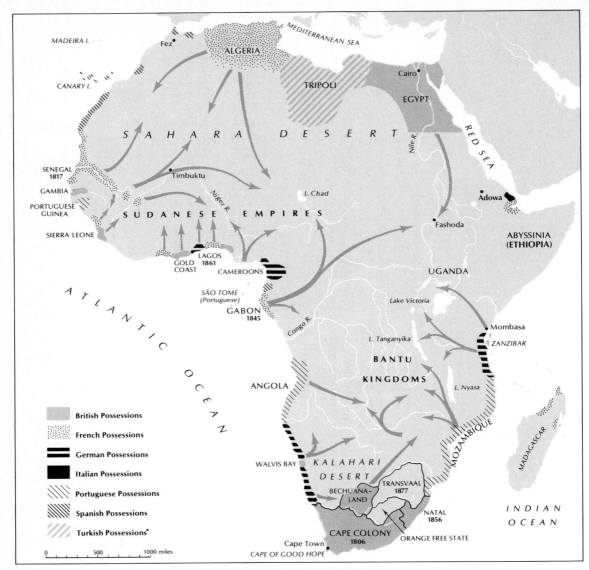

**MAP 26.1 AFRICA 1885**

general staff. The confrontation ended when the French, divided at home over the Dreyfus affair, chose to give way.

In South Africa, Cecil Rhodes typified the interconnection of local politics, private interest, and visions of empire. Confident of white and, indeed, Anglo-Saxon superiority, he schemed and propagandized relentlessly, stretching old claims, using trading companies and his own wealth to establish new ones. He died during the Boer War, but the British victory paved the way for the estab-

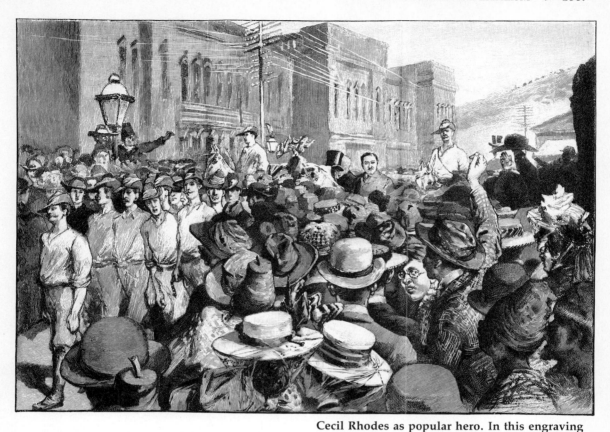

**Cecil Rhodes as popular hero. In this engraving of 1897 Rhodes is shown leaving the Cape Town railway station, his carriage drawn by a private army (called the Matabili boys—after the Zulu warriors) through a crowd that is meant to depict the romance and color of empire.** (Photo: The Granger Collection)

lishment of the Union of South Africa in 1910, a partial fulfillment of Rhodes's ambitions.

As the European states were drawn into the scramble, they sought through diplomacy to lessen the clear danger that clashes in Africa would lead to war in Europe. At Berlin in 1885 the powers established rules for one another. The most important was that coastal settlement by a European nation would give it claim to the hinterlands beyond if it controlled them. Straight lines drawn from haphazard coastal conquests cut across the little-known indigenous cultures, but they restrained the anarchy of European ambition. The powers also agreed at Berlin to prohibit slavery; and five years later they banned liquor and limited arms in the zone between the Sahara and the Cape Colony. Humanitarian considerations had not been wholly forgotten, and by the turn of the century, the ruthless exploitation of the Belgian Congo was considered an international scandal. Those who bravely planted their flags and wrote out treaties for chieftains to sign did not doubt that theirs was a beneficial achievement to be measured by mission hospitals and schools, new roads and political order as well as profit. By 1912 only Liberia and Ethio-

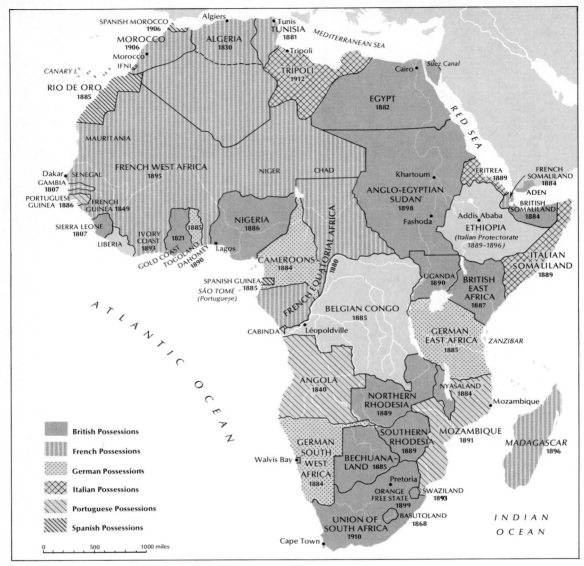

**MAP 26.2 AFRICA 1914**

pia were formally free of European domination (see Map 26.2). The social, cultural, religious, and political life of Africans was everywhere submerged under an imposed European order based on raw power and used for prestige and profit whatever its other intentions.

## Asia

For more than a century the decline of the Ottoman Empire had been a major theme of international relations, one clearly demarked by the independence of Greece early in the century, the Crimean War at midcentury, and then by the growing turmoil in the Balkans and the British occupation of Egypt. As British, French, Russian, and German interests competed for political privileges and economic concessions (that the Germans won the right to build a railroad from the Bosporus to Baghdad was recognized as a major diplomatic triumph and a troubling challenge), it almost seemed as if those rivalries were what held the Ottoman Empire together.

In the East beyond the Ottoman Empire, Great Britain and Russia were the main contenders for influence (see Map 26.3). Persia had felt their competition since the 1830s and by the 1870s had conceded control of the Imperial Bank of Persia to British interests. Russia competed by exerting military pressure along Persia's northern frontier and in the 1890s by offering a large loan and related concessions in an effort to reduce Britain's dominance. As part of a general entente reached in 1907 (see below), the two European powers agreed on spheres of influence: the British sphere would include the area of the Persian Gulf, in the south, and Russia's, the north. Their competition, by limiting the intrusions of either power, had helped the Persian state preserve a nominal independence, but their presence increased its instability, and revolution erupted in 1905. The technique of playing off Russian and British ambitions was less successful in Afghanistan, where the emir's efforts to use the Russians as a counterweight to British influence could not match Britain's determination to use its economic and military power to guarantee the security of India on Afghanistan's southeast border.

India remained the jewel of the British Empire, the envy of all imperial powers. As a British trading partner, India stood on a par with France (only the United States ranked higher). Its wealth and the prestige of its culture made India the very symbol of empire, a special status recognized in the proclama-

tion of Queen Victoria as empress of India in 1876. Many of the leading figures of British political life made their reputations in the India service, and their techniques of administration through local lords and British courts were often proclaimed as models of enlightened rule. Yet the growth of trade and industry did not prevent devastating famines in the 1890s, and concessions to local government only stimulated increasingly organized and nationwide demands for a native voice in political life.

East of India and south of China only Siam (Thailand) preserved its independence of European control through its willingness to modernize—that is, to adopt European forms of political and economic organization—and through the countervailing pressures of the three European powers in neighboring realms, who, in effect, constrained one another. The British annexed upper Burma in 1886 and part of Malaya in 1896; the Dutch were on the island of Borneo; and French influence had steadily increased in Cambodia and Cochin-China (both parts of Indochina) during the 1860s, despite the indifference of the governments in Paris. Whenever Christians were attacked or a trader murdered, the local commander pressed native rulers for further political concessions without waiting for instructions from home. The French themselves seemed unable to constrain the extension of their authority. Even the modest goal of providing their enclave a secure frontier—a European conception that ignored social realities—usually led to war and expansion into another ancient realm. France in this way eventually found itself at war with China in 1883; and though parliament voted down the government of Premier Jules Ferry, France's leading imperialist, the war nevertheless resulted in a French protectorate, reorganized in 1887 as French Indochina.

The weakness of China and the strengthening of Japan were the central realities of

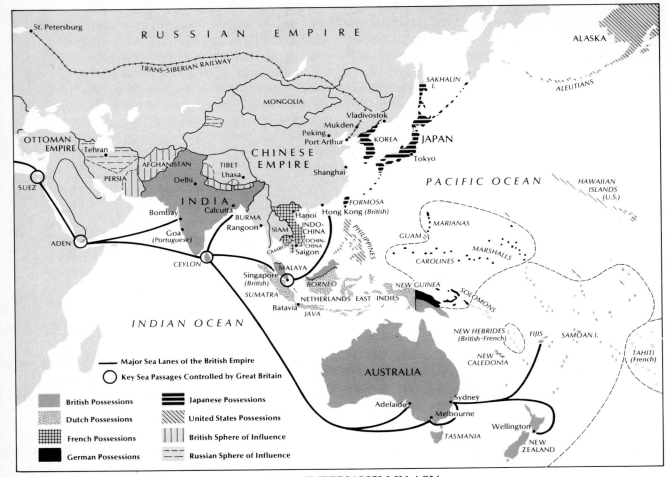

**MAP 26.3 IMPERIALISM IN ASIA**

Southeast Asian history in the second half of the nineteenth century. Both proud nations had sought to keep intruding Europeans at a distance, and both failed, but with contrasting results. For the huge Chinese Empire, its administrative system threatened by inefficiency and provincial warlords, Western missionaries and traders were especially disruptive. When the Chinese attempted to restrict the importation of opium, which was as expensive and demoralizing for them as it was profitable for the British traders who brought

the opium from India, the result was a brief war that led to the cession of Hong Kong to Britain (1841) and of special foreign trading rights in a number of Chinese cities. The impact of missionaries contributed to the Taiping Rebellion (1850–1864), in which a Chinese-led millenarian movement incorporating elements of Christianity and social discontent produced revolts that threatened the empire. Battling for survival, the government was forced to grant new concessions to Britain, the United States, France, and Russia for trade, the protection of missionaries, and extraterritorial rights. In 1860 British and French forces occupied Peking and burned the summer palace in retaliation for the seizure of their envoys, and Russia took Vladivostok—a step recognized by China's Department of Foreign Affairs, a ministry not needed before.

Thus the French gains in Indochina, the extension of Russian interests in Manchuria, the arrival of more and more missionaries, and further trading concessions were all part of a continuing process. Again and again, a local riot, a missionary murdered, or a contract broken would lead to renewed demands and military pressure from Western powers. In 1898 inland waters were opened to foreign shipping (mainly British), and the Germans laid claim to Kiaochow Bay, as Germany and Japan now joined the competition for claims on China. Chinese efforts to raise revenues, reform administration, and stimulate railroads required, in turn, further loans from and concessions to Western nations. The Boxer Rebellion of 1900–1901, a complicated response by local militias outraged at foreigners and the weakness of their own government, brought another round of violence. Scores of Western missionaries, agents, and some diplomats were killed, prompting heavy military intervention, especially by Russia and Germany. When order was restored, China agreed to a large indemnity. Popular risings in Africa and Asia were treated by Europeans simply as a breakdown of order requiring their further intervention. The only defense against European imperialism even in a great and ancient nation appeared to be a westernization that deepened European influence. For China, that also meant the revolution of 1911, led by Sun Yat-sen, and the establishment of the Chinese Republic.

Japan, which for centuries had preserved its isolation, was in 1853 successfully pressed by Commodore Matthew Perry of the United States to permit commerce with the West, an opening quickly followed by a series of treaties permitting trade and protecting the rights of foreigners. There followed the familiar pattern of misunderstandings, broken agreements, antiforeign feeling, and renewed Western demands; but domestic political transformation came quickly in Japan. A new generation of leaders joined with the emperor, after a brief civil war, in carrying out the Meiji Restoration (1868). The essentially feudal system that had lasted seven centuries was ended, and Japan embarked on a systematic policy of adapting Western industry, technology, education, laws and governmental institutions, including a constitutional system (much influenced by Germany's) in 1889. The resultant economic growth, efficient administration, and modern army enabled Japan, like the nations of the West, to attack China and win easy victories in the war of 1894–1895. Japan's gains included Formosa and the control of Korea. As in its victory over Russia (1904–1905), Japan showed that successful imperialism, like the ambitions and power from which it stemmed, need not be limited to Europeans. With the United States in control of the Philippines, as a result of the Spanish-American War (1898), the Western system of power relations dominated Southeast Asia and encircled the globe.

## II. THE COMING OF WORLD WAR
❊
### Realignments in the Bismarckian System

Despite many dangerous moments after 1870, there was no war between major states for more than 40 years. Remarkably, European governments appeared able to juggle competing worldwide interests abroad and

# ❄ EXPERIENCES OF DAILY LIFE ❄
## *The British in India*

Service to the empire offered an attractive career for many a young Englishman. If he was fortunate enough to have a solid secondary education (which normally meant the expense of a private school) yet needed to work for a living, and if he lacked the taste or talent for law or medicine, then employment in some imperial service beckoned. This might mean the army, but civilian service generally paid better. The Indian Civil Service was the most prestigious choice. Large and well-organized, the ICS developed from the reforms that followed rebellions against the British in 1857–1858. Its members saw themselves as an elite corps, and they were, in practice, the effective rulers of India, almost unchallenged in their local authority (until further reforms on the eve of World War I granted the Indian elite more of a voice). New officers in the ICS were selected through an open competition that included a "literary examination" and interviews. It helped, of course, to have some cousins, uncles, or more distant relatives who had served in India. Successful candidates were especially likely to be the younger sons of country squires, men who added to their social connections and proper manners a fondness for the outdoors, skill as horsemen, and self-confidence.

Of the 30 or so who passed the examination each year in the 1880s, the youngest might be only 18; and, with a job assured, they might spend a few more years in England, perhaps at a university, before traveling through the Mediterranean, the recently opened Suez Canal, and on to India— a matter of at least three weeks by steamship. In the order of their rank on the examination, the new Civilians, as members of the ICS were called, picked from the posts available. All would start as the subordinate of a district officer, the administrator of a region about the size of an English county. Of the nine provinces of British India, the Madras region was considered the least desirable, not because of its hot summers or recent famine (1879) but because opportunities for advancement appeared more limited there. Although a capital, Madras was not impressive. Even the small coastal steamers had to drop anchor off shore until a new marina was built in the 1890s. The newly arriving Civilian would be rowed to the beach in a dingy (horses were delivered to Madras by being dumped overboard and shooed ashore). Even the best shops along the principal street—Orr's, Spencer's, or Smith's—were only one-story wooden affairs (replaced by more impressive stone buildings by the end of the century).

The new ICS officer would nevertheless remain in the city a couple of months before being sent out to his first post; his initiation into imperial life began in the provincial capital. The hotels were poor, and their English guests stayed only until a local English family invited them into a private home. The Madras Club, on the other hand, was said to be the best in India. So there, the new Civilian would spend as much of his time as possible. Membership in the Club was exclusive. No Indians could belong, although some smaller, local clubs did sometimes elect a few natives who were judged to have suitable social positions. Not for a long time had any English businessmen been elected to the Madras Club. By the 1880's merchants who were full partners in wholesale firms might expect a favorable vote; retailers continued to be blackballed until the end of the century.

These careful distinctions of status among the English were most clearly measured in a social life administered by women. Merchants' wives called on officials' wives (if permitted social intercourse at all); and the wives of officials sent invitations to one another in an order that, like their demeanor, reflected their husbands' rank as precisely as any insignia or title. The new ICS officer was expected to spend much of his time in top hat and gloves, leaving his calling card at the ladies' homes, perhaps having tea with them, and then waiting to be invited for dinner. The speed with which such invitations arrived involved complex assessments of his lineage, manners, and appearance, an important first measure of his prospects. These wives, surrounded by servants, were of course white and nearly always English; only Englishmen of the lower classes married "women of color." Social life also included dances and amateur theatricals to which some Indians might be invited (there was debate, however, about the wisdom of allowing Indians to see English women in undignified stage roles). Polo matches, riding to the hounds (with a variety of animals substituting for foxes), horse races, and gymkhanas were the other favorite social activities that might prove important to a Civilian's career. And such occasions would be fondly recalled at the annual dinners of the ICS amid many toasts to the queen and the "Spirit of the Service."

On his first assignment, the new official might work at the headquarters of a district officer, called with admirable directness the collector, before being sent to his own, more isolated and subordinate post. He thus began with little formal training but after an initiation that prepared him to rule by "prestige of race" as much as by direct power. Indeed, he might be the only white man at his station except for a low-ranking army officer or a trader, and there he had the daily responsibility to see that order was maintained, that local disputes were adjudicated, and that taxes were properly assessed and collected. The ablest officers would regularly tour the area under their command, despite the lack of roads or accommodations, and even learn the local language. In due time, promotion would bring a better salary and more opportunities to hunt, dance, and take tea "with his own kind," who even in modest towns lived in an English enclave some distance from the native center. Eventually, the Civilian might become the collector himself; probably he would rise no higher. After some 30 years of service, he would retire to England, which he might have visited but three or four times since his school days. There he would remember with pride and a certain nostalgia having once held the power of life and death over millions of people, but the real point of his stories about quaint or dangerous native customs was the glory of empire and England's destiny to rule. ✳

**A young British official on camelback, Lahore.** (Photo: The Bettmann Archive/BBC Hulton)

complex social changes at home, including the altered bases of power created by industrialization and democracy. Between nations, this flexibility was managed through a traditional diplomacy conducted by gentlemen, most of them aristocrats, in secrecy and according to elaborate rules. Only later did it become clear how limited the efficacy of that diplomacy was. Gradually, the experience of imperialism and the greater importance of public opinion altered what could be negotiated and how negotiations were conducted, and foreign policy came to be more directly constrained both by military imperatives and domestic politics.

Bismarck had established the German Empire as the arbiter of Continental peace at the Congress of Berlin in 1878, and to preserve that position, he relied first of all on Germany's alliance with Austria-Hungary. Central Europe was thus secure, and Austria-Hungary's ties to several of the Balkan states combined with the Three Emperors' Alliance (a treaty among Russia, Germany, and Austria-Hungary) to reduce any danger from the East. Italy was then added to this network when France occupied Tunisia, and Bismarck took advantage of Italian resentment to form the Triple Alliance of Germany, Austria-Hungary, and Italy. Signed in 1882, the pact had a five-year term and could be renewed. Finally, in 1887 Italy and the United Kingdom made a vague mutual commitment to preserve the status quo in the Mediterranean.

At its height, therefore, the Bismarckian system achieved the diplomatic isolation of France, good Anglo-German relations, a formal understanding with Russia, an alliance with Italy and Austria-Hungary, as well as additional ties extending into the Balkan and Iberian peninsulas. These accomplishments required great skill; Italy and Russia, for example, had more reasons for conflict with Austria-Hungary than with anyone else. Although the precise provisions of such treaties were secret and defensive, they were understood to imply far more than they specifically provided, and they placed Germany in a position of influence rare among sovereign states in peacetime.

Even before Bismarck fell from power, however, the system showed signs of weakness. The Three Emperors' Alliance, renewed in 1884, was allowed to lapse in 1887 because a flare-up of conflict among the Balkan States had reawakened suspicion between Austria-Hungary and Russia, a serious danger to Bismarckian diplomacy that could not be overcome. With characteristic flexibility, Bismarck repaired the damage by immediately signing a separate Reinsurance Treaty with Russia, providing for the neutrality of either power if the other was at war. To preserve the Triple Alliance, which also came up for renewal in 1887, it was necessary to add recognition of Italian ambitions in the Balkans, Africa, and (in case of war with France) Corsica and Nice. Ironically, the weakest member of the Alliance could maneuver more freely than its powerful friends.

From the Germans' standpoint, the keystone of the Bismarckian system was the alliance with Austria-Hungary. Beyond that, their confidence rested on the assumption that enmities between France and Great Britain, Great Britain and Russia, and Italy and France would prevent any of them from aligning against the Second Reich. It was easy from Berlin to overlook one factor that might draw these powers together—common fear of Germany.

### The Shifting Balance 1880–1905

An expression of German power, these treaties were supposed to provide security, but it required Bismarck's supple skill to offset the menace of sudden attack they advertised. With his fall, the system he had constructed broke down. German diplomacy after 1890 was poorly coordinated, often inconsistent, and disruptive.

Bismarck's successors did not renew the understanding with Russia; instead, a traditional dislike of Slavs reinforced by Junker objections to heavy imports of cheaper Russian grain led high German officials to prefer to keep the Triple Alliance uncluttered by a treaty with Russia.[1] France seized the opportunity to break out of diplomatic isolation and pressed the Russian government—hesitant but already turning to France for loans and arms purchases—for an alliance. The understanding the two nations reached in 1891 became a full alliance in less than three years, a major shift in European military commitments. Russia agreed to support France if it should be attacked by Germany or by Italy with German aid, and France agreed to support Russia if it was attacked by Germany or by Austria-Hungary with German aid.

An accord between the Russian autocracy and the French republic had seemed politically impossible. But the tsar now greeted French delegates while a band played the "Marseillaise," previously prohibited as too revolutionary to be heard in Russia, and the Franco-Russian agreement was to last as long as the Triple Alliance.

German diplomats, in response, sought to foster some understanding with Great Britain and to demonstrate their country's place in world affairs. Those aims conflicted. The "new course" of *Weltpolitik* ("world policy"), backed by imperial claims and navy building, appeared more threatening with each of the verbal explosions for which the emperor became famous.

In 1896 William II sent a telegram of congratulation to S. J. P. Kruger, president of the South African Republic, after the Boers had defeated a raid on the Transvaal by a small private army organized by Englishmen who hoped to stir a revolution there. The message, deeply resented in Great Britain, was meant to show the British how much they needed German friendship; instead, it encouraged distrust of Germany. During the Boxer Rebellion the kaiser's enthusiastic talk of the "yellow peril" and instructions for his soldiers to behave like the barbaric Huns of old did nothing to enhance his reputation for stability or lessen the atmosphere of menace. Germans proclaimed the "natural" alliance between the Teutonic and Anglo-Saxon races but also took soundings about a possible Continental coalition against the United Kingdom. The navy they were building, which looked like a direct challenge to Great Britain and a threat to its empire, became the central issue in all efforts at some rapprochement between the two powers. When the Germans demanded a formal alliance before they would limit their shipbuilding, the British were convinced that the German fleet was aimed at them.

During the difficult years of the Boer War, the United Kingdom had found its diplomatic independence no longer so splendid and was, as the Germans hoped, beginning to look for new international understandings. In 1902 it broke its long tradition of refusing peacetime alliances by signing a treaty with Japan. Its overall aim was, of course, to guard the empire through alliance; its immediate purpose was to prevent France from supporting Russia's expansion into East Asia.

The colonial clashes between Great Britain and France in the last decade of the century had seemed some of the gravest threats to European peace. When the French had withdrawn from the confrontation at Fashoda in 1898, Foreign Minister Théophile Delcassé had set about turning humiliation into gain by seeking a broader understanding with Great Britain. France had learned not to demand too much, and its delegation of extraordinarily able diplomats worked steadily for

---

[1] Renewal of the Reinsurance Treaty was one of the issues that led to the break between Bismarck and William II in 1890. The charge that it was incompatible with the Triple Alliance was at least technically incorrect, for the promise of neutrality was not to apply if Russia attacked Austria.

the reduction of conflicts. By the turn of the century, France had dropped its resistance to British domination in Egypt in return for recognition of French interests in North Africa, particularly Morocco.

Similarly, France had won Italian acknowledgment of its interest in Morocco by recognizing Italian ambitions in Libya, and in 1902 the two nations pledged neutrality if either was attacked by a third power. Although the Triple Alliance was renewed in the same year, Italy, in fact, sat on the fence between the Franco-Russian and the Austro-German alliance. The culmination of France's policy was the Anglo-French Entente Cordiale of 1904. In one sweeping effort, France and Great Britain sought to eliminate all the major issues of imperial conflict between them. From Siam to Newfoundland, the Niger River to North Africa, they agreed on their spheres of influence and dominant interests.

Formally, the Entente Cordiale was nothing more than an understanding, but France was right in seeing it as a major break in the diplomatic encirclement Bismarck had created around it. Without demanding very formal guarantees, France was achieving a great deal. Edward VII's visit to Paris in 1903 and the French president's to London that year and to Rome in 1905 testified to France's new place in European affairs. These understandings came in the nick of time, for they helped prevent the Russo-Japanese War of 1904–1905 from leading to conflict between France and Great Britain and effectively countered German efforts to break up the Franco-Russian alliance.

### Hardening Alliances 1905–1912

Germany's diplomatic position remained strong—Britain and France were not allied; Russia's defeat at the hands of Japan and its subsequent revolution greatly reduced its influence; the chances of an Anglo-German understanding remained; and the Triple Alliance was intact. An assertive policy, German leaders reasoned, would enable them to capitalize on this situation. But the tenor of international relations was changing. Imperial ambitions, which had often threatened European relations in the preceding decades, were no longer so certain a source of antagonism as to prevent a coalition against Germany. The experience of imperialism and the politicians' increased concern for public opinion tended to transform international claims (and reactions to the Kaiser's bluster) into dangerous, if vague, issues of national honor. As armaments increased and treaties proliferated, each power became more obsessed with its own security. Thus within seven years, three diplomatic crises—each of which at first seemed a victory for Germany—in fact, brought its opponents closer together.

The first great crisis arose over Morocco. France had carefully won the acquiescence of each interested power, except Germany, in its designs on Morocco. The French planned to deal with Germany last; and the Germans, who had little direct interest there, intended to get the highest price possible for French annexation of the decaying sultanates. Wanting to test the loose understandings by which the French had improved their diplomatic position, the German chancellor, Bernhard von Bülow, demanded an international conference, for which there was solid basis in prior guarantees, and belligerently threatened France. Delcassé, the architect of French foreign policy, was forced from office, but the chancellor then sought more than this symbolic triumph. He reasoned that in a conference the other Triple Alliance nations would stand behind him, Russia and Great Britain would be won to the Germans' "correct" position, and a humiliated France would be left isolated once more.

The conference that met at Algeciras in

1906 did, in fact, produce a compromise, recognizing both international status for Morocco and the primacy of French interests, but it was a disaster for German diplomacy. Only Austria-Hungary loyally voted with its European neighbor. Italy, Russia, Great Britain, and the United States (now a regular participant in such international agreements) supported France. The German bludgeon led to military talks between French and British officials and a far stronger sense of mutual interest.

After Algeciras, Anglo-German competition for supremacy on the seas grew more serious. Both sides increased their plans for naval construction despite two great conferences at The Hague in 1899 and 1907 on disarmament and compulsory arbitration. In fact, no power was willing to sacrifice any of its strength, but it was the German delegates who bluntly accepted the onus for rejecting any limitation on the sovereign right to make war. Such actions, combined with its militarism and the threats of its diplomacy, made Germany increasingly appear the major danger to peace. When an interview in the London *Daily Telegraph* quoted Kaiser William complaining that England was ungrateful for his nation's neutrality in the Boer War, the reaction was sharp and angry. British statesmen and journalists indulged in public recriminations that heightened tension while the efforts to settle naval questions broke down.

Also in 1907, a series of agreements showed again that imperial issues, which the Germans expected would keep their antagonists apart, were not necessarily divisive. France and Russia each reached an accord with Japan, defining the areas of preeminent Japanese interest and agreeing to preserve the integrity of China. These understandings with Britain's Asian ally opened the way for an entente between Great Britain and Russia in which the two nations resolved points of contention from the straits controlling access to the Black Sea, to Persia, Afghanistan, and Tibet. An informal coalition of France, Russia, and Britain, the Triple Entente, now balanced the Triple Alliance. Its major beneficiary was France, which had long worked for this accommodation between its two European allies. The European powers were finding it surprisingly easy to mark out and limit their spheres of interest so long as they could ignore the internal politics of the places where they competed for influence.

Internal politics, however, could be neither ignored nor controlled in the Balkan States, and here the second crisis of the period arose. Serbia, led by a new king and a radical nationalist government, became Austria-Hungary's primary Balkan antagonist, and revolution in the Ottoman Empire in 1908—led by the Young Turks, whose movement sought to modernize the nation—foreshadowed a revival of Ottoman influence in the Balkans as well. Ever mindful of the dangers of nationalism, Austria-Hungary decided to strengthen its position there and at home by annexing Bosnia and Herzegovina, which it had occupied since the Congress of Berlin in 1878. Austria-Hungary claimed it had Russia's agreement, but Russia, whose Slavophiles were infuriated by the annexation, demanded an international conference. Britain and France supported the call, even though they suspected the Russian foreign minister, Izvolsky, of some double dealing. Germany, angered by the precipitateness of Austria-Hungary's action, nevertheless stood by her ally. Diplomatic crises were becoming tests of alliances (and it was significant that Italy expressed resentment at not being consulted by Austria-Hungary rather than loyalty to the Triple Alliance).

The third major crisis once again involved Morocco. Both Germany and France were prepared to reach some definitive agreement, but the Germans thought to speed things up by sending the gunboat *Panther* to the Moroccan port of Agadir in 1911. They then asked for all of the French Congo in exchange for French annexation of Morocco. Both the proposal and the method seemed excessive, and in Great Britain, David Lloyd George publicly decried them. The powers concerned eventually reached a compromise: France would cede parts of its Congo lands and bits of its other African territories adjacent to German colonies. But the fact of the settlement counted for less than the rising tension in Europe and the growing distrust of the Germans. After a final effort at naval agreement failed, Britain decided in 1912 to withdraw its battleships from the Mediterranean, concentrating them in the North Sea, while France sent its fleet to replace them. With the crisis and the confrontation of 1908, the loose Triple Entente was becoming at least as binding as the Triple Alliance.

### Two Wars in the Balkans

The Balkans became the focal point for the interplay of the forces of European imperialism, nationalism, and power politics. In Serbia, Bulgaria, Rumania, and Greece, social conflicts and the strains of modernization led to governments that won support by embracing nationalism. At the same time, the Balkan policies of Austria-Hungary and Russia had become enmeshed in each country's own bitter domestic divisions, which further reduced diplomatic flexibility. Moreover, Germany, through railway concessions in Turkey, had also developed interests in the peninsula, as had Italy, whose victory over the Ottoman sultanate in 1912 (part of her conquest of Tripoli—see Chapter 25) encouraged Greece, Bulgaria, Serbia, and Montenegro to join forces against the empire. They drove the Ottomans from all their remaining European holdings except Constantinople. The great powers then pressured the belligerents to accept peace, but the tension between

Austria-Hungary and Russian-backed Serbia sustained the ferment. Serbia also had territorial designs on weakly organized areas of Albania and Montenegro, and each Balkan state had boundary disputes with the others. These conflicting claims erupted in a second Balkan war within a few months when some Bulgarian troops launched an attack on Serbian and Greek forces. Bulgaria had gained more territory in the earlier war than had the other Balkan States; and although the Bulgarian government quickly disavowed this latest move, Serbia, Greece, Rumania, and Turkey declared war on Bulgaria and quickly defeated it. When threats from Austria-Hungary forced Serbia to abandon some of its gains, Serbian nationalists replied by proclaiming their concern and sympathy for their fellow Slavs who were subject to Austrian rule in Bosnia and Herzegovina.

Thus tensions were high when on June 28, 1914, Archduke Francis Ferdinand, the heir to the Austrian and Hungarian thrones, paraded in Sarajevo, the capital of Bosnia. It was an act of some courage. One bomb just missed killing the archduke, and his car passed other conspirators who lost their courage and failed to fire. Then the car made a wrong turn; and as it backed up, a young Bosnian revolutionary fired point-blank, killing both the archduke and his wife.

For the Austro-Hungarian government, convinced the Serbian government was involved in the assassination, here was a challenge that required strong action. It sent a special emissary to Berlin, where the German government, with a lack of reflection that remains remarkable, promised full support to Austria. On the other side, the French president and prime minister went to Russia to declare their country's loyal backing of its ally. On July 23 the Austrians sent Serbia an ultimatum meant to be unacceptable: They gave Serbia 48 hours in which to apologize, ban all anti-Austrian propaganda, and agree

**This painting dramatizes the assassination of Archduke Francis Ferdinand and his wife; the incident provided the immediate cause for World War I.** (Photo: Bildarchiv der Österreichischen Nationalbibliothek, Vienna)

to Austro-Hungarian participation in Serbia's investigation of the plot against Francis Ferdinand—in effect, to a voice in its internal government.

Serbia replied with great tact, accepting all terms except those that diminished its sovereignty and offering to submit even these to arbitration. It seemed even to Berlin that another crisis would pass. Great Britain, wanting to reduce tensions further, proposed an international conference, to which France and Russia reluctantly agreed. The Germans then declared the controversy a matter for

Austrians and Serbians alone, and on July 28 Austria-Hungary declared war on Serbia.

Austria-Hungary was, in fact, not yet ready to fight, and both Germany and Great Britain still hoped the Austrians would limit themselves to occupying Belgrade and then accept a conference. But Russia, explaining that it could not allow an occupation of Serbia, on July 29 ordered a partial mobilization, making clear that it was aimed only at Austria-Hungary; the following day the Russians discovered they lacked the organization for a partial call-up and announced a general mobilization instead. On July 31 Germany declared itself in a state of readiness, sent Russia an ultimatum demanding demobilization within 12 hours, and asked France what course it would take in case of a Russo-German war. France answered that it would act in its own interests and then mobilized, but it held its troops 10 kilometers (about 6 miles) from the frontier to prevent any incidents. The Germans, who had planned next to demand the surrender of France's border fortresses as a guarantee of neutrality, were unsatisfied with this response and planned their moves for the next several days accordingly.

Germany mobilized on August 1 and declared war on Russia; and convinced this meant fighting on the Western front as well, it invaded Luxembourg and sent an ultimatum to the Belgians demanding unobstructed passage for its troops. On August 3 Germany declared war on France and began invading Belgium. The following day the British declared war on the Germans, and within 48 hours each nation had 2 million soldiers under orders. World War I had begun.

## The Origins of the War

The question of what caused the Great War—or, more simply, who was to blame—soon became a major issue in European politics.

The Allies blamed Germany so insistently that they wrote its guilt into the treaty of peace, a view that most historians have considered one-sided at the very least and that German scholars rejected with special force, which explains the furor that first greeted the recent work of the German historian Fritz Fischer, who finds strong evidence that Germany's leaders had, in fact, looked forward to war and nurtured almost boundless ambitions for military dominance. But the question remains without a final answer, for the causes adduced depend very much on how long-range a look one takes.

The immediate cause, the assassination, almost did not happen. The tensions that made it so significant were more deeply rooted. The Balkan States, struggling to establish their authority and to win support at home, played on the competition among the major nations, who, in turn, treated Balkan affairs as matters of their own prestige. Serbia's policy, like its nationalism and its effort to modernize, challenged Austria-Hungary. Austria-Hungary was apprehensive about its declining power and thus set on teaching the Serbians a lesson while there was still time. Individual statesmen can be blamed for Austria-Hungary's untoward haste, Germany's irresponsible support of Austria-Hungary, Russia's clumsy and confused diplomacy, France's eagerness to prove to the Russians that it was a good ally, Britain's unwillingness to admit it was tied to one side and its consequent inability to warn the Germans that an attack on France meant war with Britain as well.

Such an analysis may, however, make the statesmen seem to have been more autonomous and therefore more to blame than they were. The system of alliances with which each state sought security decreased the diplomats' freedom. Every European power believed in the summer of 1914 that its very survival depended on maintaining its alliances which meant, in practice, that each alliance would follow its least responsible member.

The fear that cemented these commitments was related to the foreign-policy goals of the major nations: Britain's conviction that empire required supremacy at sea; France's determination to revenge the defeat of 1870 and regain Alsace-Lorraine; Russia's 150 years of expansion toward the West, the Balkans, and East Asia; Italy's need to show itself a great power; Austria's dependence since Metternich on foreign policy to sustain a shaky regime; the desire of a powerful Germany fearful of encirclement for prestige abroad that might reduce conflict at home.

The arms race itself contributed to the outbreak of war. In 1889 Great Britain had adopted the principle that its navy must equal in size the two next-largest fleets combined, and in 1906 it had launched the *Dreadnought*, the first battleship armed entirely with big guns. By 1914 Britain had 29 ships of this class afloat and 13 under construction, and the German navy had 18, with 9 being built. The French and German standing armies doubled between 1870 and 1914, and all able-bodied men had some military responsibilities from the age of 20 to the late fifties. Germany's victory over the French in 1871 had been understood in all Continental countries to prove the superiority of the Prussian system of universal conscription, large reserves, and detailed planning. Furthermore, it was believed that technology gave an attacker overwhelming advantages. But it required immense organization and took days to locate millions of reservists, get them to their proper units, equip them, and then effectively deploy them. Mobilization—in the eyes of some diplomats, a cumbersome but effective show of seriousness—was considered by military men in each country to be an essential act of self-defense; but it had become by 1914 tantamount to war. Even slight disadvantages in numbers of men, quality of weapons, speed of deployment, or

**By 1912 this Krupp factory at Essen was devoted to an arms race that consumed an increasing proportion of Europe's energy and wealth.**
(Photo: Archiv für Kunst und Geschichte, Berlin)

tactical foresight might prove fatal. Thus each increase in manpower and weapons was quickly matched, though in some cases only with enormous effort; France, for example, had but 60 percent of Germany's potential manpower and yet equaled its rival through more burdensome conscription. The arms race, justified by the fear that it was meant to allay, fed on itself.

Such expenditures of money and resources, however, had to be justified to parliaments. Thus, ultimately, these enormous forces, like foreign policy, rested on domestic politics. In every country political parties now competing for broader popular support found nationalist programs to have effective appeal and to offer the chance of reaching across social, religious, and regional divisions. Special interests associated with the military and empire could thus join with all

who feared a rising tide of socialism in dramatizing issues of national honor. This was especially the case in Germany where the very economic growth that made it powerful threatened the dominance of Prussia and of the Junker class in a still insecure new state. Throughout Europe domestic conflict and the politics of nationalism thus had an important part in the statecraft that led to World War I.

Few Europeans really wanted war; yet its outbreak was hailed with joy everywhere. The strain of economic, demographic, and imperial competition prepared many to welcome with relief the open and total confrontation of armed conflict. Its excitement provided the unity and common purpose so long

**Summer hats in the air, an August crowd in London's Trafalgar Square cheers the declaration of war on Austria. War on Germany had been declared a week earlier; similar scenes throughout that week of 1914 occurred in Paris and Berlin.** (Photo: The Bettmann Archives)

missed. In immediate terms, world war could have been avoided; in a larger sense, it was a product of the social structures it nearly annihilated.

## III. THE COURSE OF THE WAR
❈
### The First Years of War

For decades European military staffs had prepared detailed plans for the eventuality they now faced. The French intended to drive into Alsace and Lorraine in carefully coordinated and dashing maneuvers that reflected their almost mystic belief in élan. The Germans' strategy rested on the Schlieffen "swinging door" plan, first adopted in 1905 to meet the awful challenge of fighting on two fronts simultaneously: Using minimum forces against the Russians in the East and the expected French attack in Alsace, they would send their main armies wheeling through Belgium down on Paris and knock France out of the war before Russia could bring its massive armies into play or British aid could make a difference. That strategy, with its invasion of neutral Belgium, further labeled Germany as the aggressor and determined Britain's entry into the war.

All the belligerents in 1914 assumed that

modern war would be swift, with the advantage to the offense. But the first few months of hostilities established that the war being fought was not the one planned, though commanders were slow to admit it. Increased fire power gave defensive forces unexpected strength, cavalry was ineffectual, and the common soldier proved able to absorb more punishment than anyone had thought possible. After slight gains, the French offensive in Alsace was stopped, with heavy losses to both sides. The Germans were more nearly successful—the French command had underestimated by half the number of troops that would be immediately engaged in battle—and within a month they drove to within 30 miles of Paris (see Map 26.4).

But the German army was as battered as the defenders, its casualties were as high, and its lines of communication and supply were dangerously stretched. These factors, added to unanticipated Belgian resistance, infuriated and worried German commanders. And the Schlieffen plan was altered in practice by a small British force that had joined the French sooner than expected and by unanticipated Russian advances toward eastern Prussia. Extra German troops were sent to Alsace in hope of a breakthrough following earlier successes there, while, frightened by the Russian gains, the indecisive German chief of staff, Helmuth von Moltke (nephew of the field marshal who had led Germany to victory in 1866 and 1870), ordered to the East troops intended to be in the West. Overwhelming though they were, the German forces that cut east of Paris, instead of running beyond it, were considerably fewer than their strategy had called for.

After each bloody encounter, the Allies had retreated, but they were not routed; and German officers were surprised to take so few prisoners. The French commander in chief, Joseph Joffre, kept his forces together even in defeat, imperturbably confident of the ultimate success of a great French drive.

In September the French launched a counteroffensive along the Marne River that saved Paris and hurled the Germans back to the natural defenses of the Aisne River. There, despite repeated Allied attacks, the Germans held. In the next few months the armies tried to outflank each other but succeeded only in extending the front northward to the sea. With changes of only a few miles, the battle lines established by the end of 1914 would remain those of the Western front for the next four years. France had not been knocked out of the war, but Germany held a tenth of its territory and nearly all of Belgium (see Map 26.5).

On the Eastern front, Russian armies scored important gains in early August, taking eastern Galicia from Austria-Hungary and beginning an invasion of eastern Prussia in the north. Moltke talked in panic of a general retreat until the victories of Generals Paul von Hindenburg and Erich von Ludendorff, who soon became Germany's greatest war heroes. At Tannenberg late in August, their forces surrounded and destroyed a Russian army; and German troops pushed on almost to Warsaw before being stopped. In the south, Austria-Hungary halted the Russian advance with German aid, and despite the able fighting of the Serbian army, Austrian armies took Belgrade. By the end of 1914, the Central Powers had made impressive gains at every hand, and the Ottoman Empire's entry into the war on their side extended the threat to the Allies all the way to Suez.

## War of Attrition

On the Western front especially, the great armies found themselves bogged down in a terrifying kind of siege warfare. Artillery became increasingly important, and shells were fired at rates unimaginable a few months before, devastating the pockmarked land and making any movement in it still more difficult. Dug into trenches and clinging to pill-boxes, neither side could be uprooted. Military units worked out complex systems of communication by laying cables, building bridges, and maintaining roads and railways. For the first time, poison gas was used, but the German troops could not follow up the momentary gains it permitted.

Again and again, the Allied armies attempted to mount a great offensive, only to be stopped after gaining two or three miles and losing hundreds of thousands of men.

Battles were now numbered—the Second Battle of Ypres (April–May 1915), the Second Battle of Artois (May–June), the Second Battle of Champagne (September–November), the Third Battle of Artois (September–October); and after a year's bloodshed, the Western front remained essentially the same.

Italy's entry into the war had not broken the stalemate. Italy had declared its neutrality on the ground that Austria-Hungary's attack on Serbia was an offensive action and thus did not fall within the terms of the Triple

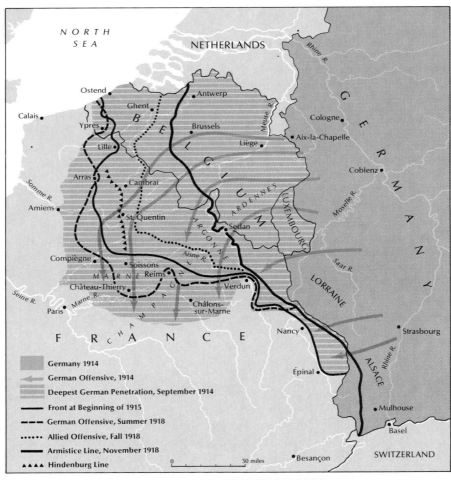

MAP 26.4 THE WESTERN FRONT

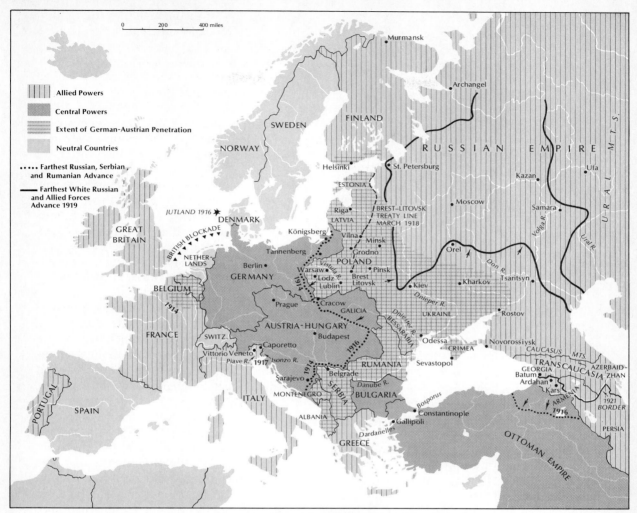

**MAP 26.5 WORLD WAR I**

Alliance, and this had kept it free to negotiate with both sides. Geography and Austria-Hungary's reluctance to give up territory the Italians sought had led them to favor the Allies. In April 1915 Italy had signed a secret agreement with Great Britain, France, and Russia, the Treaty of London, committing itself to the Allied side in return for the promise of lands along its border with Austria-Hungary (the southern Tyrol, Istria, Trieste,

and Gorizia—see Map 26.6), important Dalmatian islands, and expansion of its colonial holdings. Italy declared war on Austria-Hungary in May and soon advanced to a line along the Isonzo River. At that line, 11 battles were fought in the next two years without significant gain.

The fighting in France in 1916 brought no decisive changes either. Early in the year the Germans launched an all-out offensive

**The living looked lonely as a few Allied soldiers moved between trenches on the battlefield at Ypres.** (Photo: Imperial War Museum/ Photosearch)

against the French fortifications at Verdun. Knowing the French would be determined to hold, their aim was more to bleed the enemy than to take territory. For days shells poured down, and then the Germans attacked in overwhelming numbers. From February to July the fighting continued at full pitch. German forces captured two outlying forts, but the French managed a brief counterattack. Verdun held; and though the French losses, more than 300,000 men, weakened the subsequent Allied offensive, Germany casualties were only slightly less. The Allied attack in the Battle of the Somme, from July to November, brought still heavier casualties and a maximum advance of seven miles.

For two years each side had believed its offensives about to succeed only to see them halted by some unexpected flaw. The doctrine of the offensive, like general morale, was sinking in gore. If the brilliant tactics of rapid maneuver planned at war's outset could not guarantee victory, then attrition, systematically exhausting men and resources, seemed the only feasible alternative.

On the Eastern front (see Map 26.5) Austro-German forces launched an offensive through Galicia in May 1915, pushing forward a hundred miles, and followed it with a general offensive in July. By late September the Russians had lost Poland and Lithuania; and as the Central Powers massed on a line from Riga in the north to the easternmost part of Hungary, their new ally, Bulgaria, pressed into Serbia. The following year, however, General Alexis Brusilov, in one of the few really well-conducted Russian campaigns, regained a large part of those losses. But the effort cost Russia a million men, and it lacked the organization, the supplies, and the leadership to do more. The Russian offensive brought Rumania into the war on the Allied side, but Austria-Hungary took Bucharest at the end of the year.

Naval strength did not, in itself, produce military success for either side during the war. The single large-scale attack by sea, the landing of Allied forces on the Gallipoli peninsula in April 1915, was a failure. Having hoped to open the Dardanelles for shipping to Russia and to force the Ottoman Empire out of the war, the Allies were grateful to withdraw in December without serious loss.

Great Britain had nonetheless effectively maintained a blockade of Germany that was beginning to hurt. The Germans had tried to counter in 1915 by announcing a submarine blockade of Britain, but the angry reaction of neutrals led by the United States had forced them to abandon the tactic. The sinking of passenger ships—most sensationally, the *Lusitania*, killing more than a thousand civilians—gave way in 1916 to attacks on armed merchant ships and then, in the face of American warnings, to the renunciation of "unlimited" submarine warfare.

The one great naval battle of the war, at Jutland in May 1916, was indecisive. British and German fleets lost the same number of ships, though the British tonnage sunk was twice as great. Thereafter Admiral Alfred von Tirpitz's great fleet stayed in its harbors and did not threaten Allied control of the sea.

## The Home Front

By every measure, this was war on an unprecedented scale, and adjustment to its demands strained the very fabric of society. At first the fighting produced not only enthusiasm but also a euphoric spirit of national unity. In Great Britain the Liberal government gave way within a year to a coalition; the emergency left little room for party divisions. The French hailed their "sacred union," and the leading socialist militant took a post in the cabinet. The German parliament unanimously voted war credits, and though some Germans were shocked at the invasion of Belgium, the citizenry was convinced that the nation was fighting a just and defensive war. In Russia the government seemed almost popular.

War brought immediate dislocation. As factories closed, unemployment rose despite conscription; there then followed a labor shortage as war production became crucial to survival. Everywhere agricultural output dropped, contributing to the food shortages of subsequent years. Prices rose rapidly and consumer hoarding further strained faltering systems of distribution.

In response to domestic and military crises, the powers of governments to move men; censor the press; and control the railroads, the telegraph, and shipping; and even to direct the economy were extended as never before. Unprepared for their armies' requirements of ever more ammunition and supplies, governments quickly learned to use paper money, rationing, and central planning. In this and other ways, modern warfare involved the full participation of the civilian population. The refugees from Belgium pouring into France (and the German reprisals against Belgian civilians) were only the first and clearest symptom of this pervasive change. Just as unlimited submarine warfare, poison gas, and a blockade that treated consumer goods as contraband burst the rules of warfare among civilized nations, so the need to mobilize the home front overrode the restraints on which liberal society had depended.

In Great Britain the government, which was granted unparalleled power over the lives of civilians, requisitioned supplies and forced industry to new efficiency. Its professional army shattered, Britain, despite voluntary enlistments that raised the largest army in its history, had to adopt conscription in 1916, a step that Winston Churchill considered "the greatest revolution in our system since the institution of feudalism under William the Conqueror." Rebellion in Ireland that Easter was quickly put down; yet it was a serious diversion for British troops and a disturbing reminder of how cruelly war tested every weakness in the social structure.

Germany, deprived of critical raw materials, developed the most fully controlled economy of any of the combatants. Under the brilliant direction of Walther Rathenau, German resources were allocated and its industry deployed to the needs of war. Private firms were organized into sectors of production so that the most important could be favored, inefficient firms closed, and national planning enforced. The chemical industry developed ways of making rubber substitutes, manufactured fertilizers from nitrates in the air and textiles from wood pulp, and culled aluminum from local clays. Substitutes, which made *ersatz* an international word, included chestnut flour and clover meal used in the "war bread" that, like meatless days and conscription, soon made the civilian population feel the burden of all-out war.

In the first weeks of the fighting, half of

"Through Our Army—the Freedom of the Seas"

"Freedom Loan"

Everywhere war propaganda facilely combined the call for patriotic courage with images of the soldier as national symbol and words about freedom. (Photo: upper left, Imperial War Museum; upper right, Imperial War Museum; lower left, Private Collection)

"Freedom, Lads!"

Casualties of the Battle of the Marne. (Photo: René Dazy)

France's iron ore and coal fields and more than half its heavy industry were captured or destroyed. Joffre exercised virtually dictatorial powers, and the French, too, began to develop techniques for mobilizing a whole society. Quotas and priorities were established by government and industrial committees, and supplies were allocated according to comprehensive plans. Production steadily increased. Although censorship was severe, the tradition of political dispute was in large part preserved; and if the custom of reshuffling cabinets was a source of some inefficiency, it also eased the task of recruiting men competent to undertake new administrative tasks. In France, as in Great Britain, civilian authority had begun to reassert itself in 1915.

These three were the states that adjusted most effectively to the revolutionary requirements of fielding huge armies while increasing industrial production and maintaining intricate networks of supply. They did it with governments that had the will and the capacity to organize their nations. Civilians were disciplined to all-out war through propaganda, compulsion, and systematic economic controls.

These were feats that the Austro-Hungarian and Russian empires could not match. Not only was their industry relatively sparse but its development was uneven, and even modern plants worked at less than capacity, hampered by lack of supplies and trained manpower. Neither government knew how or dared to squeeze from the economy the overwhelming quantities of food, ammunition, or clothes that war required. Russian armies increasingly showed the effects of fighting ill-fed and ill-shod, with inadequate weapons and ammunition, and without good communication. (Orders to Russian troops were broadcast uncoded, which contributed to Ludendorff's reputation as a great tactician.) Austria-Hungary could not rely in adversity on the continued loyalty of subject peoples, and soldiers were carefully dispatched to zones far from their homes so as not to be fighting against people who spoke their own tongue.

By the winter of 1916–1917, the grave strains were visible to all. Everywhere on the bloodied Continent, Europeans were thinner and more shabbily dressed, overworked, and grieved by the endless losses of husbands, sons, and homes. Poor crops and overloaded transportation systems reduced the diet further; this was the Germans' "turnip winter," when the best organized of the domestic war economies could barely keep its people healthy.

The strains of war were changing society. The queue became a kind of public rite as many of the subtler distinctions of social class disappeared. Each government awkwardly tried to restrict the consumption of alcohol and worried about rising rates of illegitimacy. Just as rationing had spread from nation to nation, becoming ever more restrictive, so did the need to employ women. British women were asked in 1915 to take any jobs they could, and by 1917 the government denied contracts to employers unwilling to hire women. The French government forbade hiring men for certain jobs that women could do; and the Krupp works, which had no women employees in 1914, counted 12,000 by 1917. In munitions industries in particular, the number of women workers steadily rose to become one-third or more of the total; and women tilled the soil, served as bus conductors, fire fighters, and office workers in addition to more direct war work. Although labor agitation remained below prewar levels, signs of growing discontent had to be taken seriously. Trade unions were treated with new respect, and officials began to talk of the benefits to be granted after the war to those making such heavy sacrifices now. Even the Kaiser spoke of ending the three-

**After the siege that bled both armies, the ruins of Verdun stand like a broken tombstone.**
(Photo: Wide World Photos)

class voting system in Prussia and hinted at a government responsible to parliament, while the House of Commons in a notable reversal declared its support in principle for women's suffrage. Meanwhile, month upon month of bloodshed in muddy, disease-filled trenches took a psychological as well as physical toll. Morale was sinking.

### Changes in Leadership

There were some hints in that terrible winter of the possibility of peace. In December 1916, after having gained the initiative on the Eastern front, the Central Powers indicated willingness to discuss a settlement; but the Al-

lies' terms, stated a month later, were wholly unacceptable. Meanwhile, both sides had been seeking to strengthen themselves by changes in leadership.

In the fall of 1916, Hindenburg had received overall command of German troops and with Ludendorff had taken charge of campaigns in the West. To destroy the shipping on which Britain's survival depended, the Germans returned to unlimited submarine warfare in January 1917. They were aware that this might bring the United States into the war, but they calculated that American power could not make itself felt before

Britain would have to sue for peace. Britain and France also sought the formula for victory in new leadership. Joffre's intolerance of civilian leaders brought his downfall in December 1916; and General Robert Georges Nivelle, politically more tactful and personally more dashing, succeeded him as commander in chief of the French armies. He planned a massive offensive, and this one, he assured his government, would break through German defenses.

Changes in high political offices were more significant. Lloyd George, who was made minister of war in June 1916, became British prime minister in December. Eloquent and energetic, once a radical orator who had terrified the upper classes, he now seemed the kind of decisive leader who could galvinize the British into a well-organized effort to win. The French turned to the fiery Clemenceau, who became premier again in November 1917 after French morale hit a dangerous low. Change had come to Russia too—through revolution. In March 1917 the tsar had abdicated, and a new provisional government had proclaimed sweeping democratic reforms while promising to continue the war. Both sides knew that Russia was now more vulnerable than ever but that its immense resources had yet to be effectively tapped.

For the Allies these changes, especially in Russia, gave the war itself new meaning. Now democracies were fighting together against authoritarian governments dominated by the aristocracy and the military. A war that involved the people more fully than any before, it took on an ideological meaning. In April the United States declared war on Germany, resentful of the sinking of its ships and of German overtures to Mexico promising the return of Mexican lands taken by the United States. American entry added to the Allies' sense of democratic purpose as well as their military strength.

## The Great Trials of 1917–1918

In the fighting itself, however, neither new leaders nor shared ideals seemed to make much difference. On the Western front, Nivelle launched his great offensive in April and May 1917 despite multiple handicaps. The Germans had strengthened their defenses along the Hindenburg line, near the French-Belgian border, and disagreements had arisen between the British and French commands. But most dangerous of all, there was grave disaffection among the French troops. Some refused to fight, and those who remained in the trenches were dispirited by two years of endless death on the same barren hills and slimy plains. Thus the offensive (the Second Battle of the Aisne and the Third Battle of Champagne) brought a toll as great as that of its predecessors and even slighter gains.

Nivelle was replaced by General Henri Philippe Pétain, the hero of Verdun, who began a concerted effort to raise morale by recognizing many of the soldiers' grievances and by instituting regular leaves; and the government took severe measures against agitators who talked of peace. The results were encouraging, but it would be months before France dared another offensive.

The British went ahead with plans for an attack in the north, spurred by the desperate need to knock out at least some of the Germans' submarine bases, for the U-boats were sinking such enormous tonnages that the Admiralty openly wondered how many months Great Britain could last. With only weak assistance from the French army, the British fared no better in the Third Battle of Ypres (July–November) than had the French in their spring offensive. The noise of battle could be heard in England, and hundreds of thousands of men fell, but there was no breakthrough. British morale, too, was shaken.

On the Eastern front, Russian advances

in July turned into almost constant retreat in the next few months. In November the Bolsheviks, a faction of the Social Democratic party, took over the government, invited all nations to join in peace without annexations or indemnities, and entered into independent negotiations with the Central Powers. The most populous of the Allies had been defeated. In October German troops had joined Austro-Hungarian troops in a concentrated attack on the Italian front that issued in an overwhelming victory at the Battle of Caporetto. Italy's armies collapsed as tens of thousands died, surrendered, or deserted. But the Italians regrouped along the Piave River while Britain and France rushed in reinforcements, and the Austro-German onslaught was slowed and then stopped.

German reserves of manpower and resources were nearing exhaustion. Submarine warfare had come close to its goal of defeating Britain; but though Allied losses remained serious, they had dropped to a tolerable level with the development of the convoy in mid-1917. The convoys, enlarged by American ships, brought tons of supplies and toward the end of the year, even some fresh troops.

In February 1918 the Russians stopped fighting, a gesture of peace the Central Powers did not reciprocate; they continued their breathtaking eastward march. In the Treaty of Brest Litovsk, signed in March, Russia surrendered not only Russian Poland and the Baltic provinces but also the Ukraine and Transcaucasia. When it needed them most, Germany had acquired the invaluable wheat and oil of the Ukraine and a respite on one front. But the gains were so immense that merely patrolling them took great numbers of badly needed troops, and the incredibly harsh terms of the treaty stiffened the resistance of the enemy elsewhere. Both Lloyd George and President Wilson, in his Fourteen Points, now stated formal war aims that expressed their confidence in victory and put

revolutionary emphasis on the right to self-government.

In March, also, the Germans opened a great offensive on the Western front. With careful strategy, improved tactics, heavy artillery, and gas, they made the greatest advances seen on the Western front in four years. But the Allies held, and they sought to correct the weakness of divided command by naming General Ferdinand Foch supreme commander.

From March through June 1918 the Germans attacked British, French, and now American troops in sector after sector, scoring suprising successes; but the Allies were retaining their reserves while the Germans exhausted theirs. Enemy guns once more bombarded Paris as the Second Battle of the Marne and the Allied counteroffensive began in July. Slowly, then faster, the Germans were driven back over the familiar and devastated landscape. By the end of August, German armies had retreated to the Hindenburg line; and the Allies continued their push in battles of the Argonne and Ypres in September and October, gaining less rapidly than hoped or expected but now inexorably.

Elsewhere the Central Powers collapsed more dramatically. Meeting a large offensive begun in Palestine in September, Turkish and German troops were defeated by British and Arab forces led by T. E. Lawrence, whose exploits became part of the romantic lore in which this war was poorer than most. In October the sultan was deposed, and a new Ottoman government sued for peace. From Salonika, combined Serbian, French, British, and Greek forces under French leadership drove up the Balkan Peninsula. Bulgaria surrendered at the end of September, and the Allies moved toward Rumania.

The Austro-Hungarian Empire was disintegrating. Throughout 1918 Czech, Yugoslav, Rumanian, and (Austrian) Polish movements for independence had gained

**British gas masks used by Indian soldiers in 1917 express the faceless horror of trench warfare.**    (Photo: Gernschein Collection, Humanities Research Center, University of Texas at Austin)

strength, encouraged by the Allies. On the Italian front, Austria-Hungary attacked once more but withdrew after heavy losses. Defeated at the Battle of Vittorio Veneto at the end of October, its armies began simply to dissolve as the various nationalities left the

III. THE COURSE OF THE WAR ❊ 1095

battle field for home and revolution. Czechoslovakia and the kingdom later called Yugoslavia both declared their independence, and in November Austria-Hungary would surrender unconditionally to the Italians.

Ludendorff had demanded that Germany seek an armistice at the end of September, and in October a new government, under liberal Prince Maximillian of Baden, asked for peace on the terms of President Wilson's Fourteen Points. But Wilson now insisted on the evacuation of occupied territories and a democratic German government with which to negotiate. While German leaders hesitated, they faced the threat of revolution at home. Ludendorff resigned his command at the end of October; Kaiser William II abdicated on November 9 after a mutiny in the German fleet and revolution in Munich; and a German armistice commission met with Foch and agreed to terms on November 11. By then Allied troops were approaching the German borders in the West and had crossed the Danube in the East, taken Trieste on the Adriatic, and sailed through the Dardanelles. And revolution was sweeping Central Europe.

## The Effects of World War I

The war itself had some of the effects of revolution. Its psychological impact is not easy to demonstrate, but there were endless examples among intellectuals of what one historian has called "minds scorched by war," and among the populace, a cynical distrust of leaders and institutions seems to have spread after years of wartime promises. There was a cleavage, too, between those who had fought and those who stayed home, those whose lives were transformed and those who had more nearly maintained business as usual. And there was bitterness about the inequalities of sacrifice that surfaced in denunciations of war profiteers. Throughout society, there was after World War I a tendency to expect instability and change in social mores and structure. At the same time, few forgot and some would yearn for the thrill of combat, the sense of common purpose, and the vision of national unity that war had brought.

Some of the psychological and social changes showed in public behavior and even in dress. Gentlemen had abandoned their top hats when forced to use public transportation, and women's clothes grew simpler and their skirts shorter. Women of the working class took to cosmetics, high-heeled shoes, and smoking and drinking in public, as did their middle-class sisters. These changes, even more than the increase in violent crime and juvenile delinquency, shocked moralists for whom they were related to casual encounters between the sexes, increased illegitimacy, and the popularity of dance halls. Such signs pointed to a more mobile and fluid society in which old customs and patterns of proper behavior had been so disrupted that they might never be recaptured. Millions of refugees represented a deep displacement, but millions more (especially peasants and women) would choose not to return to their old way of life.

Political life was directly affected, and not just where revolution triumphed. In Germany ex-soldiers joined *Freikorps* ("free corps"), mercenary squads available for street fighting and marauding that preserved the camaraderie of arms. Throughout Central Europe political conflict adopted the techniques of force. Even in the West solid men of the older parties watched with apprehension the revival of the left. Clemenceau, Lloyd George, and Wilson, the spokesmen of victory, had all been vigorous reformers who understood and spoke to public opinion (even when the enthusiasm of patriotic unity came to seem a little hollow) as more traditional politicians did not. Even the most conservative governments had shown that the state could use its inflated bureaucracies and increased power to shape the economy, and no one could now deny that governments might improve the lot of the poor, recognition that resulted in a spate of postwar legislation on housing, education, and pensions. Having shown the capacity to mobilize society for war, governments would now be held more responsible than in the past for society's needs in peacetime.

The relative position of the various social classes was also altered. Inflation lessened the purchasing power of aristocrats and members of the middle class who lived on investments, especially in land. Taxes (particularly in England) and the relative decline in land values also weakened the aristocracy, whose power was further lessened even where there was no open revolution by the general democratization of political life. Members of the middle class, especially those on salary or fixed income, also suffered relatively more from inflation than those on workers' wages. Middle-class life became less lavish, with fewer servants (some 400,000 English women left domestic service in the course of the war) or occasions for ostentation. A middle class confident in 1914 found itself after the war exposed and vulnerable, its savings threatened, its possibilities limited, its values challenged. Workers, particularly the skilled, were on the whole relatively well off. Although rates of pay had usually run behind inflation, the years of full employment and more jobs for women had increased family income, and trade unions used their greater influence to maintain gains of shorter hours and higher pay. Peasants, though declining in numbers, were also often better off since inflation and the demand for food had helped them pay off their debts and own more land free and clear.

The war affected economic life in other ways. The employment of new technologies was stimulated by their wartime use, as happened with automobiles and airplanes, radio, and some chemicals. Not only had world trade been disrupted, but Europe's place in it also had been permanently altered. In 1914 Europe had been the world's greatest lender of money; in 1918 its states were debtors. The physical destruction of property, aside from the billions lost in war material, was greatest in Belgium and France. In France alone, thousands of bridges, thousands of factories, and a million buildings were destroyed. Total European production in the 1920s would fall below the level of 1913.

All this required enormous adjustments. So did the war's simplest accomplishment: the killing of from 10 to 13 million people, perhaps one-third of them civilians. Moreover, for every soldier who died, two or three were wounded; millions were maimed for life. The casualty figures tell much about the history of the first third of the twentieth century (see accompanying table).

Among the armed forces, casualties ran about 50 percent for the major combatants except France, whose losses were higher. The weakness of Russian organization shows in the fact that a smaller percentage of the population was mobilized—about 7 percent, as compared with 16 percent of the German and 19 percent of the French—and that the fatalities can only be estimated. The high percentage of mobilization in France and Germany is a measure of the desperate efforts they made. Whole classes from the elite schools of each nation were virtually wiped out. For France, with its older population and low birth rate, the war was a demographic catastrophe in which a large part of an entire generation disappeared on the Western front. And throughout Europe, the one-armed, the one-legged, and the blind would live on, supported by pensions and performing menial tasks, in silent testimony to the cost of total

**MILITARY FATALITIES IN WORLD WAR I (MAJOR POWERS)**

| | |
|---|---|
| Germany | 1,900,000 |
| Russia | 1,700,000 |
| France | 1,400,000 |
| Austria-Hungary | 1,200,000 |
| British Empire | 900,000 |
| Ottoman Empire | 700,000 |
| Italy | 600,000 |
| United States | 100,000 |

war. With all this before them, the leaders of exhausted nations sat down to make a lasting peace.

The gigantic effort victory required had been fueled by a vision, welded in the war-ring, of a better world in which governments would use their increased powers to ensure greater justice and fuller democracy. With Wilson as its Presbyterian voice, democracy—meaning popular participation in public life and opportunity for all—seemed a guarantee of peace. Not only would autocratic governments be doomed and states be forever prevented from making war for selfish reasons, but there would also be an end, Wilson suggested, to the old secret diplomacy that juggled spheres of influence and national interests without regard for public opinion. To many, such vague promises seemed radical enough, but they paled beside the revolution rolling from the East.

## IV. THE RUSSIAN REVOLUTION
❋
### The February Revolution

Nothing in their experience had prepared Western statesmen for the rapid triumph of Communism in Europe's largest nation. With the outbreak of war in 1914, many Russians realized that to meet this challenge, govern-

ment would have to be more efficient and in closer touch with Russian society. The Duma, called into brief sessions in 1915, established a committee to help coordinate the war effort, and local zemstvos made valuable contributions. But when the Cadet party demanded liberal reforms sought since 1905, the Duma's session was suspended. Resentful that the war could be used for political ends—they still did not see the connection—the tsar and his officials became more isolated from the country. Nicholas II, no more skilled as a military strategist than as a head of state, grandly departed to command his army, leaving Tsarina Alexandra to oppose any program for reform. Her chief confidant was Grigori Rasputin, an ignorant and corrupt mystic, whose influence symbolized the decadence of this regime.

Throughout 1916 signs of failure accumulated. Production and transportation were undependable, refugees filled the roads, inflation soared, and food shortages became critical. The resulting discontent reached into the highest circles. In November in the reconvened Duma, Pavel Milyukov, the Cadets' leader, courageously delivered a bitter attack on the government; one group of nobles murdered Rasputin in December, and others talked of the need to depose the tsar. Little seemed to change. Strikes spread; and, except for the Cossacks, the soldiers called out to quell them were increasingly inclined to join the workers.

In March 1917, when strikers again filled the streets of Petrograd (St. Petersburg's new name),[2] their economic demands quickly broadened to political issues, and troops could not be relied on to oppose them. Instead, much as in 1905, the Soviet of Workers' and Soldiers' Deputies became the voice of

[2] "St. Petersburg" was a German name, and in 1914 Nicholas had changed it to the Russian "Petrograd." The capital until 1918, the city would become Leningrad in 1924.

revolution. This council of working-class leaders joined a Duma committee (the Duma itself was not then in session) in favoring a provisional government, and soviets organized the effective defense of Petrograd against tsarist forces that might be sent to put down the insurgents. Helpless, Nicholas II abdicated. The February Revolution, as it was dated by the Russian calendar,[3] seemed an almost easy transition in the chaos of war; and the news from Petrograd was hailed with joy and relief throughout the country.

The prime minister of the provisional government was the bland and moderate Prince Georgi Lvov, but its central figure was Milyukov. The only socialist included was Aleksandr Kerensky, a member of the Social Revolutionary party, who led the labor representatives in the Duma and was vice-chairman of the Petrograd soviet, the most important center of political power in the capital.

On many matters the new government's policy was concrete and clear: It quickly established broad civil liberties, an amnesty for political prisoners, and the end of religious persecution; it favored a constitution for Finland and independence for Russian Poland, an eight-hour day for workers, and the abolition of class privileges. Beyond these points, however, the political terrain was less known, and the provisional government left most social issues for a constituent assembly, which it promised to call soon.

The revolutionary political parties were divided. The Cadets, who dominated the provision government, came to accept the idea of a republic, political democracy, and

distribution of land with compensation to former owners. To their left, the Social Revolutionaries and the Social Democratic Mensheviks, especially strong in the soviets forming across the nation, demanded more. Some of these socialists wanted drastic reforms but were willing to postpone them until after the war, which, like the Cadets, they still meant to win. The more radical stressed an early end to the war, though they did not yet advocate an immediate armistice, and were contemptuous of merely political changes. The soviets were willing, for the time being, to allow the provisional government its chance, but they refused to be implicated in it, watching instead from the outside, ever ready to criticize. To the left of all these groups stood a small number of Bolsheviks.

### The Bolsheviks

Russian Marxists had secretly formed the Social Democratic party in 1898, but its life centered mainly in the conspiratorial world of exile. At the party's second congress, held in Brussels and London in 1903, it had split into two groups, called the Bolsheviks ("majority") and Mensheviks ("minority"); in fact, the Bolsheviks rarely had a majority, but these nicknames stuck. The points of debate between them were theoretical, organizational, and personal. The theoretical issues echoed many of those that engaged Marxists everywhere, debated with the special intensity and intransigence of revolutionaries untainted by any political office, far from home or power. On the whole, the Menshiviks emphasized the importance of winning popular support, the need to remain close to the workers, and the value of parliamentary institutions and democratic procedures. Given Russia's backwardness, that implied cooperation with other parties. The Bolsheviks stressed instead the role of a revolutionary party, insisting that it must be a disciplined

---

[3] The Julian calendar, which the West had abandoned in favor of the Gregorian calendar, was still used in Russia (and today continues to be the calender of the Orthodox Church). The revolutions that in the Gregorian system occurred on March 8–12 and November 7, 1917, each fell 13 days earlier according to the Julian, and they continue to be called the February and October revolutions.

**The main street of Petrograd, July 1917, as the Bolsheviks open fire, a rising quickly defeated.** (Photo: Wide World Photos)

elite rather than a looser mass party. The party should instruct and lead rather than bow to the shortsighted wishes of the masses, always inclined to settle for immediate aims and ignorant of the larger, historic possibilities. European revolution was the goal; once achieved, no matter how, it would create the conditions for establishing socialism. These differences extended to the way discussion was conducted and allies recruited, with the Bolsheviks, led by Georgi Plekhanov and V. I. Lenin, impatiently and intolerantly denouncing enemies, dividing and isolating all who did not join them. Questions of procedure, Marxist theory, or economic analysis all became occasions for name-calling, settling old scores, and deepening divisions. Only later would these party

battles in foreign cities prove significant for Russian history.

Lenin's conception of iron discipline allowed little room for Plekhanov's independent efforts to heal the breach between the two camps, and he, too, was soon consigned to the Menshivik camp. In the bitter loneliness and doubts of exile, Lenin continued from Switzerland to organize selected followers, denounce the heresies around him, and develop his Marxist interpretation of European and Russian affairs. He remained distant from events in Russia. Neither Mensheviks nor Bolsheviks had played a central part in the Revolution of 1905, and the socialism that spread in Russia thereafter had been mainly that of the Menshiviks (who held most of the Social Democrats' seats in the Duma) and Social Revolutionaries, who were less consistently Marxists and closer to the peasants. Much as he had extended Marxism to explain that imperialism was a symptom of capitalist decay, so Lenin expanded on the role a militant party should play in a country like Russia that was just achieving modern capitalism. That, he argued, required recognizing the revolutionary potential in the peasants' hunger for land—a topic most Marxists had found uncongenial.

Lenin's total rejection of World War I as a civil war among capitalists suggested to the Germans that his agitation might be useful behind Russian lines, and in April 1917 they arranged for him to be sent by sealed train through Germany and Scandinavia to Russia. At this time the Bolsheviks were the smallest of the socialist groups, their differences from the left wing of the Mensheviks no longer very clear. Since all the socialists welcomed the revolution but considered it bourgeois, they were uncertain of their roles.

Lenin resolved this question, too, with the broader view that the Russian Revolution was part of a larger revolution about to sweep all of Europe. Free of local patriotism, he asserted that socialists had no interest in capitalistic war; and he argued that with the correct tactics, they could push the revolution beyond its bourgeois phase to a "second stage." This he soon declared to be the surrender of power to the soviets as the true representatives of the revolutionary class. The Bolsheviks thus had to capture the soviets. Historians have emphasized Lenin's tactical flexibility, but in April his views seemed impossibly dogmatic even to radicals. It was the force of his personality, his political skill, and his oratory that kept him leader of the Bolsheviks.

## Summer Crisis

Issues of war policy and land reform and the many disagreements among those who had overthrone the tsarist regime were not the only problems the provisional government faced in 1917. Strikes continued as workers sought some immediate benefit from revolution; nationalist movements in Latvia, Georgia, and the Ukraine threatened a disintegration of the Russian state; and the bureaucracy, like the police, had largely disappeared. The government was still pledged to pursue the war, but its connections to the institutions that make a society function were weak and its policies had little to offer peasants and workers. The soviets meanwhile were developing truly popular appeal and a national organization that claimed authority among the troops and over railroads and telegraph lines. The soviets distrusted the war policy and suspected the military of counterrevolutionary intentions. In March the Petrograd soviet issued its famous Order Number I: Officers would be chosen by their men, and the military would be run by elected committees. The measure was adopted in most units, and the government, which merely watched as a good part of the army melted away, lost control over much of the rest.

Pressure for peace forced the provisional government to clarify its war aims. In May it declared that Russia had no intention of dominating other peoples; but even this vague formula was compromised by a secret addition promising that Russia would fulfill its commitments to the Allies. The split grew wider between the Cadets, convinced that honor required the country to continue the war, and the soviets, whose renewed demonstrations caused a change in the government. Milyukov resigned, four more socialists joined the cabinet, and Kerensky, as minister of war, became its leading figure, assuming the prime ministership in August. Although Social Revolutionaries and Mensheviks held a majority of the cabinet posts, the soviets still withheld their full support, demanding clear policies for ending the war and redistributing land. Kerensky, an energetic leader and effective orator, recognized that he had to seek broader backing, which meant support from outside the soviets.

The Bolsheviks, too, were feeling some frustration. At the first all-Russian Congress of Soviets in June, they had succeeded in weakening the remaining support for Kerensky, but with just over 100 of the more than 800 delegates, they had not been able to gain full control. The revolution seemed to be proceeding without them. In July they had attempted a coup in Petrograd, but it had been decisively defeated; many Bolshevik leaders had been arrested, and Lenin had fled to Finland. The Bolshevist threat seemed over, and Kerensky tried to escape the dominance of the soviets which seemed too radical and untamable to these men of government. He called a great national congress of all other groups. But Kerensky had no real program to offer, and the overtures he made merely exposed how divided these groups were.

At the front, the July offensive, for which Kerensky had great hopes, failed after brief gains. The military situation, despite months of promising efforts at reorganization, became more desperate. In the countryside, manor houses were burned and landlords murdered as the peasants rioted for land, and cities were torn by strikes and demonstrations. The social tensions of 50 years were exploding in an atmosphere of anarchy.

Convinced that a strong military hand was needed, the army's commander in chief General Lavr Kornilov decided in September to lead an attack on Petrograd; and Kerensky asked the soviets to defend the provisional government against this new danger. The Bolsheviks were released from prison, and the defense of the capital was vigorously prepared. The threat passed quickly—most of Kornilov's men had refused to follow his orders—but the provisional government was more than ever dependent on the soviets. In six months in office, it had resolved few of the issues left pending in March, and Bolshevist propaganda was gaining ground with simple slogans about peace, land, and bread. These were issues at the heart of daily life, pressing problems for which the provisional government had no clear solutions.

The Bolsheviks won control of the Moscow and Petrograd soviets, and Leon Trotsky was elected chairman of the latter. Trotsky had worked with Lenin in exile, but until recently, he had stood somewhat aloof from both Bolsheviks and Mensheviks. Now he was firmly in Lenin's camp, and from his position in the soviet, he proceeded to organize the armed forces in Petrograd. When the Social Revolutionaries, fearful of losing their strong peasant following, supported peasant expropriation of land, the provisional government was left politically alone in a city it could not control trying to rule a nation in chaos and still at war.

## The October Revolution

To the dismay of many in his party, Lenin boldly decided to seize power. The second all-Russian Congress of Soviets was scheduled to meet on November 7, and Lenin planned to greet it with a new government. A few days before, Kerensky began to take countermeasures, but he was too late.

The revolution in November (October, according to the Russian calendar) was not the amorphous, general rising of March but rather a carefully planned and executed coup. Red Guards (squads of armed workers), sailors, and soldiers of the Petrograd garrison captured the Winter Palace on November 6 while comrades efficiently seized strategic points and offices throughout the city. A simultaneous movement began in Moscow, and though fighting there lasted more than a week, the outcome was hardly in doubt. On the afternoon of November 7, Lenin announced to the Congress of Soviets that the Bolsheviks held power. A young officer was sent to take command of the armies, and at each stop, the noisy acclaim of the troops dissuaded their commanders from resisting. Kerensky, who had escaped the capital, tried to muster armed support, but the one group of a few hundred Cossacks who moved on Petrograd was soundly defeated. Shaky though it was, the world's first Communist government had taken office.

"All power to the Soviets!" had been one of the Bolsheviks' most effective slogans, and the Congress of Soviets readily approved the one-party cabinet Lenin presented it. The rudiments of a new form of government emerged: the Congress of Soviets, which replaced parliament; the Central Executive Committee, elected from the Congress to give advice when the larger body was not in session; and the Council of People's Commissars, the cabinet ministers. Bolshevik rule from the very first was not representative in the traditional sense, and the government did not, in fact, depend on any elected body. Elections for the promised constituent assembly, held at the end of November, provided the last open competition among Soviet parties for more than 70 years. The Bolsheviks won a quarter of the seats, other socialist parties more than 60 percent, and conservatives and liberals the rest. As the assembly met on its second day, the guards told it to adjourn, explaining that they were tired. A minority party had ruthlessly grasped the power of the state.

Photographed as a proletarian sitting on a bench in Gorky Park in 1923, Lenin still looks enigmatic and powerful. But in its deliberate contrast with most political portraits (and especially those of fascist leaders), the pose is a reminder of the appeal of the Soviet Revolution and of its leader. (Photo: Keystone Press Agency, Inc.)

That ruthlessness was warranted in the Bolsheviks' thinking because of their historic role. Lenin had provided a basis for Bolshevist policy in his pamphlet "The State and Revolution," written in Finland in the summer of 1917. It kept the Marxist conception of the state as the coercive organ of the ruling class but argued that with the Bolsheviks in power, the proletariat would become the ruling class. Since backward Russia was barely ready for so advanced a revolution, only a dictatorship of the proletariat could provide the needed strength. By this reasoning, Lenin accomplished three things: He justified the establishment of an authoritarian government free from the restraints of parliamentarianism; he gave theoretical sanction to dictatorship as a transition stage during which Russia's transformation would be directed by the Bolsheviks; and he preserved the Marxian vision of Communism as a higher historical stage in which the state would no longer be necessary. During the dictatorship, socialism would be achieved through the nationalization of land and factories. Communism would come once everyone had learned to work for the good of society and economic production could meet the needs of all.

In the interim, the single party, the "vanguard of the proletariat," would have a special role. Model, teacher, and guide, it would prevent backsliding with its tight discipline; through it the masses would be heard. Lenin imagined that public criticism in party sessions would maintain efficiency and probity, combining the benefits of mass participation and dictatorship. Equality and justice remained explicit goals but sufficiently abstract to leave government unimpeded. Enthusiasm for a great cause would enable people to accept the hardships and sacrifices of the present for a glorious future.

The incongruous fusion of Marxist ideas and peasant demands that brought Communism to power in the least industrial of the great nations surprised most Marxists. And ruling in such a country required an extension of socialist theory to deal with issues not foreseen in the writings of the previous 50 years. Thus Lenin, the principal architect of the first socialist state, ranks with Marx himself as a theoretician of modern Communism.

## The First Communist Government

The efficiency with which the Bolsheviks seized and wielded power went beyond theory. It rested rather on the revolutionary fact of millions of workers, soldiers, and peasants determined to seize their moment to pull down the structures that had oppressed them and on the political failure of any other group to mobilize these masses or effectively address their demands. The Bolshevik triumph rested, too, on the fanatical self-confidence of able leaders hardened by years of revolutionary activity and ready now to snatch their historical moment, on the enthusiasm and dedication of hundreds of party members, and above all, perhaps, on the decisive energy of Lenin and Trotsky.

The day after taking the Winter Palace, the new government decreed that land, livestock, and all farm equipment belonged to the state but was to be held "temporarily" by peasant committees—this legitimized the rural revolution. No peasant was to work for hire, and committees of the poor would supervise the allocation of land and the distribution of agricultural produce.

In the next few months, railroads, banks, and shipping concerns were nationalized; foreign trade became a state monopoly (though there was precious little of it); and Russia's bonded debts were repudiated. Workers' committees were to share in the management of factories, and everyone was to be paid according to the work done—the leading Bolsheviks assigned themselves laborers' salaries. All social titles and military ranks were abolished. "People's tribunals" replaced tsarist courts and workers' militias, the police. Church and state were separated, and equality of the sexes was decreed, symbolized by the regulation that couples could obtain a divorce by mutual consent. The various nationalities of Russia were not only declared equal but also granted the right of

## CHRONOLOGY OF THE RUSSIAN REVOLUTION

| | | |
|---|---|---|
| 1917 | *February Revolution* | |
| | March | Strikes, soviets and Duma committee call for provisional government, troops support them |
| | March 12 | PROVISIONAL GOVERNMENT: Cadets dominate (Milyukov principal figure) |
| | March 14 | Petrograd Soviet issues Order Number I |
| | March 15 | Nicholas II abdicates |
| | | Government grants civil liberties, independence of Finland and Poland, autonomy of Estonia; promises victory in war and (April 30) constituent assembly and land reform |
| | April 17 | Lenin and other Bolsheviks arrive in Petrograd; calls for peace, land to the peasants, political rule by the soviets |
| | | Strikes, nationalist movements in Latvia, Georgia, Ukraine |
| | May 14 | Milyukov resigns |
| | May 16 | PROVISIONAL GOVERNMENT: socialists dominate (Kerensky principal figure) |
| | June 29–July 7 | Russian offensive against Germans fails |
| | July 16–18 | Bolshevik attempt at coup defeated |
| | September 9–14 | General Kornilov attacks Petrograd, government defeats him with aid of soviets, Bolsheviks gain control of Pegrograd and Moscow soviets |
| | *October Revolution* | |
| | November 6 | Bolsheviks rise, fight in Petrograd and Moscow, capture Winter Palace, win troops' support |
| | November 7 | SOVIET GOVERNMENT: Second All-Russian Congress of Soviets names new government, Bolshevik minority dominates (Lenin principal figure) |
| | November 25 | Elections for Constituent Assembly |
| 1918 | January 18 | First meeting of Constituent Assembly dispersed by Red Guards Nationalization of land and enterprise, sweeping changes |
| | March 9 | Treaty of Brest-Litovsk; Finland, Georgia, Ukraine independent; Germany to decide disposition of Russian Poland, Lithuania, Latvia, Estonia |
| | July 10 | Constitution of R.S.F.S.R |
| 1918–1920 | | Civil War: Soviet government fights Cossacks, Czechs, White Russians, Allies, Poland |

secession, and Finland severed itself from Russia in December 1917, though the Bolsheviks struggled to prevent the Ukraine and the Baltic Regions from following suit. Even the alphabet was reformed and the Gregorian calendar adopted.

These revolutionary measures ratified the dissolution of traditional society. They made way, too, for a regime of terror. A new secret police, the Cheka, differed from the old in determination more than method. The citizens who sat on committees of the poor or the army or on the new tribunal often combined a useful revolutionary enthusiasm with personal ambition and vengeance against old enemies. Tens of thousands lost their property, their rights, and their lives for failing to perceive in a time of revolution the dangers of "mistaken" alliances, "false" ideas, or "suspicious" gestures.

Such radical policies won the Bolsheviks increased support and weakened potential opposition, but they also heightened the difficulties of operating any government at all. The old bureaucrats were gone, their replacements often ignorant and incompetent. Officials were dismissed and promoted with disrupting frequency as political suspects disappeared and talented men were transferred to meet some new crisis.

External dangers were even more pressing. Almost immediately on taking power, the Bolsheviks had asked all nations to accept peace without annexations. When rebuffed, they shocked the world by publishing secret Allied agreements. Forced to negotiate alone with the Central Powers, Russia, whose delegation was headed by Trotsky, proposed in February 1918 a policy of no peace, no war—Russia would stop fighting without a treaty. The Germans advanced to within 100 miles of Petrograd.

Desperate, the Russian government agreed to the Treaty of Brest Litovsk in March. Russia surrendered more than 1 million square miles of territory, including a third of its arable land, a third of its factories, and three-quarters of its deposits of iron and coal. It granted the independence of Finland, Georgia, and the Ukraine; left to Germany the disposition of Russian Poland, Lithuania, Latvia, and Estonia; and ceded parts of Transcaucasia to the Ottoman Empire.

The Bolsheviks had met the demand for peace, but they had done so at incredible cost. Although buoyed by confidence that revolution in Germany would nullify the Kaiser's gains, they could not be sure they would survive so serious an amputation.

Quickly the government set about legitimizing its position. In July a new constitution was promulgated. It met the problem of nationalities by declaring Russia a federation—the Russian Soviet Federated Socialist Republic (R.S.F.S.R.); Great Russia, extending through Siberia, was, of course, the largest member. Political power rested with the local soviets, organized by occupation, which elected delegates to the congress of soviets of their canton, the smallest administrative unit. Each canton's congress, in turn, sent delegates to a congress of soviets at the next administrative level, and the process continued by steps up to the all-Russia Congress. Suffrage in the local soviet was universal for men and women but excluded members of the clergy, former high officials, and bourgeois "nontoilers." Since the public elected higher congresses only indirectly, the possibilities for control were great.

Not mentioned in the constitution was the Russian Communist party, as it was now named, which soon became the real center of political authority. Its Central Committee elected the smaller Politburo, which, with the governing Council of People's Commissars, shared ruling power in Soviet Russia. In Politburo and council, Lenin was the dominant figure.

The Bolsheviks, however, remained surrounded by enemies. To the Allies, the Treaty of Brest Litovsk appeared an act of treachery, as did Russia's repudiation of its debts. In March Allied troops in small numbers had landed in Murmansk, Archangel, and Vladivostok to prevent supplies sent to Russia earlier from being taken by the Germans, but it was clear that those detachments might also be used to support a change of regime.

In addition, the government had reluctantly permitted a Czech brigade of some 30,000 men to travel the Trans-Siberian Railroad from the Eastern front to Vladivostok so they might then sail around the world to continue fighting on the Western front. As the Czechs made the long train journey, they clashed with some Hungarian prisoners of war. The fighting spread, and the Czechs, aided by Russian anti-Bolsheviks, captured one station after another along the railway.

Struck by the case of the Czech successes, Allied leaders decided not to let their opportunity pass and ordered the Czechs to move back along the railway toward the center of Russia. At the same time, a number of tsarist generals, among them Kornilov and others who had escaped from prison, were preparing to lead a small but excellent army of Cossacks. It was the beginning of a civil war that would last for two terrible years.

While Trotsky undertook to organize a Red army, opponents of the new regime formed fighting units in the Ukraine, the Caucasus territory, the Baltic region, and Siberia, aided by reinforcements and supplies from the Allies. But the civil war was not just a battle of armies, for anti-Bolsheviks of every stripe—even the Social Revolutionaries, who had now gone underground—organized in hundreds of villages and towns. Food riots, battles over land, and skirmishes between workers and bourgeois added to the violence. The first Communist government in modern history was facing its gravest threat.


## V. THE PEACE
❋
### The Revolutionary Situation

Russia's was the most important revolution that resulted from World War I, but there were many others; and among the defeated nations, only Bulgaria's government survived. By default as well as victory, the Allies seemed free to set the terms they liked and to construct the Europe of peaceful democracies implied in so many wartime statements. Instead, the diplomats assembled at the Paris Peace Conference found their task complicated by the very extent of victory and beset by more interests than they could satisfy. So grand an undertaking fed the extremes of hope and disillusionment, while far from Paris, more direct means were being used to shape the postwar world.

From Ireland to Asia Minor, nationalist movements sought to capture power, and the peoples suddenly released from Hapsburg and Russian rule fought to define the boundaries of their new nations. In the Baltic lands, Lithuanian, Estonian, and Latvian republics marked their independence by war with Russia, but Lithuania was also at odds with the new republic of Poland. Poland, in fact, faced conflict on all its other borders as well—against Russians, Ukranians, Czechs, Germans. The creation of Czechoslovakia and the new Kingdom of Yugoslavia led to renewed warfare as Czechoslovakia was attacked by Hungary, and in the Balkans the kind of hostility that had preceded World War I broke out again when Rumania attacked both Hungary and Yugoslavia.

Soviet Communists had good reason then to hope revolution would sweep from East to West, and Marxists throughout Europe looked to the miraculous events in Russia as the beginning of the socialist future they had so long imagined. In March 1919 delegates from a score of countries met in Moscow to establish the Third International. Communists were active in the Baltic states, and Lenin's friend Béla Kun was to hold power as head of a Hungarian soviet in 1919 until Rumanian armies ended his brief reign. There was Communist agitation in Vienna, where the provisional government of truncated Austria looked forward to union with the new German republic.

But Germany itself was the major Communist goal. Marxists had long paid special attention to that highly industrialized nation with its class tensions and strong socialist movement. Defeat and a new government seemed the fulfillment of old portents. In January 1919 a Communist revolt broke out in Berlin, and in the following spring another managed for a few weeks to make Bavaria a Soviet republic. Both uprisings were quickly defeated by remnants of the Germany army. So Russia remained the center of the Communist world, but the chance remained that other revolutions would succeed.

## The Conference Decisions

Peace had come so suddenly that there had been little time for discussion of specific terms. But through the pressure of public opinion, the German understanding of the armistice, and American influence, President Wilson's Fourteen Points had won acceptance as a basis for defining a new European order.

In many respects similar to the programs of other statesmen, Wilson's plan dealt mainly with territorial adjustments, but it raised such changes to the level of principle, associating them with the self-determination of peoples and a democratic peace. The remaining points cautiously yet courageously set forth a vision shared by the moderate left everywhere in the West. The removal of trade barriers and free navigation of the seas had long been part of the liberal canon. International attention to the welfare of colonial populations, the reduction of armaments, and open diplomacy were more radical suggestions; but by 1918 the belief was common that had steps been taken on these issues earlier, the world's most terrible war might have been averted. Wilson's final point, and the one closest to his heart, called for a League of Nations to guarantee the safety of all. In subsequent statements, the American president had enlarged on the need for "impartial justice," "peace that will be permanent," and covenants that are "sacredly observed." His language and ideals caught the imagination of the world.

At the Paris Peace Conference, it was readily agreed that the mistakes of the Congress of Vienna must not be repeated. No defeated nations would take part in the early discussions—no German Talleyrand would divide the Allies. The atmosphere was one of sober business; the elegant aristocrats of 1815 had given way to commissions of expert advisers for every important issue, who were to provide the major negotiators with the detailed information they needed.

Thirty nations had joined the Allies at least formally,[4] but it was soon established that the momentous decisions would be taken by the five big powers—France, the United Kingdom, Italy, Japan, and the United States. In practice, since most questions did not directly concern Japan, primary authority resided in four men: Clemenceau, Lloyd George, Premier Vittorio Orlando, and Wilson.

Soon after the conference opened, in January 1919, disagreements among the principal representatives of the Big Four powers became the center around which the negotiations turned. All were elected leaders, skilled in appealing to public opinion and sensitive to its demands. All were faced with grave domestic problems and worried by the turmoil in Central and Eastern Europe. They had to hurry.

### The Treaty with Germany

To settle by May the complicated terms for peace with Germany was a remarkable achievement. Haste itself probably made the treaty more severe than it might otherwise have been. Commissions, assuming their proposals would be subject to later bargaining, tended to begin with maximum terms, but these were often simply written into the treaty itself.

The territorial provisions were not extremely harsh; Germany lost Continental lands as well as colonies, but it was preserved

---

[4] Yugoslavia, Czechoslovakia, and Poland were treated as Allies; the new republics of Austria, Hungary, and Germany as the defeated Central Powers.

**When Woodrow Wilson paraded through the streets, Parisians cheered the representative of a new democratic era as well as an ally in victory.** (Photo: The Granger Collection)

as a great state. The new European boundaries, however, were the sort to give continuing difficulty (see Map 26.6). France got Alsace-Lorraine but not the left bank of the Rhine or the establishment of an autonomous Rhineland state, which it also wanted. Instead, the Allies were to occupy the Rhineland for 15 years and the French to direct the coal-producing regions along the Saar River, but the latter were to remain under German sovereignty unless a later plebiscite determined differently. Plebiscites would also decide whether Germany would surrender part of Schleswig to Denmark or of upper Silesia to Poland.

The Polish provinces of eastern Prussia, where Germans formed about 40 percent of the population, were immediately ceded to Poland. Far more controversial, however, was the creation of a Polish corridor to the sea. Within the corridor, a majority of the population was Polish, but its outlet was the port of Danzig, a German city, which was restored to its ancient status as a free city. Worse, the corridor awkwardly separated

**Legend:**
- Allied Occupation Zone
- Demilitarized Zone
- New States Created in 1919
- Areas ceded by Austria-Hungary
- Areas ceded by Bulgaria
- Areas ceded by Germany
- Areas ceded by Russia
- Plebiscite Areas
- Boundaries at 1926

0   100   200 miles

**MAP 26.6 TERRITORIAL SETTLEMENTS 1919–1926**

eastern Prussia from the rest of Germany, and Poland would always feel insecure with an arrangement Germans never accepted.

Naturally enough, the Germans were required to disarm, and though the terms were stiff, this would not have seemed unreasonable if it had proved to be a first step toward general disarmament, as the treaty implied. Germany was to have no large artillery, submarines, or military air force, and its army was to be limited to 100,000 men on long-term enlistment. The lists of matériel Germany was to deliver to the Allies were more punitive: horses and railway carriages, quantities of coal, most of its present ships, and some new vessels to be specially built.

Most burdensome of all were the provisions for reparations. Despite fine talk of not requiring an indemnity, the Allies declared that Germany should pay for civilian damages. The claims of Belgium, a neutral attacked without warning, were easily justified; and Clemenceau could argue that the most destructive fighting had occurred in Belgium and France. But Lloyd George had campaigned on a platform of making Germany pay, and he insisted, over American objections, on including Allied military pensions as civilian costs. Pandora's box was opened. Germany was made liable for sums unspecified and without foreseeable end and forced to swear to accept "responsibility" for losses from a war "imposed . . . by the aggression of Germany and her allies." It was true that Germany had attacked first, and in the liberal view, its militarism had been the great disruptive force in European politics for a generation. But it was false, as historians soon established, that it had deliberately planned and instigated the war just fought. The "war guilt clause" thus became a subject of controversy in every country and of bitter resentment, official and private, in every part of Germany.

Finally, in German eyes, the terms of the treaty made it intolerable as a *Diktat*, a dictated settlement the country's delegates were not given a chance to dispute until it was already drafted; then only minor objections were met. Although in fact the Allies had made no clear commitment regarding terms, the Germany military had left it to the civilian government to make an armistice on the basis, they said, of Wilson's Fourteen Points. Faced with the terms set at Versailles, the German government resigned, and parliament at first rejected the stipulation of war guilt; but when the Allies held firm, parliament angrily accepted the *Diktat*. The treaty was signed on June 28, 1919, the fifth anniversary of the assassination at Sarajevo, in the Hall of Mirrors at Versailles, where Bismarck and William I had announced the German Empire 48 years before—the symbolism was complete.

### Treaties with the Central and Eastern States

For the Big Four, the most difficult question after the treatment of Germany was the Italian boundary. All agreed that Italy, for strategic reasons, should be given the Tyrol south of the Alpine Brenner Pass, a German-speaking area formerly held by Austria; but Wilson was determined to prevent those further violations of the principle of nationality incorporated in the Treaty of London of 1915 (which promised Italy a great deal more, including much of the Slavic-speaking lands of the Dalmatian coast). By stubbornly demanding more than they expected to get, the Italians stimulated unkind references to their record in the war. Then, too, Wilson made a serious tactical error: In a Paris interview he, in effect, asked the Italian people to reject the position of their negotiators, and the Italian delegation withdrew from the conference in protest to a great outpouring of nationalist feeling at home. Eventually, a compromise

Orlando, Lloyd George, Clemenceau, and Wilson look the very epitome of their respective nations as they face the camera rather than one another in this photo, which contrasts interestingly with the picture of the Congress of Vienna in Chapter 22.   (Photo: The Granger Collection)

was reached, but from that time on, Italy was another of the dissatisfied states resentfully seeking a revision of the treaties.

With the signing of the Treaty of Versailles, the Big Four dispersed to attend to their pressing domestic concerns, leaving the details of the remaining settlements (commonly named after the place where they were signed) to their foreign offices. The treaty with Austria signed at St.-Germain-en-Laye in September was closely modeled on the treaty with Germany. Provisions for reparations and demilitarization, including naval restrictions, hardly seemed appropriate

for the shaky little landlocked Austrian republic. In addition to the southern Tyrol, Italy was given the Istrian Peninsula and some islands but not Dalmatia, and boundaries with the other new states were settled on the basis of nationality in some cases and strategic needs in others. Treaties with Bulgaria (signed at Neuilly in November) and with Hungary (signed at the Trianon in June 1920) followed. Bohemia was given to Czechoslovakia on historical grounds, but Hungarian claims to a historical kingdom were largely ignored. Like Austria, Hungary lost almost three-quarters of the lands it had ruled in 1914. Although Bulgaria had surrendered relatively little territory, its resentment over its borders equaled that of the other defeated Central Powers.

Every state of Eastern Europe could claim injustice, usually with exaggerated statistics and with tales, too often true, of inhumane treatment. Railway lines and economic relationships, "natural" boundaries for defense, historical claims, and nationality simply did not coincide. At each point, one consideration had to be sacrificed to another; and since the final dispositions were frequently influenced by favoritism, external political factors, or sheer ignorance, the inconsistencies were blatant. A major role in making these arrangements work would fall to the new League of Nations.

A number of oral agreements and the very creation of the Reparations Commission provided for by the Treaty of Versailles implied that the treaties might be modified, as logic and equity argued they should; the reparations required from Austria, for example, were divided among the defunct empire's former lands in a gesture of fairness that left some new states paying reparations to others. Many territories were to be assigned only after a plebiscite, and many others were ceded to the Allies to be dealt with later. Provisions promising minorities just treatment, an expression of the Allies' decent intent, struck sensitive states as an insulting infringement on their sovereignty. The issues for future conflict were without limit.

The final treaty was one with Turkey, not signed until August 1920 at Sèvres; much of it never went into effect. The Allies, who had encouraged Arab nationalism, were embarrassed when the Soviet regime released their secret plans for partitioning the Ottoman Empire. Now they faced indigenous movements as complex and uncontrollable as those in Eastern Europe. A Turkish revival under Mustafa Kemal assured the territorial integrity of Turkey itself despite the principle of autonomous states adopted at Sèvres. In addition, Syria was to be under French influence, while a vaguely defined area—carved into Palestine, Trans-Jordan, and Iraq—was to be subject to British authority.

Aside from recognizing the presence of Britain and France, the quickly buried Treaty of Sèvres settled little, and more durable boundaries were achieved only through the conflicts and the diplomacy of the next few years. There was confusion in particular about what the British intended by separating Palestine from Trans-Jordan. In 1917 the British foreign secretary, Arthur Balfour, had promised that a "national home" for Jews would be created in Palestine; but the Balfour Declaration, exemplifying the nationalistic propaganda and humanitarian concern of that difficult year, had also guaranteed the rights of the Moslems there. Subsequent British statements had been neither clear nor consistent. The independence of Arabia was recognized in the Sèvres agreement, but competition among native rulers left its status uncertain and the boundaries of the new state undefined. For Egypt, the peace terms ratified its separation from Ottoman sovereignty and confirmed British authority—that, too, contested by local movements.

The Allied enthusiasm for dividing the Ottoman Empire both abated and seemed more suspect now that neither the Russian nor the Austro-Hungarian Empire remained on the scene to demand a share. But the recognition of French and British interests in the region led to an important innovation. Colonial territories were declared "mandates'' of the League of Nations and assigned to classes. The parts of the Ottoman Empire newly placed under British or French rule—Palestine, Trans-Jordan, Iraq, and Syria—were Class A mandates, states considered on the verge of self-government. Most of the reassigned African territories were Class B mandates, ones in which European rulers were to guarantee freedom of religion, prohibit trade in liquor and arms, refrain from subjecting natives to military training, and encourage commerce. Class C mandates were primarily Pacific islands, to be ruled essentially as colonies. In every case, the mandate power had to submit annual reports to the League of Nations for review. Like much else in the treaties, the system of mandates can be seen as an expression of conscience and growing responsibility toward the rest of the world or as an effort to legitimize continued European dominance and wrap hypocrisy in legalism. In operation, the system justified both interpretations.

## Built-in Weaknesses

By 1920 it was clear that the war to make the world safe for democracy, as the Allied leaders had labeled it, had not quite accomplished that. Yet the terms of peace did concertedly promote democracy in their call for self-determination and plebiscites, provisions for the League of Nations (carefully written into each treaty at Wilson's shrewd insistence), and the development of the system of mandates. Allied victory had spurred the establishment of representative regimes throughout Central Europe, almost requisite for admission to Allied favor. Like the diplomats at Vienna a century before, the statesmen at Paris saw an integral relationship between the form of domestic government and international peace. The treaties showed the influence of democracy less happily in their responsiveness to Allied public opinion that

expected a peace punitive enough to justify the war.

Not since 1848 had liberal conceptions so thoroughly dominated European politics, but the revolutions of World War I quickly went beyond nineteenth-century liberalism. The men at Paris found it hard to cope with revolution. They never managed a place for Russia at the conference nor even agreed on a consistent response to Communist governments. Believers in democracy, they were baffled and frightened by the turmoil unleashed by wars for democracy. Although they supported self-determination and therefore nationalism, they were more aware than their forebears that nationalism is not necessarily democratic. They took little account, however, of the social complexities of Eastern Europe, where land division was more explosive an issue than political forms and nationality itself no more important than the antagonism between peasant and lord. Living in a revolution they helped make and largely welcomed, the statesmen who forged the peace were not revolutionaries. If they encouraged revolutionary changes, they wanted to limit their part to legal formulas; and slogans that sounded radical in November 1918 gave way to frightened insistence on order a few months later.

Much that was accomplished at Paris reflected a cold assertion of national interest and a realistic appraisal of power. Inevitably, the treaties were compromises. But it was the Allies who had asserted that their handiwork should be measured by the standards of high principle and who had injected ideology into matters of power politics. Woodrow Wilson was the most dedicated and by his lights the most consistent spokesman of this new moral and democratic politics.[5] And

[5] Yet he returned to the Paris Peace Conference after a trip home insisting that the Monroe Doctrine be written into the Covenant of the League of Nations.

| International and Military History | Political History |
|---|---|
| | 1868  Meiji Restoration in Japan |
| **1870** | |
| 1875  Disraeli buys shares in Suez Canal | |
| 1878  Congress of Berlin | |
| 1879  Dual Alliance, Germany and Austria–Hungary | |
| 1881  Three Emperors' Alliance (Russia, Germany, Austria–Hungary) | |
| 1882  Britain into Egypt; Triple Alliance (Germany, Italy, Austria–Hungary) | |
| 1885  Berlin Conference | |
| 1886  Britain annexes upper Burma | |
| 1887  Establishment of French Indochina | |
| 1890  German–Russian Reinsurance Treaty dropped | 1890s  Accelerated arms race among major European powers |
| 1894  French–Russian alliance | |
| 1896  British annexation of part of Malaya; William II sends Kruger telegram | |
| 1898  Fashoda crisis; Spanish–American War | |
| | 1900–1901  Boxer Rebellion in China |
| 1902  Anglo–Japanese alliance; France and Italy pledge neutrality | |
| 1904  Entente Cordiale, Great Britain and France | |
| 1904–1905  Russo–Japanese War | 1905  Revolution in Russia; revolution in Persia |
| 1906  Algeciras Conference | |
| 1907  Triple Entente (France, Russia, Great Britain) | |
| 1908  Austria annexes Bosnia–Herzegovina | 1908  Revolt of Young Turks |
| 1911  Agadir crisis | 1910  Establishment of Union of South Africa |
| 1911–1912  Italian–Turkish war | 1911  Revolution in China |
| 1912  First Balkan War (Bulgaria, Montenegro, Serbia, and Greece against Turkey) | |
| 1913  Second Balkan War (Greece, Rumania, Serbia, and Turkey against Bulgaria) | |
| 1914  War declared | |
| 1915  Treaty of London, Italy joins Allies } World War I | |
| 1916  Battles of Jutland, Verdun | 1916  Lloyd George prime minister in Britain |
| 1917  United States enters the war | 1917  Clemenceau, French premier; revolution in Russia |
| 1918  Armistice | 1918  Kaiser William abdicates |
| 1919  Paris Peace Conference | 1919  Revolts in Germany, Hungary |
| **1920** | |

| Social and Economic History | Cultural and Intellectual History |
|---|---|
| **1870** | |
| **1890s** Strikes increase in size and number; greater importance of trade unions and socialist parties | **1890s** Height of the popularity of Kipling (1863–1936); popular press often stridently imperialist |
| | **1902** Hobson (**1858–1940**), *Imperialism: A Study* |
| **1915** Greatly increased employment of women in industry | |
| | **1916** Lenin (**1870–1924**), *Imperialism: The Last Stage of Capitalism* |
| **1918** Destruction of World War I includes 10 to 13 million killed | |
| **1920** | **1920** Keynes (**1883–1946**), *Economic Consequences of the Peace* |

critics blame him for many of the weaknesses of the treaties, charging that he was intransigent or yielding in the wrong places and that he sacrificed too much to gain his dream of the League of Nations in the belief that liberal procedures would produce liberal policies.

But Wilson is more responsible for arousing hopes than betraying them. If his doctrinaire approach often meshed unfortunately with Clemenceau's skepticism and Lloyd George's easy flexibility, there were far more fundamental difficulties. Perhaps the greatest was that none of the leaders yet fully understood how much had changed. Although they created a tiny and weak Austrian republic, they could not forget the wealth and power of the Austrian Empire and therefore forbade the union of Austria, now thoroughly German, with Germany. They did not see that the deep economic, social, and psychological dislocation following the war would continue to threaten democracy and peace no matter how many representative governments were established.

### Contemporary Criticism

Some signs of weakness in the treaty settlements appeared very early among the drafters themselves. In March 1920 the Senate of the United States rejected the documents for the final time. The most powerful nation in the world, having claimed moral leadership, would not enter the League of Nations. The United States thus joined Italy in rejecting the terms of peace, and in the process, it added France to the list of aggrieved states. The French had abandoned demands that Germany be further weakened in return for a joint guarantee from the United States and Great Britain against German aggression. When the United States refused to honor that agreement, France felt betrayed. Moreover, France had also wanted the league to have a peacekeeping force of its own, but its allies

had opposed this. Out of its dissatisfaction and alarm, it would seek to make the League of Nations not a flexible instrument for modifying the war settlements but rather an agency for rigidly maintaining the status quo.

China refused to sign the treaties because of terms that gave Japan, in addition to other gains, almost a protectorate over it. Japan was offended by the conference's refusal formally to declare all races equal. For Asian, Middle Eastern, and African peoples, it was hard to believe that European diplomacy was much more principled than in the past.

The reparations clauses were soon blamed for the economic difficulties of numerous countries—those forced to pay them and those granted much less than anticipated. But the very concept had many opponents. In a brilliant and influential pamphlet, the English economist John Maynard Keynes castigated the Carthaginian peace the victors had exacted, attacking reparations in particular.[6] He argued that the Allies owed one another more money than Germany could pay and that reparations would merely slow the recovery of Europe's economy. His analysis helped undermine confidence in the terms of peace, but his prescriptions—cancellation of international war debts and recognition that the international economic system was essentially artificial—were heresies as utopian in their way as any of Woodrow Wilson's points.

Keynes was right that policies toward Russia, Germany, and the successor states were contradictory; but his criticisms, like those that for decades would ring from party platforms in every country, tended to exaggerate how much of the postwar world could be shaped by worried statesmen quarreling in Paris.

[6] John Maynard Keynes, *The Economic Consequences of the Peace*, 1920; and the famous rebuttal, Etienne Mantoux, *The Carthaginian Peace: or the Economic Consequences of Mr. Keynes*, 1946. The reference is to the harsh peace terms that Roman senators demanded upon the defeat of Carthage in the Third Punic War, 149–146 B.C.

# SUMMARY

Although the European nations did not fight one another between 1871 and 1914, peace was precarious as imperialism abroad and tension at home encouraged militant posturing and an accelerating arms race. As foreign policy, economic competition, and domestic politics became more closely interrelated, any social or political conflict was likely to have international repercussions. One spark in the changing Balkans was sufficient to trigger the elaborate mechanisms of world war.

The war at first seemed to heal divisions in every nation, but the industrialization and democratization of the previous 40 years had altered the nature of war. It required more in wealth, organization, manpower, and morale than any society could afford and more than the Austrian and Russian empires could provide. Defeat unleashed the divisions war had briefly masked between ideologies, classes, and neighboring nationalities; and social strain exploded into open, violent revolution in Central and Eastern Europe. Revolution

in Russia, which began as an opening to democracy the West could welcome, quickly went beyond familiar concepts to bring the Bolsheviks to power. By war's end, death and destruction, the changed relations of social groups, and weakened economies made even the victors appear more like the survivors of a revolution.

It fell primarily to Great Britain, France, and the United States to define international order and set the terms of peace for a torn and ravaged continent in which insecure new nations faced one another suspiciously and Communism was now a reality. Led by the nonsocialist left, the great democracies approached the task bearing hopes resonant with the best in nineteenth-century optimism. Before the task was finished, disillusionment, confusion, and exhaustion measured how little freedom statesmen had to mold a new world. Like the great revolutions, World War I created a gulf between past and present that marks the beginning of a new era.

# RECOMMENDED READING

## Studies

Becker, Jean-Jacques. *The Great War and the French People*. 1985. Shows how the war was a turning point in French life.

*Carr, E. G. *The Bolshevik Revolution 1917–1923*. 3 vols. 1985. The most comprehensive single study.

Carsten, F. L. *Revolution in Central Europe, 1918–1919*. 1972. An important treatment of these significant outbreaks following the war.

*Craig, Gordon. *Germany: 1866–1945*. 1978. A well-written and capable analysis that stresses the failure of liberalism to overcome preindustrial forces.

Falls, Cyril B. *The Great War*. 1961. Skillful account by a noted military historian.

Feldman, Gerald D. *Army, Industry and Labor in Germany, 1914–1918*. 1966. A fundamental analysis of the war's effects on institutions and power in Germany.

*Ferro, Marc. *The Great War, 1914–1918*. 1973. This stimulating, outspoken essay emphasizes economic and social factors.

*Fischer, Fritz. *Germany's Aims in the First World War*. 1967. The reassessment that became a center of controversy among Germany historians.

Fitzpatrick, Sheila. *The Russian Revolution, 1917–1932*. 1982. A valuable, fresh overview that emphasizes social conditions.

*Fussell, Paul. *The Great War and Modern Memory*. 1975. Outstanding study of the cultural impact of the war.

*Joll, James. *The Origins of the First World War*. 1984. Draws upon the vast literature dealing with a question that was once extremely controversial to establish a perspective for our era.

Kocka, Jürgen. *Facing Total War. German Society 1914–1918*. Barbara Weinberger (tr.). 1984.

Marwick, Arthur. *War and Social Change in the Twentieth Century: A Comparative Study of Britain, France, Germany, Russia and the United States*. 1975. Develops the case for the revolutionary effects of World Wars I and II on domestic society.

*Mayer, Arno J. *Politics and Diplomacy of Peacemaking: Containment and Counterrevolution at Versailles, 1918–1919*. 1967. Argues that fear of Bolshevism shaped the peace.

*Mommsen, Wolfgang J. *Theories of Imperialism*. P. S. Falla (tr.). 1980. An admirably clear and concise guide to a century of debate, including a discussion of colonialism today.

*Nicholson, Harold G. *Peacemaking, 1919*. 1965. The analysis of a disappointed participant.

*Owen, Roger, and Bob Sutcliffe (eds.). *Studies in the Theory of Imperialism*. 1972. Telling essays evaluate current and older theories, while case studies treat particular historical examples; a heterogeneous collection, both Marxist and non-Marxist.

*Pipes, Richard. *The Formation of the Soviet Union*. 1964. A clear and comprehensive treatment.

*Robinson, Ronald, John Gallegher, and Alice Denny. *Africa and the Victorians: The Climax of Imperialism*. 1961. An important revision that has opened up fresh perspectives on imperialism.

Thompson, John M. *Revolutionary Russia, 1917*. 1989. A good overview of what the revolution meant for ordinary life.

*Ulam, Adam B. *Lenin and the Bolsheviks*. 1969. Combines the study of ideas and policy to explain Lenin's triumph.

Wehler, Hans-Ulrich. *The German Empire 1871–1918*. Kim Traynor (tr.). 1985. A comprehensive structural analysis that synthesizes the most recent empirical research.

Williams, John. *The Home Fronts: Britain, France, and Germany, 1914–1918*. 1972. Pulls together a variety of evidence of the war's domestic impact.

Winter, J. M. *The Great War and the British People*. 1986. A balanced assessment of the effects of the war on British society.

* Available in paperback.

# ❄ CHAPTER 27 ❄

# DEMOCRACY
# AND DEPRESSION
# 1920–1933

# ❄ CHAPTER 27 ❄

# DEMOCRACY
# AND DEPRESSION
# 1920–1933

❊ ❊ ❊ ❊ ❊

The great question was what kind of world the postwar world would be. As war had disrupted society, so peace brought the opportunity for further, more desirable change. Among the victors, those changes were expected to bring fuller democracy and solid prosperity; in lands that had known defeat, they were hammered out in revolutions and civil wars. The immediate result appeared to be a general triumph of democracy. States were more solidly identified with a single nationality and their citizens given greater voice in government than ever before in Europe's history. Where industrialization had been slight, social and political changes encouraged its development. The institutions of parliamentarianism had spread almost everywhere, and on the whole, they seemed to work. Revolution more radical than that was defeated everywhere except in Russia.

❊

International affairs centered at first on the economic problems left by the war and on the machinery of the League of Nations. Moderation prevailed in these matters too, and the principles represented by Woodrow Wilson came as close to realization as such peaceful dreams ever had. Great Britain and France dominated the postwar world not merely through their international power but through the influence of their political style as well.

❊

In domestic and international politics, a confident, progressive liberalism seemed dominant, but European culture reflected—and stimulated—a growing malaise. New learning questioned old values and theories, while the arts rejected convention. Beneath the economic recovery of Western society, a wide array of social issues had yet to be addressed. Much as the system of international relations had suddenly failed in 1914, the system of intricate financial structures collapsed with the crash of 1929.

❊

The financial crisis added immeasurably to more localized ailments of the European states. The postwar spread of democracy had not preserved political freedom in Italy or stability in much of Eastern Europe or brought about disarmament, and representative governments had left critical issues, both international and domestic, unresolved. And then they failed to maintain prosperity. Efforts at international negotiation for economic cooperation as well as for disarmament broke down. The Great Depression, a disaster in the lives of millions, was also a disaster for the political and economic institutions of Western liberalism.

## I. THE POSTWAR POLITICAL ORDER

❊

Nothing appeared clearer at the end of the war than that European political life would henceforth be very different, for people everywhere seemed determined to make it so. How fundamental these changes should be was the issue at stake as the left gained strength even in the West, as revolution and civil war spread across Europe east of the Rhine, and as in Russia, the Bolsheviks struggled to keep power. By the early 1920s, the picture was clearer. Germany established the sort of democracy the Allies had hoped for; and between its borders and Russia's, 13 nations, mostly new, established domestic institutions and international ties sufficient for survival. Despite all the political and economic complications, postwar Europe broadly resembled the world envisioned at the Paris Peace Conference. Uncertainty centered on Russia, the great exception—but the Soviet Union remained weak and isolated—and on Italy, whose turn to Facism was the great surprise.

## The Consolidation of Soviet Rule

The Bolsheviks had made peasants' demands their own, arranged a costly peace, and prevented anyone else from capturing power; but now they faced civil war and attack from experienced armies, foreign and domestic. In a land already devastated by war and defeat, in which communications were poor and the economy near collapse, the Bolsheviks adopted "War Communism," a desperate effort to gather the nation's remaining forces. They extended the nationalization of industry and requisitioned crops from the more affluent peasants. And they ruthlessly used terror, police repression, and propaganda to extract from a country in chaos just enough men and supplies to fight a war. With the firm leadership of Lenin, the military talent of Trotsky, and above all, the mistakes of their enemies, they were able to win.

The major threat remaining by mid-1919 was the armies gathered under former tsarist officers in Estonia, southern Russia, and the Urals. Early in the summer the army in the Urals pushed toward Moscow, but this assault from the east was stopped before troops

under General Anton Denikin moved up from the basin of the River Don to take Kiev in August and reach within 300 miles of Moscow by October. At that time, other "White" forces, as the "Red" Communists' internal enemies came to be called,[1] stood only 30 miles from Petrograd (see Map 26.5). Thereafter the tide turned, for the antigovernment armies could neither penetrate farther nor maintain a long siege against the Communists.

The White forces, even at their peak, were unable to coordinate their attacks effectively because of dissension and conflicting ambitions. Vague about the political solutions they sought, many of them behaved suspiciously like men intent on a tsarist restoration. Battlegrounds were often ill-defined, contested by units hardly more than marauding bands. And the areas under White control experienced a terror less efficient but possibly more brutal than in Red sectors. While the Communists appealed to peasants, workers, and the various nationalities, the Whites antagonized everybody, losing the popular support that was their only hope. With each defeat, more of their troops melted away, and their sympathizers (including the Allies) became more cautious.

By the end of 1919 the White armies were in general retreat. The most important group, under Denikin, withdrew to the Crimea early in 1920; there a new commander, General Peter Wrangel, stubbornly fought on before finally heeding Allied advice and evacuating his remaining armies in November 1920.

---

[1] The term *White Russian* is used in two completely unrelated senses. For centuries before the Bolshevik revolution, and still today, it has referred to one of three major divisions of the Russian people—Great Russians, Little Russians, and White or Byelo Russians. The "White Russians" inhabit the district around Minsk in western Russia and possess a language and a literature of their own, closely related to, but still distinct from, those of their Great Russian neighbors. This use of the term has no connection with "Whites" used to identify the opponents of the Bolsheviks during the civil war.

The Communists were also successful against Poland. An Allied commission had proposed to place the Russo-Polish border along the Curzon Line, so named for the British statesman who advocated it, which assigned to Poland most areas in which ethnic Poles were clearly a majority. But cultural and historical arguments made Poland insist on a boundary that had existed in 1772, well to the east. Rejecting Russian proposals for compromise, Poland sent an army into the Ukraine in March 1920. Within a month it took Kiev, but the Ukranian nationalists who had fought against the Russians were unwilling to fight for the Poles. In August the Red army, by now a relatively efficient military machine, launched an assault that soon threatened Warsaw. An effective Polish counterattack led to terms set in 1921, establishing a frontier between Poland's demands and the Curzon Line.

Russia's western border was now fixed. In Transcaucasia an agreement in 1921 between Russia and Turkey ignored local independence movements and assigned Armenia and Georgia, where anti-Communists had been strong, to the Soviet federation and Kars and Ardahan to Turkey. In Asian Russia the Bolshevik's opponents were not entirely defeated until 1922, after the Japanese agreed to withdraw from eastern Siberia. The Soviet Union was firmly in Soviet hands. A revolutionary Communist government had succeeded against great odds and almost all predictions in winning sufficient support and creating a government and an army that could hold power and win wars.

## The New Economic Policy

In some ways, these troubles aided the new government. Like their cession of territory, the Bolsheviks' economic difficulties made them less frightening to other nations; and chaos itself made it easier for them to effect revolutionary changes in landholding, social structure, and political power. Now it was time to take stock.

Under War Communism, regimentation and bloodshed were the means of survival, and by using them, the Communist party had become an increasingly disciplined and powerful body. The militant arm of a new order, it paralleled the regular government in organization. Some saw in this a pattern for effective rule. Others argued that the loose terror had gone too far (most of the countryside was still subject to the whims of local party officials and roving bands of armed men) and that continuing crises required new policies. Cities were partially empty; a million Russians had gone into exile; tens of millions more had died; less than one-sixth as many manufactured goods were produced in 1920 as in 1913, and the level was far lower in some critical areas of heavy industry. Foreign trade had almost ceased. Poor harvests left the nation faced with famine, and the continued requisitions of what food there was spurred unrest and even revolt. Black markets flourished, and bureaucratic bungling, political maneuvering, and perpetual suspicion retarded economic reconstruction in a country more lacking than ever in machinery and technicians. Thus the mutiny of sailors at the Kronstadt naval base in March 1921, though put down in a few weeks, was an ominous sign. These were just the sort of men who had made the October Revolution possible, but their demands—civil liberties, a secret ballot, and better treatment of peasants—were now rejected. Still Soviet leaders, especially Lenin, recognized the need not to depend on repression alone.

In the spring of 1921, he announced the New Economic Policy (NEP), a major turning point in the development of Communist Russia. Lenin's gift for clear and courageous analysis underlay this dramatic reversal of policy. To some Communists and many foreigners, the NEP seemed a departure from Marxism, but the failures Lenin recognized were not failures of Marxist theory. Russia, he argued, was a special case, what today would be called an underdeveloped country; and the "citadel of capitalism"—a characteristic military metaphor—had been rushed too fast. Old habits and practices could not be uprooted overnight. Furthermore, Russia lacked the cadres of technical specialists and managers a modern economy required. With noteworthy pragmatism, Lenin proposed the sort of moderate course the Bolsheviks would earlier have opposed.

Under the NEP, peasants were no longer subject to requisitions but rather to a tax in kind, and they could sell their surplus for profit on the open market. Retail concerns and manufacturers employing fewer than 20 workers could be run as private businesses. Even the larger industries, though they remained nationalized, could be leased to foreign entrepreneurs as a way of training Russians in efficient methods and new techniques. Fiscal reforms of the sort capitalist economists might have recommended guaranteed the stability of the currency, helping Russia's external trade to emerge from the pattern of barter into which it had fallen.

Even with these new practices, economic recovery was slow. Millions died in the famine of 1920–1921 despite the extensive aid of the American Relief Administration, and not for another six years would production reach pre-war levels. The NEP represented a surrender of the hope of creating Communism all at once, but it was also a reaffirmation of Communist determination. Foreign trade, fiscal policy, large industry, wholesale commerce, and natural resources remained firmly in the hands of the state.

## Creating a Communist Society

Meanwhile, every social institution was recruited to help create a stable new society. The already numerous cooperatives for the sale of agricultural products and for consumer purchases were encouraged, as were trade unions. Both kinds of organization were used to strengthen allegiance to the government, teach efficiency, and instill a sense of class and national pride. Persecution of the Church and organized campaigns against religion notwithstanding, by 1923 a certain relaxation permitted the Orthodox Church to function in a restricted fashion.

Russia's inadequate school system, which had nearly collapsed during the years of war and revolution, was improved and extended. Not until 1923 did enrollments pass prewar levels, but thereafter the rise was steady and impressive. The curriculum stressed official doctrines, and workers' children were favored for admission. Old practices of rote learning and ceremonial deference to teachers were to be abandoned. Higher education, on the other hand, developed more slowly, inhibited by the government's insistence that all subjects be taught in Marxist terms and by the emigration of many of Russia's best scholars.

The problems of ruling over multiple nationalities eased somewhat with the cession of so much territory; three-quarters of the remaining population could be called Russian. Still, non-Russian nationalities were, in fact, encouraged as never before. The four great Soviet republics—the Russian Soviet Federated Socialist Republic, the Ukranian, Byelorussian, and (after 1922) Transcaucasian Soviet republics—were themselves divided into numerous regions for the various minorities. In theory at least, each of these smaller constituent republics retained considerable autonomy under a new constitution that established the Union of Soviet Socialist Republics (U.S.S.R.).

Legally, the authority of the government stemmed from the hierarchy of soviets described in Chapter 26. The largest, the all-union Congress of Soviets, consisted of some

**Trotsky praises the historic role of the Red army at the 1922 meeting of the Third International, held in Moscow to celebrate the anniversary of the Bolshevik Revolution.** (Photo: Wide World Photos)

2000 representatives. The system of indirect universal suffrage that elected them heavily favored urban voters, though rural constituencies had five times the population. At infrequent and largely ceremonial meetings, the Congress elected the 750-member Central Executive Committee, which was more nearly the equivalent of a Western parliament, though it had only advisory powers. The Committee selected both the Council of People's Commissars and the Presidium, a directorate, whose chairman was the chief of state. Precise lines of authority among competing groups were left vague, and little distinction was made between legislative and executive functions.

In practice, the Communist party, which remained a restricted elite, was the most important instrument of rule. Not all officials were party members, but it dominated the upper reaches of government, and through a tightly organized hierarchy that paralleled the bureaucracy, it reached into every aspect of Soviet public life—factories, hundreds of new centers for adult education, and youth associations that soon had millions of members. These organizations stirred patriotic enthusiasm, explained the policies of the government, and prodded Russians in thousands of ways to create a modern industrial society.

At first, Western artistic movements as well as technology had been welcomed and energetically adopted, but the challenge of creating a new society discouraged tolerance. In 1922 cultural activities were placed directly under the Ministry of Education. The books printed and art works exhibited were those that met the current definition of communist aesthetics: realistic in style, popular in appeal, and useful to the new order. The issues of how to translate ideology into practice, what technologies to use, and how bureaucracies should function were thrashed out within the government and the party. To be on the losing side in any of these disputes was politically and sometimes personally fatal. Experience thus led Communists to caution, and this, in turn, contributed to an atmosphere of apparent calm.

Even in foreign relations, the Soviet Union, preoccupied with domestic problems, gave signs of accepting the world order despite the existence of the Third International. By 1924, the year of Lenin's death, every major power except the United States had recognized the new regime. And the bitter struggle for succession made it appear that even if Communism remained firmly entrenched in the Soviet Union, that need not seriously disturb international relations. The new Communist state became a source of inspiration and hope for the far left; and although it remained an object of fear to liberals and conservatives, most governments could accept a status quo that included an isolated and weak Soviet Union.

## The New Regimes of Eastern Europe

From Finland to the Balkans, most of the postwar states of Eastern Europe were newly created by-products of the battle among the giants who had previously dominated these lands. Recognized as independent in the peace settlements, the new states represented the Allied commitment to self-determination, and most of them had new constitutions reflecting the latest fashions and the deepest hopes of democracy.

But in nearly every case, statehood had brought war with neighboring regions; and independence, universal suffrage, and civil rights offered few solutions to the problems of conflicting nationalities and economic crisis. In most of the new states, peasant revolution or military takeover threatened almost constantly, and most of the elected leaders depended on aroused national feeling for what consistent support they could muster. Peasant parties were dominant in most of these countries as they never had been in the West, and these parties often combined agrarian radicalism with distrust of urban values, modernizing changes, or parliaments.

These social conflicts in Eastern Europe intersected with ethnic and religious differences to increase centrifugal pressures. The German minorities in Poland, Czechoslovakia, Hungary, and Bulgaria were generally among the resented well-to-do. Anti-Semitism was especially virulent in Poland and Rumania, partly an expression of rural hostility toward urban finance. Town-country antagonism also often set rural Slovaks at odds with the Czechs of industrialized western Czechoslovakia. In Yugoslavia the claims of Greek Orthodox Serbians to be the "national" people angered the Roman Catholic Croatians and Slovenes. Macedonians, divided among Yugoslavia, Greece, and Bulgaria, kept up an organized agitation that added to the instability in all three countries and produced chaotic insurrection in Bulgaria from 1923 to 1925.

Rising populations, widespread illiteracy, and lack of capital plagued economic development in the new states. Only Austria and

Czechoslovakia had advanced industries of a size that could compete in European markets; elsewhere, land remained the central economic issue. Independence brought the eviction of "foreign" landlords and the breakup of large estates in the Baltic countries; Bulgaria, Rumania, and Czechoslovakia also instituted significant land reforms. Everywhere, however, new policies proved less effective than expected. Resentment rose with any favored treatment given to specific nationalities and regions. Conservative peasants holding small plots generally proved the most resistant to agricultural modernization. In Poland and still more in Hungary (where 40 percent of the peasants were landless and the next 50 percent held less than three hectares each), the great estate owners succeeded in protecting the interests of a native aristocracy.

Each state erected tariff barriers that interrupted the flow of trade that had been established within the former empires. Furthermore, the successor countries began their existence burdened with a share of the debts of the Hapsburg Empire and with complex schedules of payments owed to one another for lands gained or lost. Only intensive help from the League of Nations kept these claims from crippling them and enabled the financial system to function at all.

Yet, gradually, stable patterns emerged. The disappearance of the Russian, Austrian, and Ottoman empires had opened the way for systematic efforts at modernization. Schools were built by the thousands and functioned fairly effectively despite the issues of language and nationality to which they gave rise. On the whole, the traditions of the Austrian bureaucracy served its heirs well, and Turkey, which became a republic under Mustafa Kemal in 1923, borrowed Western dress and institutions as avenues to national strength. The next year the Greeks, defeated by the Turks in the last of the Balkan conflicts that followed World War I, replaced their monarchy with a republic that achieved relative stability despite the continued danger of military intervention in domestic politics.

In general, the socialists and agrarian radicals prominent in the first postwar years had given way to more conservative politicians. By 1920 the defeat of Béla Kun's brief Communist regime in Hungary had led to authoritarian rule under Admiral Miklós Horthy, acting as regent for an empty throne, who abolished the secret ballot in rural areas as part of the reassertion of Magyar dominance. But most of the governments of Eastern Europe worked more or less within their constitutions; and Czechoslovakia, under President Tomáš Masaryk and Foreign Minister Eduard Beneš, became a model of the order, freedom, and prosperity democracy was supposed to bring.

## The Weimar Republic of Germany

Pressures for a more democratic and responsible German government were powerful even before the armistice. Twice in 1917 Kaiser William II had promised to make his cabinet subject to a majority in the Reichstag; and in October 1918, to begin this transformation from above, he appointed Prince Maximilian of Baden chancellor.

Prince Max symbolized a compromise that might have worked earlier, but he was not able to stem the uprisings sweeping through much of Germany in the name of peace, democracy, and socialism during the last weeks of war. Not only the political system but also the very nation Bismarck had created threatened to break apart, and Prince Max pleaded with William to abdicate. When revolt had spread to Berlin, he announced the abdication without awaiting the Kaiser's approval. Then this liberal aristocrat who favored constitutional monarchy, this non-Prussian nobleman who opposed the dominance of Junkers and army, handed his office (quite unconstitutionally) to Friedrich Ebert, the leader of the Social Democrats. The provisional government, the first German government to include socialists, was established just in time to sign the armistice.

It talked proudly of the German "revolution," and it promulgated decrees in November promising democracy, freedom of speech, a return to the eight-hour workday, and measures to improve social security. Concerned first of all simply with survival, the provisional government avoided tackling the question of land reform lest disruption increase the real danger of starvation. Frightened of a Bolshevik revolution, it quickly reached an accommodation with the army— an army already recovering some of its confidence. Ludendorff, who had insisted that Germany had to sue for peace, later talked of holding out; and even before the terms of peace had been published, the legend began to spread of a valiant army stabbed in the back by radicals at home.

Although the German military had, in fact, been defeated, the nucleus of military strength remained intact. General Wilhelm Groener, who replaced Ludendorff in late October 1918 as Hindenburg's principal aid, promised to assist the new government provided it would not meddle in the army's affairs. Ebert accepted those terms, and when an uprising of left-wing Marxists called Spartacists brought most of Berlin under their control in January 1919, the army crushed the revolt and shot its leaders. The Spartacists had failed to win a large following, and Lenin's best hope for a Communist revolution in Germany died with them.

Germany's new leaders remained committed democrats, and they held elections in January 1919 for a constituent assembly to meet in Weimar, a pleasant city associated with Goethe that recalled the culture of preindustrial Germany. Nearly three-quarters of the delegates elected were intent on installing a republic (Social Democrats held 40 percent of the seats), and with admirable dispatch they wrote a thoroughly democratic constitution that joined proportional representation to universal suffrage. The president, directly elected for a seven-year term, would nominate the chancellor, or prime minister, who would then have to be approved by the Reichstag. The Reichsrat, as the upper house was now called, would still represent the single states, but its authority was reduced. In the new Germany, government would be responsible to parliament, minorities would be fairly represented, and the aristocracy would hold no political privilege. Both civil rights and private property were specifically guaranteed. With women voting, the Social Democrats in power, and a broad spectrum of parties, German politics appeared to be launched on a distinctive new course.

The government, however, continued to face grave threats from the left and an essentially independent army on the right. In addition, Allied policies had effects quite contrary to those intended. The victors' insistence that a civilian government be immediately established had allowed the generals to escape publicly acknowledging their defeat and left the founders of the new republic to bear the onus of the harsh treaty terms. The decision not to occupy Germany but to maintain the blockade made military collapse less visible than Allied severity. Thus resentment combined with social and economic distress and with the unfinished business of reparations and plebiscites to feed the strength of right-wing nationalists.

In March 1920 some of these tried a revolt of their own. Wolfgang Kapp, a lesser official and outspoken nationalist, led some *Freikorps* (the independent small armies that formed in the chaos of defeat) and others in a march

**Poverty in Berlin, 1922; a family begging.**
(Photo: UPI)

on Berlin. When the army, so ready to repress revolt from the left, declared its unwillingness to fire on "fellow soldiers," the government abandoned the capital. Its last-minute call for a general strike, however, produced the greatest demonstration of loyalty the Weimar regime would ever win. Workers across the nation left their jobs. In a matter of days the economy came to a halt, and the Kapp "government" gave up.

The Weimar Republic was making its way between the political extremes, but the Social Democrats lacked the strength to pursue the reforms their victory implied. The bureaucracy was not democratized. Nor was the army reformed, and its officer corps, though severely limited by the Treaty of Versailles, preserved its cohesion and reached another timely understanding with the politicians. The lack of reprisals following Kapp's fall contrasted strangely with the treatment of the Spartacists. Socialist talk of nationalizing some industries produced few concrete results, and the republic could not be certain of the workers' support in future crises.

New elections showed a shift to the right, which promised order, and brought in ministries resting primarily on the Catholic Center and the People's parties, the latter dominated by industrialists who had belonged to the right wing of the former National Liberals. Although the *Freikorps* were at last outlawed, many of their members merely went into hiding; they remained prominent in the political violence that characterized the Weimar years. Scores of politicians were assassinated, including Matthias Erzberger, the Center party leader who had signed the armistice, and Walther Rathenau, a brilliant organizer of the German economy during the war and, as foreign minister in 1922, a vigorous defender of Germany's interests, shot primarily because he was a Jew. By 1924 the conservative National People's party was second in size to the Social Democrats.

The gravest problem of these years, however, was inflation. Early in 1923 French and Belgian forces occupied the Ruhr district because of Germany's failure to make coal deliveries required as reparations, and the local populace responded with passive resistance, a kind of general strike, that made the occupation fruitless. The resulting dislocation and scarcity also drastically accelerated the already serious inflation. The German government, which from 1920 on found it easier to print more money than to raise taxes, continued that practice in 1923 as its expenses rose and its revenues declined.

The German mark, valued at 4 to 1 U.S. dollar in 1914 and 9 to 1 in 1919, was exchanged at 500 to 1 by 1922. Its subsequent fall was cataclysmic. One dollar was worth 18,000 marks in January 1923; 350,000 marks in July; nearly 5,000,000 in August. Inflation rates then accelerated much more in each of the next three months. New money was run off the presses at top speed, and old notes with additional zeros printed on them were rushed to the banks before they, too, became valueless. Prices changed within hours, always upward; by November a newspaper could sell for nearly 100 billion marks.

By the end of the year a restructuring was begun. The government imposed stringent new financial measures, aided by foreign loans, a moratorium on reparations, and a subsequent new schedule of payments. A slow recovery began. Some fortunes had been made, especially by speculators and financeers during the inflation; many large industries and property owners had fared quite well. Small businesses were more often hurt, as were nearly all wage earners. Savings held in cash had been wiped out.

At the height of the Ruhr crisis, a nationalist *Putsch* was attempted in Munich, led by a little-known man named Adolf Hitler, the revolt was more notable for Ludendorff's participation. It was quickly defeated, though

**German firms in 1923 needed a handcart to carry the weekly payroll.** (Photo: Wide World Photos)

the plotters' punishment was ludicrously light: Ludendorff was acquitted and Hitler given a five-year sentence in comfortable prison quarters, where he composed *Mein Kampf* ("My Struggle") in the 13 months he actually served. It was reasonable to think in 1924 that Germany was on the road to stability. If democracy had not exactly taken root, the forms were operative; better relations with other powers now seemed possible, and the threat of internal revolution had faded.

The second half of the 1920s was a period of notable prosperity in the Weimar Republic. But the divisions in German society, briefly obscured by defeat, had grown sharper. German workers felt that socialist governments and a republican regime had done little to benefit them. The middle class could not forgive the inflation. Prosperity brought moderate policies and relief from the assassina-tions and revolts of the earlier years, but it produced no significant group with primary loyalty to the existing regime.

The leading statesman was Gustav Stresemann, who sat in every cabinet, usually as foreign minister, from 1923 to his death, in 1929. Stresemann was closest to the businessmen of the center-right, who had few idealistic illusions and who saw the need for Germany to maintain good relations with its neighbors. If he acquiesced in the army's violations of the disarmament clauses of the Versailles treaty, its stringent limitations were at least partly to blame. Although Stresemann was a nationalist, a stance essential to his effectiveness, the right denounced him for his conciliatory tone toward former enemies and for bringing Germany into the League of Nations.

Throughout this period of relative calm, the political extremes were growing at the expense of the center. When President Ebert died, in 1925, a rightist coalition elected General von Hindenburg as his successor, defeating the candidate supported by both the Center and the Social Democratic parties; significantly, the two million votes drawn to the Communist nominee would have been sufficient to defeat Hindenburg. Moreover, the elections of 1930 brought Adolf Hitler's National Socialists to prominence; the Weimar Republic was far from secure.

## The Fall of Liberal Italy

At the outbreak of the Great War, the Kingdom of Italy had lived by the rules of liberal politics and economics for more than half a century, a fact that had made it seem fitting for Italy to join the Allied side. The least industrialized of the major Western powers, it had but barely met the demands of total war, and peace brought inflation and unemployment that further weakened the economy. In many places peasants simply confiscated land long promised them; and when in 1920 industrialists began to meet growing waves of strikes with lockouts, workers answered by occupying factories. Italian institutions, strong enough to survive the war, were strong enough still to prevent revolution, but social issues largely ignored for 20 years were undermining them in an atmosphere of bitterness, fear, and violence. In Italy, as in Germany and Eastern Europe, the end of war revealed a society in which much that upheld the established system had then undermined and in which revolution was suddenly a possibility.

For Italy, the peace treaty was as disillusioning as modern war. Although granted considerable territory, it got less than it had expected, and its treatment at Paris was often humiliating. Disposition of the Dalmatian port of Fiume was still being argued when in 1919 a private expedition led by Gabriele d'Annunzio dramatically captured it for Italy. The nation's most famous living poet, d'Annunzio ruled Fiume for more than a year at the head of an "army" of the unemployed, whose nationalist frenzy and vulgar slogans were a welcome contrast to the wordy frustration of diplomacy. Eventually, the Italian government evicted its filibustering poet (who had declared war on Italy), but the affair showed the appeal and the effectiveness of direct action.

The Fascist movement was born amid these crises. The term *fascio*, meaning "bundle," comes from an ancient Roman symbol of authority—a bundle of sticks, individually weak but strong in unity. Echoes of imperial Rome remained part of the Fascist party mystique. The movement centered around Benito Mussolini, whose polemical skills had earlier carried him to the top of Italy's Socialist party; he was editor of the party newspaper and led its intransigent wing until expelled in 1915 for favoring Italian intervention in the war. He had then become one of Italy's noisiest nationalists. After the war, Mussolini continued to agitate, using the rhetoric of the left to denounce liberalism and parliamentary indecision, while using the cries of nationalism to castigate Marxists and the Allies. Inconsistencies of doctrine and tactics hid beneath activism and symbols; the party militants in their black shirts seemed a small army.

At first the Fascists had little success—they did not win a single seat in the elections of 1919—but the hesitancy and confusion of others would soon give them an advantage. The two largest political groups, the Socialists and the Popular party, were well-organized mass parties opposed to the old politics and to each other but divided internally. Left-wing Socialists split off to form a Communist party, inspired by the Bolsheviks' success. Competition from the left increased the Socialists' reluctance to cooperate with bourgeois regimes. The Catholic Popular party demanded thoroughgoing reforms, but much of its real strength came from rural and conservative groups. The aging Giolitti, returning to the prime ministry in 1920, tried in the old ways to patch together a governing majority. In preparation for the elections of May 1921—the first held under a system of universal manhood suffrage—he brought the Fascists into a "national bloc" of candidates. The alliance, however, benefited only the Fascists, who won 35 seats in the new Chamber of Deputies; Giolitti's own Liberal supporters remained a poor third behind the Socialists and the Popularists. During the campaign, Fascist squads had planted bombs, beaten up opponents, and disrupted meetings, enjoying violence and intimidating moderates, while denouncing Marxists as a threat to order.

When left-wing unions called a general strike in 1922, which many believed would rapidly turn into revolution, Mussolini's Black Shirts increased their threats and open

**Mussolini poses triumphantly with his chiefs after the Fascist march on Rome in 1922.**
(Photo: Wide World Photos)

violence and began taking over town councils by force. The government of Luigi Facta—a caretaker prime minister who was holding office because no one could win a majority—resigned, and the Fascists staged their march on Rome in October. Motley squads of party militants moved on the capital in a grand gesture of revolt while Mussolini cautiously waited in Milan. At the last minute, Facta asked for martial law, but King Victor Emmanuel III refused—the gesture of revolt had been enough. Mussolini dashed to Rome, preserving his claims to both perfect legality and forceful conquest.

At 39, Mussolini, invited by the king to form a cabinet, became prime minister of a coalition government, the violent man of order won from a desperate legislature the majority—and an overwhelming one—denied to parliamentary politicians. In the elections of 1924, Fascists won a massive victory. Intimidation and open violence contributed to this success, as did some fraud, but most Italians were willing to give the new party a chance.

In the following year, it became clearer what a Fascist regime would mean. Giacomo Matteotti, a Socialist who bravely enumerated Fascist crimes before the entire Chamber, was subsequently murdered in gangland style. As public condemnation mounted, Mussolini's government seemed about to topple, but the opponents of Fascism were no more able to unite now that they had become a parliamentary minority than when they had been stronger. On the contrary, the Fascists gradually isolated first the Socialist and then the Popular party. By 1925 all opponents had been expelled from the legislature, and newspapers either printed what they were told or risked suppression. The Fascist period had begun.

To most of the world outside Italy and to many Italian moderates, it seemed merely that the country had at last found a strong and antisocialist leader, one who could run it effectively and whose verbal excesses would undoubtedly be tempered by experience. Reasonable people found it hard to believe that a party whose program contained so many contradictions—the radical rhetoric of Fascism promised revolution and a strong state, defended property and social change, praised order and violence—could be dangerous for long.

## International Plans for Reparations and Peace

Gradually, the remaining boundary disputes had been resolved one after another, sometimes by force, more often by complex negotiations, and occasionally with the aid of the plebiscites called for in the peace treaties. By the early 1920s, reparations rather than territory presented the most troublesome international problems. There was little agreement, for example, on how to evaluate payments in kind, which the Reparations Commission allowed Germany to offer as part of its total obligation; this was the issue that had led to the French and Belgian occupation of the Ruhr in 1923. That step, however, was disastrous for all, leaving France isolated and Germany the victim of runaway inflation.

As Germany fell behind in its payments, the Allies took the position that they, in turn, could not pay their war debts to the United States. Some compromise was essential, and in 1924 the nations involved accepted the proposals of an international commission of financial experts, headed by the American banker Charles G. Dawes. The Dawes Plan fixed Germany's reparations payments on a regular scale, established an orderly mode of collection, and provided loans to Germany equal to 80 percent of the reparations payment due the first year of the plan—1 billion gold marks ($250 million; reparations would increase to 2.5 billion marks annually in the fifth year).[2] The plan did not, as many Europeans thought it should, admit any connection between Allied debts to the United States and German reparations to the European victors, but it did end the worst of the chaos. For the next six years, Germany, fed by loans largely from the United States, made its reparations payments on schedule. The issue seemed forever resolved with the adoption of the Young Plan in 1929, which finally set a limit to Germany's obligations (59 years), reduced annual payments, and ended foreign occupation of the Rhineland. Under the leadership of American bankers, the interests of international capital had come to shape policy in the name of economic necessity.

From 1924 to 1930 the conduct of international affairs did really reflect some of the idealism of the Paris Peace Conference. The League of Nations, formally established in 1920, successfully resolved a number of disputes. Some of its procedures were impractically elaborate, and its authority was restricted by the absence of the United States, by Britain's greater concern for its empire than for the League, and by France's tendency to use the League for its own security. The League thus dealt best with disputes in which no major power had a direct interest. Its special commissions made notable contributions, helping the disjointed economies of the new and contentious states of Eastern Europe, aiding refugees, and reporting on matters of public health and working conditions. This recognition that peace was related to social conditions was in itself an achievement, the liberal vision at its best. In the late 1920s at least, the decisions of the Permanent

Court of International Justice, organized at The Hague under the League, were treated with great seriousness; and people could imagine a world in which commonly accepted rules and evenhanded justice would greatly reduce the threat of war.

### The Locarno Era

Both the League of Nations and the dominant Western democracies were inclined to make general principles a subject of international agreement. Efforts to outlaw war foundered on definitions of aggression, but they led to a series of treaties known as the Locarno Pact in 1925. The major agreement, which was entered into by Germany, Belgium, France, Great Britain, and Italy, secured Germany's western frontier; Germany and its neighbors promised to arbitrate their disputes. In addition, France pursued a more traditional diplomacy by signing a mutual-defense alliance with Poland and Czechoslovakia. A Continental war caused by German aggression now seemed impossible; France and other nations could lay aside their fears.

The Locarno era, the name given to this brief period of international optimism, was capped by the Kellogg-Briand Pact of 1928. The French had suggested that the American entry into World War I be commemorated by a friendship pact, and the Americans proposed that the accord be extended to others as well. More than a score of nations immediately signed the pact, which renounced war "as an instrument of national policy." These ill-defined declarations, accompanied by no provisions for enforcement, soon proved empty, but they expressed the hope, the belief in law, and the confidence in public opinion that marked the Locarno era.

Disarmament provided another broad path to maintaining peace, and from 1921 on, some League commission was always soberly studying the problem. Naval disarmament

---

[2] The United States having waived its claims, the apportionment of reparations among the Allies had been decided on in 1920: 52 percent to France, 22 percent to the British Empire, 10 percent to Italy, and 8 percent to Belgium.

**Germans returning to the city in 1923 after a potato raid into the countryside, where they could steal some precious food.**   (Photo: Wide World Photos)

seemed especially promising. Britain no longer commanded sufficient resources to maintain a fleet twice the size of any other country's, given the enormous cost of capital ships; the expense of a sizable navy, in fact, made very nation hope to avoid unnecessary competition. At the Washington Conference of 1921–1922, called by President Warren G. Harding, Wilson's successor, the United States, Great Britain, Japan, France, and Italy had agreed after some difficulty to fix their relative strength in capital ships at current levels,[3] not to expand their naval bases, and even to scrap some of their larger vessels. About smaller ships there had been less agreement, but the Washington Conference had produced tangible results as well as statements of good will. Never again did disarmament discussions prove so fruitful. At Geneva in 1927 and London in 1930, Italy (citing the special needs of its geography) and France (arguing that all forms of disarmament should be discussed together) refused to accept a treaty. By 1935 Japan would reject even the Washington accord.

[3] This was defined as parity between the United States and Great Britain at 525,000 tons apiece in capital ships, 315,000 tons for Japan, and 175,000 tons each for France and Italy.

Attempts to limit land and air arms were even less successful. League commissions could not agree on which were offensive weapons, whether a professional army was comparable to a reserve force, and whether limitations should be expressed in terms of budgets, weapons, or men. Proposals from Germany and Russia that their military weakness provide a standard for other nations to reach by disarming only aroused suspicion. When the conference on general disarmament that these commissions prepared was finally called in 1932, the dream of arms restrictions was more remote than ever. Discussions continued at length, but before agreements were reached, Hitler had come to power in Germany, and a new arms race ensued.

## The Dominant Democracies

The international order characterized by the League of Nations, reparations, the Dawes and Young Plans, and the Locarno spirit rested on the policies and influence of France and Great Britain and on the prosperity of the United States; and so, less directly, did the stability of German democracy, the maintenance of constitutional governments in Eastern Europe, and the effective isolation of the Soviet Union. The caution with which these democracies exercised their international role, in turn, reflected some unease within their own societies. Although much was changed after the war, few of the promised benefits had materialized. Society had not been radically reformed; indeed, radicals had been as effectively defeated at the polls in Britain and France as by force in Germany and Italy. In every country the most militant Marxists felt strengthened by the presence of the Soviet Union as an international homeland for the proletariat. But that allegiance, and the founding of Communist parties that

followed from it, split and weakened the left in domestic affairs.

The real social changes of this period were usually not the result of deliberate policy. Employment in services such as sales and office work increased more rapidly than in industry (and the proportion of those who were domestic servants declined). In most countries more women were gainfully employed than before the war at those jobs thought suitable for women, despite a sharp decline from the wartime peak and despite the strong tendency for women to leave work upon marriage. The number of (middle-class) youths enrolled in universities increased sharply, and the automobile, especially in Britain and France, began to alter middle-class life. Generally, the central government now spent a higher proportion of national wealth; and although most of that went to the military and to service debts and pay pensions left from war, some of it was used to lay the basis for broader measures of social security for all. Politically, both business interests and labor unions exercised a more direct influence, essentially supporting the effort to recapture economic stability. Yet despite periods of prosperity and a genuine boom in certain industries, the 1920s did not provide the steady growth of the prewar decade. Economic uncertainty, increased by inflation and unemployment, tended, like the disillusionment over reparations or the specter of Bolshevism, to stimulate a conservatism that was essentially defensive.

### France

Life in France quickly returned to prewar patterns after 1918, including the political combination of a weak executive and moderate domestic policies. Raymond Poincaré, in office since 1913, was perhaps the strongest president the Third Republic had ever had, and his term expired in 1920. Clemenceau was a likely successor, but Parlement chose a safe and colorless man instead, a French version of the "normalcy" the United States sought in Harding. The Chamber of Deputies elected in 1919 at the height of patriotic pride in victory was the most conservative since the founding of the Third Republic.

For the next decade the leading figures of French politics were Aristide Briand, Eduoard Herriot, and Poincaré, each of whom was premier twice, with Briand heading the ministry of foreign affairs in 1925–1932. Briand, who after a radical youth had become a moderate, led a number of short-lived compromise cabinets, reflecting in his skillful flexibility something of both the best and the worst in the French tradition of governing. Herriot was a characteristic figure of the center-left, a believer in democracy, individualism, and moderate social programs. Poincaré, the strong-willed man of integrity, made the decision to occupy the Ruhr in 1923 and was called back in 1926–1929 to head a state dedicated to saving the franc, which by then had slipped to one-fifth its former value.

France had become *par excellence* the land of the lower-middle class, the artisan, and the peasant proprietor fiercely attached to a tiny plot of land. Such people were loyal to their nation and proud of their heritage. Though the cornucopia of reparations they had expected never materialized, they accomplished miracles of reconstruction, carefully making their new buildings look as much as possible like those destroyed—but it took extraordinary political courage to raise their taxes. Poor financing, beginning with inadequate taxes during the war, underlay the crisis of the franc, which had been one of the world's stablest currencies for a century before its postwar depreciation, and few things were as important to French citizens as their life savings. Demographically, France had been hardest hit of all nations by World War I, and that fact as well affected its post-war psychology. France epitomized the tendency common throughout the West to live as if World War I and the revolutions following had made but a temporary difference.

Competent French leaders thus presided during a period of prosperity over governments whose policies allowed domestic stagnation and encouraged rigidity in foreign affairs. Poincaré's concern for national honor and a stable currency appealed to a cautious middle class much as Briand's complicated maneuvers did to parliamentarians, but neither encouraged the French to face more difficult long-term issues of working conditions, social inequality, or mass culture.

### The United Kingdom

In the United Kingdom also, the 1919 elections—the first in which women (those over 30) were allowed to vote—produced an overwhelming victory for the leaders who had promised to extract enough from Germany to make winning the war worthwhile. Lloyd George remained prime minister, but even in its modest social legislation—which included an increase in unemployment benefits—his government was essentially conservative, and his conflicts with other liberal leaders added to the Liberal party's decline. Dumped by the Conservative party in 1922, Lloyd George never returned to power. For most of that decade, Britain was led by Stanley Baldwin, who had the gift of making dullness seem statesmanship. In 1924 new elections brought the Labour party (which two years before had outpolled the Liberals) briefly to power. Except for recognizing the Soviet Union, it did little to recall its leftist origins.

Throughout the period, the government met problems of unemployment, Irish nationalism, and empire by extending previous policies. Although the Conservatives expanded social welfare measures, a crisis in the coal industry led to a 10-day general strike in 1926. Frightened by the bitter class conflict the work stoppage vented, Britons were quick to praise the restraint used by both sides. Nevertheless, the fervent interest of the well-to-do in maintaining essential services (and breaking the strike), like the anti-labor legislation that followed, did much to deepen the resentment of the British working class.

Home rule, promised to Ireland before the war, had been suspended, and the Easter Rebellion of 1916 had been firmly suppressed. In 1919, however, the most militant Irish nationalists, led by the Sinn Fein (meaning "We Ourselves") party, refused to take their seats in the House of Commons and met instead at Dublin in a parliament of their own, the Dail Eireann, where they declared Ireland independent. To this defiance the London government responded slowly and ineptly, finally electing to suppress the Sinn Fein party and with it, Irish independence. To support this action, the government sent reinforcements to the Royal Irish Constabulary in numbers sufficient to spread the fighting without ending it, and they soon became the most hated symbol of British repression. The Irish terrorists who resisted these British forces were by then named the Irish Republican Army. Against these civilian terrorists, the British could look only foolish or brutal; and by 1920s the two sides were fighting a bloody war.

Faced with mounting pressure at home and abroad to find a settlement, the British government in 1920 passed an Ireland act, which set up two Irish parliaments, one in the predominantly Catholic areas of the south and west, and the other in the predominantly Protestant counties of the northeast (six of the nine counties of Ulster). A Council for Ireland was to coordinate policies between the two Irish governments. This concession of home rule did not, however, appease the leaders of the Sinn Fein, who opposed both the division of the island and the continuing ties with the British crown. Almost two more years of fighting and negotiating followed. In December 1922, the Irish parliament at Dublin proclaimed, with British acquiescence, the existence of the Irish Free State, which included all Ireland except the six counties of Ulster; Northern Ireland, as the six counties were called, maintained its traditional union with Great Britain. An uneasy peace was achieved, although the political division of Ireland would remain a source of tension and conflict.

Only in imperial affairs did habits of flexible compromise produce impressive success. Canadian complaints led the Imperial Conference of 1926 to a significant new definition of all dominions as "autonomous communities . . . equal in status . . . united by a common allegiance to the crown and freely associated as members of the British Commonwealth of Nations." The dominions, in other words, were recognized as completely autonomous in all domestic and foreign affairs; their ties to the British crown were entirely volitional, based on common traditions, loyalty, and friendship. Given legal sanction by the Statute of Westminster in 1931, this definition laid the foundation for a remarkable adaptation of empire to new conditions.

## The Other Democracies

Democracy fared rather better during the 1920s in some of the smaller Continental countries than it did in Italy and the Weimar Republic. Belgium, despite the war's destruction and conflicts over language and religion, recaptured its place among Europe's most prosperous and freest countries. The tensions between Czechs and Slovaks did not prevent Czechoslovakia from remaining a model of democratic stability and economic growth. Although the Netherlands faced nationalist unrest in its colonies, especially the

**Dublin, 1921; Barbed wire obstructs Castle Street in preparation for the British occupation of the city.** (Photo: The Bettmann Archives/BBC Hulton Picture Library)

East Indies, such problems hardly threatened democratic institutions at home; and the Scandinavian countries, while often at odds among themselves, continued to find in liberal institutions the means to imaginative foreign and domestic programs. There (Norway, 1907; Denmark, 1914; Sweden, 1919), in Weimar Germany, and in Great Britain, women's suffrage had not destroyed the family; nor had it cleansed politics, but it seemed a natural expansion of democracy. For Europe as a whole, however, the flood tide of constitutional government that had followed the war had clearly begun to ebb. Nevertheless, constitutional democracy was the political norm, and many were convinced that even the Soviet Union and Italy would in due time become more like their neighbors. Economic recovery had proved slower than expected and more difficult, but by the mid-1920s a general prosperity contributed to the electoral victories of moderate and conservative parties.

## II. TOWARD A DISTINCTIVE TWENTIETH-CENTURY CULTURE
❋

There were concrete reasons for satisfaction as middle-class Europeans bought their first car, or looked forward to a paid vacation while many millions bought their first radio and flocked to the motion pictures. Intellectuals, too, shared a sense of excitement as cultural institutions—from brash, commercial ones to the more staid and formal ones—flourished. Yet the most stimulating new ideas tended to be disquieting, building on trends apparent in the decade or so before World War I. The new directions of Western thought—the ones we identify as central to twentieth-century intellectual history—cannot therefore be said simply to result from the experience of total war; yet the currents most characteristic of the new era—the radical departures in psychology, physics, and philosophy as well as in art and literature—do fit with and reinforce attitudes that the war made almost commonplace: a nightmare sense of shock at what modern societies might do, skepticism toward accepted pieties, and reliance on personal feeling as a guide to conduct more than on formal doctrines based on reason or religion. The criticisms of liberal society developed in the previous generation were turned with increased animus against the bourgeois complacency and prosperity of the postwar era. Literature and the arts seemed more than ever at odds with society and traditional norms of behav-

ior, and this tension was disseminated (sometimes in popularized form) in print, on the radio, and in art, theater, and motion pictures.

## Freudian Psychology

No figure of the period just before and after World War I disturbed established thinking so deeply as did Sigmund Freud. A Viennese physician whose clinical studies had taken

**Although Freud's theories were intended to be universally valid, his consultation room in Vienna is unmistakably an expression of the European upper-middle class of the late nineteenth century.** (Photo: Edmund Engelman)

# ❄ EXPERIENCES OF DAILY LIFE ❄
## *Motion Pictures*

At the Grand Café in Paris on December 28, 1895, Auguste and Louis Lumière showed a motion picture. It was the beginning of a new entertainment industry. A month before, a motion picture was made part of a vaudeville act at Berlin's Wintergarden, and five months before that, a four-minute clip of a prize fight had been shown in the United States; but the attention given the Paris showing, the entrepreneurial skills of the Lumière brothers, and the quality of their technology mark the effective start of commercial film. They demonstrated their *cinématographe* in London, Stockholm, St. Petersburg, and Moscow in the next few months. The reaction to the flickering images was universal. Crowds of every social class and age in every country gasped at a locomotive that rushed straight at spectators and laughed at boys dowsing startled officials with a garden hose. For a decade or more movies kept their association with the cheapest forms of popular entertainment. They were shown primarily in penny arcades and shooting galleries in the United States, at cafes and bistros in France, in special wagons that traveled to carnivals and fairs in Germany. The films were always brief; and they featured startling effects, humorous sketches, and public ceremonies. In London, the American George Hale, who had once been a fire chief in Kansas City, made a fortune with Hale's Tours, a movie house where the audience sat in simulated railway cars, swaying to the sounds of steam engines, as scenery passed along the screen.

After the turn of the century, movies were increasingly shown in halls with fixed seating, and many lasted a full hour or more. Charles Pathé and Léon Gaumont estblished competing companies in 1906 to build permanent theaters, make films, and distribute them. By 1914 some 90 percent of the world's motion pictures were made in France, but every industrial country made some. In Russia, Sweden, Italy, and Germany, as well as France, leading actors, artists, and poets took part.

Sarah Bernhardt, aging and lame, gave a fiery performance as Queen Elizabeth, grateful that theater's ephemeralness had suddenly been overcome. The Italian film, *Cabiria*, with avant-garde sets and a script by D'Annunzio, created an international sensation in 1913. Motion pictures were now recognized as an exciting international form; yet each nation seemed to have its own style and to emphasize its own cultural traditions and historical lore. Film makers were thus ready to make propaganda films during World War I.

Then in the 1920s, in a kind of cultural explosion, motion pictures became more popular and more profitable than any other form of entertainment had ever been. Movie theaters were built on the most elegant streets of Paris, London, and Berlin, gaudily combining the exoticism of a worlds fair with reassuring luxury. Egyptian and Greek motifs, marble columns, fountains, mirrors, and statues reinforced the fantasies on the screen. The Graumont Palace built in Paris in 1919 became an international model, with its 5000 plush seats and an orchestra pit for 80 musicians. Berlin's 300 cinemas included the Sportspalast, redone for motion pictures in 1920, which boasted of being the largest movie theater in the world. Old theaters were converted and new, bigger ones built not just in the great capitals but also at the center of every city and most towns. By the mid-twenties, Britain, France, Germany, and Italy each counted their movie theaters in the thousands.

And the people came. Crowds of workers and clerks and good bourgeois attended the same movies; went, for the most part, to the same theaters; and even sat in the same seats. Tickets cost considerably more in the splashiest of the big houses, but prices remained low compared with most other forms of entertainment. Neither cost nor cultural content supported the class segregation far more visible at concerts and plays. Children and the elderly came almost as naturally as they would have to a village festival; and women came, with boy friends and husbands but also by the mid-twenties, without male escorts.

The pictures themselves changed, and so did the business of making and showing them. Feature films were the norm, and in presentation as well as plot, they were moving away from traditional theater. There were some extravaganzas (for scenes shot in the Stockholm opera house, 800 extras were used in the Swedish picture, *Erotikon,* a comedy about flirtation, which was a great box office success in 1920) and lots of stories ostensibly set in ordinary life, in which new techniques were used to suggest the flow of time or heighten suspense. Relatively fewer ventures both attracted a mass audience and used contemporary trends in the arts as had the German expressionist film, *The Cabinet of Dr. Caligari.* Reviews and movie magazines helped to provide the publicity essential to success in a business that used the star system and vast distribution networks to guarantee the profits from its short-lived product. American companies did all this very effectively, filling screens around the world. The United States made more films than any other country. Japan was second, Germany third, and the German combine, UFA, became Europe's largest film maker. In Europe a dynamic industry rapidly made the transition to talking pictures between 1929 and 1930, a change that underscored national differences.

Attracted to the revenue from entertainment taxes, governments also worried about the moral and political effects of so popular a medium. In 1919 an English Watch committee condemned a film of the Johnson-Jeffreys fight, fearing it could "demoralize and brutalize the minds of young persons." Sunday showings were an issue for years in Britain until generally forbidden, and every country had some ministry empowered to monitor the presentation of sex and violence, sometimes banning films, more often requiring certain scenes to be cut. Many, perhaps most, popular movies were in some sense about adaptation to modern life, their popularity as much a reflection as a cause of social change. If in the 1920s middle class and working class families were more likely to be talking about some of the same things, workers in the cities and the countryside could more easily imagine a different and better life, and women were more aware of opportunities to have friends and aspirations of their own, the motion picture was part of the way of life that expressed such changes. ❊

**A marquee advertising the new film, *Fredericus Rex,* lights this Berlin street in 1936; the theater was built in 1919, one of the first designed specifically for motion pictures.** (Photo: Archiv für Kunst und Geschichte, Berlin)

him gradually from neurology to psychiatry, he followed the method—close and detailed observation—of medical science, and his theoretical statements are as careful in their internal consistency as in their literary elegance.

Freud had done his most important work before 1914, and in many ways he was old-fashioned. For the most part, he accepted as socially necessary the norms of behavior of the nineteenth-century middle class. He was deeply influenced by ideas of evolution, and his metaphors and assumptions betray the liberal economist's conception of human nature.[4] His interest in the phenomenon of hysteria, his use of hypnosis, and his first ideas of the unconscious had grown from the work of French doctors with whom he had studied, but it was his genius to synthesize his particular observations into a general theory, a universal statement about the human mind, that could be tested in practical application.

In treating neurotics, Freud found that they often experienced relief of their symptoms by recalling under hypnosis events they had otherwise forgotten. He deduced that it is the recollection and not the hypnosis that is crucial, later adding that though the events remembered may not actually have happened, they are the psychic reality with which the patient has been living. The center of psychic forces in the unconscious he labeled the id. Here the basic desires universal among human beings (very similar to what were called instincts) seek satisfaction, and increasingly, he found the most troublesome and psychologically significant desires to be sexual. The ego tries to channel and control these desires as it is directed to do by the superego, which, rather like the conscience in more traditional conceptions, expresses a person's socially conditioned sense of what is acceptable behavior. Thus mental life is marked by perpetual tension between the id and the superego.

Most of this conflict, which is uncomfortably mediated by the ego, is unconscious. Indeed, one of the mind's techniques for dealing with the id is repression from consciousness of the id's desires. Repression, however, is an enormous strain that often finds outlet in neurotic behavior. As the patient comes to face and understand what is being repressed, his or her neurosis is relieved.

From this conception of the human psyche, Freud developed an elaborate and subtle theory. It was a shocking one, which ascribed sexual lusts to every person at every age. The idea of infant sexuality was especially offensive, but so was the notion of the Oedipus or Electra complex, the boy's angry competition with his father, the girl's with her mother, a competition that could produce an unconscious but guilt-ridden wish for one parent's death in order to win possession of the other. Victorian convention could not tolerate this supposition, asserting that decent people have no such base desires. Freudian theory proclaimed such people merely the most repressed, considered religion the satisfaction of infantile and obsessive needs, and explored the greatest achievements in the arts in terms of sublimation, the diversion of the demands of the id to other and higher purposes. Psychoanalysis, the name Freud gave his body of theory and his therapeutic technique, calls on the analyst to pass no judgments but rather to help the patient discover and say things about himself or herself that proper society held to be quite simply unmentionable.

Freud's ideas encouraged a shift in aesthetic and intellectual perceptions. He had replaced hypnosis in treatment by free association, which allows the mind to make the

---

[4] This point is superbly developed in Philip Rieff, *Freud, the Mind of the Moralist*, 1961.

connections it wishes by its own mysterious processes without the intervention of objective logic. He considered psychic reality to be as important as any other, and he discovered that dreams or slips of the tongue furnish significant signs of psychic conflict. Here was a rationale for taking dreams and fantasies as seriously as external events and for understanding both literature and life on several levels at once in terms of unconscious ends. And Freud himself provided the model in essays that are persuasively organized, stylistically sensitive, and philosophically suggestive.

### Implications of Freudian Theory

In the 1920s the broad implications of Freud's discoveries were beginning to gain wide public recognition. They were cited again and again as evidence of how close humanity remains to the primitive. If repression leads to neuroses, one extrapolation went, then greater sexual freedom and, above all, greater candor will produce healthier people. This remains perhaps the most widespread popular notion drawn from Freudian teaching, though it was not a view he held. Related to this is the belief that guilt is evil, a kind of Christian perversion of human nature. Freudian insights encouraged literary and personal introspection and supported the view that childhood is the most important phase of life. Although his theories stimulated new visions of a freer and happier life, Freud's dark conclusion was that "the price of progress in civilization is paid in forfeiting happiness." For civilization is based upon the repression of primitive and still very powerful drives, which at any moment might lead to revolt; Freud, who feared the revolt he foresaw, died in 1939, driven into exile by Nazi anti-Semitism.

Freud, and to a lesser extent his disciples, developed his ideas with a wealth of examples and terminology, but psychoanalysis won more outrage than respectability during its creator's lifetime. Moreover, its followers strove with Freud to maintain the doctrine whole, treating deviations as heresies. Among these were the ideas of the Swiss C. G. Jung, who broke with Freud and developed the theory of the collective unconscious, a psychic inheritance shared by human beings everywhere and reflected especially in the symbols and rituals of religion. Jung's somewhat looser and more mystical perspectives have fascinated and influenced philosophers, theologians, and artists.

Indeed, the concepts of psychoanalysis have been applied, often loosely, to works of art, periods of time, and whole civilizations. It may even be that Freudian procedures and theories have so changed behavior that they are less apposite now than when he formulated them. Only today, in fact, are systematic modifications of Freudian theory beginning to find acceptance in psychoanalysis.

## The Humanities

Some artists in the postwar period—the Surrealists with their dreamlike canvases are an example—applied Freudian ideas directly, and in his manifesto of Surrealism (1924), the writer André Breton proclaimed the liberation of the subconscious. Quite independent of Freud, explorations of the irrational within the human mind and in society fairly exploded in prose and poetry. The novels of Proust, Kafka, and Joyce most clearly mark the change in style and content. Marcel Proust died in 1922, soon to be hailed as one of the great stylists of the French language. His long novel, *Remembrance of Things Past*, built an introverted and delicately detailed picture of upper-class Parisian life into a monumental and sensitive study of one

A modernist aesthetic shines through the clean geometry of this workshop built in 1925–26 for the new headquarters of the Bauhaus, a group of architects and artists whose functionalist architecture and design would for nearly 50 years define the International style and influence the "modern" look of objects, houses, offices, and factories around the world. Part of the explosive creativity of the Weimar period, the Bauhaus broke up with the advent of Hitler; and many of its members, like Walter Gropius, who designed this building, emigrated to the United States. (Photo: Gropius, Walter. *The Bauhaus 1925–26*. Dessau, Germany. Photograph courtesy, The Museum of Modern Art, New York)

man's quiet suffering, which became a model of interior monologue, of the novel in which the subject is not action seen from the outside but feelings observed from within. Franz Kafka, who wrote in German though born in Prague, died in 1924, leaving instructions for his manuscripts to be burned. They were not, however, and his works have come to be accepted as quintessentially modern, with their realistic and reasonable descriptions of fantasies that convey the torture of anxiety. In *The Trial* the narrator tells of his arrest, conviction, and execution on charges he can never discover, an exploration of the psychology of guilt that also seems to fore-

shadow the totalitarian state. James Joyce's international fame came with the publication of his novel *Ulysses* (1922), the presentation on a mythic scale of a single day in the life of a modest Dubliner written in an exuberant, endlessly inventive game of words in which puns, clichés, parody, and poetry swirl in a dizzying stream of consciousness.

Not all of the most important writers turned away from objective, chronologically precise narrative. But even those who made use of more familiar techniques tended, like Thomas Mann in Germany, André Gide in France, and D. H. Lawrence in England, to explore topics and attitudes offensive to convention. Shock and offense seemed at times to be a form of creative expression. A movement called Dada that had originated during World War I put on displays, part theater and part art exhibition, of noisy nonsense and absurd juxtapositions to infuriate the Parisian bourgeoisie. Italian Futurists had promised to build a new art appropriate to a technological age—"The world has been enriched by a new beauty: the beauty of speed"—but balanced such positive feelings with a call to "Burn the libraries . . . demolish the venerated cities" in their manifesto of 1909. The

Fauves in France and the Expressionists in Germany and Scandinavia gloried in their reputation for wildness in style, content, and conduct. Where more sober traditions prevailed, as in the carefully constructed, cerebral poetry of William Butler Yeats, pessimism and obscurity were still the elements most readily noted. In every language, serious poetry as much as serious art and music became more difficult for the lay person to appreciate. Cubist and Expressionist painters, like composers using the 12-tone scale and dissonance, deliberately eschewed the merely decorative or pleasant. The approaches that excited artists wove a frightening violence and amorality into their contemptuous disregard for tradition. Today we confidently admire works from this period as part of a continuous development, but to contemporaries, the frenzied new forms were both a source and a voice of serious malaise. They undermined confidence in reason, positivistic science, and bourgeois civilization while widening the chasm between the "serious," creative art of "high culture" and the popular culture most intellectuals disdained.

The philosopher most widely read in the 1920s was Oswald Spengler, whose *Decline of the West* appeared in 1918. Spengler treated whole civilizations as biological organisms, each with a life cycle of its own, but his book won fame less for its interesting method than for its prediction of the West's deterioration, a prediction that labeled the world war the beginning of the final act and considered the very institutions liberals had hailed as progress to be symptoms of decay. José Ortega y Gasset's *The Revolt of the Masses*, published in 1930, was hardly more optimistic. The masses, he feared, were destined as they rose in power to destroy the highest achievements of Western civilization. Other philosophers, like contemporary artists, made much of humanity's irrationality, and scores of minor works that were vaguely Nietzschean, religious, or determinist rained scorn on a vapid, directionless culture.

The most striking innovation in philosophy came, however, from another tradition entirely. It found its first major expression in the *Principia Mathematica* (1910), by Bertrand Russell and Alfred North Whitehead, a cornerstone of what has come to be called Analytic Philosophy. On the Continent a group known as the Vienna Circle developed a related system, Logical Positivism; and the work of Ludwig Wittgenstein, especially his *Tractatus Logico-Philosophicus* (1921), became a major influence on both schools of thought. Wittgenstein attempted in a series of numbered propositions "to set a limit to thought." He sought to define, in other words, the areas of thought in which certainty could be achieved and those in which it could not. According to Wittgenstein and others of his school, logicians and philosophers should concern themselves only with what is precise and demonstrable, and their methods, based on symbolic logic, should be analogous to mathematical reasoning. The principles and techniques of symbolic logic have come to dominate philosophy in the universities of Great Britain and the United States.

Like the earlier positivists, analytic philosophers consciously set about to learn from the methodology of the natural sciences, but what they stress is the lean language of mathematics rather than observation or experiment. The philosopher's task is to analyze every statement, stripping away connotations and values that may appeal but do not convey precise meaning. "My propositions," Wittgenstein concludes in the *Tractatus*, "serve as elucidations in the following way: anyone who understands me eventually recognizes them as nonsensical. . . What we cannot speak about we must consign to silence." At its most radical, such an approach rejects from consideration most of the issues theologians and moral philosophers have argued about for centuries as too imprecise to merit debate. Philosophy, like the other disciplines, was turning from matters of general interest to its own specialized tasks.

## The Sciences

Science also had moved beyond the lay person's comprehension long before the Great War. Discoveries in the physical and life sciences were communicated and put to use with increasing rapidity, and those in one discipline were applied in related fields, often giving birth to new hybrids such as biochemistry and biophysics. Progress in these studies represented a harmonious if accelerated continuation of the work of centuries past. But from the realm of the older natural sciences came mystifying reports of theoretical advances that would upset several venerable certainties.

### Relativity and the Nature of Matter

One line of investigation stemmed from an experiment by two Americans, Albert A. Michelson and Edward W. Morley, in 1887. It had been assumed that the universe was filled with a motionless substance called "ether," because waves of light (or waves of any kind) could not pass through an empty space. This motionless ether presumably also provided a base from which motions of all sorts in the universe could be measured. But Michelson and Morley showed that the speed of light rays emanating from the earth was the same whether the rays traveled in the direction of the earth's movement or against it (the expected result had been that rays would travel faster in the direction of the earth's movement). The implications of this discovery had been explored in a variety of ways over the following decade and a half; then in 1905 Albert Einstein proposed an answer in his first, or special, theory of relativity (his second, or general, theory of relativity, expanding the insights of the first was announced in 1915). His mathematical formulations led to striking conclusions of the highest philosophical interest: Space and time are not absolute but must be measured in relation to the observer; and they also may be considered, on the most fundamental levels, as aspects of a single continuum.

As Einstein developed his theory of relativity, physicists were also achieving a new understanding of matter. Here, a principal stimulus came from Wilhelm Roentgen's discovery of x-rays in 1895, which gave the first important insight into the world of subatomic particles. Within two years the English physicist J. J. Thomson showed the existence of the electron, the subatomic particle carrying a negative electrical charge. The atom was clearly not the basic unit of matter. By the turn of the century Pierre and Marie Curie, among others, had found radium and other materials to be radioactive; that is, these materials emitted both particles and a form of electromagnetic radiation. Soon, largely through the work of Ernest Rutherford, radioactivity was identified with the breakdown of heavy and unstable atoms. The discovery that the atom was composed principally of electrically charged particles made it possible to link the structure of atoms with Dmitri Mendeleev's periodic table of elements (see Chapter 25). Elements that possessed chemically similar properties were also similar in their atomic structures. These important discoveries promised for a time to simplify and clarify the understanding of matter.

But continuing research soon revealed phenomena inexplicable in terms of Newtonian physics. In 1902 the German physicist Max Planck challenged the scientific world with the announcement of the "quantum theory" of energy. Energy in the subatomic

**Einstein's face remains one of the best known of the twentieth century, a symbol both of universal genius and of Jewish exile.** (Photo: © Karsh, Ottawa/Woodfin Camp and Associates)

world was released or absorbed not in a continuous stream but in discrete, measurable, and apparently irreducible units, which Planck called quanta. Energy, in effect, possessed many of the properties of matter, and the theory implied that matter and energy might be interchangeable. Einstein later incorporated this insight into his theory of relativity, proposing the famous equation, $E = mc^2$. Energy, he concluded, is equivalent to mass times the square of the speed of light; at least in theory, small quantities of matter could be turned into enormous amounts of energy.

In 1919 Rutherford established that bombarding nitrogen with subatomic particles produced changes in the structure of the nitrogen atom. The ancient dream of the alchemists—the transmutation of one material into another—was now possible, although not in the ways the alchemists had envisioned. With accelerating rapidity, other atomic changes were produced in the laboratory, while the study of cosmic radiation related the structure of terrestrial matter to that found in the universe beyond.

By the mid-1920s, however, scientists contemplating the expanded knowledge of matter had to face troubling anomalies. Planck's quantum theory, though apparently verified in numerous experiments, assumed among other things that particles behave in probabilistic rather than absolutely regular patterns—a concept Einstein himself could never wholly accept. Furthermore, electromagnetic radiation, of which visible light is one form, had to be treated for some purposes as a flow of particles and for other purposes as a wave, that is, a disturbance of particles in a medium that does not cause an advance of the particles themselves. The German physicist Werner Heinsenberg argued that no fixed model of the atoms of a given element was possible; only its approximate and likely structure could be described, through complex equations. In a few years matter had been found to consist mostly of empty space and not to behave with absolute regularity. Moreover, it proved impossible to measure simultaneously both the energy and the mass of a subatomic particle, because the measurement of one altered the apparent values of the other—a disturbing effect that Heisenberg appropriately named "the uncertainty principle." In the subatomic world, as in the stellar universe, the position and the purposes of the observer fundamentally affected what he observed.

Physicists who chose to philosophize about such matters now spoke in humbler and more tentative tones, describing the implications of abstract ideas more than a fixed reality. But the new theories, especially perhaps the discovery of a constant relationship between energy and mass, proved powerful tools. Physics became one of the most prestigious and highly organized (and most expensive) of human activities. Research uncovered new and special particles in bewildering number, leaving the baffled lay person apprised of merely the most publicized technological results: x-ray technology, television, the electron microscope, and eventually, the controlled fission of atomic energy.

The majority of physicists lived fairly comfortably with the contradictions and incompleteness of their theories. Newtonian principles, they often insisted, still obtained in most cases, as solid and predictable as ever. But the Western world had long looked to the sciences for support of its philosophy and even its theology, and it suffered a sense of loss in learning that physical laws were relative and that the very scientists who manipulated them were uncertain about what an atom looked like or what a particle was. In the twentieth century no Voltaire could build a view of society on a popularized version of the now wholly specialized disciplines. Coupled with developments in astronomy, which grappled with innumerable universes in a potentially infinite reach of space, the revolution in the understanding of matter left the world a little less certain. Some, occasionally even physicists, argued for a new mysticism or a turning to religion for the kinds of answers no longer available from science.

## The Biological and Social Sciences

There was no comparable revolution in the biological and social sciences, but advances in these fields were rapidly unveiling the mysteries surrounding the human condition. Heredity had come to be better understood with the rediscovery around 1900 of the theory put forth in 1866 by Gregor Mendel, the abbot of a Silesian monastery, a theory that distinguished between dominant and recessive characteristics and showed how they were passed on from parents to offspring. The isolation of viruses, first achieved in the 1890s, continued at a more rapid pace; and a range of important new drugs was synthesized, most notably penicillin, discovered by Sir Alexander Fleming and Sir Howard Florey in 1928. Just before the war, Sir Frederick Gowland Hopkins had identified organic substances in food that were later named vitamins A, B, C, and D. The others were discovered in the 1920s and their functions identified, findings that have made a major contribution to human health.

The other behavioral sciences were not so radically transformed during this period as psychology was by Freudian thought, but the work of the two giants of modern sociology, the Frenchman Emile Durkheim and the German Max Weber, had begun to change their own and related disciplines. Although very different sorts of scholars, they shared a concern for finding systematic and objective approaches to the study of society, and questions of methodology have remained central to the social sciences since. Durkheim, following the positivist tradition, explored the power of statistical tools, particularly in his investigation of suicides; and Weber's concept of the "ideal type" as a special form of generalization has led to the wide use of theoretical models. Both probed the social functions of apparently irrational custom and stressed the importance of religion. Weber's classic *The Protestant Ethic and the Spirit of Capitalism*, like Durkheim's concept of anomie—the disoriented condition of society when group norms have broken down—reflect the importance they also assigned to shared values as a cohesive factor in society, the very condition many feared the twentieth century had lost.

Similar themes emerged during the 1920s in anthropology (the discipline that had benefited most from imperialism) and history, though both fields remained primarily empiricist. And the idealism of the Italian philosopher-historian Benedetto Croce also contributed to the assumption that the values of any society are relative to its time and place as well as to a broadening of the range of human behavior that social scientists study.

The creative ferment of the 1920s seemed less troubling when it went hand in hand with technology. The public began to accept the architecture and applied design of Walter Gropius's Bauhaus school in Germany, with its emphasis on relating form to function, and the still more daring endeavors of Le Corbusier in France to envision the modern city. In motion pictures, just now winning credentials as an art form, the distortions of time and perspective through flashbacks and close-ups were less disturbing than when conveyed through words or on canvas. Even the frothiest romance or adventure story of the silent screen could express (and perhaps mold) subtle subliminal themes of social or national concern—characteristically, themes of abandonment in France, betrayal in Germany.[5] Only in this decade did Berlin ever rival Paris as an artistic center—proof of the benefits of democracy, one might argue—but intellectuals generally expressed doubts about the future of Western civilization.

That the values of Western culture were changing few denied by the late 1920s. The recognition of humanity's irrationality, the new scientific knowledge, and the violence that could accompany popular participation in public life were all threatening; the arts and philosophy as well as science had not

[5] Paul Monaco develops this view in *Cinema & Society: France and Germany During the Twenties,* 1976.

only moved beyond the average person's understanding but had also, in large measure, rejected traditional assumptions and beliefs. In essays and sermons, the public was warned of a crisis of values that neither art nor science could help, a crisis apparently related to the materialism of capitalism, the dull legalism of liberal forms, and the empty gentility of the middle class.

## III. THE GREAT DEPRESSION

❋

### Europe's Economic Vulnerability

Disturbing though they were, the attacks on familiar conceptions in the realms of the creative arts and natural phenomena did not unduly alarm average Europeans. Their daily life was secure from war and generally from want; a world of democratic nations at peace seemed to have achieved an impressive prosperity. The major nations reestablished prewar ratios between their currencies and gold, and productivity surpassed prewar levels. Then in October 1929 the American stock market crashed, inaugurating the most severe, widespread, and long-lasting of depressions in the modern history of the West. The gaps in postwar recovery were suddenly exposed, and waves of misery and instability challenged Western society and mocked liberal visions.

The dislocations of war—the destruction of plants, shifts of capital, and movements of men—had been accentuated by sudden demobilization and then by economic development itself. Not all wartime industries had been able to convert to peacetime enterprises nor all workers to regain their jobs; the prosperity of the 1920s rested heavily an new processes and on new products such as automobiles and synthetic fabrics, so that significant sectors of manufacturing declined.

Italy and Great Britain, whose coal and textile industries had entered even before the war into a period of chronic depression, never fully shared in the postwar boom. Large industrial combines, closely tied to money markets, controlled concomitantly sizable shares of overall production and employment, restricting the diversification of businesses across the economic base. More people, men and women, worked in service activities such as sales and distribution, which were susceptible to cutbacks.

This economic fragility was underscored by certain long-term trends. Old trade patterns had not revived. Goods traveled less freely within Europe, particularly the East, where debt-ridden and underdeveloped new countries—their industries often separated by national boundaries from traditional sources of capital—forced trade to find new routes. Germany's inflation as well as Russia's withdrawal from commerce had increased these difficulties, which had been only partly offset by industrialization in the new states and assistance from the League of Nations.

Moreover, Europe did not regain its prewar percentage (about half) of world trade; its firms had lost many of their overseas markets to competitors, especially Americans, during the war. So also with foreign investments: Britain had lost a quarter of its $18 billion, France half of its nearly $9 billion (primarily in Russia), and Germany all of its $6 billion. American investments in Europe, on the other hand, had multiplied seven and a half times in seven years to reach $15 billion in 1920, and they continued to rise thereafter. Furthermore, a dangerous part of Europe's apparent prosperity rested on the unproductive passing of paper from the United States to Germany as loans, from Germany to the Allies as reparations, and from the Allies to the United States as payment of war debts. The United States not only dominated world

**The Dole—a government clerk, from behind the desks of officialdom, hands out checks to some of Britain's unemployed.** (Photo: The Bettmann Archive)

trade and demanded payment of war debts but also raised tariffs in 1922 and again in 1930 to levels that made it nearly impossible for Europeans to earn dollars by selling goods to it.

The turmoil in Eastern Europe and Russia had led to increased imports of grain from Canada and the United States, where more land was turned to wheat and improved technology brought larger yields. By 1925 Europe's agricultural production had recovered, but only to face a glutted market and sluggish demand because of reduced population growth and the preference for meat over grains that accompanied rising standards of living. Throughout the West, agricultural surpluses became a problem, driving down prices and pushing governments to increase subsidies and tariffs. Demographic patterns added other strains. Population expansion

was considerable only in Eastern and Southern Europe, but new policies in the countries of immigration, especially the United States, discriminated against nationals from just those countries where overpopulation was critical. Overseas migration slowed to a trickle while pressures of numbers built up.

The war and the disruptions of the postwar years had made people as well as economies less resilient. The demographic deficit because of casualties and a low birth rate had left the population in Western Europe somewhat older and more dependent on pensions. The trauma of war had been followed by the shocks of instability, inflation, and unreliable currencies. Those whose social status depended on savings, pensions, or salaries, especially in Germany, faced poverty in the early 1920s, while those who owned real property or industry went on to greater wealth. Debtors benefited while creditors were ruined, and the sense of insecurity was never wholly lost even in the good times of 1924–1929.

## From Panic to Depression

Such dislocations did not slow the economy of the United States, now the world's wealthiest nation. Speculation in stocks and real estate had been running wild, driving purchase prices unreasonably high. Then suddenly, on October 24, 1929—the notorious "Black Tuesday" of American financial history—the price of stocks on the New York Exchange began to plummet. The crash was partially precipitated by the British decision to raise interest rates in order to bring back capital that had flowed to America, but it was more deeply rooted in the growing uneasiness among investors that the speculative inflation of stock prices had gone too far. Day after day tens of millions of dollars in paper assets disappeared. Such panics were not new to capitalism, and on several occasions in the previous century, a collapse of the New York market had spread to Europe. But in the next few months, the financial panic settled into full-scale depression. Banks had invested heavily in stocks and real estate, and some failed, causing runs on others. Businesses cut back, consumption declined, capital became more scarce, factories closed, and unemployment rose.

The crisis in the United States was soon felt abroad. European banks and exchanges were immediately shaken; more gradually, world trade declined, and the American government and businesses began to call in their investments and loans. At first, however, it seemed that the panic might be kept from affecting the entire European economy. Then in May 1931 the Austrian bank that held two-thirds of the nation's assets nearly went under, and this precipitated a run on Austrian and German banks that spread the now familiar cycle to other sectors of the economy and to other nations.

By 1932 the world's industrial production was two-thirds of what it had been three years before. Unemployment climbed to more than 13 million in the United States, 6 million in Germany, and nearly 3 million in Great Britain. Among leading industrial nations, only France, with its balanced economy, demographic stability, and relative scarcity of labor, escaped unemployment of crisis proportions.

Political leaders hoped that tested techniques of international cooperation could prevent economic disaster. One major problem disturbing financial relationships was that of war debts and German reparations. France and England maintained that they could pay their debts to the United States only if they received reparations from Germany. Although successive conferences and the Dawes and Young plans had evolved a workable system for the payment of reparations, this system, too, broke down amid the world economic crisis. The United States had never admitted a connection between reparations and war debts, but President Hoover's proposal in 1931 that all intergovernment debts be suspended was quickly accepted (most European states were already making only token payments, and France had defaulted). Meeting at Lausanne in 1932, the European powers, in effect, agreed to abandon reparations altogether. Although the moratorium originally proposed by Hoover was supposed to be temporary, any hope that the debts or reparations would ever be paid had become an illusion.

When Austria's major bank teetered on

the edge of bankruptcy in May 1931, threatening all Central European finances, it had been saved by British loans. Amid the deepening Depression, this and other financial burdens forced Great Britain to abandon the gold standard, no longer guaranteeing that pounds could be converted into gold at a fixed rate. The important bloc of countries trading in sterling quickly followed suit. This was tantamount to devaluation, as the value of the pound fell at once below the former, officially supported exchange rate with gold. Devaluation of this principal currency, in turn, threatened to throw international monetary exchanges, and the trade dependent upon them, into chaos.

But international understanding might once more prevent others from rushing to devaluate. To that end, the League of Nations sponsored a World Economic Conference that met in London in 1933. Begun with visions of high statesmanship, it ended in failure. Debts to the United States were removed from the agenda at American insistence, and no agreements for reducing tariffs could be reached until international exchange rates were stabilized.

When the United States, too, went off the gold standard, an elaborate structure of credit and exchange that had been one of the signal achievements of liberal finance fell. France was the last major country to abandon gold. Less dependent on international trade, hit later and less suddenly by the Depression, and strongly attached to the traditions of stable finance, it resisted until 1936. A historic era in which nations, like so many bankers, supported international financial stability by honoring the laws of liberal economics had ended.[6]

[6] Karl Polanyi has elaborated the significance of the abandonment of the gold standard in a famous essay, *The Great Transformation: The Political and Economic Origins of Our Time.*

## National Policies

The interrelationship between politics and economics had come to be well understood in the nineteenth century; but whereas tariffs and taxes were acknowledged to be political issues, most governments had wished to leave large spheres of economic activity alone. During World War I, however, governments were forced to direct much of the economy, and in the following years issues of reconstruction, reparations, and currencies had drawn them more deeply into matters of economic policy. Business increasingly turned to the state for assistance, and voters who had witnessed the miracles of wartime mobilization expected the state to lead them out of the Depression. By the early 1930s it was clear that each government had to act on its own to save its national economy.

On the whole, however, the measures taken had the effect of sinking nations deeper into the Depression. Austria and Germany in 1931 proposed a customs union, but French opposition led the World Court to forbid the step. Instead, nearly everywhere tariff barriers rose higher and import quotas were gradually extended to more and more items. The effect was a still further reduction in trade. Domestic programs varied, but the tendency was to protect interests that were politically strong, to shore up inefficient industries, and to support uncompetitive sectors of the economy—measures that slowed lasting recovery.

Such policies violated accepted economic precepts, but liberals were at a loss as to what else to do. Nor were socialists better prepared to solve the problems of declining commerce, insufficient capital, and unemployment, though they displayed a certain satisfaction at this new evidence of capitalism's weakness. They had a part in the governments of Germany, Austria, Sweden, Czechoslovakia, and Great Britain and were a leading force in

| International and Military History | Political History |
|---|---|
| **1920**  League of Nations | **1920**  Wrangel evacuates his armies from Soviet Union; Bela Kun defeated in Hungary; Kapp Putsch in Germany |
| **1920–1921**  Russo–Polish War | |
| **1921**  Russo–Turkish agreement | **1921**  Kronstadt Mutiny in Russia; NEP |
| **1921–1922**  Washington Naval Conference | |
| | **1922**  Fascist March on Rome; Irish Free State |
| **1923**  Belgian and French occupation of the Ruhr | **1923**  Turkish Republic of Mustafa Kemal; Munich Putsch of Hitler |
| | **1923–1925**  Bulgarian insurrections |
| | **1923–1929**  Stresemann Germany's foreign minister |
| **1924**  Dawes Plan | **1924**  Labour to power in Great Britain |
| **1925**  Locarno Pact | **1925**  Matteotti Crisis and consolidation of Fascist power in Italy; General von Hindenburg elected president of Germany |
| **1926**  Imperial Conference | **1926–1929**  Poincare prime minister of France |
| **1928**  Kellogg–Briand Pact | |
| **1929**  Young Plan | |
| **1931**  Statute of Westminster; Hoover moratorium | |

| Social and Economic History | Cultural and Intellectual History |
|---|---|
| | **1918** Oswald Spengler (**1880–1936**), *Decline of the West* |
| | Sigmund Freud (**1856–1939**) |
| **1920–1921** Famine in Russia | Max Weber (**1864–1920**) |
| | Albert Einstein (**1897–1955**) |
| | **1921** Wittgenstein, (**1889–1951**) *Tractatus Logico–Philosphicus* |
| | Marcel Proust (**1871–1922**) |
| **1922** Fordney–McCumber Tariff in United States | **1922** James Joyce (**1881–1941**), *Ulysses* |
| **1923–1924** Inflation in Germany | |
| | Franz Kafka (**1883–1924**) |
| **1924** United States limits immigration | **1924** André Breton (**1896–1966**), manifesto of Surrealism |
| **1926** General strike in Britain | |
| | **1928** Penicillin discovered by Sir Alexander Fleming (**1881–1955**) and Sir Howard Florey (**1898–1968**) |
| **1929** Stock market crash in United States: Great Depression begins | |
| **1930** Smoot–Hawley Tariff in United States | **1930** Ortega y Gasset (**1883–1955**), *The Revolt of the Masses* |
| **1931** Austrian Bank (Credit–Anstalt) nearly fails; Great Britain abandons gold standard | |
| **1933** World Economic Conference | |

most other countries; but their favorite nostrum, the nationalization of industry, was barely relevant. In practice, socialists showed again the extent to which they had absorbed the orthodoxies of classical economics. They, too, usually thought governments had to reduce their budgets and ensure that exports exceeded imports. At the same time, Socialist parties closely tied to labor unions, supported whatever palliatives for unemployment could be suggested, though the dole, the most common one, strained the budgets they wanted to see balanced. As liberals and socialists tried one new measure after another, they were embarrassed by growing Communist parties, which let no one forget that while a whole system had been collapsing, Soviet production had been advancing at a steady pace.

Gradually, conditions did improve. By 1937, production in Germany, Britain, and Sweden was well above the 1929 level of each, though it remained below that mark in the United States, Italy, Belgium, and France. Technological progress continued, and government intervention changed both economic and political life. But these changes were as socially divisive as the Depression itself, as the democracies that had dominated Europe faced the double threat of Communism and fascism with a heavy burden of failure.

## SUMMARY

In 1919 much of Europe had been in the throes of revolution; yet the western powers led the way to reasonable stability. New nations and a world order were created in their image, looking to democratic constitutions and the League of Nations as the means of organizing power. Despite the effects of war, social turmoil, and inflation, the new European order seemed by 1924 on its way to increased freedom and prosperity. Within a few years these achievements and the optimism that accompanied them were overshadowed by the calamity of the Depression. Liberal ideas and institutions appeared to be losing their capacity to deal with such problems as Europe was now facing, and the hopes of the 1920s quickly seemed foolish.

In retrospect, the failures became clear. Britain, France, and Germany, in their different ways, had turned to cautious domestic policies that postponed rather than met the deepest social and economic issues. In less wealthy nations, constitutions that did little to resolve conflicts of class and nationality were soon violated, while very different regimes in Russia and Italy moved with welcome dispatch. The League and the World Court showed themselves clearly most effective when the interests of no major power were at stake. Laborious negotiations for disarmament and monetary controls were often overrun by events, and the guardians of stability maintained their military forces while talking of reducing them and abandoned the gold standard while proclaiming its importance.

Individual liberty, democracy, and international law had seemed deeply rooted in Western culture when reaffirmed in the ruins of war; but those roots were not strengthened by the intellectual life of the 1920s, which turned inward to academic specialization or directly affronted the rationalism and genteel inhibitions on which bourgeois society was thought to rest. Those values, like capitalism itself, would be on the defensive throughout the next decade.

## RECOMMENDED READING

### Studies

*Bernstein, Jeremy. *Einstein*. 1973. A brief introduction of exemplary clarity.

*Craig, Gordon A., and Felix Gilbert (eds.). *The Diplomats, 1919–1939.* 1965. Separate essays on major figures uncover the connection between international relations and domestic affairs.

*Gamow, George. *Thirty Years That Shook Physics*. 1966. A leading physicist, Gamow is also an able popularizer.

*Gay, Peter. *Weimar Culture: The Outsider as Insider*. 1968. Sensitively explores the insecurity within German culture even in a period of great creativity.

*Graves, Robert, and Alan Hodge. *The Long Weekend: A Social History of Great Britain, 1918–1939*. 1963. A poet and a scholar recapture the feel of daily life among the middle classes.

*Hartnack, Justus. *Wittgenstein and Modern Philosophy*. Maurice Cranston (tr.). 1965. A good introduction to the topic.

*Kahler, Erich. *The Tower and the Abyss*. 1967. Uses his learned understanding of the arts across Europe to discern the elements of decay in contemporary culture.

*Kindleberger, Charles P. *The World in Depression, 1929–1939*. 1973. A clear account of how the Depression spread and affected the world economy.

Kolb, Eberhard. *The Weimar Republic*. 1988. An analysis that emphasizes elements of continuity with the Nazi period.

Lyttleton, Adrian. *The Seizure of Power: Facism in Italy, 1919–1929*. 1973. The best study in English of the complicated process that brought Facism to power.

*Maier, Charles S. *Recasting Bourgeois Europe: Stabilization in France, Germany, and Italy in the Decade After World War I*. 1975. Uses the details of economic policy and political conflict to show the period as one of bourgeois defensiveness.

*Marks, Sally. *The Illusion of Peace: Europe's International Relations, 1918–1933*. 1976. Makes use of work done in recently opened archives.

*Rogger, Hans, and Eugen Weber (eds.). *The European Right: A Historical Profile*. 1965. Separate chapters delineate the formation and political role in various European countries of the increasingly vigorous right.

*Rothschild, John. *East Central Europe Between the Two World Wars*. 1973. Now the best survey of the area in its critical era of independence.

Schuker, Stephen A. *The End of French Predominance in Europe*. 1976. Analyzes the diplomacy, domestic relations, and international finance that led to the Dawes Plan and efforts to deal with reparations.

*Sontag, Raymond J. *A Broken World, 1919–1939*. 1971. A senior historian's contribution to the best historical series on modern Europe.

*Stern, Fritz. *The Politics of Cultural Despair: A Study in the Use of the Germanic Ideology*. 1961. Focuses on three figures to assess the impact on politics of cultural attitudes.

*Stevenson, John. *British Society 1914–1945*. 1984. Reflects the altered view of Britain that results from recent scholarship and the hindsight of the last 40 years.

Trachtenberg, Marc. *Reparation in World Politics: France and European Economic Diplomacy, 1916–1923*. 1980. Presents the rehabilitation of the French position found in much of the most recent scholarship.

*Von Laue, Theodore H. *Why Lenin? Why Stalin?* 1979. Provocative essay on the stresses imposed by rapid industrialization and competition with the West.

*Wollheim, Richard. *Freud*. 1971. A concise introduction to the man and his ideas.

* Available in paperback.

# ❄ CHAPTER 28 ❄

# TOTALITARIANISM TRIUMPHANT AND WORLD WAR II 1924–1941

❊ ❊ ❊ ❊ ❊

Democracy was in retreat within less than a decade after the Paris Peace Conference. By 1929 authoritarian regimes had violated or eliminated the liberal constitutions of Hungary, Spain, Albania, Portugal, Lithuania, Poland, and Yugoslavia as well as Italy. By 1936 political liberty had been suppressed in Rumania, Austria, Bulgaria, Estonia, Latvia, and Greece as well as Germany. Most of these countries were among the poorest in Europe, but their political difficulties illustrate the broader trend. Divided over issues of social reform, nationality, and religion, they suffered increased disruption with each economic crisis and foreign threat.

❊

As the newer and poorer nations abandoned democratic forms of government, they were drawn to the political experiment unfolding in Italy, where Fascism promised to mobilize all society and to combine mass politics and industrialization with stability and order. Fascist groups appeared throughout Europe, and in Germany the most radically violent of these movements took power. Fascism, which fed on all the tensions of postwar society, presented itself as the only alternative to Communism and benefited from widespread fear of the radical left, which took the Soviet Union as its model. In Russia, however, the effort to restructure a whole society rapidly led to comparable techniques of rule. Twentieth-century ideologies, the potentialities of industrial society, and the strains of social change had generated a new political form: totalitarianism.

❊

Even in the prosperity of the 1920s, the great democracies of the West had had difficulty finding consistent policies to meet domestic demands for social justice or the threatening problems of international relations. The worst depression of modern history had created an economic disaster that free governments did not know how to repair. The social and ideological divisions within the Western democracies were further deepened by the direct international challenge from Germany and Italy and more indirectly from the U.S.S.R. From 1935 to 1939 the fascist states maintained the initiative in a series of mounting diplomatic crises. By 1939 those crises produced a war that Britain and France had desperately tried to avoid and for which Germany was psychologically and militarily far better prepared. Germany and its allies marched from conquest to conquest until they controlled the Continent by the end of 1941, when Russia and the United States were forced to fight at Britain's side.

## I. THE RETREAT FROM DEMOCRACY

❊

The transition to an authoritarian regime in European countries tended to follow a similar pattern and was usually marked by support from at least three groups. The army, concerned about external threats and domestic turmoil, favored a strong government. A more amorphous group of middle-class politicians and influential religious leaders, fearful of socialism, also supported authoritarian rule to preserve established institutions. Often they formed Catholic parties that combined promises of rural reform and the preservation of traditional society. Distrusting democratic politics and the urban masses, they rejected liberalism as having unleashed attacks on religion and opened the door to socialism. Nationalists were a third and overlapping group, and they were often very successful at winning popular support. They demanded a strong state to right old defeats, appealed to people in all social classes who felt themselves victimized by recent change and yet (like the military) wanted the benefits of industrial growth. Each of these groups thus sought selective modernization, controlled change along lines that would not threaten its own influence.

The sacrifice of parliamentary government was merely the first step. Authoritarian regimes also needed some popular support and soon found themselves at odds with various established interests, often the very conservatives who had brought them to power. Thus while some regimes adopted fascist techniques, others returned in the late 1930s to a limited constitutionalism. The political turmoil that accompanied both solutions was an important part of the crises leading to World War II.

## Authoritarian Governments

Hungary had turned to authoritarian rule relatively early, preserving the facade of constitutional institutions and relying heavily on the support of traditionally conservative groups. Once the Communists under Béla Kun were defeated, the Magyar aristocracy used a rigged electoral system to maintain its political dominance, protect its privileges, and stifle land reform. Ardent opponents of the Paris treaties, Hungary's leaders had

drawn closer to Italy. Admiral Horthy, who had become head of state in 1920, kept that office, but monarchists and fascists put successive cabinets under severe pressure. As the Depression reached Hungary, fascist trappings increased, and successive governments became more anti-Semitic, restricting the number of Jews permitted in business or the professions. Hungary would be quick to take what territory Hitler's policy in Eastern Europe permitted, yet wary of German and Italian plans. Because established institutions and groups, including the aristocracy, retained considerable influence, Hungary never became a full-fledged modern dictatorship. Belatedly, some of the fascist parties were dissolved in 1939.

In Poland, domestic political divisions were complicated by the fact of powerful neighbors, and Poles disagreed on whether their national interest lay with Germany, Russia, or France. Socialists and Catholics, conservative landowners and radical peasants all had political strength, and the resulting instability brought Marshal Jozef Pilsudski to the fore. A former Socialist, he took power in 1926 with the aid of a military revolt, serving as premier. He resigned after defeats at the polls in 1928. His supporters learned to assure safer elections in the future by persecuting the opposition. From 1930 on, Poland was ruled by men from the military. Constitutional changes in 1935 granted the president increased authority and gave the government a voice in the nomination of parliamentary candidates. Securely in power despite Pilsudski's death in 1935, Poland's military men strove valiantly to strengthen a nation badly hurt by the Depression and threatened by both Russia and Germany. The noisy conflicts of fascists and socialists, however, measured the regime's failure to establish a firm popular base.

When the monarchs of Eastern Europe attempted authoritarianism, they often flirted with fascism on the Italian model, only to find the game so dangerous that they returned to more constitutional forms of government. In Yugoslavia, Alexander I, who had ascended the throne of the new kingdom in 1921, assumed dictatorial powers in 1929 in an effort to tame the divisive forces of Croatian, Slovenian, and Serbian nationalism. But as these conflicts continued, he tried a restricted parliamentarianism. After his death in 1934, the regent, Prince Paul, pursued a similar course: Drawn at first to Germany and Italy, he decided by 1939 that Yugoslavia's international position and internal stability would best be served by a federal and democratic system. In Bulgaria a military coup ended parliament, parties, and free speech in 1934, and the regime moved closer to fascism as it sought both urban and rural support. But by 1936 the king was restricting the military, banning some fascist groups, and talking of constitutions.

Rumania's liberal government had begun to give way late in the 1920s before pressures from its ruling classes. Carol II, called to the throne in 1930, admired Mussolini and secretly subsidized the Iron Guard, a fascist organization whose political violence and anti-Semitism imitated the worst of fascism in other countries. In seeking popularity, Carol's government became more extreme; the imposition of martial law and tight censorship was followed by an anti-Semitic campaign that stripped most Jews of land and citizenship. These policies, however, proved disruptive and brought protests from Britain and France, and by 1938 the king was leading the way in suppressing fascist activities and attempting to make a new constitution work.

## The Trend to Fascism

The appeal of fascism was not limited to poor nations without parliamentary traditions, for the very lack of precise doctrine made its promise—that a strong state could marshal a mass following in behalf of social order—applicable anywhere. In Britain, Sir Oswald Mosley, once considered a likely Labour prime minister, founded the British Union of Fascists. In Belgium, fascism benefited from the antagonism between Catholics and anticlericals and between Walloons and Flemings. The Flemish speakers thought of themselves as a deprived group, dominated by the French-speaking Walloons in business, Church, and government. Largely rural and conservative, the Flemings came to feel considerable sympathy for fascism and especially for the Nazis, whose language was close to their own. In the Netherlands, also, a National Socialist movement rose to prominence in the 1930s.

There were a number of fascist and protofascist movements in France, of which the *Action Française* had the longest history and broadest influence. It had become prominent in the furor of the Dreyfus case, but remained primarily an intellectual movement appealing especially to monarchists and Catholics. Under the editorship of Charles Maurras, the *Action Française* maintained a biting critique of the bourgeois republic and developed doctrines useful to fascist parties everywhere but did not become a full-fledged fascist movement. It failed to achieve the common touch of the most successful fascist groups, and its conflicts with the papacy helped restrict its effectiveness. But it served as an important bridge between disaffected rightists, including intellectuals, and the uniformed young militants who filled the streets of Europe in the 1930s.

## *The Greek and Austrian Republics*

The republican government of Greece proved particularly vulnerable to fascism. Eleutherios Venizelos, the leader of the nation's liberals, dominated the republic's brief life, which lasted little more than a decade from its founding in 1924. Yet his party had been gradually losing ground to the monarchists even before the Depression deprived Greece of vital agricultural markets and forced Venizelos to resign in 1932. Republicans attempted a coup to ward off the restoration of the monarchy but were defeated, and a manipulated plebescite brought King George II back to the throne in 1935. When Liberals made gains in the 1936 elections, General Joannes Metaxas proclaimed himself dictator. He then clung to power in fascist style by balancing severe censorship and the abolition of political parties with extensive social welfare, public works, and armament.

In Austria the sharp division between a Catholic German countryside and a cosmopolitan imperial Vienna without an empire to administer undermined the republic. The Socialists, out of power since 1926, had little strength beyond the city, while the Christian Socialists, whose nineteenth-century programs of welfare, nationalism, and anti-Semitism had influenced the young Hitler, moved steadily toward fascism. In the 1920s each party had established its own paramilitary organization, and their violent clashes became a regular part of Austrian politics. Within the Christian Socialist party, older Catholic politicians vied for influence with German nationalists and the party army.

Prohibited by the Western powers from economic union with Germany as well as the Anschluss—the political "consolidation" desired by Nazis and others on both sides of the frontier—Austria survived financially after 1931 through foreign loans. Chancellor Engelbert Dollfuss drew Austria closer to Italy and ruled by decree, suspending parliament, outlawing Communists, and banning party uniforms (a measure aimed at the Austrian Nazis). In 1934 all parties except those in the Fatherland Front, which supported Dollfuss, were abolished. The Socialists called a general strike, and the government responded as for war. When the army bombarded Karl Marx Hof, the public housing that Viennese Socialists had been so proud of, that act symbolized the end of Austrian democracy.

A new constitution, elaborately corporative and claiming direct inspiration from papal encyclicals, was announced in 1934 but never really put into operation, and a concordat gave the Roman Catholic Church control of Austrian education. Austria's Nazis, however, remained dissatisfied, and in July a group of them assassinated the chancellor. They expected the Anschluss to follow, but a quick movement of Italian and Yugoslav troops to the frontier prevented it. For the next few years, Austria depended on Italian support, and Kurt von Schuschnigg, Dollfuss's successor, maintained a relatively mild dictatorship as he attempted to dominate the sordid squabbles for leadership within the Fatherland Front. Having destroyed the left, Austria's authoritarian government had little basis from which to resist the growing Nazi pressure.

## Dictatorship and the Spanish Republic

Alfonso XIII had kept Spain neutral in World War I, sparing it the direct ravages of war. But political and economic frictions were building toward a civil war that broke out in 1936.

Long before that date, Spain's political system had begun to break down and its economy to suffer from the lack of capital investment and unresolved problems of land tenure. In Catalonia, the center of commercial and industrial activity, a vigorous regionalist movement flourished, drawing together various groups that opposed Madrid's policies. The army, overstaffed with ambitious officers, became increasingly active in politics; and discontented workers, divided among anarchists, socialists, and a faction soon to be called Communist, staged frequent strikes that often ended in violence.

It was thus a strife-torn nation whose army in 1921 had been routed while attempting to subdue the Riffs, Berber tribes of Spanish Morocco. In the process, Spain lost most of the territory it had acquired since 1909, and an embarrassed government had promised a full report, apprehensively awaited by the army. Just before it was due, in 1923, General Miguel Primo de Rivera issued a *pronunciamiento* in time-honored style and forced the king to appoint him prime minister—an office he assumed as de facto dictator.

Although he began without a clear program, Primo de Rivera used the themes of modern antiliberalism to denounce soulless materialism and petty politics. With Mussolinian techniques, he built his personal prestige, assuaged the complaints of socialists and further divided the left with extensive welfare programs, and established a political party of his own. By 1926 the regime was able to claim a number of accomplishments. It had defeated the Riffs, albeit with help from France, and it had made extensive use of expert engineers and economists and adopted a corporative code, giving its domestic program a progressive flavor.

Nevertheless, the dictator's simplicity and candor had begun to lose their charm; his censorship antagonized intellectuals, threats of state ownership frightened business, and the government's propensity for meddling worried both Church and army. When a constituent assembly proposed not merely a corporative legislature but a kind of fascist council of ministers that the king could not dissolve, Alfonso lost his taste for imitations of Mussolini. As the Depression began to be felt in Spain, Primo de Rivera's government faltered, and in 1930 he went into exile, where he died a few months later. The king now presented himself as the protector of traditional liberties and appointed as prime minister another general, this one old and cautious enough to alarm no one. Spain's government tried both martial law and the promise of constitutionalism, but all the old problems remained. When republicans and socialists scored impressive victories in the municipal elections of 1931, Alfonso also chose exile.

The second Spanish republic presented a democratic revival. Under the republican leader, Manuel Azaña, a government of the left tried to hold its divergent supporters together with progressive labor legislation and welfare programs, but these measures were ill-adapted to Spain's economic and social structure. Granting Catalonia autonomy, one of its most successful decisions, did not end regional conflicts, and land reform based more on general principles than on specific conditions proved difficult to administer. The separation of church and state and the secularization of education infuriated half of Spain without satisfying anticlericals, many of whom continued to practice independent harassment of religious institutions and activities. Elections in 1933 installed a more conservative government with more traditional policies, but the left drew together in the popular front that triumphed in the elections of 1936.

For the five years of the republic's struggle to survive, the left had grown more radical, and antirepublicans had been preparing action of their own. A movement called the Falange had been founded by José Antonio Primo de Rivera, the dictator's son, in direct imitation of Italian Fascism; and systematic street violence was commonplace by 1936, when a group of generals announced their revolt. The Spanish Civil War, which followed, was seen from the first as part of the European battle between the fascist right and the Marxist left. The insurgent officers counted on support from Italy, Germany, and Portugal, where Antonio de Oliveira Salazar had already established his dominance over a single-party, corporative, conservative, and Catholic state.

### The Common Pattern

Whether they won power or not, Europe's fascist movements had much in common. Generally influenced by Italian Fascism, they looked and sounded similar. They liked uniforms, starting with a shirt of one color; cheap to buy and easy to adopt, it made a group of supporters (however few or poor) look like a movement, a historical force. They used paramilitary organization that promised decisive action to remake society through discipline and force. They created drama in the streets—noise, marches, colorful demonstrations, symbolic acts, and real violence—that undermined convention while advertizing fascism as something new and powerful. They borrowed heavily from workingclass movements and used all the devices of democratic politics, while seeming to stand outside the corrupting process of compromise and responsibility. Populist tactics were thus attached to the promise of order. They used nationalism, nostalgically evoking the enthusiastic patriotism of World War I, to offer simple solutions to real problems. The disruption and inequity of capitalism, class conflict, a faltering economy, and aimless governments were the fault of enemies—liberal politicians, Marxist revolutionaries, Jews, and foreigners. Although ridiculed and denounced in fascist propaganda and rallies, those enemies were credited with hidden powers. Fascist force was needed to overcome them and make the nation a single, orderly, prosperous community.

The psychological appeal of fascism is easy to understand. There was more to these movements, however, than their simple myths, their camaraderie and sense of importance, their demonstrations and uniforms, and their sinister attraction to violence. Fascists addressed real fears. They spoke to rural society threatened by urbanization, to small business people threatened by the competition of large corporations and to all business people threatened by workers' demands and government intervention, to a middle class threatened by socialism, to the privileged threatened by democracy, to the unemployed threatened by continuing economic depression, to the religious threatened by a secular society. Everywhere, they played upon fear of a communist revolution.

They could do all this by borrowing freely from ideas current throughout Europe. With a wealth of ideas on which to draw, and a remarkable lack of concern for consistency, fascist movements were intellectually as well as tactically flexible. They used socialist criticisms of liberalism and capitalism, conservative values of hierarchy and order, intellectual denunciations of modern culture, the widespread contempt for parliamentary ineffectiveness, doctrines of race developed in the nineteenth century and reinforced by war and imperialism, and the nationalism to which every government laid claim. At the same time, fascists admired technology and organization. They proclaimed theirs a new kind of movement that would create a new kind of society; modern change would be welcomed but controlled.

This ability to intersect with familiar social theories was illustrated by the connection to corporatism, a set of ideas with a long intellectual history. In its modern version, it advocated the organization of political life in terms of occupations, grouping people by trade or industry. A society so structured, the argument went, would preserve natural hierarchies while avoiding the divisiveness characteristic of parliamentary systems, which amplified differences of class and ideology; this vision of social integration gained attractiveness during the Depression. Moreover, in

1931, the fortieth anniversary of Leo XIII's *Rerum Novarum*, Pope Pius XI issued another influential social encyclical, *Quadragesimo Anno* ("In the Fortieth Year"). It went further in rejecting both the injustices of capitalism and the solutions of Marxism, calling instead for a harmonious society based on religion and cooperation through corporative organization. Many anxious people found in that papal pronouncement a sympathy for fascism that seemed to justify overlooking its deeply antireligious quality. Thus fascism tested the social cohesion and established institutions, the values and habits of European society west of the Soviet Union, and few societies could wholly resist its multiple appeal.

## II. TOTALITARIANISM
❈

Dictatorship has been recognized since ancient times as a particular political form, one way to maintain political order. But there was enough that was new and different about the most important dictatorships of this period to merit a separate term. In Italy, Germany, and the Soviet Union, governments used a single political party, devotion to a single leader, mass communications, economic control, and armed force in the name of an imposed, official ideology with the declared purpose of transforming an entire society. These massive efforts have been labeled *totalitarian*, and (despite historical precedents from ancient Syracuse to the French Revolution) totalitarianism can be recognized as distinctly new. With the aim of ideological unanimity and social coordination, totalitarian governments set new standards of oppression, making terror a tool of power, demanding agreement and not just acquiescence, establishing an unparalleled concentration of arbitrary power in party and state, claiming the right to reach into every aspect of life, and crushing "enemies" defined not by what

they did or thought but by the external characterstic of membership in groups identified by race, occupation, region, or religion.

Useful as the concept of totalitarianism is, it has also come under heavy criticism for a number of reasons. Scholars disagree as to how widely the term is applicable; some exclude Mussolini's Italy; most would not extend it to Franco Spain or the fascistic regimes of eastern and southern Europe. The concept tends to ignore important differences; the values promulgated in Soviet Russia and Nazi Germany were not at all the same, nor were their policies either in theory or practice. If understood as a literal description of reality rather than as the definition of a form, totalitarianism can be seriously misleading. In practice, none of the totalitarian regimes achieved total control of society. Political processes continued, and authorities often bent in the face of habits or institutions they could not afford to offend. Negotiation and compromise with important interests and entrenched groups proved unavoidable; inefficiency and duplication were characteristic. Fascist and Nazi rule relied heavily on existing institutions and structures, working with business, bureaucracy, and the army, and impinging cautiously on religion. Officials and party members often disagreed and bickered among themselves even while using the instruments of totalitarianism to squelch others. Even so, totalitarianism, with its limitless claims, thought control, secret police, vast armies, and bloodshed forever marked the twentieth century and changed the definition of what governments can be.

### Fascist Italy

Mussolini had moved slowly to institutionalize his power. A series of special laws passed by 1926 assured his control of Italy. The Duce ("leader") of Fascism was declared head of state and granted the right to deter-

**Mussolini and his Black Shirt bodyguard give the Fascist salute.**   (Photo: Wide World Photos)

mine the Chamber's agenda and to govern by decree. For 20 years, nearly all the laws of Italy would be issued in that way. Opposition parties were outlawed, scores of potential opponents arrested, and the civil service and judiciary purged of unreliable men.

Mussolini had a rare gift for propaganda, and Italy's newspapers were filled with unsmiling pictures of him, always in poses of command—awing visitors, captivating vast throngs, leaping hurdles on horseback, flying airplanes, harvesting grains. No story was too silly to be circulated for some effect: The Duce recited the cantos of Dante from memory; he worked all night (the light in his office

was carefully left on); he inspired philosophers and instructed economists; American razor blades were inadequate to the toughness of his beard; his speed in race cars frightened experts; his stern but tender love for his subjects knew no bounds. Neither did the audacity or vulgarity of such propaganda. Disseminated day after day, it appeared to work, for Mussolini and Fascism were gradually placed beyond the range of normal criticism.

Slogans such as "the Duce is always right" or "Believe, Obey, Fight" soon covered walls from one end of Italy to the other, and mediocre party officials were humorlessly labeled *supermen* and *saviors*. The victory of an Italian athlete or the birth of a child to a prolific mother became an occasion for hailing the new order. Through the cheap theatricality of parades and balcony speeches, Mussolini's machine pumped pride and confidence into a troubled nation. Most Italians probably maintained their distrust of any government, but the good news of the propaganda was nevertheless welcomed and some of the enthusiasm was real. Even in its cynicism, Mussolini's sensitivity to the masses brought to Italian government a popular touch that it had lacked. The nation responded to his energy, his skillful borrowing of ideas and programs, and his arrogant confidence.

The authoritarian single party, parallel to and even competing with the state, became a hallmark of totalitarian regimes; and the Fascist party, completely subordinate to the Duce, reached into every city and town. A warning presence to other authorities and to individual citizens, the party had its own militia, secret police, and tribunals. Recruited in its early years mainly from among the unemployed and alienated, it had soon won hundreds of thousands of new members eager for the advantages of influence with the regime. There were associations for Fascist teachers, workers, and university students. In the youth organizations established for every age group over four years old, the next generation wore black shirts, marched, and recited official slogans. But the party never became the elite it claimed to be, and the policy of encouraging wide membership was abandoned in the 1930s in favor of fewer, more disciplined militants. Even so, the party remained more an instrument of patronage than the disciplined hierarchy described in propaganda.

Fascist doctrine, used primarily as propaganda, was neither fully practiced nor wholly consistent; but official ideology, essential to the very nature of totalitarianism, colored every aspect of life. Fascism declared itself the antithesis of the principles of 1789

yet also truly the regime of the people. While ridiculing the idea of majority rule, Fascists were extremely concerned with public sentiment and found a façade of representative institutions indispensable. The conservative principle of authority was reduced to simple obedience to the Duce. Authority was deemed purer when arbitrary than when circumscribed by rules, more effective if kept visible rather than subtle, and traditional arguments for social responsibility justified the omnipresence of the state. Crude force, the secret police, and acts of official brutality were well advertised as fulfilling the slogan: "Nothing against the state, nothing outside the state." Citizens were to replace the handshake with the extended right arm of the Fascist salute,[1] and regulations etablished the Fascist names to give one's children and the form of address to use with one's friends. There was said to be a Fascist style in art and philosophy, sport and war; and the state provided academies, uniforms, medals, and pensions for those who adopted it, while threatening the critical with unemployment, exile, or prison. A candid irrationalism suspicious of intellectuals and traditional culture stressed the virtues of intuitive "thinking with the blood." Revitalized by a new-found joy in war, Italians would reclaim the heritage of Imperial Rome. As the antithesis of the decadent materialism of Britain, France, and the United States, Italy would influence the world through the spread of Fascism, its millions of migrants in other lands, and its own might and empire.

Fascism promised a new society, and the government, like all totalitarian regimes, was loquacious about the new kind of person it was creating—obedient, tough, efficient. Fascists, and Mussolini himself, seemed embar-

---

[1] The salute was a stylized form of the greeting used in ancient Rome and portrayed in the statue of Marcus Aurelius that now stands on the Capitoline Hill in Rome, where Michelangelo designed a piazza to frame it. The salute quickly became an international symbol.

"Sons of the Wolf," six to eight years old, parade past Roman ruins. They have begun their Fascist military training. (Photo: Wide World Photos)

rassed by the stereotype of Italians as affectionate, volatile, inefficient, and artistic. Rome rather than the Renaissance, Machiavelli rather than Cavour, technology rather than opera were the traditions to be stressed.

Yet the new order in its 20 years did not remake Italy. Inconsistent policies and conflicts between party and bureaucracy added new inefficiencies, and neither government nor party overcame local customs of patronage or personal kindness. Despite the talk of discipline and sacrifice, Fascist rule produced the worst orgy of peculation Italy has ever known. The crude tyranny of Italian Fascism was not by twentieth-century standards outstandingly brutal, and the anti-Semitic policies borrowed from the Germans in the late 1930s never really took root. But freedom was crushed, the jails filled, hundreds of prominent figures exiled to dreary southern towns or desolate islands. The measure of the regime lies as much in the goals it sought as in its failure to achieve them.

## Social, Religious, and Economic Policies

The government hoped to halt the rapid migration of peasants off the land into cities (a policy with clear appeal to rural employers), tried against all the best advice to increase the birth rate, and strove to make the Italian economy self-sufficient. But at the most, it merely slowed the opposing trends. The regime did bring off some notable achievements, which it vigorously advertised. The Mafia was suppressed; the Pontine Marshes near Rome were drained and farmers moved into newly constructed houses there; new railroads were built and the service improved; some superhighways were started. An enormous amount of construction was sponsored by the state, usually in a monumental style, and archaeological excavations were favored as evocations of a glorious past. All these projects contributed to employment. In addition, an elaborate program to enrich workers' leisure-time activities provided recreation halls, meeting rooms, and libraries in most towns as well as vacations for workers at seaside or mountain resorts. Family bonuses gave the poor an increased sense of security, and reforms of the educational system put more people in school for longer periods.

But Fascism's most publicized accomplishment was its accommodation with the Vatican. Although Mussolini and most of his early followers were thoroughly anticlerical, they soon found it worthwhile to appease Catholic interests. Crucifixes reappeared in the classrooms, chaplains were appointed to the Fascist militia, and the budget for clerical salaries and church repairs was increased. Until 1929, however, the regime had garnered only intangible benefits—the good will of many prominent Catholics and the Church's refusal to support anti-Fascist movements.

Then, after lengthy and difficult negotiations, the Lateran agreements of 1929 were announced to the world. A formal treaty ended 60 years of conflict over Rome by establishing the tiny area of Vatican City within the capital as an independent state under pa-

pal sovereignty. And a concordat established religious teaching in Italian public schools, guaranteed that marriage laws would conform to Catholic doctrine, promised to restrict Protestant activities, and fixed a sum of more than $87 million as an indemnity to be paid by the state for Church property confiscated during the unification of Italy.

Fascist prestige was at its height. The new agreements resolved a dispute that had seared the consciences of millions of Italians. Abroad, the treaty seemed to suggest that Fascism had won special favor from the papacy, and this impression was little dimmed by the sharp warning in an encyclical of 1931 against the paganism of worshiping the state or by subsequent conflicts over Catholic activities that competed with those of Fascist youth organizations. These conflicts were bitter, and relations between Church and state never regained their former warmth. Still, Catholics and the Vatican were on the whole more generous in their attitude toward Mussolini's regime than they had been toward its liberal predecessors. The reduction of nineteenth-century hostilities between Church and state remained one of Fascism's most important assets.

When Fascism came to power, two general principles seemed to govern its economic policy. The first was autarky, or national economic self-sufficiency, which emphasized industrialization and technological progress as the basis of military strength. The second, borrowed from socialism, favored national ownership while distrusting big business and a free market. Although this attitude was soon attenuated, the Fascist government remained more willing to intervene in the economy than its predecessors.

The government very early set the value of the lira to equal the French franc, a bid for prestige that hurt Italian exports. The accompanying import duties and credit restrictions then led to a painful deflation. In the interest of self-sufficiency and a more favorable balance of payments, the government launched its famous battle of grain in 1926. With enormous hoopla and a whole range of new incentives, Italy doubled its grain production by 1940—but only at the cost of more competitive agricultural production. Exports declined more than imports, and the official policy of autarky had a regressive effect. Output per capita declined in the Fascist era.

As for big business, Fascist government proved in practice a sympathetic ally. In 1925 the leaders of Italian industry agreed to recognize only Fascist-led unions and were assured their traditional monopolistic autonomy in return. Generally, the industrial giants in steel, automobiles, rubber, and chemicals found it easy to deal with (and often to manipulate) Fascist bureaucracy. At the same time, subsidies to weak industries, financed through the Institute for Industrial Reconstruction established in 1933, led to a significant extension of government ownership. The redistribution of land and tax reform were considered in high circles but not seriously attempted. By 1940, despite the early return to the nine-hour workday, real wages were down in both industry and agriculture, and the bureaucracy accepted a cut in salary though taxes remained high.

### The Corporative State

Fascist theory and economic practice came together in the Corporative State, the most discussed aspect of fascism. By 1926 great confederations, or corporations, were established for major sectors of the economy (agriculture, commerce, industry, and so forth), each including a syndicate of employers and a syndicate of employees, a kind of official union. Both strikes and lockouts were prohibited, replaced by a grievance procedure through the corporations. The heads of syndicates were party members appointed by the government, and negotiations to establish industry-wide scales of wages were dominated by government and business. There was some basis for the Marxist charge that fascism was a device for protecting capitalists.

In 1928 the Fascist Grand Council—which included party chiefs, the heads of ministries, and leaders of parliament—became an organ of state whose duties included drawing up the list of candidates for election to the Chamber of Deputies, a list that the electorate (reduced to its wealthiest one-third) could only accept or reject as a whole. And in 1934 the number of corporations was fixed at 22, each representing an entire sphere of production from extraction of raw material to manufacture and distribution.[2] For each corporation, the Duce appointed a council consisting of delegates representing the syndicates and the separate phases of production (with Mussolini council president in every case), and all the councils together formed the National Council of Corporations. In many respects a mere façade, these institutions, which never attained real autonomy, were further undercut by preparations for war and Mussolini's habit of legislating by decree. In principle, this elaborate organization eliminated class conflict by unifying owners and workers behind the state; but the employers' syndicates maintained their traditional form and autonomy, whereas the workers' syndicates were not an extension of old unions but new organizations directed by the party. Within both the corporations and the Chamber, the Fascist party was dominant, but Mussolini, in turn, was shrewdly

[2] The comprehensive intent of this organization is shown by the breadth of the 22 corporations, which were divided into three groups: I—grains, fruits and vegetables, wines, edible oils, beets and sugar, livestock, forestry and lumber, and textiles; II—metals, chemicals, clothing, paper and printing, construction, utilities, mining, and glass and pottery; III—insurance and banking, fine arts and liberal professions, sea and air transportation, land transportation, public entertainment, and public lodging.

alert to prevent the party from acquiring interests or policies of its own.

### Resistance to Fascism

At first, the new regime managed to associate some distinguished Italians with Fascism, men such as the poet Gabriele D'Annunzio, the sociologist Vilfredo Pareto, the composer Giacomo Puccini, and the playwright and novelist Luigi Pirandello. But relations with leaders in the arts and scholarly disciplines remained uneasy; many continued, as did Benedetto Croce, a quiet and safely intellectual opposition. Some, of whom the conductor Arturo Toscanini, the historian Gaetano Salvemini, and the physicist Enrico Fermi are best known to Americans, went into exile. In 1929 university rectors and deans had been required to join the party, and by 1931, when the government demanded that all professors sign a loyalty oath, only 11 refused. The government frightened most people into silence and broke up organized resistance; the remaining underground was centered in France and some secret Communist groups in Italy. Internal opposition ceased to be a threat.

Within the country, even the most skeptical were baffled by Mussolini's apparent successes and felt isolated and uncertain of what to believe. Indeed, most Italians probably shared some pride in their nation's heightened prestige. Outside Italy, important groups in all European and many South American nations sang the praises of Fascism's "bold experiment" that ended petty squabbling, ran the trains on time, kept order, and eliminated the threat of Communism.

### Nazi Germany

The Nazi regime was the most complete and terrifying achievement of totalitarianism, the beneficiary of an advanced economy and a strong administrative tradition in a society that emphasized status, regional particularism, and reciprocal distrust among Junkers, bureaucrats, professional men and workers. Philosophies of the state were more fully developed and more widely accepted in Germany than elsewhere, as were theories that probed the weaknesses of liberalism, individualism, and rationalism. Racist ideas, current throughout Europe in the nineteenth century, won particular prominence and respectability there.

More immediately, Nazism profited from the unparalleled series of shocks German society had suffered since 1918. Defeat had brought charges of war guilt, a revolution, and a republic beloved by few. The drastic inflation of the 1920s had been followed by depression and the most extensive unemployment in Europe. German politics resounded with nationalist themes and cries of treachery, and the Weimar governments never managed to subordinate the army to civilian authority.

### The Background of Nazism

Nazism itself differed from kindred movements elsewhere in its extraordinarily effective and daring leader, its simpler and more coherent ideology, and its well-organized party. As a young man, Adolf Hitler had gone to Vienna to become an artist. Rejected by the Academy, he had impressed those who knew him mainly by his bitterness and wild visions of vengeance. World War I had been a kind of salvation for him, providing comradeship, a sense of purpose, and some status—he had been promoted in the field. After the war he found brief employment in Munich spying on the small German Worker's party, which the army considered dangerously radical. Hitler took to addressing party rallies and began molding in the beer halls of Munich the speaking style and the

"We construct," a Nazi election poster of 1932, contrasts "Our building blocks—work, independence, bread" with the "Building plans of the others": A middle-class figure offers "Promises—civil service cuts, unemployment emergency degrees"; and a worker proposes "Welfare jobs, corruption—terror, hounding, lies." (Photo: Archiv für Kunst und Geschichte, Berlin)

from nationalists. With none of Mussolini's experience in the world of ideological battles, he did not pretend to sophistication or subtlety. At the core of his vision were his concepts of race and universal struggle. The German people were suffering from vast conspiracies mounted by foreign powers, businessmen, Marxists, and Freemasons, but above all, Jews—the gutter anti-Semitism he had absorbed in Vienna was used to feed distrust of social change and provide simple explanations for any misfortune. The Jews were behind war profits, reparations, inflation, and depression; but Marxism was also Jewish, and Communists were agents of the Jewish conspiracy. Internationalism and pacifism were Jewish ideas intended to destroy Germany as the bastion of Western (Aryan) civilization. Life was a desperate struggle won by the ruthless, and Germany must awake to its destiny. In Hitler's harangues Germany's defeat in World War I, the Versailles treaty, the weakness of the Weimar Republic, economic disasters, Red revolution, Jews, moral decay, and abstract art were somehow all connected in opposition to the German *Volk*, the people whose manly and primitive virtues must be welded into an irresistible force behind one leader. Admirers of an older culture, monarchists, and believers in order were invited to join the angry patriots and the unemployed in the new movement.

When in 1923 Hitler had led the party (now called the National Socialist German Workers' party) in the Munich *Putsch,* Germany was racked by many similar movements; yet the revolt had been an immediate failure. The book Hitler wrote in prison, *Mein Kampf,* became the party bible. More self-exposure than anything else, it is a turbulent and repetitious outpouring of his political views intermixed with naive but demoniac statements about how human beings are manipulated by fear, big lies, and simplistic ex-

personal party that in 1933 would make him Führer. His oratory combined brutal accusations with a messianic tone and repeated simple themes over and over in a spiraling frenzy, each sentence delivered with utter conviction and the menace of controlled violence.

Hitler borrowed ideas from the left and

planations. Even in its cynicism, *Mein Kampf* touched on all the frustrations of modern German life while deemphasizing the party's earlier more leftist program. In prison and after his release in 1925, Hitler worked to reorganize and strengthen the party. He added the SS, an elite corps in black uniforms serving as his bodyguard and as a special police force, to the SA, the brown-shirted storm troopers who were one of the more fearsome of the street armies. Some ideas and useful phrases were contributed to Nazi thought by Moeller van den Bruck, a literary figure respected in conservative circles, whose *The Third Reich* advocated revolution in behalf of a new, corporative and nationalist regime. The party established its own newspaper, edited by Alfred Rosenberg, which propagandized vigorously; and in 1930 Rosenberg would expand the canon of Nazi doctrine with his *The Myth of the Twentieth Century*, a wordy, turgid exposition of Hitler's racist ideas.

Nazism thus developed an ideology and the organizations to express it; yet until 1933 its crude appeal enjoyed only modest success. In 1928 the party's 60,000 members were still not enough to have much weight in German politics. It had some notable assets, however, and was establishing more. General von Ludendorff had joined Hitler in the 1923 *Putsch*, and there remained the possibility that other officers would cooperate, despite their contempt for the rabble to whom the Nazis appealed. Some circles of Bavarian conservatives and Rhineland industrialists showed interest in the movement, and in 1929 the Nazis gained national prominence by loudly promoting the petition against the Young Plan. Four million Germans declared it high treason not to renounce the "war guilt clause" of the Versailles treaty or to agree to any further reparations.

Hitler's intensity, fits of temper, and frequent bad manners offended many, but others felt the fascination of a personality that radiated power and could at times be charming. Early in the movement's history he gathered that small group of absolutely loyal men who would rule the Nazi state until its defeat: Hermann Göring, an air ace; Joseph Goebbels, journalist and party propagandist; and Henrich Himmler. Dedicated fanatics, they worked ceaselessly to enlarge the party, orchestrate the impressive rallies, terrorize their opponents, and spread Nazi doctrine.

The Nazis were gaining. In 1930 they became the second-largest party in the Reichstag, and the following year Hitler reached an understanding with a group of Rhineland industrialists who promised to pay the party's election deficits and to provide funds for its growing armies. (Leading Nazis critical of capitalism were shunted aside.) Like Mussolini, whom he greatly admired, Hitler combined the attractions of revolution and social order, appealed to the lower classes, and reassured the respectable. To a society broken by the Depression, the party promised recovery, with higher agricultural prices for the peasants and more employment for workers (tens of thousands of whom found jobs in the SS and SA). Hitler guaranteed as well to rebuild the army and save society from the Reds. Scholars have given a great deal of attention to the question of what groups were first drawn to the Nazis. By the 1930s, the party was broadly based. Workers were probably the biggest single group among its members, but they constituted a much smaller proportion of the Nazis than of society as a whole. Most workers continued to support socialists and Communists. Disproportionately large numbers of Nazi supporters were small business people and trades people, civil service employees, and (to a lesser extent) farmers.

In 1931 right-wing nationalists, some industrialists, and an important group of mili-

A sea of fascist salutes from the floor of the Reichstag greets the announcement by Chancellor Adolf Hitler on September 1, 1939, that German troops have begun the invasion of Poland in response to Polish fire. At the same time, Hitler named Hermann Göring (standing at the podium as Reichstag president) as his eventual successor. (Photo: UPI)

tarists joined the Nazis in a manifesto denouncing the "cultural Bolshevism" of the Weimar Republic and the threat of Marxism, hinting that when the Nazis seized power, they would protect only those who joined them now. They had learned to speak simultaneously like a government already in office and an underworld gang. Their propaganda and their menace increased, and they expressed their seriousness of purpose by beating up Jews and socialists.

## Collapse of the Weimar Republic

The Social Democrats, who had gained in the elections of 1928, led the government that faced the Great Depression. Without great imagination, they did the best they could, but their majority in the Reichstag was shaky, and President von Hindenburg refused to authorize decree powers. In 1930 the government resigned, to be replaced by the Center party's Henrich Brüning, a cautious, sober man with little popular appeal whom Hindenburg allowed to rule by decree for most of his years as chancellor. The elections of 1930 increased by over a hundred the number of Nazi deputies contemptuously ready to disrupt the Reichstag, and Hitler was so impressed with these successes that he became a presidential candidate when Hindenburg's term expired in 1932. Worried politicians persuaded the field marshal to run for reelection, and he won handily, but Hitler had over 13 million votes on the second ballot against the senile, 84-year-old Hindenburg, now pathetically cast as the defender of the constitution. When Brüning proposed the expropriation of some East Prussian estates as part of a program of financial reform, the president dismissed him. Brüning, who proved to have been the Weimar Republic's last chance, had lost the confidence of nearly every segment of the Reichstag.

The subsequent period of palace intrigue led to Hitler. Hindenburg turned to Franz von Papen, a self-confident friend of important army officers and Junkers. Hoping to establish a conservative coalition of industrialists, Junkers, and the military, von Papen lifted Brüning's ban on the SA and SS, named four barons and a count to his cabinet, and declared martial law in Prussia, a step that was in effect a coup d'état to unseat the socialist government there.

Hindenburg then called new elections, which produced a Nazi landslide. With 230 seats, they constituted some 40 percent of the Reichstag's membership and thus by far its largest party. He could find no chancellor but Hitler, who insisted on full decree powers. The field marshal refused and sent the nation to the polls again, but while the Nazis lost some seats, they remained the largest party. Hindenburg next appointed as chancellor General Kurt von Schleicher, a conventional army man who made an easy target for the abuse of Nazis, Communists, and the disgruntled von Papen. Hoping to use Hitler's popularity, von Papen then led the men of Hindenburg's coterie in urging Hitler to serve as chancellor in a coalition government. The unsuccessful leader of a Munich *Putsch* 10 years before took the oath of office late in January 1933.

Although he came to office legally, Hitler's arrival marked a further breakdown in the German political system. The Nazis increasingly won the votes of the right, and while the ballots cast for Marxist parties remained nearly constant, the Communist share increased. The moderates were losing out, and no party now seemed capable of establishing a reliable majority in the Reichstag. Of the 12 men in Hitler's cabinet, only 2 others were Nazis, and the men around Hindenburg imagined they could use the demagogue and then discard him. Instead, the Nazis established their dictatorship within two months.

Seeking to increase the party's strength, Hitler called for another election almost immediately on assuming the chancellorship. The campaign that followed was one of sys-

tematic terror, especially in Prussia, where Hermann Göring was now minister-president and the police were used as principal electoral agents. The climax came with the burning of the Reichstag, a fire that the Nazis loudly blamed on the Communists. Hindenburg agreed to issue special laws, Ordinances for the Protection of the German State and Nation, that ended most civil liberties, including freedom of the press and assembly. The voters gave the Nazis 44 percent of the seats, which, when combined with those of nationalist allies in other parties, assured them a bare majority.

Hitler pressed on. Communists were expelled from the Reichstag, conservatives wooed with calls to nationalism, and Center party members won over with promises to respect the privileges of the Catholic Church. In March Hitler dared to demand a special enabling act giving him as chancellor the right for four years to enact all laws and treaties independent of constitutional restraints. Of the 566 deputies left in the Reichstag, only 94 Social Democrats (out of 121) voted no. Blandishment and terror had done their work, but the tragedy went deeper: German politics offered no clear alternative to Hitler.

The Nazi regime moved quickly. It established concentration camps, first on private estates and then in larger and more permanent institutions. By July all parties except the National Socialist had been outlawed, and soon all other political organizations disappeared. In the elections of November 1933, the Nazis won more than 90 percent of the vote. They proceeded to restructure the administration of government, purge the civil service and judiciary, outlaw strikes, and clamp stricter controls on the press. In a few months Hitler had won fuller power than Mussolini had managed in years.

At this point the chancellor's most serious potential opposition was within his own party. Hitler's solution was barbarically sim-

**The Nazi salute greets the entry of the Hitler Youth into Nuremberg stadium on Party Day, 1933.** (Photo: Archiv für Kunst und Geschichte, Berlin)

ple. On a long weekend in June 1934, Ernst Röhm and Gregor Strasser, leaders of the Nazi left wing who took seriously the socialist aims of a Nazi revolution, were shot or stabbed. So, among hundreds of others, were General von Schleicher and his wife, some Catholic leaders, some socialists, and some taken by mistake. The Night of the Long Knives, directed primarily by the SS, meant the destruction of any serious leftist element within the party. Hitler admitted to some 74 deaths; subsequent estimates raise the figure to as many as a thousand. That summer weekend proved that any horror was possible, and the purge, like the noisy accusations of homosexuality that accompanied it, estab-

lished the tone of Germany's new totalitarianism. When Hindenburg died in August, Germans voted overwhelmingly in a referendum to unite the presidency and the chancellorship in the person of Hitler, who took the occasion to assume officially the title of Führer (''Leader'').

## Administrative and Economic Policies

The government undertook a systematic administrative reorganization. Called *Gleichschaltung* (''coordination''), the plan extended to all national functions and could be used against any institution or individual considered likely to inhibit the Führer's will. The federal states lost their autonomy, and the Nazi party extended its function, establishing administrative *Gaue* (''regions''). The party Gauleiter, or regional director, might or

**Party troops march out carrying Nazi victory banners, "Germany Awake," Nuremberg Party Day, 1933.** (Photo: Archiv für Kunst und Geschichte, Berlin)

might not be the appointed governor. This duplication of state organizations was carried further in Germany than in Italy; the party even formed its own office of foreign affairs as well as a secret police, the Gestapo, which infiltrated both the bureaucracy and the army. A law of March 1933, which had expelled Jews from public service and universities, had made all government employees appointees of the Führer. New people's courts heard secret trials of cases of treason, now very broadly defined, and rewritten statutes allowed prosecution for intent as well as for overt acts. Arrest and detention without charge or trial became a regular practice.

In its economic policies the Nazi regime scored impressive successes, especially at first. Unemployment, the crying problem of German life, dropped steadily as the result of great public works projects—the construc-tion of highways, public housing, and government offices, the reclamation of swamps and reforestation—many using special labor battalions, in which one year's service was soon made compulsory. Later the burgeoning armaments industry and a growing military establishment eliminated the problem of joblessness entirely. By spending money while more traditional governments thought it essential to balance their budgets, the Nazis reduced unemployment more effectively than any Western nation. But such programs were expensive, and they were paid for in several ways.

The government restricted internal movements of workers and goods and controlled

### NUMBER OF WORKERS OFFICIALLY LISTED AS UNEMPLOYED AS A PERCENTAGE OF WORKING-AGE (15-64) POPULATION

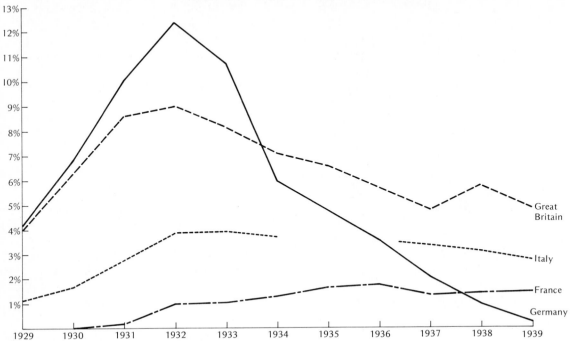

There were variations in the definition of unemployment, but the curves can be taken as one indicator of social distress. Because most women did not seek jobs, those actually out of work were a much higher proportion of the normal work force than shown here.

foreign trade, directing that payments be made with special marks whose value altered according to the goods and the nations involved. This currency scheme was largely the work of Hjalmar Schacht, a financial wizard who, though never a Nazi, contributed his skills to the new Germany. Imports were reduced, which lowered the living standard in some sectors and raised costs in many others, as part of a policy intended to make Germany as economically self-sufficient as possible. Trade thus became an explicit weapon in international relations; Germany bought pro-

duce and raw materials from the Balkan countries, for example, at prices well above the world market but with marks redeemable only through the purchase of German manufactured products. Tantamount to barter, this system increased Germany's influence in countries dependent on it for trade.

The Nazis gained additional revenues out of property confiscated from Jews, high taxes, forced loans, and carefully staged campaigns urging patriotic Germans to contribute their personal jewelry to the state. A four-year plan launched in 1936 was directed toward economic self-sufficiency rather than domestic wealth, for by then the German state was organizing for war. Ultimately, the government would cover these growing costs by printing paper currency, the effects of which would long be hidden by a war economy and the exploitation of conquered lands. By 1945 the mark had fallen to about 1 percent of its 1933 value.

Labor policies also produced visible gains while increasing government control. Outlawing strikes reassured business without gravely damaging wage levels that unemployment would have kept from rising. The National Labor Front, which included all workers and management, froze wages and directed personnel in the interests of business and government, but it was accompanied by an extensive array of benefits. All welfare programs, including plans previously regional or private, were taken over by the state, which claimed full credit for the funds and services provided from them. A Strength Through Joy program sent German workers to summer camps or on special cruises, furnishing pleasures once available only to the well-to-do. The workers' share in an expanding economy may have declined, but workers were grateful for jobs and vacations and perhaps for the sense of their own importance all the propaganda conveyed.

The professional military had reasons of its own for gratitude to the Nazi regime: Disregarding the disarmament clauses of the Treaty of Versailles (he would repudiate them formally in 1935), Hitler had set about openly and rapidly rearming Germany on becoming chancellor. While regular officers remained resentful of Nazi paramilitary organizations and disdainful of their social inferiors who now directed the state, they nevertheless appreciated the emphasis on fighting strength, and they accepted the oath of personal loyalty Hitler required of them after he had won the presidency. With the return of universal compulsory service in 1935 and the creation of an air force, Germany was soon spending several times as much on arms as Britain and France combined.

In 1938, strengthened by his diplomatic successes, Hitler asserted control more directly, removing the minister of war, the chief of staff, and more than a dozen generals. They were not merely fired but disgraced amid public tales of private vice. Baron Konstantin von Neurath, a nationalist of the old school who had been foreign minister since 1933, was replaced by Joachim von Ribbentrop, a good Nazi and no aristocrat at all. The Nazi hold on both the foreign service and the army, traditional strongholds of conservatives and aristocrats, now seemed secure.

### Religious and Racial Policies

The churches presented a less tractable problem. A concordat with the Vatican in July 1933 gave the state some voice in the appointment of bishops while assuring the Church that Catholic orders and schools would be unmolested. The Protestant denominations agreed to form a new body, the Evangelical Church, under a national bishop; but when the bishop Hitler chose tried to "Aryanize" it, dissidents formed the separate Confessional Church. In 1935 the minister for Church Affairs was given the power to confiscate ecclesiastical property, withhold funds, and have pastors arrested. Thereafter the state's primary tactic against the churches was the steady harassment of individual ministers conducted by local authorities.

Some priests and ministers cooperated with the regime, enthusiastically supporting war, race, and Reich. But most resisted at least the more outrageous demands made of them, and individual voices spoke out against Nazism clearly and courageously. In 1937 Martin Niemoeller, the leader of the Confessional Church, was arrested for his opposition to Nazism; and Pope Pius XI condemned both the deification of the state and Nazi racial doctrine. In the following years some Catholic churches were burned, members of religious orders were frequently

**Nazi propaganda against the Jews, Catholics and wealthy reactionaries who would subvert the Führer was disseminated by earnest young party members.** (Photo: Keystone)

brought to trial on morals charges, and the claims of the Hitler Youth—the Nazi organization for adolescents—challenged religious education. The churches, although not centers of organized resistance, still permitted individuals some escape from the incessant pressures of totalitarianism.

The relentless logic and dynamism of totalitarianism showed most clearly in the government's racial policy. Nazism had always made much of its anti-Semitism, and the Nuremberg laws of 1935 not only removed Jews from the public service (anyone with one or more Jewish grandparents was considered a Jew) but declared Jews no longer citizens and prohibited marriage or sexual intercourse between Jews and Aryans. Subsequently, Jews were expelled from one activity after another, required to register with the state and to give their children identifiably Jewish names. The murder of a German diplomat by a young Jewish boy in 1938 touched off a new round of terror. Many Jews were arrested, and the SS led an orgy of violence in which Jews were beaten and murdered, their synagogues burned, their homes and businesses smashed. A fine of 1 billion marks was levied on the Jews of Germany, and this was followed by still further measures to humiliate and isolate them; they were barred from the theater and concerts, forbidden to buy jewelry, forced to sell their businesses or property, denied access to certain streets, and made to wear a yellow star. Worse would come, for totalitarianism could never fulfill its vision of unanimity and total security any more than it could forgo violence.

From the beginning, the Nazis' publicity

had been flamboyant, their posters striking, and their rallies well staged; after the movement came to power, propaganda became a way of life.

Still, there was much to win the regime acceptance. For most Germans, life went on much as before but a little better, a welcome contrast to years of inflation and heavy unemployment. Factories were booming, and the standard of living rising. Employers were glad that strikes had disappeared. If there were those on official occasions, at club meetings, or even in beer halls who insisted on giving the Nazi salute, that extra enthusiasm was part of the new era. In fact, the rhetoric of patriotism came easily to most local officials, teachers, magistrates, and professors. It was not safe to criticize the government, but only a minority—Jews, labor leaders, radicals, some intellectuals, and those in exposed positions—lived in daily fear. For the rest, torchlight parades, chorused shouts of *"Sieg Heil!"* ("Hail to victory!"), book burnings, the evocation of Norse gods, schoolyard calisthenics, the return to Gothic script, a thousand such events sought to give each citizen a feeling of participating, of being swept up—and implicated—in some great historical transformation. Joseph Goebbels at the Reich Chamber of Culture saw to it that cinema, theater, literature, art, and music all became instruments for promoting Nazism. Things primitive and brutal were praised as Aryan; one who opposed or even doubted the Führer ceased to be German. Warfare was for the new regime its natural condition.

As part of its anti-Semitic policy the German government forced Jews to wear yellow stars on their clothing for immediate identification. It was the mildest of the government's discriminatory tactics.   (Photo: The Bettmann Archive)

## Communist Russia

Fascists insisted that only they could prevent the triumph of Communism, but they learned much from the Soviet example of a revolutionary movement using dictatorial powers to direct an entire society. For Communists, on the other hand, dictatorship was incidental and supposedly temporary; and to many in Russia and in the West, the Soviet Union remained the antithesis of fascism and its only consistent opponent. There was a real question as to how the Soviet regime would develop when Lenin died in January 1924. In retrospect, that was a turning point; for as issues of policy and leadership were slowly resolved, Joseph Stalin emerged as one of history's most effective dictators.

For more than a year, Lenin had been nearly incapacitated, but his prestige had precluded any public scramble for power, and many expected a more relaxed government by committee to follow. In a famous letter, Lenin had assessed two likely successors: Trotsky, whom he called the best man in the Politburo, though overconfident; and Stalin, whom Lenin found "too rude" though an able organizer (Stalin already held enormous power as general secretary of the party's Central Committee).

Over the next three years, Russia's leaders publicly debated the complex issues of Communist theory and practical policy. Trotsky led those who clung to the traditional vision of revolution spreading across Europe, and he thus favored an uncompromising radical program at home and abroad. Stalin's stand was that the Soviet Revolution could and must survive alone through "revolution in one country." No theoretician and little informed about the world outside Russia, Stalin was not wholly at ease in these debates with more intellectual and experienced opponents. But they, in turn, underestimated his single-minded determination. His argument was formally adopted by the Politburo in December 1925.

Stalin used his position with skill. He was the link between the Politburo and the party organization below it, and he could count on the loyalty of party officials, many of whom he had appointed. He played effectively on personal antagonisms and on the bad feelings created by Trotsky's tactless arrogance. When the Politburo elected three new members at that December meeting, all were Stalin's associates.

Leading opponents of Stalin on the left began to cooperate with Trotsky in public agitation, but Stalin made each such move seem a threat to party solidarity and Communist rule itself. Although Grigori Zinoviev had supported Stalin, his position as head of the Comintern—the Third International—gave him independent power until he and Trotsky were expelled from the Politburo in 1926 and from the party itself in 1927. The left was broken, and Zinoviev recanted his "mistake" the following year. So did Nikolai Bukharin, perhaps the party's subtlest theoretician and a leader of the right, who believed Russia's social transformation must necessarily be slow. Trotsky, who tenaciously refused to change his mind, was exiled and then deported, continuing from abroad his criticism of Stalin's growing dictatorship.

It may seem odd that these men, all veterans of the October Revolution, did not attempt to oust Stalin; even Trotsky, who had built the Red Army, never tried to use it against him. But these old Bolsheviks fervently accepted the need for party loyalty and revolutionary unity. Stalin, who favored the younger and less intellectual party members, made the most of this mystique to assure that the open debates of those years were not allowed again.

## The First Five-Year Plan: Agriculture

The First Five-Year Plan, launched in 1928, was a daring program that reflected some of the qualities that had brought Stalin to the top. It shamelessly incorporated ideas and suggestions Stalin had denounced when his opponents had put them forth just months before, but it was thoroughly his in its bold assumption that Russia could transform itself into an industrial power by mobilizing every resource.

By 1928 Russian production had regained prewar levels in most sectors, but the recovery had come through serious concessions to free enterprise. Lenin's New Economic Policy had depended heavily on private entrepreneurs in commerce, the so-called NEP men, and on peasant owners in agriculture. The task now was to change the very nature of the economy itself by socializing it on both fronts.

As a first step, the plan inaugurated the collectivization of agriculture, a measure with multiple aims: to bring socialism to the countryside; to increase production by spreading the improved techniques and the mechanization that peasants had on the whole resisted; and to give the state control over agricultural output, enabling it to feed industrial workers and to sell produce abroad so it could pay for the imported machinery industrialization required.

Although Russian peasants had many traditions of common effort, they bitterly resisted collectivization despite inducements of equipment and credit. Poor by international standards, perhaps 4 or 5 percent of them nonetheless had the means to hire labor and lend money within their villages, which gave them a hold over the entire economy. Significantly, these farmer-employers would come to be called kulaks, the old, pejorative term for grasping merchants and usurers.

As agricultural prices fell—while other prices soared—peasants withheld their goods from the market. Famine threatened, and the government, blaming the kulaks, mounted a sweeping campaign of propaganda and police action against them. It seized their grain (informers were given a quarter of any hoard uncovered), killed hundreds of thousands of kulaks, and deported untold numbers of them to till the unbroken soil of Siberia. Meanwhile, peasants destroyed crops and animals rather than let the government have them. The antagonisms of rural society were thus proving unexpectedly explosive, and Stalin had to intervene in 1930 to halt what had escalated to virtual civil war. By then, more than half the peasants had joined collective farms, but the losses in animal power and able farmers had hurt production se-

verely. Serious famine in 1932–1933 showed how badly the First Five-Year Plan had failed to reach its goals in agriculture.

The pattern of collectivization that then emerged proved to be a durable compromise. Even on collective farms peasants were permitted individual plots and privately owned tools. Larger machinery was concentrated at Machine Tractor Stations, which became the rural base for agricultural agents and party officials—modernization and political supervision went hand in hand. By 1933 output was sufficiently controlled to permit the government to concentrate on the central aim of the plan: the most massive and rapid industrialization in history.

## The First Five-Year Plan: Industry

According to the five-year forecast, industrial production was to double in less than five years and in some critical areas, such as electrical power, to increase sixfold. More than 1500 new factories were to be put into operation, including large automobile and tractor plants; and there were projects on a still grander scale, among them a Dnieper River power station and a great coal and iron complex in a whole new city, Magnitogorsk. These goals would be met somewhat ahead of schedule, and there would be only slight exaggeration in the government's proud claim to have made Russia an industrial nation almost overnight.

All this had to be financed internally, and it was paid for primarily by the dead, displaced, and collectivized peasants. Indirect tolls were levied on the rest of the populace as well. Workers' wages were increased only slightly, and the plan postponed improvements in even such basic facilities as housing and rail service. Food and then most consumer items were rationed, with allotments varying according to one's contribution to the plan.

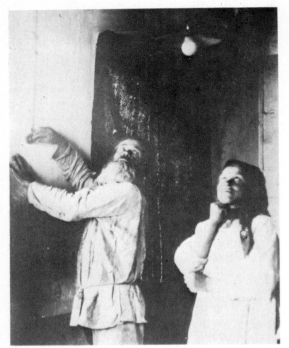

**Russia's First Five-Year Plan was responsible for the look of anticipation on the faces of these villagers; they are about to switch on the first electric light bulb ever to appear in Bryansk Province (1928).** (Photo: Novosti Press Agency)

Most Russian laborers, unskilled or poorly trained, were unaccustomed to the pace now required; thus their rate of turnover was high, the quality of their work poor, and their output per man-hour low. The state resorted to a continuous work week—multiple shifts kept the precious machines going—and moved special "shock brigades" of abler workers from plant to plant as a stimulus to higher production. Women and young people were urged into industrial jobs. "Socialist competition" pitted groups of workers and whole factories against each other for bonuses and prizes, and piecework payment, once a hated symbol of capitalist avarice, became increasingly common. Violators of shop

rules were fined; indolence, malingering, pilfering, and sabotage, often loosely defined, became crimes against the state. Punishment frequently included time in a "corrective" labor camp, so that what had initially been a mode of prison reform became another means of getting more work done.

Many of the essential managers and engineers were foreigners, but the government was eager for Russia to supply its own talent. Special courses were established in factories, and the numbers enrolled in the higher technical schools trebled. This training, like the quality of goods produced, was often inferior, but it laid a base for the future.

The plan's sober goals required a stability and discipline that led to the sacrifice of some earlier enthusiasms. In schools, the formal examinations, homework, and academic degrees, once abolished, began to return; and classroom democracy gave way before the strengthened authority of the teacher. By the 1930s the virtue of marriage was being emphasized, divorce and abortion discouraged, and prolific families specially rewarded.

The five-year programs, which had taken years to devise, had to be constantly amended, requiring the development of new skills, detailed reports on every sector of the economy, and above all, increased authority for the planners themselves.

The great venture mobilized every aspect of society. Associations of writers, musicians, and artists worked with party help to establish the themes and styles of propaganda useful to the plan. Mass organizations of youth and workers met for indoctrination, and kulaks and Church were subject to renewed attacks. Within the party itself, criticism or even skepticism about any aspect of the plan was akin to treason; hundreds of thousands of party members were expelled, and new recruits were carefully screened for absolute reliability. Much of the support for Stalin, especially among able young party members

was very genuine; and the state used propaganda, mass organizations, and secret police to create unanimity. "Overfulfillment"
was announced in 1932, but the miracle of
industrialization also marked the creation of
a Russian totalitarianism holding together a
society rent by rapid change. The very purpose of society seemed to lie in the statistics
of production quotas met.

### Growth in the Prewar Decade

The Second (1933–1937) and Third (1938–
1942) Five-Year plans were continuations of
the First at somewhat lower pressure. Although the emphasis on industrialization
continued, the rate of capital investment was
reduced, consumer goods became more
available, and rationing was eliminated by
1936. Standards of quality rose, and there
were new undertakings as well. Dramatic improvement in transportation, especially domestic aviation, made previously remote territories accessible and led to the serious
exploitation of Arctic regions. Partly for reasons of military security, industrialization
east of the Ural Mountains was stressed.

By 1939 Soviet Russia ranked third among
the world's industrial producers, behind only
the United States and Germany. That year it
produced 24 times more electrical power and
5 times more coal and steel than in 1913.
Housing and clothes were improving,
though the Russian standard of living remained low compared with that of the West.
Seven years of compulsory schooling for all
remained a goal yet to be met, but the literate
population had grown from less than 50 percent of those over school age in 1926 to
more than 80 percent in 1939; enrollment in
higher schools had trebled, and the number
and size of libraries and hospitals more than
doubled. In these years one-seventh of the
population moved to the cities, where a
higher proportion lived than ever before, and
over 90 percent of peasant households were
on collective farms serviced by the Machine
Tractor Stations.

The Soviet Union, the government proudly announced, had reached the stage of socialism and this justified a new constitution
in 1936. The changes it made were mainly
formal. Direct voting by secret ballot replaced
the cumbersome indirect elections, the government explained, now that the reactionary
classes had ceased to exist. The body thus
elected was the Soviet of the Union, one of
two houses of the Supreme Soviet; the other,
the Soviet of the Nationalities, represented
the republics. The Supreme Soviet elected the
Presidium, which legislated most of the time
and whose chairman was head of state, and
the Council of Ministers, the executive arm
(the revolutionary term Commissars thus
passed away). The constitution divided some
of the larger federal republics, making 11 in
all, and on paper at least, left them considerable autonomy. It provided social and political guarantees that Communists hailed as
the most democratic in the world, and it officially noted the special position of the Communist party as "the vanguard of the working people." When new elections were held,
96 percent of the population voted, 98 percent of it for the single list the party presented in most constituencies.

### Stalinism

With the new constitution, many expected
an easing of political controls. Amnesty had
been granted some political prisoners in 1935,
and the sinister secret police, in operation
since 1922, had been replaced by a somewhat
more controlled political police, the NKVD.
The campaign against religion was abating,
and the white-collar classes and leaders generally were being honored—the military had
officers again, and foremen were returning

to factories. Opportunities for advancement in this modernizing society were great, and special awards recognized those who excelled. But tyranny remained, justified by the dangers of "capitalist encirclement."

Soviet art and literature became timid; writers, Stalin commented ominously, were "engineers of human souls." Music perhaps fared better, notably in the sophisticated and dynamic works of Dmitri Shostakovich and Sergei Prokofiev. If intellectuals were harassed less in the later 1930s than during the First Five-Year Plan, they had long since learned the necessity of caution. The Russian Academy of Science, as lavish in its support of some kinds of research as it was arbitrarily unfriendly to others, was never far from politics.

At the center of Soviet society stood Stalin, increasingly adulated. He was honored as leader and expert in every activity; works of art were dedicated to him, factories named after him, his picture everywhere. His authority was virtually absolute, even though until 1941 he held no official position other than party secretary. Patriotism overshadowed the socialist internationalism of an earlier generation, and Soviet achievement was presented as the culmination of a long Russian development. Stalin was taking his place with Ivan the Terrible and Peter the Great among the molders of Russia.

That his power exceeded theirs showed in the great purges of the late 1930s, directed against very disparate people—engineers, Ukrainian separatists, former Mensheviks, party members—accused of being counterrevolutionaries. They were touched off by the assassination in 1934 of Sergei Kirov, who had been close to Stalin, and a member of the Politburo. An event treated as part of a large conspiracy (Kirov was hated by those who admired some of Stalin's old opponents, especially Zinoviev), the assassination was probably sponsored by Stalin himself. Then Zinoviev and members of the "left opposi-

tion" were tried for treason and imprisoned in 1935, tried again, and executed in 1937. Their trials were followed by others, always public: party leaders and army officers in 1937 and members of the "right opposition," Nikolai Bukharin and other old Bolsheviks, in 1939.

To the outside world, the indictments seemed vague and the evidence unconvincing; yet the accused consistently confessed—and disappeared. Perhaps their admissions of guilt were merely the result of torture, but they also seemed a final act of faith by men who had always believed that anyone resisting the inevitable course of history was "objectively" a traitor.

Russia was profoundly shaken by the purges and the reign of terror, which, like the earlier campaign against the kulaks, swept the country—as much an expression of local hatreds, ambitions, and vendettas as of national policy—until in 1939 Stalin once again called a halt. The dead were countless; jails and labor camps were bursting with prisoners—perhaps 10 million. More than twice that many had gone into exile. Russia's leaders, except for Stalin, were primarily from a new generation who had made their whole careers under Communism. And the institutions and techniques of Soviet totalitarianism had grown ominously like those of Germany and Italy, even though their raison d'être was a much more fundamental transformation of society. Only in the values it professed did Russia remain closer to the humane traditions of European civilization, and it was not clear in 1939 what part the isolated and untested nation would play as Western democracy faced its greatest challenge.

## III. THE DEMOCRACIES' RESPONSE
❈

Where democracy survived the Depression, the results were unimpressive. Parties of the right center pursued sound finance with re-

**The ubiquitous Stalin: his picture was encountered everywhere, even afloat at this Russian beach resort.** (Photo: Sovfoto)

sults that embittered the unemployed; liberals reluctantly jettisoned old principles to support higher tariffs and subsidies for business and agriculture; socialists resentfully compromised welfare projects for better-balanced budgets. Even where strong at the polls, the left was politically weakened by the fratricidal conflict between Communists and socialists. If voters turned toward the militant left or the radical right, the political system became unworkable, and governments resorted to decree powers and bans on extreme parties. By the mid-1930s, when there were some promising signs of new ideas, policies, and political coalitions, international dangers brought further divisions and worse crises. In fact the democracies were not doing so badly in their economic and social policies compared with the fascist regimes. They,

however, propagandized brilliantly and seemed dynamic and united. As England's Lord Tweedsmuir dryly noted, "But for the bold experiment of Fascism the decade has not been fruitful in constructive statesmanship."

## Social Change and Political Uncertainty

Slow economic recovery underscored important social changes. Agriculture was becoming more productive as it became more mechanized and scientific. These changes required more capital, favored larger holdings, and

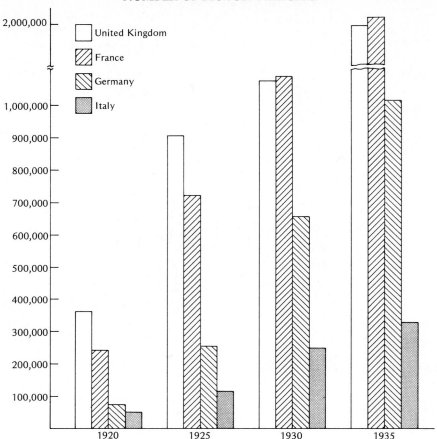

**NUMBER OF MOTOR VEHICLES**

The number of automobiles in a society reflects its general wealth, adaptation to a consumer economy, and changing patterns of communication. (Note that the United Kingdom, France, and Italy each had about 40 million people; Germany had 65 million.) This graph gives evidence of impressive prosperity and change; by 1935 France and the United Kingdom had one vehicle for every 20 people.

employed fewer people than in the past. Better transportation, mechanical refrigeration, cheaper clothes, and more leisure were clearly raising standards of living as well as changing life styles. Workers looked to unions and the parties of the left to support the government programs and pry from employers the better wages that would allow them a part of these improvements. Throughout Europe, the middle classes recouped much of the status and security threatened by inflation and depression. University enrollment, still a privilege of class, rose higher than ever before—highest in France, it rose to almost 2 percent of college-age youth in Scandinavia, Britain, Italy, and Germany (where it dropped sharply after the Nazis came to power). But small business and craft industry had suffered much more than the larger corporations, the first to benefit from the economic upturn. Economic life was clearly dominated by large-scale production and large organizations, including trade unions and governmental agencies. Women, though usually paid less than men, were now an accepted part of the industrial work force, their incomes often as important to their families' well-being as it had once been to its survival. If workers generally enjoyed a 40-hour week with more leisure time and more ways of spending it, work itself was more subject to "American" efficiency; supervisors maintained relentless discipline to keep production moving at a pace set by machines.

To many, technology now seemed a mixed blessing. Talking motion pictures and radio were enthusiastically taken up by the general public, and they did much to bridge the gap between urban and rural life and to build a popular culture common to all classes. Hailed as new art forms by a few, their frothy commercialism and adaptability to the propaganda at which the totalitarian regimes excelled worried others. The very form of prosperity thus stimulated discontent among intellectuals disdainful of mass culture, small-business owners frightened at their precarious position, and workers who disliked the conditions under which they worked and resented their limited share of national wealth. The transformation of Soviet society or even the symbolic gains of better-lit factories and vacation resorts for workers glorified through propaganda in Germany and Italy, seemed to many to offer a striking contrast between the purposeful, orderly societies of a single party and the aimless dislocation and dissension in the democracies. Wherever freedom permitted, political conflict both reflected and contributed to social division.

Among the smaller democracies, Switzerland, socially the most conservative, and Sweden, which combined social welfare programs and a mixed economy, fared the best. On the other hand, Finland and Czechoslovakia, whose economic growth and political freedom had made them models of the new postwar nations, suffered from divisions almost as grave as those that would drive Spain to civil war. At the same time, Britain and France were beset by fumbling governments that made an embarrassing contrast with the dynamic totalitarian regimes.

### Great Britain

The British political system in the 1930s was able to resist the drift to extremes, but domestic moderation resulted as much from a breakdown in party structures as from political skill. The elections of 1929 had made Ramsay MacDonald prime minister again in a Labour cabinet, but neither Labour nor its Liberal allies could find acceptable remedies for the Depression. A special commission in 1931 recommended drastic economies, as financial experts in the 1930s usually did, but these required cuts in welfare and unemployment payments intolerable to most of Labour. The cabinet itself divided, and then MacDonald announced to his stunned followers the formation of a national government, including members of all three parties. MacDonald and his supporters were expelled from the Labour party, his "treachery" a source of recriminations that nearly destroyed it.

Helped by ineffectual opposition, the national government won overwhelmingly in the subsequent elections; but the coalition had become a disguise for conservative rule. MacDonald nonetheless remained prime minister, weathering riots and a mutiny that greeted reduced budgets and battling the economic crisis with controls on foreign exchange and increased tariffs that split the Liberal party. When MacDonald resigned in

### APPROXIMATE NUMBER OF RADIOS LICENSED FOR EVERY 100 PEOPLE IN 20 SELECTED COUNTRIES (1938)

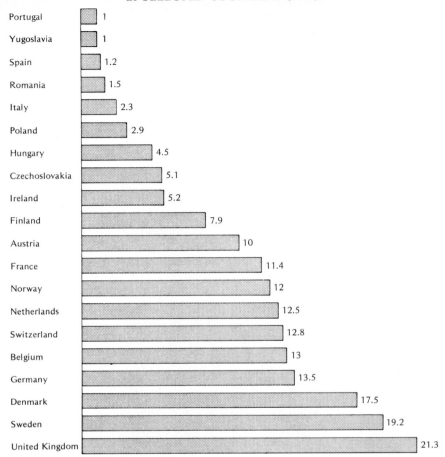

| Country | Radios per 100 people |
| --- | --- |
| Portugal | 1 |
| Yugoslavia | 1 |
| Spain | 1.2 |
| Romania | 1.5 |
| Italy | 2.3 |
| Poland | 2.9 |
| Hungary | 4.5 |
| Czechoslovakia | 5.1 |
| Ireland | 5.2 |
| Finland | 7.9 |
| Austria | 10 |
| France | 11.4 |
| Norway | 12 |
| Netherlands | 12.5 |
| Switzerland | 12.8 |
| Belgium | 13 |
| Germany | 13.5 |
| Denmark | 17.5 |
| Sweden | 19.2 |
| United Kingdom | 21.3 |

**Radio was an important new instrument of communication and propaganda. These statistics suggest that most families in the United Kingdom had a radio, that nearly everyone could sometimes listen to the radio in Finland and Austria, and that from Italy to Portugal, millions of people heard the radio only on special occasions when speakers blared in public places.**

1935, tired and unloved, his government had overseen a slow recovery of the British economy, redefined imperial relations, and initiated some cautious steps toward government planning. It had done so by pursuing others' policies and in the process struck a devastating blow to the proletarian movement to which MacDonald had devoted his life.

MacDonald was followed by the Conservative Stanley Baldwin, who returned for his third prime ministership armored in the complacent virtues of the middle class. His considerable political gifts masked a habit of indecision, but he easily won the elections of 1935 thanks to a divided opposition and to strong statements in favor of the League of Nations, in which he actually had little deep interest. The Parliament elected the same year would continue through 1945, the longest-lived in modern history, and the impressive talent it would prove to contain testified to the continued vitality of British political life.

But the lack of imaginative leadership in the 1930s was remarkable. As international affairs grew more ominous, the uncertainty of British policy further weakened democratic governments in Europe. One issue, however, was resolved with vigor. King Edward VIII, who acceded to the throne in 1936, was determined to marry an American divorcee; and when he abdicated, as Baldwin and the archbishop of Canterbury insisted he must, the transition to George VI went smoothly, an assertion of tradition that averted the crises widely predicted. When Baldwin retired in 1937, his successor was his earnest chancellor of the Exchequer, Neville Chamberlain, who was convinced that from his high office he could preserve peace in Europe.

### France

The Depression hit France later and less severely than other highly industrialized countries, but when the decline came, it lasted. Politically, France faced not so much a single crisis as a myriad of smaller problems that exhausted the older answers and undermined confidence. By the mid-1930s the French seemed more bitterly divided than at any time since the Dreyfus affair.

The left won the legislative elections of 1932 as the economic slump began to be felt, but the socialist members refused to partici-

pate in bourgeois governments. The Radical Socialists (who were really moderate republicans) remained the dominant party and sought allies toward the center and the right. Ironically, the left's electoral victory thus produced unstable governments committed to reducing expenditures and protecting established interests. Outside the chambers, rightist factions, including the fascist Croix de Feu ("Cross of Fire"), grew increasingly noisy. Demonstrations led by their uniformed militants before the Chamber of Deputies building on February 6, 1934, produced more bloodshed than Paris had seen since the Commune; many believe that the Third Republic nearly died that day.

The crisis arose suddenly over the revelation of a gigantic investment swindle perpetrated by one Serge Stavisky, whose scheme, it became clear, had relied on important political connections and a strange reluctance to prosecute him. His suicide encouraged scurrilous charges that became the basis of a campaign against bourgeois government, in which protofascist groups used all the familiar devices, including uniforms, anti-Semitism, demonstrations, and propaganda. To meet the emergency, Gaston Doumergue, a former president of the republic, was recalled from retirement to take the premiership and given full power to govern by decree. The sober old man was supported by every party except the royalists and Marxists, and held office for nine calming months before losing his majority. But when he proposed that presidential power be permanently enlarged, many deputies were indignant. The republic still rejected strong presidents, while its weak governments based on centrist coalitions paled in comparison with the angry, noisy politics of the streets and newspapers.

Working-class movements had long sought increased cooperation among the parties of the left, and when the Comintern dropped its insistence that Communist parties remain independent of all others, that became a possibility. Communists were now encouraged to join antifascist coalitions, and so a Popular Front formed in time for national elections in 1936. Radical Socialists, Socialists, and Communists agreed not to run against each other on the second, or run-off, ballot. Such rare solidarity won them a resounding victory, with the Socialists for the first time gaining more seats than the Radical Socialists and the Communists ending a sizable delegation to the Chamber. France had its first Socialist premier, Léon Blum, a learned, humane intellectual and a Jew— qualities that made conservatives distrust him all the more.

The Popular Front and the political campaign that produced its victory represented in part a great rallying to the Republic and to French radical traditions, but the hopes it aroused were soon dispelled. Even as the new government took office, it was faced with a wave of strikes by workers intent on collecting the fruits of their victory. They occupied factories, which to many of the French smacked of dreaded revolution. With difficulty, the government negotiated an accord, passing legislation that provided for a general 12 percent increase in wages, two-week paid vacations, a 40-hour work week, and compulsory arbitration. Other reforms were soon added, public works were launched; the Bank of France (long the object of the left's suspicion) was restructured to give public representatives a controlling vote; and the arms industry was nationalized. The government increased pensions for veterans and subsidies for small business people and farmers both to stimulate the economy and to win still wider support.

But each of these measures, like the devaluation of the franc, which in 1937 could no longer be avoided, frightened the business classes. New programs proved easier to institute than to finance and the economy more accessible to regulation than stimulation. Blum's government—one of the Third Republic's most admired and most hated— had hardly begun the tax reforms needed to underwrite its plans when, after a year in office, it was defeated in the conservative Senate. The Popular Front itself soon broke up.

Subsequent governments rested on the Radical Socialists and the parties of the center, with Édouard Daladier prime minister from 1938 to 1940. French politics, while sensitive to popular sentiment and capable of innovative progress, could not give sustained direction to a society rent by multiple factions and bitter slander. Meanwhile, France's carefully constructed international position was collapsing.

## The Ideological Struggle

The inability of the established democracies to resolve social tensions or provide convincing political policies and the apparent vitality of the totalitarian nations put old and tested values on the defensive. All of Europe seemed divided in a great ideological battle. Intellectual positions and newspaper articles alike took on apocalyptic tones in which the bland decencies of bourgeois democracy were easily lost. If the strident claims of radicals and fascists dominated the debate, it is all the more important to note that there was at the same time an important revival of the commitment to freedom, expressed by four major groups.

The most prominent was Marxist. The Russian Revolution had enthralled millions of Europeans with visions of economic progress in a backward nation and of social equality and high culture in a mass society. This appeal grew as capitalist economies staggered, and it reached a peak with the Soviet constitution of 1936. At the same time, socialists and even Communists belatedly learned from fascism that all bourgeois governments were not the same. Many of the left renewed their dedication to the principles of liberty while asserting that dictatorship in the Soviet Union was a special case.

In Christian thought, traditional arguments against the idolatry of the state gained new meaning. The Protestant Karl Barth and the Catholic Jacques Maritain built on firm theological orthodoxy—Barth's Pauline, Maritain's Thomist—to stress the importance of individual freedom and social justice. Similar concerns emerged in the writings of Nikolai Berdyaev, Russian Orthodox, and Martin Buber, Jewish.

Many artists and writers in the 1930s espoused themes of social responsibility. Poets and novelists such as W. H. Auden, Thomas Mann, or André Malraux stressed human dignity, social justice, the dangers of power, and the evils of war. Much that was written was narrowly ideological, closer to political tracts than lasting art; but where they were free to do so, most European intellectuals clearly identified with the humane tradition now threatened.

Nor were liberals silent. Most vigorous in the politics and universities of Britain and France, they were heard even in Italy. In his important *History of European Liberalism*, Guido de Ruggiero probed the liberal tradition of England, France, Germany, and Italy, arguing even as he explained the decline of liberal values that—amended yet again—they could offer much to modern people. A decade later Benedetto Croce's historical and philosophical writings highlighted the theme of liberty as the meaning of progress, a brave perspective in 1938.

Liberal economic theory, still dominant in the academic and business worlds, was given a major restatement by John Maynard Keynes, whose *The General Theory of Employ-*

*ment, Interest and Money* appeared in 1936. Keynes rejected the classical view of economic man and the self-regulating economy. Few people, he argued, consistently act in their own financial interest, for no one is free of ideas, values, and tastes that shape actions. Nor do iron economic laws inexorably dictate a pattern of booms and busts. The kind of unemployment facing Britain, which Keynes called simply intolerable, demonstrated that a free economy is not necessarily efficient and may stabilize in unproductive and unacceptable ways. At the same time, he dismissed Marxism as outmoded, a vision from a time already past.

In lucid prose, Keynes presented a sophisticated theory that correct governmental policies can smooth out the economic cycle. When the economy lags, the government should lower the interest rates charged to borrowers, especially businesses, to encourage production, while spending money on public works and social welfare to put more money in circulation and thus stimulate consumption. As the economy expands, the opposite policies should be followed to check inflation and excessive speculation. Thus he formulated the theoretical foundation for practices already partially adopted under Swedish socialism, the French Popular Front, and the American New Deal, President Franklin D. Roosevelt's program of social and economic reform inaugurated in 1933. More important, Keynes made the case for a free economy while rejecting social evils traditional thinkers had accepted. Both socialists and liberals would apply his principles when next they had the chance to direct an economy in peacetime.

Neither malaise nor conflict seemed to inhibit cultural creativity, as the new directions of the 1920s became less shocking a decade later. But two trends characteristic of the 1930s stand out. Science, social science, and the arts, where not restricted by the state, became more international. This was the result in part of better communication and easier mobility. But much of it was also tragically involuntary, as exiles brought the achievements of Russian ballet, Bauhaus architecture, science and scholarship from Russia, Germany, and Italy to Paris, London, and most of all, the United States. And culture generally became more politicized, more ideologically divided. In Paris, the Spanish painter Pablo Picasso became the dominant figure of twentieth-century art, restlessly experimenting with one new style after another. But his most famous work, *Guernica* (see also his *Weeping Woman* of the same year—Plate 63), was a searing comment on war prepared for the Spanish pavilion at the Paris world's fair of 1937. Social scientists, poets, and novelists not only probed the themes of alienation and faceless mass society but also actively organized to do battle in the political conflicts of the period, believing that art and social engineering could change the world. Some defended the "experiments" of Hitler and Mussolini; far more joined Marxist groups to combat the injustices of capitalist society and aid the cause of workers, minorities, or the Spanish republic. Their poetic visions tended to the apocalyptic:

> Financier, leaving your little room
> Where the money is made but not spent,
> You'll need your typist and your boy no
> more;
> The game is up for you and for the
> others. . . .[3]

W. H. Auden, the British poet who chose to live in America, was as confident with socialist anger that the world would have to be remade as was T. S. Eliot, the American poet who chose to live in Britain, in his Christian outrage: "The term 'democracy' . . . does not contain enough positive content to stand alone. . . . If you will not have God (and He is a jealous God) you should pay your respects to Hitler or Stalin."[4]

## International Tensions

In retrospect, the diplomacy of the 1930s was a contest between those seeking radical changes in the international balance, led by Italy and Germany, and those attempting to maintain the postwar international order, led by Britain and France. To contemporaries, however, the lines did not seem so clear. The isolation of two great powers—Russia, effectively ostracized, and the United States, absorbed in domestic affairs—made European diplomacy somewhat unreal, and the divergent policies of Britain and France often obscured their common interest. Hitler played skillfully on a certain bad conscience among the World War I victors about the Versailles treaty, and Western diplomats were ill-prepared for the shrill propaganda and shifting demands of dictatorships. Foreign policy in the democracies was further weakened by reversals in domestic political platforms: The left, previously committed to disarmament and supporting the League of Nations, favored strong measures against fascist aggression, whereas the right, heretofore readier to defend national interest with a show of force, was more inclined to advocate patient compromise with fascist powers.

Even before the advent of Hitler, Wilsonian internationalism had clearly begun to fail. The complicated claims for reparations and war debts had simply been abandoned rather than resolved by negotiation, and interna-

[3] W. H. Auden, "Consider This and In Our Time," in *A Little Treasury of Great Poetry,* Oscar Williams (ed.), Charles Scribner's Sons, 1947, p. 689.

[4] T. S. Eliot, *The Idea of a Christian Society,* Harcourt Brace, 1960.

tional conferences on disarmament had proved no more successful. A Far Eastern clash weakened the League of Nations still further. In 1931 Japanese troops in Manchuria occupied the major cities of the south, and China's protests led a League committee to investigate. Painfully deliberate, it recommended in 1933 that Japan be ordered to withdraw, but Japan withdrew from the League instead. The next year it renounced international limitations on its naval strength, undoing the laboriously wrought understanding of the 1920s. A four-power pact of 1933 signed by Germany, France, Italy, and Britain, reaffirming their Locarno agreements, was so obviously empty as to be wishful thinking. Later in the same year, Germany withdrew from the disarmament conference that had opened in 1932 and from the League of Nations as well.

Efforts to restrain the growing German threat through a more tightly drawn balance of power were only slightly more effective. The Eastern European nations, as frightened of the Soviet Union as of Germany, were disinclined to take unnecessary risks. The Little Entente—an alliance of Czechoslovakia, Yugoslavia, and Rumania, each also allied with France—had established a permanent council to provide fuller diplomatic and military cooperation, and Greece and Turkey were added to this French sphere by the Balkan Pact of 1934. But Hungary and Bulgaria remained outside it, authoritarian states attracted to Italy, impressed by German resurgence, and vulnerable to the economic pressures of German trade.

Austria's Nazis abandoned their attempt at a coup in 1934 when Yugoslav and Italian troops were rushed to the border to prevent the Anschluss, and for a year Italy seemed the key to the European balance of power, a position Mussolini enjoyed immensely. He encouraged the so-called Stresa Front, formed by Italy, France, and Great Britain

after Germany renounced the disarmament clauses of the Versailles treaty in 1935; but the fragility of the tripower alignment showed in their separate moves thereafter. France signed a mutual assistance pact with the Soviet Union, which worried Britain, frightened Poland, and bothered so many of the French that it was never given real strength. Britain reached a naval agreement with Germany, establishing that the German navy, excluding submarines, was not to exceed 35 percent of the British fleet; such dealings with Germany outraged France. And Italy was preparing all the while for an invasion of Ethiopia.

The Western powers had protested and the League of Nations condemned Germany's formal negation of the disarmament clauses, but everyone knew Germany had long since been rebuilding its fighting forces, and so, after all, had everyone else. In 1936 German troops marched into the Rhineland, demilitarized by the Versailles treaty, and this time Italy did nothing. France, unwilling to act alone as it had in 1923, consulted the British, who urged acquiescence. The German troops were widely cheered. Only the year before, France had returned the Saar to German control after a plebiscite had shown an overwhelming preference for German rule. The initiative belonged to the fascist powers.

## The Ethiopian Crisis

In October 1935 Italy began an invasion of Ethiopia, seemingly an old-fashioned imperialistic venture that followed careful understandings with Britain and France. But the style of the operation, marked by enthusiastic bombings of defenseless populations and racist propaganda, signaled something new. Europeans were shocked, and the League, declaring Italy an aggressor, promptly banned the sale of essential war materials to it.

Only a few countries[5] refused to impose these sanctions, but even Germany and the United States, though not members of the League, prohibited increased shipments of restricted items. Most of Europe seemed united in this crucial test of the League's peacekeeping powers. But while the embargoes angered Italy and caused some hardship, they did not stop the war, partly because oil, the most important commodity of all, was not included on the list.

The French foreign minister, Pierre Laval, determined on a hidden course divergent from France's public position. In his successful political career, he had drifted steadily to the right, earning along the way the respectful distrust of all parties. He now sought to keep Italy a useful friend against Germany, and in secret meetings with Sir Samuel Hoare, his British counterpart, he arranged for a settlement of the Ethiopian crisis that would, in effect, give most of the country to Italy. When the plan was leaked to the press, public outrage swamped it and its sponsors; Hoare was dismissed, and Laval soon fell from power. The plan, however, not only delayed a decision on the crucial question of adding oil to the list of sanctions but also undermined confidence in the two democracies. By May 1936 Ethiopia had capitulated, and a few months later Italians celebrated the League's formal lifting of the bans. The League of Nations could no longer be taken seriously as a force for peace.

### The Spanish Civil War

Shortly after the conquest of Ethiopia, a nationalist revolt broke out in Spain led by the military. Both Italy and Germany quickly proffered their support to the insurgents, and

before the end of the year, the two fascist poweres signed an agreement creating the Rome-Berlin Axis, which Germany followed with the Anti-Cominterm Pact between itself and Japan. The Spanish Civil War immediately deepened Europe's international and ideological division into competing camps.

Many times previously, the Spanish army had claimed to represent the national will, but this civil war seemed to one side the defense of democracy against fascist aggression and a battle for social justice against reactionaries, while to the other, the war was a crusade of traditional society and religion against the ravages of anarchists and Communists. Through Europe and America the public was sharply divided; and idealistic young men went to Spain by the thousands to fight as volunteers in national units like the Lincoln or the Garibaldi Brigade (whose greatest moment was the defeat of regular Italian troops sent by Mussolini).

Spain's government had the support of republicans, socialists, Communists, anarchists, labor groups, and Catalan and Basque nationalists organized in a loose coalition and calling themselves Loyalists. They were never fully controlled by the government, and local groups often went far beyond official policy in launching the radical changes the republic had promised. As the war progressed, the Loyalists became increasingly dependent on the Soviet Union for supplies; by 1938 this and the Communists' greater organizational skills made them prominent in a government dangerously divided.

The Nationalists were dominated by the army, which held somewhat aloof from the monarchists, fascistic Falangists, and clericals who flocked to the insurgents' standard. The accidental death of the general who had led the uprising left General Francisco Franco their leader. He had commanded the units stationed in Morocco—the revolt had, in fact, begun there—that were the Nationalists' best

---

[5] They were Austria, Hungary, and Albania. Switzerland was exempt from having to impose sanctions, a recognition of its formal and permanent neutrality.

Photographs helped make the Spanish Civil War a divisive reality for all Western civilization. Robert Capa, who took this shot of a Loyalist soldier carrying a wounded comrade, became famous for his pictures of the war. (Photo: © Robert Capa/Magnum)

troops; and though little interested in doctrines or ideologies, he recognized the utility of a modern mass appeal in building a disciplined movement.

Most of the Spanish navy remained loyal to the republic, and one of the insurgents' first problems was getting their armies from Morocco to the mainland, where many garrisons had risen in their favor. By July, Italian and German planes were providing the needed transport. The help of the fascist powers—Italian troops in significant numbers and military advisers, planes, tanks, and ammunition from both states—remained essential to the strength of Franco's cause. Mussolini welcomed the chance to enhance Italian prestige, and Hitler used the opportunity to test new military technology.

Only the Soviet Union gave reliable if limited aid to the Loyalists—until 1938, when Stalin decided to cut his losses. Blum's government in France favored the Loyalists but feared the domestic and international consequences of openly aiding them; Britain's Conservative government shared France's caution, but with a deeper distaste for the radicals of Madrid and a greater hope for good relations with Italy. The democracies thus chose neutrality and thought thereby to lead Germany and Italy to the same position. An international commission formed to prevent foreign intervention merely upheld the ponderous legalism that starved the republic while helping to hide the active role of the Fascist powers.

# ❄ EXPERIENCES OF DAILY LIFE ❄
## *International Brigades in the Spanish Civil War*

The origins of the Spanish Civil War lay deep in Spanish society and politics, and its tragedies melded with the beauty of Spain to add to its fascination. Yet from the first, foreigners responded to it in ideological and apocalytic terms. Most newspapers in France, Britain, and the United States took sides. The Archbishop of Westminster declared the fight in Spain to be "a furious battle between Christian civilization and the most cruel paganism that has ever darkened the world," and many Catholic publications filled pages with accounts of how priests and nuns had been murdered and Churches burned, concluding that it was a sin not to support the Nationalists. Yet Catholics were not unanimous, and in France they debated heatedly when Jacques Maritain noted that the Basque provinces, among the most pious areas of Spain, were overwhelmingly loyal to the Republic. Most intellectuals probably supported the Loyalists. An English literary magazine's question to famous writers received replies from 5 who favored the Nationalists, more than 100 for the Loyalists, and only 16 who declared themselves neutral. In the United States, Ernest Hemingway, John Dos Passos, and Archibald MacLeish worked together on a propaganda film in behalf of the republican cause.

Ordinary men and women joined in this passionate partisanship, collecting funds, demonstrating (and sometimes fighting) in the streets, holding meetings, and filling lecture halls to cheer indignant speakers. Nor was it just talk. Beginning in the Fall of 1936, a steady stream of foreign volunteers went to Spain to fight for the Republic. Over the next two years about 40,000 men made that extraordinary commitment. They came, in all, from 53 countries—about 10,000 from France and Belgium, some 5000 from Germany and Austria, 3300 from Italy, almost that many from the United States; a thousand or more from Scandinavia, Yugoslavia, Canada, Hungary; sizable contingents from Poland, Greece, Czechoslovakia; smaller ones from Bulgaria, Rumania, Latvia, Ireland, and Mexico. The international brigades were a kind of twentieth-century crusade.

The movement to send volunteers was highly organized, and the principal organizers were Communists. Most of the volunteers were not party members. They came for a variety of reasons, personal and political. Many had marched in so many demonstrations against unemployment, for better wages or welfare, and for peace that it seemed natural to keep right on. Most truly believed that if fascism was not defeated in Spain, it might never be stopped. On instructions from the Comintern, an office was set up in Paris to receive volunteers for Spain, although France, Britain, and the United States continued to insist on neutrality and would not grant visas to young men going off to fight in Spain.

Most of the volunteers came through France, nevertheless, and most arrived illegally, armed only with a code word and a street address, usually of a union office where the men could gather and be interrogated by party members to make sure of their commitment. They might then be sent (with elaborate instructions for avoiding the police, a false passport, and a beret or coat intended to make them look French) to a dingy hotel where they might wait for a week or more, several to a room, until enough men had collected to make an expedition worthwhile. Then by separate routes down back streets they would go to the train station. Warned not to identify each other in any way, they would stare past acquaintances and probable comrades, board the train, and hunch down in a third-class compartment. Throughout the trip, a party supervisor would walk through the train, whispering of the need for caution or naming the town near the border where they should get off. If all went according to plan, a truck would be waiting to take the volunteers to a path over the Pyrenees. It was the most difficult part of the trip; and for hours they would climb, scratching and sliding over boulders, before crossing the border, bloody and bruised. After a few weeks of training, they would be sent into battle.

Training camp and political affairs were more or less run by the party, and sooner or later many a volunteer became disillusioned with party discipline and Communist intolerance. In his brigade the fresh volunteer also felt the tough camaraderie as former factory hands, professors, dock workers, students, miners, and the like, made themselves understood through the confusion of different languages. None who heard it ever forgot the sound of Paul Robeson's deep voice singing spirituals that echoed up and down a Spanish valley. Many of the German volunteers were veterans of World War I who, after having escaped from the Nazis, still marched with precision. Like them, most of the Italians had fought fascists before, in the streets, and were ferocious about doing so again. Most of the French were workers, often party members, hardened by unemployment and prior tangles with bourgeois police. The American contingent included a number of blacks; and one of the commanders of the Washington brigade, Oliver Law, was an African-American.

The brigades played an important part in a number of crucial battles, and their casualties were high (perhaps one-third of them were killed), but they were never numerous enough to counterbalance the foreign armies that fought for the Na-

tionalists. In the fall of 1938 the brigades were disbanded by international agreement. Their chief importance lay in what they had represented. Some of the most famous poets, novelists, and essayists of the era (including André Malraux, Arthur Koestler, and George Orwell) wrote powerful accounts of their experiences. Most of the veterans returned home with some of the doubts and scars that veterans often carry. Those from fascist countries had nowhere to go (they were not welcome in Russia) and so waited in France until interned or allowed to join another military unit. Some, like Josip Broz and Palmero Togliatti, principal organizers of the brigades, remained party militants. The former, as Marshall Tito, would win his next civil war to become dictator of Yugoslavia; the latter would be the skillful postwar leader of the Italian Communist party in competition with socialists also led by a veteran of the Spanish war. The Americans who served in the Abraham Lincoln Brigade would be required in 1955 to register as having belonged to a communist front. ❄

**With the fall of the Spanish republic, a French gendarme leads format members of the International Brigade who have made it to safety across the French border.** (Photo: © Robert Capa/Magnum)

Foreign aid, trained troops, better military organization, and modern weapons made the victory of Franco's forces almost inevitable. They nearly won Madrid and the war itself in the summer of 1936, but the Loyalists held on and in a last-minute counterattack broke the Nationalists' assault. For more than two years, despite poor equipment and internal conflict, the republicans would show occasional spurts of skill and élan.

Franco's troops spread slowly from their capital, Burgos, in the north, and also up from the south against the Loyalist strongholds of Madrid, Valencia, and Barcelona; but to the disgust of his Axis supporters, the general conducted a war of attrition. Not until the spring of 1939, when Soviet supplies had ceased to come and Britain had signed special treaties of friendship with Italy, did the Spanish republic finally fall. Thousands of refugees wearily crossed into France while Franco filled Spain's capacious prisons with potential enemies, undid radical measures, and restored the power of the Church over education. Franco then joined the Anti-Comintern Pact and took Spain out of the League of Nations.

The civil war had cost more than a million Spaniards their lives, many of them at the hands of firing squads and mobs. The bombing of Guernica by German aircraft in 1937 made people shudder before the vision of what war now meant for civilians, and the conflict between the democracies and the Axis was established as fundamental. But the democracies, fearful and divided, accepted defeat while the Axis acted.

### The Anschluss and the Czech Partition

During the course of the Spanish Civil War, attention shifted to the center of Europe. In February 1938, Hitler summoned Austria's chancellor Kurt von Schuschnigg to Berchtesgaden, the Führer's fortified mountain retreat, and after a long, humiliating harangue won his promise to include Austrian Nazis in his cabinet. Feeling braver after he returned home, Schuschnigg called for a plebiscite. He hoped it would rally the people to save Austria's independence, though he could hardly hope for Socialists to forgive the government's suppression of their party; moreover, Italy warned that it would no longer offer military backing. Hitler was furious at Schuschnigg's action, and while Austrian Nazis rioted, Germany massed military units on the border and sent an ultimatum demanding that the plebiscite be postponed and that Schuschnigg resign.

Friendless, the Austrian chancellor had no choice; he was replaced by Artur von Seyss-Inquart, a Nazi, who invited German troops to restore order. They did so on March 13, and within a month Austria's annexation to Germany was almost unanimously approved in a plebiscite run by the Nazis. The dream of Anschluss had been fulfilled (see Map 28.1). Hitler's popularity at home rose still higher, and German influence spread more deeply into the Balkans. The lesson was clear: Germany was Europe's greatest power; alliances with the Little Entente were of small value; and when Hitler moved, Britain and France merely protested.

Two weeks after the plebiscite in Austria, Hitler demanded autonomy for the Sudetenland, an overwhelmingly German-speaking section of Czechoslovakia. The parallel with Austria was lost on no one, though the challenge to the Czech republic was far more daring, for Czechoslovakia was a prosperous industrial state protected by a respectable army, well-fortified frontiers, and mutual-aid treaties with both France and Russia. Supported by its allies, Czechoslovakia mobilized, and Hitler ordered Konrad Henlein, the Sudeten Nazi leader, to quiet down.

Internal divisions as well as geography made Czechoslovakia vulnerable. It was barely able to maintain the loyalty of the Slo-

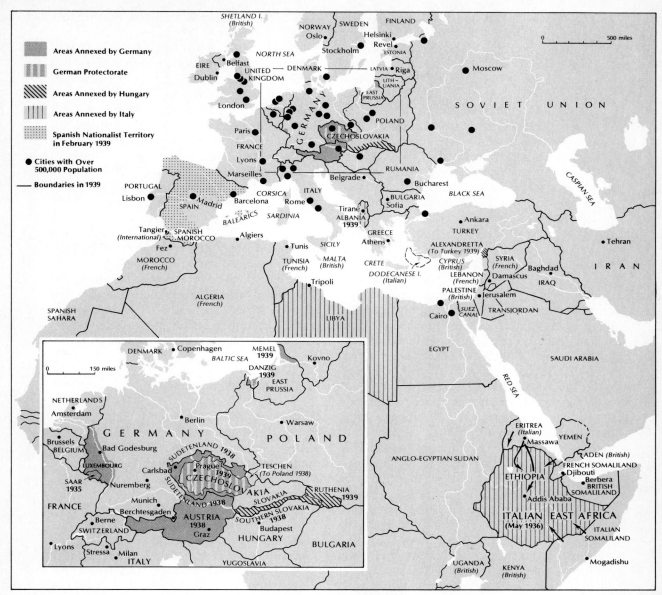

**Areas Annexed by Germany**

**German Protectorate**

**Areas Annexed by Hungary**

**Areas Annexed by Italy**

**Spanish Nationalist Territory in February 1939**

● **Cities with Over 500,000 Population**

— **Boundaries in 1939**

**MAP 28.1 EUROPE 1935–1939**

vaks and had met the threat of a pro-Nazi party—which in the elections held in 1935 had won more votes than any other—only by restricting political parties. Nor were the great powers united in their reactions to Hit-ler. Determined to prevent war, Chamberlain wanted to parlay directly with Germany, be-lieving that no nonnegotiable British interest was at stake in the Sudetenland, and he re-jected suggestions from the United States and the Soviet Union for a meeting to consider means of restraining the Nazi dictator. Many in France and England, deeply alarmed at how close to war they were, wondered whether Czech sovereignty over a German population was worth such a risk.

Throughout the summer, Sudeten Nazi leaders negotiated with the Czech state while demonstrations there and in Germany heated the atmosphere. In August, Chamberlain, with French concurrence, sent his own emissary to mediate while German troops held maneuvers on the Czech border and Hitler pointedly toured Germany's fortifications in the west.

In September the pressure increased. Hitler's speeches became more bellicose, and war seemed imminent. Chamberlain decided, once again with French support, to visit Berchtesgaden. When he met with Hitler there on September 15, the Führer raised the stakes—demanding annexation of the Sudetenland. After a few days Britain and France advised Czechoslovakia to submit. Desperately, the Czechs sought some escape, but only the Soviet Union was ready to support resistance. On September 22 Chamberlain flew back to Germany with the good news that Czechoslovakia had agreed to Hitler's terms only to find them changed again: German troops must occupy the ceded territory immediately, leaving the Czechs no time to provide for citizens who wished to escape Nazi rule or to move factories and military supplies. A shocked Chamberlain said no, and for five days the world listened for war.

Then, persuaded by Mussolini, Hitler agreed to a meeting with Britain, France, and Italy. The brief conference took place on September 29 in Munich, where just 15 years earlier Hitler had failed to capture the town hall. Now he dealt with nations. Hitler, von Ribbentrop, Mussolini, Chamberlain, and Daladier talked for an afternoon and evening; and Hitler was granted all he asked. Neither the Soviet Union nor Czechoslovakia was consulted. The next day Czechoslovakia submitted to the terms of the Munich Pact and to the demands added by Poland and Hungary, for the Teschen region and a piece of Slovakia, respectively. At a single stroke Czechoslovakia surrendered one-third of its population, its best military defenses, and much of its economic strength. Central Europe's strongest democracy was reduced to a German dependency and a keystone of France's Continental security shattered.

In the democracies, however, where people could speak freely, the horrors of World War I remained a vivid memory. And there was plenty of evidence that the next war would be worse, with cities and civilians the target of aerial bombardment. As Daladier's plane circled the Paris airport bringing him back from Munich, he watched the crowd below with dread. But it cheered him, and in Britain, Chamberlain became a hero. Peace, the papers echoed, had been preserved.

## The Path to War

Europe was shaken by the Munich Pact and by the brutality and anti-Semitism goose-stepping troops carried with them into expropriated territory. Inspired by the democracies' ready capitulation, Italy began a noisy campaign to get Nice and Corsica from France.

German might, Hitler's speeches, the news of life in lands annexed or in Germany itself—all gave Jews, non-Aryans, peoples along the German borders, and whole nations reason for terror. To hold such fear in check there stood the sane temptation to believe that even the Nazis, even Hitler, could not want another world war. Then early in 1939, following the now-familiar pattern of agitation, Germany occupied all of Czechoslovakia (except for part of the Carpatho-Ukraine, taken by the Hungarians) and in the same month annexed the seaport of Memel from a terrified Lithuania. The pretext of absorbing only German peoples had now been abandoned. Chamberlain, still ready to risk personal and national honor in the hope of winning Germany to a responsible place in European councils, led those who believed that concessions could appease Hitler. But by this time most of the English and the French had resigned themselves to the necessity of stopping the Nazis with force.

The summer of 1939 brought more alarms. Italy invaded and annexed Albania, and the Italo-German Axis was formally tightened into the "Pact of Steel." Germany kept chancelleries quaking with demands for nonaggression agreements. Late in August the leader of the Nazi party in Danzig declared that his city must be returned to the fatherland. Everyone now knew what to expect; denunciations of the Versailles boundaries and of the persecution of Germans within the Polish corridor—cries that would once have won a sympathetic hearing—clearly meant that Poland was next. As they had all summer, Britain and France renewed their pledges to assist the Poles.

The summer's most important contest, however, was for the allegiance of the Soviet Union, and Hitler won that too: A Russo-German nonaggression pact was suddenly announced at the height of the Polish crisis. Russia had made overtures to Britain and France for some time, suggesting that they join in guaranteeing the territorial integrity of all the states between the Baltic and Black seas. But the Western powers had not been ready to grant the Communist nation so extensive a zone of influence and had responded weakly to Soviet approaches, sending lesser officials rather than their foreign ministers, who had been invited to meetings in Moscow during the summer. Despite Soviet policy—which since 1935 had advocated disarmament, supported the League of Nations (Russia had entered it just as Germany had left), supplied the republican government of Spain, and offered support to Czechoslovakia—Chamberlain, like most Western statesmen, remained more willing to talk with Hitler than with Stalin.

In May 1939, Maxim Litvinov, the eloquent spokesman for this pro-Western policy, had been replaced by Stalin's tougher and less cosmopolitan friend and premier, Vyacheslav Molotov, as minister of foreign affairs. Stalin suspected the democracies would welcome a war between Germany and the Soviet Union, whereas Hitler had offered just what Russia asked: an understanding that if Germany sought any changes in its eastern border, Russia was to have a free hand in Finland, Estonia, Latvia, eastern Poland up to approximately the old Curzon Line, and the Bessarabian portion of Rumania. The Russo-German agreement was a masterpiece of cynical accommodation between the sponsors of antifascist fronts and the authors of the Anti-Comintern Pact and shocked a world still unaccustomed to totalitarian flexibility.

The last days of August resounded with formal warnings and clarifications between the Western powers and Germany, but to no avail. Hitler invaded Poland on September 1, and Britain and France mobilized and sent him an ultimatum, determined in this world conflict to make their intentions clear. On September 3, 1939, they declared war, offering battle to defend an authoritarian Poland just one year after surrendering Czechoslovakia.

# IV. WORLD WAR II: 1939–1941
❈
## Hitler's Quick Victories

Appeasement had failed, not simply because it was a policy of weakness—the appeasers insisted that theirs was a serious effort to resolve differences—but because Hitler wanted war, preferably in the short bursts he was likely to win. It made sense to try diplomacy, compromise, and reason. Even the hardest heads recognized the need to buy time, and appeasement had seemed to accomplish that even though Britain and France did not always use the time well. They commanded great industrial and military power, and they were now regretfully rearming. If the democracies had been slow to build the kind of united and firm front that might have made Hitler hesitate, there were many reasons. They lacked confidence in each other, not only for traditional reasons (old resentments, competing interest, and their own ambitions) but because they knew so much about each other's domestic problems. They looked and sounded weak in part because they were democratic. Where people could speak freely, memories of world war made it harder to prepare for another. Still recovering from the Depression, their own political conflicts had been exacerbated by the contrasting decisiveness of the totalitarian powers. In both countries, Italian and even German fascism held real attraction for many on the right, who admired order, hated Communism more than anything else, and feared that mobilizing against Germany would strengthen the left at home. For the left, too, consistent focus on the fascist threat proved difficult. Socialists and Communists warily watched each other while feeling the magnetic appeal of Soviet accomplishments. To favor rearmament risked sacrificing social goals and some domestic support while cooperating with middle-class parties and the military. Slowly, the requisite consensus was taking shape, but time was running out. For two years the Axis would score one victory after another (see Map 28.2).

The Germans had prepared carefully for the invasion of Poland, and they attacked with overwhelming force. Even so, the speed of their victory was suprising. Poland fell in less than a month under the impact of Europe's first blitzkrieg, and the Soviet Union hastily marched in to claim its share. More nervous than ever about the trustworthiness of its fascist partner, Russia pressed Finland for territory that would move the Soviet frontier a safer distance than the 20 miles from Leningrad where it then lay. The Finns, willing to negotiate, refused to cede all the Russians demanded, and in November, the Red Army marched. Finnish resistance against such odds won worldwide admiration and a brief respite during the winter but could not prevent defeat the following spring. Russia, having regained boundaries close to those the last tsars had enjoyed, could afford to wait.

The Western powers had been waiting too. Hitler suggested that with Poland gone there was no longer reason to fight, but few were tempted by his hints of peace. On the other hand, the British and French commanders were resolved not to risk their precious planes too soon or to launch the pointless assaults of World War I. Since Hitler refrained from attacking along the French border, the Allies followed suit. This was the so-called phony war, during which arms production and mobilization speeded up, the world waited, and little happened. The strain was bad for morale. French Communists now thought the war a mistake and said so loudly, even though their party had been suppressed, but the democracies searched, as they had in the previous war, for more effective leaders. Paul Reynaud, energetic and determined, replaced Daladier as premier. Chamberlain resigned in May after a wide-ranging debate on his whole conduct of the war (Norway had just fallen). Britain's new government included all parties under the firm hand of Winston Churchill, a Conservative who believed in empire and old-fashioned sonorous sentences, a political maverick who had been both a reformer and a defender of national interest through 40 years of political life. An opponent of ap-

**Sequence of German Expansion to 1942**
1. Austria, Czechoslovakia, Poland, 1939
2. 1940, Denmark, Norway
3. 1940, Low Countries, France
4. 1940-1941, Balkans
5. 1942-1943, Russian Front
6. 1942, Vichy

Axis Powers, 1939

Greater Germany, 1942

Areas of Axis Control, 1942

Neutral Countries

Areas Annexed by Russia, 1939-1940

Pre-1939 Political Boundaries

Axis Allies

**MAP 28.2 THE HEIGHT OF AXIS POWER 1942**

peasement now given his chance by disaster, Churchill would prove one of England's greatest leaders.

The war had again become terribly real.

The Allies were beginning to prepare the defense of Norway, an obvious target, when Germany attacked, taking Denmark in a day, April 9, 1940. Norway's most strategically im-

**In Warsaw, German tanks, fresh from their lightning destruction of the Polish army, pass in review before Adolf Hitler on October 5, 1939.** (Photo: Wide World Photos)

portant points were captured in short order, giving Germany a dangerous base for numerous assaults on British ships and cities.

## The Fall of France

On May 10, and without warning, German troops flooded the Netherlands and Belgium. The Dutch, who had expected to escape war—as they had since Napoleon I—surrendered in 5 days; the better-prepared and larger Belgian army held out for 18. On May 14 a skillfully executed German offensive broke through the Ardennes forest, thought to be impervious to panzer tactics, reached Sedan, and drove to the Channel, trapping the Belgian and British forces fighting there and much of the French army. The Luftwaffe controlled the air, and only Hitler's greater interest in taking Paris and the Allies' own fortitude permitted them their proudest achievement in the battle for France: Between May 26 and June 4, most of their 340,000 troops pinned against the sea were evacuated from the port town of Dunkirk and bravely carried across to the British Isles in a motley flotilla of naval vessels, commercial ferries, and private sailboats.

Hitler seemed invincible and the blitzkrieg some terrible new Teutonic force, a totalitarian achievement other societies could not hope to equal. In fact, however, many of the tactical ideas on which it rested were first put forward by British and French experts, including General Charles de Gaulle, an advocate of military mechanization and especially tank warfare; but German officers had the experience of defeat, which makes armies more open to new ideas, and they trained their forces well. The blitzkrieg was the result not so much of new technology as of new strategy. It combined air attacks with rapid movements of motorized columns to overcome the advantages defensive positions had previously enjoyed.

In a blitzkrieg, tanks roared through and behind enemy lines, a maneuver nearly forbidden in older theories and requiring great speed and careful drill. In the flat terrain of Poland, the panzer divisions were able to encircle the enemy; in France they often assaulted troops so far in the rear that the defense was unprepared for battle. The aim was less to capture ground than to break up communications, a task furthered by the air force, which was used to disorient and terrify the retreating army. Even the machine-gunning of French roads clogged with refugees and the bombing of Rotterdam thus had their place in the campaign to demoralize.

Clearly, the German tactics worked. It does not follow, however, that France's military inferiority was so great as its defeat. French commanders were able but a little too rigid and, like their nation perhaps, too in-

**Norwegians silently observe the arrival of German army reinforcements at Oslo station in 1940.** (Photo: Wide World Photos)

clined to think in defensive terms. They preferred larger tanks—not necessarily an unsound attitude—but they lacked the time to deploy them for maximum effect. French strategists were too slow perhaps to recognize the full importance of air power, and their air force was temporarily weakened by being in the midst of changing models. More fundamentally, Britain and France had allowed Germany years of massive arming, but their own planning was incomplete.

Excessive reliance on the Maginot Line, France's system of fortifications extending from the Swiss to the Belgian border, was a fatal temptation in a country of unstable governments, a tax-conscious electorate, and demographic decline that had lost so many men in the offensives of World War I. That supposedly impregnable line, which gave a false sense of security, stopped at the Belgian border. The French had not wanted to wall out Belgium and Holland, whose reassertion of neutrality made joint planning impossible. As a result, too much was staked on Germany's maintaining a similar sensitivity to the rights of neutrals. When Germany invaded the Low Countries in May, the defending armies were poorly coordinated. Defensive strategies lost their meaning when panzer divisions crashed through forests expected to stop them, leaving defenders no time to regroup or restore communications.

And morale in France was not high, though the phony war and the rout of what many thought to be Europe's best army have perhaps made it seem worse than it was. Suspicions of the British, of the army, of the politicians, of the left—like the miscalculations of its officers and the inexperience of its troops—might have faded if the lines had held; they increased with failure.

The Allied defense of France was broken after Dunkirk, and the Germans renewed their attack on June 5. They took Paris in a week. Mussolini attacked France on the tenth, anxious lest he miss the war entirely;

and he had, in fact, but barely demonstrated the inferiority of his forces before France surrendered, on June 16. The armistice was signed in the railway car used for Germany's surrender in 1918. More ironic still, the man who chose to sign for his people was the World War I hero of Verdun and marshal of France, Henri Philippe Pétain.

Pétain, who had replaced Reynaud as premier following the fall of Paris, believed France must now make its way in Hitler's Europe. He accepted terms that put three-fifths of the country under Nazi occupation and allowed French prisoners of war to be kept in Germany. For a moment the nation turned to the octogenarian marshal with stunned unanimity. The unoccupied southeastern part of France was to have its own government. Its headquarters were established the following month at Vichy, where a reconvened parliament maneuvered by Pierre Laval named Pétain chief of state.

The new regime, a confused coalition of militant fascists and the traditional right, was never to be really independent of Germany. After adopting bits of corporatism and some fascist trappings, an often willing collaborator in Hitler's new order, it settled into a lethargy of its own, ruling a truncated state as rife with intrigue, personal ambition, and shifting alliances as the Third Republic it so heartily denounced. New laws and policies aimed at creating a French fascism could not mask the sullenness of defeat nor the threat of further German demands. The abler politicians of the Third Republic drifted away from Vichy, while the few convinced totalitarians preferred the more efficient atmosphere of Nazi-occupied Paris.

### The Battle of Britain

Great Britain stood alone. While German officers—themselves unprepared for such victories on the Continent so soon—planned an invasion, their bombers roared over England in air attacks that many believed would in themselves force Britain to sue for peace. Instead, in September the projected invasion was postponed, and by the following spring the air raids were letting up. Merely to survive from June 1940 to June 1941 was a kind of victory, which Churchill proudly called Britain's "finest hour."

There had been signs that such resilience was possible. During the Norwegian campaign, which had otherwise cost Germany so little, its navy had suffered enough damage in encounters with the British to reduce its effectiveness and make it more cautious. The Dunkirk evacuation had testified to the resourcefulness of the thousands of civilians who lent the military eager assistance. And in the man-to-man air battles, British fighters, particularly their newer designs, proved at least the equal of the German.

Thus the waves of German planes flying over the island kingdom sustained losses far greater than those of the Royal Air Force, losses increased by new techniques of antiaircraft defense, including radar, an English development that was the most critical addition to military technology displayed in these years. German attacks concentrated at first on ports and shipping, then on airfields, and finally on cities, leaving great burning holes in London and destroying Coventry. But the diversity of targets dissipated the economic and military effects of the bombing, and the citizens of London reacted very differently from refugees on a crowded highway to terror from the skies. Britain's morale rose as, ever better organized, it fiercely carried on.

## War in the East

The Battle of Britain was Hitler's first serious check, but Germans could be reassured by fascist victories elsewhere. They did not come easily. Italian forces, launching an offensive into Egypt from Libya in September 1940, were driven back in a successful British counterattack until the British themselves had to withdraw into Egypt because of the Axis challenge in the Balkans. When Italian forces invaded Greece from Albania in October, the Greeks pushed them back, and Hitler had to bail out Mussolini.

The Balkan States were rapidly losing their independence. Russia stretched previous agreements to annex Bessarabia in June 1940, and Germany promised to defend what remained of Rumania (after Hungary and Bulgaria each took a bit). Rumania, Hungary, and Bulgaria, all implicated in Hitler's mapmaking, were closely tied to the Nazi Reich. It was no great step for them to welcome German troops in March 1941 and to join Hitler in attacking Yugoslavia, which had hesitated too long, and Greece, which had fought Mussolini too well.

The attack was launched in April and swept through both countries within the month. Some Greek and British forces pulled back to Crete, only to be forced out almost immediately by history's first large glider and paratroop attack. The Allies retreated to Egypt, which was now seriously endangered by the Axis domination of the Mediterranean. Hitler still appeared invincible in the summer of 1941.

Germany's expansion into the Balkans disturbed the Russians, but a confident Hitler suggested they interest themselves in Iran and India instead. Both sides anticipated conflict, and Stalin assumed the premiership in May as part of the preparation for war. Yet when the Germans attacked the Soviet Union on June 22, 1941, the Russians appeared genuinely surprised—at least by the timing and the size of the attack. The assault, in three broad sectors, was the largest concentration of military power that had ever been assembled.

Once more the blitzkrieg worked its magic, though everyone now understood

| International and Military History | Political History |
|---|---|
| **1924** | **1924** Greek republic founded; death of Lenin, rise of Stalin |
| | **1925** Consolidation of Fascist regime in Italy |
| | **1926** Pilsudski to power in Poland |
| | **1928** Fascist Grand Council established in Italy |
| | **1929** Lateran Treaty, papacy and Italy; Alexander I assumes dictatorial powers in Yugoslavia |
| | **1930** Carol II to throne in Rumania, profascist |
| **1931** Japan invades Manchuria | **1931** Second republic in Spain; MacDonald's national government in Britain |
| **1933** Germany and Japan withdraw from League of Nations | **1933** Hitler chancellor of Germany |
| **1934** Attempted Nazi coup in Austria | **1934** Coup in Bulgaria; Austrian opposition parties abolished; Night of Long Knives in Germany; Stavisky riots in France |
| **1935** Germany denounces disarmament clauses of Versailles treaty; Italy invades Ethiopia | |
| **1936** German troops enter Rhineland<br>**1936–1939** Spanish Civil War | **1936** Soviet constitution; Blum Popular Front government in France; Metaxas dictatorship in Greece; Civil War in Spain |
| **1938** Austria annexed to Germany; Munich Conference | |
| **1939** Italy annexes Albania; Russo–Finnish War; Outbreak of World War II | |
| **1940** Germany takes Norway, Denmark, Netherlands, Belgium; fall of France | **1940** Reynaud prime minister in France; Churchill in Great Britain |
| **1940–1941** Battle of Britain | |
| **1941** Germany invades Yugoslavia; Japan absorbs French Indochina; Germany invades U.S.S.R.; Atlantic Charter; Japan attacks Pearl Harbor | |

*Events in parentheses are discussed in other chapters.

| Social and Economic History | Cultural and Intellectual History |
|---|---|
| **1924** | **1924** Hitler writes *Mein Kampf* |
| **1925–1929** General prosperity | |
| **1926** Strikes effectively prohibited in Italy | |
| **1928** First Five–Year Plan in U.S.S.R.; collectivization of agriculture | |
| (**1929** Onset of Great Depression)* | |
| | **1930** Rosenberg's *The Myth of the Twentieth Century* |
| | **1931** *Quadragesimo Anno* of Pope Pius XI |
| **1933** Collective bargaining abolished in Germany | |
| **1934** Unemployment drops by one-third in Germany | |
| **1935** German Nuremberg laws | |
| **1935–1939** Purge trials in Soviet Union | |
| | **1936** Keynes, *General Theory* |
| | **1937** Picasso's *Guernica* |

how it operated. German armored divisions ripped through Russian lines and encircled astonishing numbers of troops. Quickly they crossed the vast lands Russia had acquired since 1939, taking Riga and Smolensk in July, reaching the Dnieper in August, claiming Kiev and the whole Ukraine in September. Then the pace slowed; but while one German force lay siege to Leningrad in the north, a second hit Sevastopol in the south and moved into the Crimea, and by December still another penetrated to the suburbs of Moscow.

There the German advance stopped temporarily, halted by an early and severe winter, by strained supply lines, and at last by sharp Russian counterattacks. Germany now held territory that had accounted for nearly two-thirds of Russia's production of coal, iron, steel, and aluminum; 40 percent of its grain and hogs. The December snows, however, raised the specter of a continuing two-front war, which Hitler had sworn to avoid. For all its losses of men and territory, the Red Army was intact, and the Germans had little to live on in the wasteland the Russians systematically created as they retreated. The battle for Russia was not over as Hitler's timetable predicted it would be.

### Strains on the Axis

By mid-December 1941, the Axis faced great threats from within the vast lands they ruled, from the Soviet Union, from the British Empire, and from the United States, the world's most powerful nation.

Despite its deep partisanship for France and Britain, the United States remained technically at peace in 1940. With the intention of keeping the country out of European conflicts, Congress had passed the second Neutrality Act in 1937. The law, which had helped withhold armaments from republican Spain, had been amended in 1939 to permit governments to buy war materials from American suppliers if the purchasers paid in cash and carried the goods on their own ships. That, everyone knew, could benefit only one side of the European conflict. In 1940 the American government sold weapons to private corporations for transfer to Great Britain and traded 50 old American destroyers for the lease of British bases in the western Atlantic, thus reducing the areas Britain needed to patrol.

A year later the United States formally accepted the role of "the arsenal of democracy," and began extending loans, first to Britain and then the Soviet Union, to help them pay for desperately needed supplies. In August, Winston Churchill and Franklin Roosevelt met at sea to draft the Atlantic Charter, which looked forward in very Wilsonian terms to a world "after the destruction of the Nazi tyranny" in which there would be collective security and self-determination for all nations so that "all the men of all the lands may live out their lives in freedom from fear and want."

Even so firm an ideological commitment, however, did not bring the United States into the war. Japanese airplanes did that. Tension between the two nations had reached a new high when Japan absorbed French Indochina in 1941. Then on December 7, confident that the Soviet Union was so occupied as to be no threat and that the United States could be rendered nearly harmless in one blow, Japan attacked the Hawaiian port of Pearl Harbor, a key U.S. naval base. The effects of the attack were devastating, and three days later Germany and Italy declared war on the United States. American entry into the war would prove fatal to the Axis, but Hitler had fallen into the habit of underestimating his opponents.

In late 1941 he ruled virtually the entire Continent from the Atlantic to the Ukraine

**American servicemen survey the ruins on an airfield at Pearl Harbor; the United States had entered the war.** (Photo: Navy Department/ National Archives)

in the name of a new order, and he had found sympathizers and allies in every country, from Vidkun Quisling in Norway to Francisco Franco in Spain.[6] But the Nazis alienated those they conquered by their labor conscription, their racial policies, and their oppressive brutality. A high percentage of Ukrainians, for example, had been inclined to welcome liberation from Russian rule, but brief acquaintance with how Nazis treated "inferior" Slavs ended any enthusiasm for

cooperation with the Germans and cost them an invaluable asset.

By the end of 1941, organized resistance movements in most countries were harassing the Nazi order. Mussolini, perhaps the one leader Hitler truly admired, had weakened the Axis with his misjudgments of his own strength. Although no contemporary could yet know it, the Axis had begun to lose the war.

[6] Only Sweden, Spain, Portugal, Switzerland, and Eire remained even technically neutral by grace of geography.

# SUMMARY

The democracy so optimistically extended after World War I fared badly in the following 20 years. Not only did it fail in poor and strife-torn new nations, but in the most advanced, it also fumbled before the social crises of the Depression and mass politics. Totalitarianism offered alternatives that fed on disenchantment with bourgeois culture and liberalism. Its fascist forms appealed to all those who had been the "losers" in the growth of the liberal, secular state, all who had been hurt or alienated by rapid change. The fear of Soviet Communism strengthened the view that the future lay with those who could ruthlessly mobilize masses. Ideologically and in terms of force, fascism challenged the traditional institutions and values of European culture.

Western leaders faced the challenge only slowly. By the time they had abandoned the illusion that they could buy peace, they had lost the initiative (and much of Europe), and uncertain nations faced another world war. Within two years the Axis had conquered the European Continent. Japanese airplanes then brought the United States into World War II as German submarines had done in World War I. In this most global of wars, the Allies once again stood for democracy—a democracy more socially aware and less confident than 30 years before. If Russia was as embarrassing an ally in 1941 as in 1914, the humane traditions of Western civilization clearly rested with the Europeanized societies—Russia, the Americas, and the British Empire—that set out to reconquer Europe.

# RECOMMENDED READING

## Studies

*Allen, William S. *The Nazi Seizure of Power: The Experience of a Single German Town, 1930–1935.* 1965. A much-used microcosmic study.

*Bracher, Karl D. *The German Dictatorship.* Jean Steinberg (tr.). 1970. A major synthesis of work on the origins, structure, and impact of the Nazi movement.

Branson, N., and M. Heinemann. *Britain in the 1930s.* 1971. Ably demonstrates the interrelationship between the social and economic stress of the period and political life.

Broszat, Martin. *The Hitler State.* 1981. An excellent account of the complexity and confusion of Nazi rule.

*Bullock, Alan. *Hitler: A Study in Tyranny.* 1971. The best biography of Hitler and one that gives an effective picture of Nazi society.

Carr, Raymond. *The Civil War in Spain.* 1986. Comprehensive and unusually balanced.

Carsten, F. L. *The Rise of Fascism.* 1967. The careful synthesis of a distinguished scholar.

Colton, Joel C. *Léon Blum: Humanist in Politics.* 1966. Particularly useful for the period of the Popular Front.

*Fitzpatrick, Sheila. (ed.). *The Cultural Revolution in Russia.* 1978. Essays treating varied aspects of the effort to create a new culture.

Gilbert, Martin. *The Second World War: A Complete History.* 1989. Pulls together the latest research.

Kater, Michael H. *The Nazi Party. A Social Profile of Members and Leaders, 1919–1945.* 1984. An impressive analysis of the relevant statistical data.

Kershaw, Ian. *The Nazi Dictatorship: Problems and Perspectives of Interpretation.* 1985. A significant assessment that provides an excellent introduction to a vast literature.

Koonz, Claudia. *Mothers in the Fatherland: Women, the Family, and Nazi Politics.* 1987. Reveals a great deal about the nature of Nazi rule and German society.

Lewin, Mosche. *The Making of the Soviet System: Essays in the Social History of Interwar Russia.* 1985. Shows the complex roots and limitations of the regime in a period of revolutionary change.

*Liddell-Hart, Basil H. *History of the Second World War.* 1980. The crowning work of this renowned strategist and military historian.

Mack Smith, Denis. *Mussolini.* 1981. An informed, skeptical account of the leading English scholar of modern Italy.

*Milward, Alan S. *War, Economy and Society 1939–1945*. 1977. Examines the interdependence of economic planning and military strategy.

*Nettl, J. P. *The Soviet Achievement*. 1967. Effectively tackles the task of assessing both the economic development of the U.S.S.R. and its social cost.

*Nolte, Ernst. *Three Faces of Fascism*. Leila Vennewitz (tr.). A learned effort to trace the intellectual history of fascism in France, Germany, and Italy.

*Nove, Alec. *An Economic History of the USSR*. 1982. A compact survey through the Brezhnev years, which concentrates on the formation of economic policies.

*Schoenbaum, David. *Hitler's Social Revolution: Class and Status in Nazi Germany, 1933–1939*. 1966. An important study of the social policies, in theory and practice, of the Third Reich.

Tannenbaum, Edward R. *The Fascist Experience: Italian Society and Culture, 1922–1945*. 1972. A wide-ranging effort to recapture the meaning in practice of Fascist rule.

*Tucker, Robert C. *Stalin as Revolutionary, 1879–1929: A Study in History and Personality*. 1973. Sensitively explores the shaping of Stalin's character.

Weinberg, Gerhard L. *The Foreign Policy of Hitler's Germany*. 1970. A major study by a leading American diplomatic historian.

*Woolf, S. J. (ed.). *Fascism in Europe*. 1981. An excellent collection of essays on particular countries.

*Wright, Gordon. *The Ordeal of Total War, 1939–1945*. 1968. A thoughtful and stimulating assessment of the psychological, scientific, and economic aspects of the war as well as a balanced account of its course.

* Available in paperback.

# ❊ CHAPTER 29 ❊

# WORLD WAR II
# AND THE SURVIVAL
# OF EUROPE
# 1941–1958

❊ ❊ ❊ ❊ ❊

The continent of Europe had been all but conquered—and by the most barbaric, systematically brutal rulers in all of European history. For 10 years Nazi power had spread in an unending series of successes; terror, looting, rapine, and genocide became not merely incidents of conquest but public policy. The peak of that power came in 1941, in retrospect, the great turning point. With the German invasion of Russia and the Japanese attack on the United States, most of the remaining industrial world was mobilized against the Axis, which controlled great sweeps of territory in Asia as well as Europe. Thus the liberation of Europe began in the depths of Russia, on the sea lanes, and in North Africa, requiring enormous feats of organization and terrible sacrifice. The occupied Continental nations could contribute little more than the old-fashioned heroic work of small, secret bands. In the next three years the people of Europe would suffer far more before World War II came to an end.

❊

The immediate aftermath of the war was a kind of social collapse that reduced political, economic, and social organization to a skeleton. In terms of international power, Europe appeared to have been all but conquered by the Russians and the Americans. Those two giants were themselves, in large part, products of European history. Their conflicts of power and ideology were extensions of the European experience, but now they shaped the conditions of postwar reorganization. The Eastern European countries freed by the Soviet Union could not prevent the Russians from dominating their internal affairs; the Western states, heavily reliant on economic aid from the United States, cautiously fell back on old institutions and parliamentary forms as the basis on which to rebuild. It was not certain that such structures could be adequate to postwar needs.

❊

Yet Europe accomplished a remarkable recovery. Politically, an enforced moderation gave some stability to the rapidly changing world. In the West, prosperity eased the accommodation to altered conditions, and the Eastern states gradually achieved an equilibrium between the relaxation of tyranny and the preservation of dictatorship, between Communist alliances and national autonomy. Uunprecedented increases in productivity, new techniques for directing the economies, and new policies for broadening social welfare suggested that European societies might move in directions distinctly their own. In global terms, however, it was not clear how independent a role European states could play.

## I. THE END OF WORLD WAR II
❆
### The Shifting Balance

At the beginning of 1942, Nazi power was at its height. Germany ruled most of the people and controlled most of the wealth of the Continent (see Map 29.1). Its military power that spring consisted of between 7 and 10 million men in ground forces, a superb air force, and a significant navy, including more than 150 submarines, which in the four summer months would cost the Allies nearly 400 ships. Italy added sizable forces to the Axis that were especially important in Africa. Yet Axis dominance was short-lived.

From the 1930s on, the fascist powers had held the initiative in politics, international relations, and war. The two years of staggering military defeat (1939–1941) that left England alone in Europe followed a long string of political, economic, and diplomatic failures for the liberal democracies. In retrospect, however, it is possible to see that in 1942 the tide was beginning to turn. Britain was becoming stronger; Russia remained a formidable foe, most of its military might still intact. Unless the Allies were driven from the seas, the industrial and military power of the United States would be able to tip the scales. Despite the advantage of shorter lines of communication, Germany had little time to consolidate its vast gains, and the system that took so naturally to ruthless conquest was less well adapted to the mobilization of the enormous resources under its control. The brutal realities of war made propaganda less effective, and Germany was losing the advantage of superior preparation and surprise. The Germans were unaware, of course, that in London the secret codes they believed to be unbreakable had been cracked as early as 1940 by a project code-named Ultra, a triumph of devices that foreshadowed the computer. Confidently, German officials (and especially those of the Luftwaffe) continued to transmit orders and plans that left the Allies increasingly well informed, an advantage that would be more important as the war progressed.[1] Germany was racing against time. To secure its massive victories it had to knock Russia out of the war.

### The Eastern Front

Neither the lengthening siege of Leningrad nor the attack on Moscow had achieved that. In the summer of 1942, the Germans drove farther into southern Russia, taking Sevastopol and depriving the nation of ever more desperately needed grain. But the crucial battle of the Eastern front took place from August to October at Stalingrad (now Volgograd), a major communications center, where a breakthrough would open to Hitler the oilfields of southern Russia.

By September the Germans had penetrated the city, where they battled the Russians at such close quarters that sometimes the enemies fought from within the same building. But the German offensive weakened as supplies dwindled, and Russia's heroic defense had allowed time to amass more troops than the Germans believed available for a counterattack, which broke through and encircled the German army. Hitler frantically ordered his army to stand its ground; and when it surrendered, in February 1943, less than one-third of its 300,000 men were left. The giant Russian pincers pushed on until March, costing the Germans more than half a million casualties. Stalingrad was the turning point of the European war.

---

[1] The secret of Ultra was not revealed until long after the war, and historians are still assessing its impact. The information the Allies gained through Ultra appears to have been especially important in the Battle of Britain, the protection of Atlantic shipping, the war in Egypt, and above all, in the Normandy landing.

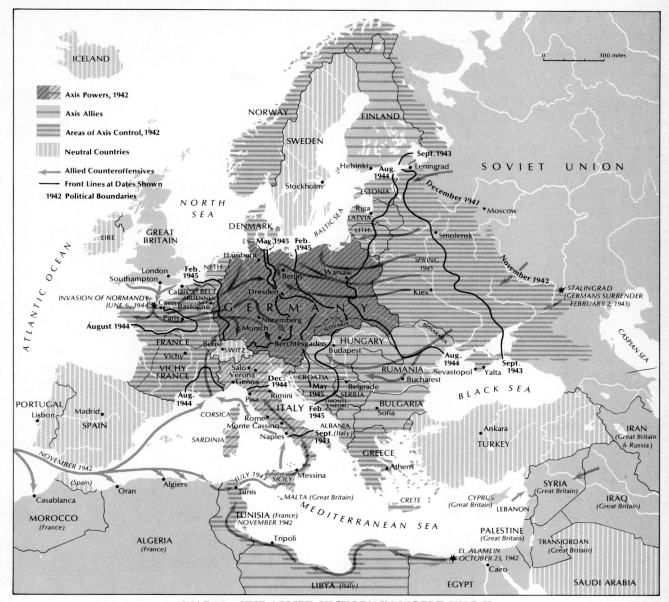

**MAP 29.1 THE ALLIED VICTORY IN WORLD WAR II**

### The War in the West

The dominant Axis position in the West was deteriorating as well. By early 1943 the worst threats from U-boats had been overcome, and the air supremacy Great Britain had won over its own islands extended to the Continent by the time the Germans invaded Russia. Thousands of tons of explosives fell on Germany each month in 1942, and five times as much was dropped in 1943. The Americans favored pinpoint bombing of strategic targets; the British preferred nighttime area bombing, with a city itself as the target. The firebombing of Hamburg in 1943 created a holocaust, but its horror would be exceeded two years later with a yet more massive raid that leveled Dresden, a city of miserable civilians and refugees and without significant industry. Indifference to the suffering of noncombatants had become a common quality of modern war.

For the Allies, the major strategical dispute of the war was becoming critical: how to attack Hitler's "fortress Europe." The Russians repeatedly urged the opening of a second front on the Continent, and most of the American military favored an immediate invasion, whereas the British warned against the dangerously high cost of such an operation. With Roosevelt's support, Churchill prevailed, and it was decided to invade Morocco and Algeria, the lightly defended western regions of North Africa then under the control of Vichy France. Success would end the Axis threat to Egypt and open southern Europe—the "soft underbelly" of the Continent, as Churchill called it—to Allied assault.

### North Africa and Asia

Until 1942 the battle lines in North Africa had ebbed and flowed, as two skilled commanders—Erwin Rommel, the German "desert fox," and the British general, Bernard Mont-gomery—parried each other's thrusts in the deserts between Libya and Egypt. Then in October 1942 the British defeated the German *Afrikakorps* at El Alamein in Egypt, barely 70 miles from the Nile delta. As at Stalingrad, so, too, at El Alamein the Nazi tide reached a high point and then began to recede. In November 1942, in the largest amphibious action yet attempted, British and American forces landed in Morocco and Algeria and attacked the *Afrikakorps* from the west. The campaign was an important test for the still green American troops; it was also a test of Allied strength and coordination, ably directed by an American commander, General Dwight D. Eisenhower. By May 1943 and after heavy losses, the Axis powers had been pushed out of Africa.

In July another mammoth amphibious assault carried Anglo-American forces into Sicily. As they advanced across the island, the Fascist Grand Council voted Mussolini out of office; and in September Allied forces landed in southern Italy. In the year since Stalingrad and the North African invasion, the course of the war had changed. Hitler still controlled most of Europe and much of the heaviest fighting lay ahead, but the eventual outcome no longer seemed in doubt.

Japan meanwhile had made sweeping gains in East Asia and the Pacific (see Map 29.2). Shortly after Pearl Harbor, Roosevelt and Churchill had agreed to give their fight against Germany priority over the war in Asia. The decision acknowledged the bonds of Western culture, the importance of European industrial power, and the danger that Russia might not long survive without massive help. In effect, the policy required the United States to postpone revenge for its defeats in the Pacific. It had lost the Philippine Islands after dramatic and costly defensive stands at Bataan and Corregidor early in 1942. Later in May a naval engagement in the Coral Sea, just north of Australia, ended with

**MAP 29.2 WORLD WAR II IN THE PACIFIC**

no clear-cut victory but reduced the immediate threat of further Japanese gains. In June the Japanese landed in the Aleutian Islands, but American air power drove off their attempt to invade Midway Island. By the end of the year, U.S. forces had taken the first steps in their slow progress back through the Pacific territories.

## The Demands of Total War

In this total war, which required the coordination of entire national economies, long-range planning, and the cooperation of every sector of society, Germany, the state in theory most devoted to militarism, managed in practice less well than its enemies.

## The Allies

The Soviet Union suffered the heaviest losses of any combatant, whether measured in terms of people killed by war and starvation or in terms of the capacity for agricultural and industrial production that was lost. Accustomed to central planning, the Soviets quickly mobilized every resource, subjecting civilians to severe rationing and factory workers to military discipline and to increased hours of labor. Even before 1939 Stalin had adopted the policy of industrializing the more backward and safely distant regions east of the Urals, and in the months before Hitler's attack in 1941 hundreds of factories had been dismantled and moved piece by piece, and some 3500 new industrial enterprises were established there. From this base the Soviet Union was able throughout the war to produce most of the military supplies it needed, aided by the established practice of employing women (who were over half the industrial work force by war's end). The prodigies performed despite hardship and defeats testify to sustained morale. Patriotism of a rather old-fashioned and bourgeois sort became the dominant theme of Soviet public life.

Great Britain responded more slowly; not until the fall of France did the grim meaning of the war make itself felt at home. The bombing of Britain, however, seemed to stiffen civilian morale; and gradually the government developed a capacity to coordinate and command national resources with an efficiency any dictator could have admired. Although the number of workdays lost to strikes increased in the course of the war, so did production; and, as in World War I, the end of unemployment (a million workers remained without work in the first year of the war), better wages, the employment of more women, and higher taxes somewhat narrowed class differences. The United States also mobilized its full economic resources for this war, producing by the end of 1942 more war matériel than all its enemies combined. Ships, planes, arms, and munitions poured from American factories and, with food from American farms, flowed across the oceans to Britain and the Soviet Union. In this war of total economies, where organization was more important than brilliant strategy or even technological discoveries, the Allies were clearly superior.

## Nazi Rule

Until 1943 German civilians experienced few real hardships and nothing comparable to the sacrifices of the Soviets or the lowered standard of living of the British, which allowed those countries to squeeze the maximum war production from their economies. Nor was German output much greater than at the war's outset. This changed when Albert Speer was given increased powers to direct the economy, as he had been demanding. In mid-July 1943 German production was twice what it had been in 1939, despite Allied bombing, and a year later it was three times the prewar level. By then, however, advancing Allied armies were rapidly reducing the resources available to the country.

The delayed and incomplete social and economic mobilization of Nazi Germany stemmed from the very nature of the regime. The illusion, supported by breathtaking successes and official propaganda, that the war would soon be over encouraged interim measures rather than long-range planning. Disdainful of intellectuals and distrustful of established interests, the Nazis failed to achieve the effective cooperation with science and industry that marked the British and American war effort. In their incessant battles for power, the party, the army, and local officials often pursued conflicting or self-defeating policies. Europe's Nazi rulers had an unparalleled opportunity to bend the Continent to their purposes. Yet the much-advertised New Order remained curiously ill defined, while policies of terror and destruction reduced efficiency and undermined even its clearest goal, the exploitation of conquered territory.

Truly totalitarian control in subject lands proved beyond the German reach. Content with ruthless terror and intermittent demonstrations of their power, Nazi administrators tended in most areas to leave day-to-day affairs to established institutions and local officials. Despite the fear they induced, the conquerors never felt secure. Their rule was most severe and most destructive in Eastern Europe. The French, although relatively better treated, suffered severe deprivations after unoccupied France, governed from Vichy, was taken over in November 1942. Food rations provided about half the minimum needed for decent health. Having stockpiled critical supplies and gained access to more through conquest, Germany's most crucial need was for workers. Slave labor was the answer chosen in accordance with Nazi racial theory. The "Aryan" populations of Nordic lands and the "mixed races" of the industrial West were generally better treated and encouraged to maintain production (although a million French, including 220,000 Jews, were taken to Germany). Slavs were rated much lower on the Nazi racial scale, and they were driven from the German borders in "population transfers" that vacated land for German settlers; eventually some 5 million Slavs were shipped like cattle to labor in Germany. By 1944 the 8 million foreign workers in Germany constituted one-fifth of the work force.

But the hysteria of racial hatred dominated rational planning. Brutalized and starved workers could hardly be efficient; transporting and guarding them became an enormous, corrupting, and expensive enterprise. Hounding Jews and Gypsies or cramming Jews into ghettos was not enough; in 1942 a meeting of the regime's high officials adopted, in a phrase the century will never forget, "the final solution of the Jewish question." That solution was extermination. By 1945, nearly 6 million Jews and probably as many others—Poles, Gypsies, and Magyars especially—had died in places like Auschwitz, Buchenwald, and Dachau. These camps were also supposed to be centers of production. A Krupp arms factory, an I. G. Farben chemical plant, and a coal mine were part of

German soldiers prepare to execute a Jew near Lodz, Poland. The doomed man has had to dig his own grave. This was one of many photographs found in German headquarters after the Allies invaded Poland.  (Photo: UPI)

the Auschwitz complex. But its chief product was corpses, at a rate that reached 12,000 a day.

The extermination camps remain the ultimate nightmare of modern history. Beating and torturing prisoners was not new, although the scale was unprecedented; but the industrial organization of death in those Nazi camps raises terrifying questions about modern civilization. Hundreds of thousands of people were involved in operating those camps and in rounding up men, women, and children to be shipped to them. At first, the victims were primarily Slavs and Jews from the conquered lands of Eastern Europe, then Jews from Western Europe were hunted down and added to the flow. They came by trainload, huddled in boxcars, hungry, thirsty, frightened, and confused. Upon arrival, the weakest and least "useful" were sent to "showers" that proved to be gas chambers. The others were given uniforms, often with patches to distinguish in neat categories the common criminals, political prisoners, Communists, Jehovah's Witnesses, Jews, and Slavs from all the others. Many were literally worked to death or killed when they could work no longer. The prisoners themselves, reduced to blind survival, were caught up in this corrupt world of beatings, limited rations, constant abuse, and contempt, in which gestures of cooperation or shrewd selfishness might gain another day of life. German clerks and bureaucrats kept elaborate records of names, stolen possessions, and bodies disposed of. Corpses were efficiently stripped of gold fillings and useful hair before being turned to ashes that could be used as fertilizer. Doctors invented new tortures under the guise of medical experiments to benefit the Aryan race. Yet even the SS guards—let alone camp commandants, those who scheduled the trains, or business people who bid for contracts giving detailed specifications for gas ovens—used euphemisms rather than acknowledge what was really happening, perhaps the sign of some residual conscience. Similarly, people in nearby towns rarely discussed what was carried in the trains rumbling by or asked about the odor that settled over the countryside from crematoria smokestacks. Nor did the Allies quite believe or choose to act on the stories that filtered out of Germany about atrocities on a scale too terrible to comprehend.

### Resistance Movements

For contemporaries who did not know the full extent of Nazi policies, there was nevertheless plenty in public practice to stimulate opposition to Nazi rule; that opposition gradually and against great odds evolved some organization, its every act a declaration of heroic confidence that the Nazis must someday fail. Small cells of resisters formed loose networks that spread through each nation and assumed an importance far beyond their power or steadily growing numbers. Always based on a small minority, the partisan movements achieved particular strength in Denmark and Norway, the Netherlands, France, and Yugoslavia. A number of them received material help and direction from their formal or unofficial governments in exile operating from London, which also commanded whatever fighting men had been able to escape the occupied homelands, the most notable of which was the Free French national committee, headed by General Charles de Gaulle.

Millions of Europeans came to rely on the BBC for encouragement and reliable news, for the Germans were losing the propaganda war as well. Some of the most active resistance fighters were simply individual members of neighborhood groups, but most were attached to parties with developed ideologies describing a better postwar world. The resistance movements thus revived faith in democracy and social justice even as they echoed prewar politics; in France, for example, moderates, Christian Democrats, Socialists, and Communists each had their organization. Generally, the Christian Democrats and especially the Marxists developed the largest and most effective groups, thus laying the basis for powerful postwar parties.

The Nazis levied the harshest of reprisals for acts of resistance. When Czechs assassinated the new "Reich protector of Bohemia and Moravia" in June 1942, the Germans retaliated by wiping out the village of Lidice, which they suspected of hiding the murderers—every man was killed, every woman and child deported; and on a single day in 1943, the Germans put 1400 men to death in a Greek village.

Yet the underground movements continued to grow, and their maneuvers became a barometer of the course of the war. In France, partisan activities expanded from single exploits—smuggling Allied airmen out of the country, dynamiting a bridge, or attacking individual German officers—to large-scale operations closely coordinated from London. Norway's resistance helped force the Germans to keep 300,000 troops there and away from the more active fronts. In Yugoslavia, the partisans, divided between two political groups, maintained an active guerrilla war; and the British decision to support the group led by Tito as the more effective all but assured his control of the country at the end of the war. After the Allied invasion of Italy, partisan groups there maintained an unnerving harassment of Fascist and Nazi forces. Even in Germany itself some members of the army and the old aristocracy began to plot against Hitler, and in July 1944 a group of conspirators planted a bomb under the table at which the Führer stood to conduct a conference with his staff. Hitler escaped serious injury, but the sense of his doom had spread to the heart of Germany.

## The Politics of Coalition

Almost until the end, however, Hitler remained firmly in command, and Nazi strategy was wholly committed to holding off Germany's enemies. Mussolini, a victim of his own propaganda who had consistently overestimated Italian strength and yet was reluctant to demand that Italians make the sacrifices of total war, had little influence on German plans. With his fall, the Italian Peninsula, too, came under the direct control of the German army. There was no such unanimity among the Allies. Although the nature of Nazism and its fearful power provided one

simple common purpose, the Allies said less about their long-range goals than they had in World War I. And their mutual distrust complicated the conduct of the war itself.

## War Aims

When Anglo-American successes in North Africa were not followed by invasion of the Continent, the Russians suspected that they and the Germans were being left to annihilate each other. The Americans continued to favor a direct attack on the mainland, but the British still argued in terms of tightening the blockade in the west and of encircling Germany by means of more limited assaults from the eastern Mediterranean. Churchill, it became clear, would like to have his troops so placed as to give the Western powers a voice in the disposition of Eastern Europe.

Stalin insisted that the Soviet Union should regain the Polish territory taken in 1939; Poland could be compensated to the west at the expense of a defeated Germany. The British rightly warned that the Americans would find this unacceptable; and, in fact, the Anglo-American powers never forgot that Communists had encouraged revolution from Moscow to the Rhine after World War I or that Russian imperialists had sought to expand into Eastern Europe since the eighteenth century. In London the exiled leaders of the Eastern European countries agitated for their various nationalist aims while Stalin's ominous references to the need for "friendly" governments along Russia's borders made everyone shudder.

With such issues before them, Roosevelt and Churchill met at Casablanca in January 1943. There they agreed to invade Sicily (to the Russians' disgust) and to demand the unconditional surrender of Italy and Germany, an expression of moral outrage against fascism that has been heavily criticized since for strengthening the Axis powers' determination to resist. Its main purpose, however, may well have been to reassure the suspicious Allies that none would seek a self-serving, separate peace.

## Sponsored Regimes

Leaders of the powerless governments in exile viewed what they could learn about the meeting with some misgivings, for in practice, the Anglo-Americans were not above dealing with regimes that bore a fascist taint. At the time of the North African invasion, for example, Admiral Jean François Darlan, a former vice premier of Vichy and then commander of its armed forces, had happened to be in Algiers. Eisenhower's staff had quickly negotiated an agreement with him so that his forces would not resist the invasion, in return for which Darlan had been named governorgeneral of French Africa. De Gaulle was outraged. Since his call for continued resistance in 1940 and his organization from London of the French forces fighting with the Allies, the general had pressed his claim to represent the voice of France. His hauteur, his persistent demand for a French part in Allied policy, and his considerable success in winning support in French colonies had made his relations with Britain and the United States cool at best. Darlan's assassination in December 1942 reduced tension a bit, although both the British and Americans continued to deal with Vichy and the authorities in French North Africa even after the Germans occupied all of France.

The issue of what governments to foster soon extended to Italy. In July 1943, two weeks after the landing in Sicily, Italy's Fascist Grand Council met in a hasty session, voted Mussolini out of office, and had him arrested, naming Marshal Pietro Badoglio prime minister. A new coalition of monarchists and more moderate Fascists then sought an armistice. The Committees of National Liberation, composed of anti-Fascists from liberals through Communists, were now prominent throughout Italy, however, and they wanted nothing to do with the marshal, a Fascist hero who had led the campaign in Ethiopia, or with the king, who had bowed to Mussolini for 20 years.

Again the Allies were divided. Britain favored the monarchy and feared leftist influence in the Committees of Liberation; the Americans leaned toward the committees but shared the British concern about Communist influence and so joined in excluding the Russians from active participation in the Allied military government installed in Italy. Stalin accepted this, recognized the new Italian regime, and encouraged Italy's Communists to pursue a policy more flexible and accommodating than even the Socialists could swallow. But arguments about spheres of influence and the need for military control that were used against the Russians in Italy would soon be used by them elsewhere.

All this bargaining had occurred without an actual encounter among the Big Three. Finally, in December 1943, Roosevelt, Churchill, and Stalin met for the first time, at Teheran. Whereas the British had earlier served as mediators between the United States and the Soviet Union, it was the Americans who now appeared closer to a middle position. The conversations were not easy, but they provided a basis for continued cooperation. Churchill proposed an invasion of the Dardanelles, but this move was rejected and an invasion of France agreed to for the following year. There was tentative understanding that Russia would accept a boundary with Poland nearly the same as that proposed in 1919, and the nature of the postwar Polish government was left open. Stalin also promised to declare war on Japan as soon as Germany surrendered. The Big Three maintained their unity largely by postponing action on difficult and divisive issues; but that

Stalin, Roosevelt, and Churchill, meeting for the first time at Teheran, reached an understanding that laid the groundwork for Allied cooperation in pursuing the war.   (Photo: UPI)

at least assured the continued, vigorous prosecution of the war.

## The Road to Victory

By late September 1943 the Allies were well entrenched in Italy and rapidly amassing still greater power. Germany could not hope to win but might prevent cataclysmic defeat by taking advantage of its shortening lines of communication and defensive strength. Meanwhile, the Allied air assault subjected Germany to constant pounding, and the war in Russia was exhausting the German capacity to fight.

## The Italian and Eastern Fronts

Although the Allies captured Naples in October, their campaign in Italy was bogged down in difficult terrain where an insufficient number of troops faced fierce German resistance, while the Allies' main forces were assigned to the forthcoming invasion of France. It took the Allies five months to fight their way past a costly new beachhead at Anzio; not until May 1944 did they finally seize the old Benedictine abbey of Monte Cassino, less than 75 miles inland, and then only after a destructive bombardment. Rome, the first European capital to be liberated, fell in June.

Mussolini, who had been rescued from prison the previous September in a daring maneuver by German troops, had proclaimed a Fascist republic in the north and was now frankly a German puppet. For Italians, with their country a battleground for foreign armies, the war also became a civil war against Fascism. In December 1943, King Victor Emmanuel III announced his intention to abdicate in favor of his son (though he did not actually do so until 1946), and Badoglio gave way to a cabinet drawn from members of the Committees of National Liberation. The new government joined the Allied cause, and the slow push northward was aided by partisan risings against Nazi occupation. German resistance now converged on the so-called Gothic Line, running from Pisa to Rimini. Not until this line was pierced, in September 1944, could further drives lead to the capture of Ravenna (in December), Bologna, Verona, and Genoa (in April 1945). At that point German resistance ceased.

Russia's successes were more spectacular. In the spring of 1943, the Germans still had vitality enough to launch an offensive of their own, but it slowed within weeks. In July the Russian army began a relentless advance that continued with few setbacks for almost two years. Its armies now outnumbered the Germans, and it enjoyed a growing edge in matériel as well. Soviet forces reached the Dnieper and Kiev by November. In February 1944 they were at the Polish border; they retook the Crimea in the spring; in August Rumania surrendered; Finland and Bulgaria fell a few weeks later. When the Allied leaders met next, at Yalta in February 1945, Russian troops held part of Czechoslovakia and stood on the German frontier of Poland.

### The Western Front

The opening of the final act of the war in Europe was the Allied invasion of France across the English Channel. The Germans knew that such an attack must come, but they believed that it would concentrate on the area around Calais, the shore closest to England. The Allies encouraged this belief through various feints and then actually landed in Normandy to the west of Caen on June 6, 1944. The operation was enormous: it called for putting 150,000 men ashore within two days, supported by 5000 ships and 1500 tanks. But the Anglo-Americans were now expert in amphibious assaults, they held overwhelming control of the air, and the Germans failed to coordinate their defenses.

In a complex series of costly landings, Eisenhower's Allied force poured onto the French beaches, the first of more than a million men to disembark within a few months. In July they broke through the German defense and began a series of rapid drives through France. A second amphibious attack, in southern France in mid-August, led to swift advances inland greatly aided by well-organized French resistance groups. On August 24 the Parisian underground rose against the Germans, and French forces under Charles de Gaulle quickly entered the cheering city. Brussels fell a week later, and 10 days after that, American troops crossed the German frontier.

Hitler's desperate replies to the Allied blows included the launching in June of a new "miracle" weapon, the relatively ineffective V-1 pilotless plane, followed in September by the far more dangerous V-2 rocket. Had the Nazis earlier recognized the potential of this new weapon and pushed its development, its effects might have been devastating. The V-2 flew faster than the speed of sound and was almost impossible to intercept; but these rockets were hard to aim, too few, and used too late to be decisive. More threatening was a counterstroke in December through the Ardennes on either side of Bastogne that rocked the Allied line back. The Battle of the Bulge, which cost about 70,000 men on each side before the Allies

**Charles de Gaulle, the symbol of French resistance, greeted by Parisians on the day of the city's liberation in 1944.** (Photo: © Robert Capa/Magnum)

regained the initiative in January, was the last offensive the Germans would mount.

## Competing Allies

As Allied troops drove farther into the Continent, the Big Three met again, this time at Yalta, for their last wartime conference; and the decisions they made that February, though widely hailed at the time, have become the most controversial of World War II. The hurried meeting dealt with four broad issues:

1. The creation of a United Nations Organization. The U.S.S.R.'s request for 16 votes to counterbalance the votes of the British Commonwealth and of U.S.-dominated Latin America was reduced to 3, and the veto it also demanded was restricted slightly.

2. Russian entry into the war against Japan. Russia agreed to declare war against Japan within 90 days after the defeat of Germany; it was to receive in compensation the territories it had surrendered to Japan in 1905 and was guaranteed a sphere of influence in Manchuria. The agreement clearly strengthened Russia's position in Asia.

3. The treatment of Germany. The assignment of zones of occupation to each of the Big Three presented little problem, and Russia reluctantly accepted the proposal that France also be given a zone to occupy.

But the reparations and "labor services" the Russians demanded were enormous, and the agreements on specific terms had to be postponed.

4. The establishment of new governments in the liberated nations. This, the most difficult issue of all, could not be postponed much longer; and yet every effort at accord merely exposed the distrust between the Soviet Union and the Western powers.

By this time, the form of Italy's government had been largely set, and de Gaulle was reasserting the independence of France; but the degree of Soviet dominance in Eastern Europe was an open question. There were indications that Soviet leaders might show restraint. In most of the Eastern nations they occupied, the Russians were tolerating all the old antifascist parties and seemed to support fairly broad coalitions, but Soviet officials rejected participation by the Western powers in the affairs of the new governments and restricted Allied observers. Four months earlier, when Churchill visited Moscow, he boldly proposed that Russia should have overwhelming predominance in Rumania and the largest influence in Bulgaria, that the British be given a free hand in Greece, and that Russia and Britain have an equal interest in Yugoslavia and Hungary. And Stalin, in fact, did nothing when Churchill strongly intervened in the civil war raging in Greece, routing the leftists.

Such crude understandings, however, offered little protection against the cold self-interest Russia had shown on other occasions. As Soviet troops had approached Warsaw in August 1944, the Polish underground arose against the Germans. But these partisans were closely tied to the anti-Communist Polish government in London, and the Russians had simply halted their advance until the Germans wiped out the Polish resistance fighters.

At Yalta no real agreement could be found about the borders of Poland or the independence of its government. The general formula adopted, with its references to democratic governments and assurances of free elections for all liberated nations, would prove subject to many interpretations. An adamant Stalin, a pugnacious Churchill, and a weary and ill Roosevelt turned back to the wars they still faced in Germany and against Japan.

## The End of the War

As the Allies pushed into Germany from all sides, it became clear that Berlin would be the final battle. Eisenhower feared that Hitler intended to make a last desperate stand in his famed mountain redoubt at Berchtesgaden in the south German mountains (in fact, German resistance was everywhere collapsing); he therefore halted the eastward advance of American and British armies at the Elbe River in preparation for the battle in the south, which was never joined. The Russians took Berlin. Hitler had characteristically ordered the German garrison to defend the capital to the death, which assured the maximum destruction of the city. Hitler himself committed suicide on April 30, 1945; his aides burned the body, and the remains have never been found. Four days later a group of German officers signed the final, unconditional surrender. The war in Europe was over.

But in Asia the world conflict continued. Despite massive bombing and repeated naval victories, progress toward Japan had been agonizingly slow the past three years. Hundreds of islands in the Pacific and thousands of miles of jungle had to be laboriously reconquered in the face of fierce resistance.

As the American forces, commanded by Douglas MacArthur, closed in on Japan, they unleashed an air bombardment of unprecedented intensity. During the three months after Germany's surrender, the raids obliter-

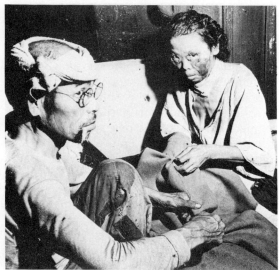

**Hiroshima: The Japanese were victims of one of science's great achievements and the beginning of the atomic age. They suffered both human and environmental destruction.** (Photo: Wide World Photos; UPI)

ated Japan's navy, industrial plants, and large parts of its cities—nearly 200,000 people were killed in Tokyo in just one week. But still the Japanese would not surrender.

On August 6 the new president of the United States, Harry Truman (Roosevelt had died in April), authorized the use of a new weapon, developed after years of secret research, the atomic bomb. In one blow, half of the city of Hiroshima was wiped off the face of the earth and a quarter of its 320,000 inhabitants killed. Two days later the Soviet Union declared war on Japan, and on August 9 the Americans dropped an even more powerful atomic bomb on the city of Nagasaki.

Faced by total annihilation, the Japanese surrendered unconditionally on September 2. Remarkable accomplishments in science and technology, sustained by great wealth and reinforced by scores of European scientists driven to sanctuary in the United States, had permitted a great democracy to end World War II by unleashing a new order of terror upon humanity. Later, some would question the decision to use so terrible an instrument; but even in the jubilation of victory, leaders busily reordering a shattered world had to recognize that another war could mean the end of civilization.

## II. THE CIRCUMSTANCES OF PEACE
❊
### The Europe that Survived

Wartime conditions did not disappear for years. It took the better part of a decade for the millions of refugees and displaced persons to find settled lives; the rationing of food and clothes continued in many countries into the 1950s; some of the most severely bombed cities, such as London and Dresden, were still engaged in reconstruction in the 1960s. Moreover, troops from the two world pow-

ers, the United States and Russia, swarmed over the Continent, symbols as well as instruments of a new era of foreign domination.

### The Devastation

In contrast to World War I, a majority of the fatalities in World War II were civilians, killed by bombs, conquerors, or concentration camp officials. Russia alone lost about 20 million people, and the Germans murdered more than 12 million in concentration camps, half of them Jews who had never seen combat. Elsewhere the casualties were not on this scale—perhaps 5 million Western Europeans and a similar number in all other theaters of war (the number of noncombatants who died in China is unknown). For every person killed, two were either wounded or taken captive. But civilian deaths are harder to categorize than those of soldiers, and often there was no one who could or cared to do the counting. So the total casualties of World War II—dead, wounded, or crippled by inhumane treatment—remain an estimate, a number hard to comprehend: some 55 million people.

The physical destruction was likewise unprecedented. In 1945 Europe's industrial capability, crippled by the obliteration of factories, communications facilities, and large segments of cities, was perhaps half of what it had been in 1939. In France alone, some 2 million buildings needed reconstruction, and only one-tenth of the country's vehicles were usable. Less than half of such major cities as Frankfurt, Dresden, Brest, and Toulon were still standing. The Continent's most important ports, bridges, and rail lines had been destroyed by Allied bombs. Ironically, Germany's industry was in better shape than any other on the Continent west of Russia, its fixed assets higher in 1945 than in 1939 despite Allied bombing.

Agriculture was also hard hit: France's

cattle population had been reduced by half, and large areas of farmland in France, Italy, and Germany could not be cultivated. The need for food was so urgent during the first months of peace that supplies were sometimes dropped by parachute to speed distribution; in the winter of 1945–1946, starvation stalked the Continent, and in some places, such as Vienna, thousands died—many of them children—before sufficient food arrived. Disease was also an ever-present danger, although a newly developed drug, penicillin, did help limit the epidemics that erupted as a result of inadequate sanitation and medical facilities.

Some experts estimated that it would take 20 years for the Continent to regain its prewar prosperity. The very necessities of life were in desperately short supply, and Europeans had few means of producing goods themselves. Often only an illicit black market made essential supplies available to the few who could affort them. Impoverished and ravaged nations thus looked to the United States and the Soviet Union for relief.

### The Disruption

Normally, the killing and destruction of war leaves great holes in societies that themselves remain intact—families survive despite missing members, local institutions remain despite major changes. World War II brought with it not only more deaths than any previous war but especially in Eastern Europe, unprecedented disruption of social ties. Nazi rule evicted 100,000 French from Alsace-Lorraine and 1,500,000 Poles from "German" areas, and forced 8 million foreigners to work in Germany by war's end. In the Balkans and Hungary hundreds of thousands of people were expelled or fled under the Germans. On a similar scale, Stalin had driven Germans from occupied Poland in 1939, a large proportion of whom returned when the Germans took Poland, only to flee again when

Russia recaptured the country. Untold numbers of German and Polish civilians and of German POWs were interned or murdered by Soviet armies. The millions of refugees who fled bombings and conquering armies toward the end of the war were added to those already displayed. The ethnic conflicts and the problems of "minorities" that had plagued Eastern Europe after World War I culminated, by the end of World War II, in the greatest dislocation of populations in European history. In 1945, some 12 million Europeans were officially recognized as displaced persons, separated from home, kin, and possessions and facing disease and starvation before they could know how or where to reconstruct their lives.

Millions more, not officially called displaced, found themselves without property or employment in societies that were barely functioning. Whether the Germans had ruled directly or through local authorities, their reign had brought extensive purges and fundamental changes in social and political institutions. When those rulers diappeared (often followed by more purges and massacres), a vacuum was left, to be filled by armies of occupation—the Soviet army in Eastern Europe, the other Allied armies in Germany and Italy. Military rule, a reminder of war, was thus a peacetime necessity while political groups and social institutions vied for a role in shaping a new society.

### The Settlement

Unlike the treaties prepared at the Paris Peace Conference after World War I, the settlements of 1945 were limited, relatively informal and indeterminate arrangements. Although the leaders of the Soviet Union, Britain, and the United States met at Potsdam for two weeks in July 1945, they hardly hammered out broad new policies. Indeed, they barely knew one another, for of the Big

# ❄ EXPERIENCES OF DAILY LIFE ❄
## *Refugees*

Refugees are a symptom of society in disarray, and in the middle of the twentieth century there were more of them than ever before in European history. Refugees moved along roads in an anonymous flood; they were herded by train; they escaped from camps and were gathered in camps again. Whatever the political change that pushed them forward, whatever their personal histories, refugees throughout Europe had in common their vulnerability and desperation. Usually they carried with them all the possessions to which they could still lay claim, the more fortunate in a cart, others in an old suitcase or two or in still smaller bundles. Often they could not speak the language of the lands through which they passed. Bit by bit they lost touch with some of the people who had started out with them, as neighbors, friends, or relatives were shunted in other directions. Many—especially, of course, the elderly and the very young—died from disease or malnutrition and many others from bullets or accidents. Always there were soldiers and police to fear on the journey toward soldiers in other uniforms and different police who might protect them. Refugees learned to watch out for thieves and for the chance to buy, beg, or steal a little food; they learned to trust no one and to depend on total strangers. Survival became the single goal, but one could never know when that had been won.

There had been homeless Europeans before in modern history: the migrants of the nineteenth century, civilians escaping from the armies of World War I, Greeks and Turks whose only plebiscite on nationality was to move away, exiles from the new nations in Eastern Europe and in the next 15 years from the new regimes in Russia, Italy, Spain, and Germany. Nevertheless, the phenomenon took on new dimensions during World War II and its aftermath. The last year of the war was by far the most destructive of property, and millions of homes were destroyed by air raids and massed armies. At war's end there were millions of civilians, especially women and children, without shelter. Germans seeking refuge in Denmark constituted 4 percent of that nation's population. There were 8 million slave laborers in the Third Reich and millions from all over Europe in concentration camps who with liberation were put on trains headed for where their homes had been. They arrived (in Paris, for example) hollow-eyed and dazed, the stench of dirt and disease still upon them. There were German prisoners of war in West and East and Allied prisoners, including more than 7 million Soviet citizens, in Germany. Many of these latter were defectors, many dreaded a forced return to their homeland and summary justice. Perhaps 60 million European civilians had been forced to move by World War II.

The end of the war did not stem the flow. Turmoil in the Balkans pushed millions to seek refuge in Greece or Italy and Austria. Rumanians drove out Hungarians; Czechs drove out Hungarians and Germans (especially from the Sudetenland, whose Aryan claims had once so concerned Hitler). The more than 2 million Poles and Czechs who returned from prison and forced labor in the Soviet Union joined the millions of Ukrainians and Poles who moved west to stay on the other side of a shifting border from Russia. The boundary between Poland and Germany was, in turn, moved to the west, and millions of Germans were forced to leave what was now Poland, including those transplanted to the region just a few years before as part of the Nazi program for Germanization. Other Germans were driven by force or terror or the reputation of the Soviet army from places where their grandparents had been born. The question of where national boundaries should be drawn, which had so troubled the peacemakers of Versailles, was settled now by first drawing the lines and then pushing inconvenient nationalities across it.

Mixing in with all these victims of the past were "unaccompanied children," common criminals, ex-Nazis, and deserters. Against this crush, soldiers of the conquering armies attempted to maintain some order, establishing nice distinctions between refugees (homeless people in or near their own nation) and displaced persons, between the stateless and citizens of particular states, and between war criminals or collaborators and all others. Although now in short supply, Jews who rejected any other nationality and wanted to go to Palestine posed a special problem. We will never know how many people moved from one place to another at the end of the war (perhaps another 20 million); refugees tried not to leave records and

learned to change their identity to avoid prejudices at each checkpoint. We will never know how many of these people were abused or murdered, although we can be sure the proportion of women was high because so many men had been conscripted and killed already.

Armies and governments tried to deal with these homeless people as best they could, and those who had not snatched a place to settle soon found themselves in camps. Abandoned factories and warehouses, even former concentration camps were used to house the homeless. When facilities were specially built, they were crude barracks, usually without plumbing or electricity, for they were meant to be temporary. Bit by bit the fortunate were assigned a destination, and then they experienced new doubts and fears as they left for places they did not know, carrying with them few reserves of strength and none of wealth. Those left behind included especially the disabled and the aged. Some refused emigration rather than leave a relative behind. By 1960 there were still 32,000 refugees in 107 camps in Europe, sharing tiny quarters and communal toilets. Some had lived in such places for 15 years; there were children who had grown up there, speaking the polyglot language mixed nationalities had invented. Some were married and gave birth to their children in the camps.

The miracle is that so many millions did survive to tell their stories and to start their lives anew despite visible and invisible scars that did not seem likely to heal. Thanks to penicillin and DDT, there were not the devastating epidemics that would have occurred in any other era. Thanks to something deep in human nature, the concepts of family and loyalty and normal life still appeared to be intact in European society when the great forced movement of populations had subsided. ❇

**Jewish refugees aboard immigrant ship** *Josiah Wedgwood.* (Camera Press)

Three, only Stalin was also present at the Yalta Conference five months before. President Truman had been in office only three months, and in the midst of the meeting, Winston Churchill was defeated in the British elections and replaced by Clement Attlee.

Nevertheless, the Allies did agree on basic regulations for the future of Germany: the dissolution of all Nazi institutions, the restoration of free speech and democratic politics, the abolition of all armaments production, and the control of heavy industry. For a while the Americans had leaned toward a plan that would have banned industrial activity, but in the end, the Potsdam conferees took no such radical measures.

### The Peace Terms

The resolution of most political issues was left to unspecified future meetings. Ostensibly, Allied forces were merely occupiers and were not to influence local politics except to repress Nazism. In fact, the distrust between the Soviet Union and the Western powers led unintentionally to a peculiarly harsh retribution—Germany was not only occupied but effectively divided into two states. But the absence of definitive decisions at Potsdam long continued to bedevil the Allies, particularly in regard to Berlin; divided into four occupation zones and originally administered by an Interallied Control Council, the city was isolated in the midst of the eastern (Soviet) sector of Germany to be the focus of contention for more than 20 years.

The major political penalty imposed on Germany at the conference was the relocation of its eastern border to the west, at the rivers Oder and Neisse, which thus enlarged Poland. This shift produced huge new flows of refugees, which increased when Czechoslovakia, independent again, expelled all its Germans.

It was agreed that a Council of Foreign Ministers of the four principal Allies (France was now included) would continue to meet after Potsdam; and though the council soon became a forum for quarrels between the Russians and the others, it did draft a series of peace treaties in 1946. The nations that had fought the Axis in Europe gathered in Paris early in 1947 to sign treaties with Germany's cobelligerents: Italy, Rumania, Hungary, Bulgaria, and Finland, each of which ceded minor territories to its neighbors. Austria, however, like Germany, obtained no formal treaty and remained divided in four occupied zones, with the difference that the Austrians held their own capital, Vienna, from which to establish a unified government that could prepare the way for eventual independence.

The Potsdam conference also laid down the terms of the peace with Japan. The Soviet Union would get some territory and the European nations would regain their colonies in Asia. But the prime beneficiaries were China and, above all, the United States, whose troops occupied Japan and most of the other strategic islands in the Pacific. Little account of Europe needed to be taken in these arrangements.

Within Europe, the first concern was to root out fascism. In the lands the Germans had occupied, this took the form of summary executions of ordinary collaborators and, notably in France, emotional prosecutions against leading figures like Pierre Laval and Marshal Pétain. In Germany itself, however, the vastness of the problem made enforcement of anti-Nazi regulations difficult against all but the highest leaders. Millions of forms were filled out and hundreds of trials held. But the energy needed to sustain the drive against former Nazis soon waned, and only those prosecuted early received significant punishments.

To signify that their massacres and geno-

An American lieutenant colonel talks to some two hundred German civilians forced to observe a scene inside Landsberg concentration camp. (Photo: Wide World Photos)

cide had gone beyond the limits that a civilized world could endure, even in wartime, the Allies created an international tribunal to try Hitler's closest associates for crimes against humanity. Held in Nuremberg in 1945 and 1946, the trials were also intended to inform the German people of the full horror of Nazi rule and to establish some acceptable standards of warfare. Yet to many, trials not conducted by some neutral body seemed a veneer for vengeance and without juridical basis. The appalling revelations of those solemn hearings were nonetheless followed by restrained judgments—only 12 of the 22 prime defendants were condemned to death, and 3 were acquitted.

## The United Nations

Although the League of Nations had failed, the creation of some organization for effective international cooperation had become an official Allied aim; the Atlantic Charter, issued in 1941 by Great Britain and the United

**Hermann Goering on the witness stand at the Nuremberg trials, May 13, 1946, in a courtroom ringed with Allied soldiers.** (Photo: The Bettmann Archive)

States, led gradually to the creation of the United Nations Organization.

Its first agency, the United Nations Relief and Rehabilitation Administration (UNRRA), established late in 1943 to aid countries reconquered from the Axis, came to play a major role in the reconstruction of postwar Europe. The following year Italy, though a former enemy, was allocated $50 million, mainly in medical supplies. A related effort concentrated on economic rehabilitation. To avoid the devastating inflation that had followed World War I, the United Nations Conference at Bretton Woods, New Hampshire, in 1944 created an International Monetary Fund and an International Bank for Reconstruction and Development. Those institutions, with nearly $20 billion in assets, proved important in maintaining the stability of currencies and international exchange after the war.

But the main aim of the United Nations was much grander. At a meeting at Dumbarton Oaks in Washington, D.C., in 1944, representatives of the United States, the Soviet Union and the British Commonwealth agreed to create an international organization to preserve peace throughout the world. A few months after the discussions in 1945 at Yalta, 51 countries approved the United Nations Charter at a special conference held in San Francisco. The charter established a General Assembly of all members to determine policy; a decision-making Security Council of 11 members to supervise ''the maintenance of international peace''; and various economic, social, and legal agencies. Permanent Security Council seats were reserved for the great powers—the United States, the Soviet Union, China, Great Britain, and France—with the remainder rotating by election from among the other member states. But the Big Five were given, at Russia's insistence, the right to veto any council action, and Soviet opposition to much that was proposed eventually shifted some of the initiative to the General Assembly, where a two-thirds majority could overrule a veto. In this maneuvering, both Russia and the United States needed the support of the so-called Third World, the nations of Asia, Africa, and Latin America that were not formally tied to one of the two major blocs.

Despite the position of Britain and France on the Security Council, therefore, and the election of Scandinavians as the UN's secretary general (chief executive officer) until 1961, most of the organization's attention was focused on Asia and Africa after 1945, and many major decisions depended entirely on the United States or Russia. Even the UN's relief work after 1945 was primarily an American undertaking. Thus the United Nations, though structurally similar to the League of Nations, in fact, represented a redistribution of international power that left Europe no longer dominant.

## Europe Divided between East and West

Liberation resulted in a battle for domestic power throughout Europe. Nearly everywhere, Communists had played a leading part in the resistance movements, frequently as their very core. They emerged at war's end with their prestige high to take the lead in denouncing fascists and profiteers. Although socialist and centrist resistance movements joined the Communists in demanding a new era of democracy and equality, these groups

came to distrust each other and to seek the support of foreign powers, a practice that often determined what liberation would mean. Europe, whose political and ideological divisions in the 1930s had led to world war, became in the postwar world more sharply divided than ever.

## Eastern Europe: The Politics of Puppets

Nowhere was the direct influence of foreign domination more visible than in Eastern Europe. In 1945 Soviet troops held the entire area from the Adriatic to the Baltic just short of a line stretching between Trieste and Hamburg. In the Soviet Union, whose economic future would largely determine the recovery of all of Eastern Europe, industrial production was less than two-thirds of its prewar level. The Five-Year Plan announced in 1946, which was designed to increase Russia's industrial output by more than 50 percent over what it had been in 1940, depended openly on its ransacking East Germany and the other occupied areas for materials. Three formerly independent states, Estonia, Latvia, and Lithuania, became Soviet republics, and Russia further extended its western border with the annexation of East Prussian, Polish, Hungarian, and Rumanian territory. Elsewhere the subordination of local institutions to Communist orthodoxy soon became no less blatant.

The Russians restrained the forces of revolution in Eastern Europe, more explosive in 1945 than in 1918, that were fed by long-ignored issues of land distribution and industrial development. But they used these issues, skillful political maneuvers, and the crudest coercion to establish Communist governments subservient to the Soviet Union. The exclusion of leading anti-Communists from a ruling coalition was usually the first step in the common procedure, followed by propaganda campaigns, electoral pressures, and sudden arrests that eliminated non-Communists from positions of power. Finally, a heavy-handed dictatorship set about creating a Soviet satellite with purge trials and secret police.

Rumania was first to feel the full weight of these techniques, and late in 1947 King Michael was forced into exile by the Communists. Poland, where the Communists were weakest, had explicitly been promised free elections; but when these were held in 1947, a series of repressive measures against the minority National Peasant party left the dominant Independent Socialists with an overwhelming majority. The United States and Britain complained but to no avail. A few months later the leader of the National Peasant party fled to London, and his followers were purged. The Catholic Church was persecuted, the Independent Socialist party subordinated to the Workers' party (Communist), and a Russian placed in command of the army. In short order, Poland was firmly tied to the Soviet Union economically and politically.

A similar pattern developed elsewhere. Hungary's coalition government at first had an anti-Communist majority, but another dubious election, in 1949, gave the Communists complete control, and close links with Russia were quickly established. With one exception, even where popular support gave Communist dominance considerable legitimacy, results were much the same. Albania and Bulgaria became solid members of the Communist bloc by 1950. Czechoslovakia, with a notable democratic tradition, did not succumb so easily. The Communists constituted the largest postwar party but not a majority, and the president and foreign minister, Eduard Beneš and Jan Masaryk, were heirs to the liberal politics of prewar Czechoslovakia. But in 1948, when peaceful means had proved unsuccessful, the Communists threatened with Russian support to take over

the country by force. Bowing to this pressure, Beneš placed the government under Communist control; a month later Masaryk died in a mysterious fall from a window; and late in the year a one-party election gave the Communists complete ascendancy, and Beneš resigned.

Yugoslavia, however, did not meekly follow the Russian lead, though Communists dominated its government after Marshal Tito easily won the 1945 national election. Tito had had close contacts with the West throughout the war, and he resisted the Soviet Union's repeated efforts to control his foreign policy and interfere in domestic affairs. An open break came in 1948. Yugoslavia had joined with Russia and other Eastern European states the previous year to create the Cominform, an agency designed to coordinate international Communist political activity, but it was now expelled from the organization and denounced by its neighbors, who also severed economic relations. While remaining Communist in politics and ideology, Yugoslavia established ties with the West that gave it an independence not enjoyed by Soviet allies. Tito's insubordination seemed recklessly daring, but he demonstrated how a small state could use the tense balance between the superpowers to survive without total reliance on either of them.

In the eastern zone of Germany, the Russians followed the same procedures as in the states of Eastern Europe. Early in 1946 they forced the major political group, the Social Democratic party, to merge with the Communist party, which put the Russians in complete control thereafter. Interpreting the economic restrictions imposed at Potsdam as severely as possible, they dismantled scores of factories, appropriated the Germans' postwar production, and forbade trade with the West—the latter two actions in violation of the Potsdam agreements. As West Germany began to revive economically in 1947, however, the Russians gradually allowed the eastern zone to increase its industrial activity and in 1949 gave it independent status as the German Democratic Republic. The first elections, in 1950, confirmed the Communists' dominance.

## Western Europe: The Politics of the Past

In circumstances that seemed unprecedented, each Western country was nevertheless drawn toward its prewar pattern of parliamentary life. The reestablishment of functioning institutions and the reconstruction of a viable economy took precedence over vaguer visions of reform. Before such needs, old ways were the natural recourse; however, much such conservatism belied the broader hopes of resistance movement and wartime rhetoric.

In West Germany local elections held in 1946 produced a victory for the Christian Democrats over their somewhat less conservative opponents, the Social Democrats, both parties being firmly rooted in Germany's pre-Nazi political traditions. To speed the process of recovery, the Americans and British then combined their zones into a single economic unit and soon relaxed restrictions on economic activity. Early in 1949 the area occupied by the Western powers was granted its independence, the ad hoc division of Germany thereby acknowledged with the proclamation of the Federal Republic of Germany.

West Germany's federal structure, reinforced during the occupation period, allowed considerable autonomy to local states. But the truncated new state was more centralized and its political system (dominated by the two large parties) more stable than the old Weimar Republic, which it otherwise strongly resembled. The chancellor for the next 14 years was the Christian Democratic leader Konrad Adenauer, who was 73 years old in 1949 and who had been mayor of Cologne from 1917 to 1933. Under his firm and conservative leadership, West Germany, closely allied with the United States, rapidly prospered in an atmosphere of efficient calm.

In France, the new Fourth Republic looked much like the Third. Political life was shaped by three large parties—the Communists, the Socialists and a new Catholic party of the left, the MRP (Popular Republican Movement). They soon forced de Gaulle out of office as provisional president despite economic policies that included the nationalization of many important industries. And whereas de Gaulle favored a strong president directly elected, the left wrote a constitution providing for a single representative chamber intended to dominate the executive—a position traditional to the left—only to have it rejected in a national referendum. The constitution narrowly adopted in 1946 then returned to the familiar bicameral system with most executive authority in the hands of a prime minister responsible to parliament (its only major innovation, the granting of a larger voice to colonial representatives). Governments were once again dependent on unstable coalitions, an instability increased by the fact that the Communists, the largest party, were the least tempted by compromise. The political balance thus shifted toward the shaky center as cabinets confronted strikers and agitation on the left and a dramatic revival of de Gaulle's popularity on the right.

In Italy more than 54 percent of the electorate voted in 1946 to replace the monarchy with a republic; and subsequent governments were dominated by the Christian Democrats, a sprawling Catholic party that combined much conservative sentiment with a more radical core inherited from the pre-Fascist Popular party. From 1945 to 1953 the leader of the Christian Democrats and the central figure of Italian politics was Alcide De Gasperi. Prime minister during most of this time, he ostracized the Communists and took advantage of divisions among Socialists to bring Italy into close alliance with the United States. In the crucial elections of 1948, the Christian Democrats, aided by extensive American pressure, won an absolute majority, and the threat that Italy's Communist party, the largest in the West, might obtain power began to fade. With a program of moderate reform, including efforts to revitalize the economy of southern Italy and stimulate industry in the north, and a strong parliamentary leader manipulating a diffuse coalition of interests, Italy returned to the unheroic political traditions subverted by Fascists in the 1920s.

Among the smaller nations of Western Europe, the resumption of old ways was equally evident. Spain and Portugal, ostracized for their links with the Nazis, remained defiant dictatorships. In the democracies the traditional parties reemerged, though they were often faced by active Communist minorities and forced to promote domestic welfare through interventionist social and economic policies. Belgium, for example, retained its monarchy and returned to a government of shifting alliances as the old Socialist and Catholic parties jockeyed for power. Although the antagonism between the Walloons and Flemings persisted, the Belgians were nonetheless able to begin a rapid economic recovery and to provide broadened welfare services. The Netherlands and the Scandinavian countries, where the Communists were generally not strong, underwent a similar growth of prosperity and social programs guided by usually fragile coalition governments, most often led by Socialists.

In many respects, postwar politics brought greater change in Great Britain than in Continental countries where the regimes themselves were new. Winston Churchill's defeat in the elections of 1945 was a turning away from wartime unity and sacrifice, for the Labour party won its enormous majority by promising to launch domestic reforms long postponed. Under Clement Attlee, who had led the party since 1935, it nationalized the Bank of England and a wide range of major industries and services, including the coal-mining, transportation, electrical, and—after great controversy—iron and steel industries. It also instituted extensive welfare programs and established public housing, national insurance, and free medical care for all Britons. At the same time, the government began to withdraw from the overseas empire to which men like Churchill had been so attached, granting India independence in 1947.

## The International Context

In the postwar atmosphere of dislocation, domestic instability, and colonial revolt, the world dominance of either the Soviet Union or the United States seemed at stake in nearly every political conflict. The Soviet government was, from the first, determined that the menace from the West of German power, fascism, and capitalist distrust must be forever prevented from mounting devastating attacks like those just overcome. The United States and its allies increasingly braced to meet what was seen as a worldwide Communist conspiracy. Each of these dominant powers professed a comprehensive ideology held to be universally valid and deeply rooted in the European experience. The struggle between Russian Communism and American democratic capitalism reached the intensity of war without open battle and was quickly nicknamed the Cold War.

### The Cold War

President Truman increasingly agreed with his advisers (and with Churchill) that only the strongest measures could stop Soviet ex-

**In a little less than a year, 277,264 flights were completed in the Berlin airlift.** (Photo: Fenno Jacobs/Black Star)

pansion, and he determined to devote the full weight of American manpower and money to containing Russian influence. The Western powers began to encourage the economic recovery of Germany, and the Russians, fearing that Berlin would be an outpost of the West German economy, countered in June 1948 by closing off overland access to Berlin. War seemed imminent. For nearly a year all supplies to West Berlin were ferried to the city in a remarkable airlift. By the time the crisis was resolved and the Soviets backed down, West and East Germany had become autonomous republics bearing the political trappings of the alliance to which they belonged.

In 1947 the American president also announced the Truman Doctrine, promising military and economic aid to nations threatened by Communist takeovers. At that moment, Greece and Turkey were the areas at conflict. Britain had announced it could no longer afford to sustain its traditional dominance in the eastern Mediterranean, and the

United States was, in effect, taking over. Money and supplies at once poured into Greece, rent for nearly a year by a recurrence of civil war in which the Communists were being helped by neighboring Yugoslavia. The American response, combined with Yugoslavia's break with Russia, enabled the Greek government to crush the opposition by 1949. Turkey, slowly moving toward the establishment of democratic institutions, received similar assistance. Opposition to Communism and Soviet influence had become the focus of American policy.

A few months after the announcement of the Truman Doctrine, U.S. Secretary of State George Marshall unveiled a more imaginative plan. To stimulate European recovery—and eliminate the economic conditions in which Communism prospered—he offered massive economic aid to all nations still struggling to recover from the effects of the war. But Russia forbade the Eastern European states from participating in the American-sponsored program and established its own Council of Mutual Economic Assistance (Comecon) instead.

This competition entered Europe's domestic politics as well. Communist parties throughout the West opposed the Marshall Plan despite its obvious benefits. In the East, the last vestiges of non-Communist political activity were removed, and in the West, Communists were excluded from coalition governments in France and Italy in 1947 (in part at least, as a result of strong American pressure) and from all government positions in Switzerland in 1950; West Germany banned the party itself in 1956.

Local issues were thus tinged by international implications. Trade agreements became a litmus test of a country's ideological leanings; strikes were denounced as Communist-inspired attempts at subversion; spy scandals made sensational headlines; and travel between East and West became almost impossible. The relatively limited question of

whether the city of Trieste belonged to Italy or Yugoslavia became the subject of intense great-power maneuvers. Unmistakably, Europe had become a battleground in the Cold War.

And the two halves of Europe followed the lead of their powerful patrons. When the news arrived that the Soviet Union had tested its own atomic bomb in 1949, it was seen as a direct challenge to the United States, and Truman met it by announcing that American scientists were working on an even more devastating version, the hydrogen bomb. But the loss of the U.S. monopoly over atomic weapons made ground forces seem essential to deter further Soviet aggression without resort to the total annihilation of atomic war. Consequently, in 1949 the North Atlantic Treaty Organization (NATO) was created to coordinate the military planning of the United States, Canada, and 10 Western European states,[2] which, in effect, now received U.S. military aid. The Russians replied with the Warsaw Pact in 1955, which performed the same function for the Eastern Europeans.

At first, the Cold War had been primarily a conflict over Europe, a competition for public opinion as well as international policy. Divisions over any number of domestic issues continued to form along lines of pro-American or pro-Soviet positions. But with Eastern Europe isolated behind what Churchill called the "iron curtain" and with Communists excluded from political power in the West, the focus of the Cold War shifted. When the Communist North Koreans invaded South Korea in 1950, the United States at once asked the United Nations to intervene, and in Russia's temporary absence, the UN called

[2] Great Britain, France, Belgium, the Netherlands, Luxembourg, Italy, Portugal, Denmark, Norway, and Iceland were the European members. Greece and Turkey would be added in 1952 and West Germany, in 1955.

for an international army to stop the North Koreans. The Cold War was now worldwide (see Map 29.3). Even when centered on Europe, the Cold War had marked the lessened autonomy of the European nations, and that became clearer as the conflict between Soviet and American influence dominated colonial issues and shaped events in the Middle East and Asia.

## The Loss of Empire

The most dramatic evidence of the decline in European power was the rapid dwindling of colonies and influence overseas. World War II had severely shaken the colonial empires, which no longer had the material means to suppress the increasingly powerful demands for independence in their overseas possessions. For a few months after the war ended, Great Britain and France enjoyed the luxury of their old rivalries in the Middle East. But in 1946 both withdrew from the new states of Lebanon and Syria, Trans-Jordan became independent, foreign troops left Iraq and Iran, and negotiations began for British forces to depart from Egypt and the Sudan.

At the same time, despite Arab hostility, Great Britain undertook concrete planning for the establishment of separate Jewish and Muslim states in Palestine. Mounting terror campaigns from both sides notwithstanding, the British decided to remove all their troops in May 1948, and the United Nations, eager to give Jews a refuge following Hitler's persecutions, endorsed the creation of the state of Israel. The Arabs invaded the day the British left but were driven back despite a huge numerical superiority, and UN mediators were able to bring about a shaky truce that confirmed Israel's existence.

Colonialism weakened in Asia as well. The French recognized Vietnam as a free state in 1945; Ceylon and Burma gained their independence from Great Britain in 1948; and Indonesia won its freedom from the Dutch after a long struggle in 1949. Where they failed to grant true autonomy, however, as in Indonesia and Vietnam, Europeans found themselves fighting wars they could not win. In Vietnam, for instance, a French-educated Communist leader, Ho Chi Minh, organized a brilliant guerrilla campaign that became a serious and costly war, culminating in the capture of a major French base at Dien Bien Phu in 1954 and French withdrawal.

Throughout Asia the end of European domination left a heritage of ties to international capitalism, of bureaucracy and parties organized on Western models, and of nationalist and socialist ideas increasingly tempered by local traditions and such indigenous forms as passive resistance, developed to a fine political art by India's religious leader and social reformer Mohandas K. Gandhi, whose spiritual message and personal qualities won worldwide admiration. Local cultures often remained decisively important, and the prospect of Indian independence led to serious conflict only gradually reduced by dividing the subcontinent, with most Muslims giving allegiance to the newly created state of Pakistan and most Hindus loyal to India.

The resolution of all these struggles was outside European control. The creation of Israel, for example, depended primarily on UN intervention and, above all, on the diplomatic recognition of the new nation by the United States and the Soviet Union. Similarly, the critical conflict in Iran was between the Russians, whose influence rapidly waned, and the Americans, whose economic aid rose with equal speed. Although Africa was less directly affected by the Cold War, the competition between the great powers encouraged formal independence there as well.

As the Europeans withdrew from these lands long under their hegemony, the U.S.–Soviet conflict remained. Pakistan committed itself to the West; India tried to steer a middle

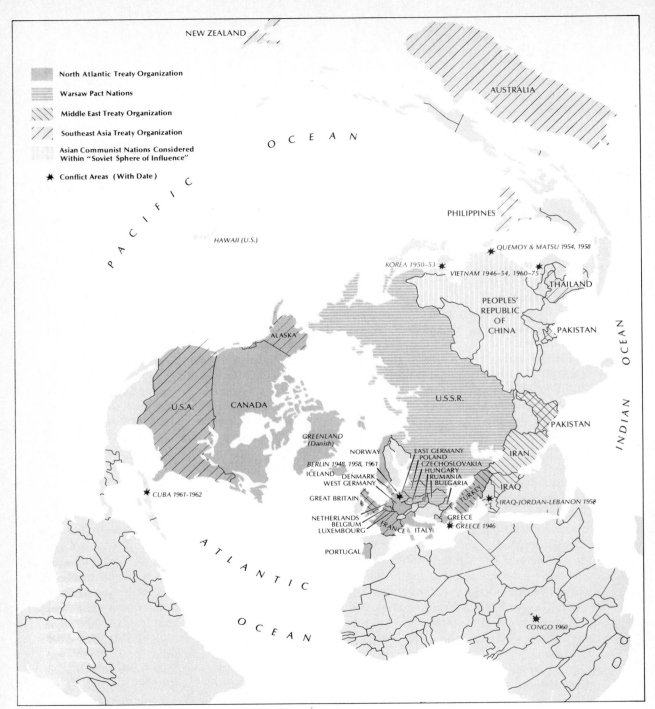

**Legend:**

- North Atlantic Treaty Organization
- Warsaw Pact Nations
- Middle East Treaty Organization
- Southeast Asia Treaty Organization
- Asian Communist Nations Considered Within "Soviet Sphere of Influence"
- ★ Conflict Areas (With Date)

NEW ZEALAND

AUSTRALIA

OCEAN

PACIFIC

PHILIPPINES

HAWAII (U.S.)

QUEMOY & MATSU 1954, 1958

KOREA 1950–53

VIETNAM 1946–54, 1960–75

THAILAND

PEOPLES' REPUBLIC OF CHINA

PAKISTAN

INDIAN OCEAN

ALASKA

U.S.A.

CANADA

U.S.S.R.

PAKISTAN

GREENLAND (Danish)

NORWAY

EAST GERMANY
POLAND
CZECHOSLOVAKIA
HUNGARY
RUMANIA
BULGARIA

IRAN

BERLIN 1948, 1958, 1961

ICELAND

DENMARK
WEST GERMANY

CUBA 1961–1962

GREAT BRITAIN

TURKEY

IRAQ

IRAQ-JORDAN-LEBANON 1958

NETHERLANDS
BELGIUM
LUXEMBOURG

FRANCE  ITALY

GREECE

★ GREECE 1946

PORTUGAL

ATLANTIC

OCEAN

CONGO 1960

**MAP 29.3 THE COLD WAR OF THE 1950s**

course; and a major Communist revolt broke out in Burma immediately after independence. In Vietnam the French were encouraged by the United States, while Ho Chi Minh was strongly supported by Russia and by the most formidable of the newly Communist states, China, where, after long civil conflict, the Communists under Mao Zedong consolidated power in 1949.

As a counterweight to these advances in Asia, the United States promoted the economic revival of a now democratic Japan and gave strong economic and military support to Taiwan (a large island off China still held by the Chinese nationalists). The American government also founded the Southeast Asia Treaty Organization (SEATO), a Pacific equivalent to NATO, in which Britain, Pakistan, Australia, New Zealand, and various Asian states joined with the United States in common defense. The creation of SEATO marked the further institutionalization of the Cold War on a worldwide scale.

In all these developments, Europeans could be little more than spectators. Great Britain did attempt to use the Commonwealth of Nations, binding together all its former colonies under technical allegiance to the royal family, as a means of continuing its influence. But it was little more than a grand international club, incapable even of restraining conflicts among its members (between India and Pakistan, for example) and rejected by the fiercely anti-British republic of Eire, which the British formally recognized in 1949. The main accomplishment of a similar French organization, the *Union Française,* was the survival of France's language and culture in its former colonies. Although right-wing elements within Europe resented these many losses, most Europeans were reconciled to the disappearance of worldwide possessions by a political and economic revival at home that could hardly have been foreseen during the late 1940s.

# III. EUROPEAN RECOVERY
❄
## The Basis of Economic Revival

In economc affairs, in contrast to domestic and international politics, renewed vitality led to innovations that eventually transformed society. Initially, however, in economic matters, too, Europe's debt-ridden and disrupted nations appeared dependent on the superpowers. But it still had extraordinary resources, and the decade between 1947 and 1957 was one of amazing economic growth as well as sharply defined limits on political change. Europe, the homeland of the Industrial Revolution, had populations which possessed high levels of experience and skill. World War II, for all its destructive impact, had in many respects promoted the efficient use of these resources, taking up the considerable slack left by a decade of depression.

Full production and employment in wartime were related to another notable social phenomenon: The number of births remained steady and in some countries even increased. During World War I the birth rate had plummeted, reducing the size of the generation that followed. Western Europe, at least, had a nearly opposite experience in World War II. The birth rate in France, for example, had declined by 45 percent in 1914–1918, and through the 1930s deaths had outnumbered births so persistently that many observers thought the country was embarked on a path of "national suicide." But during World War II the birth rate increased 11 percent over the preceding decade. Similarly, England's birth rate had fallen by 25 percent in the First World War but showed a relative increase of 18 percent during the Second. The figures rose as well in almost all the neutral countries (Ireland, Spain, Sweden, Switzerland), whose economies had benefited from sales to the belligerents. In Germany itself the birth rate had dropped by 50 percent in World War I but by only 22 percent in World War II, despite the mobilization of millions of men and the death of more than a million. The Italian patterns were similar.

In sum, in the midst of the fighting, Western Europe witnessed the beginnings of a "baby boom," comparable to though never so large as that which occurred in the United States during the same period. Relatively high birth rates were maintained until 1963, when a slow decline ensued. Given the war losses and Europe's sustained industrial potential, the increase in births undoubtedly helped stimulate and sustain economic recovery.

In 1945 Europe, like the United States, also had access to a large backlog of unexploited technology, much of which derived from military research. Atomic power, the jet engine, the rocket engine, television, computers, antibiotics, and frozen and dehydrated foods are only the best known of technical advances destined to have major economic impact. And the increased economic importance of advanced technology benefited a Europe richer in technology, experience, and organization than in natural resources.

Finally, even the destruction and dislocations caused by the war contributed to recovery in that rebuilt factories could utilize the best available machinery and methods. The millions of refugees, some highly skilled, formed a large and usually cheap increment to the labor force; and the need to construct thousands of factories, offices, housing units, and other buildings was a powerful stimulus to economic growth. Defeated Germany also enjoyed the negative benefit of having no large military expenditures. Thus, in the depths of distress during the early years of peace, the Europeans, who never lost their resilience, established the basis of subsequent prosperity.

## The Role of the Soviet Union and the United States

The recovery of Eastern Europe depended heavily on the Soviet Union, which through strenuous efforts was able to reach and surpass its prewar industrial output by 1953, and leaders such as Politburo member Nikita Khrushchev confidently predicted that the U.S.S.R. would exceed America in industrial production by 1970.

Impressive as these achievements were, the very size of Russia's economy raised unexpected problems that have persistently slowed the relative rate of growth. As Soviet production and wealth expanded, the costs of administration increased disproportionately, and the inefficiencies of the nation's centralized management became more pronounced. The absence of a free market deprived planners of an effective means of judging costs, profits, and performance. In several critical areas the "command economy" of the U.S.S.R. proved less successful than the West's mixed economy, combining national planning and private enterprises. Russian agriculture, in particular, has been a major disappointment. In 1953 the cereal harvest was only slightly larger than in 1913, when the population had been smaller by a quarter.

Nevertheless, the growth of Russian industry and its developed technology provided an important market for and stimulus to production in the countries of the Communist bloc. After 1945 these states attempted to organize their economies on the Russian model. All but Poland collectivized farmlands, and all instituted five-year plans to achieve rapid industrialization. In varying degrees, these governments adopted elements of a mixed economic system—"goulash socialism," as Hungary's compromise has been called: The state retained ownership of most means of production, but managers operated within the structure of a largely free market. The formula first proved most successful in the already advanced economies of Czechoslovakia and East Germany. Even under the new conditions, a prewar heritage of economic and social modernization proved an invaluable asset; and Eastern Europe, though dramatically less prosperous than the West, had the highest rate of economic growth in its history by the 1950s.

The Western European nations, looking across the Atlantic for help, found the United States slow to appreciate the depth of their plight in 1945. In 1946 the United States extended to Great Britain a long-term credit of $4.4 billion and subsequently provided a credit of $1.2 billion to France. Following these steps, several developments—aside from the escalating competition for international power with the Soviet Union—persuaded the American government to adopt the systematic policy of aid embodied in the Marshall Plan. The economies of the European countries continued to founder; currency reserves were nearing depletion, which would have halted imports, removed all limits to inflation, and dealt a final blow to hopes of steady recovery.

Dramatically announced in 1947, the Marshall Plan, unprecedented in scope and breadth of vision, was initiated with the massive sum of more than $5 billion appropriated by Congress in 1948. The distribution of the aid reflected not the alliances of World War II but the alignments of the Cold War—in 1948, for example, Italy received more than $600 million to finance a broad program of industrial reconstruction. Over the next four years, the Marshall Plan channeled into Europe more than $15 billion under the direction of the Organization for European Economic Cooperation (OEEC), which 18 Western states established for this purpose. Subsequently, the European Payments Union (1950–1958) was created to regulate currency exchanges; and imports from the United States, made possible by credits under the Marshall Plan, benefited the United States while helping the OEEC countries to rebuild their industries and to lay the foundations for rapid recovery.

In 1948, 1949, and 1950, the combined gross national product of the OEEC participants spurted at an annual rate of 25 percent and by 1952 was approximately half again as large as it had been in 1938. In spite of a bigger population, per capita income increased by more than a third. Western Europe had never been wealthier, and this was only the basis for further advances. In the decade of the 1950s, Europe achieved the highest rate of growth it had ever recorded. The Marshall Plan was a spectacular economic success that demonstrated the value of the experience and renewed enthusiasm of the Western European peoples.

### Government Policies in Western Europe

In stimulating and sustaining their nations' recovery, the policies of the OEEC governments were of major importance. Nearly everywhere in Europe the state was expanding the public sector of the economy and assuming leadership in planning for economic growth. The United Kingdom's Labour government began its program of systematic nationalization of industry, starting with the coal mines, in 1947. The French government in 1945 and 1946 took over the Bank of France and other major banks, large insurance companies, utilities, coal mines, and the Renault automotive works (made vulnerable by its owner's collaboration with the Germans). Italy, through a legacy from the Fascist regime, already controlled the biggest publicly held complex of industries anywhere in Western Europe. Two huge, state-owned aggregates—the Institute for Industrial Reconstruction, which consisted of more than 100

**In the prosperity of the late 1950s, a German couple escapes for a picnic in the mountains, taking their new car and portable radio.**
(Photo: Archiv für Kunst und Geschichte, Berlin)

companies, and the National Hydro-carbon Corporation, which directed the production of gas, oil, and other energy sources—dominated the economy. West Germany alone made no effort to expand the number of publicly owned industries, but there, too, the government had an important role (as it had during the war, under Speer) in coordinating economic growth that would come to be known in the late 1950s as the German miracle.

In one sense, nationalization proved a disappointment, as state ownership gave no assurance of efficient management, good labor relations, or a high return on capital. But it helped governments develop all-encompassing economic plans that would guide both public and private enterprises to function in the general interest. Through the Monnet Plan (1946–1950) and subsequent designs for balanced economic growth, France set the model of loose but effective control. Utilizing refined methods of national income accounting, economists and other "technocrats" were able to turn the flow of investments in directions favored by the government. In doing so, they successfully built on institutions and policies many of which had developed under the Vichy regime. Britain created a National Economic Development Council in 1961 and adopted a five-year plan in 1962 for similar purposes. Comparable plans overseeing the operations of a mixed economy were devised and followed in almost all European and Mediterranean countries from Sweden to the new state of Israel. In West

Germany a private trade association with close government ties, the Federation of German Industries, as well as a number of the largest banks exercised effective influence over the economy.

The policies of European governments were closely comparable in another respect: All undertook to promote the welfare of their citizens and, in particular, to protect workers and their families against sickness, impoverished old age, and unemployment. Great Britain provided the earliest and (Sweden excepted) probably the most complete example of what has come to be called the welfare state. Its cornerstone was the National Health Service, inaugurated in 1948, which assumed nearly the total cost of medical, dental, and hospital care for all residents of the United Kingdom. The Continental governments instituted similar programs, including such benefits as family allowances—payments for the support of minor children—which, in turn, may have helped sustain the birth rate.

Welfare programs had considerable economic impact. They relieved people of the need to save in anticipation of sickness and old age. At the same time, to meet welfare costs, the state developed more efficient methods for collecting taxes. The government thus accumulated large monetary reserves, which it could invest according to its economic plans, further enlarging its role in leading the nation to recovery.

### The First Steps toward Integration

From 1948 on, the OEEC sought to coordinate the policies of participating governments, recognizing that the free international movement of the factors of production—capital and labor—as well as of finished products was critical to high domestic growth rates. But efforts to change this organization into a tariff union failed, except for a small "common market" established in 1948: Benelux, a customs union embracing Belgium, the Netherlands, and Luxembourg. At the same time, an important group of Western leaders urged that the European states take steps toward political integration. A meeting at The Hague in 1948, chaired by Winston Churchill, to discuss the formation of a Council of Europe, led to the creation of a Council of Ministers and a Consultative Assembly, with headquarters at Strasbourg. The new organization's powers were very limited, however; and it became clear that few governments, least of all Great Britain's, were willing to surrender any sovereignty or significant decision-making power to a supranational authority.

Two leading French integrationists, the economist Jean Monnet and Foreign Minister Robert Schuman, then decided to proceed by working for fuller integration in one limited sector at a time. Their efforts led to the creation of the French-German Coal and Steel Authority in 1950 as an imaginative solution to problems that had plagued relations between the two countries. In 1952, propelled by the euphoria of recovery, these two nations joined with Italy and the three Benelux states to establish the European Coal and Steel Community (ECSC), the real kernel of a common market. Each member appointed a representative to the ECSC's executive body, which was then left significantly autonomous in planning and coordinating the production and distribution of the coal and steel critical to industrial growth. As the union proved its economic value and steadily increased its authority, it excited renewed visions of economic and political federation.

### The Limits of Political Change

By the early 1950s, recovering from the war was no longer the focus of European life, and that in itself was a striking achievement. In-

## PERCENT OF ANNUAL INCREASE IN GNP 1950–1960 AT CONSTANT PRICES IN SELECTED COUNTRIES

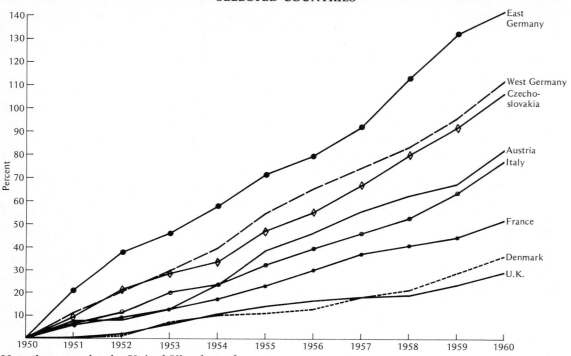

Note that even for the United Kingdom, the growth rate averaged about 3 percent a year about the same as in the period of industrial "takeoff" in the nineteenth century. Growth rates tend to be higher, of course, where the starting point is lower.

stead, economic growth and the consumer goods it brought were giving European society a new look of health and stability. Not surprisingly in such an atmosphere, the political balance shifted toward the center and center right. Of course, a move toward the political center or simply more relaxed rule meant something quite different in Franco's Spain, Great Britain, or the Soviet Union. But everywhere the business of daily life in peacetime seemed to take precedence as

prosperity, based on sophisticated technology and expanding trade, became again a common European goal.

Having adopted extensive welfare measures and accepted a large governmental role in economic planning (often including the nationalization of major industries), European society seemed resistant to further or more fundamental change. And this resistance was strengthened by the pressures of the Cold War, which even in domestic affairs divided and isolated much of the left. In the Soviet Union, too, a somewhat comparable shift occurred. In Eastern and Western Europe, moderate governments in stable societies were tempted to assert themselves; but the effect of such assertiveness in the years 1956–1958 was to establish once again Europe's secondary position on the world stage.

### Western Europe

In Britain the Conservatives regained power in 1951 and held it for the next 13 years despite Churchill's retirement in 1955. Although rationing ended and taxes were lowered, the new measures introduced by the Labour government were not undone, the Conservatives promising rather to accomplish similar ends with an administration that would be more effective and less intrusive. In 1953 the coronation of Queen Elizabeth II seemed to mark the beginning of a new and more pleasant era.

West Germany under Adenauer vied with Britain as America's primary European ally, joining NATO in 1955 and winning diplomatic recognition even from the Soviet Union. In a notable easing of international tension, a peace treaty with Austria was signed by all the former Allies in the same year. That quickly led to the withdrawal of occupation forces and to the full recognition of Austria's sovereignty. In Italy, the formation of political coalitions became more complex after the fall of De Gasperi in 1953; the Communists remained the nation's second largest party, but the Christian Democrats dominated every government. Within that party, the factions of the center and the right increased their strength, and programs of social reform and public welfare tended to be subordinated to the party's ties to business, the Catholic Church, and the United States.

The dictatorships of Spain and Portugal, bolstered by good relations with the United States, faced minimal domestic oppositions. Only in Europe's smaller democracies—the Scandinavian and Benelux countries and Austria—were Socialist parties (firmly anti-Communist) able to remain in office in the 1950s. The stability bravely hoped for in the Marshall Plan was achieved with unexpected speed; the threat of chaos and despair had clearly passed, taking with it the likelihood of political revolutions.

### The Soviet Union

Equally remarkable, a comparable relaxation occurred in the Soviet Union after the passing of Stalin, whose dictatorship had grown even more intense and repressive in the years following World War II. Intellectuals and artists had been required to follow more closely the official view, whether socialist realism in the arts or the fallacious genetic theories of Trofim Lysenko. Clearly, the regime had been anxious to counteract the effects of wartime appeals to regional sentiment and of postwar contacts with the West. But the tough intolerance, like the ugly touches of anti-Semitism, also reflected the personality of Joseph Stalin. There were signs suggesting a new wave of purges when he died of a stroke in 1953.

After 30 years of dictatorship, such a loss was necessarily traumatic in itself; and the problem of succession, always difficult in an absolutist system, was one the Soviet Union had faced but once before. There were other issues too. Shortly before his death, Stalin himself had hinted that the pace of industrialization might be slowed in favor of other needs, since Russia was meeting the high goals of the current Five-Year Plan, and he had implied the possibility of less contentious relations with the West.

The succession went surprisingly smoothly. Party and state officials performed their duties, and at the very top, a form of collective leadership emerged even while its members engaged in intense competition for power. Only in 1956–1957 did it become clear that Nikita Khrushchev was emerging victorious.

Khrushchev's triumph showed again that

control of the Communist party was central to political power in Russia, but it had to do with policies as well. Some of his competitors, initially more powerful, had favored a sharper break with old policies than officialdom could accept (emphasizing the needs of consumers, for example, or the advantages of more decentralized decision making). Khrushchev took a more conservative position. And though the infighting was ruthless and included executions as well as sudden dismissals, his preeminence was marked not by the purge of his opponents but by their assignment to minor and distant positions—steps approved by majority votes in the Presidium and Central Committee. The political forms of the Soviet Union now worked for moderation.

Khrushchev's rise within the government was most dramatically signaled by his speech at the Twentieth Party Congress in 1956. He launched a full attack on the "cult of personality" that had been devoted to Stalin, presenting a kind of bill of particulars of his excesses, his paranoid distrust, his interference in the conduct of war, his responsibility for the purge trials of the 1930s. Nothing like this had occurred before in the Soviet Union; myths that for a generation had been central to a great nation's enormous sacrifices were being attacked by its own leader. Khrushchev's charges circulated widely in secret and then more openly, with effects in the Soviet Union and Eastern Europe and among Communist movements everywhere still being seen. Suddenly, streets and squares were renamed; statues and pictures disappeared. With the thaw[3] following Stalin's death, a freer, more open society appeared in prospect.

Built-in counterpressures quickly made themselves felt. The needs of the party, the problems of administering a vast socialist state, rumblings of excitement from other peoples of the Soviet bloc who believed a real thaw might mean autonomy for them—all this led Khrushchev to clamp controls on criticism once more. But the restraints were never again so rigid or so arbitrary as under Stalin. When in 1957 the Soviet Union celebrated the fortieth anniversary of the Russian Revolution by launching the world's first space satellite, Russia's status as one of the most powerful and stable nations was dramatically confirmed.

## Forays at Independence

On the Continent, prosperity and peace raised the prospect that European nations might pursue policies quite independent of American or Soviet influence. The effort, led by the United States, to strengthen European defenses clearly pointed to the rearming of Germany, a measure the French could hardly welcome and Russia was determined to prevent. As a safeguard, the French proposed in 1952 the creation of a European Defense Community, in effect, a common European army that would benefit from German strength without the risks of a separate German military force.

The proposal was accepted by most of the European members of NATO and pushed hard by the United States; but its implication of permanent Continental engagement was distasteful to the British, and growing doubts, increased by resentment of extraordinary pressure from the United States, led the French Parlement to reverse itself and reject the EDC in 1954. There was, in short, a limit to how far European governments could be pushed, and American intransigence in the face of Khrushchev's professed

---

[3] The metaphor of the thaw, which has come to be generally applied to these changes, is derived from a novel of that title by the noted Russian fiction writer and journalist Ilya Ehrenburg.

desires to improve relations (John Foster Dulles, secretary of state under President Dwight D. Eisenhower, Truman's successor, considered even Churchill a bit weak in his opposition to the Communist menace) only strengthened that view.

## The Suez Crisis

With a kind of stalemate in Europe, the more immediate confrontations of the Cold War shifted to other parts of the world, particularly those in which European dominance had recently been overcome. Great Britain, its economy beginning to lag badly behind those of other European countries and fearful of losing its special role as America's primary ally, attempted one dramatic foreign venture. In Egypt, once a crucial part of the British Empire, Gamal Abdel Nasser's government raised growing distrust in the West by its domestic policies and its turning to the Communist bloc for help in industrialization. When the Western powers, following the United States, refused aid for the construction of a high dam across the Nile at Aswan, Nasser announced the nationalization of the Suez Canal, still owned by a British-controlled company. Britain led in demanding strong measures and, after international efforts at compromise broke down, conspired with Israel and France to take military action. Israel's attack on Egypt in October 1956 was followed by an Anglo-French bombardment and occupation of the canal banks. Within a week, however, the protests of the Soviet Union and the opposition of the United States enabled the United Nations to force a ceasefire. Shortly afterward, foreign troops withdrew.

Nothing had been gained by this sudden outburst of an outdated imperialist mentality, and much was lost in prestige and in good relations with Arab states and the whole Third World. Although Britain soon became the third nation to possess a hydrogen bomb, it was increasingly dependent even for its own defense on American policy.

## The Nations of the Soviet Sphere

Until 1953 the Communist governments of Eastern Europe outdid themselves in mimicry of the Soviet fatherland, including the idolization of Stalin and the ruthless use of secret police and internment camps. But the Soviet Union's open exploitation of its neighbors' resources to aid its own industrial growth was inevitably resented, and Stalin's death allowed that resentment to show.

Within three months, the workers of East Berlin were in the streets proclaiming a general strike in protest against increased production quotas that they believed to be primarily for the benefit of the Soviet Union. Russian tanks rushed in to put down the revolt, but it had long-lasting effects. Walter Ulbricht became the new leader of East Germany; and while strengthening the party's dictatorship, he offered a reform program of higher wages and better living conditions. He also won from the Russians recognition of East German sovereignty and the end of occupation. Still tightly tied to the Soviet Union and limited in its autonomy, East Germany developed a voice of its own in the councils of Communist countries and expanded its trade with West Germany and other states outside the Soviet orbit.

A far more serious outburst erupted in Poland following Khrushchev's speech attacking Stalin in 1956. This, too, began as a workers' protest, but it quickly gathered support from the growing faction of the national Communist party critical of Russian policies in Poland. Again Soviet forces intervened, to be jeered and sometimes attacked, and the Polish party elected Wladyslaw Gomulka party secretary in preference to the pro-Russian candidate. Gomulka, who remained the

**Soviet tanks occupy the streets of Budapest after the revolt had been crushed.**   (Photo: UPI)

dominant figure in the government until 1970, was a firm Communist who insisted, however, that socialist states must follow somewhat different paths from Russia's in accordance with their national traditions. He convinced Soviet leaders of his loyalty to the Russian alliance, a loyalty he subsequently proved on many occasions, and he thereby won their acquiescence to his more independent course. Russia and Poland began to deal with each other more nearly as sovereign equals. The presence of Russian troops was limited; Poland demanded and got a share of the reparations Germany paid; and it negotiated economic aid from the United States. Gomulka also mitigated the repression of the Catholic Church, and by the 1960s he conceded greater independence to Polish intel-

lectuals and allowed increased contacts with the West.

Another revolt in 1956 ended more tragically. Riot broke out in Hungary in October following a series of conflicts within its Communist party. From the outset, the uprising was even more markedly anti-Russian than Poland's, and at first, the Russians withdrew, seemingly disposed in this case, too, to accept increased national autonomy. But then Imre Nagy, who had been arrested the year before for "right-wing deviationism," was recalled as premier. Bowing to popular pressure, he showed that he was willing to break the alliance with Russia and favor neutrality. The Russian attitude hardened, and then the Soviet army attacked in force to crush the revolution in 10 days of bitter fighting.

Many in Hungary expected Western aid, for which rebel radio stations pleaded, but none came. Indeed Washington, hurling denunciations of Russian imperialism, was embarrassed by the fact that while Russian tanks were crunching across Hungary, the troops of three American allies were invading Egypt. Russia had made it clear that the satellite states would not be permitted to break their alliance with the Soviet Union; and the West had confessed that a Russian sphere did indeed exist. A wave of refugees left the country, and Nagy himself was kidnaped by the Russians and executed in 1958. Hungary was punished with harsh repression, a heavy-handed Soviet presence, and a general worsening of working conditions, but its premier, Janos Kadar, who had supported the more moderate phase of the rising, slowly led it on a more national course.

Czechoslovakia fared no better. The most industrialized of the states in the Russian orbit, it had not taken easily to Communism. After trials and purges in the 1950s, the regime was secure and the economy prospered but without the technological transformation or growth in consumer goods so apparent in the West. The divisions between the dominant Czechs and the Slovaks hardened.

Geography aided some of the other Communist nations to achieve greater autonomy Albania, the most backward country on the Continent, increasingly allied itself to mainland China in diplomatic and dogmatic opposition to Russia. Rumania, which with Bulgaria had been among the most Stalinist of the satellite regimes, found the adjustments to Soviet policy after 1953 more difficult to make. While maintaining a strict domestic dictatorship, its insistence on an independent foreign policy made it the most venturesome of the Russian-dominated regimes in establishing good relations with Western powers.

Yugoslavia had never been a satellite state. After its expulsion from the Cominform in 1948, it improved its relations with its non-communist neighbors and benefited from American aid. Reconciliations with Khrushchev in 1954 and 1957 did not reduce its independence or its trade with the West nor diminish Tito's prestige as a leader capable of dealing with both the Soviet Union and the United States. Partly of necessity, Yugoslavia developed a Communism of its own that by the 1960s was relaxing central economic controls and encouraging local participation in decision making. No other Communist nation was able to move so far from the common model.

## New Starts: The Fifth Republic

The launching of Sputnik in 1957, remarkable enough in itself, had also signaled the continued advance of the superpowers. The suppression of revolt in Eastern Europe had, like the debacle at Suez, further defined the limits constraining single European states. And almost simultaneously, two events reflected distinctly different responses to this situation: the fall of the Fourth Republic in France and the founding of the European Common Market.

Under the Fourth Republic the French government had in many respects performed very well—how well would become clear only in the prosperity of the 1960s. But coalition governments also shared the best-known weaknesses of the Third Republic. With the Communist party ostracized since 1947 but still sizable, the other three large parties—the Socialist and more often the Radical Socialists and the MRP (Popular Republicans)—had to seek alliances to capture a parliamentary majority. It appeared briefly in 1954 as if the able Radical Socialist Pierre Mendès-France could continue to make the system work, as so often happened (in the nick of time) in the past. With the backing of a huge majority, he promised to finish off the negotiations that would extricate France from Indochina and then launch a dynamic program of political reform and social modernization. He accomplished the first, but even

| International and Military History | Political History |
|---|---|

<table>
<tr><td>1942, Apr.–May</td><td>Philippines fall to Japan</td><td></td><td></td></tr>
<tr><td>1942, July</td><td>Sevastopol falls to Germans</td><td></td><td></td></tr>
<tr><td>1942, Aug.–Feb., 1943</td><td>Battle of Stalingrad</td><td></td><td></td></tr>
<tr><td>1942, Oct.</td><td>British win at El Alamein</td><td></td><td></td></tr>
<tr><td>1942, Nov.</td><td>British and Americans land in North Africa</td><td>1942, Nov.</td><td>Germans occupy all of France</td></tr>
<tr><td>1943, Jan.</td><td>Casablanca Conference</td><td>1943, July</td><td>Mussolini ousted; Badoglio government</td></tr>
<tr><td>1943, July</td><td>Allies land in Sicily</td><td></td><td></td></tr>
<tr><td>1943, July–Aug.</td><td>Intense bombing of Hamburg</td><td></td><td></td></tr>
<tr><td>1943, Oct.</td><td>Allies take Naples</td><td></td><td></td></tr>
<tr><td>1943, Nov.</td><td>Russians reach Dnieper and Kiev</td><td></td><td></td></tr>
<tr><td>1943, Dec.</td><td>Teheran Conference</td><td>1943, Dec.</td><td>Badoglio out, Italy joins Allies</td></tr>
<tr><td>1944, Feb.</td><td>Russians reach Polish border</td><td></td><td></td></tr>
<tr><td>1944, June</td><td>Allies take Rome, land in Normandy</td><td>1944, July</td><td>Attempt on Hitler's life</td></tr>
<tr><td>1944, Aug.</td><td>Allies take Paris, Warsaw; Rumania, Bulgaria, Finland surrender</td><td></td><td></td></tr>
<tr><td>1944, Dec.</td><td>Battle of the Bulge</td><td></td><td></td></tr>
<tr><td>1945, Feb.</td><td>Firebombing of Dresden; Yalta Conference</td><td>1945, Apr.</td><td>Hitler commits suicide</td></tr>
<tr><td>1945, May</td><td>Berlin falls, Germany surrenders</td><td>1945</td><td>Tito wins control of Yugoslavia, Labour government in Great Britain</td></tr>
<tr><td>1945, July</td><td>Potsdam, Conference</td><td></td><td></td></tr>
<tr><td>1945, Aug.</td><td>Atomic bombs on Hiroshima, Nagasaki</td><td></td><td></td></tr>
<tr><td>1945, Sept.</td><td>Japan surrenders</td><td></td><td></td></tr>
<tr><td>1946</td><td>Estonia, Latvia, Lithuania become Soviet republics; United Nations established; Great Britain and France withdraw from Middle East</td><td>1946</td><td>Constitution of Fourth Republic in France; Italian Republic; Communist government in Soviet zone of Germany</td></tr>
<tr><td>1947</td><td>Peace treaties signed in Europe; Truman Doctrine; Berlin blockade; Marshall Plan; Cominform of Communist parties; India independent</td><td>1947</td><td>King Michael of Rumania into exile; Poland establishes Communist government; Communist parties ousted from government coalitions in West</td></tr>
<tr><td>1948</td><td>Council of Europe; Yugoslavia breaks with U.S.S.R.; recognition of Israel</td><td>1948</td><td>Communist government in Yugoslavia</td></tr>
<tr><td>1949</td><td>Republic of Eire; Communist government in China; NATO; SEATO; U.S.S.R. explodes atomic bomb; Indonesia independent</td><td>1949</td><td>Establishment of Federal German Republic (West Germany) and German Democratic Republic (East Germany); Communist government in Hungary</td></tr>
<tr><td>1950–1953</td><td>Korean War</td><td>1950</td><td>Albania and Bulgaria join Communist bloc</td></tr>
<tr><td></td><td></td><td>1951</td><td>Conservatives regain power in Great Britain</td></tr>
<tr><td>1954</td><td>France rejects EDC; French defeated at Dien Bien Phu</td><td>1953</td><td>Death of Stalin; coronation of Elizabeth II; Berlin workers revolt</td></tr>
<tr><td>1954–1958</td><td>Algerian revolt against France</td><td>1954</td><td>Mendes–France prime minister in France</td></tr>
<tr><td>1955</td><td>West Germany in NATO; Warsaw Pact</td><td></td><td></td></tr>
<tr><td>1956</td><td>Suez War</td><td>1956</td><td>Polish revolt; Hungarian rising put down by Soviet troops; Khrushchev criticizes Stalin</td></tr>
<tr><td>1957</td><td>U.S.S.R. launches Sputnik</td><td></td><td></td></tr>
<tr><td>1957–1958</td><td>Treaty of Rome establishes European Economic Community (January 1, 1958)</td><td></td><td></td></tr>
<tr><td>1958</td><td></td><td>1958</td><td>DeGaulle establishes Fifth Republic in France</td></tr>
</table>

World War II (1942–1945)

## Social and Economic History

**1942**

**1943**  Speer takes control of German economy,
          establishment of UNRRA

**1944**  Bretton Woods Conference leads to
          establishment of International Monetary Fund
          and International Bank

**1945**  National economic planning launched in Britain
          and France (**1946–1950** Monnet Plan)
**1945–1947**  Nuremberg trials
**1945–1947**  Effects of war: devastation and mass
          movements of peoples

**1947**  Beginning of European recovery; OEEC;
          collectivization of Eastern European economies
**1947–1957**  Economic "miracle" in Germany and Italy
**1948**  Benelux tariff

**1950**  French–German Coal and Steel Authority
**1950–1958**  European Payments Union

**1952**  European Coal and Steel Community

**1958**  European Economic Community

before those treaties were completed, nationalist violence in Algeria captured public attention and permitted Mendès-France's opponents to build a new alliance that soon overturned his government. Always more popular in the country than in parliament, he was probably the Fourth Republic's best chance; instead, his vision of a France transformed remained untested. Colonial questions, like the debate over the EDC, raised patriotic feelings and brought pressure from allies (especially the United States) that put added strain on parliamentary coalitions by creating new divisions. In a nation ambivalent about further social change, the center parties found themselves increasingly challenged on the left and right. A rising Gaullist movement threatened the MRP, and in the elections of 1956 an angry movement of small shopkeepers and farmers—people bypassed by the benefits of modernization—sounded vaguely fascist as it shouted its way into prominence; at the same time, the Socialists lost votes and the Communists gained.

Short-lived cabinets of decent men followed each other in dreary succession. Parliament passed laws, many of them admirable, and listened to speeches that were often highly intelligent; but government seemed unable to grasp a major issue and resolve it. Meanwhile, the most pressing issue was rising from outside France in the growing revolt against French rule in Algeria. Beset by colonial uprisings in Africa and Asia since 1945, the French army had expended itself in repressive measures only to have "the politicians" concede autonomy or independence.[4]

[4] In 1958 in Africa alone, eight new states chose to be autonomous within the French Union: Senegal, Mali, the Ivory Coast, Mauritania, Niger, Upper Volta, Cameroun, and Gabon. French Somaliland (Afars and Issas Territory) preferred to remain a territory; and Guinea, Togo, the (Brazzaville) Congo, and the Central African Republic chose full independence.

In the spirit of the Cold War, many officers saw themselves fighting alone against Communist conspiracy around the world, and they were determined not to permit their efforts to be scuttled in Algeria, a French colony since 1830, in which a sizable French population had lived for generations. At the same time, leftists and intellectuals expressed outrage at the atrocities committed by a furious army and at the kind of democracy that waged war against Algerians seeking to govern themselves. From 1954 to 1958 the Algerian question brought down more French governments than any other issue.

Then in 1958 a group of French army officers turned from the fight against Algerian nationalists to seize political control of Algeria, and they threatened to move against the indecisive government of metropolitan France. Uncertain that any ordinary ministry could effectively resist, a majority of the National Assembly preferred de Gaulle to the military insurgents. They welcomed his announcement that he would serve and invested him with extraordinary powers for 6 years. He led France for the next 10. Only a few even on the left found in the practices or the constitution of the Fourth Republic something worth fighting for.

Long convinced that France needed a stronger political system, de Gaulle had been shrewdly ambiguous in his pronouncements on Algeria. The army, the center, and the right all found him acceptable, and he used his strength to consolidate support and win France to a new constitution. Overwhelmingly approved by popular referendum in September 1958, it established the Fifth Republic as a presidential regime whose chief executive would be indirectly elected for a seven-year term. De Gaulle was chosen president two months later, and Gaullists became by far the largest party in parliament, where the Communists were reduced to a handful.

The president moved cautiously on the Algerian question, quietly weakening and dispersing the leaders of the military revolt. Only gradually did it become clear that de Gaulle accepted Algerian self-determination, a proposal approved by three-quarters of the voters in a referendum held in January 1961. Effectively isolated, the most intransigent of the officers formed the Secret Army Organization (OAS) and for 18 months indulged in terrorism in France and Algeria. But the French president, having arranged peace with the Algerian rebels, declared war on the army rebels. By the end of 1962, they had disbanded, Algeria was independent, and France's presidential regime could turn to other questions.

### The European Economic Community

None of these dramatic developments was to have greater long-range importance than the establishment of the European Economic Community, known as the Common Market, in itself a kind of practical compromise between grand visions of a united Europe such as lay behind the formation of the Council of Europe in 1948 and the concrete achievements of the Coal and Steel Community founded four years later. The six nations be-longing to the latter—Belgium, the Netherlands, Luxembourg, France, Germany, and Italy—in 1957 signed the Treaty of Rome (Britain, among others, declined to do so), which created the new Community to go into effect January 1, 1958. Formally, it was a limited agreement, an addition to the Coal and Steel Community establishing an agency to coordinate the development of atomic energy and binding the six nations to a careful series of steps leading to the elimination of tariffs between the member states and to a common tariff toward all other nations. The France of the Fourth Republic, which long favored the creation of international European agencies with independent authority, had played a leading part along with the three smaller states in pressing for the new agreement. "Europe," the French government said at the time, "will not be made all at once, or according to a single, general plan. It will be built through concrete achievements." That larger hope was still far from realization, and it would take some time to tell what the Fifth Republic would mean for the new initiative or whether the opening words of the new treaty would ever have more than rhetorical weight. It declared its signatories "Determined to establish the foundations of an ever closer union among the European peoples."

## SUMMARY

The defeat of Fascist Italy and Nazi Germany meant the preservation of much of what European civilization had stood for. Afterward, the European nations recovered from war with astonishing speed and on the whole adjusted realistically to the loss of empire and international preeminence. But there was disillusionment, too. Prosperity and political stability were accomplished by accepting the loss of a major independent voice in world affairs. Europe was divided by the Cold War and dominated by the greater power of the United States and the Soviet Union. Neither the Communists nor the democratic opponents of fascism had managed in victory to create the societies they promised, and prosperity did not itself resolve old conflicts. Political leaders operating in a prewar style attempted domestic compromise and the assertion of national autonomy in international affairs, but that led to a test of power no European state save the Soviet Union could meet. Rapid development was no longer a Western monopoly, and it was unclear what Europe's economic, social, and cultural place in the modern world should be. The contrived stability of de Gaulle's Fifth Republic and the optimism of the founders of the European Economic Community, uncertain as the prospects were for either, at least implied the possibility of trying other approaches.

## RECOMMENDED READING

### Studies

Allsop, Kenneth. *The Angry Decade: A Survey of the Cultural Revolt of the 1950s.* 1969. Captures very well postwar disillusionment.

*Aron, Raymond. *The Imperial Republic: The United States and the World, 1945–1973.* 1974. A leading French thinker analyzes the period of American dominance.

Brown, Colin, and Peter J. Mooney. *Cold War to Détente, 1945–1980.* 1981. A largely narrative account of relations between the superpowers.

Calvocaressi, Peter. *The British Experience 1945–1975.* 1978. A comprehensive account of British life in a period of imperial decline and economic difficulty.

*Crossman, Richard H. (ed.). *The God That Failed.* 1950. The moving testimony of former Marxists about their lost faith in the era of Stalin and the Cold War.

*Crouzet, Maurice. *The European Renaissance Since 1945.* 1971. An optimistic essay on the politics, society, and culture of postwar Europe.

*Dahrendorf, Ralf. *Society and Democracy in Germany.* 1969. A German sociologist assesses the special qualities of German society.

Dawidowicz, Lucy S. *The War Against the Jews, 1933–1945.* 1976. A full and balanced assessment of the twentieth century's greatest horror.

*DePorte, A. W. *Europe Between the Superpowers.* 1979. A stimulating assessment of Europe's place in the postwar bipolar system.

Fejto, François. *A History of the People's Democracies: Eastern Europe Since Stalin.* 1971. A careful study of the conflicts and variety among Eastern European states under Soviet dominance.

Grosser, Alfred. *The Western Alliance: European-American Relations Since 1945.* 1983. A clear-headed account of how international relations have worked.

*Hoffman, Stanley, et al. *In Search of France.* 1965. A group of distinguished scholars attempts to define the unique patterns of French political and social life.

*Laqueur, Walter. *Europe Since Hitler.* 1972. One of the ablest of the surveys of contemporary Europe.

*Maier, Charles S. *In Search of Stability: Explorations in Historical Political Economy.* 1987. Essays relating economic interests to the ambitions and limitations of European politics.

Michel, Henri. *The Shadow War: The European Resistance, 1939–1945.* 1972. Combines recent scholarship in a solid study of the most attractive (and romanticized) aspect of World War II.

Middlemas, Keith. *Power, Competition and State. Vol. I: Britain in Search of Balance, 1940–1961.* 1986. A clear assessment of the pressures that shaped British society and politics.

Milward, Alan S. *The Reconstruction of Western Europe, 1945–1951.* 1984. Concludes that the economic boom of the fifties and sixties began as early as 1945, through the role of government policy in establishing international economic interdependence.

*Neff, Donal. *Warriors at Suez.* 1981. Well-researched and comprehensive, this dramatic account by a journalist focuses on the political leaders of the nations involved in the highly significant crisis of 1956.

*Paxton, Robert. *Vichy France: Old Guard and New Order, 1940–1944.* 1972. Stresses the continuity and lasting significance for French society and institutions of this twilight period.

*Payne, Stanley G. *The Franco Regime, 1936–1975.* 1987. A fair-minded account that sees the bases of Spain's subsequent transformation in Franco's later years.

Postan, Michael M. *An Economic History of Western*

*Europe, 1945–1964.* 1967. A noted economic historian analyzes the roots of European recovery.

Rioux, Jean-Pierre. *The Fourth Republic, 1944–1958.* 1987. A close look at and a critical assessment of the politics of the period.

Sherwin, M. J. A. *A World Destroyed: The Atomic Bomb and the Grand Alliance.* 1975. A scholarly and balanced account of this controversial and complicated subject.

*Ulam, Adam B. *Expansion and Coexistence: The History of Soviet Foreign Policy, 1917–1973.* 1974. An expert appraisal of the consistent patterns and political pressures underlying Soviet policy.

Wilkinson, James D. *The Intellectual Resistance in Europe.* 1981. A wide-ranging and sensitive assessment of the content and legacy of the resistance and its place in contemporary thought.

* Available in paperback.

# CHAPTER 30

# THE PRESENT IN HISTORICAL PERSPECTIVE

❖ ❖ ❖ ❖ ❖

By 1957 European survival and recovery had ceased to be in doubt. The open questions were, instead, about continuing ideological and social divisions, about whether Europe's future lay within individual nations or would lead to larger multi-national groups, and about whether either way would enable Europe to maintain its own unique culture and have an independent role in the world. In the last generation, Europe has embraced the social organization and high technology said to mark "advanced industrial societies," including the United States, Canada, and Japan, and that distinguish Europe as a privileged zone compared with most of the rest of the world. In the first decade of this period, economic growth was the overwhelming reality, and in important respects, the nations of Europe became more alike. Understood as a self-sustaining process of modernization, European development presented less fortunate countries with two kinds of models: the democratic capitalism of the West and the state socialism of the East. Then in 1968 and for the next several years, a wave of revolutionary discontent brought to the fore complex social and cultural problems that also appeared to be characteristic of advanced societies. Responses to these problems varied, however—most sharply between Eastern and Western Europe, but also within each country, according to its political realities, social traditions, and economic potential, so that older regional and national differences once again showed their importance. The varied attempts to deal with these problems had an intermittent rhythm as new initiatives were followed by compromise and cautious retreat. But the overall direction became clearer in the late 1980s, with the focus in Western Europe on making the European Community into a single economy by 1992 and in Eastern Europe on the political freedom that would permit restructuring the economy.

❖

One important point lay in what did not happen. The recession of the 1970s and early 1980s challenged visions of endless economic growth but did not become another great depression. Neither did the upturn of the 1980s solve the problems of declining heavy industries and large pockets of endemic unemployment. Social change proved less destructive of traditional values, institutions, or conflicts than predicted. There has been no major war, no use of atomic weapons; yet Europe was pulled along in a frightening and wasteful arms race. Relative stability made it easier to see beyond the limits of familiar practice. In Western Europe's domestic politics, old rigidities were breaking up. International constraints were also weakening. As international economic ties became more important and Western Europe more prosperous, the interests of American capital became less decisive. When tensions between the United States and the Soviet Union relaxed in the 1960s and 1970s, European states pursued more independent foreign policies and renewed their ties to the developing and underdeveloped nations. Their freedom of maneuver remained limited, however; only collectively could European countries expect to match the power and influence of the superpowers. Thus the growth of the European Community, in some respects a product of the Cold War, raised the possibility of a more truly independent Europe. The economic prospects alone generated far-reaching economic and political changes (and significant resistance). Then more surprising change began to unfold in Eastern Europe. Facing an economic crisis, Soviet leaders concluded that it could be met only by restructuring their social and political system. That soon meant tolerating somewhat comparable steps in Eastern Europe, where national feeling added explosive pressures. As the Soviet Union made clear that it would not intervene, more concessions had to be made. In the fall of 1989 an accelerating chorus of great popular movements brought down the old Communist regimes, and the governments of Eastern Europe began awkwardly transforming themselves into free, multiparty democracies. Suddenly, the Soviet bloc was no more; disarmament and independence were real possibilities.

❈

Despite the excitement and euphoria of the miracle of 1989, attitudes toward the future remain ambivalent. The prospects for the EEC and the societies of Eastern Europe are as mixed as ever, justifying visions of a world truly safe for democracy but also of a continent dominated by Germany, renewed nationalism, and ruthless competition. One reason for studying the past is to better understand the present, and the tendency for Westerners to see themselves in terms of their place on some scale of historical evolution has grown stronger in the last two centuries. The French Revolution, industrialization, theories of liberalism and progress, World War I, the Russian Revolution, totalitarianism, and World War II not only have made social change a central preoccupation of modern life but also have opened a continuing debate about the direction in which it leads. Predictions that society is steadily, even inevitably, marching toward greater individualism, democracy, and wealth have been countered by equally confident predictions of dehumanization, cultural and moral decline, and loss of freedom. In every case, predictions rest on the assessment of social organization, technological development, and human rationality that the commentators draw from history; for the present is always understood as a period of transition to a different future.

## I. THE NATURE OF ADVANCED SOCIETIES
❈

### Social Effects

Europe's economic growth since the mid-1950s has probably been greater than at any other time in history. Often the triumph of a mixed economy, of that combination of private enterprise and state planning practiced in most European states, this growth has produced far-reaching changes. In advanced societies, adults are literate and families small. Because people live longer, the population tends to become older. Leisure time increases for everyone, and more women work for wages. Steadily increasing productivity requires high rates of investment and frequent

## ACTIVE WORK FORCE

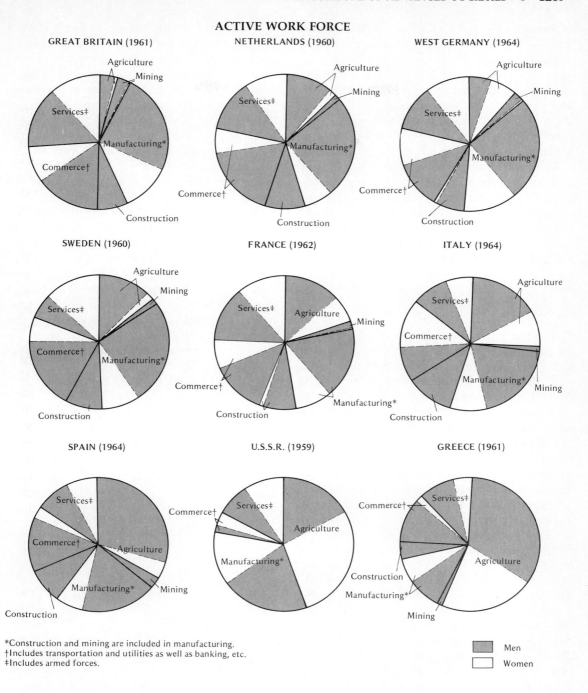

**GREAT BRITAIN (1961)**
Agriculture
Mining
Services‡
Manufacturing*
Commerce†
Construction

**NETHERLANDS (1960)**
Agriculture
Mining
Services‡
Manufacturing*
Commerce†
Construction

**WEST GERMANY (1964)**
Agriculture
Mining
Services‡
Manufacturing*
Commerce†
Construction

**SWEDEN (1960)**
Agriculture
Mining
Services‡
Manufacturing*
Commerce†
Construction

**FRANCE (1962)**
Agriculture
Mining
Services‡
Commerce†
Manufacturing*
Construction

**ITALY (1964)**
Agriculture
Services‡
Commerce†
Manufacturing*
Mining
Construction

**SPAIN (1964)**
Services‡
Commerce†
Commerce†
Agriculture
Manufacturing*
Mining
Construction

**U.S.S.R. (1959)**
Services‡
Agriculture
Manufacturing*
Construction
Manufacturing*
Mining

**GREECE (1961)**
Commerce†
Services‡
Agriculture
Construction
Manufacturing*
Mining

*Construction and mining are included in manufacturing.
†Includes transportation and utilities as well as banking, etc.
‡Includes armed forces.

Men
Women

changes in production and marketing, which reduce costs while adding new products, releasing workers to the service sector of society, which becomes steadily larger. Standards of consumption rise throughout society, and the cycle of growth continues. In all this, European traditions of technical skill, high levels of education, ease of communication, effective government, and social flexibility have been important advantages. Such rapid growth, however, threatens to transform society in disagreeable ways through pollution, urban crowding, and the weakening of old social ties. It also raises fundamental questions about how the benefits of prosperity should be distributed.

## Urbanization

While the inner core of older cities may lose population (exacerbating problems of urban decay), the agglomeration grows, and in effect, the larger cities continue to spread. In France one person in five and in Great Britain nearly that proportion lives within an hour's drive of the capital city. Volgograd stretches for 45 miles along the river after which it was named, and some 14 cities in the Soviet Union have a population of over a million. In general, the new highways, extended subways, and bus lines that push the city outward rarely keep pace with the congestion of traffic at its core. As similar skyscrapers rise in the centers (along with criticism of them), similar residential districts sprawl across the outskirts. In the 1950s new housing tended, East and West, to look like dreary concrete barracks and often provided few of the services necessary to create a sense of community. In nearly every country, efforts at better planning led to the creation of whole new cities, often bleak and artificial, surrounding the metropolis; 5 towns of 24,000 people each were planned around Paris, 24 such towns now surround Moscow.

The more recent trend has been toward new urban hubs on a smaller scale, carefully planned to have shopping, recreational, and cultural centers of their own as well as some light industry so that most of the working population need not commute. Many of these, especially perhaps in Scandinavia (Tapiola, outside Helsinki, being one of the most successful), have proved very attractive, mixing large and small modern buildings, pleasant streets, and restful green spaces.

Thus, despite the uneven results and the absence of wholly satisfactory solutions, Europe contains the world's most interesting experiments in urban planning. Cities like Rome and Vienna have found that banning traffic from the narrow, medieval streets of the old centers of the city can lead to a renewal that makes those sections among the most attractive (and most expensive) for shops and housing. Although loud laments

### SOME OF EUROPE'S LARGEST CITIES
*(1971–1979 estimates)*

|  | City | Metropolitan Area |
| --- | --- | --- |
| Moscow | 7,831,000 | 10,001,000 |
| London | 6,970,000 | |
| Paris | 2,317,227 | 8,612,531 |
| Leningrad | 4,073,000 | 4,588,000 |
| Madrid | | 3,200,067 |
| Rome | 2,897,505 | |
| Kiev | 2,144,000 | |
| Budapest | 2,091,360 | |
| Bucharest | 1,858,418 | 1,934,000 |
| Berlin | 1,909,706 | |
| Milan | 1,706,268 | |
| Hamburg | 1,663,305 | |
| Warsaw | 1,542,500 | |
| Munich | 1,296,970 | |
| Athens | 867,023 | 2,101,103 |
| Cracow | 1,444,000 | |
| Gorky | 1,344,000 | |
| Naples | 1,225,227 | |
| Barcelona | | 1,742,355 |
| Glasgow | 832,097 | 1,727,625 |
| Lisbon | 829,900 | 1,611,887 |
| Stockholm | 653,929 | 1,380,426 |

The results of the rush to meet the demand for new housing in these Parisian suburbs range from crowded new houses meant to evoke Norman cottages to high-rise apartments on a bleak hilltop. The remaining trees mark the forests displaced, and the smog hints at the great city beyond. (Photo: Viva/Woodfin Camp and Associates)

Communist Europe good housing remains scarce, and there are long waiting lists for cramped apartments; in capitalist Europe the renovation of city centers continues the process that pushes all but the well-to-do to distant and often faceless suburbs. Although the price paid in terms of social cohesion and convenience is still disputed, in the narrow terms of living space and hygiene, far more Europeans are far more comfortably housed than ever before.

### Communication and the Environment

In many parts of Western Europe, canals continue to carry significant quantities of cargo, and air travel is especially important across the distances of the Soviet Union; but ground transportation remains the heart of commerce. In the 1960s every nation launched new road-building projects, and by 1980 the most important of these were completed nearly everywhere in the West (except Great Britain and the Iberian peninsula). Superhighways run from Stockholm to south of Valencia and from Naples to Hamburg; already many of the older highways have become overcrowded and in need of repair. In Europe railroads are valued for passenger travel as well as for transport, although nowhere are they expected to turn a profit. In 1981 French trains, which hold world speed records, began to carry passengers from Paris to Lyons at 165 miles per hour.

Western European nations have also been technological leaders in electronic communication, experimenting with interactive uses of computers that permit home subscribers to pay bills, consult encyclopedias, or record their opinions by means of their television sets. Although the international broadcasts of the Western European television network have had far greater success with sporting events than with drama or politics, politicians and governments worry about the internationalization of information and culture. In

accompanied the closing of Les Halles in Paris, the great sheds built in the Second Empire for the provisioning of the capital, the efficiency and improved traffic that resulted were (like the controversial but exciting new cultural center and apartments that replaced them in the 1970s) undeniable benefits. In London, Covent Garden, too, became a cultural center; and Billingsgate, the fishmarket that gave the language another word for verbal abuse, closed in 1981. In the West private stations have, in effect, ended the state's monopoly, and in much of the East it proved impossible to prevent audiences from turning to foreign stations. In some senses, Europeans now know each other better and have been drawn closer together than ever before. Yet, despite increased travel and information, ethnic and regional differences have not lost their hold.

The most obvious by-product of industrial growth is the pollution that contaminates air, waterways, and countryside, pouring from factories and automobiles and littering the landscape. Especially shocking in Europe, where monuments and scenic places revered for centuries have become seriously threatened, the problem calls for coordinated planning and severe restrictions that governments intent upon encouraging growth have been reluctant to take. The Rhine is one of the most polluted of international waterways, and high concentrations of mercury have been recorded in Geneva's Lac Leman. It is dangerous to bathe in or eat fish from much of the Baltic and Mediterranean seas. Escaped industrial gases have caused illness and death in the outskirts of Milan, and the magnificent palaces of Venice were discovered to be slowly sinking, apparently because the earth beneath their pilings gives way as underground water is pumped up on the mainland for industrial use. The remaining monuments of ancient Greece and Rome and the ornate façades of Gothic churches show signs in city after city of crumbling and cracking from the vibrations and fumes of modern traffic.

There are, of course, signs that humankind and modern technology can clean up as well as pollute. Through stern regulations Great Britain has eliminated the smog that plagued London since the sixteenth century and killed thousands of people as recently as 1952. The Thames has become a clean river for the first time in centuries. Nearly every building in Paris was cleaned in the 1960s and 1970s, stripping away the somber, dark patina of soot accumulated through 150 years of industrialization. Huge demonstrations against nuclear power, like the ecological movements (especially in Germany, the Low Countries, and France), testify to a growing concern. Green parties, which emphasize environmental problems and their connection to other social issues, have become important both in their own right and for their wide influence. However belatedly, governments have responded, and several international agencies are pledged to press for enforceable European standards for protecting the environment. Pollution in Eastern Europe during the last 40 years combined many of the worst effects of nineteenth- and twentieth-century industrialization. Everywhere the scale of the problem is huge, and it remains too early to say whether increased sensitivity will continue to shape policy even when it slows economic growth or how much prior damage can be undone.

## The Distribution of Benefits

As advanced nations increase their wealth, they by no means distribute it equally; but by any measure—real wages, per capita income, or consumer expenditures—the standard of living of the working classes has risen impressively in the past two decades. The gap between wage earners and the very rich has narrowed only slightly in the West (income distribution is least uneven in Sweden and the Netherlands); and in Communist Europe professional people and officials live at a much higher standard and with far greater freedom of choice than workers or peasants, an important element in the unpopularity and downfall of those governments. Throughout Europe, the full impact of these inequalities has been softened, however, by complex provisions for social security, free education, subsidized or free medical care, and a wide variety of family benefits and services. Such benefits provide an important part of income for all but the very rich as well as a guaranteed minimum for the poor.

Social differences are more acceptable in periods of rapid economic growth when nearly everyone's lot is improving. In the 1970s, however, unemployment began to rise steadily in the West, exposing the weak position of those in declining industries—many of them the very ones on which industrialization had been built—and small-scale agriculture. Women, the young, and, above all, foreign immigrants have been hardest hit. As unemployment virtually disappeared in the industrial zones in the 1960s, large numbers of people from the less developed periphery had moved to the more prosperous regions—southern Italians to northern Italy, Switzerland, and Germany; Spaniards, Portuguese, and North Africans to France; Yugoslavs and Turks to Germany; Caribbean and African blacks from former colonies to England. In general, they found employment as domestic servants, street sweepers, and the least skilled industrial workers—by the 1970s contributing 17 percent of the work force in Switzerland, some 8 percent in Germany, and only slightly less in France. Often different in physical appearance, language, and culture, these migrants were drawn together and forced by poverty to live in crowded slums that quickly became ghetto subcultures, resistant to and misunderstood by the larger society. Without the full protection of citizenship, resented by native workers competing for jobs and higher pay, despised as sources of crime and heavy welfare costs, these migrants recreated some of the gravest social problems of the early nineteenth century, now exacerbated by prejudices of race and color.

There are, of course, other groups that have not fully shared in the general prosperity. In every country, whole regions labeled as backward have been made the target of special subsidies and tax incentives intended to encourage their industrialization, often with disappointing results. Neither, in general, do women receive equal pay or equal opportunity for advancement, despite the fact that 36 percent of the work force are women in Britain, France, and Germany, with the proportion higher in Sweden and Finland, lower elsewhere. On the average, women workers earn between two-thirds (in Britain) and three-fourths (in France) as much as men. Although in Sweden, France, and Britain women have leading roles in many occupations of high prestige, nowhere are they more than a small minority in such positions except for the medical profession in the Soviet Union, which they dominate.

## Education

Access to the professions and important managerial positions is restricted even more by education than by sex. Traditionally in Europe, secondary education has been the great dividing point, at which a small fraction of young people were admitted to schools that prided themselves on the demanding and usually classical curriculum required for admission to a university. Many more students attended a somewhat more vocational secondary school whose graduates did not normally go on to universities, and half or more of all students beyond the ages of 12 or 14 went directly to work. Throughout Europe, the elites shared high formal culture, access to which was, with few exceptions, first a matter of social class and only second a matter of academic inclination. After World War II, the Communist regimes of Eastern Europe gave preference to the children of workers and party members but only slowly enlarged the total number allowed entrance into college-preparatory programs. In the West the proportion of school-age youths undertaking the more prestigious education has steadily increased. And that change has been accompanied by a move toward "comprehensive" schools, more like the American high school, which less sharply segregate the college-bound.

In each country such reforms in the late 1960s and early 1970s were the subject of controversy, often even riots and demonstrations. Education in advanced societies was tied to social changes that prolonged the period of youth and occupational changes that made formal education the key to social mobility. Reform at the secondary level meant more students entering universities and demands for reform at that level too. Despite the creation of hundreds of new institutions, often with American-style campuses, enrollments in many places have swollen beyond their capacity. The particular pattern in each nation reflects its own traditions of culture and class distinction, but the emerging tendency is clear. Those European nations with the highest proportion of 20- to 24-year olds enrolled in universities (roughly 15 to 20 percent) are the Netherlands, Sweden, Denmark, France, Italy, and Norway, where traditions of democratic access if not equality are stronger. Those with the lowest proportion (less than 10 percent in Yugoslavia, Spain, and Portugal) are the poorest. And nearly all the rest of Europe, both East and West, falls in between. The expansion of educational opportunities largely ceased in the 1980s, and cutbacks in government spending (especially severe in Great Britain) reopened unresolved issues of fair access, quality, general culture, and prospects for employment.

### Social Welfare

In most of Europe, universities charge no tuition, and the state subsidizes other forms of culture. But as the battles over education made clear, the citizens of Europe's advanced societies also look to the state as a major instrument of social justice. In practice, this has meant less the elaboration of utopian programs for social change, even in Eastern Europe, than efforts to guarantee a minimum standard of living. In the Communist nations, for example, housing and transport have been relatively cheap, and in the West governments extensively subsidize both (about one-third of new housing in Germany is government sponsored, one-half in Great Britain, two-thirds in Sweden and France). Social welfare payments of wide-ranging variety are an important part of the family economy for nearly everyone, not just the poor. Similarly, a high proportion of private medical expenses are paid through the state in most countries, and governments have encouraged a steady increase in the number of physicians and hospital beds available. Not surprisingly, rates of infant mortality have declined and rates of longevity have improved so that they are the highest in the world among Europe's most advanced nations. The variations among countries and among regions and classes within the same country reflect, on the other hand, important and troublesome disparities. These government expenditures in addition to those for other services and for defense mean that taxes are relatively high (between 21 and 24 percent of the GNP in the wealthiest nations of Europe). When social policy dictates, as in theory it usually does, that taxes should fall most heavily on the rich (although in practice, they often do not), that can, as many economists are quick to argue, discourage investment, thereby creating yet another incentive for government planning and the nationalization of critical industries.

### The Economic Base

Although the coal fields of Britain, West Germany, and Eastern Europe, the iron ore fields of France and Sweden, and the newly discovered North Sea oilfields remain important, Europe's industrial economy rests primarily upon the efficient transformation of raw materials, much of which must be imported. Wealth comes from productivity, which requires heavy investment, advanced technology, able managers, skilled and willing workers, efficient marketing, and high consumption. Governments from one end of Europe to the other have sought to stimulate these components of productivity through general policies and by exercising direct control, enacting specific measures (such as taxes or tariffs), and providing the infrastructure on which they rest (communication and education, for example). These policies worked to some extent in the boom years of the 1960s, as growth everywhere but in Great Britain was impressive. Sweden, with the most socialist economic system, and Switzerland, with the most thoroughly free market one, achieved the highest per capita income in the industrial world. The most consistently high growth rates, however, belonged to the six states of the original European Economic Community as per capita productivity increased at an amazing rate of over 4 percent a year (compared with 2.5 percent in the United States).

In Eastern Europe, although various countries could point to impressive increases in single sectors, there were no such examples of consistent, overall growth. The exuberant consumerism that filled the shops of Western cities with material goods was not a Communist goal; but even the sober quotas for increased consumer consumption announced in most plans, following Khrushchev's of 1958, were usually not quite met. The contrasts between East and West were even greater in agricultural production. In the West, the number of people who worked the land continued to decline (in Ireland, one of the West's least developed nations, 60 per-cent of the work force was employed in agriculture in 1960, only 20 percent in 1980), but production increased. Nearly one-half the tractors in use in the world are in Europe. With only about 3 percent of the world's farmland, Western Europe produces 15 percent of the world's eggs, potatoes, and wheat (of which France alone is the fifth-largest producer, after the U.S.S.R., the United States, China, and India) and nearly one-third of the world's dairy products and sugar beets. In the Soviet Union, by contrast, agricultural production has tended to stagnate and the crucial wheat crop, in particular, has been disappointing nearly every year. Agricultural production has generally been less disappointing in Yugoslavia and Poland, which may be related to the fact that large proportions of their farmlands remained in private hands.

As these trends continued, they brought about a far-reaching difference in kind. Competitive pressures to increase productivity and adopt new technologies were familiar enough even if they appeared to be getting more intense, but productivity and profits now rested on something more. They required information, instantaneous and open communication, quick and flexible responses, highly trained managers and technicians as well as transistors, robots, and microchips. Many European managers who had been hesitant before became convinced that completion of the European Community was needed to make Western Europe the kind of modern society that could meet the challenge from the United States and Japan. For the Communist countries of Eastern Europe, the problem was far graver. By the 1970s, their economies were no longer doing very well by older standards. Falling further behind Western Europe in wealth and failing to produce adequate consumer goods were dangerous enough, but the shift from heavy industry to information technology and a premium on flexibility implied a change in the very structure of their societies.

## II. EUROPE'S PLACE
## IN THE WORLD
✿
### Wealth and Power

One of the world's superpowers, the Soviet Union, can be considered a European state much of whose power and influence since World War II was associated with its hegemony over Eastern Europe. Western Europe, the second-wealthiest region of the world, has been gaining on the first, North America; and in 1979, for the first time, the GNP of the nine members of the European Community exceeded that of the United States. Europe's population grows less rapidly than do populations in most other parts of the world, but Europe's international importance is assured both by its great wealth and by the fact that this wealth depends very heavily on trade. It is not surprising that Europeans play so great a role in international economic organizations such as the International Monetary Fund, the Organization for Economic Cooperation and Development, or the Trilateral Commission, a privately based group of business and political leaders from Europe, the United States, and Japan.

At the end of World War II, the European powers had generally recognized the independence of their former colonies and protectorates in the Middle East and Asia, but the comparable process in Africa took longer. There, most of today's states won their independence between 1960 and 1965. Often that change was less abrupt than it might appear, some self-government having been followed by autonomy within the British Commonwealth or the French Community before actual independence. The long African struggle and the European resistance to it left much bitterness and suspicion, but not all ties were broken. Bureaucracies, courts, churches, and educational systems; patterns of trade and investment; and political interests and sentiment all guaranteed continuing connections. Britain played a major role in the transformation of white-ruled Rhodesia into black-ruled Zimbabwe, in 1979; and France intervened during civil strife in Chad and the Central African Republic in the 1980s. But colonial issues are no longer the major preoccupation of European foreign ministries.

### European Foreign Policies

Important ties around the world, including former colonies, were very different from old claims to worldwide empire. The concessions of independence to nation after nation continued almost annually throughout the 1950s, 1960s, and 1970s. These victories for native rule were often the outcome of long conflict, for Europeans on the scene—officials, business people, and residents—usually resisted as long as they could. In Europe, however, this continued disintegration of empire no longer carried the kind of trauma that had marked the "fall" of India, Indonesia, Indochina, and Algeria, blows in terms of wealth and prestige deeply felt in the domestic life of England, the Netherlands, and France. That was one respect in which foreign relations were different from the late 1950s on. Relations with the superpowers also changed in tone. Recovery from wartime devastation was no longer the issue. For the Communist governments of Eastern Europe, the invasion of Hungary had demonstrated their dependence upon the Soviet Union for internal stability as well as economic assistance. American opposition to the Suez venture of the British and French had similarly shown that Western European governments would have to recognize limits the United States would

The Brandenburg gate in Berlin had been erected as a monument to Prussia's past military achievements. Blocked by barbed wire in 1961, it was the dividing line between East and West. (Photo: Wide World Photos)

set. Militarily, the Warsaw Pact and the NATO alliance institutionalized this dependence while keeping the Cold War the focus of foreign policy.

East-West tension seemed to have become a permanent fact of life when in 1961 the government of East Germany built a great gray wall across the center of Berlin to keep its citizens from leaving for the West. The long crisis over the division of Germany and the terms of a formal peace treaty was cast in stone, unresolved. There were a number of such crises. In 1961 the United States had sponsored an invasion of Cuba aimed at the

overthrow of Fidel Castro, who allied himself more and more closely with the Soviets; in the following year the Russians began to base some missiles on Cuba. They were soon withdrawn under severe pressure from the United States, but for a moment, war had seemed quite possible. Both crises, however, underscored the mutual interest in not disturbing the balance of power. These experi-

## WORLD POPULATION, 1986, ESTIMATED

|  |  | Annual Growth Rate in Percent |
|---|---|---|
| World | 4,935,000,000 | 1.7 |
| Asia | 2,985,000,000 | 1.7 |
| **Europe** | 682,000,000 | 0.3 |
| Africa | 562,000,000 | 3.0 |
| North America | 404,000,000 | 1.6 |
| South America | 275,000,000 | 2.3 |
| Oceania | 27,000,000 | 2.0 |

ences and the sharp rift between the Soviet Union and China (supported only by Albania among European Communist governments) that became more public and threatening after 1960 demonstrated a need for diplomatic exchanges in which general issues could be considered.

European governments favored East-West negotiations at summit conferences or on specific matters and promoted agreements on space exploration in 1967, the beginning of the Strategic Arms Limitation Talks in 1969, and their extension to human rights issues at the Helsinki Conference in 1975. Through trade, loans, and technical agreements, the governments of Western Europe also encouraged those of Eastern Europe toward whatever autonomy they were willing to attempt. At the same time, each of the Western nations also tended to emphasize its own traditional policies and interests. Great Britain was generally most supportive of United States policy (and has been most favorably treated by it); France stressed its ties to Eastern Europe and the Third World; Germany has, on a number of occasions, asserted a more independent policy toward the East, and the Scandinavian countries have been especially active in the United Nations.

The most flamboyant search for an independent policy was de Gaulle's. Resentful of American policy toward France and determined that the loss of empire need not result in loss of influence, he set upon an independent course that by 1966 led to the withdrawal of French forces from NATO command (and of NATO forces from French soil), although France remained a member of the alliance. He persisted in building from scratch a French nuclear force, and began an exchange of visits with Eastern European leaders that contributed to increasing cultural and economic ties between the two parts of Europe. De Gaulle also emphasized the importance of aid to developing nations, making France second only to the United States as a grantor of foreign aid and bringing Europe into the worldwide competition for the sale of arms to less industrial nations. Although much of the rhetoric that accompanied these policies soon seemed dated, the policies themselves continue as an important part of the French and European diplomatic arsenal.

Germany, too, gradually came to assert some of the political weight its wealth implied. Through his close allegiance to the United States and then his close cooperation and friendship with de Gaulle, Adenauer had made his pariah nation respectable and even trusted. Thus, when the Social Democrats came to power, Willy Brandt, less committed to the inevitability of the Cold War, was able to use his negotiating skill in a new opening to the East. By then East Berlin had been absorbed into an East German state that had established itself as a loyal and relatively prosperous member of the Soviet bloc. The resulting treaty between West Germany and the Soviet Union, signed in 1970, was a milestone, for which Brandt was awarded the Nobel peace prize. While the treaty left open the possibility of a peaceful reunification of Germany, it ratified the Oder-Neisse Line as Germany's eastern boundary, pointed to a normalization of Berlin's status, and paved the way for extensive relations between the governments of Eastern Europe and the Continent's second-most-powerful nation, after the Soviet Union. Germany's *Ostpolitik* no⁺

## CHRONOLOGY OF FORMAL INDEPENDENCE FROM EUROPEAN RULE

| Date | Colonial Ruler | Country |
|---|---|---|
| 1947 | Britain | India, Pakistan |
| 1948 | Britain | Burma |
| 1949 | Britain | Bhutan, Sri Lanka (Ceylon) |
| | France | Laos |
| | Neth. | Indonesia |
| 1951 | Fr./Br. (Italy) | Libya |
| 1953 | France | Cambodia |
| 1955 | France | Vietnam (North Vietnam) |
| 1956 | France | Morocco, Tunisia |
| 1948–1957 | Britain | Malaysia |
| 1957 | Britain | Ghana (Gold Coast) |
| 1958 | France | Guinea |
| 1960 | France | Benin (Dahomey), Central African Republic, Chad, Congo, Gabon, Ivory Coast, Upper Volta (Burkina Faso), Madagascar, Sudanese Republic (Mali), Mauritania, Niger, Senegal, Togo |
| | Belgium | Zaire (Belgian Congo) |
| | Britain/Italy | Somalia |
| 1961 | Britain | Sierra Leone, Kuwait, Tanzania |
| 1960–1961 | UN/France | Cameroon |
| 1962 | Britain | Uganda, Jamaica |
| | UN/Belg. | Rwanda, Burundi (Urundi) |
| | France | Algeria |
| 1963 | Britain | Kenya |
| 1964 | Britain | Malawi, Zambia |
| 1965 | Britain | Gambia, Maldives, Singapore |
| 1966 | Britain | Botswana, Lesotho |
| | France | Guyana |
| 1967 | Britain | South Yemen (Aden) |
| 1968 | Britain | Mauritius, Swaziland |
| | Spain | Equatorial Guinea |
| 1970 | Britain | Fiji, Tonga |
| 1971 | Britain | Bahrain, Qatar, United Arab Emirates |
| 1974 | Britain | Grenada |
| | France | Comoros |
| | Portugal | Angola, Guinea-Bassau |
| 1975 | Portugal | Cape Verde, Sao Tome and Principe, Mozambique |
| | Neth. | Suriname |
| 1976 | Britain | Seychelles |
| 1977 | France | Djibouti |
| 1978 | Britain | Domenica, Solomon Islands, Tuvalu |
| 1979 | Britain | St. Lucia, Saint Vincent and the Grenadines, Kiribati (Gilbert Islands) |
| 1965–1980 | Britain | Zimbabwe, Vanvatu (New Hebrides) |
| 1981 | Britain | Belize |
| 1983 | Britain | Brunei, St. Christopher and Nevis (St. Kitts) |

\* The chronology of formal independence indicates how rapidly these movements spread, essentially from Asia to Africa to even the smallest territories. In some instances, formal freedom came after long and bloody struggles, in some with relative ease and after a period of increasing autonomy. Many of these new nations maintain strong ties to their former rulers both by choice and from economic necessity. Nearly all of these governments operate through parliamentary institutions of a European type.

only stimulated trade (culminating in the 1981–1982 agreements for a natural gas pipeline from Russia to Germany, Italy, and France) and strengthened permissible diversity among Eastern European governments but also encouraged some of the European left, especially in the Low Countries and Germany, in their call to have Europe declared a nuclear-free zone—that is, exempt from the nuclear weapons of either side. Such possibilities no longer depended on the superpowers alone.

### The European Community

Among themselves, the Western European nations[1] had achieved something quite unprecedented, beginning with the founding of the Council of Europe in 1949. Its Ministerial Committee and Assembly can pass no binding legislation, but they can provide important forums. The Council's statutes require its members to uphold individual and political freedom and the rule of law—provisions that effectively excluded the Eastern European states as they did Spain, Portugal, and Greece when ruled by dictators. Its Human Rights Commission hears petitions from individuals as well as nations and can have practical effect, as when in 1977 the attorney general of Great Britain admitted Irish charges that torture had been used against members of the Irish Republican Army and promised to punish the guilty. The Council

has not sustained a consistent influence in European affairs, yet it represents a widely shared vision of common European values, one neatly symbolized in the popular use of the Council's flag as a sticker on automobiles, indicating the owner's sense of belonging to Europe as well as a single nation, and by the Council's choice of Beethoven's "Ode to Joy" as its anthem.

By far the most important political and economic development in Western Europe has been the steady growth of the European Economic Community. In retrospect, its founding seems another reason to consider the late 1950s the beginning of a different era. The product of painfully negotiated compromises at every stage, its accomplishments have come so slowly that they can easily be underestimated. When the Common Market was first established, Great Britain refused to join. Reluctant to accept permanent involvement in the political affairs of the Continent or to loosen its Commonwealth ties, it led in the creation of a counterpoise to the European Economic Community (EEC), joining with Sweden, Norway, Denmark, Austria, Switzerland, and Portugal in the European Free Trade Association (EFTA), which had more limited goals (free trade but not a common tariff among its members), a looser structure, and less success than the EEC. In the decade of the 1960s, the "inner six" enjoyed nearly unprecedented growth and prosperity and in 1968 abolished all tariffs against one another's goods. In contrast, the United Kingdom remained at the bottom of the list of major European countries in the rate of economic expansion. Successive British governments sought to join the EEC in 1961–1963, 1967, and 1971, but the first two times, Britain's desire for special terms with regard to the Commonwealth nations, differences over agricultural policies, and de Gaulle's opposition prevented agreement. Following the French president's resignation

---

[1] Geographers list 19 nations as belonging to Western Europe: Austria, Belgium, Denmark, Finland, France, Greece, Iceland, Ireland, Italy, Lichtenstein, Luxembourg, Netherlands, Norway, Portugal, Spain, Sweden, Switzerland, the United Kingdom, and West Germany. All of these save Finland now belong to the Council of Europe, which also includes Cyprus, Malta, and Turkey.

Belgium, Denmark, Iceland, West Germany, Italy, Luxembourg, Netherlands, Norway, Portugal, Turkey, the United Kingdom, Canada, and the United States belong to NATO, as do France and Greece, although their armed forces no longer are under NATO command.

**The headquarters of the European Community in Brussels—a modern architecture for Community officials in quasi-Baroque spaces of imperial grandeur.** (Photo: J. Messerschmidt/Leo de Wys)

and concessions from both parties, Great Britain, accompanied by Ireland and Denmark, formally joined in 1972. In a surprising referendum, Norwegians voted not to follow suit, but in a British referendum held in 1975, two-thirds of the voters supported the decision to enter the European Community. The Communist nations of Eastern Europe countered with their own agency for economic coordination, Comecon, but by the 1970s they were vying with one another for increased trade and loans from the EEC. (See Map 30.1.)

The Community's progress has often been slow and disappointing. Although the elimination of trade barriers evolved more rapidly than planned, the goals of further integration were not met on schedule. Agricultural prices and subsidies have been the greatest difficulty, resulting in huge and costly stockpiles of produce as each nation presses for the protection of its own farmers. For Britain, which imports most of its food from outside the EC and has fewer farmers at home to protect, the Community's agricultural policies were costly. Britain's share of EC farm subsidies was far greater than EC expenditures in Britain until 1981 when the vigorous protests of the British government forced adjustments that have gradually led

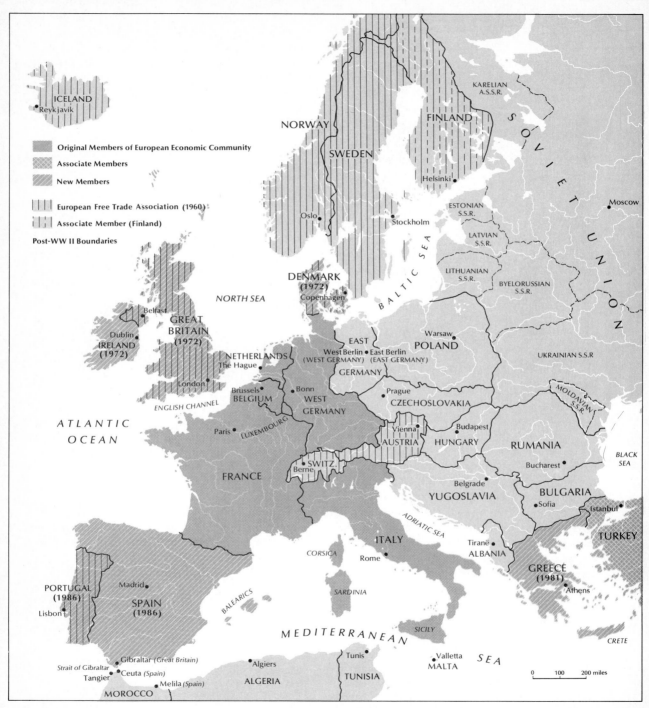

**MAP 30.1 EUROPE SINCE WORLD WAR II**

to reform of the agricultural program. It remained a difficult issue, however, the subject of renewed pressure in 1986 as a result not just of British objections but of the addition of Spain and Portugal to the Community, following the accession of Greece in 1981. Expansion to 12 members risked making agreement more difficult to obtain, despite the considerable autonomy granted the Community's executive to carry out policies previously agreed to.

The process of integration continued nevertheless. At the suggestion of the French president, in 1972 the heads of government of the EC countries began the practice of meeting four times a year, and in 1985 negotiations began for exempting some decisions from a single nation's veto. The Community's affairs are administered by its Council, a large bureaucracy located in Brussels; and increasingly EC officials acted as an independent executive on complicated economic and legal matters. In 1979, for the first time, citizens of the member nations voted directly for delegates to the Community's parliament, where the representatives sit according to party rather than nationality.[2] That step, one of its negotiators declared, "marks the birth of the European citizen." Decisions of the Community's Court of Justice led to increasingly uniform regulations (on standards of quality for products, insurance, environmental issues, and so forth) and legal protections, defining, for example, the rights of migrant workers. And special programs, including significant expenditures intended

to bring poorer regions such as the northwestern part of the British Isles and southern Italy as well as the economies of newer members closer to the Community's general level of prosperity, gave it a voice in matters long considered the exclusive concern of national governments.

## 1992

This step-by-step expansion in the EC's significance has developed in three ways. The most visible are the agreements among the member states, with new ones now set forth at nearly every one of the meetings of the heads of government, held every six months (the chairmanship rotates with these meetings, and it is often a matter of pride to use one's term to press a particular program). The most criticized are the policies and regulations on a widening range of matters set forth by the Community's administrators, regulations that can affect many aspects of economic and social life. The most significant may be the changing attitudes among the citizens of the member states. The preamble to the 1957 treaty that established the Economic Community expressed the desire "to lay the foundations of ever-closer union among the peoples of Europe . . . [and] to ensure economic and social progress by common action. . . ." Such lofty rhetoric was frequently ignored by politicians and ridiculed by journalists over the next 30 years, for the conflicts over minute interests and general principles often made such aims seem impossible. Half a dozen times in the 1960s and 1970s, Community leaders set forth proposals for a common foreign policy, for monetary union, for uniform regional and social programs, and even for political union. Each time these programs, however carefully worked out and eloquently presented, were eventually shelved.

Great Britain, particularly with Margaret

---

[2] The complexities of representation are exemplified by the fact that France, Great Britain, Italy, and West Germany each was given 81 representatives (a large enough number to assure Scotland and Wales more representatives than Denmark or Ireland); the Netherlands was allotted 25 but Belgium, 24 (having surrendered one so that the Flemings and Walloons would have equal representation); Denmark's 16 includes the gift of a representative from Belgium.

Thatcher as Prime Minister, and Denmark have usually led the resistance in the name of national sovereignty and the dangers of an international bureaucracy. Thus it was no surprise that Jacques Delors seemed to meet almost total rejection from Prime Minister Thatcher in the meeting of December 1985. He proposed that the EC discuss the possibility of strengthening its institutions, creating monetary union, establishing a common defense, and completing a single market over the next seven years. As President of the Commission (the administration of the EC), Delors has played an unusually active and effective role. The acrimony at that meeting was widely reported as another defeat for his ambitions. As often before, however, discussion continued, language was softened (the goal would be to "harmonize" the cherished practices of individual states), and, in effect, a compromise was reached. It called for an intergovernmental commission to establish a more precise program. From that developed the Single European Act, to come into effect by the end of 1992. The measure was so far-reaching that it had to be separately approved by each nation's parliament (in England the House of Lords briefly threatened to resist) and in Denmark and Ireland was also subject to a national referendum (winning 56 percent of the votes in the former and 70 percent in the latter).

The members of the Community had agreed among other things that they would, by 1992, cooperate on foreign policy, establish joint research programs in several areas of high technology, set binding minimal standards for environmental protection, and take further steps to reduce regional disparities in wealth. But for the lives of ordinary citizens, the most important measures by far are those to assure the free movement of "goods, persons, services, and capital." In 1990 all border checkpoints between Germany, Belgium, the Netherlands, Luxemburg, and France were abolished. By 1992 citizens of the Community will carry a community passport, cross national boundaries without restriction, be able to open a bank account or take out a mortgage anywhere in the EC, and practice their professions in any EC country as the licences and university degrees of one will be recognized in all the others. Important as each measure is, and there are many others, their greater significance may lie in the way the member societies responded. Individual decisions quickly ran ahead of legislation. By 1989–90 more than 200,000 university students from EC nations were studying in other EC countries, and businesses of every type (including the small and medium-sized businesses for which there are special protections, largely at British insistence) quickly made it a policy to anticipate a unified Community in all their plans. Its promise was similarly felt by socialists who think the power of government should be used to increase equality and by liberals who believe in the liberating effect of free exchange.

By far the world's greatest trader, the European Community had become an important element in world affairs and one that exercised considerable influence on the democratization of Greece, Portugal, and Spain. In fact, most trade barriers between the Community and other Western European nations have been eliminated, and formal ties to individual Eastern European states, beginning with Yugoslavia, have grown each year. As the Communist regimes of Eastern Europe began to fall, one immediate response was talk of creating an EC development bank to channel Western aid. Fear of exclusion from the Western European market, which had contributed to reform in the Soviet Union, also stimulated American and Japanese corporations to seek further European connections. From the first, members of the Community recognized both a desire and an obligation to sustain something of the older trade patterns with their former colonies, and this led to preferential trade agreements and the creation of associate status for such countries, arrangements subsequently extended under various terms to more than 50 states. When in 1972 the EEC offered preferential tariffs to all Mediterranean nations, every country but Libya responded favorably. Agreements with most of the nations of sub-Saharan Africa and with present and former colonies in the Caribbean and Pacific grant them access to the markets of the Community, often with guarantees to stabilize their export income while protecting their domestic industries. In addition, the Community provides sizable aid to developing countries. Thus in relations between North and South—that is, between developed and developing nations—as well as between East and West, the European Community has an important role.

## III. THE POLITICS OF PROSPERITY
❈
### Representative Democracy

The kind of political system advocated by liberal democrats in the nineteenth century and all but imposed at the Versailles Peace Conference has become universal in Western Europe. Since World War II, parliamentary government, multiple parties, and universal suffrage have thrived in countries like Germany and Italy that loudly eschewed them earlier in the century and have been more recently adopted in every nation that could exercise the choice. In the 1960s, most governments lowered the voting age to 18 and in other ways encouraged increased political participation.

### Alternating Parties: Great Britain and Germany

Formally, at least, the British and West Germany political systems have been models of stability, in which two dominant parties have smoothly alternated in power and pursued policies of an underlying continuity. In Britain the Conservatives (in office from 1951 to 1964, 1970 to 1974, and since 1979) placed greater emphasis on the role of the private sector in economic matters but largely accepted the extensive welfare programs and mixed economy they inherited. Conversely, the Labour governments were severely constrained by the plight of the British economy, pressuring their trade-union constituents to accept wage limits and cutting public expenditures in an effort to balance the budget sufficiently to halt the fall of the value of the pound and to reassure such creditors as the International Monetary Fund, whose loans imposed the strings of international finance.

Until the 1980s, all these governments shared in the efforts to improve public services, especially transportation, and to make education more democratic by encouraging comprehensive high schools and an impressive expansion of higher education. Each party, however, divided internally on the newer issues of joining the Common Market, protecting black immigrants from discrimination, and allowing Scotland and Wales to have local representative assemblies. Britain's overwhelming problem, however, remained economic. Plants were not modernized nor productivity improved at the pace required to compete with the leading industrial nations, while inflation threatened to reduce further the rate of investment. Analysts have found it easier to lay the blame—on the enormous cost to Britain of World War II, unimaginative and weak managers, an inadequate educational system, the selfish conservatism of labor unions, the high costs of welfare and defense—than prescribe the solution. Even membership in the European Community and the development of the rich oilfields of the North Sea provided no automatic solution.

Neither did the established parties. In office during the peak of the recession of the 1970s, the Labour party bore the brunt of the public reaction. Once out of office, it became more bitterly divided and more ideologically leftist. The Conservatives, under the firm and effective leadership of Margaret Thatcher, at the same time became more doctrinaire in their advocacy of free enterprise. The effects of the government's austere policies were, at best, mixed, and its popularity rested rather on its decisive style and the nationalist fervor roused during Britain's successful war with Argentina, which attacked the Falkland islands in 1983. As the distance between the two parties spread, a third rose to prominence—the Social Democrats, a coalition of Liberals and the right wing of Labour. The search for new policies still seemed to founder on old divisions, however, and the prospects for a third party faded as Labour moved toward more moderate policies. Judgments on the Thatcher years (a longer period than any other Prime Minister had won in this century) remain similarly mixed. The British economy was restructured, and both productivity and prosperity increased in the late 1980s under her tough medicine. Meanwhile, high unemployment and reductions in social services, including education, exacerbated some of the fundamental problems of British society.

In economic terms, the contrast with West Germany could hardly have been greater, and within the Federal Republic (which surpassed even the United States in world trade), political issues tended to be overshadowed by the satisfying fact of prosperity. Even the significant change in government from the Christian Democrats to the Social Democrats in 1969 did not lessen the commitment to encouraging investment, expanding trade, and preventing inflation. Often surprisingly conservative in their economic policies, the Social Democrats nevertheless pursued democratization in other ways, carrying through educational reforms and expanding social services (steps that have incidentally brought greater centralization and given the bureaucracy more power). Their most venturesome measure required all firms with more than 2000 employees to have a central board of directors, half of whose members are elected representatives of labor. Yet even as Germany won a more central place in European affairs, dissension was growing within both major parties; and the discovery that one of Willy Brandt's aides was a Soviet spy forced Brandt's resignation in 1974 in favor of the firmly centrist Social Democrat, Helmut Schmidt.

When the Christian Democrats regained office in 1982, under Helmut Kohl, they cut expenditures on social services without eliminating them and proved almost as eager as their predecessors to maintain good relations with the East. In the face of such continuity, the new concerns in German politics were associated with the Greens, a group whose environmentalist and antimilitary program recalled the student movement of the 1960s, and a small but worrisome nationalist movement. Kohl's cooperative role in the European Community proved valuable in 1989 as he balanced between the EC and sudden pressures for German unification.

### Including the Opposition: Italy and France

The Italian Republic, whose economic miracle was perhaps even more remarkable than Germany's, has always had a national government dominated by the Christian Democrats, a party far more heterogeneous than its German counterpart. In fact, elements of Italy's Christian Democratic party were closely tied to most of the nation's other major political currents, so that the process of coalition building always began within the semisecret confusion of the dominant party.

**An expanding market for consumer products was an important part of the economic boom in Europe in the 1960s and early 1970s. These washing machines are being tested at a factory in Italy, one of the world's largest exporters of home appliances.** (Photo: Tony Howarth/ Woodfin Camp and Associates)

While the Christian Democrats sought allies from among smaller parties in the center, the Communists—Italy's second-largest party— and a smaller group of monarchists and neo-Fascists on the right maintained loud and often effective opposition.

Room for maneuver was thus limited, and until 1958, the center coalitions supported governments that postponed most major reforms and left the most important economic initiatives to the state-owned holding companies. While the economy boomed, politics often sank into immobility beneath labyrinthine deals. From 1958 on, however, there was growing talk of an "opening to the left," an understanding that would woo Socialists from their Communist allies and permit a left-center coalition. Italy's rapid moderniza-

tion, the need for administrative reform, and the change in Catholic attitudes associated with Pope John XXIII all pointed to this course.

Finally achieved in 1963, the new coalition lasted until 1972, and it accomplished some of the promised changes. But the Socialists were more divided than ever, and the Christian Democratic factions lost none of their autonomy; the process of compromise remained infinitely complex; and few ministries survived a whole year. Unprestigious governments and a sprawling, inefficient bureaucracy nevertheless maintained a tension-filled nation in reasonable peace and freedom during a period of rapid social transformation. The Communist party, well-organized and skillfully led, had been making steady gains with its pungent criticisms and practical programs. When the regional governments the constitution had promised were finally established in the 1970s, the Communists gained office in many of them and in most of Italy's largest cities. There they enhanced their reputation for probity, efficiency, and reasonableness in initiating progressive programs. The time had come, Communists argued, for a "historic compromise," a coalition of Communists and Christian Democrats to rule in the name of reform. For several years that step seemed all but inevitable. Instead, the small parties between the Communists and the Christian Democrats showed new vigor. In 1982 one of their number became the republic's first prime minister who was not a Christian Democrat, although that party remains the most important in any governing coalition. The following year, Bettino Craxi, a wily politician who had rebuilt the Socialist party, became prime minister. Despite scandals and economic difficulties, Craxi established one of Italy's longest-lasting governments before giving way again to the Christian Democrats. Italy's complicated political system continued to produce moderate programs that balanced conflicting interests.

The growing influence of the left in France was a somewhat more surprising outcome of the years of Gaullist supremacy, for by 1962, when his followers won a firm majority in the Chamber of Deputies, Charles de Gaulle seemed to have established the stability and even the popularity of the Fifth Republic. France had become the fourth nation in the world to have nuclear weapons and exercised an independent position in world affairs. At home, too, the regime had a style all its own, centered in the powerful personality of de Gaulle. Economic and social policy was firmly in the hands of able, even brilliant, technocrats; not only was parliament docile but the bickering and factionalism of traditional political life seemed dead as de Gaulle relied instead on plebiscites and public relations to maintain presidential government's tie to public opinion. That France prospered in such stability was tangibly apparent on every side. Nevertheless, the presidential election of 1965 (the first since 1848 conducted by direct universal suffrage) required a run-off vote before de Gaulle could win a majority over François Mitterrand, the rising leader of the left. The opposition was strengthened by discontent among workers convinced they were not receiving their share of France's prosperity, by a broader dissatisfaction with many of the effects of rapid economic growth (including urban problems, inadequate housing, and the neglect of underdeveloped regions), and by criticisms, especially from intellectuals, of an often arbitrary bureaucracy and of de Gaulle's sometimes pompous paternalism.

In May 1968 the regime was nearly toppled by the surprisingly effective revolt of students in the Parisian universities, a revolt that began with specific objections to an overcrowded, excessively centralized, and outmoded educational system but quickly became a broader attack on the society of consumption and the technocratic policies Gaullists represented. As the students occupied buildings and battled with police, millions of workers went on strike. With firmness and political skill, the storm was weathered; most workers, ambivalent at best toward the students, who appeared rich and privileged to them, were interested rather in higher wages. And the Communists somewhat uncomfortably kept their distance from the student radicals, whose rising so fright-

A French missile-firing nuclear submarine is launched at Cherbourg. More than other European nations, France sought to maintain an independent, technologically advanced military force. (Photo: Wide World Photos)

ened much of French society that Gaullists were able to gain impressively in the elections held that June. But the Fifth Republic was never the same. The government promised and carried out extensive reforms of education, increasing options and access and giving students and parents a larger voice at every level; it reformed much in its own administration and turned to broader programs of welfare and social improvement, including somewhat vague plans to give workers a role in factory management. A few months later, de Gaulle put forth a complex set of propos-

als for administrative reforms leading to some regional decentralization. Characteristically, the proposals were both far-reaching and vague, and the electorate was asked to approve them in a referendum, while leaving all the details to the president. This time the voters refused, and in April 1969 de Gaulle resigned.

His successor, Georges Pompidou, was a

firm Gaullist whose new government was both more open and more willing to reconsider established policies. The election of Valéry Giscard d'Estaing as president in 1974 marked a further evolution. A member of the government's majority but not of the Gaullist party, he had campaigned with a direct informality that seemed to promise a more accessible, democratic, and relaxed administration, one that might even lead to a new coalition of the center, reaching from reform-minded Gaullists to the Socialists. Instead, the Socialists stayed closer to the Communists with whom they had contracted a common electoral program in 1972, one that demanded nationalization of many industries, more even distribution of income, and better housing. Significantly, in addition to these more common Marxist goals, it also called for more decentralized political authority and steps to assure greater opportunities for leisure, a more vigorous cultural life, and pleasanter cities. French political life, despite the fact that most voters appeared closest to the center, remained organized in terms of a Marxist left and a technocratic right of about equal strength.

The left got its chance when the presidential election of 1981 was won by the Socialists and Communists led by Mitterrand. Their followers danced in the streets, and the new government began with dramatic measures that nationalized many industries and most banks, raised wages and benefits, and increased social expenditures. Many of the accompanying reforms were clearly popular, but the daring gamble in stimulating economic growth failed as a result of its own mistakes, distrust within the business community and the fall of the franc, and an unfavorable international economy marked by high interest rates. Having been effectively isolated, the weakening Communists withdrew their support in 1984 as Mitterrand turned to policies of austerity, deflation, and

investment in high technology that were more like his predecessors' than his own platform. When the Socialists lost their parliamentary majority in 1986, France began an experiment new to the Fifth Republic, with the president and prime minister from different parties. To the surprise of some, that balancing worked quite well, winning Mitterrand reelection and the Socialists a renewed majority in 1988, to pursue their program of economic modernization, military strength, and support of the European Community.

## The Chances of Revolution

For a few weeks in May 1968 it had seemed as if the students of Paris might recapture the revolutionary spirit of 1848, as their barricades of paving stones and trees, imaginative posters, and endless slogans paid homage to a revolutionary tradition. In France, Germany, Italy, Great Britain, and the United States students during 1968–1969 behaved as an independent political force, mounting attacks on university regulations that became denunciations of middle-class and capitalist society, which they portrayed as hypocritical and repressive. Inspired by the values and successes of national liberation movements in the Third World and appalled by the war in Vietnam, the students voiced criticisms of national foreign policy and of the military that became an indictment of continuing imperialism. They proclaimed that history was at a turning point, but once again history failed to turn. In general, these protests led to reforms of education and amended government policies in other spheres, but in the short term at least, they strengthened the old order. Labor unions and parties of the left were suspicious of youthful anarchy, while reformers and liberals were as offended as conservatives by the violence and indifference to legal procedure. As revolutions, these movements thus failed in a cloud of angry rhetoric disproportionate to their strength, but in the long term, they influenced a style of protest that others would take up and publicized criticisms that remain in the modern consciousness about the society of consumption, the value of work and competition, the trustworthiness of elites, and the injustices of hierarchy. These concerns are now at least acknowledged in the programs of the left in nearly every Western country, while fear of disorder and of a declining belief in traditional values has increased among conservatives.

Students were active as well in the movement that briefly transformed Czechoslovakia in 1968, where Alexander Dubček, as first secretary of the Communist party, led the adoption of a program calling for freedom of speech, assembly, and religion and the granting of greater autonomy to Slovakia. These liberal and nationalist goals, very much like those expounded in the revolutions of 1848 but now called "Communism with a human face," were seen in Moscow as an intolerable danger, and Czech resistance to Soviet pressure was overcome in August by the armed invasion of troops from the Soviet Union, East Germany, Hungary, and Poland. It was the largest military operation in Europe since World War II; and within a few months all the liberal reforms save a grant of Slovakian autonomy had been reversed, the Soviet troops invited to remain, and Dubček ousted from office.

### Greece, Portugal, and Spain

Despite the enormous concentration of power in the hands of the modern state, revolutions nevertheless remained a possibility. In Greece they have come primarily as military coups, first in 1967, when a group of army officers overthrew the unstable parliamentary system and eventually the monarchy itself, and then in 1973 when the military, in turn, gave way to civilian leaders who arrested the officers and restored democracy. Despite harsh, even brutal, repression, Greece's military rulers had found it necessary gradually to restore freedoms that further exposed their unpopularity. Having to strengthen a fragile but modernizing economy, weakened by conflict with Turkey over control of Cyprus, they had to draw closer to Western Europe but found little disposition there to treat with Greek dictators. Political tensions remained high, and the socialist government that won victory in 1981 often stridently asserted its independence, especially of American policy, before falling on charges of corruption in 1989. Yet, with all the domestic battles, the problems of uneven economic growth, and the conflicts with Turkey, the main course of Greek development has been toward a more fluid society with closer ties to Europe.

The restoration of political freedom in Portugal and Spain was even more remarkable. Less dictatorial than the Salazar regime, which it succeeded on his incapacitation in 1968, the government of Marcello Caetano continued along essentially the same lines. But although opposition at home was effectively stymied, that proved impossible in Portugal's African colonies. The last of Europe's colonial powers to hang on to its empire, Portugal used force and cruel repression in Portuguese Guinea, Angola, and Mozambique only to see liberation movements there grow stronger. Portugal was subject to increasing condemnation in the United Nations, among African states and other European nations, while the government's political and economic strength at home was sapped despite censorship and further restrictions on the right of assembly. Suddenly, in April 1974 a group of Portuguese army officers seized control, ousting the old regime, promising full freedom and civil rights at home and self-determination for the colonies. Crowds filled the streets to dance and cheer before smiling soldiers whose rifles were decorated with flowers.

The euphoria could not last as Portugal came to grips with a series of staggering problems. A poor and backward country hoping to modernize, Portugal faced raging inflation and declining production with its agriculture in disarray as peasants claimed the land they had long coveted, socialist and Communist unions competed to capture a following in critical industries, many of the nation's skilled managers sought employment in Switzerland and Brazil, and rural and business groups battled to make their interests heard. The army leaders themselves were divided ideologically (among Communists, socialists, Christians, and conservatives) and over policy, both domestic and colonial. Seven governments in little over two years tried to cope with these problems. Extensive nationalizations of banks and industry were followed by free elections in 1975 and 1976. A series of attempted revolts of the left and the right, usually led by military factions, have all been defeated; and since 1976 and the election of the moderate General António Ramalho Eanes as president, there has been reasonable stability. The Socialists are the largest party, though not a majority, and both their minority government and more centrist coalitions have succeeded in drawing Portugal closer to the other governments of Western Europe than ever before—a tendency reinforced in the elections of 1985–1986 that accompanied Portugal's joining the European Community. Mario Soares, a socialist and former prime minister, became Portugal's first democratically elected civilian president in 60 years.

The political transformation in Spain has been less dramatic, but it follows on the most rapid industrial growth in Europe. Not until the 1950s did Spanish production exceed the level of 1935, so slow was the nation's recovery from the years of civil war. By the 1960s, however, the money attracted through tourism, the encouragement of efficient large-scale agriculture at the expense of the small producer, and systematic government programs of industrialization on the familiar European model all began to have effect. The gross national product of 1960 had increased fivefold 15 years later; and a new generation of leaders in business, the professions, and the Church kept some distance from the old pieties of the Franco regime while sporadic strikes and demonstrations (in which Basque nationalists and priests were prominent) expressed a growing discontent with the government's corruption, suppression of freedom, and social conservatism. Still, the aging Franco skillfully kept his hand on power even after his retirement from the conduct of daily affairs in 1973 and the formal naming of Juan Carlos, the son of the Bourbon claimant, to the throne and as Franco's successor. When Franco died in 1975, the revolution many feared did not take place; and the new king proved both more flexible and more adept than most anticipated. Political repression and censorship were steadily relaxed, and successive prime ministers edged toward genuinely representative government.

With freedom, old antagonisms reappeared in public, and there was dark talk of a return to the 1930s and civil war. That did not happen. An attempted coup d'état by army officers in 1981 was put down, and the king received much credit for his role in the preservation of democracy and the relative calm that followed. With the granting of regional autonomy, Basque terrorists became more isolated, although still active. The divided Communists have been eclipsed by the Socialists led by the extremely popular Felipe Gonzales, whose moderate program favored the restructuring of industry (at the cost of many jobs) and the acceptance of NATO (Spain had joined in 1982). Although opinion polls indicated that most Spaniards had come to oppose membership, the referendum on that issue held in 1986 produced a victory for the proponents of NATO and a personal victory for Gonzales. It followed quickly on Spain's entrance into the European Community, which was presented as the end of a long isolation and the achievement of a healthy, modern democracy.

## The Shadow of Recession

Predictions of the future, however, had tended to be more confident early in the 1970s than in the 1980s. To be sure, reforms continued to be made, particularly in education as the French university system was decentralized and German students were given an official voice in university affairs. Catalans seemed pleased with the increased autonomy granted them in 1977, and agitation in the Basque provinces declined after the concessions granted there two years later. Ecological movements had some effect at the polls, and there was even an echo of the 1960s in the demonstrations against placing nuclear warheads in Western Europe that in 1981 saw nearly half a million young people marching in Bonn and perhaps another million in other capitals. Except for a rising regionalism, however, public life was largely dominated by more conventional concerns and duller issues. Although often willing to admit that the traditional programs of left and right were losing relevance, established parties remained uncomfortable with these new issues. Instead, governments were forced to grapple with problems that appeared embedded in their social and economic systems and that were complicated by international connections.

### Energy, Inflation, and Recession

The clearest challenge came in October 1973, when the oil-exporting nations (mainly in the Middle East) first banded together to raise international prices, for Europe imported nearly two-thirds of its energy in the form of petroleum. Only the Soviet Union could meet its own energy needs through domestic production. Subsequent development of North Sea oilfields made Norway self-sufficient and Britain nearly so, and the Netherlands has benefited from developing Europe's largest fields of natural gas. Although the hope of making Europe energy-self-sufficient by 1985 proved illusory, the collapse of oil prices in 1986 reduced the economic pressures resulting from Europe's rapacious demand for energy. That hoped-for self-sufficiency depended heavily on nuclear power (in 1976 over half of the world's nuclear power plants in operation and of those under construction were in Europe), which has been more costly than anticipated and raised serious questions of pollution and safety. In 1986 the meltdown of a reactor at Chernobyl in the Soviet Union sent radioactive clouds over much of Central Europe, briefly disrupting agriculture while strengthening the antinuclear movement.

A second and more complicated but related problem was inflation (rising to an annual rate of increase in 1975–1976 of over 20 percent in Britain and Italy, 30 percent in Portugal) that undermined planning, savings, and trade, while squeezing salaried employees and many workers between rising costs and lagging incomes. Only West Germany among major capitalist nations consistently managed to hold the rate of inflation below 5 percent. The general causes of the inflation are well known—governments spending more than their income, more money in circulation, the higher prices of imports, the tendency of businesses to maintain or increase profits by raising prices rather than increasing efficiency, the assumption on all sides that prices are bound to go up—but the solution is difficult. Government expenditures reflect social policies and political pressures not easily reversed, and organized workers are not inclined to absorb the losses that would follow from not seeking higher wages. In fact, the debate as to what interests should be sacrificed can easily become an exercise in social conflict, as it has tended to do in Britain and Italy.

By the 1980s the advanced economies of Western Europe were facing other difficulties too. Increased competition from the Japanese and from new plants in other parts of the world (often ones built with European capital) gave dangerous competition to the now-aging industries of Europe. From Denmark to California, tax revolts threatened many long-established governmental programs, while a significant proportion of the work force (its size could only be guessed) worked for barter or for cash that went unreported, to avoid both taxes and regulations intended to improve the standard of living. Only in Italy was the proportion of this "underground economy" thought to approach the size it reached in the United States (where estimates of its value ranged from 7 to 25 percent of GNP), but the underground economy was believed to account for nearly 10 percent of GNP in a number of European countries. Above all, it was clear that, like the threat of new competition, the problems of energy, inflation, and monetary policy were international in scope.

Then a new word, *stagflation*—the paradoxical combination of economic stagnation and rising prices—gave way in economic discussions to an ominous older one, *recession*. Everywhere unemployment was rising. The classic tight-money policies insisted upon by Britain's Prime Minister Margaret Thatcher had slowed inflation—although it remained high—but at the price by 1982 of having 12 percent of the work force without jobs. Elsewhere, slightly less draconian measures (reinforced by high interest rates in the United States and declining oil prices) succeeded in slowing inflation. But in France and Italy,

too, unemployment rose to about 8 percent, levels not experienced since World War II; even in Germany, the rate climbed to 6 percent. Foreign workers were hardest hit, which meant that the recession rapidly extended to poorer countries. And within Europe, unemployment was second highest among the young, a fact of frightening political and social implications.

Where socialists held office in the mid-1980s, they often found themselves (somewhat as they had in the Great Depression) governing at a time when their programs for increased social services, better education, more vacation time, and a greater voice in the workplace for employees came to seem unaffordable. Instead, it fell to them to push policies more congenial to their opponents, abandoning industries no longer competitive and pressing for investment in new technologies. The economic upturn that followed the recession left large pockets of endemic, long-term unemployment with bleak prospects for whole regions and for all who had worked there in unskilled labor or practicing skills no longer needed. That sort of unemployment was a social and political problem that showed its effects in vandalism, drug addiction, and racial conflict as well as political frustration. The demands of an international economy had moved beyond the range of established political programs.

### Terrorism

Some small, radical groups, rather than abandon the fading hope for revolution, turned to terrorism. Modern society, in its very complexity and urban anonymity, seemed especially vulnerable to such tactics. In the demimonde of international crime and espionage and arms deals (all regular beneficiaries of the Cold War), the necessary skills and equipment were not hard to come by; and if governments could be provoked into

A crowd gathers at the spot in Rome where the body of Aldo Moro was found, and two women in an ancient gesture reach out to touch the picture of Moro on posters put up by the Christian Democratic party, declaring "his faith in liberty lives in our hearts." (Photo: Wide World Photos)

repressive responses, they might alienate their own citizens. Until they were largely defeated by the severe but efficient measures of police and government, German terrorists made business leaders as well as politicians their targets. The more extensive activities of Basque terrorists, which brought death to numbers of officials and lesser-known victims, shook several Spanish governments and led many, especially in the military, to decry the weakness of a democratic state. In Italy, Marxist and neo-Fascist underground bands accompanied shooting, kidnaping, and bombings with their proclamations of revolutionary rhetoric. Groups such as the Red Brigades heightened tension and inse-

curity; and when in 1978 they followed a series of dramatic actions by the kidnaping of Aldo Moro, the whole nation held its breath. The police were unable to locate Moro, until his bullet-riddled body was left in a car in central Rome. Yet the public responded with remarkable firmness and unanimity, and the state neither turned to repression nor collapsed. Thus terrorism was on the wane when the Red Brigades captured an American NATO commander in 1982. This time the police, armed with information garnered from years of trials and investigations, were able to free the American and to capture a sufficient number of terrorists to deal a serious blow to their movement. Such incidents, like the shooting of Pope John Paul II by a Turkish terrorist in 1981, provoked outcries about modern society—for the alienation that produces terrorists, the values that condone violence, and the technology that makes such acts easy—but changed society very little.

Terrorism was most effective when it fed regional or religious animosities, as when supporters of the Palestine Liberation Organization killed Israeli athletes at the Munich Olympic Games in 1972 or in Northern Ireland, where terrorism rose to the level of a continuous war. There, the Irish Republican Army, an underground organization repudiated by the Irish Republic, and extremist Protestant groups have killed hundreds of innocent people and pushed the British government to abandon its program for local rule by both Protestants and Catholics. Centuries of religious and national conflict, discrimination, and repression had enabled the most fanatic on both sides to win support against the political policies and military efforts of the British government as the number of martyrs mounted. By 1985 there was some increased willingness to seek workable compromise in Northern Ireland, and in Europe as a whole, the continued incidents of terrorism (whether in Paris stores or aimed at American tourists) were more often associated with the conflicts of the Middle East or Africa than an expression of internal social tensions or a vision of revolution.

## Flight from Communism

### Eurocommunism

Europe as a whole offered an extraordinary variety of experiments in social systems ranging from the capitalism of Switzerland and West Germany to the mixed economies of Western Europe, the market Communism of Yugoslavia, and the other varieties of Communism in Eastern Europe and the Soviet Union. Europe's least-developed nation, Communist Albania, completed the spectrum; it was China's best ally outside Asia until the late 1970s when China turned to a more moderate course. This variety of experiments aimed at combining a directed economy with social justice and political freedom stimulated the development within Western European Communist parties known as Eurocommunism. By combining democracy and pluralism with the traditional goals of Communism, the movement sought not only to broaden its base and win elections but to strengthen the forces for change in Western Europe and perhaps even transform the nature of the governments of Eastern Europe. The failure of Eurocommunism was thus significant for later failures elsewhere.

Italy's Communist party, the largest in the world in a non-Communist country, was its model and major proponent. In Antonio Gramsci, who died in a Fascist prison, the party had one of the ablest of modern Marxist theoreticians; his emphasis on the importance of local history and culture in determining the path to Communism gave the party's flexibility a justification beyond mere tactics. And through the years of opposition and close ties to the Italian Socialist party, the Communists developed, under the leadership of Enrico Berlinguer, a suave and attractive politician, a detailed program for the reform of Italian society, which accepted the principles of formal democracy—including civil rights, multiple parties, and free elections.

The successes of the Italian party increased its influence at home and abroad and led the French Communist party, traditionally among Europe's most Stalinist, toward a similar stance. Both parties denounced the

Soviet invasion of Czechoslovakia in 1968. The Italian party even accepted NATO, and the French one not only ceased to oppose France's nuclear weapons but, determined to prove its respect for free elections, in 1976 officially rejected the dictatorship of the proletariat as an item of party dogma. With the liberalization in Spain after the death of Franco, the Spanish Communist party, under Santiago Carrillo (whose years of exile were spent in the United States rather than the Soviet Union), adopted similar views and moved even closer toward democratic socialism.

This form of Communism, ready to cooperate with other parties on single points and insistent on its own democratic convictions, appeared to have been accepted by most Western European Communist parties (with the notable exceptions of Portugal's and Finland's).[3] Despite heavy Soviet pressure and public denunciations of these Western Communists as ''bourgeois ideologists,'' the Russians were unable to restore the unity of European Communism. On the sixtieth anniversary of the Russian Revolution in 1977, Eurocommunism thus marked a third schism in the Communist ranks; and part of its Western appeal was its claim to seek Europe's independence from both Soviet and American influence. Many voters even on the left remained skeptical, however, of the Communists' dedication to liberal freedoms, noting that the parties themselves remained highly centralized, intolerant, suspicious of the European Community, and in foreign affairs, closely tied to Soviet and anti-American positions. Instead in the 1980s it was the socialist parties of Italy, France, Spain, Portu-

gal, and Greece that gained power, often at first in alliance with the Communists, who outside Italy were left smaller and more isolated than before. While the Communists, unable to sustain cross-class appeal and satisfy their old hardline militants, faced the decline of their traditional base. Even the Italian party, weakened by the death of Berlinguer in 1985, looked again to Moscow for new inspiration from Gorbachev.

## The Soviet Sphere

The Soviet presence remained the central fact of politics in Eastern Europe, with ties to the U.S.S.R. the keystone of each nation's foreign policy and Soviet approval the measure of domestic orthodoxy. Yet differences once submerged came to seem increasingly important, and each country enlarged its particular ties to Western Europe through cultural exchanges, communication, and trade. Bulgaria sought better relations with other Balkan States, and Rumania formed economic ties with Yugoslavia and attempted to establish itself as a nonaligned state, while East Germany, the second industrial power among Communist states (the seventh in Europe and the eleventh in the world), oscillated between friendlier relations and renewed tensions with West Germany and between repression and concessions at home to meet the sort of discontent expressed in bloody riots in the early 1970s.

Although the invasion of Czechoslovakia was followed by efforts to strengthen Comecon and by the enunciation of the ''Brezhnev doctrine,'' which declared a ''threat to socialism'' in one country to be a threat to all, that policy was rejected by Rumania as well as by Yugoslavia and by the Italian Communists. Not content to be a Russian granary, Rumania launched its own course of industrialization. The Rumanian leader Nicolae Ceausescu was welcomed in the west for this independence, but at home he became an

---

[3] Communist parties have traditionally attracted nearly a third of the electorate in Italy, one-fifth in France and Finland, one-eighth in Spain, and much less elsewhere: about 5 percent in Sweden, 4 percent in Denmark, 3 percent in Belgium, 2 percent in Greece and the Netherlands, and less than 1 percent in West Germany and Great Britain.

## Party Festivals

In Italy an important event in a working-class district was the *Festa dell'Unità*. Arrangements might be planned for months. Tasks had to be assigned, some men found to make the booths and others to set up tables and chairs. Neighborhood women prepared most of the food, and everyone, men and women together, would help with the cooking that had to be done during the *festa*, in tents if it was held outdoors. Men did most of the serving, and for a big *festa* the local representative might return to his home district to wait on tables. The food was the main thing, pasta and sausages and cakes made by the people there and typical of the region. Families sat for hours at the long tables savoring each course and drinking the local wine. Some of the games were regional, too, and there were also booths for games of chance and throwing darts (in the 1970s the face of Richard Nixon was a likely target) and races in which the contestants' legs were tied together or they carried a glass of wine they must not spill. Later, there would be dancing and sometimes even fireworks.

The *Festa dell' Unità* was an important event in the life of the neighborhood but also in the life of the Italian Communist Party, the Party had begun holding them in 1945 and it encouraged party members in every district to put on at least one *festa* a year. The local Party paid the workers for the food they prepared and bought the wine; the city or regional Party usually sent around a truck with wood for the booths, bunting, hundreds of red flags, lights to string across the grounds, some banners and posters with current slogans, and maybe even a public-address system. The Party thought there should be speeches, although few people really listened to them, but it was nice to have music coming over the loudspeakers when nobody from the neighborhood was playing a guitar or accordian. Although there was no fee to get in, nearly everyone gave a donation at the entrance. The Party kept any surplus once all the expenses were paid. Mainly, the *festa* was a neighborhood event, and nearly everyone except the

priest came. Even though most were not Party members, they liked the sense of community and the praise of the working people who had to fight for what they got.

There were also regional and even national *feste*. In all, the PCI had sponsored some 700 of these various *feste* each year during the 1940s. The number rose to 6,000 in the 1970s and to 8,000 in the early 1980s. The local ones became a little more informal and maybe less serious with more music and lights. In the 1940s and 1950s it was an important political statement to be seen carrying the party banner or singing the "Internationale," and it provided a strong sense of belonging and purpose.

The regional and national *feste* were huge, with the size of the crowd at the main event often estimated (the numbers varied somewhat with the politics of the reporter) to reach 350,000 people or more, and they went on for a week and sometimes longer. These bigger *feste* also changed greatly over the years. In the 1950s they featured great masses of people marching through city streets, carrying banners with slogans for peace and disarmament or expressing the Party's position on a particular bill in parliament. There were also flags and banners to identify workers from different trades and the enterprises they came from, and sometimes there were farmers on tractors and peasants in regional costume to show the people united. There was a lot of dancing and picnicking at these *feste* of the 1950s, and the drinking and talking would go on for hours in scores of cafes. In the style of the time, a "Miss *Festa* of ———" might even be on display, and there were exotic goods for sale, foods and musical instruments primarily, from Communist countries around the world. Basically, though, these were very serious occasions. Huge pictures of Italian and Soviet Communist leaders (Khruschev and Eisenhower together, in honor of their first summit in 1957), hundreds of hammers and sickles and red stars, and thousands of red flags would direct the crowd and the eye toward the giant podium. There, invited guests from Communist parties in Africa and Asia as well as Europe would sit with the principal speakers of the day.

In the 1960s design became more important. There were stunning posters and striking pagodas and arches using Party symbols. Even the parades seemed a little more relaxed and the marchers better dressed. The *festa* now took over a number of buildings across the city, and there were attractive exhibits and displays of books and magazines featuring Party publications (including its childrens' and women's magazines, its intellectual and literary quarterlies, and its national and local newspapers). The most popular themes attacked American imperialism in Vietnam (with heartrending photographs), imperialism in general, and fascism in Greece and Latin America and Italy. There were also displays giving statistics of the arms race, showing the progress being made in the Soviet Union, and analyzing the evils of racism (especially in the United States; yet every poll showed that the two countries most admired by members of the PCI were the U.S.S.R. and the U.S.A.). In the 1970s the practice developed of assigning each big *festa* some central theme, such as workers' housing or women in society (sessions about, women became a part of every major *festa*); and there were special conferences, study groups, concerts, and ballets. The intellectual and cultural tone was high. The Party could still turn out huge crowds, and there were members who remained dedicated to an older concept of the *Festa dell'Unità*, like the group that paraded with a banner describing their achievements in the Tuscan town of Poggibonsi, "26,000 inhabitants, 18,125 votes for the PCI, 5,500 party members, 400 subscribers to *l'Unità*, [the party newspaper], and 16,000 copies sold each month." They got a round of applause and a smile for their provincial old-fashionedness.

By the 1980s, the Party's great *feste* had elements of an industrial exhibit and a rock concert with lectures and seminars on the side. The spectacle and the content were impressive, but there was less sense of community. This Party did not seem to define a whole subculture or expect to be at the center of its members' lives. The tone had become less doctrinaire, and there was much less about the Soviet Union than there had been 20 years before. To be sure, by the end of the decade there were portraits of Gorbachev and encouraging messages from him to be read aloud. He, after all, might understand why the PCI had asked to sit with the Socialists and not the Communists in the European parliament and why they debated changing their name and removing the hammer and sickle from their flag. At those discussions, some of the older militants who had spent their lives in the Party had tears in their eyes. ❄

**Even with tens of thousands in attendance, mealtime kept some of the atmosphere of a family picnic at the National *Festa dell' Unitá* held in Florence in 1988.** (Photo: Red Giorgetti)

In a scene that, except for the television camera, is reminiscent of the long history of industrial labor movements, Lech Walesa addresses Polish workers outside a factory in Zyrardow, not far from Warsaw, in October 1981. (Photo: Giansanti/Sygma)

increasingly brutal and repressive tyrant. Private ownership continued to have an important role in the economies of Poland and of Hungary, which developed one of the strongest and most consumer-oriented of the Eastern European economies. The Catholic Church, influential in Hungary, Czechoslovakia, and Poland, became especially outspoken in the last, where opinion could be more openly expressed. Protests, demonstrations, and even riots against the police or over the price of food served as a constant reminder to the Communist leaders of Eastern Europe

of the need to maintain a balance of cooperation with the Soviet Union and a firm grasp of domestic power, on the one hand, with concern for public opinion, on the other.

This conflict was sharpest in Poland, where riots in 1976 forced a postponement of higher food prices and where strikes in 1980–1981 led to the recognition of Solidarity, an organization of independent trade unions led by Lech Walesa, who became a national hero. This movement, which received strong support from the Catholic Church, even led to a change of government, but the new party head, General Wojciech Jaruzelski, soon clamped down on Solidarity and ruled for two years by martial law. Amidst continuing expressions of discontent and severe economic crisis, the dominance of the Communist party and Poland's ties to the Soviet Union remained intact.

Each country thus cautiously evolved foreign ties and domestic policies that reflected something of its history and traditional culture. Yugoslavia, the maverick among Communist states, cautiously established better relations with its more orthodox neighbors while firmly maintaining its independence. Domestically, too, it stood between East and West, combining something of a market economy and decentralized factory management (in which workers were given large voice) with state ownership, elections allowing more than one candidate for each office within a single party, and greater freedom for dissent—despite crackdowns on figures like Milovan Djilas, a lifelong Communist who paid with years of imprisonment for his systematic and Marxian critique of Soviet society and of party officials as a new ruling class, or like the professors associated with the theoretical journal *Praxis*, the only officially tolerated voice of criticism, who all were suspended from their positions in 1975. Yet, by a timely strengthening of its federal structure, the state held together after the death of Tito in 1980. Ominously, though, the economy began a steady downward spiral. The measures that had seemed so promising were not enough to permit the continuing restructuring and new investment a modern economy requires. Nor was limited freedom sufficient to prevent a rise in crippling ethnic and political tensions.

## The Miracles of 1989

A pattern was emerging. Some loosening of repression and encouragement of independent economic activity could stimulate the economy, as had happened in Poland and Hungary; but that was rapidly followed by further stalemate when institutional blockage stifled further economic renewal and the tolerance of some dissent stimulated demands for greater freedom. Poland was a clear example. The threat of economic disaster had not been reduced by martial law. Instead of disappearing, Solidarity propagandized with wit and daring from the underground. The visit of the Polish Pope, intended to appeal to patriotic and religious feeling, became the occasion for more demonstrations. General Jaruzelski then relaxed martial law and released some political prisoners. Anger and frustration increased; the economy worsened. But one thing had changed. Moscow seemed to favor further reform. In February 1989 the government was willing to recognize Solidarity once again, but the union now demanded free elections. When the government hesitated, Gorbachev signaled that Poland was on its own. Thus in April a pact was signed that recognized Solidarity and promised free elections. When they took place, Solidarity won almost all the seats. Communist party members, stunned and frightened, had little leverage when negotiations began about forming a new government; and after various formulas had failed to work, Solidarity took over the cabinet in August, the first non-Communist government in what for 40 years had been called the Soviet bloc.

These changes might have been expected to begin in Hungary, where political discussion and the economic activity were generally more open than in other Communist countries, and Hungarians were well aware of events in Poland. By April even some Hungarian Party officials talked of the need for free speech, civil rights, and the protections of private property. On May Day the official demonstration was dwarfed by another sponsored by the oppositions, and the anniversary of the death of Imry Nagy, who had led the 1956 rising, became the occasion in June for another huge demonstration, which even some members of the government chose to attend. Ever flexible, the Hungarian Communist Party met in October to change its name to the Socialist Party, while parliament promised that free elections would be held the following year.

Suddenly the power of people aroused seemed irrisistible. There were plenty of old-line leaders who remained convinced, of course, that a show of strength would be enough; but that was becoming difficult. In East Berlin, Erich Honecker, party leader and prime minister, had his troops beating and arresting demonstrators even in October, the week before he resigned; but options were limited. Gorbachev said he disapproved; censorship was of little use because everyone could watch West German television, and the nation seemed simply to be emigrating. Every day hundreds of people, especially the young and those with marketable skills, abandoned the country. They went to Hungary and mobbed the West German embassy seeking visas until embarrassed governments arranged for special trains. The situation was out of control when Honecker's successor, Egon Kranz, stunned everyone by bravely announcing that East Germany's borders would be opened that very day, November 9, 1989. The guards could not at first believe their orders. Then late at night they shrugged and stepped aside as hoards of people pushed through the gates of the Berlin wall. Hundreds cheered and waved from atop that symbol of oppression before strolling past the well-stocked shops of West Berlin. The celebrations continued in front of the television cameras for days, even after work crews began dismantling the wall. But the flow of people did not stop, and perhaps one-third of them, thousands each day, had decided to try a different life in West Germany. Throughout East Germany, in a few weeks meetings once held in secret had moved into churches under the wary eyes of the police, then out into public squares as the police withdrew. Pleas for order, familiar promises,

even revelations of past corruption were overshadowed by individual frustration and the possibility that the two Germanies might be united.

Only the harshest of the East European governments, Czechoslovakia, Bulgaria, and Rumania, remained unscathed. But there had already been a number of demonstrations in Prague during that amazing year, and in October, 40,000 gathered in Wenceslas Square to protest against an unyielding government. In what was becoming a familiar rite, slogans were written on walls, posters appeared, political groups formed. After riot police beat up on demonstrating students, 200,000 people filled Wenceslas Square and a few days later, 300,000 came to shout and sing and jingle keys as a good-humored suggestion that it was time to leave. By December the now well-organized Civic Forum held power and had elected as its president a popular playwright, Vaclav Havel, whose plays had long been banned and who, like so many others of Eastern Europe's new leaders, had served his time as a political prisoner. Bulgaria had responded to the challenge even more promptly, partly as the result of public pressure and partly from the shrewdness of a party still sensitive to its supporters. In November, Todor Shivkov, Party secretary since 1954 and head of state since 1962, was forced from office, then jailed. The fact that Bulgaria's politicians, more than their neighbors, still looked to the Soviet Union even as crowds demanded democracy had eased the transition there. Only Rumania had to suffer heavy bloodshed to rid itself of Communist rule. The most deprived (more than one 40-watt light bulb per room was illegal) and arbitrarily ruled of the Eastern European countries, it was also the last to mount an effective resistance. When crowds gathered in December, the government did not hesitate to shoot; and we may never know how many died. Still the crowds formed, and Ceausescu tried to make his escape. Caught, he was executed by firing squad on Christmas day, following a brief trial; but it took a week to end the fighting between the last of the special police loyal to Ceausescu and the army, which supported the new leaders. Everywhere Rumanian flags waved, a conspicuous hole in their center where the communist insignia had been. The last Communist government west of the Soviet Union (except for Albania) had fallen.

After 45 years, the end came with surprising suddenness. There had, of course, been many signs of resentment and resistence in previous years; but they had been no match for Soviet power. Gorbachev's attitude was thus crucial, and in 1988 he had announced before the United Nations that the Soviet Union would allow its allies to go their own way. Those governments had held power for more than a generation; officials, administrators, police, and Party members were all native sons and daughters. They had once offered hope to many and commanded significant loyalty. The dissipation of all that was remarkable. Economic failure and Soviet policy explained a good deal, but there was something more. Workers and Catholics in Poland, party members and entrepreneurs in Hungary, students and intellectuals in Czechoslovakia had joined with nationalists and millions of others in the conviction that these regimes must end—rarely does politics produce failure on such a scale. As ordinary people had gathered to express that conviction, they had quite naturally waved banners, held hands, sung songs, and carried candles in rituals adapted from demonstrations elsewhere by students, the women's movement, the American civil rights movement, Christians, and Greens. Everywhere, stimulated by the television images and instant news of their neighbors, people had believed their cause was universal but also attached it to memories of their own history, heroes, and special needs. Eastern Europe in the fall of 1989 had experienced one of those magic moments when ordinary people really do exercise power. They had seized it to demand the end of one-party government, meaningless elections, official ideology, censorship, arbitrary police, scarcity, and hopelessness.

Within months, the meaningful elections and unaccustomed freedoms that promised the beginning of a new era also resurrected old divisions—ethnic, social, and ideological. They illumined not only the appalling failures and corruption of the fallen regimes but also the awesome problems still to be faced and the disagreements yet to be resolved. All at once, Eastern Europe in 1990 looked rather like the Eastern Europe of the 1920s. Moderate conservatives gained the lead among the multiple parties of Hungary and watched resentfully at the treatment accorded the Hungarian population in Rumania. Czechoslovakia, with the internationally admired Havel elected president of the republic, found itself debating yet again the relations of Czechs and Slovaks. As Poland risked the drastic medicine of sudden conversion to a market economy, rifts appeared within Solidarity. In Bulgaria, Communist party members won most of the seats in free elections, and in Rumania leaders who no longer claimed to be Communists showed little willingness to allow real democracy. East Germans voted for those who promised the most rapid assimilation into the German Federal Republic, transfixed by the economic implications. The conversion to the West German mark in July (on fairly generous terms) went smoothly, but no one knew whether the promise of heavy investment from the West could rectify the drastic rise in unemployment. It took considerable international negotiation (and a heavy subsidy to the Soviet Union from West Germany) before German unification could be officially accomplished in October; but by then that monumental step, which had seemed all but impossible a few months earlier, had become a mere formality.

All the new regimes would have to deal with a lack of consumer goods in feeble economies liable to sharp inflation as they turned to a market economy. They would have to employ suspect elites and dubious institutions, while facing ethnic divisions and maybe even border disputes. Where restructuring the economy produced long-term hardship or the confusion of freedom looked like chaos, many might then remember with nostalgia the job security, subsidized housing, and health care of Communist rule. Against that stood the challenge of the Western European model of international cooperation, prosperity, and freedom and the excitement of peoples suddenly at liberty to determine what their aspirations were.

## The Soviet Union

In the 1960s in Western Europe, small groups of Maoists had criticized and harried the large Communist parties in the name of the principles represented by Chairman Mao Zedong, but the Soviet Union remained the model of European Communism. Its most impressive achievement, admired throughout the world, was its industrial growth. By the 1960s the Soviet economy was second in overall production and wealth only to that of the United States. In 1961 it sent the first man into orbit around the earth; and as the world's largest producer of steel, iron, and more recently, oil, the U.S.S.R. was apparently gaining on the West. With this basis for confidence, Khrushchev, brash and outspoken, became an international personality who did much to humanize the image of the Soviet government. His foreign policy suggested that the Soviet regime had no desire to risk its achievements and its empire in a world conflagration. At home, the very success of heavy industry led to increased demand for consumer products, higher standards of quality, and adequate housing.

These pressures, like the logic of de-Stalinization, opened the possibility of a new evolution in Soviet rule, but it proved difficult to accomplish. Khrushchev's plans to increase agricultural production through the application of the latest technology and by the cultivation of millions of acres of land in Asian Russia did not achieve the desired result. Soviet agriculture remained a perennial disappointment, and the question of whether to invest in consumer goods or heavy industry revived long-standing conflicts within the highest circles. Many Kremlin leaders worried, as well, about the restiveness in Eastern Europe and the growing rift with China. When, in the process of solidifying his authority, Khrushchev antagonized the military, they and his opponents in the Politburo and the Central Committee felt strong enough to speak against him. He was voted out of office in 1964 and sent into quiet retirement. The Soviet Union was developing practices that, though preserving dictatorship and a tradition of internal battles for power, permitted orderly transitions.

Khrushchev's successors were cool and tough party technicians, Aleksei Kosygin and Leonid Brezhnev. A firm grip on power, strengthened as Brezhnev emerged as the dominant figure, provided no simple resolution of the problems that had weakened Khrushchev. The cold-blooded invasion of Czechoslovakia established the limits to freedom or autonomy to be allowed in Eastern Europe, but hardly guaranteed stability. The relatively low yield of Russian agriculture continued to produce crises in bad years and had to be met in 1972 and 1975 by huge purchases of grain from the United States (made possible by better relations with the administration of President Richard M. Nixon). At the same time, the emphasis on consumer production was partially reversed as the Soviet Union turned for the latest technology to Western firms, particularly in Italy and France, to build huge new plants in Russia.

**The Soviet Union gained immense prestige as the first nation to launch a space vehicle in 1957, initiating a peaceful, but frenzied, race for preeminence in space between the superpowers. The atmosphere of détente in the 1970s led to exhibits like this one held in Los Angeles in 1977.** (Photo: Wide World Photos)

The issue of civil rights for at least some forms of dissent proved impossible to squelch either in world opinion or at home. When Boris Pasternak was awarded the Nobel prize for literature in 1958, he was forbidden permission to go to Stockholm to receive it. But his work, especially the novel *Doctor Zhivago*, had, like Khrushchev's denunciation of Stalin, done much to disseminate a view of the seamy and repressive aspects of Soviet life. The case of Alexander Solzhenitsyn caused still more international furor. His *Gulag Archipelago* was a haunting account of the terrors of the Soviet concentration camps, and he, too, was prevented from receiving the Nobel prize awarded him in 1970. Four years later he was arrested and then deported, to become an outspoken critic of the Soviet regime, thereby joining his voice to those of a score of Russian writers and scientists whose denunciations, widely published outside the U.S.S.R., came to be increasingly known in their own country. To this was added the plight of Soviet Jews, subject to discrimination and attack, then intermittently permittd to emigrate. Although international conventions (and American policy under President Jimmy Carter) underscored the demands for greater liberty, they neither shook the Soviet regime nor undermined its place in world affairs.

The international appeal of the Soviet Union as a model of socialism declined further as Brezhnev was succeeded by Yuri Andropov (1982–1984) and Konstantin Chernenko (1984–1985), elderly and ailing party figures whose presence emphasized the bureaucratic grayness of Soviet rule. Thus the promotion to general secretary of the Communist party in 1985 of Mikhail Gorbachev, at 54 the youngest man to lead the Soviet Union since Stalin, seemed to mark a new era, even if it began with the familiar problems of stifling inefficiencies, absenteeism, and alcoholism in an economy sapped by heavy military expenditures.

Having promised to follow the path of his predecessors, Gorbachev gradually revealed a personality and intellectual courage that led him in startling new directions. Recognizing dangerous stagnation in the Soviet economy, he called for more decentralized decision making. Seeing the implications of that, he sought to reduce the Party's dominance throughout society and to make it more responsive by encouraging discussion and debate. *Perestroika*, political and economic restructuring, and *glasnost*, greater openness, soon became international words; for in his frequent interviews and trips at home and across Europe, Gorbachev expressed new hope with a warmth and charm that won him admirers around the world. At home he maneuvered with great political skill, increasing his own power and control even while prying open institutions long accustomed to secrecy and domination. In international affairs as well, he seemed prepared to take a fresh, realistic look. Soviet troops had been fighting in Afghanistan since 1979 to support a Communist government entangled in a bloody guerrilla war against rebel groups heavily supported by the United States. Large increases in Soviet forces and tougher tactics had only escalated both the war and the destruction of villages and towns. Soviet losses in men, matériel, and money had become a painful drain; and outside the Soviet Union commentators pointed to the parallel with the American experience in Vietnam. Recognizing the dangers, Gorbachev in 1987 ordered a staged withdrawal. At a summit meeting with President Ronald Reagan, he similarly outran conventional approaches, proposing breath-taking reductions in nuclear arms and nearly won Reagan's acquiescence before aides hurriedly dissuaded him with reminders of uncontrolled danger, treaty obligations, and strategic aims. Wherever he turned, Gorbachev seemed ready to cut some Gordian knot; and that was his approach to Eastern Europe. *Perestroika* and *glasnost* at home seemed to argue for similar programs in Eastern Europe and would certainly be hurt by opposition to them. Keeping those countries in line was costly to the Soviet Union in prestige (as the case of Poland and nationalist protests revealed) and money. The barter arrangements that shored up those economies, in effect, gave them oil at prices below the world market, a potential source of hard currencies the Soviet Union needed, while saddling the Soviet Union with Eastern European products that often were not what it needed most.

Until it happened, many in Eastern and Western Europe doubted that Gorbachev could accept the overthrow of neighboring Communist regimes or requests for the removal of Soviet troops; realism argued that the international and domestic pressures on him would be too great in the face of such passivity. Instead, by accepting such sweeping change, he preserved important connections with those recent allies, prevented a new drain on Soviet resources, increased the likelihood of significant disarmament, and reinforced the movement for change within the Soviet Union. It was not a movement easy to direct, and Gorbachev found himself in a still more difficult balancing act: facing open and covert hostility from hardliners in the government, unprecedented public criticism from those who demanded more rapid change and greater freedom, and most dangerous of all, an amazing wave of nationalist unrest. In 1988 there were nationalist demonstrations, some of them bloodily repressed and some continuing for months. The most important of these extended all along the Soviet Union's eastern frontier, in Georgia, Moldavia, and the Ukraine, but most threateningly in the North and South. The Baltic republics of Latvia, Lithuania, and Estonia, with relatively recent memories of independence to build upon, not only staged fervent, magnificently restrained demonstrations but began to rewrite their laws and constitutions as if already independent. Gorbachev talked with them, held out some promises and reminders of the benefits the U.S.S.R. had to offer, and delayed.

In the South there was tragic violence as Arzerbaijanis attacked Armenians in Baku, and the two regions errupted into open war. Their hatred fed on many sources: ethnic (Azeri and Armenians had fought for centuries), religious (Shi'a Muslims and Armenian Orthodox Christians), social (the Armenians had generally been wealthier and better educated), political (disputed territories and relations with Moscow), and economic (the oil industry of Arzerbaijan was in a slow decline). Even so, the absence of integrative Soviet ties, of institutions, practices, and feelings that could restrain such violence cast doubt on the viability of the state. Finally, Soviet troops were sent to force their way into the region to restore order. It was characteristic of the new era that Arzerbaijanis and Armenians continued to protest and demonstrate (there was a general strike in Baku) in the occupied regions and in Mos-

cow, that Gorbachev was criticized for intervening and for doing so too late, that Latvia offered to arbitrate, and that expressions of grave concern came from the Muslim population along the Southern tier of the Soviet Union. Throughout most of the U.S.S.R as well as in its largest republic, Russians have long enjoyed privileged status; and among them, too, some nationalists mobilized in the name of culture (with appeals to the Orthodox Church), order (attractive to the military and some Party members), and race (including virulent anti-Semitism). With the election of Boris Yeltsin, Gorbachev's outspoken populist opponent, to the presidency of the Russian republic and its declaration of autonomy, the future of the Soviet empire had become uncertain. Among the problems Gorbachev's daring venture had to face, nationalism was as grave a challenge as bloated bureaucracy and empty shelves.

### The Familiar and the New

For much of the 1980s it seemed as if the lives of individuals had changed more than the political and social systems in which they lived. That was true of the majority who were ever more prosperous and of the minority left behind, of women who had more opportunities for education and careers, of the elderly who lived longer and received help from the state, of the young who followed international fashion in dress and music. It was true of everyone who worked shorter hours in cleaner places, moved to the city or suburb, traveled, watched television, or received medical care. That was true, in short, of most Europeans; yet they did these things in societies in which old prejudices, social distinctions, and institutions remained strong.

In international affairs, too, Europe had held on to familiar uncertainties. Cold War had stiffened with the Soviet Union's invasion of Afghanistan and crackdown on dissidents at home and with the harsher rhetoric and more belligerent stance of President Ronald Reagan. Europeans generally expressed doubt about his program for creating new defensive weapons in space and then essentially acquiesced. While the arms race between the superpowers went on, European nations competed around the world for the sale of arms. Strains in NATO, the problems of recession, and a slowing of the drive for European unity all seemed to stiffen the resistence to political change. Even when the Soviet Union appeared eager to abandon any dreams of dominating Europe, western governments worried about the loss of old certainties more than they welcomed new opportunities. Yet the Community's agencies continued gradually to expand their authority, European monetary policy did ease the effects of the oil crisis, and European public opinion had an important role in encouraging Gorbachev and Reagan to reopen talks in 1985 about an arms agreement. To many politicians, journalists, and ordinary citizens, however, it was frightening and frustrating to find that after so many years of breathtaking change, so much remained disappointingly familiar. Experts, of course, were quick to explain that this had to be; then 1989 proved again that history never stops.

Within a few months, the Soviet threat ceased to shape—or justify— global policies. Conflicts in Africa, Latin America, and Asia could no longer be understood or manipulated in the simplistic terms of Cold War strategies. As Soviet forces retreated from Eastern Europe, the United States had no choice but to rethink its huge military budget and its costly engagements in the politics of other nations around the world. The pressure for German unification did not come from diplomatic conferences, and politicians could only hurry to respond, knowing that such momentous changes would test institutions and social fabric in ways no one could pre-

dict. The Europe now again at center stage was a Europe of many nations and interests acting with an autonomy not experienced since 1939 to situations beyond the control of power politics.

## IV. A NEW ERA
✤
### The Sense of Change

A concern, almost an obsession, with where we stand in historical evolution is part of the self-awareness of modern humanity. In every country politicians are fond of forecasting what "history will say" about their even quite minor decisions; change seems so central a trait of current life that the word *revolution* becomes commonplace, and we speak easily of contemporary "revolutions" in everything from world politics to the roles of the sexes to food processing. At least in part, this expresses a fear for the future and an effort to predict or even control it by extending an imaginary line from some point in the past through the present and on to the decades ahead. In part, it follows from the hopes and the habits of thought of the past two centuries.

Analysts of how the world today differs from the past emphasize various aspects of society, but most commentators write of a present that is as distinct from the past as the periods of nineteenth-century industrialization, the Enlightenment, and Renaissance, and the Middle Ages were from each other. Some analyses begin with politics as the organization of power within and between nations. Some focus on economic distribution and the modes of production. Others concentrate on social structures and institutions. Finally, some stress changes in social values, attitudes, and ideas. Yet all these emphases tend to concur that a major historical change has occurred in the last few years.

**The Berlin Wall, November 10, 1989—West Berliners climb the wall to join others in peering over the other side, a political demonstration and the celebration of a new era.** (Photo: Reuters/ Bettmann)

If one dates the new era from the 1940s, the Axis domination of Europe then marks the tragic end of one epoch, Russian and American influence and European recovery the beginning of another. To put the date in the late 1950s places more emphasis on social change and prosperity but points to the same evidence of European societies that no longer directly dominate the world. The watershed, some would argue, lies in the 1960s, with the increasing strength of the Common Market and the autonomy of Europe after a long period of European self-doubt and floundering extending back to the eve of World War I. Or

the year 1968 can stand as the symbol of worldwide changes, led by North America and Europe, in values, outlook, and life style. Seen in any of these ways, our own era becomes one in which a new age is taking shape. Many are already convinced that 1989 will stand as one of history's great turning points.

The varied role of European nations in world affairs is one obvious indication of change. In 1940 France dropped from the ranks of the world's most powerful states; Germany did so five years later; and in the 1950s even victorious Great Britain could no longer sustain a position comparable with that of the United States or the Soviet Union. Russia alone among the European states attained the position of a superpower. The economic crises of the postwar period and the loss of colonial empires confirmed a process of relative decline in Western Europe's strength. And many shared the Spenglerian gloom of Arnold Toynbee in his multivolume *Study of History* in placing this decline on a world-historical scale as the end of the European millennium.

### The Locus of Power

Subsequent recovery has not restored Europe's former international dominance. The countries of the European Community exceed by only a little the United States or the Soviet Union in population and productive capacity, but they are not one nation. Accustomed to exercising their diplomatic influence in the interstices of Cold War competition, the European states now must decide what more independent courses they wish to pursue individually (maybe even in conflict with each other) or collectively. The Soviet Union found a limit to the effectiveness of its power even in Eastern Europe, and the United States could not prohibit Communism in Cuba or defeat it in Vietnam; and both superpowers, faced with economic problems at home and concerned over the rising stength of China and Japan, will continue to seek good relations with the nations of Europe even as the terms of those relationships change.

Economic expansion is now a universal goal, one that in Western Europe has pulled nations closer together. But that effect is not automatic, and it will meet new obstacles with the changes in Central and Eastern Europe. European relations with less developed and non-European countries also continue to change. For some years, the major European powers have played a somewhat more independent role in the Middle East, shown a deepening interest in South America, and established stronger economic and political connections with the independent nations of Africa. Developing nations have reason beyond cultural ties to look to Europe. The European states provide more developmental aid than either the United States or the Soviet Union, offer more models likely to seem relevant, and for a generation at least, have intruded less than Russia or the United States into the domestic politics of others.

At the same time, the increasing importance of Japan and China; the rising prosperity in much of Asia; the potential of India, Brazil, and much of South America, and the continuing conflicts and passions of the Middle East will all open new diplomatic opportunities. It is not hard to imagine on a global scale a network of international understandings much like those among European nations in the eighteenth and nineteenth centuries. In such a world, the wealth and the diplomatic skill of Europe will count for much.

Two favorite descriptions of the contemporary era have been the "Atomic Age" and the "Space Age," chosen to express the critical role technology now plays. In both fields the Soviet Union and the United States achieved rough parity in the 1960s. Although European scientists contributed much to the progress these two giants have made, no other nation can match their capacity to sustain the immense organization and expend the massive funds large atomic arsenals and space flights require. On the other hand, the utility (let alone the morality) of such weapons is increasingly questioned, and Britain and France are among the half dozen nations that produce them. Western Europe also is a leader in peaceful applications of nuclear energy and in the launching and use of satellites for communications and other purposes.

In most branches of technology, Western

Europe surpasses Russia and lags behind the United States and Japan only in specific sectors. Its automated assembly lines, refineries, and switchyards, like its computer applications and communications networks, are, in fact, often models for similar facilities in Eastern Europe and the United States. On the whole then, Europe has essentially regained the position it held on the eve of World War II but not that of the nineteenth century. Such a rapid adaptation in a period of headlong technological advance has precipitated Europe into the postindustrial age.

## Postindustrial Society

The somewhat misleading term "postindustrial society" was coined to indicate that the conditions and problems characteristic of the most advanced societies constitute a new historical stage. No longer is industrial production the dominant, absorbing activity in such countries; rather, the white-collar occupations constitute some of the largest job categories, and service activities such as sales and distribution employ as many workers as production (a fact related to the changes in "proletarian" parties).

Postindustrial society then tends to take its lead from the professional groups. Expert managers, staff specialists, and technicians, usually highly specialized in their functions and often in their training, form a very large part of society—about the same proportions as the entire middle class in the nineteenth century. Even the very wealthy tend to exercise their influence through their connections with these groups. This in itself represents a crucial change in social structure. Only recently have they become prominent in the Soviet Union (a last step in the transformation of a peasant society). Their presence, an achievement of Soviet Communism, is also a major source of pressure for change and the belief that it is possible. Furthermore,

the majority of people—members of the lower-middle class, industrial workers, and most farmers—have become more similar in standard of living and even life style. Most European families now spend less than half their income on food and could easily reduce the proportion if they chose to. At the bottom of this society and often sadly separated from the rest of it are the rural poor and urban slum dwellers. Although a far smaller proportion of the population than the "deserving poor" of the nineteenth century, they are often cruelly distinguished by lack of education and by language or race.

Both the white-collar and working classes tend to be highly mobile, ready to shift jobs and location as new opportunities arise; and this is essential for the flexible adjustment to new demands on which advanced countries depend. But increased mobility and related changes affect the very fabric of society, most clearly perhaps with regard to the family. More than ever likely to be living at some distance from grandparents or cousins, the members of a family are rarely able to work together even in the fields or factories, mines or small shops. Rather, increased leisure allows them to take their recreation together.

As domestic servants became scarce, household appliances became an essential benefit of the consumer society. Combined with smaller families, this means that women can approach salaried labor not merely as an interim measure to occupy their time until marriage or temporarily to supplement family income but as a lifelong occupation. The women's liberation movement, more prominent in America than Europe in the 1970s but now more similar on the two continents, thus results from the recognition of social opportunities as well as ideas of equality. On both counts, it seeks a redefinition of traditional social roles, challenges the emphasis on competition and aggressiveness in modern organizations, and offers a different view of the life cycle and the right to privacy. Speciali-

**The supermarket, once the key symbol of American affluence, was rapidly adapted to differing national tastes. This one is in France.** (Photo: Viva/Woodfin Camp and Associates)

zation in modern society also extends the period of training and therefore dependency; the teen-ager of today would have been considered a young adult, already working, through most of history. That creates another set of needs—social and institutional—just as increased longevity requires special provisions for the retired and the elderly.

In theory, a mobile society would identify the talents of each citizen (of either sex) and provide the training to allow those talents to be used to the full. Education would thus become the critical social filter, selecting the talent and providing the training society needs. In practice, this has proved difficult even in Communist countries, nor have European societies settled the question of what sort of education is, in fact, most beneficial to the individual and to society.

An assumption underlying the concept of postindustrial societies is that everywhere they become more alike. To Europeans, this change has seemed to come in the form of influences from the United States, and reactions to that challenge have reflected judgments about American society viewed as fluid, democratic, and open but also violent, crass, and culturally shallow. European economies, which in 1939 were barely familiar with installment buying, now enthusiastically employ easy purchase terms and credit cards to stimulate consumption. In the 1950s

Coca-Cola was attacked as lamentable Americanization, but now supermarkets, discount stores, and packaged products are common. Television has become a focal point in most homes and altered the style of politics, while Eurovision allows national networks to share Europe-wide transmissions, and American programs are almost as popular as American movies were in the 1920s. Cities continue to expand and to grow more similar in appearance. Paid vacations, often both winter and summer, and the ubiquitous automobile carry commercial blight and common behavior to the seashores and mountains, whose isolations poets praised a few generations ago. Regional and class differences are no longer so readily and publicly identified by the clothes people wear, the places they go, or the diversions they enjoy.

As this happens, new problems arise requiring concerted social action, and matters once largely resolved by custom—such as diet, dress, popular culture, or the appearance of the countryside—become the object of deliberation. More people have more choices to make about their way of life, their occupations, their housing, and their leisure; but as such choice is extended—for example in the recent spread of legislation making divorce and abortion easier throughout Europe—it can also be burdensome to the individual and a challenge to traditional social values. These concerns and the tensions to which they give rise stand as another mark of modern society.

## The Role of the State

Not only do postindustrial societies require that the state play a very active economic and social role, but that role also seems to become more similar from nation to nation. As always, the government is a final source of social stability, but this control extends far beyond mere police power to a legal and political part in labor disputes and corporate mergers, a responsibility for general welfare and the distribution of resources, and a major part in general planning for social change as well as economic growth.

In principle, the welfare state as accepted throughout Europe implies the constant reallocation of wealth from the well-to-do in favor of the poor. In practice, the middle of society probably benefits as much as the less fortunate, and the accompanying tax burden is too great to fall on the rich alone. But for most Europeans, the fear of going hungry, of facing illness without medical care, or of being destitute in old age has been greatly reduced. Public welfare appears almost as essential a part of state activity as the building of superhighways.

The state is also expected to assure the fiscal policies, at least some of the investments, the trade arrangements, the educational system, detailed information on economic and social matters, and the means of communication that postindustrial societies require. Such tasks tend to make the government bureaucracy a model of postindustrial society itself: efficiently organized for special functions; open to people of talent and technical training, who can expect promotion on merit (as well as seniority); approaching specific problems with rational objectivity. In practice, of course, no government agency is so removed from special interests and political prejudices, and this makes the bureaucracy itself a central issue of modern politics. Such tasks also lead the state into extensive long-range planning. In the French system, a planning office with a large staff of experts and a consultative assembly representing affected interests both creates long-range programs and drafts legislation for parliamentary action.

Most other Western countries have adopted similarly comprehensive arrangements and have discovered how to manage the economy indirectly through tax and fiscal policies as well as through nationalized industries and direct subsidies, much as they indirectly shape society through policies on housing, welfare, and education. In Eastern Europe the advantages of indirect controls and more decentralized decision making are now highly appreciated. Despite fundamental differences in various national systems, there is thus reason to see them drawing closer even in the roles assigned to the central governments. And the institutions with which governments deal—political parties, businesses, unions, education systems, hospitals—tend to manifest a similarly bureaucratic organization. That organization can itself become a force inhibiting change.

When the economy falters, whole groups believe themselves the victim of injustice; when social customs break down, protest focuses on the state. Not surprisingly, the wave of changes since World War II and the picture of the future that can follow from them have produced resistance and serious criticism. Just as contemporary change continues a process centuries old, so the criticisms of those changes build on a long tradition of disenchantment with claims of progress. For many, the new era threatens much that was fundamental to Western Civilization and that made European culture so vital. In that view, society since World War II offers disturbing indications that ours is an age of crisis.

## The Crisis of Society

Applied to society, the metaphor of a crisis suggests some breakdown or spasm (the term was once primarily medical) that challenges survival itself and after which nothing is likely ever to be quite the same. The idea of crisis is usually accompanied by other terms loosely used—*breakdown*, *revolution*, *depression*, *failure*; but the imprecision of *crisis*

makes it useful to describe a feeling that things cannot go on as they are and makes it appropriate to a time that seems on the eve of something drastically new. One of the favorite terms in current commentary and central to Marxist analysis, it is most often applied to the functioning of society, the state of contemporary culture, and the issue of what values people hold.

The dominant style of Western social analyses is to write as if society is a patient whose illness needs diagnosis. Such a view, common in novelists and congenial to modern psychology and sociology as well, is assumed in most contemporary assessments of our age; thus any private act, any social behavior, any publication is likely to be taken as a symptom of some larger tendency or need. Combined with an intense historical consciousness, including a fear that Western civilization may be in decline and a nostalgia for other eras, this orientation easily leads to a kind of cultural hypochondria.

Clearly, there is much that does not function well. The totalitarian regimes of the 1930s and 1940s were terrifying evidence of that; worse, part of their justification was a disgust with the civilization from which they sprang—a civilization many denounced as materialistic, torn by ideological and class conflicts, lacking in universally accepted values either aesthetic or moral. If totalitarianism has subsided, it is not certain that such criticism is now less valid. Even in democracies, the political process often seems far removed from the people, a sort of private game based on the manipulation of public opinion. And save for self-interest, the great parties have largely lost the refreshing clarity of purpose with which they emerged from the resistance movements. The Christian Democrats, who dreamed of a Christian social vision above politics and were among the first to see the promise of European unity, have become but another coalition mediating among established influences, weak in France, stronger but hardly more creative in Germany and Italy. The socialists, once sure their hour had come, remain torn between allies on the left and in the center; no longer confident of many of their old panaceas, they are neither the incisive critics nor the innovative leaders they once showed promise of being. Those newly in power in Eastern Europe search for ways to connect abstract values to functioning institutions.

On the Continent, generally, issues of civil liberties and charges of corruption still challenge the political system. In the Scandinavian countries and Britain, where such questions are less troubling, governments have hardly done better in consistently meeting the needs of a new era. Disillusionment in the Communist regimes has become all but universal, and everywhere policies that were supposed to have furthered freedom or equality can be shown merely to have left the poor and unfortunate more subordinate to the rich and powerful. Thus critics are sure of a despairing answer when they ask what Western nation is now moved by a great purpose or what government is truly free, honest, efficient, and farsighted.

### Meritocracy and Bureaucracy

Indeed, the state itself is an object of suspicion, not so much in the classic Marxist sense as the captive agent of the ruling class nor in the traditional liberal view as a threat to individual liberty, but simply in itself as a concentration of power dedicated to its own interests. And the criticism is applied with equal vigor to other large organizations, business corporations, political parties, and universities.

Max Weber saw bureaucracy, with its functional organization, uniform application of rules, and awards of status according to ability, as central to modern society. And its growth has been a result of efforts to make society more equitable as well as of the need to assemble great amounts of information and to act with rational efficiency. The undeniable achievements of such an approach encouraged a view of society itself as a meritocracy in which in every generation and in all fields new leaders would be selected by essentially objective criteria. Since the 1960s, however, this extension of a liberal vision has been subject to severe attack.

Elites that confidently claim to have earned their position may be as self-interested as and sometimes more offensive than an aristocracy born to privilege. The process of selection has remained relatively restrictive after all, and even formal criteria—examinations and superiors' recommendations—are often narrow and warped by political favoritism and social prejudice. If the virtue of bureaucracy is the even-handed application of general rules (and many deny that it accomplishes that in practice), its weakness is faceless impersonality. Citizens often find themselves helpless before regulations that defeat the purpose intended, unable to locate the source of decisions that seriously affect their lives, and treated in the dehumanized terms of multiple forms to be filled and filed. Even in societies committed to justice and freedom, the individual often cannot find any authority willing to consider the whole person and real, human needs.

The reaction against the world of meritocracy and bureaucracy, though strong, has been marked by a certain hopelessness. Political movements throughout the West have denounced the trend toward more and more social regulation; but without solutions to offer, they have appealed in the rhetoric of nostalgia primarily to groups whose importance has been waning. From Russia to the United States, politicians' promises to make government (and society) less officious have yet to produce satisfactory results. Intellectuals, artists, and students have spoken out more effectively. In England the playwright John Osborne was typical of a whole group of "angry young men" who shook the complacency of the late 1950s with their attacks on the establishment. Soviet dissidents unmasked rule in the name of the proletariat as just another autocracy. The disturbances and riots in East Germany, Poland, Hungary, and Czechoslovakia underscored that complaint; and student revolts from Berkeley to Harvard to the Sorbonne, in Britain, Germany, and Italy directly attacked all the central assumptions of meritocracy. Yet so far at least, all this outrage has produced more alienation than change in Western Europe and more change than resolution in the East.

## Alienation

To Marx, one of the great evils of industrial capitalism was the separation of workers from the product of their labor so that they were deprived of craftsmen's independence and pride in what they did. On the cleaner, well-lit, and partially automated assembly lines of the post industrial era, there is evidence that a similar alienation continues. It underlies much of the agitation even among prosperous workers; and the frequent strikes that in the 1960s were especially common in Great Britain and Italy had to do as much with issues of the workers' privileges and dignity as with their wages. Many lament the cultural loss in the disappearance of artisanship generally. Perhaps, the argument runs, a society is poorer if it has more things but almost none individually carved or blown or tailored with great care to be treasured by fabricator and owner.

Craftsmanship is not the only victim of technological unemployment, for in many fields people find themselves threatened by new methods and by younger specialists with more recent training. Perhaps new efforts to provide additional training on the job, to make factory work more interesting (in which the Swedish have pioneered), and to give workers a voice in management (something the Germans have tried extensively; the French, Italians, and Americans have experimented with; and the British Labour party has argued for) can make a real difference. The question remains whether the modern cult of efficiency leaves room for such human and aesthetic considerations, whether the rewards of leisure and wealth can compensate for a sense of alienation from one's own labor.

More troubling still are the deeper signs of a general alienation: the attraction to crime, the escapism of commercial pornography, alcoholism, and drug abuse. The very freedom prosperity provides brings a heavy burden of self-direction. Yet in large, highly organized societies, individuals today often feel powerless even though they are confronted with a more bewildering array of personal choices than most of humanity ever faced. It is significant that social control—perceived to operate through advertising, religion, and custom as well as institutions—has become a favorite subject for social research.

## The Cultural Crisis

The end of World War II and the fall of the Axis brought the sudden stimulus of ideas and artistic styles long banned, as works produced in secret could be brought into the open. In all the arts, but especially in painting, a flood of exciting works came from the United States, whose culture had been enriched by European émigrés, free there to continue their creativity. Artists already famous in the 1930s, like the painter Pablo Picasso (see Plate 63) and the poet T. S. Eliot, could simultaneously be honored as grand old figures and savored with a freshness usually reserved for the young. There was great continuity between the cultural outburst that followed liberation and the prewar world even though the new European works focused on the intervening experience of dictatorship and war.

Neo-realism flourished, especially in Italy, where the novels of Ignazio Silone and Alberto Moravia gave incisive, detailed accounts of the daily lives of little people buffeted by movements and events beyond their control, and where the films of Roberto Rossellini and Vittorio de Sica combined the harsh eye of the candid camera with sympathy for the minor characters who are society's victims and its strength. French films and the plays of the German Bertolt Brecht, who moved to East Berlin in 1949, pursued similar themes with more formal ideological purpose. The once-shocking techniques of Kafka were extended by novelists to depict Central Europe's experience of the twentieth century, with the savage satire of Heinrich Böll perhaps the most widely admired. The arts had never been more international, and works produced in one country were quickly appreciated throughout the West.

## The New Wave

The *nouvelle vague* of the 1960s in literature and film was primarily a French phenomenon, but the term can fairly be extended to describe a major and continuing shift in the arts. The novels of Alain Robbe-Grillet and the films of Jean François Truffaut, Ingmar Bergman, and Federico Fellini are more like personal essays, held together by the sensitivity and imagination of a single creator that the audience is permitted to share in whatever way it can. In painting, abstract expressionism, which dominated earlier, gave way to a great variety of styles often deliberately garish and disturbing—Pop Art, Op Art, and the satirically representational. And composers shifted their explorations from the 12-tone scale and dissonance, avant-garde interests for more than a generation, to the new sounds of *musique concurète* (using everyday noises as well as musical sounds carefully arranged on spliced tapes) and of electronic music in the manner of the American John Cage and the German Karlheinz Stockhausen. Sculpture, generally a more conservative art, experimented with the use of common objects, new materials of every sort, strange forms, and work on a gigantic scale. The Englishman Henry Moore's huge reclining figures, with their combination of clean lines, solid masses, and empty spaces (influenced by African art) are perhaps the most admired; "environmental" sculptures, tracing lines across deserts or wrapping whole buildings in various materials, have been the most controversial.

The arts insisted on being radical and adopting new modes of expression, deliberately shocking and yet highly personal, sometimes almost private (see Plate 64). But few artistic conventions remained to be burst (the inhibitions on display of sex in motion pictures eroded rapidly in the 1960s), and to do something new becomes more difficult, although, in the tradition of the avant-garde, still required. One trend is to absorb and distort technology. Thus some artists have made use of electric lights, random noise, plastics, or mechanical motion, giving them aesthetic meanings much as artists had long done with nature. Another is to break the barriers between "serious" and commercial art, for each uses the other; much that begins as formal art quickly reaches the populace in articles of mass production and slick packages or advertising. In the process, commercial art and popular movies have become more sophisticated, and some popular music, originally associated with the Beatles, has become artistically more serious and complex. This intersection of "high" and "popular" culture, lessening a division within Western civilization that has lasted for centuries, may foretell a new explosion of creativity; the more common comment is to note the decay both of folk culture and of the traditional canons of high art. Yet starting in the 1970s there was also some turning back, with a "new" taste among serious artists for ornamentation in architecture, representation in art, and lyricism in music.

### Classical and Modern

These trends are often referred to as postmodernism, a term that has clearer meaning within each field than overall. As self-definition by what it is not, postmodernism proposes a major change by pointing to what has been abandoned—an emphasis on form, abstraction, restraint, control, and rational analysis. During the Enlightenment, when the comparison of ancient and modern culture became a popular theme, writers were tempted to feel that the moderns had the better of it, combining ancient wisdom with new knowledge. Contemporary commentators are less confident.

The high-bourgeois culture of the nineteenth century remains strong. Symphony orchestras are numerous and of superb quality, their concerts well attended. Paintings old and new sell for ever higher prices. The great literary works of all ages are taught in schools and universities and still read with pleasure. Yet the tendency for such interests to be made academic, a matter of special study by experts, may suggest some decline in their power to attract. The very forms of that culture—long novels and epic poems, symphonies, operas, enormous museums— have by current standards become terribly expensive in time and money. Ironically, their cultural dominance has been least threatened in the Soviet Union, where the state was

committed to excluding much of contemporary Western culture. Nowhere is ballet more honored or more old-fashioned. But critics wonder whether people will choose to receive the long preparation, maintain the patience, or preserve the values necessary to appreciate the West's traditional culture.

Easy communication and the great number of intellectuals forced into exile, particularly from Hitler's Europe to America, have made high culture even more international. Paperback books, records and tapes, and reproductions of paintings have carried the arts more broadly into society, but the fear remains that they are not an integral part of it. To many, the signs are disturbing: the tendency for the creative life itself to become institutionalized in universities; the frenetic search for new techniques that bespeaks some deep dissatisfaction; the danger that serious culture will be eroded by the commercial, the shocking, the fashionable aspects of mass culture. The arts have expanded to encompass almost all forms of communication and fabrication. This, like the increased interest in good design and attractive cities, may mark the hope of the new era, or it may indicate a fatal loss of focus and of that common core of values and tradition on which great cultures in the past have rested.

### The Crisis of Values

On no other issue are contemporary moralists so agreed as that the lack of universally respected values is the source of serious discontent and a symptom of fatal decay. Both historical self-consciousness and the social sciences teach that values change with time and place. Once value systems are seen as relative, however, it becomes difficult to insist on imposing any particular set. This symptom of social disintegration becomes one of its causes.

## Existentialism

Existentialism, one of the most influential movements of the postwar period, offered a radical solution. Jean-Paul Sartre, French philosopher and writer, was existentialism's most important figure, but his ideas were based, in turn, on the prewar work of German philosophers, especially Karl Jaspers and Martin Heidegger. Once again the intellectual continuity across the war is striking.

Sartre extended relativism to its ultimate implication: Life is absurd, without purpose or meaning. But from this point he slowly built: People become what they are through the things they do in a lifetime; individual actions follow from decisions; and each decision to act is a moral choice. Thus Sartre constructed a radical individualism but one that keeps people morally responsible (and in the highest sense, free) whatever their fate. There is in existentialism a sense of the heroic that had special meaning perhaps to those formed in the resistance movement and that was expressed with great power in the writings of Albert Camus, most encouragingly perhaps in his early novel *The Plague*.

As a statement of the human condition, existentialism blends remarkably with the mainstream of modern thought; there were Christian existentialists and existentialist Marxists; positivists, liberals, and Freudians have also incorporated its insights. But its very breadth of appeal was also a weakness. The values an existentialist chooses rest, after all, on blind experience or some other philosophy. Like neorealism, existentialism belonged to the early postwar period and spoke more clearly to the abnormal years of terror and rebuilding than to a time of routine and prosperity.

## Older Doctrines

In the public anguish over values that has marked this period, Christian voices, individually strong, have collectively had a rather uncertain effect. After the war the leading theologians—once again, mainly men of an older generation who were already well known two decades earlier, like Jaspers, Karl Barth, and Jacques Maritain—were studied with new interest. The Protestant Paul Tillich and the Catholic Pierre Teilhard de Chardin achieved a large following with their systematic efforts to establish the relevance of Christianity to every fact of modern life and to accommodate contemporary modes of thought. Pope John XXIII was beloved as few popes have ever been by non-Catholics as well as Catholics for his gentleness, his tolerance, and his receptivity to change. All this, combined with the postwar vigor of Christian political parties and a rise in church attendance in the 1950s, suggested a major revival of Christianity.

Yet by the 1960s society seemed to have been little affected. Although some theologians hailed the benefits of the greater openness about sex in literature, dress, and practice, most found it anathema. Religion has shown its power to sustain community and hope less clearly where it has been publicly respected than in the Communist regimes that repressed it. While Western churches became socially more aware and sometimes even radical, Marxist parties and the modern state accomplished more. Civil marriages (and divorces) increased, and religious vocations declined. When Christians evoked rigid, traditional standards of morality, they could be dismissed as reactionaries; when they embraced modern psychology or worked for social change, they were accused of opportunism. But when they charged that society was in a moral crisis, they were widely heard. The election of John Paul II as pope in 1978 (significantly, a Pole and the first non-Italian pope in 455 years) clearly marked the continuing changes in the Roman Catholic Church. Although he, too, proved immensely popular, he remained resolutely conservative on theological and moral matters involving the family, sex, and the priesthood.

If Christians have been outspoken about the crisis of values in this generation, philosophers have had less to say. In Britain and the United States, philosophy has become a highly specialized, quasi-mathematical discipline inclined to view the ethical questions troubling most thoughtful people as too loosely defined to merit comment. Elsewhere, analytic philosophy and logical positivism have not been so dominant, but we still seem to take our intellectual problems very largely as formulated in the nineteenth century, by Kierkegaard, Marx, Nietzsche, and Freud. (Significantly, the nineteenth-century schools of thought less critical of Western society or more optimistic about human nature are largely ignored.) The French philosopher Michel Foucault has brilliantly exposed the elements of social control in modern cultural discourse on sanity, crime, and sex; but he has done so through the historical analysis of European ideas and perceptions without himself proposing alternative standards of conduct. Ours may be an era dominated by science, but social philosophy today—despite interesting efforts to extend new findings in biology to theories of human society—is less affected by the theories of natural science than at any time since Voltaire applied Newton to society or Hobbes sought to analyze the mechanics of politics.

There have, in fact, been few efforts at constructing grand philosophical systems in the nineteenth-century style, although the widespread revival of interest in Hegel, especially through the work of the German philosopher Edmund Husserl, has given a common vocabulary to existentialists and Marxists eager to reconcile modern views of human consciousness with respect for reason, and of the meaning of history with assertions of human liberty.

Some have suggested that the absence of systematic philosophies is in itself a historic change: the end of ideologies following from the end of class conflict in postindustrial society. But dissatisfaction has certainly not disappeared, nor has conflict. And theories of conflict tended in the 1970s to supplant the emphasis on consensus so common in the 1950s. Marxian analysis remains influential among intellectuals, although it no longer dominates European intellectual life as it did in the 1960s, spreading into much of academic history, sociology, and anthropology and stimulating a variety of literary criticism. Many of the century's most influential thinkers like Antonio Gramsci in Italy and Georg Lukacs in Hungary, were theoreticians of Marxism, but they now seem dated. Appealing in its humane concerns, Marxism is not a very reassuring source of social values, given its historical determinism and ethical relativism and the record of Marxist societies.

There are not many alternatives. The death of liberalism has been so confidently announced for so long that one may conclude it survives. In its individualism, openness, and tolerance, Western society is indeed liberal; but as a systematic doctrine, liberalism has been in dissarray. Recent criticism of Marxism, including the "new philosophers" in France, suggest that a revival of liberalism is possible. Conservative social theories, which contributed richly to Western thought, now appear primarily by implication in ideas of biological determinism or theology. The most influential aspect of conservative thought was its critique of "mass" culture and technological progress, but those concerns have also largely been adopted by the left. Thus the social theorists of the Frankfurt school combined a distaste for modern society that was common among German intellectuals with a heavy debt to Marxism in their influential writings on psychology, sociology, and philosophy. Herbert Marcuse, who, like most of the Frankfurt group, spent World War II in the United States, found himself a hero to leaders of the student revolts of 1968, although few of the new generation shared his admiration of Freud as well as Marx.

## The Social Sciences

In the West the social sciences have enjoyed an enormous increase in prestige and analytic power, primarily through the application of behavioral methods of model building, and of quantitative research, first in economics, then in sociology, political science, and history. But these methods all begin by seeking to be "value-free." Another of the important movements in social science is structuralism, and its roots, too, lie in the early part of the twentieth century in the work of the Swiss linguist Ferdinand de Saussure, who coined the term *semiology* to describe the study of the signs by which people communicate. For the French anthropologist Claude Lévi-Strauss, a leading structuralist, every aspect of supposedly primitive society—its kinship systems, customs, rituals, and myths—can be analyzed as the extension of complex, integrated structures of thought. Not consciously held, these structures nevertheless reflect the nature of the human mind. This radical subjectivism, which can lead Lévi-Strauss to an admiration of premodern societies comparable to that of many modern artists, speaks only indirectly to questions of values. In contemporary matters, Lévi-Strauss, like Sartre, whose historical relativism he opposed, considers himself a Marxist.

Linguistics in the social sciences and biology in the natural sciences have in the last generation been fields of especially exciting activity that tends to invade and synthesize neighboring disciplines. Much of the new scholarship and research does quite rapidly come to have a broad impact on society. Analytic philosophy and linguistics have made important contributions to computer languages. The identification of the genetic code in DNA by Francis Crick and James Watson, for which they received the Nobel prize in 1962, opened up whole new areas of biological engineering and medical research. But how the generation and control of information and life should be used is not the subject of the sciences that invent these powers. Never has any previous civilization supported so much scholarship, so many centers of learning, or so many artists. But there is no simple test to tell whether that achievement should be a source of comfort or is itself a sign of some dangerous dispersion. Scholars barely able to keep abreast of their own disciplines speak ominously of a knowledge explosion, and professors of humanities defensively decry the dearth of interest in the things they study. Doubt about human rationality and disdain for elites have made anti-intellectualism respectable even among intellectuals, and alienation or some eternal human quest has led to a remarkable revival of interest in the occult. Computers, after all, can also be used to plot astrological charts. Nevertheless, when Czechoslovakia came to life, it picked a playwright as President.

## The Consolation of History

Beyond doubt, there is cause for concern. The question is whether these signs mark a fatal crisis or even a fundamental transformation. Seen in historical perspective, they may not be quite so terrible nor this era so drastically different as our heightened sense of change leads us to believe. One should at least consider how many great crises Western civilization has survived and how strongly traditional values and institutions still intricately attach the present to the past.

Since every era tends narcissistically to believe its own problems the most important and therefore the gravest, the assumption needs to be carefully probed. Although Europe is a lesser force in the world than it was in the nineteenth century, it is surely not so seriously threatened as were the Greeks by Xerxes, the Romans by the barbarians, or medieval Christendom by Islam. European countries are more comparable in wealth and power to the United States than the struggling medieval principalities were to Constantinople. No twentieth-century war has been more devastating than the Black Death. It is doubtful that the ideological conflict and spiritual crisis of the present are so severe as those that followed the Reformation. Nor is it clear why centuries of peasant revolts, the alcoholism of Hogarth's London, or the highway robbery, cock fighting, prostitution, and public hangings of the eighteenth century were any less signs of alienation than the manifestations that trouble us today. If social change now is rapid, we have learned to expect and even anticipate it; the changes that followed the fifteenth century or those in the hundred years after 1760 may well have been more shocking and harder to absorb.

We should not assume that earlier ages enjoyed a comforting unanimity cruelly denied to us. At few moments in Western history has a single philosophy or set of values enjoyed undisputed hegemony. The view that other eras were informed by a single spirit is largely the product of distance, which makes outlines clearer and fissures more obscure. The rights of throne and altar or the forms of transubstantiation were once questions as socially shattering as those of public and private ownership or the right to an abortion. Neither is it certain that village life was less cruel than the impersonal city or that peasants were less materialist than the modern middle class. We do know that the crises of the past that strained and altered Western civilization ultimately left it with new vitality.

## Modern Expectations

The tendency to assume that the quality of social life has deteriorated may also reflect a rise in expectations. We have learned to smile at the simple optimism of nineteenth-century visions of progress, but we expect "autonomy" and "spontaneity" and "self-fulfillment" for every individual. Society is asked to reinforce in all people qualities Western thinkers traditionally believed to be beyond most of humankind. Today's intellectuals are not demonstrably more at odds with the mass of society than the elites of other times, but they resent it more. There is greater concern today, however badly practice lags, for racial equality, good education, and humane treatment of society's misfits than at any time in the past.

Contemporary anxiety over the family as a social institution is a good example of how higher expectations as well as changing behavior affect the perception of the present. That the family may be about to disappear or is at least threatened now as never before is a cliché rarely challenged. But it has been a cliché for centuries, hurled from thousands of pulpits; serfdom, slavery, poverty, and maybe human nature have also endangered the family. But since the eighteenth century, the demands placed on it have steadily increased. Paradoxically, this began at the very time that industrialization separated household members for nearly all their waking hours, moved millions of people to new places, and deprived the family of the traditional social support of relatives and village custom. Yet the institution survived, and the Victorians tried hard to make the family function according to the highest Christian norms

At La Grande Motts on the French Mediterranean, 32 concrete pyramids and 12,000 campsites provide space for 35,000 vacationers who crowd the beaches. With vacations available to nearly everyone, tourism has become an industry. (Photo: Henri Cartier-Bresson/Magnum)

while adding still other requirements. Marriage is now expected to be a matter of mutual choice and to be more a delightful partnership than a mere division of labor; the rearing of children lasts longer and is intended to be far more intensive. Protected by the state and honored by religion, the family is supposed to provide a secure place for happiness and mutual growth, and its joys of sex and solidity are propagandized in the mass media in utopian terms that risk making reality drab at best. That contraceptives allow more couples to postpone marriage and that laws make it easier to abandon the commitment to wedlock need not mean that the institution is crumbling. It is more likely that the family itself, its social functions, and the social roles within it are simply being yet again redefined.

## The Western Tradition

The painful questioning of values in modern society is in large part a continuation of a Western tradition. Ambivalence toward the past and toward change, for example, is an ancient one, especially pronounced since the French Revolution and the Romantic era. Similarly, the conflict between individual and society so explosive today was a theme of Sophocles and central to early Christianity, neatly dissected by Hobbes, restated in quite different terms by Rousseau, and a major preoccupation throughout the nineteenth century. Contemporary experiments in communal living and a return to nature drew on the anarchists and utopian socialists of the nineteenth century as well as a Christian practice continuous from medieval monasteries through Anabaptists to the present. The threat of the overbearing state has been a subject of endless discussion since Machiavelli.

The distrust of rationalism as a force that can inhibit creativity and the obverse, a fear of humankind's dark irrationality, twist through the novels and plays of the nineteenth century, are floodlit in the writings of Freud, and have concerned theologians since Augustine. The arguments about free will and determinism continue between Catholics and Protestants, existentialists and Marxists. When modern Westerners approach the most important issues of the day, they necessarily bring with them some part of a cultural heritage long concerned with similar problems. In this way the past is constantly reinvoked in the present, and current conflicts are given some shape and limit by the past.

### Continuity in Modernization

The impressive pattern of social change in the last 200 years has come to be called modernization—a typical Western conception that sees history moving in a single direction and tends to assume that the changes that have transformed the West will be repeated elsewhere until "developing" countries become more like their European models. Clearly, all societies are feeling the effects of expanding technology, the trend toward secularization, the increased role of the state, and the growth of bureaucracy. But Western history also continues to demonstrate, as it always has, that the specific effects of such trends will be fundamentally affected by local conditions and customs, by social systems and economic organization, by politics, and by

deliberate choice. The West has both retained its unity and preserved its diversity through these centuries of change. National and regional differences in manners and taste alter even the most similar institutions and continue to find expression in the most modernized societies. Despite greater travel and better communication, a universal technology, comparable standards of living, and an international style in dress and architecture, London, Paris, New York, Rome, Budapest, Prague, or Berlin each remains unique.

Since the establishment of the national monarchies, European governments have used sumptuary laws, mercantilist measures, and social legislation to alter the effect of economic forces. Handicrafts, for example, have often been favored by political measures and public taste although industrial competition threatened their survival; and individual farms are in most countries sustained through the social choice of subsidies as well as by rural tenacity. A sociologist has noted that the different forms and scale of organization in contemporary industries, and even the way they use technology, reflect whether those industries were founded before the industrial revolution (as were the building trades), during the nineteenth century (as was the textile industry), or in the twentieth century (as were the smaller and more decentralized electronics firms).[4] As concern now rises for the protection of the environment, public policy once more limits private interest. But then some of Europe's most famous parks can be traced back to the common lands and hunting preserves of the Middle Ages. Technological imperatives alone do not shape society.

Secularization describes the historical development whereby religion shifts from the

---

[4] A. L. Stinchcombe, "Social Structure and the Invention of Organization Forms," in Tom Burns (ed.), *Industrial Man*, 1969, pp. 153–194.

center to the periphery of public concern and functions once performed by the Church are given over to the other, secular agencies. This is primarily an institutional change and one that need not denote a decline of belief. In fact, the nineteenth and twentieth centuries have probably been more "religious" than the eighteenth. As the practice of faith has ceased to be a matter of universal custom, it has become a matter of conscious, personal choice.

Even the growth of the state, in power and in social penetration, has brought with it new restrictions on the exercise of government influence. The use of representative forms and legal codes has been one way of restraining the state, and more recently the Scandinavian device of the ombudsman paid to respond to individual complaints has come to be widely adopted. Local resistance to central control has brought new recognition of regional sentiment, from Ireland, Scotland, and Wales to Brittany and Languedoc, Catalonia, and the Basque country; from regions of Italy to the Croatian portions of Yugoslavia and the Slovak provinces of Czechoslovakia; from Sweden to the Soviet Union. Just a few years ago it was believed that the dialects and customs that the national state had tried to stamp out were now doomed to be eliminated through force of example, by radio, television, and easy travel. Instead, once isolated regions have used familiarity with dominant cultures to assert their equality. Now the fashionable question is whether the national state is by nature a machine for warmaking that has begun to lose its function.

But the most effective defense against the intrusive power of the state may be a subtle change in the boundary between the affairs considered to be properly public and those protected as private. The nuclear family and the individual dwelling have steadily widened the zone for formally sanctioned privacy. In the nineteenth century religious tolerance, security of the postal service, and the secret ballot were steps in a gradual enlargement of privacy to include one's personal convictions (steps that often required a revolution). That recognition of individualism in the twentieth century extends even to styles of dress, sexual practice, and conscientious objection to military service.

The growth of bureaucracy, another of the themes of modernization, has strengthened institutions independent of state control as well as the state itself; and these institutions have proved a major source of continuity, carrying within them old values and attitudes to be applied to new situations. The courts of justice, parliaments, churches, universities, and banks of Europe and America are powerful establishments with independent but continuous traditions that extend back often to the Middle Ages and beyond. And the tendency now is to seek ways to make all social institutions, from welfare agencies to factories, more responsive to the individual and more accessible. Many French and a few American firms now allow their employees to set their own hours, and these efforts, like the multiple schemes for worker representation on management councils, may or may not work, but any artisan of the early nineteenth century would have understood the need to try them.

The Vatican Council that opened in 1962 under the inspiration of Pope John XXIII was perhaps the most noted of all these efforts at institutional reform before *perestroika*. Dedicated to *aggiornamento* ("renewal"), the council sought to bring the Catholic Church up to date not only in its organization but also in its social policy, expressing concern for developing nations, respect for Jews, and belief in religious liberty. The Church's leadership was made more international, and the decision to say masses in the vernacular instead of Latin put the understanding of the individual believer above institutional uniform-

# 1957–1990/TIMELINE

| International and Military History | Political History |
|---|---|
| 1957 European Economic Community formed | |
| 1958–1963 Pope John XXIII | 1958 "Opening to the left" in Italy (Beginning of Fifth Republic in France)* |
| 1960 European Free Trade Association; Soviet–Chinese rift | 1964 Khruschev removed |
| 1960s Most African nations win independence from European rule | 1968 Students revolt in Paris spreads across Europe, Prague spring; incapacitation of Salazar in Portugal |
| 1961 Berlin Wall; Cuban Missile Crisis | |
| | 1969 SPD under Brandt takes office in West Germany; De Gaulle resigns |
| 1962–1965 Vatican II | |
| 1966 France withdraws from NATO | 1973 Franco retires in Spain; right–wing military coup in Greece |
| 1967 International agreement on space exploration | 1974 Revolution in Portugal; restoration of democracy in Greece |
| 1968 U.S.S.R. led armed intervention in Czechoslovakia: Brezhnev doctrine | |
| 1969 SALT | 1975 Death of Franco and beginning of democracy in Spain under King Juan Carlos |
| 1970 German Federal Republic–U.S.S.R. treaty | 1976 Riots in Poland |
| 1972 Denmark, Ireland, United Kingdom enter the EEC | 1978 Assassination of Moro in Italy |
| 1975 Helsinki Conference on Human Rights | 1979 Conservatives under Thatcher begin long period in office |
| 1978 John Paul II becomes Pope | 1980 Death of Tito |
| 1979 U.S.S.R. invades Afghanistan | 1980–1987 Emergence of Solidarity, martial law under General Jaruzelski in Poland |
| 1981 Greece joins the EEC | 1981 Mitterand elected president of France |
| | 1982 Attempted assassination of Pope John Paul II; Christian Democrats return to power in West Germany |
| 1983 Falklands war | 1983 Craxi becomes Italy's prime minister |
| 1985 Geneva conference, United States and U.S.S.R. discuss arms limitation | 1985 Mihkail Gorbachev General Secretary of Communist Party in U.S.S.R. |
| 1986 Portugal and Spain join the EEC | |
| 1988 Gorbachev tells U.N. that Eastern European nations can choose their own direction | 1989 Recognition of Solidarity and free elections in Poland; demonstrations lead to collapse of Communist rule Hungary, East Germany, Czechoslovakia, Bulgaria, Rumania; nationalist protests and independence movements in Georgia, Armenia, Arzerbaijan, Moldavia, Ukraine, Luthuania, Latura, Estonia; Gorbachev president of U.S.S.R. |
| 1989 U.S.S.R. begins withdrawal from Afghanistan | |
| 1990 Accelerated negotiations for arms reductions | |

*Events in parentheses are discussed in other chapters.

| Social and Economic History | Cultural and Intellectual History |
|---|---|
| | Antonio Gramsci (1891–1937)<br>Bertolt Brecht (1898–1956) |
| 1957 U.S.S.R. launches Sputnik | |
| | 1958 Boris Pasternak awarded Nobel prize |
| 1960s Economic boom | 1960s *Nouvelle vague*<br>Albert Camus (1913–1960) |
| 1961 U.S.S.R. sends first man into orbit | 1961 Arnold Toynbee's *A Study of History* completed |
| | 1962 Nobel prize to Crick and Watson for discovery of DNA |
| | Paul Tillich (1886–1965)<br>T.S. Eliot (1888–1965) |
| 1968 EEC abolishes internal tariffs; educational reforms throughout Western Europe | Karl Barth (1886–1968) |
| | Karl Jaspers (1883–1969) |
| | 1970 Alexander Solzhenitsyn awarded Nobel prize |
| 1973 Beginning of international oil crisis, followed by recession, stagflation | Pablo Picasso (1881–1973)<br>Jacques Maritain (1882–1973) |
| | Martin Heidegger (1889–1976) |
| 1980 Thatcher government launches cuts in services | Ignazio Silone (1900–1978) |
| 1981 Pipeline to carry natural gas from U.S.S.R. to Western Europe | Jean–Paul Sartre (1905–1980) |
| | Alberto Moravia (1907–1985)<br>Heinrich Böll (1917–1985)<br>Michel Foucault (1926–1985)<br>Henry Moore (1908–1966)<br>Claude Lévi-Strauss (1908– |
| 1986 Chernobyl meltdown | |
| 1990 | |
| 1992 EC Single Europe Act to take effect | |

**Prelates from around the world, in Rome for the Vatican Council, stand as Pope Paul VI is carried on his throne into St. Peter's, a sixteenth-century church in the city that dominated Europe two thousand years earlier. The splendid ceremonies of one of the world's oldest religions maintained their fascination for the modern world as the Church itself undertook a wide-ranging aggiornamento.** (Photo: Wide World Photos)

ity. Yet efforts to go much further, to give national or regional Church councils autonomous authority, for example, or to abandon the celibacy of the priesthood, have been firmly resisted. Even while showing impressive adaptability, Western institutions tend to slow the process of change, carefully weaving the new into the old social fabric.

Predictions of the future that take several centuries of history into account can still be wrong, but knowledge of the past should at least leave the present more comprehensible. Journalists were quick to comment that the fall of 1989 looked like the spring of 1848, when the streets filled with anger that seemed irrestible and hope that had never been forgotten. The past can still inspire. But 1849 (when armies, authorities, and institutions conspired to take back the freedoms they had granted) must be remembered, too. Even without the talk of German unification, the Eastern European scene in 1990 also contained a lot that fearfully recalled the history of the 1920s and 1930s—but the outcome then was not inevitable either. If the entire Western world cheered the cascade of freedoms suddenly proclaimed in Eastern Europe, that expressed, beyond kindred feeling and a preference for democracy, the joy at new evidence that sometimes human beings who had seemed powerless the week before can bend the direction of history and repeal the laws of power. In the light of historical experience, we have little reason to feel sorry for ourselves or to feel confident of our superiority. Every age has been a time of transition, and all have given wise prophets cause to predict an apocalypse. In our era the possibility of atomic warfare forces everyone to bear the burden of such wisdom. Over the last century Western society has dealt with many of its social needs on the assumption of ever-expanding prosperity and received reassurance from its dominance in the world. Now many believe that continued economic growth must end before nature, so long dominated, takes its revenge with an uninhabitable environment.

If wealth no longer increased, such fundamental change would make the future in important respects more like the distant past, with the significant difference that non-Western societies are likely to be more similar to the West in ideologies, social organization, and technology than ever before, adding new perspectives and possibilities to a rich and varied tradition.

## SUMMARY

In terms of well-being, creativity, or general decency, Europe as a whole and Western Europe in particular compares well with any society past or present. Yet the limits on the autonomy of its sovereign states seem to weigh more heavily than their worldwide influence. Where free expression is allowed, the inadequacies and inequities of Europe's societies produce criticism more resounding than the praise their prosperity and freedom can win, and the ideas of their extraordinary intellectual tradition and the continued creativity of their culture come to focus on defining the nature of the current crisis.

Western civilization is often said to be entering a new era troubled by many signs of crisis; yet that description could fit most of the past 2000 years. It has since Roman times been a diverse civilization, built of Greek philosophy and Roman institutions and an Eastern religion, a mixture of many races and cultures and political systems, all borrowing from and competing against each other. Such qualities have helped make the West particularly adaptable and ready to learn from the outside world. It still is. Its long history has been filled with wars and revolutions that have bred a flexible toughness in its institutions, and its future is probably no more uncertain than futures normally are. As for the present, a troubled civilization still finds nourishment and individuals still seek guidance in the Western experience.

# RECOMMENDED READING

## Studies

*Albertini, Rudolf von. *Decolonization. The Administration and Future of the Colonies, 1919–1960.* Francisca Garvie (tr.). 1982. A solid account that focuses on Britain and France.

*Ardagh, John. *France in the 1980s.* 1982. Fascinating examination of the fabric of daily life, with an eye on the development of the whole period since 1945.

Ash, Timothy Garten. *The Polish Revolution: Solidarity.* 1984. A comprehensive account of a moment that captured worldwide attention.

*Barraclough, Geoffrey. *An Introduction to Contemporary History.* 1967. A historian's assessment of the main currents of world history, making Europe no longer its dominant center.

*Beer, Samuel H. *Britain Against Herself.* 1982. A subtle and expert analysis of political and social stalemate in Britain.

Berger, Suzanne (ed.). *Organizing Interests in Western Europe: Pluralism, Corporatism, and the Transformation of Politics.* 1981. Important assessments of the political balance of power.

Brown, B. E. *Protest in Paris: Anatomy of a Revolt.* 1974. The student revolt subject to scholarly study.

*Craig, Gordon. *The Germans.* 1983. A noted historian's insightful and handsomely written assessment of German Society.

*Ellul, Jacques. *The Technological Society.* John Wilkinson (tr.). 1964. One of the most striking and influential of contemporary attacks on the effects of technology.

*Heidenheimer, Arnold, J., Hugh Heclo, and Carolyn Adams. *Comparative Public Policy: The Politics of Social Choice in Europe and America.* 1975. Studies the background and implications of the varied approaches to social policy.

*Heilbroner, Robert G. *An Inquiry into the Human Prospect.* 1980. An analysis based on the literature of modern social science.

*Helias, Pierre-Jakez. *The Horse of Pride: Life in a Breton Village.* June Guicharnaud (tr.). 1980. A compelling account of a preindustrial society about to be transformed.

Hennessy, Peter, and Anthony Seldons. *Ruling Performance: British Governments from Atlee to Thatcher.* 1987. Some contrasting perspectives on British politics.

Hoffmann, Stanley, and Paschalis Kitromilides. *Culture and Society in Contemporary Europe.* 1981. An anthology of essays by leading intellectuals.

*Hughes, H. Stuart. *The Sea Change: The Migration of Social Thought, 1930–1960.* 1977. A major study of the transatlantic roots of modern social thought.

Hulsberg, Werner. *The German Greens: A Social and Political Profile.* 1988. A systematic treatment of the strongest of the European environmental movements.

*Jay, Martin. *The Dialectical Imagination. A History of the Frankfurt School and the Institute of Social Research, 1923–1950.* 1973. A rewarding study of the founders and their influential work.

Katzenstein, Mary F., and Carol M. Mueller (eds.). *The Women's Movements of the United States and Western Europe.* 1987. Especially valuable for its broad coverage.

Keylor, William R. *The Twentiety-Century World. An International History.* 1984. A stimulating attempt to break out of the traditional national boundaries.

Lewin, Moshe. *The Gorbachev Phenomenon: A Historical Interpretation.* 1988. A brilliant analysis relating current developments to Soviet society over the last 50 years.

*Mandelbaum, Michael. *The Nuclear Revolution: International Politics Before and After Hiroshima.* 1981. A wide-ranging and insightful study that compared the postwar situation with other periods of modern European history.

Marrus, Michael R. *The Emergence of Leisure.* 1974. An historical study of one of the major modern changes.

Merkl, Peter H. *The Federal Republic at Forty.* 1989. Shows the strengths and weaknesses of a system now solidly established.

*Parker, Geoffrey. *The Logic of Unity.* 1975. A very useful analysis of the force of European unity by a geographer.

Payne, Stanley G. *Politics and Society in Twentieth-Century Spain.* 1976. Shows the roots of Spain's remarkable modernization.

Poster, Mark. *Existential Marxism in Postwar France.*

1975. An able analysis of an intellectual movement that had wide impact.

Rostow, Walt W. *The World Economy: History and Prospect*. 1977. A leading student of economic development assays the directions of the future.

Sampson, Anthony. *The Changing Anatomy of Britain*. 1983. The most recent in a series of analyses of the inner workings of British power.

*Shils, Edward. *Tradition*. 1982. An outstanding sociologist speculates on the beneficial role of tradition in shaping society in an era of change.

*Stromberg, Roland N. *After Everything: Western Intellectual History Since 1945*. 1975. A disenchanted and provocative essay on contemporary intellectual fashions.

*Williams, Raymond. *Communications*. 1976. A stimulating examination of the important role of the media.

*Willis, F. Roy. *France, Germany and the New Europe, 1945–1967*. 1968. Surveys the transformation of a traditionally bitter relationship into one of close cooperation.

*Wolf, Eric R. *Europe and the People Without History*. 1982. An interdisciplinary evaluation of capitalism and its cultural cost around the world.

* Available in paperback.

# ❆ INDEX ❆

# COLOR
## ❄ ILLUSTRATION ❄
## SOURCES

# ✳ ABOUT THE AUTHORS ✳

*Mortimer Chambers* is Professor of History at the University of California at Los Angeles. He was a Rhodes scholar from 1949 to 1952 and received an M.A. from Wadham College, Oxford, in 1955 after obtaining his doctorate from Harvard University in 1954. He has taught at Harvard University (1954–1955) and the University of Chicago (1955–1958). He was Visiting Professor at the University of British Columbia in 1958, the State University of New York at Buffalo in 1971, the University of Freiburg (Germany) in 1974, and Vassar College in 1988. A specialist in Greek and Roman history, he is coauthor of *Aristotle's History of Athenian Democracy* (1062), editor of a series of essays entitled *The Fall of Rome* (1063), and author of *Georg Busolt: His Career In His Letters* (1990). He has contributed articles to the *American Historical Review* and *Classical Philology* as well as other journals.

*Raymond Grew* is Professor of History at the University of Michigan. He earned both his M.A. (1952) and Ph.D. (1957) from Harvard University in the field of modern European history. He was a Fulbright Fellow to Italy (1954–1955), Guggenheim Fellow (1968–1969), Director of Studies at the Écoles des Hautes Études en Sciences Sociales in Paris (1976), and a Fellow of the National Endowment for the Humanities (1979). In 1962 he received the Chester Higby Prize from the American Historical Association, and in 1963 the Italian government awarded him the Unita d'Italia Prize. He is an active member of the A.H.A., the Society for French Historical Studies. He is the author of *A Sterner Plan for Italian Unity* (1963, edited *Crises of Development in Europe and the United States* (1978), and is presently the editor of *Comparative Studies in Society and History*. His articles and reviews have appeared in a number of European and American journals.

*David Herlihy*, Mary Critchfield and Barnaby Keeney Professor of History at Brown University, is the author of numerous books and studies on the social history of the Middle Ages. His most recent publications are *Opera Muliebria: Woman and Work in Medieval Europe* (1990); *Medieval Households* (1985); and, in collaboration with Christiane Klapisch-Zuber, *Tuscans and Their Families: A Study of the Florentine Catasto of 1427* (1985). He received his M.A. from the Catholic University of America in 1953, his Ph.D. from Yale University in 1956, and an honorary Doctor of Humanities from the University of San Francisco in 1983. He is a former president of several historical associations, and in 1990 served as president of the American Historical Association, the largest historical society in America. He was a fellow of the Guggenheim Foundation (1962–1963), the American Council of Learned Societies (1966–1967), the Center for Advanced Study in the Behavioral Sciences (1972–1973), and the National Endowment for the Humanities (1976). He is a fellow of the American Academy of Arts and Sciences and of the American Philosophical Society. His articles and reviews have appeared in numerous professional journals, both here and abroad.

*Theodore K. Rabb* is Professor of History at Princeton University. He received his Ph.D. from Princeton, and subsequently taught at Stanford, Northwestern, Harvard, and Johns Hopkins universities. He is the author of numerous articles and reviews, and has been editor of *The Journal of Interdisciplinary History* since its foundation. Among the books he has written or edited are *The Struggle for Stability in Early Modern Europe* and *The New History*. Professor Rabb has held offices in various national organizations, including the American Historical Association and the Social Science History Association, and is currently involved in preparing for PBS a multipart television series on Renaissance history.

*Isser Woloch* is Professor of History at Columbia University. He received his Ph.D. (1965) from Princeton University in the field of eighteenth- and nineteenth-century European history. He has taught at Indiana University and at the University of California at Los Angeles where, in 1967, he received a Distinguished Teaching Citation. He has been a fellow of the A.C.L.S., the National Endowment for the Humanities, the Guggenheim Foundation, and the Institute for Advanced Study at Princeton. His publications include *Jacobin Legacy; The Democratic Movement under the Directory* (1970), *The Peasantry in the Old Regime: Conditions and Protests* (1970, *The French Veteran from the Revolution to the Restoration* (1979), and *Eighteenth-Century Europe: Tradition and Progress, 1715–1719* (1982).

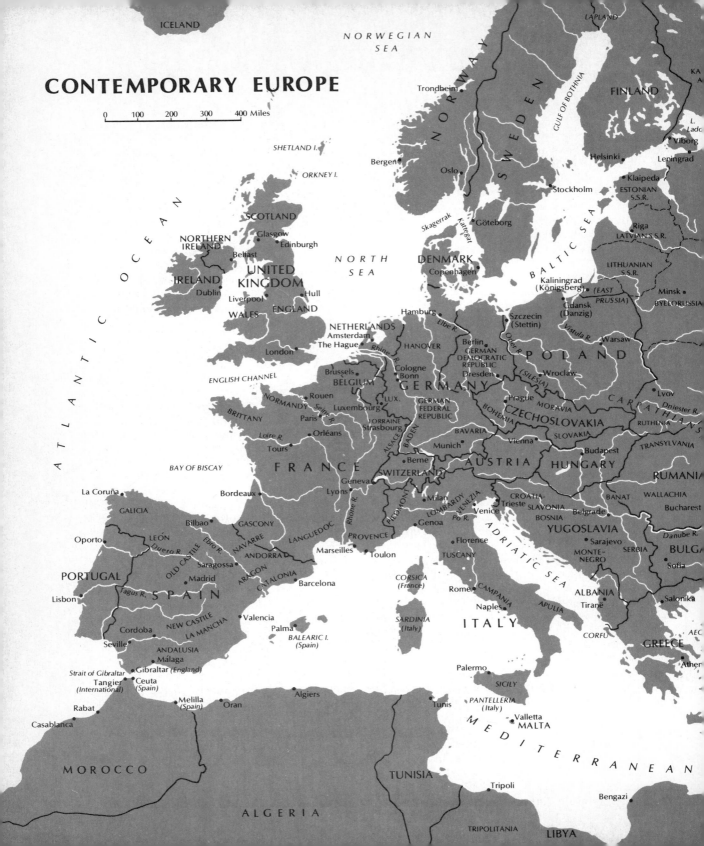

# CONTEMPORARY EUROPE

0   100   200   300   400 Miles

ICELAND

ATLANTIC OCEAN

NORWEGIAN SEA

NORWAY

SWEDEN

FINLAND

LAPLAND

L. Ladoga

Trondheim

Bergen

Oslo

Stockholm

GULF OF BOTHNIA

Helsinki

Viborg

Leningrad

Klaipeda

ESTONIAN S.S.R.

Göteborg

Skagerrak

Kattegat

BALTIC SEA

Riga

LATVIAN S.S.R.

SHETLAND I.

ORKNEY I.

SCOTLAND

Glasgow

Edinburgh

NORTHERN IRELAND

Belfast

IRELAND

Dublin

Liverpool

Hull

UNITED KINGDOM

WALES

ENGLAND

London

NORTH SEA

DENMARK

Copenhagen

Kaliningrad (Königsberg)

(EAST PRUSSIA)

LITHUANIAN S.S.R.

Minsk

BYELORUSSIA

Hamburg

Elbe R.

Szczecin (Stettin)

Gdansk (Danzig)

Vistula R.

Warsaw

POLAND

Lvov

ENGLISH CHANNEL

NETHERLANDS

Amsterdam

The Hague

Rhine R.

HANOVER

Berlin

GERMAN DEMOCRATIC REPUBLIC

Dresden

Oder R.

Wroclaw

(SILESIA)

Dniester R.

CARPATHIANS

RUTHENIA

Brussels

BELGIUM

LUX.

Cologne

Bonn

GERMAN FEDERAL REPUBLIC

GERMANY

Prague

BOHEMIA

MORAVIA

CZECHOSLOVAKIA

SLOVAKIA

TRANSYLVANIA

Rouen

Seine R.

Luxembourg

LORRAINE

Strasbourg

BADEN

BAVARIA

Munich

Vienna

Budapest

NORMANDY

Paris

ALSACE

Berne

SWITZERLAND

AUSTRIA

HUNGARY

RUMANIA

BRITTANY

Loire R.

Orléans

Tours

FRANCE

Geneva

Lyons

Rhône R.

PIEDMONT

Milan

LOMBARDY

VENEZIA

Trieste

Venice

CROATIA

SLAVONIA

BANAT

WALLACHIA

Bucharest

BAY OF BISCAY

La Coruña

Bordeaux

GASCONY

LANGUEDOC

PROVENCE

Po R.

Genoa

TUSCANY

BOSNIA

Belgrade

YUGOSLAVIA

SERBIA

Danube R.

BULGARIA

Sofia

GALICIA

Oporto

LEÓN

Dueto R.

Ebro R.

NAVARRE

Bilbao

Marseilles

Toulon

Florence

ADRIATIC SEA

Sarajevo

MONTE-NEGRO

PORTUGAL

OLD CASTILE

Saragossa

Madrid

ARAGON

CATALONIA

ANDORRA

Barcelona

CORSICA (France)

Rome

CAMPANIA

APULIA

ALBANIA

Tirane

Salonika

Lisbon

Tagus R.

SPAIN

NEW CASTILE

LA MANCHA

Valencia

Palma

BALEARIC I. (Spain)

SARDINIA (Italy)

ITALY

Naples

CORFU

GREECE

AEGEAN

Athens

Cordoba

ANDALUSIA

Seville

Málaga

Gibraltar (England)

Strait of Gibraltar

Tangier (International)

Ceuta (Spain)

Melilla (Spain)

Oran

Algiers

Tunis

PANTELLERIA (Italy)

Palermo

SICILY

Valletta

MALTA

MEDITERRANEAN

Rabat

Casablanca

MOROCCO

ALGERIA

TUNISIA

Tripoli

TRIPOLITANIA

LIBYA

Bengazi

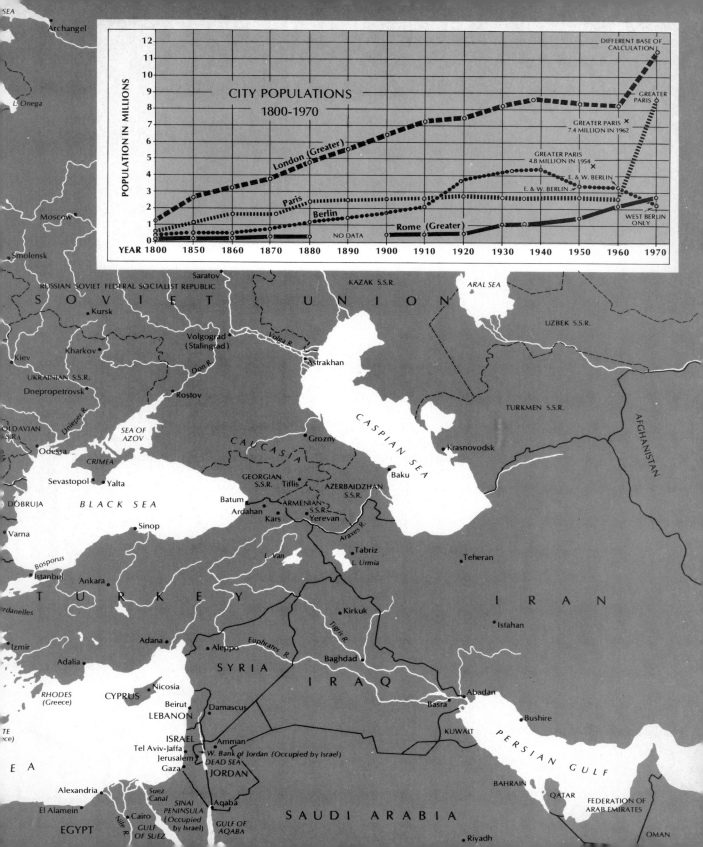

# LAND AND SOCIETY THROUGH THE AGES
## A Cartographic Essay

## MICHAEL P. CONZEN
*University of Chicago*

To accompany *The Western Experience, Third Edition,* by Mortimer Chambers, Raymond Grew, David Herlihy, Theodore K. Rabb, and Isser Woloch.

*Maps were executed by David Lindroth.*

---

## INTRODUCTION

The history of Western civilization—indeed of any civilization—can be thought of as a kind of dialogue between society and nature. In this dialogue, men and women make a complicated series of choices within the limits imposed by nature. The results of these decisions, the way a society actually *looks* in its habitat, is called its cultural landscape. In a way, then, the history of European civilization is a rich succession of layers of cultural landscape, each showing the ways human beings have tried to occupy and use space during different historical periods. This essay highlights some of the main patterns of cultural landscape that have characterized the Western experience.

Maps that show the spatial distribution of characteristic human activities can communicate much about the relationship between social organization and environmental space. A careful reading of the following maps can lead to a deeper understanding of this complex and ever-changing relationship.

## THE CLASSICAL WORLD: THE CITY-STATE

A singular achievement of Greek civilization was the city-state. This institution had a firm geographical basis as well as a political and philosophical significance. The topography of the Greek peninsula was clearly influential in the emergence of this form of government. Essentially, the city-state represented a rational effort to organize populations scattered among coastal and river basins of uncertain fertility and separated by rocky mountain ridges.

### Geographic Origins of the City-State

Between Minoan and Mycenaean times, the "polis" developed from a castle stronghold, situated on a hilltop and presiding over a territory of dispersed rural villages, into a more recognizably urban settlement with civilian housing and public spaces. Mycenae illustrates this growth well (Map A-1). Early but elaborate burials testify to the site's central importance for the surrounding region. The hilltop

# MYCENAE

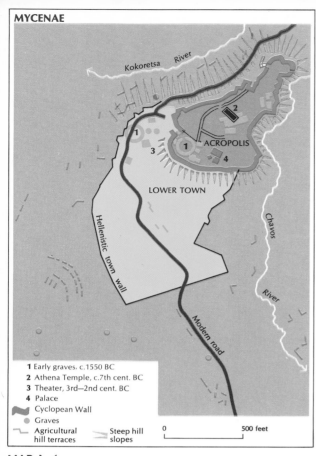

1 Early graves, c.1550 BC
2 Athena Temple, c.7th cent. BC
3 Theater, 3rd–2nd cent. BC
4 Palace

Cyclopean Wall

Graves

Agricultural hill terraces

Steep hill slopes

0          500 feet

**MAP A–1**

# SPARTA AND ITS POLIS TERRITORY

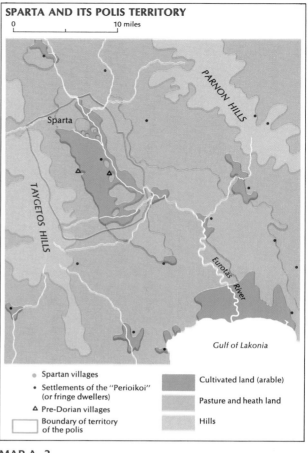

0                    10 miles

• Spartan villages

• Settlements of the "Perioikoi" (or fringe dwellers)

△ Pre-Dorian villages

☐ Boundary of territory of the polis

Cultivated land (arable)

Pasture and heath land

Hills

**MAP A–2**

**MAP A–4**

# POLIS DIFFUSION THROUGHOUT THE MEDITERRANEAN WORLD, 250 B.C.–A.D. 400

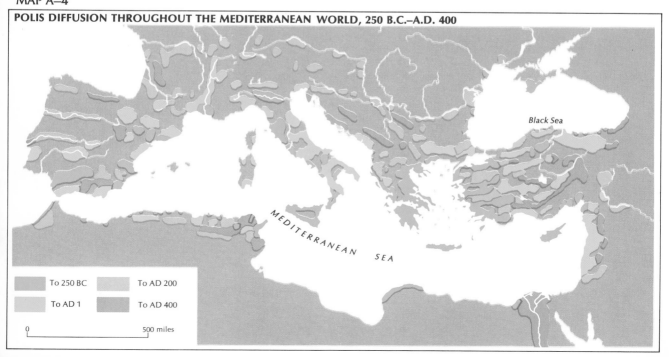

To 250 BC          To AD 200

To AD 1          To AD 400

0          500 miles

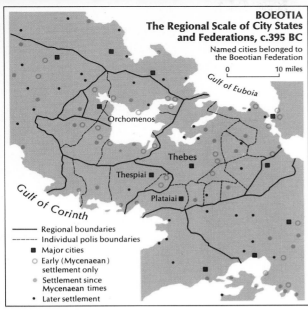

**BOEOTIA**
**The Regional Scale of City States**
**and Federations, c.395 BC**

Named cities belonged to
the Boeotian Federation

0          10 miles

Gulf of Euboia

Orchomenos

Thebes

Thespiai

Plataiai

Gulf of Corinth

—— Regional boundaries
---- Individual polis boundaries
■ Major cities
○ Early (Mycenaean)
  settlement only
● Settlement since
  Mycenaean times
· Later settlement

MAP A–3

required direct citizen participation in politics. The area shown in the Boeotia map (A-3) is no larger than that of metropolitan Chicago.

## Urbanization in the Roman Empire

Greek overseas settlement spread the concept of the polis throughout the Mediterranean, as later the idea of a city with a politically related territory penetrated every part of the Roman Empire (Map A-4). In practice this form of settlement had to be adjusted to local environments, and many areas of Europe were too sparsely populated to justify such Roman "coloniae." But the seed of an urbanized civilization, the polis, was nevertheless implanted throughout Europe.

## The City and Agriculture in the Roman Empire

In addition to establishing the continental road system, town networks, and frontier defense lines, the Romans expanded local economies

between the two rivers acquired stout defenses, a palace complex, temples, and housing. Hill terraces, evidence of Greek efforts to grow food for the town, indicate the close relationship between the town, its food supply, and the surrounding district. Gradually this fortified hilltop settlement, or "acropolis," became physically more complex as Mycenaean political power and trade grew; a lower town developed adjacent to the fortress site, also surrounded by a military defense wall.

Such a "town," however, was merely the functional center of a territory that might include hundreds of square miles. For instance, Sparta in its early stages of development occupied a small but strategic portion of the Eurotas Valley over which it had primary control (Map A-2). This territory included much of the available cultivated land in the region. Consequently, villages beyond the borders of the polis territory were tied to Sparta by special economic and political bonds.

## The Network of City-States

City-states formed a loose regional network, usually without strong domination by any one state. The polis might expand or contract, or change its shape as a result of political alliances (such as the Boeotian Federation) and the fortunes of war. But the natural environment itself had much to do with the way the polis developed. In fact, the marginal fertility of the habitat meant that the polis had to be small. This, in turn, made possible Greek "democracy," which

MAP A–5

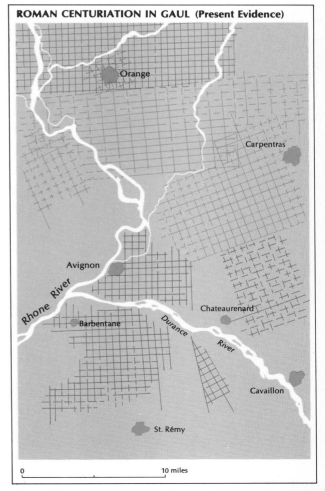

**ROMAN CENTURIATION IN GAUL (Present Evidence)**

Orange

Carpentras

Avignon

Rhone River

Chateaurenard

Barbentane

Durance River

Cavaillon

St. Rémy

0          10 miles

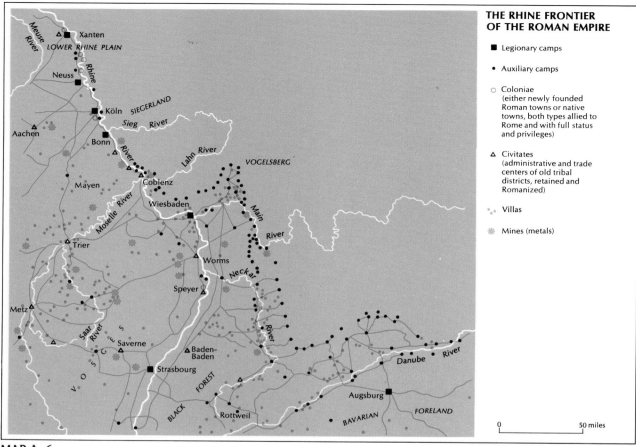

## THE RHINE FRONTIER OF THE ROMAN EMPIRE

■ Legionary camps

• Auxiliary camps

○ Coloniae
(either newly founded
Roman towns or native
towns, both types allied to
Rome and with full status
and privileges)

△ Civitates
(administrative and trade
centers of old tribal
districts, retained and
Romanized)

∵ Villas

✳ Mines (metals)

Meuse River
Xanten
LOWER RHINE PLAIN
Rhine
Neuss
Köln    SIEGERLAND
Aachen
Sieg River
Bonn
Rhine River
Mayen
Lahn River
Coblenz
VOGELSBERG
Moselle River
Wiesbaden
Main River
Trier
Worms
Neckar
Speyer
Metz
River
Saar River
V O S G E S
Saverne
Baden-Baden
Danube River
Strasbourg
BLACK FOREST
Augsburg
Rottweil
BAVARIAN    FORELAND

0    50 miles

MAP A–6

MAP A–7

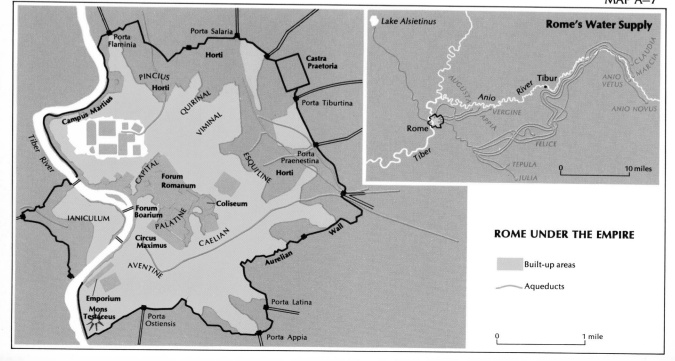

Porta Flaminia
Porta Salaria
Horti
Castra Praetoria
PINCIUS
Horti
QUIRINAL
Porta Tiburtina
VIMINAL
Campus Martius
Tiber River
CAPITAL
Forum Romanum
ESQUILINE
Porta Praenestina
Horti
Coliseum
IANICULUM
Forum Boarium
PALATINE
Circus Maximus
CAELIAN
Aurelian    Wall
AVENTINE
Porta Latina
Emporium
Mons Testaceus
Porta Ostiensis
Porta Appia

Lake Alsietinus
Rome's Water Supply
AUGUSTA
Anio    River    Tibur
CLAUDIA
MARCIA
ANIO VETUS
APPIA
VERGINE
ANIO NOVUS
Rome
FELICE
Tiber
TEPULA
JULIA

0    10 miles

### ROME UNDER THE EMPIRE

▨ Built-up areas

〰 Aqueducts

0    1 mile

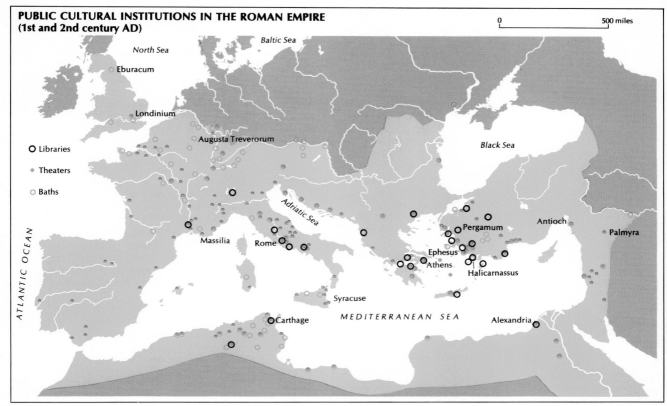

## PUBLIC CULTURAL INSTITUTIONS IN THE ROMAN EMPIRE
(1st and 2nd century AD)

O Libraries
• Theaters
○ Baths

North Sea
Baltic Sea
Eburacum
Londinium
Augusta Treverorum
Black Sea
Adriatic Sea
Massilia
Rome
Pergamum
Antioch
Palmyra
Ephesus
Athens
Halicarnassus
ATLANTIC OCEAN
Syracuse
MEDITERRANEAN SEA
Alexandria
Carthage

MAP A–8

through agricultural colonization. Whether reorganizing native farming or clearing tracts of wilderness, they surveyed large areas of arable land into a grid system of fields (a process called centuriation). Traces of this grid system are occasionally visible in present-day landscapes. The Roman sense of order is well illustrated in the grid pattern around the French town of Avignon (Map A-5). Even so, because of environmental and administrative needs the overall grid pattern was irregular.

At regional levels, Roman economic organization was strongly affected by both nature and the demands of imperial defense. In what is now central Germany, agricultural villas worked the lighter alluvial soils found in or near river valleys. Where necessary, roads were cut through dense forests to link vital frontier outposts with mining centers and the cities, such as Augsburg and Trier (Map A-6), that served as administrative centers. Not only did these imperial frontier regions define the edge of the civilized world for the Romans, but, with their natural resources, they contributed directly to the might of Rome.

## The Urban Culture of the Roman Empire: The Metropolis

Rome, begun as a union of several villages situated on neighboring hills, grew into a sprawling metropolis as it became the center of an empire (Map A-7). Repeated urban renewal cleared ground for vast ceremonial complexes of temples, public squares, market buildings, theaters, and circuses. Outside these complexes were neighborhoods of crowded buildings and irregular streets, a vibrant mixture of residences and craft shops. Aqueducts brought a vast water supply to the congested city, symbolizing Rome's dependence on outside resources for its survival and growth.

## Provincial Towns of the Roman Empire

In its provincial towns Rome built theaters, libraries, and public baths in an attempt to spread a higher culture throughout the Empire (Map A-8). Here, again, the Greek legacy is apparent. For instance, because of a long tradition of intellectual attainment there were many more libraries in Greece than anywhere else in the Empire.

# THE ECONOMY OF THE MIDDLE AGES

## Economic Life and the Monasteries

The Church played a major role in the political, economic, and social life of Europe after the decline of the Roman Empire. By the height of the Middle Ages monastic orders had proliferated throughout Europe, establishing centers of learning, extending charity, and undertaking agrarian colonization without regard for political boundaries. The Cistercians, a Benedictine reform order devoted to simple living, emerged in northeast France in the twelfth century and quickly grew as the early monasteries expanded their activities by founding daughter houses (Map A-9). Through these daughter houses, the Cistercians spread a common tradition of land colonization in agriculturally marginal areas. At many sites sacred relics drew pilgrims from far and wide. Other religious activities, however, were more regional and centralized. One site, the abbey at Einsiedeln, Switzerland, not surprisingly attracted more visitors from northern regions than from the more mountainous south. Yet the overall pattern of pilgrimage coincided reasonably well with what was later to become the broad transcontinental trade corridor between northern Italy and the North Sea.

## Rural Settlement

During the Middle Ages differences in local environments and cultural traditions produced a wide variety of rural settlement forms. Common to many regions was the open-field village shown in the Swedish example (Map A-10). The irregular area of cultivable land was divided into narrow strip plots, and most farmers had fragmented holdings. The pasturelands and woodland of the village, however, were not divided and were used by all farmers.

## Clearing the Land

Rural settlement expanded greatly in medieval times as large forest tracts between major river valleys were cleared and villages, like Otterstorpaby (see Map A-10), grew up. Occasionally the reverse happened as populations were decimated by war, famine, or disease. Many cleared areas near the Weser, for example, were lost to readvancing forests between 1290 and 1430, in the aftermath of the Black Death (Map A-11).

## The Growth of Towns

Relative political stability and a consolidating agrarian base provided the groundwork for improved trade and growth of towns (see Map A-11). This

MAP A–9

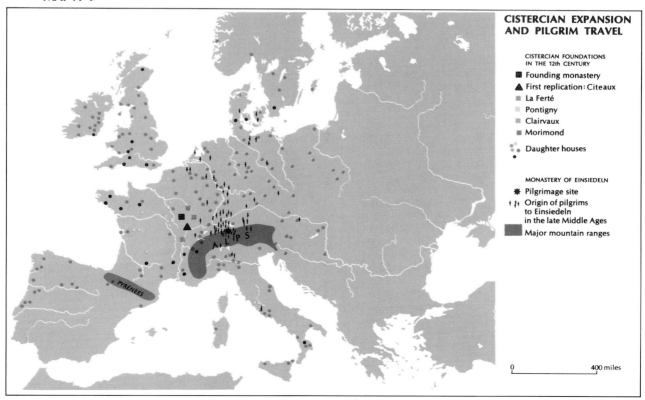

**CISTERCIAN EXPANSION AND PILGRIM TRAVEL**

CISTERCIAN FOUNDATIONS IN THE 12th CENTURY
- ■ Founding monastery
- ▲ First replication: Citeaux
- ■ La Ferté
- ■ Pontigny
- ■ Clairvaux
- ■ Morimond
- Daughter houses

MONASTERY OF EINSIEDELN
- ✳ Pilgrimage site
- † †† Origin of pilgrims to Einsiedeln in the late Middle Ages
- Major mountain ranges

0          400 miles

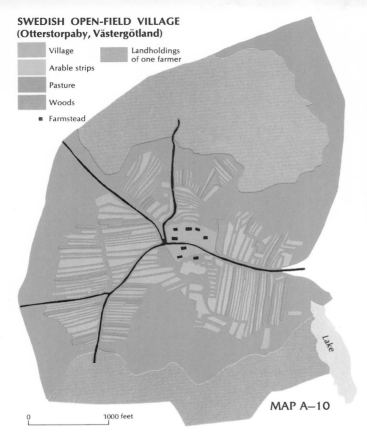

## SWEDISH OPEN-FIELD VILLAGE
### (Otterstorpaby, Västergötland)

- Village
- Arable strips
- Pasture
- Woods
- ■ Farmstead
- Landholdings of one farmer

Lake

0       1000 feet

MAP A–10

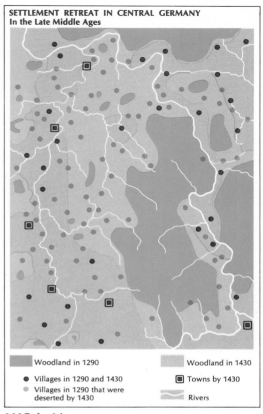

## SETTLEMENT RETREAT IN CENTRAL GERMANY
### In the Late Middle Ages

- Woodland in 1290
- Woodland in 1430
- ● Villages in 1290 and 1430
- ○ Villages in 1290 that were deserted by 1430
- ◼ Towns by 1430
- Rivers

MAP A–11

MAP A–12

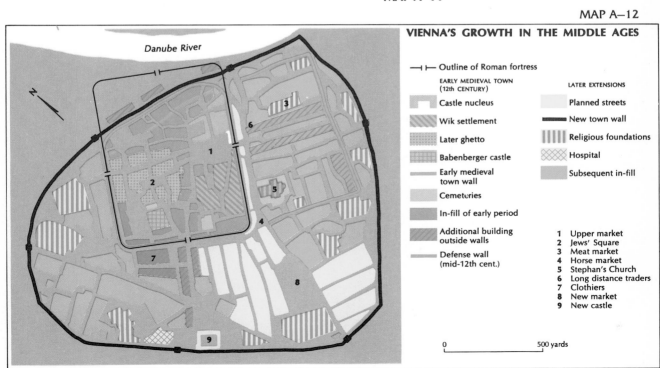

## VIENNA'S GROWTH IN THE MIDDLE AGES

Danube River

⊢ ⊦ Outline of Roman fortress

**EARLY MEDIEVAL TOWN (12th CENTURY)**

- Castle nucleus
- Wik settlement
- Later ghetto
- Babenberger castle
- Early medieval town wall
- Cemeteries
- In-fill of early period
- Additional building outside walls
- Defense wall (mid-12th cent.)

**LATER EXTENSIONS**

- Planned streets
- New town wall
- Religious foundations
- Hospital
- Subsequent in-fill

1 Upper market
2 Jews' Square
3 Meat market
4 Horse market
5 Stephan's Church
6 Long distance traders
7 Clothiers
8 New market
9 New castle

0       500 yards

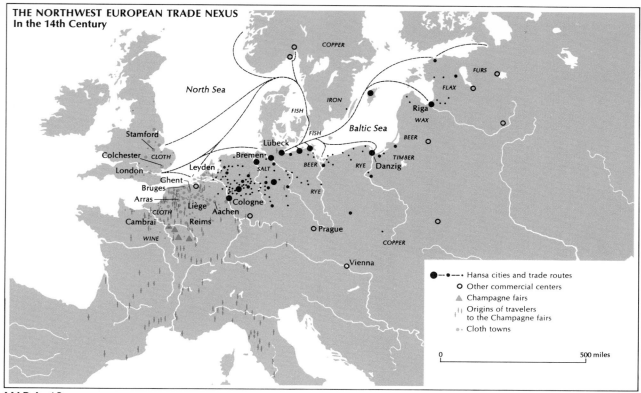

## THE NORTHWEST EUROPEAN TRADE NEXUS
### In the 14th Century

*North Sea*

*COPPER*

Stamford
Colchester — *CLOTH*
London
Bruges
Arras
Cambrai
Liège
Reims
*CLOTH*
*WINE*

Leyden
Ghent
Aachen
Cologne

Bremen
Lübeck
*SALT*
*BEER*
*RYE*
*RYE*

*Baltic Sea*

*IRON*
*FISH*
*FISH*
*FISH*

*FURS*
*FLAX*
Riga
*WAX*

*BEER*
Danzig
*TIMBER*

Prague
*COPPER*

Vienna

● ─ ● ─ ─ ─ Hansa cities and trade routes
○ Other commercial centers
▲ Champagne fairs
⊥⊥ Origins of travelers to the Champagne fairs
• Cloth towns

0 _____ 500 miles

MAP A–13

MAP A–14

MAP A–15

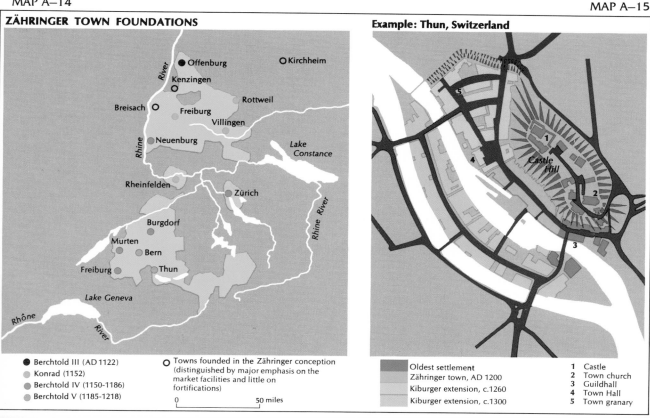

## ZÄHRINGER TOWN FOUNDATIONS

*River*

Offenburg
Kenzingen
Kirchheim
Breisach
Freiburg
Rottweil
Villingen
Neuenburg
*Rhine*
*Lake Constance*
Rheinfelden
Zürich
*Rhine River*
Burgdorf
Murten
Bern
Freiburg
Thun
*Lake Geneva*
*Rhône River*

● Berchtold III (AD 1122)
● Konrad (1152)
● Berchtold IV (1150–1186)
● Berchtold V (1185–1218)
○ Towns founded in the Zähringer conception (distinguished by major emphasis on the market facilities and little on fortifications)

0 _____ 50 miles

### Example: Thun, Switzerland

Castle Hill

5
1
4
2
3

Oldest settlement
Zähringer town, AD 1200
Kiburger extension, c.1260
Kiburger extension, c.1300

1 Castle
2 Town church
3 Guildhall
4 Town Hall
5 Town granary

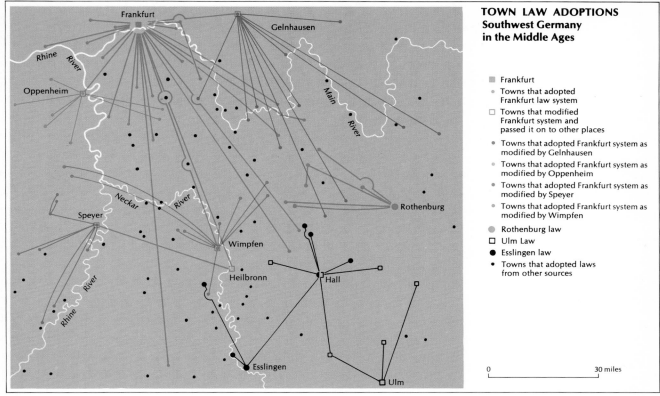

TOWN LAW ADOPTIONS
Southwest Germany
in the Middle Ages

■ Frankfurt
• Towns that adopted Frankfurt law system
□ Towns that modified Frankfurt system and passed it on to other places
• Towns that adopted Frankfurt system as modified by Gelnhausen
• Towns that adopted Frankfurt system as modified by Oppenheim
• Towns that adopted Frankfurt system as modified by Speyer
• Towns that adopted Frankfurt system as modified by Wimpfen
● Rothenburg law
□ Ulm Law
● Esslingen law
• Towns that adopted laws from other sources

0      30 miles

MAP A–16

was a slow process, as shown in the case of Vienna (Map A-12), which grew from about 12,000 to 20,000 between A.D. 1200 and 1300. On the site of an earlier Roman fortress at this important Danube River crossing point, a castle was built and a traders' district (Wik) sprang up, surrounded by a town wall (subsequently obliterated by later development). Jewish merchants gathered here, but were forced to live in a settlement outside the city walls, thus being denied the rights of municipal citizenship. Later, other merchant quarters (not necessarily Jewish) and craft districts were established outside the old walls, joined by several newly founded monasteries. There was enough room to lay out "planned" streets to the south of the old town, and a new, enlarged wall was built to enclose the whole settlement, which by then included a new and larger castle. During this period of growth and change, three of the four gates of the Roman fortress were still used as part of the medieval street system.

### Trade Routes

The prosperity of towns such as Vienna was made possible through a combination of local and long-distance trade. The axis of trade between the Mediterranean and the Low Countries was anchored at one end around the North Sea, the site of Europe's major clothmaking region (Map A-13). Lying between the Rhine and Seine rivers, this area was supported in part by wool supplies from England and from the Ardennes Hills just south of Liège and Aachen. The robustness of medieval trade was reflected in the great international trade fairs of the Champagne district, where individual merchants gathered from all over Europe. Conversely, competition, uncertain markets, and security problems in the North Sea and Baltic regions produced closed trade associations such as the Hanseatic League of north German cities, which sought to monopolize the northern market.

### Colonization

Some regions of Europe were comparatively late in being drawn into international trade or even in acquiring towns of local significance. One example of commercial town founding was the colonization of Eastern Europe by German subjects; another example, on a smaller scale, is provided by the mos-

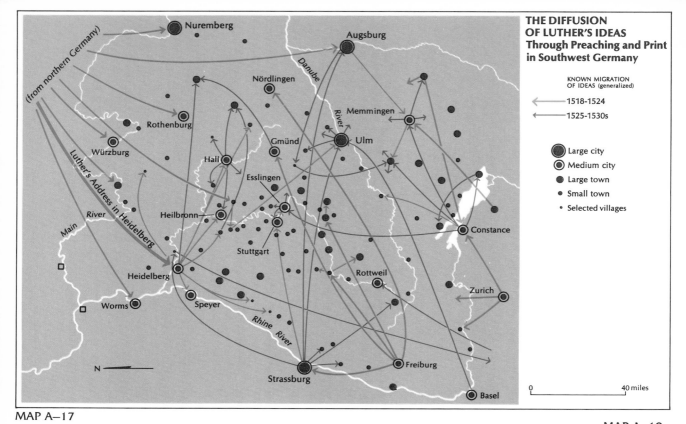

## THE DIFFUSION OF LUTHER'S IDEAS
### Through Preaching and Print in Southwest Germany

KNOWN MIGRATION OF IDEAS (generalized)

→ 1518-1524
← 1525-1530s

◉ Large city
◎ Medium city
● Large town
• Small town
· Selected villages

(from northern Germany)

Nuremberg

Augsburg

Danube

Nördlingen

Memmingen
River

Rothenburg

Würzburg

Gmünd    Ulm

Luther's Address in Heidelberg

Hall

Esslingen

River
Main

Heilbronn

Constance

Stuttgart

Heidelberg

Rottweil

Worms

Speyer

Zurich

Rhine River

Freiburg

N

Strassburg

Basel

0          40 miles

MAP A—17

MAP A—19

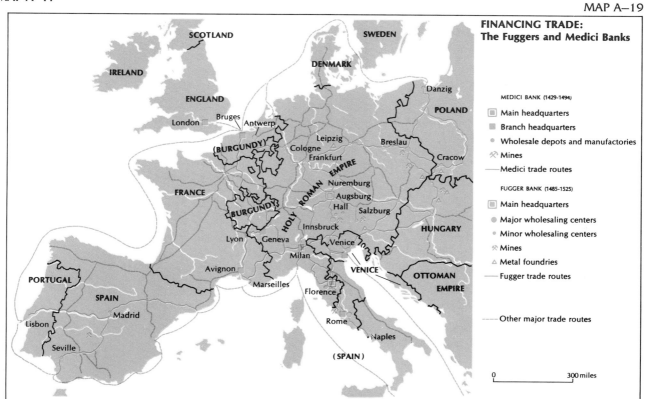

## FINANCING TRADE:
### The Fuggers and Medici Banks

SCOTLAND

SWEDEN

IRELAND

DENMARK

Danzig

ENGLAND

POLAND

London

Bruges  Antwerp

BURGUNDY

Leipzig
Cologne    Breslau
Frankfurt

Cracow

FRANCE

BURGUNDY

EMPIRE

Nuremburg

Augsburg
Hall    Salzburg

HUNGARY

Innsbruck

Lyon   Geneva

Venice

Milan

PORTUGAL

Avignon

VENICE

OTTOMAN

SPAIN

Marseilles

Florence

EMPIRE

Madrid

Rome

Lisbon

Naples

Seville

( SPAIN )

MEDICI BANK (1429-1494)
▣ Main headquarters
■ Branch headquarters
• Wholesale depots and manufactories
⚒ Mines
— Medici trade routes

FUGGER BANK (1485-1525)
▣ Main headquarters
● Major wholesaling centers
• Minor wholesaling centers
⚒ Mines
△ Metal foundries
— Fugger trade routes

- - - Other major trade routes

0          300 miles

aic fiefdom of the counts of Zähringen, knit together from sparsely settled political territories in the Upper Rhine region and central Switzerland (Map A-14).

### New Towns

Often new castles, built to control particular areas, stimulated local market and craft activities that gave rise to a new set of towns. Thun was one of these towns (Map A-15). Until 1200 it consisted of a single street tucked between the castle and the river, a pattern typical of European villages, still common even today in Austria and Romania. In the next fifty years Thun extended to the northwest, where the street pattern could branch out and there was room for a marketplace. Further expansion spilled onto the island in the river as the next most logical defensive location.

### The Spread of Urban Forms

Founding new towns involved more than choosing a site. Laws for local government had to be worked out. Since one attraction of towns was their departure from feudal ties, their founders often adopted the municipal laws and codification of rights of existing towns, either because the same overlord ruled both the new and the old towns or because settlers

from the older town had helped establish the new. This pattern of town law diffusion, characteristic of towns in southwest Germany, illustrates how urban legal "families" evolved (Map A-16).

## THE EARLY MODERN ERA

### Reformation: Preaching

The fifteenth and sixteenth centuries witnessed major changes both in the climate of ideas and in the means of communicating them across long distances. It was, in fact, during these centuries that explorers boldly extended European knowledge of the world. Of equal significance was Luther's challenge to Church orthodoxy, which rapidly transformed the religious map of northern Europe. Luther's public appearances and the subsequent movements inspired by his example disseminated the new doctrines among the generally larger towns of southwest Germany (Map A-17). In printed form, Luther's ideas swept over Germany without regard for town size. Ideas spread as readily from small towns to large towns as from large to small, although many large towns became the centers from which new ideas radiated.

MAP A–18

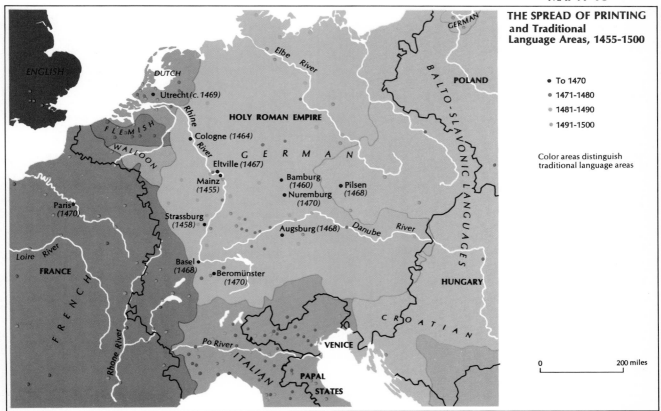

THE SPREAD OF PRINTING
and Traditional
Language Areas, 1455-1500

- ● To 1470
- ● 1471-1480
- ● 1481-1490
- ● 1491-1500

Color areas distinguish
traditional language areas

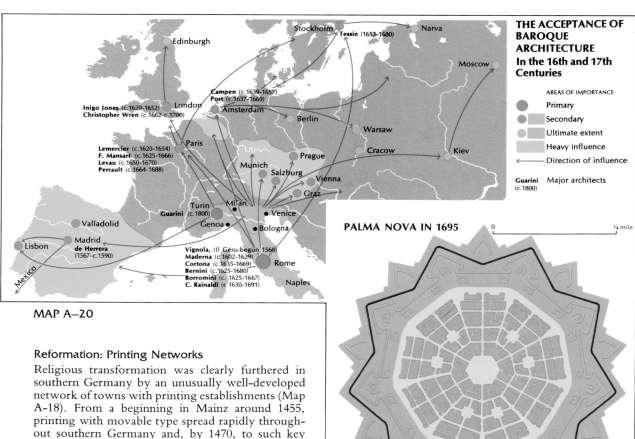

**THE ACCEPTANCE OF BAROQUE ARCHITECTURE**
**In the 16th and 17th Centuries**

AREAS OF IMPORTANCE

- Primary
- Secondary
- Ultimate extent
- Heavy influence
← Direction of influence

**Guarini** Major architects
(c.1800)

Stockholm  Narva
Tessin (1653-1680)
Edinburgh
Moscow
Campen (c.1639-1657)
Post (c.1637-1669)
Inigo Jones (c.1620-1652)    London    Amsterdam    Berlin
Christopher Wren (c.1662-c.1700)
Warsaw
Paris    Prague    Cracow    Kiev
Lemercier (c.1620-1654)    Munich
F. Mansart (c.1625-1666)    Salzburg
Levau (c.1650-1670)    Vienna
Perrault (c.1664-1688)    Graz
Turin    Milan
**Guarini** (c.1800)    Venice
Valladolid    Genoa    Bologna
Lisbon    Madrid    Vignola, (Il Gesu begun 1568)    Rome
de Herrera    Maderna (c.1602-1629)
(1567-c.1590)    Cortona (c.1635-1669)    Naples
Mexico    Bernini (c.1625-1680)
Borromini (c. 1625-1667)
C. Rainaldi (c.1630-1691)

MAP A–20

**PALMA NOVA IN 1695**    0    ¼ mile

Defense walls
Main ditch
Remaining defense system (or berms)    Town buildings

MAP A–21

## Reformation: Printing Networks

Religious transformation was clearly furthered in southern Germany by an unusually well-developed network of towns with printing establishments (Map A-18). From a beginning in Mainz around 1455, printing with movable type spread rapidly throughout southern Germany and, by 1470, to such key distant centers as Cologne, Venice, Paris, and Utrecht. During the next thirty years the further adoption of movable type created dense printing networks in northern Italy, Germany, and the Low Countries—areas long accustomed to outside influences through their mercantile traditions.

## The Spread of Renaissance Ideas: Mercantile Ties

Traditions of trade were being modified by new capitalist developments. The wealthiest merchants became bankers to monarchs and supervised vast trading systems. The Fugger family of Augsburg and the Medici Bank in Italy created wholesale trading empires, complete with their own warehouses, mines, foundries, trading posts, and fleets that stretched from Danzig to Lisbon (Map A-19).

## The Spread of Renaissance Ideas: Style

The cultural dynamism of Italy continued long after the Renaissance. Baroque art, architecture, and town planning in the seventeenth century originated from the same centers and spread across the continent along similar paths, reflecting the influences of trading ties, dynastic connections, and the tastes of rulers (Map A-20). In this case Rome's preeminence first influenced southern Germany and Paris, and later Spain and Stockholm. Paris in turn influenced the cultural climate of London and Stockholm, as London then spread the prevailing ideas of the time to Edinburgh.

## The Spread of Renaissance Ideas: The Town

The principles of town planning had meanwhile been revolutionized by the invention of firearms, and town fortifications grew to gigantic proportions. Vast earthworks of mounds, ditches, and berms (flat, grassy open spaces) were constructed outside the town walls so that the town itself was beyond the range of any attacker's cannon. Palma Nova, near Venice, provides a splendid example of new-town construction in which modern concepts of street geometry were combined with defense requirements (Map A-21). As with medieval town extensions or new foundations, walls were built to enclose areas large enough to allow for later building. But by the seventeenth century urban growth had so far outdistanced the provisions of an earlier time that many farmers were displaced as towns expanded into the countryside. In many large towns later expansion occurred completely beyond the earthworks.

# THE INDUSTRIAL ERA

## Enclosure and Demographic Changes

The greatest transformation of the cultural landscape in modern times, perhaps most conspicuous in the massive shifts of populations from countryside to city, has been associated with the new industrialism. But forces were at work in the preindustrial countryside that paved the way for these demographic changes. An agricultural revolution that was well advanced by the eighteenth century modernized many farming practices and considerably altered the look of the land. A key element of this revolution was the enclosure of traditional open-field village lands to form large fenced fields owned by individuals. This process had taken hold in England

MAP A–22

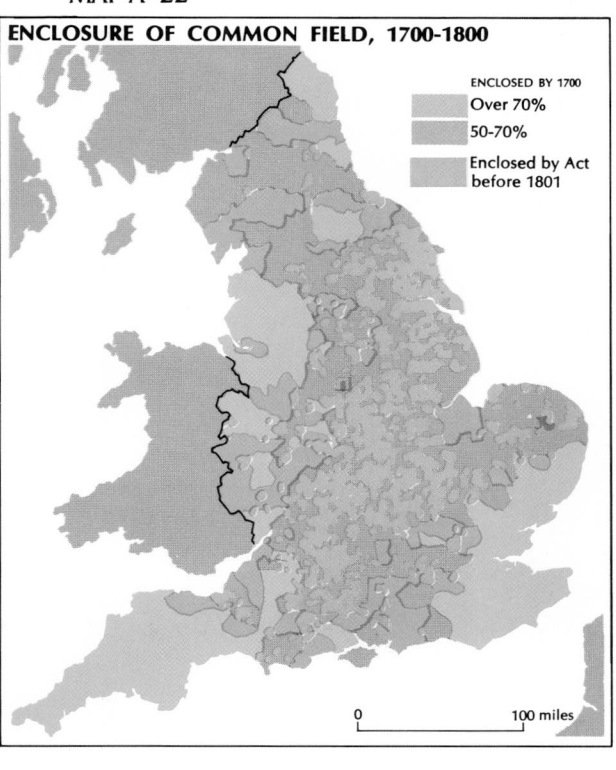

**ENCLOSURE OF COMMON FIELD, 1700-1800**

ENCLOSED BY 1700
Over 70%
50-70%
Enclosed by Act before 1801

0    100 miles

MAP A–24

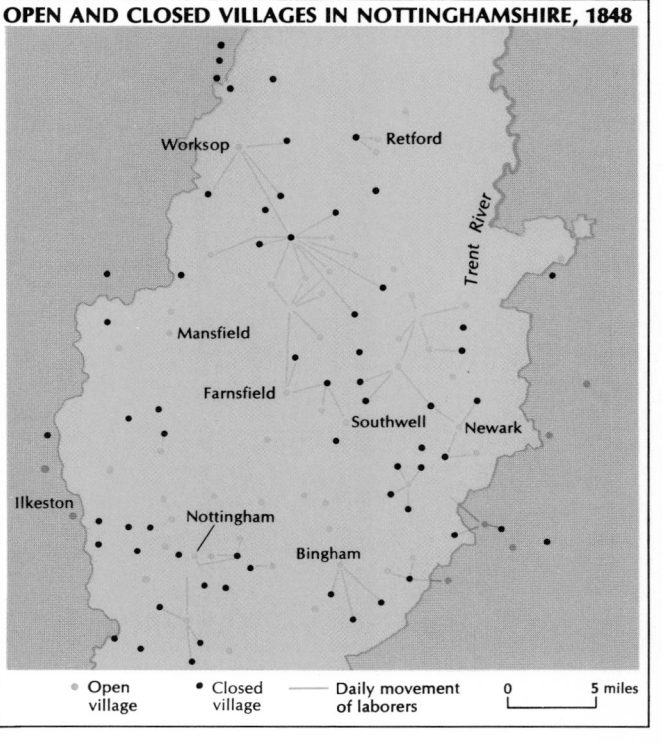

**OPEN AND CLOSED VILLAGES IN NOTTINGHAMSHIRE, 1848**

Worksop    Retford

Mansfield

Farnsfield

Southwell    Newark

Ilkeston

Nottingham

Bingham

Trent River

● Open village    ● Closed village    — Daily movement of laborers    0    5 miles

MAP A–23

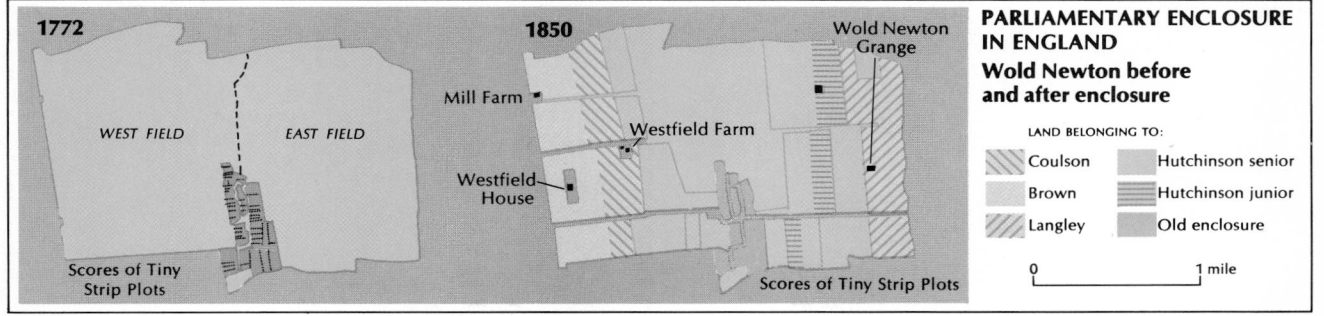

**1772**

WEST FIELD    EAST FIELD

Scores of Tiny Strip Plots

**1850**

Wold Newton Grange

Mill Farm

Westfield Farm

Westfield House

Scores of Tiny Strip Plots

**PARLIAMENTARY ENCLOSURE IN ENGLAND**
**Wold Newton before and after enclosure**

LAND BELONGING TO:

Coulson    Hutchinson senior
Brown    Hutchinson junior
Langley    Old enclosure

0    1 mile

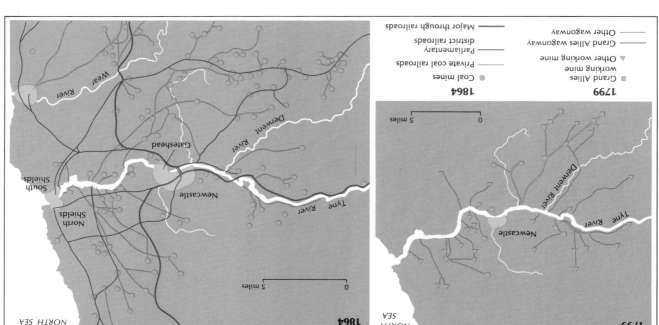

MAP A–26

## THE COAL INDUSTRY ON TYNESIDE

1799

1864

**1799**
- ■ Grand Allies working mine
- ▲ Other working mine
- Grand Allies wagonway
- Other wagonway

**1864**
- ● Coal mines
- Private coal railroads
- Parliamentary district railroads
- Major through railroads

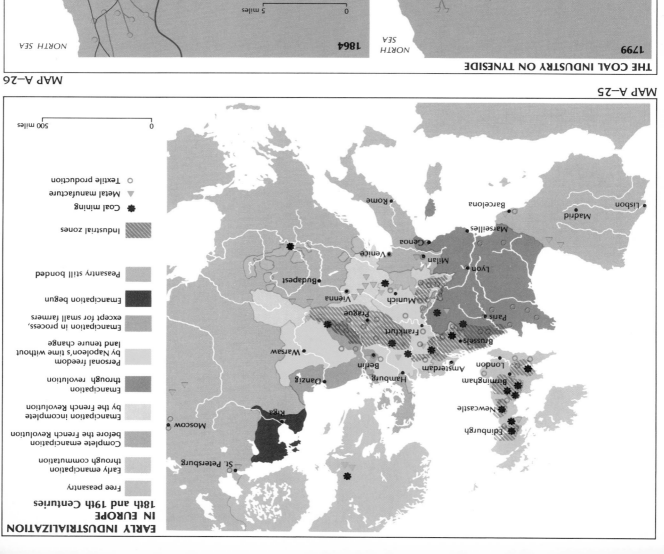

MAP A–25

## EARLY INDUSTRIALIZATION IN EUROPE
### 18th and 19th Centuries

- Free peasantry
- Early emancipation through commutation
- Complete emancipation before the French Revolution
- Emancipation incomplete by the French Revolution
- Emancipation through revolution
- Personal freedom by Napoleon's time without land tenure change
- Emancipation in process, except for small farmers
- Emancipation begun
- Peasantry still bonded

- ▨ Industrial zones
- ✳ Coal mining
- ▼ Metal manufacture
- ○ Textile production

0 ——— 500 miles